Pronunciation Table

Vowels

Symbol	Keyword
i	beat, feed
ɪ	bit, did
eɪ	date, paid
ɛ	bet, bed
æ	bat, bad
ɑ	box, odd, father
ɔ	bought, dog
oʊ	boat, road
ʊ	book, good
u	boot, food, student
ʌ	but, mud, mother
ə	banana, among
ɚ	shirt, murder
aɪ	bite, cry, buy, eye
aʊ	about, how
ɔɪ	voice, boy
ɪr	beer
ɛr	bare
ɑr	bar
ɔr	door
ʊr	tour

Consonants

Symbol	Keyword
p	pack, happy
b	back, rubber
t	tie
d	die
k	came, key, quick
g	game, guest
tʃ	church, nature, watch
dʒ	judge, general, major
f	fan, photograph
v	van
θ	thing, breath
ð	then, breathe
s	sip, city, psychology
z	zip, please, goes
ʃ	ship, machine, station, special, discussion
ʒ	measure, vision
h	hot, who
m	men, some
n	sun, know, pneumonia
ŋ	sung, ringing
w	wet, white
l	light, long
r	right, wrong
y	yes, use, music
t̯	butter, bottle
t˺	button

American English Sounds

/t̯/, /t˺/, /d̯/, /t/, /d/, and /nʃ/

/t̯/ The /t/ in *tap* or *sat* is a voiceless sound. Many Americans, however, use a voiced sound like a quick /d/ for the *t* in words like *latter*, *party* and *little*. The *t* in these words, shown in this dictionary as /t̯/, sounds like the *d* in *ladder*, *hardy* and *middle*. This sound usually occurs between vowels (especially before an unstressed vowel), between *r* and a vowel, or before a syllabic /l/.

/t˺/ This symbol means that many speakers pronounce a *glottal stop* in place of or together with /t/. A glottal stop is the sound in the middle of the expression *uh oh*. For example, in the words **button** /'bʌt˺n/ and **football** /'fʊt˺bɔl/, the *t* does not sound the same as in the word *ton* /tʌn/; it sounds more like a short period of silence. The glottal stop usually occurs before a syllabic /n/ or a consonant that begins the next syllable.

/t/ and /d/ These symbols mean that these consonants may be either pronounced or left out. For example, the *t* in **restless** /'rɛstlɪs/ and the *d* in **grandfather** /'grænd̯faðɚ/ are usually dropped in normal connected speech, even though it is considered more correct in slow, careful speech to pronounce the *t* and *d* in these words.

/nʃ/ Many speakers pronounce the sequence /nʃ/ as /ntʃ/. For example **attention** /ə'tɛnʃən/, **conscious** /'kɑnʃəs/ may also be pronounced as /ə'tɛntʃən/, /'kɑntʃəs/. Only the pronunciation with /nʃ/ is shown.

LONGMAN

Basic

DICTIONARY
OF AMERICAN
ENGLISH

Longman

Acknowledgments

Pearson Education Limited
Edinburgh Gate
Harlow
Essex CM20 2JE, England UK
and associated companies throughout the world

Visit our website:
http://www.longman.com/dictionaries

© Pearson Education Limited 1999

First edition 1999

015 014 013 012 011

ISBN 0582 33251 6 (Paperback edition)
ISBN 13: 978-0-582-33251-5

ISBN 0582 77643 0 (Cased edition)
ISBN 13: 978-0-582-77643-2

Set in Eurostile by The Pen & Ink Book Company,
Huntingdon, Cambridgeshire

Printed in China
EPC

Director
Della Summers

Editorial Director
Adam Gadsby

Publisher
Laurence Delacroix

Senior Editor
Ruth Urbom

Production Editor
Peter Braaksma

Pronunciation Editor
Rebecca Dauer

Design
Clive Russell
and
Simon Cuerdon

Production
Clive McKeough

Illustrators
Chris Simpson
Fiona MacVicar

Editorial Assistants
Susan Braund
Pauline Savill

Contents

What your dictionary tells you

different meanings of the word

set·tle /ˈsetl/ *verb* (settling, settled)
1 to begin to live in a new place: *My son settled in Los Angeles.*
2 to end an argument by agreeing to do something: *We settled our disagreement without a fight.*
3 to rest on something in a comfortable position: *I settled back on the chair and relaxed.*

definition

4 settle a bill to pay the money that you owe for something

phrasal verbs

5 settle down to become calmer and less noisy: *It took the children a while to settle down.*
6 settle in to become happier in a new place or job: *How are you settling in at the school?*
7 settle for something to accept something that is less than what you wanted: *Most of the tickets were gone, so we had to settle for what we could get.*

example

spelling

set·tle·ment /ˈsetlmənt/ *noun*
an official decision or agreement that ends an argument: *The two sides have **reached a settlement**.* (=made an agreement)

part of speech

fish¹ and fish² are separate even though they have the same spelling because one is a noun and the other is a verb. Look at **Which word?** on page vii.

fish¹ /fɪʃ/ *noun*
[*plural* **fish** or **fishes**]
an animal that lives in water and can swim, and which people eat as food

fins

gills

pictures with labels for clarity

fish² *verb*
1 to try to catch a fish

difficult past tenses

freeze /friz/ *verb* (freezing, froze, *past participle* **frozen**)
1 to become very cold and change from a liquid into a solid: *Water freezes to become ice.*

This is shown when a verb does not add **-ed** to form the past tense.

difficult comparatives and superlatives

little (**less, least**)
1 only a small amount of something: *She eats very little.* | *I have very little money at the moment.*

This is shown when the comparative and superlative is not formed with **-er** and **-est**.

difficult plurals

wom·an /ˈwʊmən/ *noun* [*plural* **women** /ˈwɪmɪn/]
an adult female person ≫ compare MAN

This is shown when a noun does not add **-s** to form the plural.

nouns with no plural

traf·fic /ˈtræfɪk/ *noun* [U]
1 the cars and people moving on a particular road: *The city streets are full of traffic.*

The dictionary tells you when a noun is uncountable. They are not used with **a** or **an**.

split¹ /splɪt/ *verb* (**splitting**, *past tense* **split**, *past participle* **split**)
2 (*also* **split up**) to divide something into parts: *We split the money **between** us.*

You can find information about which prepositions to use with a word.

prepositions

The meaning of the word is explained using simple words. Any difficult words are written IN SMALL CAPITAL LETTERS and you will always find them in the dictionary. The examples show you how to use the word.

iv

hap·pen /'hæpən/ *verb*

1 to start or continue, usually without being planned: *The accident happened outside my house.*

2 **happen to do something** to do something by chance: *If you happen to see Susan, give her this message.*

NOTE: If an event **occurs** or **happens**, it is not planned: *The explosion happened Friday evening.* If an event **takes place**, it is the result of a plan or arrangement: *The wedding will take place on June 6th.*

notes →

There are notes to help you to use a word without making mistakes.

hap·pen·ing /'hæpənɪŋ/ *noun*
an event

pronunciation →

hap·pi·ly /'hæpəli/ *adverb*
in a happy way: *They were laughing happily.*

hap·pi·ness /'hæpɪnɪs/ *noun* [U]
the state of being happy or pleased: *They've had years of happiness together.*

hap·py /'hæpi/ *adjective* (**happier**, **happiest**)
1 feeling very pleased: *I am happy to see you again.* ⇒ opposite UNHAPPY

information about other words →

2 **Happy Birthday!**, **Happy New Year!** said to someone to wish him or her good luck on a special occasion

Sometimes it is useful or interesting to know about another word which is like the word you are looking at, or to know what the opposite of a word is. You can find this information in your dictionary.

chip

chipped cups

pictures →

potato chips   *computer chip*

There are pictures to help you understand the meanings of words.

Remember, there are also 12 color pictures in your dictionary which help you understand lots of words.

chip¹ /tʃɪp/ *noun*
1 a small space or crack where a piece is missing from something: *My cup has a chip in it.*
2 a very small piece of metal or plastic used in computers to store information and make the computer work

Now look at the next page for more information on how to use your dictionary.

How to find the word you need in your dictionary

This is the English alphabet:

a b c d e f g h i j k l m n o p q r s t u v w x y z

A B C D E F G H I J K L M N O P Q R S T U V W X Y Z

A is the first letter in the alphabet and **Z** is the last.

Look at the letters below and put them in the correct order.

O D J B Q R Z T N A *A* _____

Now look at the alphabet above to see if you have the right answers.

In a dictionary, the words are in the same order as the letters of the alphabet (this is called **alphabetical order**), so that words which start with **a** are at the beginning of the dictionary and words which start with **z** are at the end.

Look at these words and then put them in alphabetical order.

alphabet	*teacher*
aunt	*orange*
afternoon	*computer*
dog	*school*
music	*yellow*

afternoon _____ _____
_____ _____
_____ _____
_____ _____
_____ _____

Now look in the main part of the dictionary to see if you have the right answers.

The word **afternoon** comes before the word **alphabet** in the dictionary. These words both begin with the letter **a**, so you must look at the second letters (**f** and **l**) to see which one comes first.

The following words all begin with the same letters. Put them in alphabetical order and then look to see if your answers are correct.

fire
fire department
firefighter
fireworks
fire engine
fireplace

_____ *fire*
_____
_____
_____
_____
_____

In this dictionary, **fire engine** and **fire department** are in alphabetical order in the same way as if they were one word instead of two, so that **fire department** comes before **fire engine** because **d** comes before **e** in the alphabet.
You can find phrasal verbs such as **pick up** and **sit down** by looking at the main verb (**pick up** is at **pick**, **sit down** is at **sit**).
If you want to find an idiom or an expression in this dictionary, look at the most important word of the idiom (= a word which is NOT **a**, **the**, **to** etc.). For example, to find the idiom **give someone a hand**, look at **hand**.

Where would you look to find these expressions?

just a minute
behind someone's back
take your time

Look in the dictionary to find the answers.

Which word?

Sometimes you will find that there are two or more words with the same spelling (look at **love**, for example).

---

love¹ /lʌv/ *verb* (**loving, loved**)
1 to care very much for someone, or have a strong romantic feeling for someone: *Mothers love their children.* ≫ compare HATE¹
2 to like something very much: *Maria loves to read.*

love² *noun*
1 [U] a strong romantic feeling for someone: *Her love **for** her husband is real.* ≫ compare HATE², HATRED

Love¹ and **love²** are separate because they are different types of words. **Love¹** is a verb and **love²** is a noun. If you are using the dictionary to find information about a new word, you need to know what type of word it is.

The sentences below have a space where a word is missing. Look at the list of words and decide which words you can put in the first sentence. For example, you can say "Their house is beautiful", so **BEAUTIFUL** is one of the words which can go in the first sentence. Then look at the second and third sentences and choose suitable words. Remember that there is more than one word for each sentence.

1. Their house is ....

2. We .... every day.

3. I have a new ....

computer	*hat*	*work*
eat	*old*	*beautiful*
big	*bicycle*	*sleep*

The words which can be used in the first sentence are all **adjectives**. An **adjective** is a word which describes someone or something. The words which can be used in the second sentence are all **verbs**. A **verb** is a word which tells you what someone or something does. The words which can be used in the third sentence are all **nouns**. A **noun** is a word which is the name of a person, place, animal, or thing.

Now look at these words and say whether each one is a noun, a verb or an adjective (write N, V, or A after the word).

blue	*A*	see	
mother		information	
loud		understand	
dictionary		boy	

Find the words in the dictionary and see if your answers are correct. Write a sentence using each word.

Finding the right part of the word

A word often has more than one meaning. Look at **as** below:

---

as /əz; *strong* æz/ *adverb, preposition*
1 used to say what someone's job is, or what something is used for: *She works as a teacher.* | *We can use this box as a table.*
2 when; while: *We sang as we worked.*
3 because: *I can't come, as I'm too busy.*
4 **as ... as** used to compare two or more: *I'm not as old as you.* | *It's just as good as the other one.*
5 **as well** also: *Can I have some milk as well?*

Which of the meanings of 'as' is being used in each of these sentences? Write the number of the meaning after each sentence.

She isn't as smart as her sister.   *4*

I spent 6 months as a student at that college.

We watched as the car disappeared.

He lived there as a young man.

They used a piece of cloth as a curtain.

How to say the word

Look at the phonetic symbols on the inside front cover. Now look at the words below and put the right word with the right sound.

c<u>a</u>t l<u>aw</u> n<u>a</u>rrow sh<u>o</u>p f<u>a</u>ther <u>o</u>ften d<u>o</u>g h<u>o</u>t h<u>a</u>nd c<u>a</u>r

/æ/   *cat*

/ɑː/   _____

/ɔ/   _____

Notice that different spellings may have the same sound.

Now look at these words beginning with 'th-' and see if you can find the pronunciation for each word.

this	/ˈθɪətər/
though	/ðer/
these	/θɔːt/
theater	/ðiːz/
thought	/ðəʊ/
their	/ðɪs/

If you look again at the pronunciation for **theater** (/ˈθɪətər/) you can see that there is a small mark like this ' in front of it. This is to tell you that you must say the first part of **theater** a little bit louder and with a little more force than the rest of the word (*THE*ater). Making one part of a word more important when you say it is called **stress**. Stress isn't always at the beginning of a word.

Do you know where the stress should be for these words? Put a ✓ next to the one which is right and an ✗ next to the one which is wrong. Say the words out loud to help you decide.

| ˈaffect | acaˈdemic | ˈaccept |
| afˈfect | aˈcademic | acˈcept |

Where should the stress be in these words? Put a ' in front of the part of the word where the stress should be.

| ex plain | ex plan a tion | dic tion ary |
| pur pose | fire en gine | |

Look in the dictionary to see if you have the right answers.

Sometimes nouns and verbs which look the same have different stress, for example **record** (noun) is pronounced 'record, but the verb **record** is pronounced re'cord.

Look at these examples and say whether the stress is the same or different.

There has been an increase in the number of students at the school.
The number of students at the school will increase next year.

Our country exports oil.
What are America's main exports?

Other ways your dictionary can help you

Look at pages 4 and 5 to find more information about how this dictionary can help you. Then see if you can name the different parts of the dictionary entry below. The first one has already been done to help you.

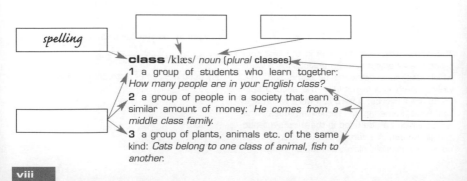

spelling

class /klæs/ *noun* [*plural* **classes**]
1 a group of students who learn together: *How many people are in your English class?*
2 a group of people in a society that earn a similar amount of money: *He comes from a middle class family.*
3 a group of plants, animals etc. of the same kind: *Cats belong to one class of animal, fish to another.*

THE
DICTIONARY
A–Z

a /ə; *strong* eɪ/
1 one or any: *There's a man at the door.* | *She was wearing a red skirt.*
2 each or every: *The candy cost 75 cents a bag.* | *He visits twice a year.*

NOTE: **An** is used instead of **a** before a word that starts with the sound of **a**, **e**, **i**, **o**, or **u** ≫ look at AN

a·ban·don /ə'bændən/ *verb*
to leave someone or something that you are responsible for: *The baby was abandoned by its mother.*

ab·bre·vi·a·tion /ə,brivi'eɪʃən/ *noun*
a short way to write a word or name: *Mr. is the abbreviation for Mister.*

ABC's /,eɪbi'siz/ *noun*
the letters of the English alphabet: *She's learning her ABC's.*

ab·do·men /'æbdəmən/ *noun*
the front part of your body between your chest and your legs

a·bil·i·ty /ə'bɪləti/ *noun* (*plural* **abilities**)
when someone can do something successfully: *A teacher must have the ability **to** keep students interested.* | *She lost her ability to walk after a car accident.*

a·ble /'eɪbəl/ *adjective*
if someone is able to do something, they can do it: *Is he able to swim?* | *I won't be able to come.* ≫ opposite UNABLE

a·board /ə'bɔrd/ *adverb, preposition*
on or onto a ship or plane: *Are all the passengers aboard?*

a·bol·ish /ə'bɑlɪʃ/ *verb*
to make a law to end something: *The government abolished slavery long ago.*

ab·o·li·tion /,æbə'lɪʃən/ *noun*
when a law is made to end something or to make something illegal: *the abolition of slavery in the 1860s*

a·bor·tion /ə'bɔrʃən/ *noun*
when someone ends a PREGNANCY so that the baby is never born

a·bout /ə'baʊt/ *adverb, preposition*
1 if one thing is about something else, that is what it describes or deals with: *She gave me a book about the local area.*
2 a little more or less than a particular number or amount: *Come at about six o'clock.*
3 almost: *Dinner is about ready.*
4 **be about to do something** to be going to do something very soon: *I was about to come and see you.*
5 **how about, what about** used when you are suggesting what to do: *How about going to the movies?*

a·bove /ə'bʌv/ *adverb, preposition*
1 in or to a higher place or over something else: *The picture is on the wall above my desk.* ≫ compare BELOW —see color picture on page 194
2 more than a particular number or amount: *The temperature went above 90 today.*
3 **above all** more than anything else: *I want you to remember this above all.*

a·broad /ə'brɔd/ *adverb*
in or to a foreign country: *My brother is studying abroad.* | *Have you ever been abroad?*

a·brupt /ə'brʌpt/ *adjective*
sudden: *There was an abrupt knock at the door.*

ab·sence /'æbsəns/ *noun*
when someone or something is not there: *Her absence was noticed by her boss.* ≫ opposite PRESENCE

ab·sent /'æbsənt/ *adjective*
not here: *He was absent from class last Tuesday.* ≫ compare PRESENT[1]

absent-mind·ed /,.. '..< / *adjective*
not noticing things that are happening around you, and often forgetting things

ab·so·lute /'æbsə,lut, ,æbsə'lut/ *adjective*
complete or exact: *Are you telling me the absolute truth?*

ab·so·lute·ly /,æbsə'lutli, 'æbsə,lutli/ *adverb*
1 very; completely: *It's absolutely beautiful.* | *Are you absolutely sure?*
2 said to say that you completely agree with someone: *"Do you think I'm right?" "Absolutely!"*

ab·sorb /əb'sɔrb, -'zɔrb/ *verb*
1 to take in a liquid slowly

2 to learn and understand something: *I haven't absorbed all the information yet.*

ab·sorb·ent /əb'sɔrb,ənt, -'zɔr-/ *adjective*
able to take in liquid: *You need a thick piece of absorbent material.*

ab·sorb·ing /əb'sɔrbɪŋ, -'zɔr-/ *adjective*
very interesting: *an absorbing novel about the Wild West*

ab·surd /,əb'səd, -'zəd/ *adjective*
extremely silly: *The story was so absurd that no one believed it.* —**absurdly** *adverb*

a·bun·dant /ə'bʌndənt/ *adjective*
more than enough in quantity: *We have an abundant supply of water.*

a·buse¹ /ə'byus/ *noun*
1 wrong or harmful use of something: *We talked about the problem of drug abuse.*
2 bad or cruel treatment of someone
3 rude and bad things that are said to someone: *He shouted abuse at me.*

abuse² *verb* [abusing, abused]
1 to do cruel or violent things to someone
2 to use something in a wrong or harmful way

ac·a·dem·ic /,ækə'dɛmɪk/ *adjective*
about or relating to work done in schools, colleges, or universities: *The academic year begins in September.*

ac·cent /'æksɛnt/ *noun*
a way of speaking that shows that someone comes from a particular place: *John speaks with a southern accent.* | *a French accent*
≫ compare DIALECT

ac·cept /ək'sɛpt/ *verb*
1 to take something that is offered to you: *Will you accept my offer?* | *He would not accept any money from us.*
2 to agree that something is true, right, or should be done: *The mayor accepted that there had been some mistakes.*

ac·cept·a·ble /ək'sɛptəbəl/ *adjective*
of a good enough quality: *It wasn't your best work, but it was acceptable.*

ac·cept·ance /ək'sɛptəns/ *noun*
when you agree to take something that is offered to you, or agree that something is true or right

ac·cess /'æksɛs/ *noun*
1 a way of being able to use or do something: *Students need access **to** computers.*

2 a way of getting to a place: *There should be access **to** the building for people in wheelchairs.*

accident

ac·ci·dent /'æksədənt, -,dɛnt/ *noun*
1 something bad, that happens by chance: *I didn't mean to break it – it was an accident!*
2 when a car, plane etc. hits something or gets damaged: *a car accident in which two people died* | *The number of accidents on roads is rising every year.*
3 by accident if something happens by accident, it is not planned but happens by chance: *Jill opened the letter by accident, thinking it was for her.*

ac·ci·den·tal /,æksə'dɛntəl/ *adjective*
not planned, but happening by chance

ac·ci·den·tal·ly /æksə'dɛntⁿli, -'dɛntəli/ *adverb*
if you do something accidentally, you do it without intending to: *I accidentally left my keys in the car.*

ac·com·mo·date /ə'kɑmə,deɪt/ *verb* [accommodating, accommodated]
1 to have enough space for something: *The room will accommodate fifty people.*
2 to give someone a place where they can live or stay

ac·com·mo·da·tion /ə,kɑmə'deɪʃən/ *also* **accommodations** *noun*
a place where you can live or stay: *Accommodation is provided for all new students.*

ac·com·pa·ny /ə'kʌmpəni/ *verb* [accompanying, accompanied]
1 to go somewhere with someone: *He accompanied me to the hospital.*
2 to play music with someone who is singing or playing another instrument: *Maria sang, and I accompanied her on the piano.*

ac·com·plish /ə'kʌmplɪʃ/ *verb*
to do something successfully: *We accomplished a lot during the day.*

ac·com·plish·ment /əˈkʌmplɪʃmənt/
noun
something that you achieve or are able to do
well: *Winning the award is quite an accomplishment!*

ac·cord /əˈkɔrd/ *noun*
of your own accord if you do something of your
own accord, you do it without being told or
asked to: *She left of her own accord.*

ac·cord·ing·ly /əˈkɔrdɪŋli/ *adverb*
in a way that is suitable for a particular situation: *If you do something wrong, you'll be punished accordingly.*

according to /.ˈ.. ./ *preposition*
because of what someone says or what something shows: *According to the map, we're very close to the lake.*

ac·count¹ /əˈkaʊnt/ *noun*
1 an amount of money you keep in a bank: *He
paid the money into his bank account.*
2 a story or description: *Can you give us an
account of what happened?*
3 **take something into account** to think about
something before you make a decision about it:
*You must take the price into account when
choosing which one to buy.*
4 **on account of something** because of something: *We stayed at home on account of the
bad weather.*
5 **accounts** [plural] records that deal with the
money that a person or company spends and
receives

account² *verb*
account for something to give the reason for
something: *I can't account for the missing
money.*

ac·count·ant /əˈkaʊntənt, əˈkaʊnᵗnt/
noun
someone whose job is to keep records of the
money spent or received by a person or a company

ac·cu·ra·cy /ˈækyərəsi/ *noun* [U]
the quality of being exactly right or correct

ac·cu·rate /ˈækyərɪt/ *adjective*
correct or exact: *an accurate description of the
events* | *The figures aren't very accurate.*
≫ opposite INACCURATE —**accurately**

ac·cu·sa·tion /ˌækyəˈzeɪʃən/ *noun*
a statement saying that someone has done
something wrong

ac·cuse /əˈkyuz/ *verb* [accusing, accused]
to say that someone has done something
wrong: *Sally accused Paul of cheating.*

ac·cus·tomed /əˈkʌstəmd/ *adjective*
be accustomed to something to think that
something is normal or usual, especially
because you do it a lot or know it well: *I'm not
accustomed to getting out of bed this early.*

ache¹ /eɪk/ *noun*
a continuous pain: *I have a stomach ache.*

ache² *verb* [aching, ached]
to hurt with a continuing pain: *Her head ached.*

a·chieve /əˈtʃiv/ *verb* [achieving, achieved]
to succeed in doing something, especially by
working hard: *She's achieved a lot since she
came to this school.*

a·chieve·ment /əˈtʃivmənt/ *noun*
something that you have worked hard for and
done well

ac·id /ˈæsɪd/ *noun*
a chemical substance that can burn things

acid rain /ˌ.. ˈ./ *noun* [U]
rain which damages trees and plants because it
contains acid put into the air by factory smoke

ac·knowl·edge /əkˈnɑlɪdʒ/ *verb*
[acknowledging, acknowledged]
1 to agree that something is true: *The hospital acknowledged that it made a mistake.*
2 to tell the person who sends you something
that you have received it: *No, they didn't
answer my letter. They didn't even acknowledge
it.*

a·corn /ˈeɪkɔrn/ *noun*
the nut of the OAK tree

ac·quaint·ance /əˈkweɪntᵗns/ *noun*
someone you know, but not very well ≫ compare FRIEND

ac·quaint·ed /əˈkweɪntɪd/ *adjective*
be acquainted with someone to know someone: *Are you acquainted with Mr. Smith?*

a·cre /ˈeɪkər/ *noun*
a measure of land that is equal to 4,840
square yards or 4,047 square meters

ac·ro·bat /ˈækrəˌbæt/ *noun*
someone who performs in a CIRCUS and does
difficult tricks with their body

a·cross /əˈkrɔs/ *adverb, preposition*
1 from one side of a place to the other: *They
swam across the river.*

2 on the other side of something: *She lives across the street from me.* —see color picture on page 194

act¹ /ækt/ *verb*
1 to do something or behave in a particular way: *You're acting like an idiot.*
2 to pretend to be someone else in a play or movie: *She's been acting since she was five years old.*
3 **act as** to do something or be used instead of someone or something else: *This room acts as her office.*

act² *noun*
1 something you do: *an act of bravery*
2 one of the parts that a play is divided into
3 something you pretend to feel or think: *She seems happy, but it's just an act.*

act·ing /'æktɪŋ/ *noun* [U]
the work done by an ACTOR or ACTRESS

ac·tion /'ækʃən/ *noun*
1 something that you do: *His quick action saved her life.* | *The police say they will not be taking any further action in the matter.*
2 **out of action** not working or broken: *My car is out of action.*

ac·tive /'æktɪv/ *adjective*
1 doing something or always ready or able to do things: *She is very active for her age.* | *He's over 80, but he's still pretty active.*
2 an active verb is one that has one person or thing doing something: *In the sentence, "John kicked the ball," "kicked" is an active verb.* ≫ compare PASSIVE

ac·tiv·i·ty /æk'tɪvəti/ *noun*
1 [U] when people are moving around, doing things etc.: *The classroom was full of activity.*
2 (*plural* **activities**) something you do, especially to enjoy yourself: *Dancing is her favorite activity.*

ac·tor /'æktɚ/ *noun*
someone who acts in a play or movie

ac·tress /'æktrɪs/ *noun* (*plural* **actresses**)
a woman who performs in a play or movie

ac·tu·al /'æktʃuəl, 'ækʃuəl/ *adjective*
real and clear: *We think he stole the money, but we have no actual proof.*

ac·tu·al·ly /'æktʃuəli, -tʃəli, 'ækʃuəli, -ʃəli/ *adverb*
1 a word used to show that you are giving real or true information about something: *I know who he is, but I've never actually met him.* | *Do you actually believe that?*

2 a word used when you are politely telling someone that they have made a mistake: *Actually, the class starts at 3 o'clock, not 4.*

A.D. /,eɪ 'di/
after the birth of Christ, used in dates: *The document was dated A.D. 1471.* ≫ compare B.C.

ad /æd/ *noun*
an advertisement

a·dapt /ə'dæpt/ *verb*
1 to change your behavior or ideas because of a new situation you are in: *The children have adapted to their new school.*
2 to change something so that it is suitable for a new situation: *This kitchen is adapted for blind people.*

a·dapt·a·ble /ə'dæptəbəl/ *adjective*
able to change and be successful in a new situation

add /æd/ *verb*
1 to put something into or onto something else: *To make the cake, mix butter and sugar, and then add flour.*
2 to put numbers or amounts together to produce a total: *If you add 3 and 4, you get 7.* | *Add up these numbers.* ≫ compare SUBTRACT
3 to say more about something

ad·dict /'ædɪkt/ *noun*
someone who cannot stop doing something harmful, especially taking drugs: *a clinic for treating drug and alcohol addicts*

ad·dic·tion /ə'dɪkʃən/ *noun*
the need to have something such as drugs because you cannot stop taking it

ad·di·tion /ə'dɪʃən/ *noun*
1 [U] when numbers or amounts are added together ≫ compare SUBTRACTION
2 someone or something that is added: *She was an important addition to the company.*
3 **in addition to something** and something else too: *In addition to English, the children also learn German and Spanish.*

ad·dress¹ /ə'drɛs, 'ædrɛs/ *noun* (*plural* addresses)
the name of the place where you live: *Please write your name and address.*

address² /ə'drɛs/ *verb*
1 to speak to someone: *The President will address the nation tonight.*
2 to write a name and address on something: *She addressed the letter to Mrs. Wilson.*

ad·e·quate /'ædəkwɪt/ *adjective*
enough: *The information you gave us was not adequate.* >> opposite INADEQUATE

ad·jec·tive /'ædʒɪktɪv, 'ædʒəktɪv/ *noun*
a word that describes someone or something: *In the phrase, "a beautiful song," "beautiful" is an adjective.*

ad·just /ə'dʒʌst/ *verb*
to make a small change in something to make it better

ad·min·is·tra·tion /əd,mɪnə'streɪʃən/ *noun*
the management or organization of a company, government etc.

ad·mi·ral /'ædmərəl/ *noun*
an important officer in the navy

ad·mi·ra·tion /,ædmə'reɪʃən/ *noun*
a feeling that someone or something is very good, beautiful, intelligent etc.

ad·mire /əd'maɪɚ/ *verb* (admiring, admired)
1 to respect and approve of someone or something: *I always admired his work.*
2 to look at something in an approving way: *I was just admiring your new car.*

ad·mis·sion /əd'mɪʃən/ *noun*
1 when you say that you have done something wrong or bad: *an admission of guilt.*
2 permission to enter a place: *Admission was free for children.*

ad·mit /əd'mɪt/ *verb* (admitting, admitted)
1 to agree or say that something bad about yourself is true: *She admitted that she was lazy.* >> opposite DENY
2 to let someone enter a place: *This ticket admits two people to the game.*

ad·o·les·cent /,ædl'ɛsənt/ *noun*
someone who is between 13 and 17 years old, and is developing into an adult >> compare TEENAGER

a·dopt /ə'dɑpt/ *verb*
to take someone else's child into your family and treat him or her as if they were your own

a·dore /ə'dɔr/ *verb* (adoring, adored)
to love someone or something very much: *She adored her son. | I adore chocolate.*

a·dult /ə'dʌlt, 'ædʌlt/ *noun*
a grown-up person: *We were in a group of 3 adults and 4 children.*

ad·vance¹ /əd'væns/ *verb* (advancing, advanced)
1 to move forward: *The army advanced toward the town.* >> compare RETREAT¹

advance² *noun*
in advance before something happens or before you do something: *You must pay in advance.*

ad·vanced /əd'vænst/ *adjective*
1 using the most modern ideas or equipment: *They sell the most advanced computers available.*
2 at a high or difficult level: *advanced learners of English*

ad·van·tage /əd'væntɪdʒ/ *noun*
something that helps you: *It is an advantage to speak several languages.* >> opposite DISADVANTAGE

ad·ven·ture /əd'vɛntʃɚ/ *noun*
an exciting thing that happens to someone

ad·ven·tur·ous /əd'vɛntʃərəs/ *adjective*
liking excitement and adventures

ad·verb /'ædvɚb/ *noun*
a word that tells you how, when, or where something is done: *In the sentence, "She spoke loudly," "loudly" is an adverb.*

ad·ver·tise /'ædvɚ,taɪz/ *verb* (advertising, advertised)
to use notices, photographs, movies etc. to try to persuade people to buy, do, or use something: *It is illegal to advertise cigarettes on TV.*

ad·ver·tise·ment /,ædvɚ'taɪzmənt/ *noun*
a short movie, photograph, notice etc. that tries to persuade people to buy, do, or use something

ad·vice /əd'vaɪs/ *noun*
a suggestion about what someone should do: *Let me give you a piece of advice. | Can I ask your advice about what classes to take?*

ad·vise /əd'vaɪz/ *verb* (advising, advised)
to tell someone what you think he or she should do: *The doctor advised me to rest for a few days.*

ae·ro·bics /ə'roubɪks, ɛ-/ *noun*
exercise done to music, usually in a class

aer·o·sol /'ɛrə,sɔl, -,sɑl/ *noun*
a container from which a liquid can be sprayed (SPRAY¹)

af·fair /əˈfɛr/ *noun*
1 a sexual relationship between two people, especially one which is secret: *Her husband was **having an affair with** his secretary.*
2 something that happens: *The party was a noisy affair.*
3 things connected with a particular subject: *government affairs*

af·fect /əˈfɛkt/ *verb*
to produce a change in someone or something: *The disease affected his breathing.* ≫ compare EFFECT

af·fec·tion /əˈfɛkʃən/ *noun* [U]
the feeling of liking and caring for another person

af·fec·tion·ate /əˈfɛkʃənɪt/ *adjective*
showing that you like or love someone

af·ford /əˈfɔrd/ *verb*
to have enough money to buy something: *We can't afford a new car.*

a·fraid /əˈfreɪd/ *adjective*
frightened of something: *Are you afraid **of** the dark?* ≫ compare SCARED

af·ter /ˈæftɚ/ *preposition, adverb*
1 later than something in time: *Tomorrow is the day after today.* | *The watch broke three days after I bought it!* ≫ compare BEFORE[1]
2 moving toward or behind someone or something else: *The child ran after her dog.*
3 used to say how many minutes past the hour it is when you are telling the time: *It's ten after four.*
4 **be after someone** to be looking for someone: *Are the police still after him?*
5 **be after something** to be trying to get something: *I think he's after more money.*
6 **after all** in spite of what you did or thought before: *Don't worry about it. After all, it's not your fault.*

af·ter·noon /ˌæftɚˈnun/ *noun*
the time between the middle of the day and the evening: *I saw Jim yesterday afternoon.* ≫ compare MORNING

af·ter·ward /ˈæftɚwɚd/ *adverb* (also **afterwards**)
later, after something else has happened: *We went to the dance and walked home afterward.*

a·gain /əˈgɛn/ *adverb*
1 one more time: *Can you say that again?*
2 **again and again** a lot of times

3 **now and again** sometimes, but not very often: *My aunt visits us now and again.*

a·gainst /əˈgɛnst/ *preposition*
1 close to or touching something: *He leaned against the wall.* —see color picture on page 194
2 not agreeing with someone or something: *I'm against killing animals for their fur.*
3 playing or competing for the other side in a game or competition: *We're playing against the blue team.*
4 in order to try to stop something happening: *a protest against the war*
5 **against the law** not allowed by the law: *It's against the law to drive too fast.*

age /eɪdʒ/ *noun*
1 the number of years someone has lived or something has existed: *Pat is ten years of age.*
2 [U] when something has existed for a long time: *The wine improves with age.*
3 **old age** when someone is old: *Who will take care of me in my old age?*
4 a period of time in history
5 **ages** a long time: *We talked for ages.*

a·gen·cy /ˈeɪdʒənsi/ *noun* (*plural* **agencies**)
a business that provides a particular service

ag·es /ˈeɪdʒɪz/ *plural noun*
a long time: *It's been ages since I've seen her!*

ag·gres·sive /əˈgrɛsɪv/ *adjective*
forceful and ready to argue with people: *Your child is too aggressive with others.*

a·go /əˈgoʊ/ *adverb*
in the past: *It happened just a few minutes ago.*

NOTE: **Ago** is used with the past tense of verbs, but you cannot use it with past tenses which are formed with **have**. Compare these sentences: *He arrived a month ago. He has been here since last month.* ≫ look at BEFORE, SINCE

ag·o·ny /ˈægəni/ *noun* [U]
very bad pain

a·gree /əˈgri/ *verb* (**agreeing, agreed**)
1 to have the same opinion as someone else: *I agree **with** you.* ≫ opposite DISAGREE
2 **agree to something** to say that you will do or that you approve of something: *He agreed to the plan.*
3 **agree with something** to believe that something is right: *I don't agree with hunting.*

a·gree·ment /ə'grimənt/ *noun*
1 an arrangement or promise between people or countries: *a trade agreement between the U.S. and Japan*
2 [U] having the same opinion as someone else: *Are we all in agreement about the plan?*
≫ opposite DISAGREEMENT

ag·ri·cul·tur·al /ˌægrɪ'kʌltʃərəl/ *adjective*
used in farming or about farming: *agricultural machinery*

ag·ri·cul·ture /'ægrɪˌkʌltʃɚ/ [U]
the activity of growing crops and raising animals for people to eat: *About 25% of the country's people work in agriculture.* ≫ compare FARMING

a·head /ə'hɛd/ *adverb*
1 in front of someone or something: *I saw her ahead of me.*
2 before an event or a particular time: *So far we are ahead of schedule.*
3 into the future: *We need to plan ahead if we are to succeed.*

aid¹ /eɪd/ *noun*
help, especially in the form of money, food, equipment etc.: *American aid to the earthquake victims*

aid² *verb*
to help someone

AIDS /eɪdz/ *noun* [U]
a very serious disease which destroys the body's ability to fight illnesses ≫ compare HIV

aim¹ /eɪm/ *verb*
1 to plan or want to do something: *We aim to win.*
2 to get ready to throw or fire something toward a person or thing: *He aimed the gun at me.*

aim² *noun*
1 something that you want to do or get: *Our aim is to provide better schools for everyone.*
2 **take aim** to put a weapon in the direction of someone or something

air¹ /ɛr/ *noun*
1 [U] the gas surrounding the Earth, which people breathe
2 **the air** the space above you: *He threw his hat into the air.*
3 **by air** in a plane: *We traveled by air.*

air² *verb*
air your views/opinions to tell someone what you think about something

air con·di·tion·er /'. .ˌ.../ *noun*
a machine that makes the air in a room or building stay cool

air con·di·tion·ing /'. .ˌ.../ *noun* [U]
a system of machines that stops the air in a building from feeling too warm

air·craft /'ɛrkræft/ *noun* (*plural* **aircraft**)
an airplane, or another vehicle that can fly

air·field /'ɛrfild/ *noun*
a place where small airplanes fly from

air force /'. ˌ./ *noun*
soldiers who fight in airplanes ≫ compare ARMY, NAVY

air·line /'ɛrlaɪn/ *noun*
a company that carries people or goods by airplane

air·mail /'ɛrmeɪl/ *noun*
letters and packages sent in airplanes

airplane

engine

wing

air·plane /'ɛrpleɪn/ *noun*
a vehicle that flies, in which people travel —see color picture on page 187

air·port /'ɛrpɔrt/ *noun*
a place that airplanes arrive at and leave from

air raid /'. ˌ./ *noun*
an attack by soldiers in airplanes, especially by dropping bombs

air·y /'ɛri/ *adjective* (**airier, airiest**)
having fresh air inside: *We were given a nice airy room.*

aisle /aɪl/ *noun*
a long passage between rows of seats

open   ajar   closed

a·jar /ə'dʒɑr/ *adjective*
a door that is ajar is not completely closed

a·larm¹ /ə'lɑrm/ *noun*
1 [U] a feeling of fear or danger
2 something that makes a noise to wake people up or warn them of danger: *a fire alarm*

alarm² *verb*
to worry someone or make them feel afraid

alarm clock /.'. ,./ *noun*
a clock that makes a loud noise at the time you want to wake up

al·bum /'ælbəm/ *noun*
1 a record, CD etc. with several songs on it: *He bought the new Michael Jackson album.*
2 a book with empty pages where you can put photographs, stamps etc.

al·co·hol /'ælkə,hɔl, -,hɑl/ *noun* [U]
drinks such as beer, wine etc. that affect your brain and can make you feel drunk: *We do not sell alcohol to anyone under 21.*

al·co·hol·ic¹ /,ælkə'hɔlɪk, -'hɑ-/ *noun*
someone who cannot stop drinking too much alcohol: *Her father is an alcoholic.*

alcoholic² *adjective*
containing alcohol: *alcoholic drinks*

a·lert /ə'lət/ *adjective*
quick to notice things

al·ge·bra /'ældʒəbrə/ *noun* [U]
a type of MATHEMATICS in which letters are used instead of numbers

a·li·en /'eɪliən, 'eɪlyən/ *noun*
1 someone who lives or works in a country, but is not a citizen
2 a creature that some people believe comes from another world: *a movie about aliens invading Earth*

a·like /ə'laɪk/ *adjective, adverb*
the same in some way: *They were all dressed alike in white dresses.* ≫ compare SIMILAR

a·live /ə'laɪv/ *adjective*
not dead; living: *Is his grandfather still alive?*
≫ compare DEAD¹

all /ɔl/ *adverb, pronoun*
1 the whole of something: *Don't eat all the cake!*
2 every one of: *Answer all twenty questions.*
3 completely: *He was dressed all in black.*
4 **all over** everywhere: *I've been looking all over for you.*
5 **not at all** not in any way: *I'm not at all hungry.*

al·ler·gic /ə'lədʒɪk/ *adjective*
if you are allergic to something, you become ill if you eat, touch, or breathe it: *I'm allergic **to** cats.*

al·ler·gy /'ælədʒi/ *noun* (*plural* **allergies**)
a condition that makes you ill when you eat, touch, or breathe in a particular thing: *His breathing problems are caused by an allergy **to** house dust.*

al·ley /'æli/ *noun* (*plural* **alleys**)
a narrow street between buildings or walls

al·li·ance /ə'laɪəns/ *noun*
an agreement between countries or groups to work together

al·li·ga·tor /'ælə,geɪtɚ/ *noun*
a large animal with a long body, sharp teeth and short legs, that lives in hot wet areas

al·low /ə'laʊ/ *verb*
to say that someone can do something: *You're not allowed **to** go in there.* ≫ opposite FORBID

al·low·ance /ə'laʊəns/ *noun*
money that you are given for a special reason

all right /,. './ *adjective, adverb*
1 good enough, but not excellent: *"How is the coffee?" "It's all right, but I've had better."*
2 not sick or in pain: *Do you feel all right?*
3 used to say "yes"; OK: *"Can I borrow this book?" "All right."*

al·ly /'ælaɪ, ə'laɪ/ *noun* (*plural* **allies**)
someone who helps you or supports you in a fight, argument, war etc.

al·mond /'ɑmənd, 'æm-/ *noun*
a flat white nut with a slightly sweet taste, or the tree on which these nuts grow

al·most /'ɔlmoʊst, ɔl'moʊst/ *adverb*
nearly: *It's almost 9 o'clock.* | *We're almost there.*

a·lone /ə'loʊn/ *adjective*
1 not with other people: *He lives alone.*
≫ compare LONELY
2 only: *She alone knows the truth.*
3 **leave someone alone** to stop annoying someone: *Leave me alone. I'm busy!*
4 **leave something alone** to not touch something: *Leave that dog alone.*

a·long /ə'lɔŋ/ *adverb, preposition*
1 following the length of something; from one end of something long to another: *We walked along the road.*
2 forward: *Move along, please!*
3 **bring someone along/come along** to bring someone somewhere with you, or to go somewhere with someone: *Can I bring my friend along?*

a·long·side /ə,lɔŋ'saɪd/ *adverb, preposition*
by the side of something

a·loud /ə'laʊd/ *adverb*
in a voice that is easy to hear: *She read the story aloud.*

al·pha·bet /'ælfə,bɛt/ *noun*
the letters of a language in a particular order: *The English alphabet begins with A and ends with Z.*

al·pha·bet·i·cal /,ælfə'bɛt̬ɪkəl/ *adjective*
in the same order as the letters of the alphabet. *The words in this dictionary are in alphabetical order.*

al·read·y /ɔl'rɛdi/ *adverb*
1 before now. *I've seen that movie twice already.*
2 by this or that time: *It was already raining when we started our trip.*

al·so /'ɔlsoʊ/ *adverb*
as well; too: *The store sells mostly shoes, but they also sell some bags. | We can also go to the museum if there's time.*

NOTE: When there is only one verb, put **also** before the verb, unless it is the verb **be** which must have **also** after it: *He enjoys football and baseball, and he also likes tennis. | She likes music and she is also interested in sports.* Where there are two verbs, put **also** after the first one: *I would also like to come. | It is an expensive sport which can also be dangerous.*

al·tar /'ɔltɚ/ *noun*
a raised table used in a religious place

al·ter /'ɔltɚ/ *verb*
to change something: *We had to alter our plans.*

al·ter·a·tion /,ɔltə'reɪʃən/ *noun*
a change to something

al·ter·nate¹ /'ɔltɚ,neɪt/ *verb* (**alternating, alternated**)
repeating first one thing, then another: *The weather has been alternating **between** sunshine and rain.*

alternate² /'ɔltɚnɪt/ *adjective*
1 first one, then another in a regular pattern: *He works on alternate Saturdays.* (=one Saturday he works, and the next Saturday he does not work)
2 able to be used instead of something or someone else. *Is there an alternate route to the stadium?*

al·ter·na·tive¹ /ɔl'tɚnətɪv/ *noun*
something you can do or use instead of something else: *They were searching for any alternative **to** war.*

alternative² *adjective*
different from something else: *an alternative plan*

al·though /ɔl'ðoʊ/
even if; in spite of something. *Although the car is old, it still drives well.* ≫ compare THOUGH

al·to·geth·er /,ɔltə'gɛðɚ, 'ɔltə,gɛðɚ/ *adverb*
including everyone or everything; completely: *There are 30 people on the bus altogether. | He has quit his job altogether.*

al·ways /'ɔlweɪz, -wɪz, -wiz/ *adverb*
1 at all times: *You should always lock your door at night.*
2 for a very long time: *I'll always remember you.*

NOTE: When there is only one verb, put **always** before the verb, unless it is the verb **be** which must have **always** after it: *We always enjoy our vacations. | It is always nice to see you.* When there are two verbs, put **always** after the first one: *You must always be careful when you cross the street. | She is always complaining.*

a.m. /ˌeɪ ˈɛm/
in the morning: *I got up at 8 a.m.* ➣ compare
P.M.

am /m, əm; *strong* æm/ *verb*
the part of the verb **be** that is used with *I*: *Am
I late for dinner?* | *I'm* (=I am) *very sorry.*

am·a·teur /ˈæmətʃɚ/ *adjective*
doing something for enjoyment, not for money
➣ compare PROFESSIONAL

a·maze /əˈmeɪz/ *verb* [amazing, amazed]
to surprise someone very much: *She was
amazed to see so many people there.*

a·maze·ment /əˈmeɪzmənt/ *noun* [U]
very great surprise: *We watched the show in
amazement.*

a·maz·ing /əˈmeɪzɪŋ/ *adjective*
very surprising and exciting: *What amazing
news!* ➣ compare INCREDIBLE

am·bas·sa·dor /æmˈbæsədɚ, əm-/ *noun*
an important person who does political work for
his or her government in another country

am·bi·tion /æmˈbɪʃən/ *noun*
1 a strong wish to be successful
2 something you very much want to do: *Her
ambition is to be a singer.*

am·bi·tious /æmˈbɪʃəs/ *adjective*
wanting very much to be successful: *a young,
ambitious businessman*

am·bu·lance /ˈæmbyələns/ *noun*
a special vehicle for carrying people who are
sick or injured. —see color picture on page 187

a·mend·ment /əˈmɛndmənt/ *noun*
a change, especially to the words of a law

A·mer·i·can /əˈmɛrɪkən/ *noun*
someone from the U.S.

am·mu·ni·tion /ˌæmyəˈnɪʃən/ *noun* [U]
something that you can shoot from a weapon

a·mong /əˈmʌŋ/ *preposition*
1 in a group of people or things: *It's nice to be
among friends.* ➣ compare BETWEEN
2 in the middle of a lot of people or things: *We
looked for the ball among the trees.*
3 between a group of people: *The candy was
shared among the children.* ➣ compare
BETWEEN

a·mount /əˈmaʊnt/ *noun*
how much of something there is, or how much
is needed: *It cost a large amount of money.*

amp /æmp/ *noun*
a measure of electricity

am·phib·i·an /æmˈfɪbiən/ *noun*
an animal such as a FROG that can live on land
or in the water

am·ple /ˈæmpəl/ *adjective*
enough or more than enough: *The car has
ample room for five people.*

a·muse /əˈmyuz/ *verb* [amusing, amused]
to make someone laugh or smile: *He was not
amused at the joke.*

a·muse·ment /əˈmyuzmənt/ *noun*
1 [U] enjoyment
2 an enjoyable thing to do

amusement park /.ˈ.. ˌ./ *noun*
a place where people go to enjoy themselves by
riding on special machines and playing games
for small prizes

a·mus·ing /əˈmyuzɪŋ/ *adjective*
making you laugh or smile: *an amusing story*
➣ compare FUNNY

an /ən; *strong* æn/
used instead of **a** before a word that begins
with the sound of a, e, i, o, or u: *an apple* | *an
orange* | *half an hour*

NOTE: You use **an** instead of **a** before words
beginning with a vowel sound, e.g. *a dog, a
girl, a house,* but *an umbrella, an elephant,
an object.* Remember that there is
sometimes a difference in the way a word is
spelled and the way it sounds. Use **an** before
words which begin with a vowel sound, but
are not spelled with **a, e, i, o,** or **u** at the
beginning, e.g. *It will take about an hour* (=
/aʊɚ/) and **a,** not **an,** with words which are
spelled with a vowel at the beginning but do
not begin with a vowel sound, e.g. *a
European* (ˌjʊərəˈpiən/) *country.*

---

a·nal·y·sis /əˈnæləsɪs/ *noun* [plural
analyses]
a careful examination of something

an·al·yze /ˈænlˌaɪz/ *verb* [analyzing,
analyzed]
to look at something very carefully to find out
what it is made of or to understand it: *He had
his blood analyzed by a doctor.*

an·ces·tor /ˈænˌsɛstər/ *noun*
someone in your family who lived a long time before you were born ≫ compare DESCENDANT

an·chor /ˈæŋkər/
noun
a heavy weight dropped down from a ship to the bottom of the water to stop the ship from moving

an·cient
/ˈeɪnʃənt/ *adjective*
very old: *ancient buildings* | *ancient history* (=about a very long time ago)

and /ən, n, ɔnd; *strong* ænd/
a word used for joining two words, phrases, or parts of a sentence: *I had a drink and a piece of cake.* | *Are John and Jill coming tonight?*

an·es·thet·ic /ˌænəsˈθɛt̬ɪk/ *noun*
a drug that stops the feeling of pain

an·gel /ˈeɪndʒəl/ *noun*
a spirit who lives with God, usually shown in pictures as a person with wings

an·ger /ˈæŋgər/ *noun* [U]
the feeling of being very annoyed

an·gle /ˈæŋgəl/ *noun*
the shape made when two straight lines meet or cross each other: *an angle of 90°*

an·gri·ly /ˈæŋgrəli/ *adverb*
in a way that shows anger: *"Go away!" she shouted angrily.*

an·gry /ˈæŋgri/ *adjective* (**angrier, angriest**)
feeling very annoyed: *I'm very angry at her.*

an·i·mal /ˈænəməl/ *noun*
a living creature that is not a person or a plant: *animals such as dogs, goats and lions*

an·kle /ˈæŋkəl/ *noun*
the joint at the bottom of your leg just above your foot —see picture at FOOT

an·ni·ver·sa·ry /ˌænəˈvərsəri/ *noun*
(*plural* **anniversaries**)

NOTE: An **anniversary** is a day when you remember something special or important which happened on the same date in an earlier year: *Their wedding anniversary is June 12th* (=they got married on June

12th). | *Today is the 50th anniversary of the end of the war.* A person's **birthday** is the date on which they were born: *My birthday is October 20th.* (=I was born on October 20th)

an·nounce /əˈnaʊns/ *verb* (**announcing, announced**)
to tell something to a lot of people, especially officially: *The captain announced that the plane was going to land.*

an·nounce·ment /əˈnaʊnsmənt/ *noun*
something written or spoken that tells people important news: *I read your wedding announcement in the newspaper.*

an·nounc·er /əˈnaʊnsər/ *noun*
someone whose job is to give people information on the radio, on television, during an event etc.

an·noy /əˈnɔɪ/ *verb* (**annoying, annoyed**)
to make someone feel angry: *You're beginning to annoy me!*

an·noyed /əˈnɔɪd/ *adjective*
angry about something: *He is getting annoyed with his sister.*

an·nu·al /ˈænyuəl/ *adjective*
happening every year: *The flower show is an annual event.* —**annually** *adverb*

a·non·y·mous /əˈnɑnəməs/ *adjective*
not known by name: *The author of the book is anonymous.*

an·oth·er /əˈnʌðər/ *pronoun*
1 one more: *Would you like another cup of coffee?*
2 a different one: *Is there another room we can use?* ≫ compare OTHER

an·swer¹ /ˈænsər/ *verb*
1 to say or write something after you have been asked a question: *"Did you see her?" "No," she answered.* | *You should answer all the questions in the test.*
2 **answer the door** to open a door when someone knocks on it
3 **answer the telephone** to pick up a telephone when it rings

answer² *noun*
1 something that you say or write after you have been asked a question: *I'm still waiting for an answer.*

2 something that solves a problem: *There are no easy answers to the problem of crime.*

an·swer·ing ma·chine /ˈ... .,./ *noun*
a machine that answers your telephone and records messages when you are not there

ant /ænt/ *noun*
a small insect that lives in groups

Ant·arc·tic /ænt'ɑrktɪk, ænt'ɑrtɪk/ *noun*
the Antarctic the very cold, most southern part of the world **—antarctic** *adjective*

an·te·lope /ˈæntəl,oʊp/ *noun (plural* antelope *or* antelopes)
a wild animal that runs very fast and has long horns on its head

an·ten·na /æn'tɛnə/ *noun*
a piece of equipment that receives radio or television signals

an·ti·bi·ot·ic /,æntɪbaɪ'ɑtɪk, ,æntaɪ-/ *noun*
a drug that fights illness in someone's body: *The doctor gave me some antibiotics for my sore throat.*

an·tic·i·pate /æn'tɪsə,peɪt/ *verb*
(anticipating, anticipated)
to expect something to happen: *We anticipate that there may be a few problems.*

an·tique /æn'tik/ *noun*
an object that is old and worth a lot of money: *This table is an antique.* **—antique** *adjective*

anx·i·e·ty /æŋ'zaɪəṭi/ *noun* [U]
a feeling of worry

anx·ious /ˈæŋkʃəs/ *adjective*
very worried about something

anx·ious·ly /ˈæŋkʃəsli, 'æŋʃəsli/ *adverb*
in a way that shows you are very worried: *They waited anxiously for news of their son.*

an·y¹ /ˈɛni/ *pronoun*
1 used to say that it is not important which of several things you choose: *Any of these restaurants is fine.*
2 a word meaning "some," used in questions and sentences: *Is there any ice cream left?* ≫ compare SOME

any² *adverb*
used in questions and sentences with "not" to mean "more," "much," "a little" etc.: *I don't know how things could get any worse.* | *Are you feeling any better?*

NOTE: Use **any**, not **some**, in questions and in NEGATIVE sentences: *I need to buy some coffee.* | *Is there any coffee?* | *There isn't any coffee.* But when you are asking for something or offering something you use **some**: *Would you like some coffee? Can I have some coffee, please?*

an·y·bod·y /ˈɛni,bɑdi, -,bʌdi, -bədi/
any person: *Has anybody seen my pen?* | *Anybody can learn to swim.* ≫ compare SOMEONE

NOTE: Use **anybody** or **anyone**, not **somebody** or **someone**, in questions and in NEGATIVE sentences: *There was somebody waiting outside.* | *Is there anybody here?* | *There wasn't anybody in the office.*

an·y·how /ˈɛni,haʊ/ *adverb*
another word for ANYWAY

an·y·one /ˈɛni,wʌn, -wən/
another word for ANYBODY: *Did you tell anyone about this?*

an·y·thing /ˈɛni,θɪŋ/
1 used in questions and sentences with "not" to mean "something": *Do you want anything?* | *She didn't want anything else* [=any other things] *to eat.* ≫ compare SOMETHING
2 used to say that it does not matter what thing you choose, do etc. because you could choose, do etc. any of them: *My dog will eat anything.*

NOTE: Use **anything**, not **something**, in questions and in NEGATIVE sentences: *I need to get something to drink.* | *Do you have anything to drink?* | *I don't want anything to drink.*

an·y·way /ˈɛni,weɪ/ *adverb*
1 in spite of something else: *The dress cost a lot, but I bought it anyway.*
2 used when you are saying something that supports what you have just said: *I don't want to go to the party. Anyway, I haven't been invited.*
3 used when you are continuing what you are saying or changing the subject of what you are saying: *Anyway, where do you want to go for lunch?*

an·y·where /ˈɛni,wɛr/ *adverb*
in or to any place: *I can't find my keys any-*

where. | *Have you been anywhere else?* (=to any other places) >> compare SOMEWHERE

a·part /ə'pɑrt/ *adverb*
1 separated by distance or time: *The two cities are six miles apart.*
2 separated into many pieces: *I had to take the lamp apart to fix it.*
3 **apart from someone or something** except for someone or something: *All the children like music apart from Joe.*

a·part·ment /ə'pɑrt⌐mənt/ *noun*
a place where someone lives, usually a group of rooms in a large building

ape /eɪp/ *noun*
a large animal like a monkey, but with a very short tail or no tail

a·piece /ə'pis/ *adverb*
each: *The apples are 25 cents apiece.*

a·pol·o·gize /ə'pɑlə‚dʒaɪz/ *verb*
(apologizing, apologized)
to say that you are sorry about something you have done: *Billy apologized for telling a lie.*

a·pol·o·gy /ə'pɑlədʒi/ *noun* (plural apologies)
something that you say or write to show that you are sorry about something you have done

a·pos·tro·phe /ə'pɑstrəfi/ *noun*
the mark (') used in writing to show that letters have been left out, such as *don't* instead of "*do not*" or with the letter "s" to show that something belongs to someone, such as "Sarah's book"

ap·pa·rat·us /‚æpə'rætəs, -'reɪtəs/ *noun* [U]
tools or other things used for a particular purpose: *diving apparatus*

ap·par·ent /ə'pærənt, ə'pɛr-/ *adjective*
easy to understand or realize: *It was apparent that he knew nothing about cars.* >> compare OBVIOUS

ap·par·ent·ly /ə'pærənt⌐li, ə'pɛr-/ *adverb*
used to say that something seems to be true, but you are not sure: *Apparently, she's living in Japan.*

ap·peal¹ /ə'pil/ *verb*
1 to ask for something urgently: *She appealed to me for help.*
2 **appeal to someone** to be attractive or interesting to someone: *That type of music doesn't appeal to me.*

appeal² *noun*
an act of asking for something, especially money: *The Red Cross is making an appeal for medicine and blankets.*

ap·pear /ə'pɪr/ *verb*
1 to seem: *She appeared to be upset.*
2 to begin to be seen: *Stars appeared in the sky.* >> opposite DISAPPEAR

ap·pear·ance /ə'pɪrəns/ *noun*
1 [U] the way someone looks to other people: *Carol is very concerned about her appearance.*
2 when someone or something arrives at a place or begins to be seen: *This is his first appearance in court.*

ap·pe·tite /'æpə‚taɪt/ *noun*
the feeling that you want to eat: *I lost my appetite when I was sick.*

ap·plaud /ə'plɔd/ *verb*
to hit your open hands together many times to show that you enjoyed a play, speaker etc. >> compare CLAP

ap·plause /ə'plɔz/ *noun* [U]
the sound of people hitting their hands together many times to show that they liked or enjoyed something

ap·ple /'æpəl/ *noun*
a round hard juicy red or green fruit that is white on the inside —see picture at FRUIT

ap·pli·ance /ə'plaɪəns/ *noun*
a machine or piece of equipment used in someone's home: *Bob works at a store that sells kitchen appliances.*

ap·pli·ca·tion /‚æplɪ'keɪʃən/ *noun*
1 a written paper asking for something: *We received ten applications for the job.*
2 a piece of computer SOFTWARE

ap·ply /ə'plaɪ/ *verb* (applying, applied)
1 to officially ask for something: *I want to apply for the job.*
2 to affect or be intended for someone or something: *The rules apply to everyone.*
3 to put something such as paint on a surface: *Apply the glue along the edge of the wood.*

ap·point /ə'pɔɪnt/ *verb*
to choose someone for a job: *I appointed her as my secretary.*

ap·point·ment /ə'pɔɪnt⌐mənt/ *noun*
a time arranged for meeting someone: *I have an appointment with the doctor on Monday.*

ap·pre·ci·ate /əˈpriʃiˌeɪt/ *verb*
(appreciating, appreciated)
to be grateful for something: *I appreciate your help.*

ap·pre·ci·a·tion /əˌpriʃiˈeɪʃən, -pri-/ *noun* [U]
something you say or do to thank someone or show that you are grateful: *I would like to express my appreciation to everyone who helped.*

ap·pren·tice /əˈprɛntɪs/ *noun*
someone who is learning a new job

ap·proach¹ /əˈproʊtʃ/ *verb*
to move closer to someone or something: *A man approached me on the street.*

approach² *noun*
a way of doing something or dealing with a problem

ap·pro·pri·ate /əˈproʊpriɪt/ *adjective*
right; suitable: *Visitors to the church should wear appropriate clothing.* ≫ opposite INAPPROPRIATE

ap·prov·al /əˈpruvəl/ *noun* [U]
when you think that someone or something is good ≫ opposite DISAPPROVAL

ap·prove /əˈpruv/ *verb* (approving, approved)
to think that something is good: *I don't approve of smoking.* ≫ opposite DISAPPROVE

ap·prox·i·mate /əˈprɑksəˌmɪt/ *adjective*
not exact: *Our approximate time of arrival is two o'clock* (=it might be just before or just after two).

ap·prox·i·mate·ly /əˈprɑksəmɪt˺li/ *adverb*
a little more or less than an exact number or amount: *Approximately half of our money comes from selling books.*

ap·ri·cot /ˈeɪprɪˌkɑt, ˈæ-/ *noun*
a round, soft, yellow fruit

A·pril /ˈeɪprəl/ *noun*
the fourth month of the year

a·pron /ˈeɪprən/ *noun*
a piece of cloth that you wear on top of your clothes, to keep your clothes clean when you cook

a·quar·i·um /əˈkwɛriəm/ *noun*
a large glass box in which fish live

arch /ɑrtʃ/ *noun*
(plural **arches**)
a curved shape at the top of a door, window etc: *The old church had large arches supporting the weight of the roof.*

ar·chae·ol·o·gist /ˌɑrkiˈɑlədʒɪst/ *noun*
someone who studies very old things and buildings made by people who lived a long time ago

ar·chae·ol·o·gy /ˌɑrkiˈɑlədʒi/ *noun* [U]
the study of very old things and buildings made by people who lived a long time ago

ar·chi·tect /ˈɑrkəˌtɛkt/ *noun*
someone whose job is to plan and draw buildings

ar·chi·tec·ture /ˈɑrkəˌtɛktʃər/ *noun* [U]
1 the shape and style of buildings: *I love the architecture of Venice.*
2 the job of planning and drawing buildings: *He studies architecture.*

Arc·tic /ˈɑrktɪk, -tɪk/ *noun*
the Arctic the most northern part of the earth, including parts of Alaska and Greenland, and the sea called the Arctic Ocean —**arctic** *adjective*

are /ɚ; *strong* ɑr/ *verb*
the part of the verb **be** that is used with **we**, **you** and **they**: *Who are you?* | *We're* (=we are) *Jane's friends.* | *They are going to be late.*

ar·e·a /ˈɛriə/ *noun*
1 a particular part of a place, city, or country: *He lives in the Boston area.* (=near Boston)
2 the measure of a surface: *The house has an area of 2,000 square feet.*

a·re·na /əˈrinə/ *noun*
a building with a large central area surrounded by raised seats, used for sports and entertainment

aren't /ˈɑrənt/
1 are not: *Bill and Sue aren't coming to the party.*
2 used in questions instead of **am not**: *I'm your best friend, aren't I?*

ar·gue /ˈɑrgyu/ *verb* (arguing, argued)
to disagree, often speaking loudly and angrily: *Mom and Dad always argue about money.*

ar·gu·ment /ˈɑrgyəmənt/ *noun*
a disagreement, especially an angry one: *They had a big argument.*

ar·id /'ærɪd/ *adjective*
very dry and getting very little rain

a·rise /ə'raɪz/ *verb* (**arising**, *past tense*
arose, *past participle* **arisen**)
to happen or appear: *Several problems arose
when I lost my job.*

a·rith·me·tic /ə'rɪθmə,tɪk/ *noun*
the science of numbers, including addition, division etc.

arm¹ /ɑrm/ *noun*
the part of your body between your shoulder
and your hand

arm² *verb*
to give someone weapons

arm·chair /'ɑrmtʃɛr/ *noun*
a chair with sides on which to rest your arms
—see picture at CHAIR

armed /ɑrmd/ *adjective*
carrying a weapon, especially a gun: *The prison
had many armed guards.* ≫opposite UNARMED

armed forc·es /,. '../ *plural noun*
all the soldiers of a country

ar·mor /'ɑrmə/
noun [U]
a covering of metal
worn as protection
by soldiers in the
past

arm·pit
/'ɑrm,pɪt/ *noun*
the place under your arm where your arm joins
your body

arms /ɑrmz/ *plural noun*
weapons such as guns and bombs: *He was
caught selling arms to the enemy.*

ar·my /'ɑrmi/ *noun* (*plural* **armies**)
the soldiers of a country that fight on land
≫ compare AIR FORCE, NAVY

a·rose /ə'roʊz/
the PAST TENSE of the verb **arise**

a·round /ə'raʊnd/ *adverb, preposition*
1 on all sides of something: *We put a fence
around the yard.* —see color picture on page
194
2 in or to different places: *They walked around
the town.*
3 in or near a particular place: *Is there a bank
around here?*

4 not exactly; about: *Come around 10 o'clock.*
5 in the opposite direction: *Let me turn the
car around.*
6 with a movement or shape like a circle: *The
Earth moves around the Sun.*

ar·range /ə'reɪndʒ/ *verb* (**arranging,
arranged**)
1 to make plans for something: *I have arranged
a meeting for tomorrow.*
2 to put things in a particular order or position: *She arranged the flowers in a vase.*

ar·range·ment /ə'reɪndʒmənt/ *noun*
a plan or agreement that something will happen

ar·rest¹ /ə'rɛst/ *verb*
to catch someone and take him or her away
because he or she has done something wrong:
*Police arrested several people for fighting in the
street.*

arrest² *noun*
when a police officer arrests someone: *The
police made three arrests yesterday.*

ar·riv·al /ə'raɪvəl/ *noun*
when a person, airplane etc. gets to a place:
After our arrival, we went to a hotel. ≫ compare DEPARTURE

ar·rive /ə'raɪv/ *verb* (**arriving, arrived**)
to get to a place: *Your letter arrived yesterday.* |
We arrived in Boston on Tuesday. ≫ opposite
DEPART

ar·row /'æroʊ/
noun
1 a weapon like a
sharp stick that is
shot from a BOW³
2 a sign that shows
direction or where
something is

art /ɑrt/ *noun*
1 [U] the skill of
drawing and painting:
He is studying art in school.
2 [U] paintings, drawings etc.: *The museum
has many **works of** art.*
3 the skill used in making or doing something:
a book about the art of cooking
4 the arts [*plural*] painting, music, literature,
movies etc.

ar·ter·y /'ɑrtəri/ *noun* (*plural* **arteries**)
one of the tubes that carry blood from your
heart to the rest of your body

ar·thri·tis /ɑrˈθraɪtɪs/ *noun* [U]
a disease that makes your hands, arms, legs etc. painful and difficult to move

ar·ti·cle /ˈɑrtɪkəl/ *noun*
1 a piece of writing in a newspaper, magazine etc.: *Did you read the article on the flood?*
2 a thing: *Police found an article of clothing by the road.*
3 the words **a** or **an** (=indefinite article) or **the** (=definite article)

ar·ti·fi·cial /ˌɑrtəˈfɪʃəl/ *adjective*
not natural, but made by people: *artificial flowers | an artificial leg*

art·ist /ˈɑrtɪst/ *noun*
someone who paints pictures, writes music etc.

ar·tis·tic /ɑrˈtɪstɪk/ *adjective*
having skill in an art, such as painting, music etc.

as /əz; *strong* æz/ *adverb, preposition*
1 used to say what someone's job is, or what something is used for: *She works as a teacher. | We can use this box as a table.*
2 when; while: *We sang as we worked.*
3 because: *I can't come, as I'm too busy.*
4 **as ... as** used to compare two or more: *I'm not as old as you. | It's just as good as the other one.*
5 **as well** also: *Can I have some milk as well?*

ash /æʃ/ *noun* (*plural* **ashes**)
the gray powder that is left after something has been burned

a·shamed /əˈʃeɪmd/ *adjective*
feeling bad about something you have done wrong: *She felt ashamed of herself.* ≫ compare EMBARRASSED

a·shore /əˈʃɔr/ *adverb*
onto the land: *Pull the boat ashore!*

ash·tray /ˈæʃtreɪ/ *noun* (*plural* **ashtrays**)
a small dish in which you put the ASH from a cigarette

a·side /əˈsaɪd/ *adverb*
to the side: *I stepped aside to let her pass me.*

ask /æsk/ *verb*
1 to say something that is a question: *"Who are you?" she asked.*
2 to try to get help, information etc. from someone: *She asked me what time it was. | If you need anything, just ask.*
3 to invite someone to go to a place with you: *John asked me to go to the dance with him.*

a·sleep /əˈslip/ *adjective*
1 sleeping: *The baby is asleep.* ≫ compare AWAKE
2 **fall asleep** to begin to sleep: *I fell asleep in front of the TV.*

as·par·a·gus /əˈspærəgəs/ *noun* [U]
a long thin green vegetable shaped like a small stick

as·pect /ˈæspɛkt/ *noun*
one of the parts of a situation, idea, problem etc.: *We are looking at several aspects of the plan.*

as·pi·rin /ˈæsprɪn/ *noun*
a medicine that makes pain go away

as·sas·sin /əˈsæsən/ *noun*
someone who kills an important person, especially for political reasons

as·sas·si·nate /əˈsæsəˌneɪt/ *verb* (**assassinating, assassinated**)
to kill an important person, especially for political reasons ≫ compare MURDER[1]

as·sas·si·na·tion /əˌsæsəˈneɪʃən/ *noun*
when someone kills an important person, especially for political reasons: *the assassination of President Kennedy*

as·sault[1] /əˈsɔlt/ *verb*
to attack or hit someone: *he was arrested for assaulting a neighbor.*

assault[2] *noun*
an attack on someone

as·sem·ble /əˈsɛmbəl/ *verb* (**assembling, assembled**)
1 to bring people together in a group
2 to fit the parts of something together

as·sem·bly /əˈsɛmbli/ *noun* (*plural* **assemblies**)
a meeting of a group of people for a particular purpose

as·set /ˈæsɛt/ *noun*
something that is useful in helping you succeed or deal with problems

as·sign /əˈsaɪn/ *verb*
to give someone a job to do: *Police were assigned to watch the President.*

as·sign·ment /əˈsaɪnmənt/ *noun*
a job or piece of work that you must do: *Did you finish your homework assignment?*

as·sist /əˈsɪst/ *verb*
to help someone

as·sist·ance /ə'sɪstəns/ *noun* [U]
help or support

as·sist·ant /ə'sɪstənt/ *noun*
someone who helps a person in their job

as·so·ci·ate /ə'souʃiˌeɪt, -siˌeɪt/ *verb*
(associating, associated)
1 to connect two things or ideas in your mind
2 **associate with someone** to spend time with someone or be connected with him or her

as·so·ci·a·tion /əˌsousi'eɪʃən, -ʃi'eɪ-/ *noun*
an organization of people with a particular purpose or interest

as·sume /ə'sum/ *verb* (assuming, assumed)
to think that something is true even though you do not know that it is: *I assumed that she was English by the way she talks.*

as·sure /ə'ʃʊr/ *verb* (assuring, assured)
to tell someone that something is true to make them feel less worried: *I can assure you that we are not closing the hospital.*

as·ter·isk /'æstərɪsk/ *noun*
the sign *

as·ton·ish /ə'stɑnɪʃ/ *verb*
to surprise someone very much

as·ton·ish·ment /ə'stɑnɪʃmənt/ *noun* [U]
when you are very surprised

as·trol·o·ger /ə'strɑlədʒɚ/ *noun*
someone who studies ASTROLOGY

as·trol·o·gy /ə'strɑlədʒi/ *noun* [U]
the study of the PLANETs and stars in the belief that they influence people's lives

as·tro·naut /'æstrəˌnɔt, -ˌnɑt/ *noun*
someone who travels in space —see color picture on page 192

as·tron·o·mer /ə'strɑnəmɚ/ *noun*
someone who studies ASTRONOMY

as·tron·o·my /ə'strɑnəmi/ *noun* [U]
the science of the study of the sun, moon, and stars

at /ət; *strong* æt/ *preposition*
1 in a particular place: *Meet me at my house around six.* | *She's at work.*
2 when something happens: *It gets cold at night.* | *The movie starts at seven o'clock.*
3 toward someone or something: *Look at me!* | *Stop shouting at the children.*
4 because of something: *No one laughed at his joke.*

5 used for showing how much, how old, or how fast: *He got married at twenty-one.* | *driving at forty miles per hour*
6 **good/bad etc. at something** able or not able to do something well

ate /eɪt/
the PAST TENSE of the verb **eat**

a·the·ist /'eɪθiɪst/ *noun*
someone who does not believe in the existence of God

ath·lete /'æθlit/ *noun*
someone who is good at sports, especially someone who takes part in sports competitions

ath·let·ic /æθ'lɛtɪk/ *adjective*
able to play a sport very well

at·las /'ætləs/ *noun* (*plural* **atlases**)
a book of maps

ATM /ˌeɪ ti 'ɛm/ *noun*
Automated Teller Machine; a machine in the wall outside a bank where you can get money

at·mos·phere /'ætˀməsˌfɪr/ *noun*
1 a feeling that a place or situation gives you: *I enjoyed the exciting atmosphere of the game.*
2 **the atmosphere** [U] the air that surrounds the Earth
3 the air in a room, building etc.: *a smoky atmosphere*

at·om /'ætəm/ *noun*
the smallest part into which a substance can be divided

a·tom·ic en·er·gy /.ˌ.. '.../ *noun* [U]
power produced by splitting an atom, used for making electricity

at·tach /ə'tætʃ/ *verb*
1 to connect one thing to something else: *This machine attaches labels to clothes.*
2 **be attached to someone** to like someone very much: *Mary was very attached to her father.*

at·tack¹ /ə'tæk/ *verb*
1 to use violence against a person or place, often using weapons: *The army attacked with no warning.* | *The rebels attacked the camp at dawn.*
2 to say bad things about someone or something; criticize

attack² *noun*
a violent action intended to hurt someone or something

at·tempt¹ /ə'tɛmpt/ *verb*
to try to do something difficult

attempt² *noun*
when you try to do something difficult: *At least she **made an** attempt **to** speak their language.*

at·tend /ə'tɛnd/ *verb*
to go to or be present at an event: *Will you be attending the meeting?*

at·tend·ance /ə'tɛndəns/ *noun* [U]
when you are present at a place: *His attendance **at** school is bad.* (=he does not go enough)

at·tend·ant /ə'tɛndənt/ *noun*
someone whose job is to take care of someone or something

at·ten·tion /ə'tɛnʃən/ *noun* [U]
1 when you look at or listen to someone or something: *May I have your attention, please?* (=will you listen to me) | *Sorry, I wasn't **paying** attention. What did you say?*
2 special care or interest that you give to someone or something: *Crime attracts a lot of attention in the newspapers.* | *Old cars need more attention than new ones.*

at·tic /'ætɪk/ *noun*
a space or room at the top of a house inside the roof —see color picture on page 186

at·ti·tude /'ætə,tud/ *noun*
the way you think or feel about something or someone: *a friendly attitude*

at·tract /ə'trækt/ *verb*
1 to make someone interested in something, or go to see something: *Disneyland attracts many visitors every year.*
2 if one object attracts another, it makes that other object move toward it: *He used a magnet to attract the metal balls.*
3 **be attracted to someone** to like someone and want to be with them

at·trac·tion /ə'trækʃən/ *noun* [U]
the feeling of liking someone or something very much

at·trac·tive /ə'træktɪv/ *adjective*
1 pretty, beautiful, or pleasant to look at: *She's a very attractive woman.* | *an attractive cottage*
2 interesting or desirable: *an attractive idea* ≫ opposite UNATTRACTIVE

auc·tion /'ɔkʃən/ *noun*
a public sale where things are sold to the person who offers the most money

au·di·ence /'ɔdiəns/ *noun*
the people watching a play, listening to music etc.

au·di·o /'ɔdiou/ *adjective*
relating to recording and broadcasting

au·di·o·vis·u·al /,ɔdiou'vɪʒuəl/ *adjective*
relating to the use of recorded pictures and sound

au·di·to·ri·um /,ɔdɪ'tɔriəm/ *noun*
a large room, especially in a school, where people sit to watch a performance

Au·gust /'ɔgəst/ *noun*
the eighth month of the year

aunt /ænt, ɑnt/ *noun*
the sister of one of your parents, or the wife of your uncle ≫ compare UNCLE

au·thor /'ɔθɚ/ *noun*
a person who writes a book, play etc.

au·thor·i·ty /ə'θɔrəti, ə'θɑr-/ *noun*
1 [U] the power to control people and make them do what you want: *The police have the authority to stop the march.*
2 **the authorities** the people who control or govern something

au·thor·ize /'ɔθə,raɪz/ *verb* (**authorizing, authorized**)
be authorized to to have the power to do something

au·to¹ /'ɔtou/ *noun*
a car

auto² *adjective*
relating to cars: *He owns an auto parts store.*

au·to·bi·og·ra·phy /,ɔtəbaɪ'ɑgrəfi/ *noun* (*plural* **autobiographies**)
a book written by someone about their own life ≫ compare BIOGRAPHY

au·to·graph /'ɔtəgræf/ *noun*
a famous person's name, written by him or her ≫ compare SIGNATURE

au·to·mat·ic /,ɔtə'mætɪk/ *adjective*
1 automatic machines work without people operating them, after being started: *The building has automatic doors.* (=doors which open and close without being touched)
2 done without thinking —**automatically** *adverb*: *I saw it out of the corner of my eye and ducked automatically.*

au·to·mo·bile /,ɔtəmə'bil, 'ɔtəmə,bil/ *noun*
a car

au·tumn /'ɔtəm/ *noun*
the season between summer and winter, when the leaves fall off the trees

a·vail·a·ble /ə'veɪləbəl/ *adjective*
able to be used or seen, used etc.: *Do you have any rooms available on the 16th?*

av·a·lanche /'ævə,læntʃ, -lɑntʃ/ *noun*
a large amount of snow or a lot of rocks that fall down a mountain

av·e·nue /'ævə,nu/ *noun*
a street in a town or city ≫ compare STREET

av·er·age[1] /'ævrɪdʒ/ *adjective*
1 usual or ordinary: *The average child enjoys listening to stories.*
2 calculated by adding several amounts together and dividing the total by the number of amounts: *The average rainfall in July is just one inch.*

average[2] *noun*
the amount you get by adding several numbers together and dividing the total by the number of amounts. For example the average of 3, 5, and 7 is 5 (3+5+7=15 — 15÷3=5).

av·o·ca·do /,ævə'kɑdou, ,ɑ-/ *noun*
a green fruit shaped like a PEAR with a large seed inside

a·void /ə'vɔɪd/ *verb*
to stay away from a person, place, or thing: *Are you trying to avoid me?*

a·wait /ə'weɪt/ *verb*
to wait for someone or something

a·wake /ə'weɪk/ *adjective*
not sleeping: *I'm never really awake until I've had a cup of coffee.* | *Your son has been awake for hours!* ≫ opposite ASLEEP

a·ward[1] /ə'wɔrd/ *noun*
a prize you get for doing something well: *He won the award for best actor.*

award[2] *verb*
to give someone an award

a·ware /ə'wɛr/ *adjective*
if you are aware of something, you know it is happening: *I was not aware of the problem.*

a·way /ə'weɪ/ *adverb*
1 to another place: *Go away!* | *He turned around and ran away.* —see color picture on page 194
2 at a distance from a place or person: *The nearest city is five miles away.*
3 not at home or at work: *I'll be away for a few days.*
4 **put something away** to put something in its correct place: *Put your toys away now.*

awe·some /'ɔsəm/ *adjective*
very impressive; extremely good: *His party was awesome!*

aw·ful /'ɔfəl/ *adjective*
1 very bad or unpleasant: *This food tastes awful!*
2 **look/feel awful** to look or feel sick

aw·ful·ly /'ɔfli/ *adverb*
very: *That poor little girl looks awfully scared.*

a·while /ə'waɪl/ *adverb*
for a short period of time: *Sit down awhile and talk to me.*

awk·ward /'ɔkwərd/ *adjective*
1 not able to move your body skillfully or gracefully: *He's very awkward. He keeps dropping things.*
2 not easy to hold or use: *The cup is an awkward shape.*
3 making you feel uncomfortable or embarrassed: *an awkward silence*

ax (axe) /æks/ *noun* (*plural* **axes**)
a tool with a metal blade on a handle, used for cutting wood

ba·by /'beɪbi/ *noun* (*plural* **babies**)
a very young child —see color picture on page 191

baby car·riage /'.. ,../ *noun* (*also* **baby buggy**)
a small bed with wheels, used for pushing a baby around outdoors

ba·by·sit /'beɪbi,sɪt/ *verb* (**babysitting, babysat**)
to care for a child while his or her parents are away

ba·by·sit·ter /'beɪbi,sɪtɚ/ *noun*
someone who is paid to BABYSIT a child

bach·e·lor /'bætʃələ, 'bætʃlɚ/ *noun*
a man who is not married

back¹ /bæk/ *noun*
1 the part of your body that is behind you and goes from your neck to your legs: *I lay on my back, gazing up at the clouds. | Jo said that her back is aching.*
2 the part of something that is farthest from the front: *It's O.K. to write on the back of your paper. | There's a pool in back of* (=behind) *our house.* ≫ compare FRONT¹
3 behind someone's back if you do something behind someone's back, you do it without them knowing and without their approval: *You shouldn't talk about Helen behind her back.*
4 be on someone's back to keep telling someone to do something in a way that is annoying: *Dad's been on my back all day about washing the car.*
5 turn your back on someone to refuse to help or be friendly with someone: *Now that he's famous he's turned his back on his friends.*

back² *adverb*
1 in the direction that is behind you: *She looked back to see if Tom was still there.*
2 to the place where something or someone was before: *Put the book back on the shelf when you've finished it. | I'll be back in an hour.*
3 in reply: *Call me back when you can.*
4 away from the front of something: *Stand back from the fire.*

5 back and forth in one direction, then in the other direction: *He kept walking back and forth across the floor.*

back³ *verb*
1 (*also* **back up** *or* **back off**) to move in the direction that is behind you or to make a vehicle do this: *She backed the car into the street. | I ran up to him, but he didn't back off.*
2 back down to accept that you were wrong about something
3 back someone up to support someone by agreeing that what they say is true
4 back out of something to decide not to do something that you had agreed to do

back⁴ *adjective*
in the back or behind something: *the back door* ≫ opposite FRONT²

back·bone /'bækboʊn/ *noun*
the line of bones going from your neck to your bottom

back·ground /'bækgraʊnd/ *noun*
1 the type of education, family etc. that you have: *Tell me something about your background. | a middle-class background*
2 [U] the area that is behind the main objects or people in a picture: *Here's a picture of Mary with our house in the background.*
3 the facts or events that have led to a particular situation: *The peace talks are taking place against a background of violence.*

back·pack /'bækpæk/ *noun*
a bag that you carry on your back —see picture at BAG and see color picture on page 188

back·up /'bækʌp/ *noun*
a copy of something that can be used if the first one is lost or damaged: *You should make a backup of your files.*

back·ward¹ /'bækwɚd/ *adverb* (*also* **backwards**)
1 in the direction that is behind you: *He took two steps backward.* ≫ compare FORWARD¹
2 starting at the end; in the opposite way to what is usual. For example, if you count backward from 5, you say "5, 4, 3, 2, 1, 0."
3 with the back part in front: *He has his T-shirt on backward.*

backward² *adjective*
1 in the direction that is behind you: *a backward glance* ≫ compare FORWARD²
2 slow to learn things or to develop

back·yard /,bæk'yɑrd/ *noun*
the area of land behind a house

ba·con /ˈbeɪkən/ *noun* [U]
meat from the back or sides of a pig, that has been salted or smoked ≫ compare HAM

bac·te·ri·a /bækˈtɪriə/ *plural noun*
living things that are so small that you cannot see them, but which can make you sick

bad /bæd/ *adjective* (**worse, worst**)
1 not good or not nice: *I'm afraid I have some bad news.* | *The weather is very bad for June.* ≫ compare GOOD¹
2 not able to do something well: *I'm bad at tennis.* | *a bad driver*
3 serious or severe: *a very bad cold*
4 not good to eat: *The milk has gone bad.*
5 be bad for someone to cause harm to someone: *Smoking is bad for you.*
6 too bad used to say you are sorry that something unpleasant has happened: *It's too bad Calvin can't come with us.*
7 feel bad to feel sorry or ashamed about something: *I feel really bad about forgetting your birthday.*
8 not bad used to say that you think something is good or acceptable

badge /bædʒ/ *noun*
a small object that you wear on your clothes, often showing your name, job etc.

badg·er /ˈbædʒɚ/ *noun*
a wild animal with black and white fur that lives in a hole

bad·ly /ˈbædli/ *adverb* (**worse, worst**)
1 in a way that is not satisfactory or successful: *She sings very badly.*
2 very much: *He wanted very badly to be a success.*
3 severely or seriously: *She was badly hurt in the accident.*

bag

grocery bag

backpack

sports bag

bag /bæg/ *noun*
a container made of cloth, paper, plastic, or leather that opens at the top, used for carrying things

bag·el /ˈbeɪgəl/ *noun*
a type of bread that is shaped like a ring —see picture at BREAD

bag·gage /ˈbægɪdʒ/ *noun* [U]
all the bags that you take with you when you travel ≫ compare LUGGAGE

bag·gy /ˈbægi/ *adjective* (**baggier, baggiest**)
baggy clothes fit very loosely

bait /beɪt/ *noun* [U]
food that you use to attract fish or animals so that you can catch them

bake /beɪk/ *verb* (**baking, baked**)
to cook food in an OVEN, using dry heat: *I'm baking a cake.*

bak·er /ˈbeɪkɚ/ *noun*
someone whose job is making bread and cakes

bak·er·y /ˈbeɪkəri/ *noun* (*plural* **bakeries**)
a place where bread and cakes are made or sold —see color picture on page 193

bal·ance¹ /ˈbæləns/ *verb* (**balancing, balanced**)
1 to keep yourself or something else steady, without falling to one side or the other —see color picture on page 189
2 to give equal importance to two things: *It is difficult to balance the time I spend at home and work.*

balance² *noun* [U]
1 the ability to stay steady without falling to one side or the other: *I lost my balance and fell down.*
2 when two things have the same importance

bal·co·ny /ˈbælkəni/ *noun* (*plural* **balconies**)
1 a place above the ground on the outside of a building where people can sit
2 the seats upstairs in a theater

bald /bɔld/ *adjective*
bald people do not have any hair on their head —see color picture on page 191

ball /bɔl/ *noun*
1 a round object that you throw, kick, or hit in some games
2 an object with a round shape: *ball of wool*
3 a large important party at which people dance
4 be on the ball to be able to think or act quickly: *You really need to be on the ball when the teacher asks a question.*

bal·let /bæ'leɪ, 'bæleɪ/ *noun*
a performance in which a story is told using dancing and music

bal·loon /bə'lun/ *noun*
a small rubber bag that can be filled with air or gas so that it floats

bal·lot /'bælət/ *noun*
a piece of paper that is used for voting

ball·point pen /ˌbɔlpɔɪnt 'pɛn/ *noun*
a pen with a very small metal ball at the end that rolls ink onto the paper

bam·boo /ˌbæm'buˑ/ *noun* [U]
a tall hard grass with hollow stems, often used for making furniture

ban¹ /bæn/ *verb* (**banning, banned**)
to say officially that something must not be done: *Smoking is banned in school.* ≫ compare FORBID

ban² *noun*
an official order which says you must not do a particular thing: *There is a ban on having dogs in the park.*

ba·nan·a /bə'nænə/ *noun*
a long curved fruit with a yellow skin —see picture at FRUIT

band /bænd/ *noun*
1 a narrow piece of material used for holding things together: *Put a rubber band around these papers.*
2 a group of people who play music together: *We want to form our own band.*
3 a group of people who are together for a particular purpose: *a band of thieves*

ban·dage¹ /'bændɪdʒ/ *noun*
a long piece of cloth that is tied on to your body to cover a wound

bandage² *verb* (**bandaging, bandaged**)
to tie a BANDAGE on a part of someone's body

Band-Aid /'bænd eɪd/ (*trademark*) *noun*
a thin piece of material that you put on your skin to cover a wound

ban·dit /'bændɪt/ *noun*
someone who robs or attacks people

bang¹ /bæŋ/ *noun*
1 a loud noise like the noise made by a gun: *The door slammed shut with a bang.*
2 when you knock or hit yourself against something: *a bang on the head*

bang² *verb*
1 to make a loud noise, usually by hitting something hard: *He banged his fist on the table.*
2 to hurt a part of your body by hitting it against something: *Joe banged his head on the car door.*

bangs /bæŋz/ *plural noun*
hair that is cut straight across your FOREHEAD
—see picture at HAIRSTYLE

bank¹ /bæŋk/ *noun*
1 a business that keeps your money safe or lends money to you etc., or the building this business is in —see color picture on page 193
2 the raised land along the side of a lake or river

bank² *verb*
1 to put money in a bank: *Where do you bank?*
2 bank on someone or something to depend on someone or something: *We're banking on you to help us.*

bank·er /'bæŋkɚ/ *noun*
someone who has an important job in a bank

bank·ing /'bæŋkɪŋ/ *noun* [U]
the business done by a bank

bank·rupt /'bæŋkrʌpt/ *adjective*
not able to pay the money that you owe

ban·ner /'bænɚ/ *noun*
a long piece of cloth on which something is written

ban·quet /'bæŋkwɪt/ *noun*
a formal meal for a lot of people on a special occasion

bap·tis·m /'bæptɪzəm/ *noun*
a CHRISTIAN religious ceremony in which someone is touched or covered with water to become a member of a church

bap·tize /'bæptaɪz, bæp'taɪz/ *verb* (**baptizing, baptized**)
to perform a BAPTISM: *Many people have been baptized in church in a ceremony performed by the local priest.*

bar

a candy bar   prison bars

bar¹ /bɑr/ *noun*
1 a place where people go to buy and drink alcohol
2 a solid piece of something, longer than it is wide: *a bar of soap*
3 a long piece of wood or metal across a window or door to stop people from going in or out
4 **behind bars** in prison

bar² *verb* (**barring, barred**)
1 to officially stop someone from doing something or something from happening: *After testing positive, he was barred from the sport for a year.*
2 to put a bar across a window or door to stop people from going in or out: *She barred the door and called the police.*

bar·be·cue /'bɑrbɪ,kyu/ *noun*
1 a meal that is cooked and eaten outside
2 a metal frame for cooking food outside over a fire

barbed wire /,bɑrbd 'waɪər/ *noun* [U]
wire with short sharp points in it: *a barbed wire fence*

bar·ber /'bɑrbər/ *noun*
a person whose job is to cut men's hair

bare /bɛr/ *adjective*
1 not covered by clothing: *Don't let the baby walk around in her bare feet.* (=without shoes and socks)
2 empty: *a bare room* (=a room with no furniture)
3 without any decoration: *bare white walls*

bare·foot /'bɛrfʊt/ *adjective, adverb*
not wearing any shoes or socks

bare·ly /'bɛrli/ *adverb*
just; almost not: *He had barely enough money to buy food.* >> compare HARDLY

bar·gain¹ /'bɑrgən/ *noun*
1 something that you buy for less than it usually costs: *These shoes are a bargain at only $10.*

2 an agreement to do something in return for something else

bargain² *verb*
to discuss the price of something, especially something that you are buying or selling

barge /bɑrdʒ/ *noun*
a large boat with a flat bottom, used for carrying things

bark¹ /bɑrk/ *verb*
if a dog barks, it makes a short loud sound

bark² *noun*
1 [U] the hard skin that covers the outside of a tree
2 the short loud sound a dog makes

bar·ley /'bɑrli/ *noun* [U]
a type of grass that is used for making food, beer, and some other drinks

barn /bɑrn/ *noun*
a large building on a farm in which animals and crops are kept

bar·racks /'bærɪks/ *plural noun*
a group of buildings in which soldiers live

bar·rel /'bærəl/ *noun*
1 a large round container with flat ends, in which oil, beer etc. is kept
2 the part of a gun that is a long metal tube

bar·ri·er /'bæriər/ *noun*
1 a fence or wall that stops people from going through a place: *The police put a barrier across the road.*
2 something such as a rule or problem that stops you from doing something

bar·tend·er /'bɑr,tɛndər/ *noun*
someone whose job is to make and serve drinks in a BAR¹ (1)

base¹ /beɪs/ *noun*
1 the bottom of something or the part something stands on: *We walked to the base of the cliff.*
2 the main place where the work of a company is done: *The company's manufacturing base is in Illinois.*
3 a place where people in a military organization live and work: *the naval base in San Diego*

base² *verb* (**basing, based**)
1 **base something on something** to develop something by using something else as the reason or starting point: *The movie is based on his earlier book.*
2 **be based somewhere** to have your main

home, company etc. in a particular place: *We're based in the city, but we spend a lot of time in the country.*

baseball

base·ball /'beɪsbɔl/ *noun*
a ball game in which two teams of nine players try to get points by hitting a ball with a round stick and then running around a specially shaped field, or the ball used in this game —see color picture on page 184

base·ment /'beɪsmənt/ *noun*
a part of a house or building that is below the level of the ground ≫ compare CELLAR

bas·es /'beɪsiz/ *noun*
the plural of the word BASIS

ba·sic /'beɪsɪk/ *adjective*
simple and forming the main or most important part of something: *People need basic skills such as reading and writing.*

ba·si·cal·ly /'beɪsɪkli/ *adverb*
said when giving the most important reason or fact about something, or an explanation of it: *Well, basically, we have to paint the wall again.*

ba·sin /'beɪsən/ *noun*
a large round bowl

ba·sis /'beɪsɪs/ *noun (plural* **bases***)*
1 the most important part of something, from which something else develops: *These ideas formed the basis of the plan.*
2 the way something is done, organized, or regularly happens: *We still meet for lunch on a fairly regular basis.*
3 on the basis of something because of a particular fact or reason: *The company hires people on the basis of experience.*

bas·ket /'bæskɪt/ *noun*
a container made of thin pieces of wood, wire etc., used for carrying things —see picture at NET

bas·ket·ball /'bæskɪt,bɔl/ *noun*
a game in which two teams try to throw a ball through a round net which is high above the ground, or the ball used in this game —see color picture on pages 184 and 185

bat¹ /bæt/ *noun*
1 a long piece of wood used for hitting the ball in baseball
2 a small animal with wings that flies at night and hangs upside down when it sleeps

bat² *verb (***batting, batted***)*
to hit a ball with a bat

batch /bætʃ/ *noun (plural* **batches***)*
a number of people or things that you deal with together: *I have a batch of papers to grade.*

bath /bæθ/ *noun (plural* **baths** /bæðz, bæθs/*)*
an act of washing yourself in a bathtub: *I take a bath every day.*

bathe /beɪð/ *verb (***bathing, bathed***)*
to wash your whole body in water

bath·ing suit /'beɪðɪŋ,sut/ *noun*
a piece of clothing that you wear when you swim

bath·robe /'bæθroʊb/ *noun*
a type of loose coat that you put on after you have had a bath

bath·room /'bæθrum, -rʊm/ *noun*
a room in a house where people wash their bodies and use the toilet —see color picture on page 186

bath·tub /'bæθtʌb/ *noun*
a large container that you fill with water and sit in to wash your body

bat·ter¹ /'bæṭɚ/ *noun*
a mixture of flour, eggs, milk etc., used for making cakes

batter² *verb*
to hit someone or something hard many times

bat·ter·y /'bæṭəri/ *noun (plural* **batteries***)*
an object that provides electricity for a radio, car etc.

bat·tle /'bæṭl/ *noun*
1 a fight between two armies, or groups of ships or planes ≫ compare WAR
2 a situation in which people are arguing or competing with each other, or struggling against something: *her battle against cancer*

bay /beɪ/ *noun*
a part of the ocean that is enclosed by a curve in the land

B.C. /ˌbi ˈsi/

Before Christ; used in dates to show how many years before the birth of Christ it happened: *It was built in 2000 B.C.* » compare A.D.

---

be /bi/ *verb*

present tense

singular	plural
I am (I'm)	We are (We're)
You are (You're)	You are (You're)
He/She/It is	They are
(He's/She's/It's)	(They're)

past tense

singular	plural
I was	We were
You were	You were
He/She/It was	They were

present participle	being
past participle	been
negative short	aren't, isn't,
forms	wasn't, weren't

(you can find each of these words in its own place in the dictionary)

1 used to describe people or things, or give information about them: *The baby's name is Peter.* | *My mother is a teacher.* | *I'm (=I am) very happy.*

2 used with the -ing form of other verbs to show that something is happening now: *What are you doing?* | *I am painting a picture.*

3 used with other verbs to show that something happens to a person or thing: *He was bitten by a dog.* | *The house was built 50 years ago.*

4 used with other verbs to show what you expect to happen in the future or what must happen: *We have to be at the airport by six.* | *I will be leaving tomorrow.*

5 there is (*plural* there are) used for saying that someone or something exists, or to say where they are: *Look, there's (=there is) Sue!* | *How many children are there in your class?*

---

beach /bitʃ/ *noun* (*plural* **beaches**)

an area covered in sand or stones next to an ocean or lake

bead /bid/ *noun*

1 a small ball of glass, wood etc., used for making jewelry

2 a small drop of liquid: *There were beads of sweat on his forehead.*

beak /bik/ *noun*

the hard pointed mouth of a bird

beam /bim/ *noun*

1 a line of light shining from a bright object: *A beam of light shone through the window.*

2 a long heavy piece of wood or metal used in building houses

bean /bin/ *noun*

1 a seed or seed container of a plant that you eat: *green beans* —see picture at VEGETABLE

2 a seed of a plant used for making food or drink: *coffee beans*

bear¹ /ber/ *verb* (*past tense* **bore**, *past participle* **borne**)

1 to support the weight of something: *That chair cannot bear your weight.*

2 to carry something or someone somewhere

3 to accept or deal with something bad without complaining: *The pain was almost too much to bear.*

4 to be responsible for something, or to accept the blame for something: *The President must bear some of the responsibility for this disaster.*

5 can't bear someone or something to dislike someone or something very much: *I can't bear people who complain all the time.*

bear² *noun*

a large strong wild animal with thick fur —see color picture on page 183

beard /bɪrd/ *noun*

hair that grows on a man's chin » compare MUSTACHE —see picture at MUSTACHE and see color picture on page 191

beast /bist/ *noun*

a wild and dangerous animal

beat¹ /bit/ *verb* (*past tense* **beat**, *past participle* **beaten**)

1 to defeat someone in a game, or to do better than them: *The Broncos beat the Cowboys 17–10.*

2 to hit someone or something many times: *In the old days, children could be beaten at school.*

3 to make a regular sound or movement: *Her heart was beating too fast.*

4 to hit against something continuously: *Huge waves kept beating against the cliff.*

beat² *noun*

one of a series of regular sounds or movements: *I could feel every beat of my heart.*

beau·ti·cian /byu'tɪʃən/ *noun*
someone who gives beauty treatments to your face and body

beau·ti·ful /'byuṭəfəl/ *adjective*
1 very attractive and nice to look at: *Marilyn was such a beautiful woman.* ≫ compare HANDSOME
2 very good: *What a beautiful day!*

> NOTE: The adjectives **beautiful** and **pretty** can be used to describe women, children and things, but they are never used to describe men. A man who is nice to look at can be described as **handsome**.

beau·ti·ful·ly /'byuṭəfli/ *adverb*
very well; in a way that looks or sounds good: *She plays the piano beautifully.*

beau·ty /'byuṭi/ *noun* [U]
the quality of being beautiful: *I admire the beauty **of** Bach's music.*

bea·ver /'bivəʳ/ *noun*
an animal with thick fur, a flat tail, and sharp teeth that it uses to cut down trees

be·came /bɪ'keɪm/
the PAST TENSE of the verb **become**

be·cause /bɪ'kɔz, -'kʌz/
1 for the reason that: *I missed the bus because I was late.*
2 because of something for this reason: *We stayed at home because of the rain.*

be·come /bɪ'kʌm/ *verb* (**becoming, became**)
1 to begin to be something: *Prince Edward became king when his father died.* | *The days are becoming warmer.*
2 whatever became of ...? used when asking what has happened to someone or something: *Whatever became of your friend in Australia?*

bed /bɛd/ *noun*
1 a piece of furniture on which you sleep: *a double bed* | *What time did you **go to** bed last night?* (=go to your bed to sleep)
2 the ground at the bottom of a river or ocean
3 make the bed to arrange the covers on a bed so that they look nice and neat
4 go to bed with someone to have sex with someone

bed·ding /'bɛdɪŋ/ *noun* [U]
the covers that you put on a bed to keep you warm

bed
single bed   double bed
bunk beds   crib

bed·room /'bɛdrum, -rʊm/ *noun*
a room with a bed where you sleep —see color picture on page 186

bed·spread /'bɛdsprɛd/ *noun*
an attractive cloth cover for a bed

bed·time /'bɛdtaɪm/ *noun*
the time when you usually go to bed to sleep

bee /bi/ *noun*
a flying insect that makes HONEY, and can sting you

beef /bif/ *noun* [U]
the meat from a cow

bee·hive /'bihaɪv/ (*also* **hive**) *noun*
a place where BEEs are kept

been /bɪn/ *verb*
1 the PAST PARTICIPLE of the verb **be**: *It has been very cold this week.*
2 have been somewhere to have visited a place and come back from it: *Have you ever been to Oregon?*

beep·er /'bipəʳ/ *noun*
a small machine that you can carry that makes a sound when someone telephones you

beer /bɪr/ *noun*
an alcoholic drink made from grain, or a bottle of this drink: *Can I have two beers, please?*

beet /bit/ *noun*
a round red vegetable that grows under the ground

bee·tle /ˈbiːtl/ *noun*
an insect whose outside wings make a hard cover for its body

be·fore¹ /bɪˈfɔr/ *preposition*
1 earlier than: *You have to leave before 8 o'clock.* | *She arrived before I did.* ⟫ compare AFTER
2 ahead of someone or something: *They called out Pat's name before mine.*
3 in front of someone or something: *He will be appearing before the Senate committee later this month.*

> NOTE: **Before** means "earlier than something else," e.g. *She left before I arrived.* | *Brush your teeth before you go to bed.* **Ago** means "in the past." Look at these sentences: *We went to Florida 3 years ago. Our second visit to New York was in 1998, and our first visit was 3 years before (=in 1995).* | *It happened many years ago. It happened before the war.*

before² *adverb*
at some earlier time: *I have never seen you before.* (=this is the first time I have seen you) ⟫ compare AFTER

be·fore·hand /bɪˈfɔrˌhænd/ *adverb*
before something else happens: *She knew I was coming, because I called her beforehand.*

beg /bɛg/ *verb* (begging, begged)
1 to ask someone for money or food because you are poor
2 to ask someone very strongly for something: *Joe can beg for forgiveness as much as he likes, because I'm never going to see him again.* | *I begged her to stay, but she wouldn't.*
3 I beg your pardon used when you did not hear what someone said and you want them to say it again, or when you are sorry because of something

be·gan /bɪˈgæn/
the PAST TENSE of the verb **begin**

beg·gar /ˈbɛgɚ/ *noun*
someone who asks people for money or food in order to live

be·gin /bɪˈgɪn/ *verb* (beginning, began)
1 to start: *The game begins at 2 o'clock.* | *It's beginning to rain.* ⟫ compare END²
2 to begin with used when talking about the first part of something: *I didn't like school to begin with, but now I enjoy it.*

> NOTE: Remember that the past tense is **began**, and the PAST PARTICIPLE is **begun**.

be·gin·ner /bɪˈgɪnɚ/ *noun*
someone who is starting to do or learn something: *a swimming class for beginners*

be·gin·ning /bɪˈgɪnɪŋ/ *noun*
the start: *We got married at the beginning of the year.* ⟫ compare END¹

be·gun /bɪˈgʌn/
the PAST PARTICIPLE of the verb **begin**

be·half /bɪˈhæf/ *noun*
on behalf of someone instead of someone or for someone: *I have come on behalf of my brother who can't be here.*

be·have /bɪˈheɪv/ *verb*
1 to do or say things in a particular way: *The children behaved very well.*
2 behave yourself to do things in a way that other people think is good ⟫ opposite MISBEHAVE

be·hav·ior /bɪˈheɪvyɚ/ *noun* (U)
the way someone behaves: *I need to talk to you about your behavior at school.*

be·hind /bɪˈhaɪnd/ *adverb, preposition*
1 at the back of something: *My brother went in front and I walked behind.* ⟫ compare FRONT¹ —see color picture on page 194
2 not as successful as someone or something else: *We're only four points behind.*
3 in the place where someone or something was before: *Oh, no! I left my wallet behind.*
4 supporting a person, idea etc.: *We need to get behind the President on this issue.*

beige /beɪʒ/ *noun* (U)
a very light brown color

be·ing¹ /ˈbiɪŋ/
the PRESENT PARTICIPLE of the verb **be**

being² *noun*
a person or living thing: *Men, women, and children are human beings.* | *a being from another planet*

be·lief /bəˈlif/ *noun*
1 the feeling that something is true or exists: *She has a strong belief in God.* | *religious belief*
2 an opinion or idea that you think is true: *He will never change his political beliefs.*

be·liev·a·ble /bəˈlivəbəl/ *adjective*
able to be believed: *The story in the book is very believable.* ⟫ opposite UNBELIEVABLE

be·lieve /bəˈliv/ *verb* (**believing, believed**)
1 to think that something is true: *It's hard to believe she's over 70.* | *I don't believe it!*
2 to think that someone is telling the truth: *Don't you believe me?*
3 **believe in something** to think that something exists: *Do you believe in ghosts?*
4 **believe in someone** to trust someone and think that he or she will succeed: *You just need to believe in yourself!*

be·liev·er /bəˈlivɚ/ *noun*
someone who believes that a particular idea or thing is very good

bell /bɛl/ *noun*
a hollow metal object that makes a musical sound when it is hit

bel·ly /ˈbɛli/ *noun* (*plural* **bellies**)
your stomach, the front part of your body between your chest and your waist

be·long /bɪˈlɔŋ/ *verb*
1 **belong to someone** to be owned by someone: *Who does this coat belong to?* (=who is the owner)
2 **belong to something** to be a member of a group or organization: *She belongs to the Girl Scouts.*
3 to be in the right place or situation: *Put the chair back where it belongs.*

be·long·ings /bɪˈlɔŋɪŋz/ *plural noun*
the things that you own: *Take all your belongings with you when you get off the plane.*

be·low /bɪˈloʊ/ *adverb, preposition*
1 at a lower place; lower than; under: *We stood on the bridge and dropped stones into the water below.* | *He lives in the apartment below mine.* ⫸compare ABOVE —see color picture on page 194
2 less than a particular number or amount: *It's ten degrees below zero outside!*

belt /bɛlt/ *noun*
a piece of cloth or leather that you wear around your waist —see picture at FASTENER

bench /bɛntʃ/ *noun* (*plural* **benches**)
a long seat for two or more people

bend¹ /bɛnd/ *verb* (*past tense* **bent**, *past participle* **bent**)
1 to move the top part of your body down

toward the ground: *She bent down to pick up a book.* —see color picture on page 189
2 to move something so that it is not straight: *Bend your knees a little.*

bend² *noun*
a curve in something: *a bend in the road*

be·neath /bɪˈniθ/ *preposition*
below; under: *I felt the warm sand beneath my feet.*

ben·e·fi·cial /ˌbɛnəˈfɪʃəl/ *adjective*
good or useful

ben·e·fit¹ /ˈbɛnəfɪt/ *verb*
to be useful or helpful to someone: *The plants benefited **from** (=were helped by) the rain.*

benefit² *noun*
something that helps you or gives you an advantage: *She knows **the** benefits **of** a good education.*

bent /bɛnt/
the PAST TENSE and PAST PARTICIPLE of the verb **bend**

ber·ry /ˈbɛri/ *noun* (*plural* **berries**)
a small soft fruit that grows on a bush or tree

be·side /bɪˈsaɪd/ *preposition*
next to or close to someone or something: *Come and sit beside me.* —see color picture on page 194

be·sides /bɪˈsaɪdz/ *adverb, preposition*
1 a word used when you are giving another reason or fact to support what you are saying: *I'm too tired to go out – besides, I don't have any money.*
2 in addition to something: *Besides going to school, he also has a job.*

best¹ /bɛst/ *adjective* (*the superlative of* **good**)
better than anyone or anything else: *He is the best player on our team.*

best² *adverb* (*the superlative of* **well**)
1 in a way that is better than any other: *She's the best dressed person in the room.*
2 most: *Which dress do you like best?*

best³ *noun*
1 **the best** someone or something that is better than any other: *You're the best!* | *She wants her children to have the best of everything.* (=the best things)
2 **do your best** to try as hard as you can to do something: *It doesn't matter if you didn't win – you did your best.*

best man /ˌ. '. / *noun* (*plural* **best men**)
a male friend who helps and supports a man
who is getting married ≫ compare BRIDESMAID

bet¹ /bɛt/ *verb* [**betting, bet**]
to risk money on the result of a game, race
etc.: *He bet me $5 that his team would win.*

bet² *noun*
an agreement to risk money on the result of a
game, race etc. ≫ compare GAMBLE

bet·ter¹ /'bɛtɚ/ *adjective*
1 the comparative of GOOD: *This book is better
than the other one.* | *I'm trying to get a better
job.*
2 not as sick as before: *Are you feeling better
today?*
3 be better off having more money, or a bet
ter position or job, than you had before: *I'm better off now than I've ever been.* ≫ compare
WORSE

better² *adverb*
1 the comparative of WELL¹. *He can sing much
better than me.*
2 more: *I like him better than his brother.*
3 had better do something should; ought to:
You'd (=you had) better go home now. | *I'd
(=I had) better be leaving soon.*

be·tween /bɪ'twin/ *adverb, preposition*
1 in the space in the middle of two people or
things: *There is a fence between his yard and
ours.* | *April comes between March and May.*
≫ compare AMONG —see color picture on page
194
2 in the period between one time and another:
The library is open between 9 and 5 o'clock.
3 more than one number or amount, but less
than another number or amount: *a number
between zero and a hundred*
4 used to say how things are shared or divided: *We can split the cost between us.*
5 used to show the relationship of two people,
events etc. to each other: *There is very little difference between the two companies.*
6 joining two places: *Are there any flights
between Boston and Buffalo?*

NOTE: Use **between** when you are talking
about something which is done or shared by
two people or things. Use **among** when you
are talking about something which is done
or shared by more than two people or
things: *She divided the cake between the
two children. The money was divided among
his brothers and sisters.*

be·ware /bɪ'wɛr/ *verb*
used to tell someone to be careful of
something because it is dangerous: *Beware of
the dog!*

be·yond /bɪ'yɑnd/ *adverb, preposition*
1 on or to the other side of something: *From
here you can see beyond the mountains.*
2 more than a particular number, amount of
time etc.: *There won't be any work for you
beyond next month.*

bib /bɪb/ *noun*
a piece of cloth that you tie under a baby's chin
to keep its clothes clean when it is eating

Bi·ble /'baɪbəl/ *noun*
the holy book of the Christian religion

bib·li·cal /'bɪblɪkəl/ *adjective*
from or in the Bible

bi·cy·cle /'baɪsɪkəl/ *noun*
a vehicle with two wheels that you sit on and
ride by moving your legs: *I got a new bicycle
for my birthday.* —see color picture on page
187

bid¹ /bɪd/ *verb* [**bidding, bid**]
to offer to pay a particular price for something:
He bid $50,000 for the painting.

bid² *noun*
an offer of an amount of money to buy something

big /bɪg/ *adjective* [**bigger, biggest**]
1 large in size: *They live in a big house.*
2 important, serious, or successful: *I have a
big test coming up today.* | *The song was a big
hit.* ≫ compare SMALL, LITTLE¹

bike /baɪk/ *noun*
a bicycle

bi·ki·ni /bɪ'kini/ *noun*
a piece of women's clothing in two parts that is
worn for swimming

bi·lin·gual /baɪ'lɪŋgwəl/ *adjective*
1 able to speak two languages equally well:
He's bilingual in French and German.
2 spoken or written in two languages: *I have a
bilingual dictionary.*

bill /bɪl/ *noun*
1 a piece of paper showing how much you
must pay for something: *How much is the
water bill?*
2 a plan for a new law: *The government is considering the new education bill.*
3 a piece of paper money: *a five-dollar bill*

bill·board /'bɪlbɔrd/ *noun*
a very large sign used for advertising something, usually next to a road

bil·lion /'bɪlyən/ (*plural* **billion** or **billions**)
the number 1,000,000,000

bin /bɪn/ *noun*
a large container for keeping things in

bind /baɪnd/ *verb* (*past tense* **bound**, *past participle* **bound**)
to tie someone or something with rope or string

bin·go /'bɪŋgoʊ/ *noun* [U]
a game that you win if numbers chosen by chance are the same as a line of numbers on your card

bin·oc·u·lars /bɪ'nakyələz, baɪ-/ *plural noun*
a pair of glasses that make things that are far away look bigger ≫ compare TELESCOPE

bi·og·ra·phy /baɪ'agrəfi/ *noun* (*plural* **biographies**)
a book about someone's life written by someone else ≫ compare AUTOBIOGRAPHY

bi·o·lo·gi·cal /ˌbaɪə'ladʒɪkəl/ *adjective*
relating to BIOLOGY

bi·ol·o·gy /baɪ'alədʒi/ *noun* [U]
the scientific study of living things

bird /bəd/ *noun*
an animal with wings and feathers that lays eggs and usually can fly

birth /bəθ/ *noun*
1 **give birth** to have a baby: *She gave birth to a baby boy last night.*
2 when a baby is born: *I wanted to be there for the birth of my son.*

birth con·trol /'. .,./ *noun* [U]
ways of controlling the number of children you have

birth·day /'bəθdeɪ/ *noun*
the day of the year on which someone was born: *My birthday is on January 6th.* ≫ compare ANNIVERSARY

bis·cuit /'bɪskɪt/ *noun*
a type of bread that is baked in small round pieces

bish·op /'bɪʃəp/ *noun*
a priest who is in charge of all the churches and people in a large area

bit¹ /bɪt/
the PAST TENSE of the verb **bite**

bit² *noun*
1 a small piece of something: *The floor was covered with bits of glass.*
2 **a (little) bit** slightly: *I feel a little bit tired tonight.*
3 **for a bit** for a short time: *Why don't you lie down for a bit?*
4 **bit by bit** slowly, a little at a time: *Bit by bit they discovered the truth.*
5 **quite a bit** a large amount: *He's willing to pay quite a bit for the car.*

bite¹ /baɪt/ *verb* (**biting**, *past tense* **bit**, *past participle* **bitten**)
to cut or injure something with your teeth: *He bit into the apple.* | *Does your dog bite?*

bite² *noun*
1 an act of biting something: *Do you want a bite of my cake?*
2 a wound made by biting: *She was covered in insect bites.*

bit·ten /'bɪt̚n/
the PAST PARTICIPLE of the verb **bite**

bit·ter /'bɪtə/ *adjective*
1 having a very sour taste: *The coffee was a little bitter.*
2 very angry: *We had a bitter argument.*
3 very cold: *There's a bitter wind tonight.*

black¹ /blæk/ *adjective*
1 of the color of the sky at night, darker than any other color: *She was wearing a black dress.*
2 having dark-colored skin: *Most of the people who live here are black.*
3 black coffee or tea has no milk in it: *I'd like my coffee black.*
4 **black and blue** having dark marks on your skin as a result of being hurt: *Her arm was black and blue after the accident.*
5 **black and white** containing only the colors black, white, and gray: *an old black and white movie* | *a black and white photo*
6 **a black eye** an eye surrounded by dark marks as a result of being hit: *He gave the other boy a black eye.*

black² *noun*
1 [U] a black color: *He was dressed in black.*
2 someone with dark-colored skin

black·ber·ry /'blæk,bɛri/ *noun* (*plural* **blackberries**)
a small dark sweet fruit that grows on bushes —see picture at FRUIT

black·bird /'blækbəd/ *noun*
a bird that is common in America and Europe. The male is black and has a yellow beak.

black·board /'blækbɔrd/ *noun*
a dark board on the wall in a school, on which the teacher writes

black·smith /'blæksmɪθ/ *noun*
someone who makes things out of iron, especially shoes for horses

blade /bleɪd/ *noun*
1 a flat sharp edge of something such as a knife or tool, that is used for cutting: *The blade of a knife needs to be sharp.*
2 a long flat leaf of grass

blame¹ /bleɪm/ *verb* (blaming, blamed)
to say that someone is the cause of something bad. *The police blamed Larry for causing the accident.* | *Don't try to blame this on me!*

blame² *noun* [U]
when someone is the cause of a mistake or something bad

blank /blæŋk/ *adjective*
1 without any writing or sounds on it: *You will need a blank piece of paper for this.* | *Do you have a blank tape?*
2 not showing any expression or interest: *She looked at him with a blank face.*

blan·ket /'blæŋkɪt/ *noun*
a thick heavy cover that keeps you warm in bed

blast¹ /blæst/ *noun*
1 an explosion: *Ten people were killed in the blast.*
2 a sudden strong movement of wind or air: *A blast of wind blew the door open.*
3 a sudden very loud noise: *I heard the blast of a trumpet.*
4 **full blast** as loudly or as fast as possible: *The television was on full blast.*

blast² *verb*
1 to break something into pieces by causing an explosion: *They blasted through the rock.*
2 to make a lot of loud noise: *I can't hear anything with that music blasting.*
3 **blast off** to leave the ground at the beginning of a space flight

blast-off /'. ./ *noun*
the moment when a SPACECRAFT leaves the ground

blaze¹ /bleɪz/ *noun*
1 a very large bright fire: *The small fire soon became a blaze.*
2 a very bright light or color: *The flowers were a blaze of color.*

blaze² *verb* (blazing, blazed)
to burn or shine strongly and brightly: *The fire was blazing through the house.*

blaz·er /'bleɪzɚ/ *noun*
a short coat, without matching pants

bleach¹ /blitʃ/ *verb*
to make something white or lighter in color: *Did you bleach your hair?*

bleach² *noun* [U]
a chemical liquid or powder used to make things clean or lighter in color

bleak /blik/ *adjective*
1 not cheerful or hopeful: *Without a job, Jim's future looks bleak.*
2 unpleasantly cold. *It was a bleak winter's day.*

bleed /blid/ *verb* (past tense **blod**, past participle **bled**)
to lose blood, especially from a wound or injury: *His nose was bleeding.*

blend¹ /blɛnd/ *verb*
1 to mix things together: *Blend the sugar and eggs together.*
2 to look attractive or pleasant together: *The colors in the room blend nicely.*

blend² *noun*
a mixture of things together

blend·er /'blɛndɚ/ *noun*
a small machine used for mixing foods or liquids together

bless /blɛs/ *verb* (past tense or past participle **blessed** or **blest**)
1 **Bless you!** something you say to someone when they SNEEZE
2 to ask for God's favor or protection for something: *The priest blessed the bread and wine.*

blew /blu/
the PAST TENSE of the verb **blow**

blind¹ /blaɪnd/ *adjective*
not able to see: *She was born blind.*

blind² *noun*
a piece of material that you can pull down to cover a window ≫ compare CURTAIN

blind·fold¹ /'blaɪndfoʊld/ *verb*
to cover someone's eyes with a cloth so that he or she cannot see

blindfold² *noun*
a piece of cloth used for covering someone's eyes so that he or she cannot see

blink /blɪŋk/ *verb*
to open and close your eyes quickly: *The bright light made him blink.* ≫ compare WINK

blis·ter /'blɪstɚ/ *noun*
a raised area of skin, filled with liquid, usually caused by rubbing or burning: *My new shoes were giving me blisters.*

bliz·zard /'blɪzɚd/ *noun*
a very bad storm with a lot of snow and wind ≫ compare HURRICANE

blob /blɑb/ *noun*
a drop of thick liquid: *He left blobs of paint on the floor.*

block¹ /blɑk/ *noun*
1 a solid piece of wood, stone etc. with straight sides: *The wall was built out of stone blocks.*
2 the distance along a street from where one street crosses it to the next: *We live two blocks from the store.*
3 something that stops things moving through or along something else: *a road block*

block² *verb*
1 to stop someone or something from moving through a place: *A car was blocking the road.*
2 to stop something from happening or succeeding

blond /blɑnd/ *adjective*
blond hair is light yellow in color

blonde /blɑnd/ *noun, informal*
a woman with BLOND hair

blood /blʌd/ *noun* [U]
the red liquid that flows through your body

blood·y /'blʌdi/ *adjective* (**bloodier, bloodiest**)
covered in blood, or involving injuries where you are losing blood: *I have a bloody nose.*

bloom¹ /blum/ *noun*
1 a flower
2 **in (full) bloom** having a lot of open flowers: *The roses are in full bloom.*

bloom² *verb*
to open out into flowers: *Lilacs bloom in the spring.*

blos·som /'blɑsəm/ *noun*
a flower on a tree or bush

blot¹ /blɑt/ *verb* (**blotting, blotted**)
to press paper or cloth onto a wet spot to dry it

blot² *noun*
a dirty mark made by a drop of liquid: *an ink blot*

blouse /blaʊs/ *noun*
a shirt for women or girls —see color picture on page 190

blow¹ /bloʊ/ *verb* (*past tense* **blew**, *past participle* **blown**)
1 to send out air through your mouth: *She blew on her soup to cool it.*
2 to move something using the force of moving air: *The wind blew his hat off.*
3 if the wind blows, it moves and makes a noise: *The wind was blowing all night.*
4 to send air into something so that it makes a sound: *The guard blew his whistle to call for help.*
5 **blow it** *spoken* to not succeed in something because you make a mistake: *I had a chance to win, but I blew it!*
6 **blow something out** to stop a flame burning by using a movement of air: *Blow out the candles on your birthday cake!*
7 **blow something up** (a) to destroy something with an explosion: *The bridge was blown up in the war.* (b) to fill something with air: *Can you help me blow up the balloons?*
8 **blow your nose** to clean your nose by making air go through it

blow² *noun*
1 a hard hit with your hand or a weapon: *He received a blow on the head.*
2 an event that makes you unhappy or shocks you: *The news of her death was a terrible blow to us all.*

blown /bloʊn/
the PAST PARTICIPLE of the verb **blow**

blue /blu/ *adjective, noun* [U]
the color of the sky when there are no clouds: *She has blue eyes.* | *a blue shirt*

bluff /blʌf/ *verb*
to pretend that you know more about something than you really do: *He said he knew all about computers, but I think he was bluffing.*

blunt /blʌnt/ *adjective*
not sharp or pointed: *The knife is too blunt to cut anything.* —see picture at SHARP

blush /blʌʃ/ *verb*
to become red in the face because you feel shame or EMBARRASSMENT

board¹ /bɔrd/ *noun*
1 a long thin flat piece of wood used for building something

2 a flat surface used for a special purpose: *Put this notice up on the board.* | *a chess board* (=for playing CHESS on)

3 a group of people who make rules and important decisions for a school, company etc.

4 on board on a ship, plane, train etc.: *Is everyone on board?*

board² *verb*
1 to get onto a ship, plane, train etc.: *Passengers should board the train now.*
2 board something up to cover a window or door with wooden boards

board·ing school /ˈ.. .,/ *noun*
a school where students live as well as study

boast /boʊst/ *verb*
to talk too proudly about yourself: *He boasted about his wealth.*

boast·ful /boʊstfəl/ *adjective*
speaking too proudly about yourself

boat /boʊt/ *noun*
a small ship: *He owns a small fishing boat.*
—see color picture on page 187

bob /bɑb/ *verb* (**bobbing, bobbed**)
to move quickly up and down, especially on water: *The boat bobbed up and down on the lake.*

bod·y /ˈbɑdi/ *noun* (*plural* **bodies**)
1 the whole of a person or animal: *I want to have a strong healthy body.*
2 the main part of a person or animal, not the head, arms, or legs: *She has a short body and long legs.*
3 a dead person or animal: *Her body was found in the woods.*

boil /bɔɪl/ *verb*
1 to make a liquid so hot that it starts to produce BUBBLEs and steam: *Boil some water for the coffee.*
2 to cook food in boiling water: *Boil the eggs for four minutes.*

bold /boʊld/ *adjective*
not afraid to do dangerous things; confident: *He made a bold attempt to catch the robber.*

bolt¹ /boʊlt/ *noun*
1 a piece of metal or wood used for keeping a door closed
2 a screw with no point which fastens into a NUT and holds two things together

bolt² *verb*
1 to close a door with a bolt
2 to run away suddenly: *The horse bolted and threw its rider to the ground.*

bomb¹ /bɑm/ *noun*
a container full of a substance that will explode, used as a weapon: *The group placed a bomb in the town's main railway station.* | *a nuclear bomb*

bomb² *verb*
to drop bombs on a place: *The airforce bombed the capital city.*

bone /boʊn/ *noun*
one of the hard parts in the body of a person or animal: *He fell and broke a bone in his leg.*

bon·fire /ˈbɑn,faɪɚ/ *noun*
a big outdoor fire

bon·net /ˈbɑnɪt/ *noun*
a soft hat that you tie under your chin

bon·y /ˈboʊni/ *adjective* (**bonier, boniest**)
very thin, so that you can see the bones: *He had long bony fingers.*

boo¹ /bu/ *verb*
to shout "boo" at someone, especially to show that you did not like a performance

boo² *noun*
1 a noise made by people who did not like a performance, person etc.: *There were boos from the audience.*
2 a word you shout when you want to surprise someone who does not know that you are there

book¹ /bʊk/ *noun*
1 a set of sheets of paper fastened together, with writing on them that you read: *What book are you reading?* | *school books* —see color picture on page 185
2 a set of sheets of paper held together for writing on: *Write this in your exercise book.* (=a book you do schoolwork in)

book² *verb*
1 to arrange to have something such as a ticket for an event or a room in a hotel kept for you, so that you can use it later: *I've booked tickets for tomorrow night's show.*
2 to ARREST someone

book·case /ˈbʊk-keɪs/ *noun*
a piece of furniture with shelves for books

book·store /ˈbʊkstɔr/ *noun*
a store that sells books —see color picture on page 193

boom /bum/ *noun*
a loud, deep sound

boot /but/ *noun*

a shoe that covers your foot and sometimes the lower part of your leg —see color picture on page 190

booth /buθ/ *noun*

a small place where one person can do something: *a phone booth*

bor·der /'bɔrdɚ/ *noun*

1 an edge: *white plates with a blue border*
2 the dividing line between two countries

bore¹ /bɔr/ *verb* (**boring, bored**)

1 to make someone feel uninterested, especially by talking too much: *He bored me all evening with his vacation photos.*
2 to make a deep round hole in a hard surface: *This machine can bore through solid rock.*

bore² *noun*

an uninteresting person or thing

bore³

the PAST TENSE of the verb **bear**

bored /bɔrd/ *adjective*

feeling tired and uninterested: *She was getting bored with her job.* ≫ compare FED UP

bor·ing /'bɔrɪŋ/ *adjective*

not interesting; dull: *It was such a boring book that I didn't finish it.* ≫ compare INTERESTING

NOTE: Do not confuse the adjectives **boring** and **bored**. If something is **boring**, it is not interesting, e.g. *a boring class.* **Bored** is used to describe the way you feel when something is boring: *The kids were bored with the game and did not want to play any more.*

born /bɔrn/ *adjective*

be born to come out of your mother's body or an egg: *I was born in Canada in 1976.*

borne /bɔrn/

the PAST PARTICIPLE of the verb **bear**

bor·row /'barou, 'bɔrou/ *verb*

to use something which belongs to someone else for a short time and then give it back to him or her: *Can I borrow your bicycle?* ≫ compare LEND

NOTE: Compare the verbs **borrow** and **lend**. If you lend something to a person, you let them use it for a while. If you borrow something from someone, you take it from

them, knowing that you will give it back to them later. The verb **lend** often has two objects (to lend **sth** to **sb**) but **borrow** just has one (to borrow **sth**): *Will you lend me some money? Can I borrow some money?*

boss¹ /bɔs/ *noun* (*plural* **bosses**)

a person who is in charge and tells other people what work to do

boss² *verb*

boss someone around to tell someone what to do in an annoying way: *My brother's always bossing me about.*

boss·y /'bɔsi/ *adjective* (**bossier, bossiest**)

always telling other people what to do in a way that is annoying: *My older sister's really bossy.*

bot·a·ny /'batⁿn-i/ *noun* [U]

the scientific study of plants

both /bouθ/

used to talk about two people or things together: *Hold the dish with both hands.* | *We both like dancing.*

both·er¹ /'baðɚ/ *verb*

1 to interrupt someone and annoy him or her: *Don't bother your father now — he's very busy.*
2 to worry someone: *I always know when something is bothering him.*
3 to make the effort to do something: *He didn't even bother to say "Thank you".* | *I'll never get the job, so why bother?*

bother² *noun*

something that annoys or upsets you

bot·tle¹ /'batl/ *noun*

a tall round glass or plastic container, with a narrow top ≫ compare JAR —see picture at CONTAINER

bottle² *verb*

to put a liquid into a bottle: *This is where they bottle the milk.* | *bottled water*

bot·tom /'batəm/ *noun*

1 the lowest part of something: *Look at the bottom of the page.* ≫ compare TOP
2 the flat surface on the lowest side of something: *The price is on the bottom of the box.*
3 the lowest position in a class, company etc.: *He's always at the bottom of the class.*
4 the part of your body that you sit on: *He fell on his bottom.*

bought /bɔt/

the PAST TENSE and PAST PARTICIPLE of the verb **buy**

boul·der /'boʊldɚ/ *noun*
a large rock

bounce /baʊns/
verb (**bouncing, bounced**)
1 to throw something against something else, so that it hits it and comes back: *He is bouncing the ball against the wall.* —see color picture on page 189

2 to move up and down because you are jumping or walking on something: *Stop bouncing on the bed!*

bound¹ /baʊnd/ *adjective*
1 be bound to do something to be certain to do something: *She is so smart, she's bound to be a success.*
2 tied up and not able to move: *He was bound hand and foot with a rope.*

bound² *verb*
to jump quickly and with a lot of energy: *The children came bounding down the stairs.*

bound³ *noun*
a big jump

bound⁴
the PAST TENSE and PAST PARTICIPLE of the verb **bind**

bound·a·ry /'baʊndəri, -dri/ *noun* (*plural* **boundaries**)
the line that divides two places: *A white line marks the boundary of the field.* ≫ compare BORDER

bow¹ /baʊ/ *verb*
to bend your head or the top part of your body forward to show respect: *Everyone bowed to the king.*

bow² *noun*
an act of bowing

bow³ /boʊ/ *noun*
1 a long thin piece of wood held in a curve by a tight string, used for shooting an ARROW
2 a long thin piece of wood with tight strings fastened along it, used for playing musical instruments
3 a knot of cloth or string: *She tied a red bow in her hair.*

bow

bow
bow
bow

bowl /boʊl/ *noun*
a deep round dish or container: *Fill the bowl with water.* | *I ate a bowl of ice cream.*

box¹ /baks/
a container with four straight sides, usually made of hard paper or wood: *I need three boxes for these books.* | *Mom bought a box of cookies.*

box² *verb*
to fight someone as a sport while wearing big leather pads on your hands

box·er /'baksɚ/ *noun*
someone who boxes as a sport or job

box·ing /'baksɪŋ/ *noun* [U]
the sport of fighting while wearing big leather pads on your hands

box of·fice /'. ,../ *noun* (*plural* **box offices**)
a place in a theater where you can buy tickets

boy /bɔɪ/ *noun*
a male child or a young man: *He went to a school for boys.*

boy·friend /'bɔɪfrɛnd/ *noun*
a boy or man with whom you have a romantic relationship: *Is Chris your boyfriend?* ≫ compare GIRLFRIEND

Boy Scouts /'bɔɪˌskaʊts/ *plural noun*
an organization for boys that teaches them practical skills —**Boy Scout** *noun*

bra /brɑ/ *noun*
a piece of clothing that a woman wears under her clothes to support her breasts

brace·let /'breɪslɪt/ *noun*
a band or chain that you wear as a decoration around your wrist —see picture at JEWELRY

brac·es /ˈbreɪsɪz/ *plural noun*
wires which some children have on their teeth to make them straight

brag /bræg/ *verb* (**bragging, bragged**)
to talk too proudly about what you have done, or what you own etc.: *He is always bragging about his new car.* ≫ compare BOAST

braid¹ /breɪd/ *verb*
to twist together three or more pieces of hair, rope, etc.

braid² *noun*
three or more lengths of hair that are twisted together into one piece: *She wore her hair in braids.* —see picture at HAIRSTYLE

brain /breɪn/ *noun*
the part inside your head that controls how you think, feel, and move

brake¹ /breɪk/ *noun*
the part of a bicycle, car etc. that you use to slow or stop it

brake² *verb* (**braking, braked**)
to make a bicycle, car etc. slow or stop using the brake: *The driver braked quickly to avoid an accident.*

branch /bræntʃ/ *noun*
1 a part of a tree that grows out from the middle
2 one part of something larger such as a business: *The bank has branches in Canada and the U.S.*

brand /brænd/ *noun*
a type of product made by one company: *What brand of soap do you use?*

brand-new /ˌbrænˈnuˑ/ *adjective*
completely new; never used before: *He won a brand-new car!*

bran·dy /ˈbrændi/ *noun* [U]
a strong alcoholic drink made from wine

brass /bræs/ *noun* [U]
a very hard yellow metal which shines brightly, made by mixing COPPER and ZINC

brave /breɪv/ *adjective*
not afraid or not showing fear: *The soldiers were very brave in the battle.* ≫ compare FEARLESS

brav·er·y /ˈbreɪvəri/ *noun* [U]
willingness to do dangerous things without feeling afraid: *The fireman was praised for his bravery.* ≫ compare COURAGE

bagel

bread

pretzel

bun

loaf of bread

bread /brɛd/ *noun* [U]
a food made by mixing flour and water and then baking it: *Do we need any bread from the store?*

breadth /brɛdθ, brɛtθ/ *noun* [U]
the distance from one side of something to the other: *The ship measured 50 feet in breadth.*

break¹ /breɪk/ *verb* (*past tense* **broke**, *past participle* **broken**)
1 to separate into two or more pieces, especially by hitting or dropping something: *The plate fell on the floor and broke.* | *She broke her leg in the accident.*
2 to damage something so that it does not work: *Be careful with the radio or you will break it!*
3 **break down** to stop working, used about large machines: *My car broke down on the way to work.*
4 **break in/break into** to get inside a place using force, usually to steal something: *Someone broke in through the window.* (=broke the window to get inside the building)
5 **break the law** to do something that the law says you must not do
6 **break a record** to do something faster or better than it has ever been done before: *She broke the world record in the 100 meters.*
7 **break out** if something bad such as a fire or war breaks out, it begins to happen: *The fire broke out at two o'clock in the morning.*
8 **break a promise** to not do something that you promised to do
9 **break up (with someone)** to end a relationship with a boy or girl friend: *Sally broke up with Jack last week.*

break² *noun*
1 a period of time when you stop working: *I'm tired. Let's take a break.*

2 a space between two things: *I could see a break in the clouds.*

break·down /'breɪkdaʊn/ *noun*
1 the failure of a relationship or system: *There was a breakdown in the peace talks.*
2 an occasion when a car stops working

break·fast /'brɛkfəst/ *noun*
the first meal of the day

breast /brɛst/ *noun*
1 one of the two round parts on the front of a woman's body that give milk
2 the part of the body, especially a bird's body, between the neck and stomach

breath /brɛθ/ *noun*
1 the air that you take in and let out through your nose or mouth: *He took a deep breath and jumped into the water.* | *I can smell beer on his breath.*
2 be out of breath to have difficulty breathing for a while because you have been running or exercising
3 hold your breath to make yourself stop breathing for a while, especially to swim under water: *How long can you hold your breath?*
4 catch your breath to begin breathing in a normal way again after you have been running or exercising: *I had to sit down to catch my breath.*

breathe /brið/ *verb* (breathing, breathed)
to take air into your body and let it out through your nose or mouth

breath·less /'brɛθlɪs/ *adjective*
having difficulty breathing, especially after exercise

bred /brɛd/
the PAST TENSE and PAST PARTICIPLE of the verb breed

breed¹ /brid/ *verb* (past bred)
1 if animals breed, they have babies: *Some animals will not breed in cages.*
2 to keep animals so that they will have babies: *He breeds cattle and horses.*

breed² *noun*
a type of animal: *What breed is your dog?*

breeze /briz/ *noun*
a light wind: *I enjoy the cool breeze in the evening.*

brew /bru/ *verb*
1 to pour very hot water over coffee or tea to make it ready to drink

2 be brewing to be going to happen soon: *It looks like a storm is brewing.*

bribe¹ /braɪb/ *verb* (bribing, bribed)
to offer someone a bribe: *He tried to bribe the police to let him go.*

bribe² *noun*
money or gifts that you use to try to get someone to do something for you, usually something that is not honest

brick /brɪk/ *noun*
a hard block of baked clay, used for building

bride /braɪd/ *noun*
a woman who is about to get married, or who has just married ≫ compare GROOM

brides·maid /'braɪdzmeɪd/ *noun*
a girl or woman who helps a bride at her wedding ≫ compare BEST MAN

bridge /brɪdʒ/ *noun*
a structure built over something to allow people or vehicles to go from one side to the other: *A new bridge was built across the river.*

bri·dle /'braɪdl/ *noun*
leather bands put on a horse's head to control its movement

brief /brif/ *adjective*
1 lasting a short time: *The meeting was very brief.*
2 using only a few words: *He gave a brief description of the man.*

brief·case /'brifkeɪs/ *noun*
a thin flat suitcase for carrying papers or books ≫ compare SUITCASE

bright /braɪt/ *adjective*
1 shining with a lot of light: *I love the bright lights of the city.*
2 having a strong, clear color: *She wore a bright yellow dress.*
3 quick at learning things; intelligent: *Susan is a very bright child.*

bright·en /'braɪtn/ *verb*
brighten up to become more sunny or lighter and more pleasant: *The weather should brighten up later.*

bril·liant /'brɪlyənt/ *adjective*
1 very intelligent: *He is a brilliant doctor.*
2 bright and strong, often used of colors: *Mary has brilliant green eyes.*

bring /brɪŋ/ *verb* (past brought)
1 to take someone or something to someone

else or to a place: *Bring me the ball.* | *Can I bring Gary to the party?*

2 to cause a particular result, or to cause something to happen: *Tourism brings a lot of money to the area.*

3 bring someone up to care for and educate a child: *She brought up three children by herself.*

brisk /brɪsk/ *adjective*
quick and full of energy: *I had a brisk walk this morning.* ≫ compare SLOW

Brit·ish¹ /ˈbrɪtɪʃ/ *adjective*
relating to or coming from Great Britain

British² *noun*
the British the people of Great Britain

brit·tle /ˈbrɪtl̩/ *adjective*
hard, but easily broken

broad /brɔd/ *adjective*
1 wide: *He has very broad shoulders.*
2 including many different types of things or people: *The talk covered a broad range of topics.* ≫ compare NARROW

broad·cast¹ /ˈbrɔdkæst/ *verb* (*past* **broadcast**)
to send out a radio or television PROGRAM: *Channel Six will broadcast the game at ten o'clock.*

broadcast² *noun*
a PROGRAM on the radio or television

broke¹ /broʊk/
the PAST TENSE of the verb **break**

broke² *adjective*
completely without money: *I can't go to the movies with you. I'm broke.*

bro·ken¹ /ˈbroʊkən/
the PAST PARTICIPLE of the verb **break**

broken
cracked
broken

broken² *adjective*
1 in pieces because of being hit, dropped etc.: *Can you fix this broken window?*
2 not working: *My watch is broken.*

bronze /brɑnz/ *noun* [U]
a hard metal, made by mixing copper and tin

broom /brum, brʊm/ *noun*
a brush with a long handle, used for sweeping the floor

broth·er /ˈbrʌðər/ *noun*
a boy or man with the same parents as you: *Peter is my brother.* ≫ compare SISTER

broth·er-in-law /ˈ.. .ˌ./ *noun* (*plural* **brothers-in-law**)
1 the brother of your wife or husband
2 the husband of your sister

brought /brɔt/
the PAST TENSE and PAST PARTICIPLE of the verb **bring**

brown /braʊn/ *adjective, noun* [U]
a dark color like coffee, wood, or earth: *Have you seen my brown shoes?*

bruise¹ /bruz/ *noun*
a mark on your skin where it has been damaged by a hit or a fall

bruise² *verb* (**bruising, bruised**)
to mark someone's skin with a bruise: *She fell and bruised her knee.*

brush

toothbrush
hairbrush
paintbrush

brush¹ /brʌʃ/ *noun* (*plural* **brushes**)
an object with strong hairs on the end of a handle, that you use for cleaning, painting etc.

brush² *verb*
to clean something or make something look neat using a brush: *Have you brushed your teeth today?* | *She needs to brush her hair.*

bub·ble¹ /'bʌbəl/ *noun*
a hollow ball of liquid containing air or gas:
There are soap bubbles in the sink.

bubble² *verb* (bubbling, bubbled)
to make bubbles: *The water was bubbling gently in the pan.*

buck /bʌk/ *noun*
1 a dollar: *Can you loan me ten bucks?*
2 a male deer or rabbit

buck·et /'bʌkɪt/ *noun*
a container with a handle, used for holding or carrying water

buck·le /'bʌkəl/ *noun*
a fastener used for joining the two ends of a belt, shoe, bag etc. —see picture at FASTENER

bud /bʌd/ *noun*
a young flower or leaf before it opens —see picture at ROSE²

Bud·dhis·m /'budɪzəm, 'bu-/ *noun* [U]
the religion based on the teachings of Buddha

Bud·dhist /'budɪst, 'bu-/ *noun*
a person who follows the teachings of Buddha

budge /bʌdʒ/ *verb* (budging, budged)
to move something heavy from one place to another: *This rock won't budge.*

budg·et¹ /'bʌdʒɪt/ *noun*
a plan of how to spend money: *We have a budget of $500,000 for the new building.*

budget² *verb*
to plan and control how much money you have to spend on something

buf·fa·lo /'bʌfə,lou/ *noun* (plural buffalo *or* buffaloes)
a large animal like a cow with a large head and thick hair on its neck —see color picture on page 183

bug¹ /bʌg/ *noun*
1 a small insect
2 a very small living thing that can get into your body and causes an illness: *There's a flu bug going around the school.*

bug² *verb* (bugging, bugged)
to annoy someone: *Stop bugging me!*

build /bɪld/ *verb* (past built)
1 to make something by putting pieces together: *The house is built of brick.*
2 to make something develop or increase: *We want to build on our earlier success.*

build·ing /'bɪldɪŋ/ *noun*
something with a roof and walls such as a house, office, or church

built /bɪlt/
the PAST TENSE and PAST PARTICIPLE of the verb **build**

bulb /bʌlb/ *noun* (*also* **light bulb**)
the glass part of an electric light that shines when it is turned on

bulk /bʌlk/ *noun*
the bulk of something the main or largest part of something

bulk·y /'bʌlki/ *adjective* (bulkier, bulkiest)
big and heavy: *The box is too bulky to lift.*

bull /bʊl/ *noun*
a male cow

bull·dog /'bʊldɔg/ *noun*
a short dog with a thick neck, large head, and flat nose

bull·doz·er /'bʊl,douzɚ/ *noun*
a powerful vehicle that moves dirt and rocks

bul·let /'bʊlɪt/ *noun*
a small round piece of metal that is fired from a gun

bul·ly¹ /'bʊli/ *noun* (plural bullies)
a person who hurts weaker people or makes them afraid

bully² *verb* (bullying, bullied)
to hurt people who are not as strong as you, or make them afraid

bump¹ /bʌmp/ *verb*
1 to hit or knock into something by accident: *I bumped my knee on the chair.*
2 **bump into someone** to meet someone by chance: *I bumped into John in town.*

bump² *noun*
a round swelling on your skin where you have hit it on something: *He had a bump on his head.*

bump·er /'bʌmpɚ/ *noun*
a bar at the front and back of the car to protect it if it hits anything

bump·y /'bʌmpi/ *adjective* (bumpier, bumpiest)
not smooth; having a lot of raised parts on it: *We had to drive on a bumpy road.*

bun¹ /bʌn/ *noun*
a small round piece of bread —see picture at BREAD

bun² *noun*
a way of arranging your hair in a small round shape at the back of your head —see picture at HAIRSTYLE

bunch /bʌntʃ/ *noun*
several things of the same kind, or a large amount of something: *He gave me a bunch of flowers.*

bun·dle /'bʌndl/ *noun*
a group of things such as papers or clothes that are tied together so you can carry them

bunk /bʌŋk/ *noun*
a narrow bed which is attached to the wall on a ship or train

bunk beds /'. ./ *plural noun*
two beds that are put one on top of the other, used especially for children to sleep in —see picture at BED

bur·den /'bɚdn/ *noun*
something heavy that you have to carry

burg·er /'bɚgɚ/ *noun*
meat that is cut into very small pieces and then made into a round flat shape before it is cooked

bur·glar /'bɚglɚ/ *noun*
a person who enters buildings, usually by force, to steal things ≫ compare ROBBER, THIEF

bur·gla·ry /'bɚgləri/ *noun* (*plural* burglaries)
the crime of entering a building by force and stealing things

bur·i·al /'bɛriəl/ *noun*
the act or ceremony of putting a dead person into the ground

burn¹ /bɚn/ *verb* (*past* burned /bɚnd/ or burnt)
1 to damage or destroy something with fire: *I burned my hand on the fire.*
2 to make heat or fire: *Is the fire still burning?*
3 **burn down/burn up** to be destroyed completely by fire: *The building burned down last year.*
4 **burn out** to stop making heat or fire because there is no wood, coal etc.

burn² *noun*
an injury or mark on your body caused by fire or heat: *He has a burn mark on his arm.*

burnt /bɚnt/
the PAST TENSE and PAST PARTICIPLE of the verb burn

bur·row /'bɚoʊ, 'bʌroʊ/ *noun*
a hole in the ground made by a small animal such as a rabbit

burst /bɚst/ *verb* (*past* burst)
1 to break open or apart because of too much pressure inside: *The children tried to burst the balloons.*
2 **be bursting** to be very full of people, activity etc.: *The little town is bursting with tourists.*
3 **burst out laughing/crying** to start laughing or crying loudly and suddenly
4 **burst into tears** to start crying suddenly

bur·y /'bɛri/ *verb* (burying, buried)
1 to put a dead body into the ground
2 to cover something with something else so it cannot be seen: *The dog buried a bone in the leaves.*

bus /bʌs/ *noun* (*plural* buses)
a large vehicle that takes people from one place to another: *Ann got on the bus downtown.* —see color picture on page 187

bush /bʊʃ/ *noun*
a short plant like a small tree —see color picture on page 188

bus·i·ly /'bɪzəli/ *adverb*
done with a lot of activity and interest: *Sharon is busily planning the wedding.*

busi·ness /'bɪznɪs/ *noun*
1 a company that provides service or sells things to earn money: *He has a furniture business in town.*
2 [U] making, buying, and selling things, or the amount of money made doing this: *Business is very good this year.* [=we are earning a lot of money]
3 **mind your own business** used when telling someone in a rude way that you do not want any help or advice: *"What are you doing?" "Mind your own business."*
4 **none of your business** used when telling someone in a rude way that you do not think he or she should know about something: *It's none of your business how she spends her money.*

busi·ness·man /'bɪznɪsˌmæn/ *noun* (*plural* businessmen /-mɛn/)
a man who works in business, especially one who owns a company or helps to run it

busi·ness·wom·an /'bɪznɪsˌwʊmən/ *noun* (*plural* businesswomen /-wɪmɪn/)
a woman who works in business, especially one who owns a company or helps to run it

bus stop /'. ./ *noun*
a place at the side of a road where buses stop for people to get off and on

bus·y /'bɪzi/ *adjective* (**busier, busiest**)
1 working or doing something so you do not have time to do other things: *He's busy writing letters.*
2 full of activity, people etc.: *We live on a very busy street.*
3 a telephone that is busy is being used: *I tried calling her, but her line is busy.*

but /bət; *strong* bʌt/
a word you use when you are saying that although one thing is true, another thing which is opposite to it is also true: *I would like to come to the party, but I can't.* | *Mom liked the food, but Dad hated it.*

butch·er /'bʊtʃɚ/ *noun*
a person who sells meat

but·ter /'bʌtɚ/ *noun* [U]
a yellow food made from milk: *Do you want butter on your bread?*

but·ter·fly /'bʌtɚ,flaɪ/ *noun* (*plural* **butterflies**)
an insect that has large wings with bright colors on them ⟫ compare MOTH —see color picture on page 183

but·tock /'bʌtək/ *noun*
one of the soft parts of your body that you sit on

but·ton /'bʌtⁿn/ *noun*
1 a small round object that you push through a hole to fasten clothes: *I lost a button on my shirt.* —see picture at FASTENER

2 a round object that you push to start or stop a machine

but·ton·hole /'bʌtⁿn,hoʊl/ *noun*
the hole for a button to be pushed through

buy /baɪ/ *verb* (**buying** *past* **bought** /bɔːt/)
to get something by paying money for it: *I bought a new radio.* ⟫ compare SELL

buzz /bʌz/ *verb*
1 to make a noise like the sound of a BEE
2 **buzz off** used when telling someone in a rude way to go away: *Buzz off and leave me alone!*

by¹ /baɪ/ *preposition*
1 near; beside: *He was standing by the window.* —see color picture on page 194
2 past: *She walked by me without saying hello.*
3 used to show who or what does something: *The house was damaged by fire.* | *We read a story by Mark Twain.*
4 using or doing a particular thing: *I earned some money by delivering newspapers.* | *Are you going by car?*
5 no later than: *Please have this ready by tomorrow.*
6 used for saying what part of something someone holds: *He grabbed me by my arm.*

by² *adverb*
past: *One or two cars drove by.*

bye /baɪ/
a word you say when you leave someone or when he or she leaves you; goodbye

bye-bye /,. '.,'. ./
another word for **bye**

Cc

cab /kæb/ *noun*
1 a car with a driver who will take you somewhere if you pay
2 the part of a truck or train where the driver sits

cab·bage /'kæbɪdʒ/ *noun*
a large round vegetable with thick green or purple leaves

cab·in /'kæbɪn/ *noun*
1 a small wooden house
2 a room on a ship or plane

cab·i·net /'kæbənɪt/ *noun*
1 a piece of furniture with shelves or drawers
2 an important group of people in a government who help the leader

ca·ble /'keɪbəl/ *noun*
1 a tube that contains wires that carry electricity or telephone calls
2 [U] a system of television that is paid for the person watching it
3 a thick rope, usually made of metal

cac·tus /'kæktəs/ *noun* (*plural* **cacti** /'kæktaɪ/ or **cactuses**)
a plant with sharp needles and a thick stem that grows in hot dry places

ca·fe /kæ'feɪ, kə-/ *noun*
a small restaurant

cage /keɪdʒ/ *noun*
a box made of metal wires in which you keep birds or animals

cake /keɪk/ *noun*
a sweet cooked food made of flour, fat, sugar, and eggs: *My mom baked a birthday cake for me.*

cal·cu·late /'kælkyə,leɪt/ *verb*
(**calculating, calculated**)
to use numbers to find an answer or to measure something: *I need to calculate the amount of material I will need for the job.*

cal·cu·la·tion /,kælkyə'leɪʃən/ *noun*
the result of using numbers to find an answer, amount etc.

cal·cu·la·tor /'kælkyə,leɪtər/ *noun*
a small machine that can add, subtract etc. numbers

cal·en·dar /'kæləndər/ *noun*
a series of pages that shows the days, weeks, and months of the year

calf /kæf/ *noun* (*plural* **calves** /kɑːvz/)
1 a young cow
2 the part of the back of your leg between your knee and your foot

call¹ /kɔl/ *verb*
1 to telephone someone: *I called my sister, but she wasn't home.*
2 to ask or order someone to come to you: *The teacher called into her room.*
3 to say or shout something: *to call for help*
4 to give someone or something a name: *Her name is Elizabeth, but we call her Liz.*
5 **call something off** to decide that an event will not happen: *The game was called off because of the bad weather.*
6 **call someone in** to ask or order someone to come and help with a difficult situation: *The President called in the soldiers to deal with the problem.*
7 **call someone back** to telephone someone again: *Can Mr. Wilson call you back?*

call² *noun*
1 an act of talking to someone on the telephone: *There's a call for you Teresa.*
2 a shout or cry: *I heard a call for help.*
3 a short visit for a particular reason: *The salesman is out on a call right now.*
4 **be on call** to be ready to go to work if you are needed: *The doctor is on call 24 hours a day.*

calm /kɑm/ *adjective*
1 peaceful, not angry or upset: *He was very calm when we told him the news.*
2 very still, or not moving very much: *We swam in the calm water.*

calves /kævz/
the plural of **calf**

cam·cord·er /'kæm,kɔrdər/ *noun*
a machine that you use to make VIDEO movies

came /keɪm/
the PAST TENSE of the verb **come**

cam·el /ˈkæməl/ *noun*

a large animal with one or two HUMPs on its back that lives in the desert and carries people and goods —see color picture on page 183

cam·er·a

/ˈkæmrə, -ərə/ *noun*

a small machine for making photographs —see color picture on page 185

camp¹ /kæmp/

noun

a place with tents where people stay for a short time

camp² *verb*

to set up a tent and stay in it for a short time

cam·paign /kæmˈpeɪn/ *noun*

a series of actions done to get a result, especially in business or politics: *There is a new campaign to stop people smoking.*

camp·er /ˈkæmpɚ/ *noun*

1 a little house on wheels that can be pulled by a car

2 someone who is staying in a tent on vacation

camp·ing /ˈkæmpɪŋ/ *noun* [U]

living in a tent for a short time, especially when you are on a vacation: *Do you want to go camping this weekend?*

camp·site /ˈkæmpsaɪt/ *noun*

a place where people can camp —see color picture on page 188

cam·pus /ˈkæmpəs/ *noun* (*plural* campuses)

the land or buildings belonging to a university or school

can¹ /kən; *strong* kæn/ *verb*

to be able to do something: *"Can she swim?" "Yes, she can."* | *You can go when you finish your work.*

can² *noun*

a container made of metal: *Do you have a can of soup?* ≫ compare BOX

ca·nal /kəˈnæl/ *noun*

a long narrow river for ships to travel along, or to bring water from one place to another

ca·nar·y /kəˈnɛri/ *noun* (*plural* canaries)

a small yellow bird that sings

can·cel /ˈkænsəl/ *verb* (cancelling, cancelling *or* canceling, canceled)

to stop something that you planned to do: *We had to cancel our trip.*

can·cer /ˈkænsɚ/ *noun* [U]

a serious illness which causes a growth to spread in the body

can·di·date /ˈkændəˌdeɪt, -dɪt/ *noun*

a person who hopes to be chosen for a job or a political position

can·dle /ˈkændl/ *noun*

a long piece of wax with a string in the middle that you burn to give light.

can·dy /ˈkændi/ *noun* (*plural* candies)

a sweet food made of sugar or chocolate, or a piece of this: *Can I have a piece of candy?* —see picture at BAR¹

cane /keɪn/ *noun*

a long thin stick that someone uses to help them walk

can·non /ˈkænən/ *noun*

a large gun, usually on wheels

can·not /ˈkænɑt, kəˈnɑt, kæ-/

can not: *I cannot understand why she is so angry.*

ca·noe /kəˈnu/

noun

a narrow, light boat which you move using a PADDLE —see color picture on pages 187 and 188

can't /kænt/

can not: *I'm sorry I can't go with you.*

can·vas /ˈkænvəs/ *noun* [U]

strong cloth used to make tents, bags, etc.

cap /kæp/ *noun*

1 a soft hat with a curved part at the front —see color picture on page 190

2 a cover for the end of a bottle or tube

ca·pa·ble /ˈkeɪpəbəl/ *adjective*

1 **be capable of something** to be able to do something: *I didn't think he was capable of murder.*

2 good at something: *She's a very capable lawyer.* ≫ opposite INCAPABLE

ca·pac·i·ty /kə'pæsəti/ *noun* [*plural* **capacities**]

1 the amount that something can hold or produce: *The bottle has a capacity **of** two pints.*

2 an ability to do something: *Paul has a great capacity **for** hard work.*

cape /keɪp/ *noun*

a long loose piece of clothing that you wrap around your neck and shoulders

cap·i·tal /'kæpətl/ *noun*

1 the city in a country where the main government is

2 (*also* **capital letter**) a large letter that you use at the beginning of a sentence: *A, D, P are capital letters; a, d, p are small letters.*

capital pun·ish·ment /ˌ... '.../ *noun* [U]

the punishment of killing someone for a crime

cap·tain /'kæptən/ *noun*

1 someone who controls a ship or airplane

2 an officer in the army or the navy

3 the leader of a team or group

cap·tive /'kæptɪv/ *noun*

a prisoner, especially in a war

cap·tiv·i·ty /kæp'tɪvəti/ *noun* [U]

the state of being a prisoner, or being kept in a small space: *They were **in** captivity for a year.*

cap·ture /'kæptʃɚ/ *verb* (**capturing, captured**)

to take someone as a prisoner: *They captured four enemy soldiers.*

car /kɑr/ *noun*

a vehicle with four wheels and an engine

card /kɑrd/ *noun*

1 a piece of stiff paper with a picture on the front and a message inside: *I sent you a birthday card.*

2 a small piece of plastic or stiff paper that has information about someone or something: *Do you have a business card?*

card·board /'kɑrdbɔrd/ *noun* [U]

stiff thick paper used for making boxes

car·di·gan /'kɑrdəgən/ *noun*

a SWEATER which has buttons on the front

care¹ /kɛr/ *verb* (**caring, cared**)

1 to feel interest in or concern about someone

or something: *Does she care **about** her work? I don't care what you do!*

2 **care for someone** to help someone who is sick: *Her son cared for her last summer.*

3 **care for something** to like or want something: *I don't really care for butter.*

care² *noun*

1 [U] the act of watching or helping someone: *Take care **of** your brother while I am away.* | *Do you need medical care?*

2 **take care** to be careful: *Take care when you are crossing the street.*

3 feelings of worry, fear, or concern

ca·reer /kə'rɪr/ *noun*

a job that you know a lot about and want to do for a long time: *He would like to have a career in banking.*

care·ful /'kɛrfəl/ *adjective*

thinking about what you are doing so that you do not make a mistake: *Be careful with that hot pan!* —**carefully** *adverb*

care·less /'kɛrlɪs/ *adjective*

not thinking about what you are doing: *Careless driving causes accidents.* —**carelessly** *adverb*

car·go /'kɑrgoʊ/ *noun* (*plural* **cargoes**)

something carried on a ship, plane etc.: *The ship carries a cargo **of** oil.*

car·ol /'kærəl/ *noun*

a Christmas song

car·pen·ter /'kɑrpəntɚ/ *noun*

a person whose job is to make things out of wood

car·pen·try /'kɑrpəntri/ *noun* [U]

the activity or job of making things out of wood

car·pet /'kɑrpɪt/ *noun* [U]

a heavy material used for covering floors and stairs ≫compare MAT, RUG

car·riage /'kærɪdʒ/ *noun*

a vehicle that is pulled by horses

car·rot /'kærət/ *noun*

a long orange root that is eaten as a vegetable —see picture at VEGETABLE

car·ry /'kæri/ *verb* (**carrying, carried**)

1 to take something somewhere: *He carried the food to the table.*

2 **carry on** to continue doing something: *They carried on talking.*

3 be/get carried away to be so excited that you do not control what you do or say: *Sorry about that – I got carried away.*

4 carry something out to do or finish something: *The soldiers carried out their orders.*

cart /kɑrt/ *noun*

a small vehicle used for carrying things

car·ton /'kɑrt⁻n/ *noun*

a paper or plastic box for holding food or drinks: *Get a carton of milk for me.* —see picture at CONTAINER

car·toon /kɑr'tun/ *noun*

a funny short movie with characters that are drawn and not real

carve /kɑrv/ *verb* (**carving, carved**)

1 to cut wood or stone into shapes: *He carved the figure of a woman from the wood.*

2 to cut cooked meat into pieces: *She carved the steak.*

case /keɪs/ *noun*

1 one example of something: *This is a typical case of poor planning.*

2 a question that is decided in a court of law: *He is involved in a murder case.*

3 in case because something might happen: *I'll take an umbrella in case it rains.*

4 in that case since this is true: *"It's cold." "In that case, we'll need our coats."*

5 a container that you store things in: *I bought a case of wine.*

cash¹ /kæʃ/ *noun* [U]

coins and paper money: *Are you paying by cash?*

cash² *verb*

to get cash in return for a check: *I cashed a check at the bank.*

cash·ier /kæ'ʃɪɚ/ *noun*

a person who takes and gives out money in a store

cash reg·is·ter /'. ,.../ *noun*

a machine in a store that shows how much you pay

cas·sette /kə'sɛt/ *noun*

a small plastic container used for playing music when put into a special machine

cas·tle /'kæsəl/ *noun*

a large beautiful house where a king, queen, or some other person lives

castle

cas·u·al /'kæʒuəl, -ʒəl/ *adjective*

1 relaxed and not worried about things

2 casual clothes clothes that you wear at home, not at work or school

cat /kæt/ *noun*

a small animal that people often keep as a pet

cat·a·log /'kætl̩,ɔg, -,ɑg/ *noun*

1 a book that has pictures and information about things you can buy from a company

2 a list of things in a particular order: *There is a catalog of all the books in the library.*

catch¹ /kætʃ/ *verb* (*past* **caught** /kɔt/)

1 to stop something that is moving through the air and hold it: *The dog caught the ball in its mouth.* —see color picture on page 189

2 to take hold of someone or something after chasing or hunting them: *The police finally caught the thief.* | *How many fish did you catch?*

3 catch the bus, train etc. to get on a bus, train etc. to go somewhere: *I caught the train to Boston.*

4 to get an illness: *Did you catch a cold?*

5 to be attached or stuck on something: *My shirt caught on the fence and tore.*

6 catch up to come up from behind someone or something and get to the same place: *I tried, but I couldn't catch up with you.*

catch² *noun*

the act of catching something: *That was a good catch!*

cat·e·go·ry /'kæṭə,gɔri/ *noun* (*plural* **categories**)

a group of people or things that are like one another in some way

cat·er·pil·lar /'kætɚˌpɪlɚ, 'kætə-/ *noun*

the young form of some insects, that looks like a worm with many legs

ca·the·dral /kə'θidrəl/ *noun*

an important large church

Cath·o·lic /'kæθlɪk, -θəlɪk/ *noun*

a Christian belonging to the church whose leader is the Pope —**Catholic** *adjective*

cat·tle /'kætl/ *plural noun*

large animals kept for their meat, milk, and skins

caught /kɔt/

the PAST TENSE and PAST PARTICIPLE of the verb **catch**

cau·li·flow·er /'kɔliˌflauɚ, 'ka-/ *noun*

a white vegetable with green leaves around the outside

cause¹ /kɔz/ *verb* (**causing, caused**)

to make something happen: *The heavy rain caused the flood.*

cause² *noun*

1 a person or thing that makes something happen: *What was the cause of the accident?*
2 an idea you believe in or care about very strongly: *They gave money for a good cause.*

cau·tion /'kɔʃən/ *noun* [U]

great care in avoiding danger: *Drive with caution.*

cau·tious /'kɔʃəs/ *adjective*

taking care to avoid danger ≫ compare RECKLESS

cave /keɪv/ *noun*

a hollow place under the ground or in the side of a mountain

CD /ˌsi 'di/ *noun*

a type of record on which high quality sound or a lot of information is kept

CD play·er /.'. ˌ../ *noun*

a special machine used for playing a CD —see color picture on page 185

CD-ROM /ˌsi di 'ram/ *noun*

a CD on which a lot of information is kept to be used by a computer

cease /sis/ *verb* (**ceasing, ceased**)

to stop: *Her mother never ceases talking about her problems.*

cease·less /'sislɪs/ *adjective*

continuing for a long time without stopping

ceil·ing /'silɪŋ/ *noun*

the inside surface of the top part of a room

cel·e·brate /'sɛləˌbreɪt/ *verb*
(**celebrating, celebrated**)

to have a special meal or party because of a particular event: *We celebrated her birthday at the restaurant.*

cel·e·bra·tion /ˌsɛlə'breɪʃən/ *noun*

a special meal or party that you have because something good has happened: *Are you coming to the New Year's celebration?*

cell /sɛl/ *noun*

1 a small room where a prisoner is kept
2 a very small part of a plant or animal

cel·lar /'sɛlɚ/ *noun*

a room under the ground in a house, where things are stored ≫ compare BASEMENT

cel·lo /'tʃɛloʊ/ *noun*

a musical instrument like a large VIOLIN which you hold between your knees

ce·ment /sɪ'mɛnt/ *noun* [U]

a powder that becomes hard like stone when mixed with water, used in building or making SIDEWALKs etc.

cem·e·ter·y /'sɛməˌtɛri/ *noun* (*plural* **cemeteries**)

an area of land where dead people's bodies are put into the ground

cent /sɛnt/ *noun*

a small coin used in some countries

cen·ter /'sɛntɚ/ *noun*

1 the middle of something: *Put the flowers in the center of the table.*
2 a place or building used for a special purpose: *Have you seen the new shopping center?*

Cen·ti·grade /'sɛntəˌgreɪd/ *noun* [U]

a way of measuring how hot or cold something is

cen·ti·me·ter /'sɛntəˌmitɚ/ *noun*

a measure of length: *There are 100 centimeters in a meter.*

cen·tral /'sɛntrəl/ *adjective*

1 in the middle of something
2 the most important

cen·tu·ry /'sɛntʃəri/ *noun (plural centuries)*

a period of 100 years: *This house was built two centuries ago.*

ce·re·al /'sɪriəl/ *noun*

1 food made from grain, usually eaten with milk: *What's your favorite cereal?*

2 a crop such as wheat, rice, or corn

cer·e·mo·ny /'sɛrə,mouni/ *noun (plural ceremonies)*

a group of special actions done and special words spoken at an important public or religious event: *Who performed the marriage ceremony?*

cer·tain /'sət⁻n/ *adjective*

1 sure: *I am certain he told me to come at two o'clock.* | *Are you certain about that?*

2 some: *You cannot smoke in certain restaurants.*

cer·tain·ly /'sət⁻nli/ *adverb*

1 without doubt: *You certainly have a lot of books.*

2 of course: *"Will you help me, please?" "Certainly."*

cer·tif·i·cate /sə'tɪfəkɪt/ *noun*

an important written paper: *Your birth certificate tells people when you were born.*

chain¹ /tʃeɪn/ *noun*

a group of metal rings joined together in a line: *She wore a gold chain around her neck.*

chain² *verb*

to use a chain to tie something to something else: *I chained my bicycle to the fence.*

chair /tʃɛr/ *noun*

a piece of furniture you sit on, with four legs and a back ≫ compare SOFA, STOOL

chair·per·son /'tʃɛr,pəsən/ *noun*

a person who controls a meeting

chalk /tʃɔk/ *noun*

a hard white stick that is used for writing or drawing

chal·lenge¹ /'tʃæləndʒ/ *verb (challenging, challenged)*

1 to offer to fight or play a game against someone: *We were challenged to a game of golf.*

2 to test or question someone: *I did not think he was right, so I challenged him.*

challenge² *noun*

1 something difficult that you need skill and ability to do: *To build a bridge in a month was a real challenge.*

2 the act of testing or asking questions of someone

cham·pagne /ʃæm'peɪn/ *noun [U]*

an alcoholic drink with a lot of BUBBLEs in it

cham·pi·on /'tʃæmpiən/ *noun*

a person who is the best at something, especially a sport or game

cham·pi·on·ship /'tʃæmpiən,ʃɪp/ *noun*

a competition to find who is the best at something: *Our team won the swimming championships.*

chance /tʃæns/ *noun*

1 a time that you use for doing something: *Now I finally have a chance to read my letter.*

2 how possible it is that something is true or that someone will succeed: *There is a good chance that I will be chosen for the team.*

3 a risk: *He is taking a chance by driving his car so fast.*

4 something that happens without being planned or caused: *I met him by chance.*

change¹ /tʃeɪndʒ/ *verb (changing, changed)*

1 to make something different or become different: *This town has changed since I was a child.* | *The leaves change colors in the fall.*

2 to stop having or doing one thing and start something else instead: *Would you change seats with me?*

3 change clothes, change your clothes to put on different clothes: *He changed when he arrived home from school.*

chair

stool

wheelchair

armchair

chair

4 change your mind to make a new decision which is different to the one before: *I was going to the store, but I've changed my mind.*

change² *noun*

1 the result when something or someone becomes different: *There has been a change in our plans.*

2 [U] money that you get back when you pay too much for something: *I gave him a dollar and he gave me 20 cents in change.*

3 for a change as something different from usual: *Let's go to a different restaurant for a change.*

chan·nel /'tʃænl/ *noun*

1 a particular television company: *What's on channel seven?*

2 water that connects two seas

cha·os /'keɪɑs/ *noun* [U]

a state of no order or no control: *After the explosion, the city was in chaos.*

chap·el /'tʃæpəl/ *noun*

a small church, or part of a church

chap·ter /'tʃæptɚ/ *noun*

a part of a book: *Open your books to Chapter 3.*

char·ac·ter /'kærɪktɚ/ *noun*

1 what a person or thing is like: *He has a strong but gentle character.*

2 a person in a book, movie, or play

charge¹ /tʃɑrdʒ/ *verb* [charging, charged]

1 to ask for money for something you are selling: *He charged me $5 for the book.*

2 to buy something, but pay for it later: *I'll charge this to my credit card.*

3 to say that a person has done something wrong: *He was charged **with** stealing a car.*

4 to run or hurry: *The little boy charged into the room.*

charge² *noun*

1 a price you pay for something: *There is a charge **for** the extra coffee.*

2 be in charge, take charge to be in a position of control and responsibility: *Mr. Davis is in charge **of** buying the goods.*

3 a statement that a person has done wrong: *He is in court on a murder charge.*

4 a hurried attack

char·i·ty /'tʃærəṭi/ *noun*

1 (*plural* **charities**) an organization that gives money, food etc. to those who need it

2 [U] money or help given to those who need it: *She is too proud to accept charity.*

charm¹ /tʃɑrm/ *verb*

to please someone very much, or make them think you are very attractive

charm² *noun*

1 [U] a pleasing, attractive quality that someone or something has: *He was full of charm and everyone liked him.*

2 a thing that brings good luck

charm·ing /'tʃɑrmɪŋ/ *adjective*

very pleasing or attractive

chart /tʃɑrt/ *noun*

1 a large piece of paper with information on it in pictures and writing

2 a map, especially of the ocean or stars

chase¹ /tʃeɪs/ *verb* [chasing, chased]

to follow someone or something quickly: *The boy chased the dog.*

chase² *noun*

the act of following someone or something quickly: *The police caught him after a long chase.*

chat /tʃæt/ *verb* [chatting, chatted]

to talk in a friendly way: *We chatted together for a while.*

chat·ter /'tʃætɚ./'ʳɔɴ‿/ *verb*

to talk a lot about things that are not important

cheap /tʃip/ *adjective*

1 not expensive, costing only a little money: *Those black shoes are cheap.*

2 of bad quality: *The pants were made of cheap material.* ≫ opposite EXPENSIVE

cheat¹ /tʃit/ *verb*

to do something which is not honest; deceive: *He always cheats when he plays.*

cheat² *noun*

a person who is not fair or honest

check¹ /tʃɛk/ *verb*

1 to make sure that something is correct, true, or safe: *Did you check the doors to see if they are locked?*

2 check in to report that you have arrived somewhere: *You need to check in at the hotel soon.*

check² *noun*

1 a careful look to make sure that something is correct, true, or safe: *The police are doing a check for drugs.*

2 a piece of paper that you write on to pay for something: *Can I pay by check?*

3 a pattern of squares: *The material had red and white checks on it.* —see picture at PATTERN

check·ers /'tʃɛkəz/ *plural noun*

a game for two people using 24 round pieces on a board of black and white squares

check·out /'tʃɛk-aʊt/ *noun*

a place in a store where you pay for goods

cheek /tʃik/ *noun*

the round soft part of your face under your eyes —see picture at HEAD[1]

cheer[1] /tʃɪr/ *verb*

1 to shout because you are pleased: *The crowd cheered when the players arrived*

2 cheer (someone) up to make someone happy: *I tried to cheer her up by buying her a gift.*

cheer[2] *noun*

a shout of happiness or support: *Let's give three cheers for the winning team!*

cheer·ful /'tʃɪrfəl/ *adjective*

happy and feeling good —**cheerfully** *adverb*

cheese /tʃiz/ *noun* [U]

a solid food made from milk

chem·i·cal[1] /'kɛmɪkəl/ *noun*

a substance, especially one made by or used in chemistry

chemical[2] *adjective*

made by or used in chemistry

chem·ist /'kɛmɪst/ *noun*

a person who studies chemistry

chem·is·try /'kɛməstri/ *noun* [U]

the science which studies substances like gas, metals, liquids, etc., what they are made of, and how they change

cher·ry /'tʃɛri/ *noun* (*plural* **cherries**)

a small round fruit with red or black skin which grows on trees —see picture at FRUIT

chess /tʃɛs/ *noun* [U]

a game that you play by moving different shaped pieces on a board of black and white squares

chest /tʃɛst/ *noun*

1 the front of your body between your neck and your stomach

2 a large box that you store things in

chew /tʃu/ *verb*

to break up food in your mouth with your teeth

chew·ing gum /'.. ,./ *noun* [U]

a sweet substance that you chew, but do not swallow

chick /tʃɪk/ *noun*

a young bird, especially a young chicken

chick·en /'tʃɪkən/ *noun*

1 a bird that people keep for its eggs and meat

2 [U] the meat of this bird: *a chicken sandwich*

chief[1] /tʃif/ *adjective*

most important: *What is the chief cause of crime?*

chief[2] *noun*

a leader of a group or tribe: *The chief of police came to the meeting.*

chief·ly /'tʃifli/ *adverb*

mostly; mainly: *He kept animals – chiefly cattle and pigs.*

child /tʃaɪld/ *noun* (*plural* **children** /rtʃɪldrɛn/)

1 a young person, older than a baby but not fully grown —see color picture on page 191

2 a son or daughter: *They have three children.*

child·hood /'tʃaɪldhʊd/ *noun* [U]

the time when you are a child

child·ish /'tʃaɪldɪʃ/ *adjective*

1 behaving in a silly way: *Don't be so childish!*

2 suitable for a child

chil·dren /'tʃɪldrən/

the plural of **child**

chime /tʃaɪm/ *verb* (**chiming, chimed**)

to make a sound like a bell: *The clock chimed three o'clock.* ≫ compare RING

chim·ney /'tʃɪmni/ *noun* (*plural* **chimneys**)

a pipe that allows smoke to go up and out of a building

chim·pan·zee /ˌtʃɪmpænˈzi/ *noun*

an animal like a monkey but without a tail, that lives in Africa

chin /tʃɪn/ *noun*

the part of your face below your mouth —see picture at HEAD[1]

chi·na /'tʃaɪnə/ *noun* [U]

a hard white substance, or the cups, plates, etc. that are made from this

chip

chipped cups

potato chips   *computer chip*

chip¹ /tʃɪp/ *noun*

1 a small space or crack where a piece is missing from something: *My cup has a chip in it.*

2 a very small piece of metal or plastic used in computers to store information and make the computer work

3 a thin dry piece of potato or other vegetable that has been fried in oil: *Open another bag of potato chips.*

chip² *verb* (chipping, chipped)

to break a small piece off something hard: *He chipped the plate when he hit it.*

chirp /tʃɝp/ *noun*

a short high sound made by some birds and insects

choc·o·late /'tʃɑklɪt/ *noun*

1 [U] a sweet brown food made from COCOA

2 a small candy covered in chocolate: *He gave her a box of chocolates.*

choice /tʃɔɪs/ *noun*

1 the chance to choose between two or more things: *I've got to **make a** choice between the two jobs.*

2 the person or thing that you have chosen: *Her choice of dress surprised me.*

3 one of several things from which you can choose: *The car comes in a wide choice of colors.*

choir /kwaɪɚ/ *noun*

a number of people who sing together: *The school choir is going on a trip.*

choke /tʃoʊk/ *verb* (choking, choked)

to not be able to breathe because of something in your throat: *She choked **on** a piece of meat.*

choose /tʃuz/ *verb* (choosing, chose)

to decide from a group of things or people the one you want: *She chose **to** study chemistry.*

chop¹ /tʃɑp/ *verb* (chopping, chopped)

to cut something with an ax or sharp knife

chop² *noun*

a piece of meat with a bone

cho·rus /'kɔrəs/ *noun* (*plural* choruses)

1 a part of the song that is repeated

2 a group of singers

chose /tʃoʊz/

the PAST TENSE of the verb **choose**

cho·sen /'tʃoʊzən/

the PAST PARTICIPLE of the verb **choose**

chris·ten·ing /'krɪsənɪŋ/ *noun*

the religious ceremony at which a baby is given its name

Chris·tian /'krɪstʃən, 'krɪʃtʃən/ *noun*

a person who follows the teachings of Jesus Christ —**Christian** *adjective*

Chris·ti·an·i·ty /ˌkrɪstʃi'ænəti/ *noun* [U]

the religion based on the teachings of Jesus Christ

Christ·mas /'krɪsməs/ *noun*

December 25, the day of the year when Christians celebrate the birth of Jesus Christ and people give and receive gifts

chuck·le /'tʃʌkəl/ *verb* (chuckling, chuckled)

to laugh quietly: *Karen chuckled at the funny story.*

chunk /tʃʌŋk/ *n*

1 a large piece of something: *a **chunk of** cheese*

2 a large part or amount of something: *Having to get a new car took a big chunk out of her savings.*

church /tʃɝtʃ/ *noun* (*plural* churches)

a building in which Christians meet and pray

ci·gar /sɪ'gɑr/ *noun*

a thick brown tube of tobacco leaves rolled together that is smoked

cig·a·rette /ˌsɪgə'rɛt, 'sɪgəˌrɛt/ *noun*
a thin tube made of tobacco rolled in white paper, that is smoked

cir·cle¹ /'sɚkəl/ *noun*
1 a round shape; a ring: *They sat in a circle around the fire.* —see pictures at DIAMETER and SHAPE¹
2 a group of people who know each other and like the same things: *She has a large circle of friends.*

circle² *verb* (circling, circled)
to draw a circle around something: *Circle the correct answer.*

cir·cu·lar /'sɚkyələ/ *adjective*
round; moving around in a circle: *Move your arms in a circular motion.*

cir·cu·late /'sɚkyəˌleɪt/ *verb* (circulating, circulated)
to move continuously around a place or system: *Blood circulates around the body.*

cir·cu·la·tion /ˌsɚkyə'leɪʃən/ *noun* [U]
the movement of blood around your body

cir·cum·fer·ence /sɚ'kʌmfrəns/ *noun*
the distance around the outside edge of a round object —see picture at DIAMETER

cir·cum·stan·ces /'sɚkəmˌstænsɪz/ *plural noun*
1 in/under the circumstances because of what has happened: *In the circumstances I think I should stay at home.*
2 in/under no circumstances never: *Under no circumstances will I vote for him.*

cir·cus /'sɚkəs/ *noun*
a show given by people and trained animals, often in a large tent

cit·i·zen /'sɪtəzən/ *noun*
a person who lives in a particular country or city and has special rights there

cit·y /'sɪti/ *noun* (plural cities)
a very large town

ci·vil·ian /sə'vɪlyən/ *noun*
a person who is not in the army, navy etc.

civ·i·li·za·tion /ˌsɪvələ'zeɪʃən/ *noun*
a way of life in which people have laws, government, and education

civ·i·lize /'sɪvəˌlaɪz/ *verb* (civilizing, civilized)
to change the way that people live together, by making laws and having government and education

civ·il war /ˌ.. './ *noun*
a war between two groups of people who live in the same country

claim¹ /kleɪm/ *verb*
1 to ask for something that you think belongs to you: *You can claim the lost ring in the office.*
2 to say that something is true: *He claimed **to** have found a cure for the disease.*

claim² *noun*
1 something that you say is true: *I don't believe his claim about how rich he is.*
2 something that you ask for because you think you should receive it

clang /klæŋ/ *verb*
to make the sound of one piece of metal hitting another: *I heard a bell clanging in the distance.*

clap /klæp/ *verb* (clapping, clapped)
to make a sound by hitting your hands together to show that you like something: *When the singer finished, the audience clapped and cheered.* ≫ compare APPLAUD

clash¹ /klæʃ/ *verb*
1 to fight or argue with someone: *The police clashed **with** the angry crowd.*
2 if colors clash, they look bad together: *His red shirt clashed **with** his coat.*

clash² *noun* (plural clashes)
1 a fight or argument with someone
2 a loud sound made by one metal object hitting another one

clasp¹ /klæsp/ *verb*
to hold something tightly: *He clasped my hand.* ≫ compare GRIP

clasp² *noun*
a small metal object that fastens two things together: *She has a gold clasp on her dress.*

class /klæs/ *noun* (plural classes)
1 a group of students who learn together: *How many people are in your English class?*
2 a group of people in a society that earn a similar amount of money: *He comes from a middle class family.*
3 a group of plants, animals etc. of the same kind: *Cats belong to one class of animal, fish to another.*

clas·sic /'klæsɪk/ *noun*
a book or movie which is very good and which people have liked for a long time: *The movie "Casablanca" is a classic.*

clas·si·cal /'klæsɪkəl/ *adjective*
classical music or art is serious and important:
I prefer classical music to rock music.

class·room /'klæsrum, -rʊm/ *noun*
a room in a school where students are taught

clat·ter /'klæt̬ɚ/ *verb*
to make the loud noise of a lot of hard things
hitting together: *The pans clattered to the floor.*

clause /klɔz/ *noun*
a group of words that contain a noun or a verb.
The sentence *"As I was walking home, I met my
friend"* contains two clauses. *"As I was walking
home"* is one clause, and *"I met my friend"* is
another clause. ≫ compare SENTENCE

claw¹ /klɔ/ *noun*
1 one of the hard sharp parts on the foot of a
bird or animal
2 the hand of a CRAB or LOBSTER

claw² *verb*
to tear something using claws: *The cat clawed
the chair.*

clay /kleɪ/ *noun* [U]
soft, sticky earth used for making pots and
bricks

clean¹ /klin/ *adjective*
1 not dirty: *Are your hands clean?* | *a clean
shirt*
2 not yet used: *a clean piece of paper*
3 not involving sex, drugs, or anything illegal

clean² *verb*
to remove dirt from something and make it
clean: *Have you cleaned the kitchen?* | *Clean up
your room!*

clean·er /'klinɚ/ *noun*
1 someone whose job is to clean houses, buildings etc.
2 a substance that is used for cleaning things:
floor cleaner

clear¹ /klɪr/ *adjective*
1 easy to understand, hear, or see: *He spoke
in a clear voice.* | *Are the instructions clear?*
2 easy to see through
3 not blocked or covered: *The road is clear
now.*
4 certain; without doubt: *It is clear that he is
to blame for the accident.*

clear² *verb*
1 to take things away from a table, floor etc.

and put them in the places they should be: *Can
you clear the dishes from the table?*
2 clear up (a) to explain or deal with a complicated problem or situation: *I think he will be
able to clear up the mystery.* (b) to get better:
I hope the weather clears up before Sunday.

clear·ly /'klɪrli/ *adverb*
1 in a way that is easy to hear, see, or understand: *Please speak clearly so we can hear you.*
2 without any doubt: *Clearly, he felt she was to
blame.*

clerk /klɚk/ *noun*
a person who works in an office or hotel and
deals with letters, keeps records etc.

click¹ /klɪk/ *noun*
a short sharp sound: *I heard the click of a key
in the lock.*

click² *verb*
to make a short sharp sound: *The door clicked
shut.*

cli·ent /'klaɪənt/ *noun*
someone who pays a professional person for
help or advice

cliff /klɪf/ *noun*
an area of high, steep rock, often close to the
ocean or at the side of a mountain

cli·mate /'klaɪmɪt/ *noun*
the weather that a place usually has

climb¹ /klaɪm/ *verb*
1 to go up something: *The two boys climbed
the tree.* —see color picture on page 189
2 to increase in number, amount, or level:
Prices are climbing every day.

climb² *noun*
the action of going somewhere: *a long climb up
the hill*

cling /klɪŋ/ *verb* (*past* **clung**)
to hold on tightly: *The baby monkey clung to its
mother.*

clin·ic /'klɪnɪk/ *noun*
a place where people go to see a doctor

clip¹ /klɪp/ *noun*
a small metal object used for holding things
together: *The letters were held together with a
paper clip.*

clip² *verb* (**clipping, clipped**)
1 to hold things together with a clip: *A small
card was clipped to the letter.*

2 to cut something with a sharp instrument, especially to make it look neater: *He is clipping his fingernails.*

cloak·room /'kloʊk-rum/ *noun*
a room where you leave coats, hats etc.

clock /klɑk/ *noun*
a machine that shows you what the time is ≫ compare WATCH

clock·wise /'klɑk-waɪz/ *adverb*
moving in the same direction as the hands of a clock ≫ compare COUNTERCLOCKWISE

close¹ /kloʊz/ *adjective*
1 near: *I live close to the school.* | *They were standing close together.* (=very near each other)
2 **close to** almost: *The temperature is close to 90 degrees.*
3 careful: *We kept a close watch on the children.*
4 liking or loving someone: *Peter and John are close friends.*

close² *verb* (closing, closed)
1 to shut something. *Please close the door.*
2 to stop being open for business: *What time does the bank close?*
3 **close in** to move nearer and try to catch someone or something

close³ *noun*
the end of an activity or period of time: *the close of day* (=the evening)

closed /kloʊzd/ *adjective*
shut: *Keep your eyes closed.* | *The store is closed on Sunday.* ≫ compare OPEN¹ —see picture at AJAR

clos·et¹ /'klɑzɪt/ *n*
1 a tall cupboard that you keep your clothes in, built into the wall of a room
2 **come out of the closet** to tell people that you are HOMOSEXUAL

closet² *adj*
closet liberal/homosexual etc. someone who does not admit in public what s/he thinks or does in private

cloth /klɔθ/ *noun*
1 [U] material made of wool, cotton etc.: *She bought some cloth to make a new dress.*
2 a piece of material used for a particular purpose: *He polished the surface with a soft cloth.*

clothes /kloʊz, kloʊðz/ *plural noun*
things that you wear on your body: *I need to buy some new clothes.*

> NOTE: **Cloth** is NOT the singular of **clothes** (look at the entry for **cloth** above). The word **clothes** is always plural and does not have a singular form. People usually use the name of the things they are talking about when there is only one, e.g. *a shirt, a dress* etc.

cloth·ing /'kloʊðɪŋ/ *noun* [U]
clothes that people wear: *warm winter clothing*

cloud /klaʊd/ *noun*
a mass of very small drops of water floating in the sky

cloud·y /'klaʊdi/ *adjective* (cloudier, cloudiest)
having lots of clouds: *It's a cloudy day.*

clown /klaʊn/ *noun*
a person who wears funny clothes and tries to make people laugh

club /klʌb/ *noun*
1 a group of people who meet each other because they share an interest: *I belong to a chess club.*
2 a large heavy stick, used in some sports: *a golf club*

clue /klu/ *noun*
something that helps you find the answer to a difficult problem: *The police are looking for clues to help them catch the killer.*

clum·sy /'klʌmzi/ *adjective* (clumsier, clumsiest)
moving in an awkward way and often breaking things: *He was very clumsy and shy when he was a boy.* —**clumsily** *adverb*

clung /klʌŋ/
the PAST TENSE and PAST PARTICIPLE of the verb cling

clutch /klʌtʃ/ *verb*
to take hold of something tightly: *She clutched her baby in her arms.*

cm
a short way of writing CENTIMETER

coach¹ /koʊtʃ/ *noun* (plural coaches)
someone who gives special lessons to a team or person: *a football coach*

coach² *verb*
to give someone special lessons: *He coaches the tennis team.*

coal /koʊl/ *noun* [U]
a hard black material dug out of the ground and burned to give heat

coarse /kɔrs/ *adjective*
not smooth or fine; rough

coast /koʊst/ *noun*
the land next to the ocean: *She lives near the Pacific coast.*

coast·line /ˈkoʊstlaɪn/ *noun*
the edge of the coast: *From the ship, they could see the rocky coastline.*

coat /koʊt/ *noun*
1 a piece of clothing that you wear over your other clothes to keep you warm outdoors: *Do you have a winter coat?* —see color picture on page 190
2 an animal's fur, wool, or hair
3 a covering of something spread over a surface: *The wall needs a coat of paint.*

coat hang·er /ˈ. ˌ../ *noun*
a curved piece of wood or plastic with a hook on top, that you can hang clothes on

coax /koʊks/ *verb*
to persuade someone to do something by talking to them gently and kindly: *His mother coaxed him into taking the medicine.*

cob·web /ˈkɑbwɛb/ *noun*
the thin net which a SPIDER makes to catch insects

co·coa /ˈkoʊkoʊ/ *noun* [U]
1 a brown powder from the seeds of a tree, from which chocolate is made
2 a hot drink made from this powder

co·co·nut /ˈkoʊkəˌnʌt/ *noun*
a large brown nut with hard white flesh and a hollow center filled with white juice

cod /kɑd/ *noun* (*plural* **cod**)
an ocean fish used for food

code /koʊd/ *noun*
a way of using words, letters, numbers etc. to send secret messages: *written in code*

cof·fee /ˈkɔfi, ˈkɑ-/ *noun*
1 a brown powder from the seeds of the coffee tree

2 [U] the hot drink made from this powder: *Would you like some coffee?*

cof·fin /ˈkɔfɪn/ *noun*
a box which is used to hold a dead body

coil¹ /kɔɪl/ *verb*
1 to twist a rope, wire etc. around and around something
2 to go around in a circle: *A snake was coiled around the tree.*

coil² *noun*
a length of rope or wire that has been twisted into a round shape

coin /kɔɪn/ *noun*
a piece of money made of metal

co·in·ci·dence /koʊˈɪnsədəns/ *noun*
a situation in which two events happen together by chance: *What a coincidence to meet you here!*

cold¹ /koʊld/ *adjective*
1 not warm or hot: *It's cold outside!* ≫ compare HOT
2 unfriendly: *She can be a very cold person.*

cold² *noun*
1 a common illness of the nose and throat: *I have a cold.*
2 cold weather: *Don't stand out there in the cold – come in!* ≫ compare HEAT¹

col·lapse /kəˈlæps/ *verb* (**collapsing, collapsed**)
to fall down suddenly: *The old man collapsed in the street.* | *The roof of the house collapsed.*

collar

col·lar /ˈkɑlɚ/ *noun*
1 the part of a shirt or coat that goes around your neck: *The collar of his shirt was dirty.*
2 a leather or metal band that is put around the neck of an animal

col·lect /kəˈlɛkt/ *verb*
1 to come together or bring things together in the same place: *A crowd collected to watch the ceremony.* | *I collect stamps from all over the world.*

2 to get money from a lot of different people: *I'm collecting for the blind.*

col·lec·tion /kə'lɛkʃən/ *noun*

a set of similar things which have been brought together: *He has a large collection of old coins.*

col·lege /'kɑlɪdʒ/ *noun*

a place where people study after they finish school

col·lide /kə'laɪd/ *verb* (**colliding, collided**)

to hit together with a lot of force: *The two trucks collided on the wet road.*

col·li·sion /kə'lɪʒən/ *noun*

a violent crash, for example between two cars

co·lon /'koʊlən/ *noun*

the sign (:) which in this book comes before an example

colo·nel /'kənl/ *noun*

an officer in the army

col·o·ny /'kɑləni/ *noun* (*plural* **colonies**)

a country that is controlled by another country

col·or¹ /'kʌlɚ/ *noun*

the quality that makes things look green, red, yellow, etc.: *What color is her hair? | My favorite color is orange.*

NOTE: The word **color** is not usually used in sentences describing the color of something, e.g. *Her dress is red.* | *He has brown hair.*

---

color² *verb*

to put color on to something: *The little girl was coloring the pictures in her book.*

col·or·ful /'kʌlɚfəl/ *adjective*

bright; having a lot of colors: *She always wears colorful clothes.*

col·umn /'kɑləm/ *noun*

1 a large post used for supporting a part of a building

2 a long, narrow, upright shape, list etc.: *Can you add up this column of numbers?*

comb¹ /koʊm/ *noun*

a thin flat thing made of plastic, metal, etc. that you use to make your hair neat

comb² *verb*

to make your hair neat using a comb: *Have you combed your hair?*

com·bi·na·tion /ˌkɑmbə'neɪʃən/ *noun*

two or more different things that are used or put together: *A combination of reasons led to the decision.*

com·bine /kəm'baɪn/ *verb* (**combining, combined**)

to join or mix two or more things together: *The two small stores combined to make one new company.*

come /kʌm/ *verb* (**coming, came,** *past participle* **come**)

1 to move toward the person speaking: *Come here, Mary. | Are you coming with me?*

2 **come about** to happen: *This situation should never have come about.*

3 **come across something** to find someone or something by chance: *I came across an old friend I hadn't seen for years.*

4 **come from** to have been born or have lived a long time in a place: *I come from San Francisco.*

5 **come on!** used when telling someone to hurry, or to come with you: *Come on, Helen, or we are going to be late!*

6 **come off** to not be on something or connected to it: *A button came off my shirt.*

7 **come back** to return from a place: *When is James coming back from England?*

8 **come down** to become lower in price, amount, number etc.: *When the price comes down a little, we will buy the computer.*

9 **come out** to become known: *Soon it came out that she had been seeing another man.*

com·e·dy /'kɑmədi/ *noun* (*plural* **comedies**)

a funny play, movie etc.; something that makes you laugh ≫ compare TRAGEDY

com·fort¹ /'kʌmfɚt/ *noun* [U]

1 a feeling of being relaxed and calm, not worried or in pain: *I take comfort in the fact that she loves me.*

2 a way of living in which you are happy and have all you need: *He lived in comfort.* [=he had enough money to live well]

comfort² *verb*

to make someone feel less worried by being kind to him or her: *She comforted the crying child.*

com·fort·a·ble /'kʌmftəbəl, 'kʌmfɚtəbəl/ *adjective*

1 pleasant to wear, sit in, or be in: *This is a very comfortable chair.*

2 with no pain or worries: *We're not rich, but we are comfortable.*

com·ic /'kɑmɪk/ *adjective*
making people laugh; funny

comic book /'.. ,./ *noun*
a small book for children, with pictures that tell the story —see color picture on page 185

com·ma /'kɑmə/ *noun*
the sign (,) used in writing to show a short pause

com·mand¹ /kə'mænd/ *verb*
1 to order someone to do something: *I command you to attack!*
2 to be in charge of people: *A general commands a large number of soldiers.*

command² *noun*
1 an order that must be obeyed
2 [U] power or control: *The officer is in command of his men.*

com·mence /kə'mɛns/ *verb*
to begin: *The evening performance will commence at eight o'clock.* ≫ compare START

com·ment¹ /'kɑmɛnt/ *verb*
to give an opinion about something: *The President is not commenting on the meeting.*

comment² *noun*
an opinion or remark about something: *Do you have any comments about the situation?*

com·men·tar·y /'kɑmən,tɛri/ *noun*
[*plural* commentaries]
a description of an event while it is happening, especially on radio or television

com·men·ta·tor /'kɑmən,teɪtɚ/ *noun*
someone who describes an event while it is happening

com·merce /'kɑmɚs/ *noun* [U]
the buying and selling of goods; business

com·mer·cial¹ /kə'mɚʃəl/ *adjective*
related to the buying and selling of goods

commercial² *noun*
an advertisement on television or on the radio

com·mit /kə'mɪt/ *verb* [committing, committed]
1 to use your time, money etc. to achieve something: *How much money are they willing to commit to the work?*
2 to do something wrong or illegal: *He said he did not commit the crime.*

com·mit·tee /kə'mɪti/ *noun*
a group of people chosen to do something, make decisions etc.

com·mon¹ /'kɑmən/ *adjective*
1 found everywhere; usual: *Dogs are a common pet.* ≫ compare RARE
2 belonging to or shared by several people: *We are all working toward a common goal.*
3 **common sense** the ability to think about things and make good decisions: *It's just common sense to plan ahead.*

common² *noun*
have something in common to have the same interests as someone else: *You and I have a lot in common.*

com·mu·ni·cate /kə'myunə,keɪt/ *verb*
[communicating, communicated]
to speak or write to someone: *If you speak English, you can communicate with a lot of people.*

com·mu·ni·ca·tion /kə,myunə'keɪʃən/ *noun*
1 [U] the act of speaking or writing to someone and being understood by him or her: *Communication between people who speak different languages is difficult.*
2 **communications** [*plural*] the ways of sending information between places, such as radio, telephone, television etc.

com·mu·ni·ty /kə'myunəti/ *noun*
[*plural* communities]
all the people living in one place: *All the children in our local community go to the same school.*

com·mut·er /kə'myutɚ/ *noun*
a person who travels to work each day

com·pact disc /,kɑmpækt 'dɪsk/
a CD

com·pan·ion /kəm'pænyən/ *noun*
a person you are with, often a friend: *He was my closest companion for many months.*

com·pa·ny /'kʌmpəni/ *noun*
1 [*plural* companies] a group of people doing business: *I work for a computer company.*
2 [U] a person or people you are with: *I can't talk now. We have company.*

com·par·a·tive /kəm'pærətɪv/
a word or a form of a word that shows that something is bigger, smaller, better, worse, etc. than something else; for example, "bigger" is the comparative form of "big" ≫ compare SUPERLATIVE

com·pare /kəmˈpɛr/ verb (comparing, compared)

to decide in what way things are alike or different: *People are always comparing me **to** my sister.*

com·par·i·son /kəmˈpærəsən/ noun

an act of saying in what way two things are alike or different: *My shoes are small in comparison **with** my brother's.*

com·part·ment /kəmˈpɑrtˈmənt/ noun

a small space inside something larger

com·pass /ˈkʌmpəs/ noun (plural compasses)

an instrument with a metal needle that always points north

com·pel /kəmˈpɛl/ verb (compelling, compelled)

to force someone to do something: *The floods compelled us to turn back.*

com·pete /kəmˈpit/ verb (competing, competed)

to try to win a race, prize etc.: *Five children competed in the race.*

com·pe·ti·tion /ˌkɑmpəˈtɪʃən/ noun

a test of who is best at something: *She won first place in a piano competition.*

com·pet·i·tor /kəmˈpɛtətər/ noun

a person who tries to win something

com·plain /kəmˈpleɪn/ verb

to say that you are unhappy or angry with something or someone: *We complained **about** the bad food.*

com·plaint /kəmˈpleɪnt/ noun

something you say which shows that you are unhappy or angry about something: *I have had a lot of complaints **about** your work.*

com·plete¹ /kəmˈplit/ adjective

1 whole; with nothing left out: *I now have a complete set of dishes.* ≫ opposite INCOMPLETE

2 total; in every way: *This is a complete waste of time.*

complete² verb (completing, completed)

to finish doing or making something: *They have completed the new school building.*

com·plete·ly /kəmˈplitˈli/ adverb

totally: *I completely forgot about your birthday.*

com·pli·cat·ed /ˈkɑmpləˌkeɪt̬ɪd/ adjective

difficult to understand; not simple: *She asked us to solve a very complicated problem.*

com·pli·ment¹ /ˈkɑmpləmənt/ noun

something nice that you say about someone ≫ compare INSULT²

compliment² verb

to say something nice to someone, or to praise someone: *She complimented Mary **on** her dress.*

com·pose /kəmˈpoʊz/ verb (composing, composed)

1 be composed of to be formed from different parts: *The book is composed of five parts.*

2 to put things together to form a song, piece of art etc.

com·pos·er /kəmˈpoʊzər/ noun

a person who writes music

com·po·si·tion /ˌkɑmpəˈzɪʃən/ noun

a story, poem, piece of music etc. that you have written

com·pound /ˈkɑmpaʊnd/ noun

a group of buildings and the land around them

com·pul·so·ry /kəmˈpʌlsəri/ adjective

having to be done because it is a rule or law: *Learning science is compulsory in our school.*

com·put·er /kəmˈpyut̬ər/ noun

a machine that stores information and can work out answers very quickly: *Do you have a personal computer?* —see color picture on page 185

computer game /.ˈ.. ./ noun

a game played on a computer

con·cen·trate /ˈkɑnsənˌtreɪt/ verb (concentrating, concentrated)

to think very carefully about what you are doing: *With all this noise, it is difficult to concentrate.*

con·cern¹ /kənˈsɜrn/ noun

worry: *He shows no concern for his children.*

concern² verb

1 to be about someone or something: *The story concerns a man who lived in Russia.*

2 to be important or to involve someone: *This letter concerns you.*

3 to worry someone: *Her refusal to eat concerns me greatly.*

con·cerned /kənˈsɝnd/ adjective

1 anxious or worried: *I'm very concerned* **about** *my mother's illness.*

2 **as far as I'm concerned** in my opinion

3 involved in something or affected by it

con·cern·ing /kənˈsɝnɪŋ/

about: *I have a question concerning the car.*

con·cert /ˈkɑnsɝt/ noun

an act of playing music in public for a lot of people

con·clude /kənˈklud/ verb (concluding, concluded)

1 to finish something: *The meeting concluded with a vote on the issue.*

2 to decide that something is true from the information that you have: *I concluded* **that** *I had no choice but to accept her offer.*

con·clu·sion /kənˈkluʒən/ noun

1 a decision that something is true from the information that you have: *My conclusion is that he is telling the truth.*

2 the end or final part of a book, story etc.

con·crete /kɑnˈkrit, ˈkɑŋkrit/ noun [U]

a gray powder mixed with sand and water, which becomes hard and is used for building

con·demn /kənˈdɛm/ verb

1 to say that you do not approve of someone or something very strongly

2 to give someone a punishment for a crime

con·di·tion /kənˈdɪʃən/ noun

1 the state of someone or something: *The car is* **in** *very* **good** *condition.* | *Weather conditions are bad today.*

2 something that must happen before something else happens: *One of the conditions* **of** *having the job was that I had to learn English.*

con·duct¹ /kənˈdʌkt/ verb

1 to do or organize something: *He conducted a test on the computer.*

2 to lead or guide someone: *He conducted us on a tour of the castle.*

conduct² /ˈkɑndʌkt/ noun [U]

the way you behave ≫ compare BEHAVIOR

con·duc·tor /kənˈdʌktɝ/ noun

a person who controls a group of people playing music

cone /koʊn/ noun

a round shape that is pointed at one end, like the end of a sharp pencil —see picture at SHAPE¹

con·fer·ence /ˈkɑnfrəns/ noun

a meeting of people to find out what they think about a subject: *She is at a scientific conference.*

con·fess /kənˈfɛs/ verb

to tell someone that you have done something wrong: *When the police questioned the man, he confessed.*

con·fes·sion /kənˈfɛʃən/ noun

something that you say or write that shows you have done something wrong: *He* **made a** *confession.*

con·fi·dence /ˈkɑnfədəns/ noun [U]

a feeling that you are sure that you can do something: *She* **has** *a lot of confidence* **in** *her ability to sing.*

con·fi·dent /ˈkɑnfədənt/ adjective

feeling sure that you can do something well: *I was confident* **that** *I had passed the exam.*

con·firm /kənˈfɝm/ verb

to say for certain that something is true or will happen: *The doctors confirmed* **that** *she had a broken leg.*

con·fir·ma·tion /ˌkɑnfɝˈmeɪʃən/ noun [U]

something that shows that something else is true or will happen

con·flict¹ /ˈkɑnˌflɪkt/ noun

a fight or argument: *There is a conflict* **between** *the two countries.*

conflict² /kənˈflɪkt/ verb

to disagree: *His story conflicts* **with** *what he said before.*

con·fuse /kənˈfyuz/ verb (confusing, confused)

1 to make it difficult for someone to know what to think or do: *His questions really confused me.*

2 to think wrongly that one person or thing is someone or something else: *I confused the two boys because they look so much alike.*

con·fu·sion /kənˈfyuʒən/ noun [U]

a state of not knowing what to think or do: *There was a lot of confusion* **over** *the new rules.*

con·grat·u·late /kənˈgrætʃəˌleɪt/ verb

to say you are pleased about a happy event: *I congratulated them* **on** *the birth of their baby.*

con·grat·u·la·tions
/kən,grætʃə'leɪʃənz/ *plural noun*

an expression of happiness or admiration for something someone has done: *Congratulations on your new job!*

con·gress /'kaŋgrɪs/ *noun*

the group of people chosen or elected to make the laws in some countries

con·junc·tion /kən'dʒʌŋkʃən/ *noun*

a word such as "and" or "but" that joins two parts of a sentence

con·nect /kə'nɛkt/ *verb*

to join two or more things together: *Connect this hose to the wall.*

con·nec·tion /kə'nɛkʃən/ *noun*

1 a relationship between two or more things, ideas etc.: *What's the connection between the two events?*

2 the joining of two or more things: *Check the pipes for any leaks around the connections.*

con·quer /'kaŋkə/ *verb*

to defeat someone in war: *Long ago, the Romans conquered the Greeks.*

con·quest /'kaŋkwɛst/ *noun*

the defeat or control of a group of people

con·science /'kanʃəns/ *noun*

the feeling inside you that tells you whether something is right or wrong: *He has a guilty conscience.* (=he feels he did something wrong)

con·scious /'kanʃəs/ *adjective*

awake and knowing what is happening around you: *He is badly hurt but still conscious.* ≫ opposite UNCONSCIOUS

con·sent¹ /kən'sɛnt/ *verb*

to agree to something, or to allow it to be done: *Her father consented to her marriage.*

consent² *noun* [U]

permission for someone to do something: *We need your parents' written consent.*

con·se·quence /'kansə,kwɛns, -kwəns/ *noun*

something that happens as a result of something else: *Think of the consequences if you quit your job.*

con·se·quent·ly /'kansə,kwɛntli, -kwənt-/ *adverb*

happening as a result of something else

con·ser·va·tion /,kansə'veɪʃən/ *noun* [U]

the saving and protecting of animals or plants: *He is involved in the conservation of trees.*

con·ser·va·tive /kən'sə·vəṭɪv/ *adjective*

not liking to change things, and having traditional ideas about politics —**conservative** *noun*

con·sid·er /kən'sɪdə/ *verb*

to think about something: *I'm considering changing my job.*

con·sid·er·a·tion /kən,sɪdə'reɪʃən/ *noun* [U]

1 thought and care for other people's feelings: *You show no consideration for anyone but yourself!*

2 careful thought and attention: *They gave the plan careful consideration.*

con·sist /kən'sɪst/ *verb*

consist of to be made up of: *The soup consists of carrots, peas, and onions.*

con·so·nant /'kansənənt/ *noun*

a written letter, or the sound of a letter, which is not a, e, i, o, or u. ≫ compare VOWEL

con·stant /'kanstənt/ *adjective*

happening all the time: *He's under constant pressure from his job.* —**constantly** *adverb*

con·sti·tu·tion /,kanstə'tuʃən/ *noun*

a set of laws governing a country, state, club, etc.

con·sti·tu·tion·al /,kanstə'tuʃənəl/ *adjective*

written in or concerning the set of laws governing a country or organization

con·struct /kən'strʌkt/ *verb*

to build or make something: *The city plans to construct a bridge over the river.*

con·struc·tion /kən'strʌkʃən/ *noun* [U]

the building of something: *The house is under construction.* (=being built)

con·sul /'kansəl/ *noun*

a person who lives in a foreign city whose job is to help people from his or her own country

con·sult /kən'sʌlt/ *verb*

to ask someone, or to look in a book for information: *You should consult your doctor!*

con·sume /kən'sum/ *verb* (consuming, consumed)

to eat or use something: *The country consumes much more than it produces.*

con·sump·tion /kən'sʌmpʃən/ *noun* [U]
the eating or using of something: *We have a plan to reduce water consumption.*

con·tact¹ /'kɑntækt/ *verb*
to talk or write to someone: *She contacted me as soon as she arrived.*

contact² *noun* [U]
1 the act of meeting or talking to someone: *We don't have much contact with other people.*
2 the touching or being close to something: *The fire started when two wires came into contact.* (=began to touch)

contact lens /'.. ,., ,.. './ *noun* (*plural* contact lenses)
a small round piece of plastic that you put in your eye to help you see clearly

con·tain /kən'teɪn/ *verb*
to have something inside: *I found a box containing the letters.*

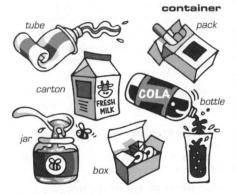

container

tube

pack

carton

COLA

bottle

FRESH MILK

jar

box

con·tain·er /kən'teɪnɚ/ *noun*
something you can put things into, for example a box, bottle etc.

con·tent /kən'tɛnt/ *adjective*
satisfied and happy: *She's content to be a writer.*

con·tent·ed /kən'tɛntɪd/ *adjective*
satisfied and happy: *My father seems more contented in his new job.*

con·tents /'kɑntɛnts/ *plural noun*
the things that are inside something: *The contents of the box fell onto the floor.*

con·test /'kɑntɛst/ *noun*
a fight or competition

con·ti·nent /'kɑntənənt, 'kɑntⁿn-ənt/ *noun*
one of the large areas of land on Earth, such as Africa, Europe, Australia etc.

con·ti·nen·tal /ˌkɑntən'ɛntl/ *adjective*
relating to a larger area of land

con·tin·u·al /kən'tɪnyuəl/ *adjective*
happening often or all the time

con·tin·ue /kən'tɪnyu/ *verb* (continuing, continued)
1 to keep happening or doing something without stopping: *She continued to work through the night.*
2 to start again after stopping: *The play will continue in 15 minutes.*
3 to go further in the same direction: *The road continues on to Miami from here.*

con·tin·u·ous /kən'tɪnyuəs/ *adjective*
never stopping: *This plant needs a continuous supply of fresh water.*

con·tract /'kɑntrækt/ *noun*
a written agreement between two people or companies that says what each one must do for the other

con·trar·y¹ /'kɑnˌtrɛri/ *noun* [U]
on the contrary used for saying that the opposite of what was just said is true: *"You must be tired." "On the contrary, I feel fine."*

contrary² *adjective*
different from or not agreeing with something: *Many people had contrary opinions about what to do.*

con·trast¹ /kən'træst/ *verb*
to compare two things and show the differences between them: *The book contrasts different ways to prepare fish.*

contrast² /'kɑntræst/ *noun*
a difference: *There is a big contrast between the rich and poor.*

con·trib·ute /kən'trɪbyut, -yət/ *verb* (contributing, contributed)
to give money or help: *We all contributed money to buy Richard's present.*

con·tri·bu·tion /ˌkɑntrə'byuʃən/ *noun*
money or help that is offered or given: *Do you want to make a contribution to the church?*

con·trol¹ /kən'troʊl/ *verb* (**controlling, controlled**)

to make someone or something do what you want: *He could not control his children.*

control² *noun* [U]

1 the power or ability to make someone or something do what you want: *The car went out of control and hit a tree.*

2 the power to rule a place, company, or country: *The army is trying to regain control of the city.*

con·ven·ience /kən'vinyəns/ *noun* [U]

the quality of being useful, helpful, or easy: *I like the convenience of living close to the city.*

con·ven·ient /kən'vinyənt/ *adjective*

useful for your needs; near and easy to get to: *The store is a convenient place to shop.* ≫ opposite INCONVENIENT —**conveniently** *adverb*

con·vent /'kɑnvɛnt, -vənt/ *noun*

a place where women who lead a religious life (NUNS) live ≫ compare MONASTERY

con·ver·sa·tion /ˌkɑnvɚ'seɪʃən/ *noun*

a talk between two or more people: *I had a long conversation with your teacher.*

con·ver·sion /kən'vɚʒən, -ʃən/ *noun*

a change from one use to another or from one religion to another

con·vert /kən'vɚt/ *verb*

to change something into something else: *That building has been converted into a school.*

con·vict¹ /kən'vɪkt/ *verb*

to decide in a law court that someone is guilty of something: *He was convicted of murder.*

convict² /'kɑnvɪkt/ *noun*

a person who has been sent to prison for doing something wrong

con·vince /kən'vɪns/ *verb* (**convincing, convinced**)

1 to make someone believe something: *He convinced me that he was telling the truth.*

2 be convinced that to be completely certain that something is true: *I was convinced that I was doing the right thing.*

cook¹ /kʊk/ *verb*

to make food ready to eat by heating it: *He's cooking dinner for me tonight.*

cook² *noun*

a person who prepares food for eating: *Sarah is a very good cook.*

cook·book /'kʊkbʊk/ *noun*

a book that tells you how to prepare different foods

cookie

cook·ie /'kʊki/ *noun*

a thin dry sweet cake

cook·ing /'kʊkɪŋ/ *noun* [U]

the activity of making food ready to eat

cool¹ /kul/ *adjective*

1 said when you agree with something or like something: *Look at those cool shoes!*

2 a little cold: *The room became cool after the sun went down.*

3 calm and not excited

cool² *verb*

1 to make or become a little colder: *Leave the cake to cool.*

2 cool down/cool off to become calmer after being angry: *I'll discuss it with her again when she's cooled down.*

co·op·er·ate /koʊ'ɑpəˌreɪt/ *verb* (**cooperating, cooperated**)

to work together with someone else to get something done: *If we all cooperate, we'll finish this by five o'clock.*

co·op·er·a·tion /koʊˌɑpə'reɪʃən/ *noun* [U]

willingness to work together: *Thank you for your cooperation.*

co·op·er·a·tive /koʊ'ɑprətɪv/ *adjective*

willing to help other people

cop /kɑp/ *noun*

a police officer

cop·per /'kɑpɚ/ *noun* [U]

a red-gold metal

cop·y¹ /'kɑpi/ *verb* (**copying, copied**)

1 to make or do something exactly the same as something else: *Can you copy this tape for me?*

2 to write exactly the same thing as someone else: *He copied his friend's answers on the test.*

copy² noun (plural **copies**)

1 something that is made to look the same as something else: *Please send a copy of this letter to Mr. Brown.*

2 one magazine, book, or newspaper of the many that are made: *Do you have another copy of this book?*

cord /kɔrd/ noun

a piece of wire or a thin rope

core /kɔr/ noun

1 the central or most important part of something: *Now we are getting to the core of the problem.*

2 the hard central part of certain fruits

cork /kɔrk/ noun

1 [U] a light substance from the outside of a particular type of tree

2 a piece of this put in the top of a bottle to keep the liquid in

corn /kɔrn/ noun [U]

a tall plant with yellow seeds that you can cook and eat

cor·ner /'kɔrnɚ/ noun

the place where two lines, walls, streets etc. meet each other: *His house is on the corner of 42nd Street and Rowan Road.*

corn·flakes /'kɔrnfleɪks/ plural noun

a breakfast food made from crushed corn, usually eaten with milk

cor·po·ra·tion /ˌkɔrpə'reɪʃən/ noun

a large business

corpse /kɔrps/ noun

a dead body

cor·rect¹ /kə'rɛkt/ adjective

right; with no mistakes: *He gave a correct answer.* ≫ opposite INCORRECT

correct² verb

1 to make something right or better: *These glasses will help to correct your vision.*

2 to fix the mistakes in something: *I've corrected your homework.*

cor·rec·tion /kə'rɛkʃən/ noun

a change that makes something right or better: *He made several corrections to the letter.*

cor·re·spond /ˌkɔrə'spand, ˌkar-/ verb

1 to be like or to relate to something else: *Your name does not correspond to the one on my list.*

2 to write to someone and receive letters from him or her

cor·re·spond·ence /ˌkɔrə'spandəns, ˌkar-/ noun [U]

letters

cor·re·spond·ent /ˌkɔrə'spandənt, ˌkar-/ noun

1 someone who works for a newspaper or television company and reports news

2 someone who writes or receives letters

cor·ri·dor /'kɔrədɚ, -ˌdɔr, 'kar-/ noun

a long narrow passage between two rows of rooms: *My room is at the end of the corridor.*

cos·met·ics /kaz'mɛtɪks/ plural noun

substances that you put on your skin and face to make you look better

cost¹ /kɔst/ noun

1 the money that you have to pay when you buy or do something: *The cost of the books has gone up.*

2 something needed, given, or lost in order to get something else: *War is never worth the terrible cost in human life.*

3 at all costs no matter what has to be given or lost: *We need that job at all costs.*

cost² verb (past **cost**)

1 to have a particular price: *How much did that bag cost?*

2 cost an arm and a leg to be very expensive

cost·ly /'kɔstli/ adjective (**costlier, costliest**)

costing a lot of money: *The ring was very costly.* ≫ compare EXPENSIVE

cos·tume /'kastum/ noun

clothes worn for a special reason, or that represent a country or time in history: *The children wore animal costumes.*

cot /kat/ noun

a narrow bed that folds up

cot·tage /'katɪdʒ/ noun

a small house in the country

cot·ton /'katⁿn/ noun [U]

1 thread or cloth made from the cotton plant: *She bought a new cotton dress.*

2 a plant grown for the white threads that cover its seeds

cotton ball /'.. ˌ./ noun

a small soft ball of cotton

couch /kaʊtʃ/ *noun (plural* **couches***)*

a long seat on which you can sit or lie ≫ compare SOFA

cough¹ /kɔf/ *verb*

to push air out from your throat and mouth with a sudden, rough sound: *She's been coughing all night.*

cough² *noun*

a sharp noise made when you cough: *Billy has a bad cough, so his mother took him to the doctor.*

could /kəd; *strong* kʊd/ *verb*

1 a word meaning "can" in the past: *He said we could come any time.*

2 used when saying what might happen: *It could take weeks for the package to arrive.*

3 used as a polite way of asking someone something: *Could you help me, please?*

could·n't /ˈkʊdnt/

could not: *I couldn't see because it was dark.*

could've /ˈkʊdəv/

could have: *He could've told me he was going to be late.*

coun·cil /ˈkaʊnsəl/ *noun*

a group of people who are chosen to make laws or decisions in a town or city: *The city council will decide where to plant the trees.*

count¹ /kaʊnt/ *verb*

1 to say numbers in the right order: *Can you count from 1 to 10?*

2 to find out how many things there are in a group: *She counted the books – there were fourteen of them.*

3 to be important or have value: *He felt that his opinion didn't count for anything.*

4 **count on someone or something** to depend on someone or something: *You can always count on me to help.*

count² *noun* [U]

1 the total that you get when you add things together: *At the last count, I'd visited 15 countries.*

2 **lose count** to forget the total of something: *I've lost count of how many people I invited.*

coun·ter /ˈkaʊntə/ *noun*

1 a narrow table in a store or bank where you go to get something

2 a flat surface in a kitchen where you can prepare food

coun·ter·clock·wise /ˌkaʊntəˈklɑk-waɪz/ *adjective, adverb*

in the opposite direction of the way the hands of a clock move around ≫ opposite CLOCKWISE

count·less /ˈkaʊntlɪs/ *adjective*

too many to count: *She spends countless hours watching television.*

coun·try /ˈkʌntri/ *noun (plural* **countries***)*

1 a nation with its land and people: *France and Germany are European countries.*

2 [U] the land that is outside a city or town: *He lives in the country.*

coun·try·side /ˈkʌntriˌsaɪd/ *noun* [U]

land outside a city or town

coun·ty /ˈkaʊnti/ *noun (plural* **counties***)*

a part of a state

cou·ple /ˈkʌpəl/

1 [U] two things, or a small number of things: *I waited for a couple of hours.*

2 two people who are married, live together, or have a close relationship: *We've invited three other couples to dinner.*

cou·pon /ˈkupɑn, ˈkyu-/ *noun*

a piece of paper that you can use to pay less money for something

cour·age /ˈkɜɪdʒ, ˈkʌr-/ *noun* [U]

willingness to do dangerous things without feeling afraid: *The soldier showed great courage in the battle.* ≫ compare BRAVERY

cou·ra·geous /kəˈreɪdʒəs/ *adjective*

brave: *It takes a courageous person to do what she did.*

course /kɔrs/ *noun*

1 **of course** certainly: *"Can I borrow your pen?" "Of course."*

2 [U] the path or direction that something takes: *The plane had to change course in order to land.*

3 a class in a particular subject: *What courses are you taking in college?*

4 one part of a meal: *We have three courses: soup, meat and vegetables, and fruit.*

5 the way that something happens or develops: *World War II changed the course of history.*

court /kɔrt/ *noun*

1 a place where someone is asked about a crime, and other people decide whether the person is guilty

2 an open space where games are played: *I'll meet you at the tennis court.*

cour·te·ous /'kɔtiəs/ *adjective*
polite

cour·te·sy /'kɔtəsi/ *noun* [U]
polite behavior

court·yard /'kɔrt⌐yɑrd/ *noun*
an open space that is surrounded by walls or buildings

cous·in /'kʌzən/ *noun*
the child of your aunt or uncle

cov·er¹ /'kʌvɚ/ *verb*
1 to put something over something else: *She covered the table with a cloth.*
2 to be spread over a particular area or surface: *The town covers five square miles.*
3 to include or deal with something: *His talk covered the subject of how to read faster.*
4 cover (something) up to hide something, or to stop mistakes from being known by other people: *She tried to cover up the news about her sister.*

cover² *noun*
1 something that you put over something else
2 the outside of a book or magazine
3 take cover to shelter or hide from something: *We took cover when the shooting started.*

cow /kaʊ/ *noun*
a large female animal that farmers keep for their milk and meat

cow·ard /'kaʊɚd/ *noun*
someone who is not brave and avoids dangerous situations

cow·ard·ly /'kaʊɚdli/ *adjective*
showing a lot of fear, not brave ≫ compare BRAVE

cow·boy /'kaʊbɔɪ/ *noun* (*plural* **cowboys**)
a man who rides a horse and takes care of cattle

co·zy /'koʊzi/ *adjective* (**cozier, coziest**)
warm and comfortable: *They have a cozy little house.*

crab /kræb/ *noun*
a sea animal with ten legs and a hard shell
—see color picture on page 183

crack¹ /kræk/ *verb*
1 to break something so that lines appear on the surface of it: *One of the cups is cracked.*
—see picture at BROKEN

2 to make a loud noise
3 crack down to become more strict when dealing with bad behavior

crack² *noun*
1 a thin line on the surface of something: *There's a crack in the wall.*
2 a very narrow space between two things: *Can you squeeze through the crack?*
3 a sudden loud noise: *I heard a crack of thunder.*
4 [U] a form of the drug COCAINE: *He was caught selling crack.*

crack·er /'krækɚ/ *noun*
a thin hard dry piece of bread with salt on it

cra·dle /'kreɪdl/ *noun*
a bed for a baby, which can swing from side to side

craft /kræft/ *noun* (**craftier, craftiest**)
1 a job or activity that you need skill to do: *He knew the craft of making furniture.*
2 a boat or plane

crafts·man /'kræftsmən -/ *noun* (*plural* **craftsmen** /-mɛn/
someone who has a lot of skill in a particular craft

craft·y /'kræfti/ *adjective*
good at making other people believe things that are not true

cram /kræm/ *verb* (**cramming, crammed**)
to force people or things into a small space: *Lots of people were crammed **into** the bus.*

crane /kreɪn/ *noun*
a tall large machine used for lifting heavy things

crash¹ /kræʃ/ *noun* (*plural* **crashes**)
1 a loud noise like something breaking or hitting something else: *The car hit the tree with a crash.*
2 an accident in which vehicles hit each other: *He was involved in a car crash.*

crash² *verb*
1 to have an accident, used for vehicles: *The car crashed into a tree.*
2 if a computer crashes, it stops working
3 to make a sudden loud noise

crash course /ˌ. './ *noun*
classes in which you learn the most important things about a subject in a short time

crate /kreɪt/ *noun*
a big wooden box

crawl /krɔl/ *verb*
to move along the floor on your hands and knees: *The baby crawled toward his father.* —see color picture on page 189

cray·on /'kreɪɑn, -ən/ *noun*
a soft colored pencil

cra·zy /'kreɪzi/ *adjective* (**crazier, craziest**)
1 foolish; very strange: *He's crazy to drive his car so fast.*
2 be crazy about to like someone or something very much: *He's crazy about her.*

creak /krik/ *verb*
to make a long high noise when pushed, stepped on, or sat on: *The door creaked as she opened it.*

cream¹ /krim/ *noun* [U]
1 the thick part of milk that you can eat with other foods: *Do you take cream in your coffee?*
2 a thick liquid that you put on your skin: *I'm trying a new face cream.* —**creamy** *adjective*

cream² *adjective, noun* [U]
a yellowish-white color

cre·ate /kri'eɪt/ *verb* (**creating, created**)
to make something new: *The government wants to create more jobs.*

cre·a·tion /kri'eɪʃən/ *noun*
something that is made

cre·a·tive /kri'eɪtɪv/ *adjective*
good at making new and interesting things

crea·ture /'kritʃɚ/ *noun*
an animal or insect

cred·it¹ /'krɛdɪt/ *noun* [U]
1 attention and approval for doing something good: *I never get any credit for the work I do.*
2 a way of buying things in which you pay for them later: *We bought the furniture on credit.*

credit² *verb*
to add money to a bank account

credit card /'.. ,./ *noun*
a small plastic card that allows you to buy things and pay for them later

creek /krik, krɪk/ *noun*
a small narrow river

creep /krip/ *verb* (*past* **crept** /krɛpt/)
to move slowly and quietly

crept /krɛpt/
the PAST TENSE and PAST PARTICIPLE of the verb creep

crest /krɛst/ *noun*
the top of a hill, mountain, or wave

crew /kru/ *noun*
the people who work on a ship or plane

crib /krɪb/ *noun*
a bed with high sides for a baby —see picture at BED

crick·et /'krɪkɪt/ *noun*
a small brown insect that jumps and makes a loud noise at night

cried /kraɪd/
the PAST TENSE and PAST PARTICIPLE of the verb cry

cries /kraɪz/
the plural of cry

crime /kraɪm/ *noun* [U]
1 an action that is wrong and can be punished by the law: *Stealing is a crime.*
2 commit a crime to do something wrong that can be punished by the law

crim·i·nal /'krɪmənəl/ *noun*
someone who has done something very wrong and is punished by the law: *The prison contains 325 criminals.*

crim·son /'krɪmzən/ *adjective, noun* [U]
a deep red color, like the color of blood

crip·ple /'krɪpəl/ *verb* (**crippling, crippled**)
to hurt someone so that they cannot use their arms or legs: *She was crippled in the car accident.*

cri·sis /'kraɪsɪs/ *noun* (*plural* **crises**)
a time when something serious, very worrying, or dangerous happens

crisp /krɪsp/ *adjective*
dry and hard; easily broken: *Potato chips only taste good if they are crisp.*

crit·ic /'krɪtɪk/ *noun*
a person whose job is to say whether art, music, movies, etc. are good or bad

crit·i·cal /'krɪtɪkəl/ *adjective*
1 looking for faults: *She was very critical of my work.*
2 very important: *This item is critical to the plan's success.*

crit·i·cis·m /'krɪtəˌsɪzəm/ *noun*
the act of saying whether someone or something is good or bad: *I listened to all her criticisms in silence.*

crit·i·cize /'krɪtə,saɪz/ *verb* **(criticizing, criticized)**

to say what is wrong with something; to find faults in something: *She's always criticizing me.*

croc·o·dile /'krɑkə,daɪl/ *noun*

a large animal with a long body, a hard skin, and sharp teeth, which lives in hot wet areas —see color picture on page 183

crook /krʊk/ *noun*

a person who is not honest

crook·ed /'krʊkɪd/ *adjective*

1 not straight; bent or curved: *We drove down a crooked road.*

2 not honest: *It sounded like a crooked deal to me.*

crop /krɑp/ *noun*

1 a plant such as wheat, corn, fruit etc. that a farmer grows

2 an amount of wheat, fruit etc. that is cut or gathered at one time

cross¹ /krɔs/ *noun* **(plural crosses)**

1 two pieces of wood put across each other, or an object shaped like this: *She wore a gold cross on a chain.*

2 a mixture between two or more things: *My dog is a cross between a German shepherd and a collie.*

cross² *verb*

1 to go over from one side of something to the other: *Be careful when you cross the street.*

2 if you cross your arms or legs, you put one over the other

cross³ *adjective*

angry

cross·roads /'krɔsroʊdz/ *plural noun*

a place where two roads meet and cross each other

cross·walk /'krɔswɔk/ *noun*

a special place where you may cross the street

cross·word puz·zle /'krɔswəd ˌpʌzəl/ *noun*

a game in which you write words into a special pattern of squares

crouch /kraʊtʃ/ *verb*

to make your body come close to the ground by bending your knees and back: *She crouched behind the wall to hide.* —see color picture on page 189

crow /kroʊ/ *noun*

a large black bird with a loud cry

crowd¹ /kraʊd/ *noun*

a large group of people: *There was a crowd of people waiting at the airport.*

crowd² *verb*

to come together in a large group: *People crowded at the doors when the movie ended.*

crowd·ed /'kraʊdɪd/ *adjective*

too full of people: *We had to wait in a crowded room.*

crown /kraʊn/ *noun*

a special hat made of gold, beautiful stones, etc., worn by a king or queen

cru·ci·fix /'krusə,fɪks/ *noun* **(plural crucifixes)**

an small object with a figure of Jesus on it

crude /krud/ *adjective*

1 in a natural or raw condition: *Crude oil has to be made pure before it can be used.*

2 rude, especially about sex: *He told a crude joke.*

cru·el /'kruəl/ *adjective*

hurting other people or animals or making them feel unhappy: *You should not be cruel to animals.* ≫ compare KIND

cru·el·ty /'kruəlti/ *noun* [U]

actions that cause pain to a person or animal

cruise¹ /kruz/ *noun*

a trip on a large boat for pleasure over the ocean

cruise² *verb*

to move along slowly: *I saw a boat cruising past on the lake.*

crumb /krʌm/ *noun*

a little piece of something such as bread or cake

crum·ble /'krʌmbəl/ *verb* **(crumbling, crumbled)**

to break apart into little pieces: *The walls of that old house are crumbling.*

crum·ple /'krʌmpəl/ *verb*
to crush something and make it smaller: *The front of the car crumpled when it was hit.*

crunch /krʌntʃ/ *verb*
1 to crush food with your teeth and make noise
2 to make a sound like something being crushed: *The stones crunched under the car tires.*

crush /krʌʃ/ *verb*
to press something so hard that it is damaged or breaks: *Some people were crushed by the falling rocks.*

crust /krʌst/ *noun*
the hard part on the outside of bread

crutch /krʌtʃ/ *noun* (plural **crutches**)
a special stick that you put under your arm to help you walk when you have hurt your legs

cry¹ /kraɪ/ *verb* (**crying**, *past* **cried**)
1 to shout something loudly: *The boy cried for help.*
2 to produce tears from your eyes usually because you are sad or hurt: *I always cry at sad movies.*

cry² *noun* (plural **cries**)
a loud shout; a call: *We heard a cry for help.*

cub /kʌb/ *noun*
a baby bear, lion, tiger, or fox

cube /kyub/ *noun*
a solid shape with six equal square sides —see picture at SHAPE¹

cuck·oo /'kuku/ *noun*
a bird that has a call which sounds like its name

cu·cum·ber /'kyu,kʌmbɚ/ *noun*
a long thin green vegetable which is usually eaten without cooking it —see picture at VEGETABLE

cud·dle /'kʌdl/ *verb* (**cuddling**, **cuddled**)
to put your arms around someone and hold him or her close to you: *She cuddled her little boy.*

cuff /kʌf/ *noun*
the end of an arm of a shirt, dress etc.

cul·ti·vate /'kʌltə,veɪt/ *verb* (**cultivating**, **cultivated**)
to prepare and use land for growing crops

cul·ti·va·tion /,kʌltə'veɪʃən/ *noun* [U]
the preparation and use of land to grow crops

cul·ture /'kʌltʃɚ/ *noun*
1 the beliefs, customs, and way of life of a particular society
2 [U] art, music, and the theater: *Paris is full of culture.*

cup   mug

cup /kʌp/ *noun*
1 a small round container with a handle, used for drinking from, or the liquid it contains: *Would you like a cup of tea?*
2 a prize, shaped like a bowl, usually made of silver or gold

cup·board /'kʌbɚd/ *noun*
a piece of furniture with shelves and a door, in which you keep plates or food

cup·cake /'kʌpkeɪk/ *noun*
a small cake for one person

curb /kɚb/ *noun*
a raised edge at the side of a street

cure¹ /kyʊɚ/ *verb* (**curing**, **cured**)
to make someone better when he or she has been sick: *I hope the doctor can cure the pain in my shoulder.*

cure² *noun*
a medicine or treatment for making someone feel better: *They are searching for a cure **for** cancer.*

cu·ri·os·i·ty /,kyʊri'ɑsəti/ *noun* [U]
the desire to know something or learn about something: *He is full of curiosity **about** the world around him.*

cu·ri·ous /'kyʊriəs/ *adjective*
1 wanting to know or learn about something: *I'm very curious **about** our new neighbors.*
2 strange or unusual: *We heard a curious noise upstairs.*

cu·ri·ous·ly /'kyʊriəsli/ *adverb*
in a way that seems strange or unusual

curl¹ /kɚl/ *verb*
1 to roll or bend something into a round or curved shape: *She curled her hair.*
2 curl up to lie or sit with your arms and legs close to your body: *She curled up in front of the fire.*

curl² *noun*
a piece of hair that hangs down in a curved shape

curl·y /'kɚli/ *adjective* (**curlier, curliest**)
hanging down in a curved shape

cur·ren·cy /'kɚ ənsi, 'kʌr-/ *noun* (*plural* **currencies**)
the money used in a country

cur·rent¹ /'kɚ ənt, 'kʌr-/ *adjective*
happening or being used right now: *Why do you want to change your current job?*

current² *noun*
a flow of water, air, or electricity: *Don't swim in the river. The current is very fast.*

curse¹ /kɚs/ *verb* (**cursing, cursed**)
1 to say or think bad things about someone or something: *He cursed the person who stole his money.*
2 to speak angry words: *I heard him curse when he hit his head.*

curse² *noun*
1 something you say which shows anger or hate, or which uses bad words
2 a word or wish that, with the help of God or some magical power, something bad will happen to someone

cur·sor /'kɚsɚ/ *noun*
a mark you can move on a computer screen that shows where you are writing

cur·tain /'kɚt ⁿn/ *noun*
a large piece of hanging cloth that can be pulled across a window or stage ≫ compare BLIND²

curve¹ /kɚv/ *noun*
a line that bends like a part of a circle: *I see a curve in the road.*

curve² *verb* (**curving, curved**)
to bend or move in the shape of a circle: *The river curved around the hill.*

cush·ion /'kʊʃən/ *noun*
a bag filled with soft material to sit on or rest against ≫ compare PILLOW

cus·tom /'kʌstəm/ *noun*
a special way of doing something by a person or group

cus·tom·er /'kʌstəmɚ/ *noun*
a person who buys things from a store

cus·toms /'kʌstəmz/ *plural noun*
a place where your bags can be searched when you leave or enter a country

cut¹ /kʌt/ *verb* (**cutting, cut**)
1 to divide or open something with a knife or something sharp: *Cut the apple in half.* | *He has cut his leg, and it is bleeding.*
2 to make something shorter: *Could you cut my hair for me?*
3 to reduce the number or amount of something: *The number of students has been cut in half.*
4 cut down to make something fall to the ground by cutting it: *We'll have to cut down that tree.*
5 cut (something) off (a) to stop the supply of something: *Our water has been cut off.* (b) to separate a person or place from the other people or places near them: *Snow has cut us off from the town.*
6 cut something up to cut something into pieces: *Could you cut up the chicken?*
7 cut something out to remove something by cutting it: *She cut a picture out of the newspaper.*
8 cut it out! used for telling someone to stop doing something: *Cut it out you two, or I'll send you to bed!*

cut² *noun*
1 an opening or wound made by something sharp: *I have a cut on my arm.*
2 a reduction in size, number, or amount: *The government promised us a tax cut.*

cute /kyut/ *adjective*
attractive and pretty: *"Oh, what a cute little dress."*

cy·ber·space /'saɪbɚˌspeɪs/ *noun* [U]
all the connections between computers in different places, the place where information, pictures etc. exist

cy·cle /'saɪkəl/ *noun*
a set of events that happen again and again

cyl·in·der /'sɪləndɚ/ *noun*
a long round shape like a tube or a pencil —see picture at SHAPE¹

'd /d/
1 had: *He'd* (=he had) *eaten all the cake.*
2 would: *I'd* (=I would) *buy a new car if I had the money.*

dad /dæd/ *noun*
father

dad·dy /'dædi/ *noun (plural* **daddies***)*
father; used by small children

daf·fo·dil /'dæfəˌdɪl/ *noun*
a yellow flower which appears in the spring

dai·ly /'deɪli/ *adjective, adverb*
happening every day: *Take the medicine twice daily.* ≫ compare WEEKLY

dair·y /'dɛri/ *noun (plural* **dairies***)*
a place where milk is kept and foods are made from milk

dai·sy /'deɪzi/ *noun (plural* **daisies***)*
a small white flower with a yellow center

dal·ma·tian /dæl'meɪʃən/ *noun*
a white dog with black spots

dam¹ /dæm/ *noun*
a wall built to hold back water

dam² *verb (***damming, dammed***)*
to build a dam across something: *There is a plan to dam the river.*

dam·age¹ /'dæmɪdʒ/ *noun* [U]
harm that has been done to something

damage² *verb (***damaging, damaged***)*
to harm something: *The cars were badly damaged in the accident.*

damp /dæmp/ *adjective*
a little wet: *My clothes are still damp from the rain.*

dance¹ /dæns/ *verb (***dancing, danced***)*
to move to music: *We danced all night at the party.*

dance² *noun*
1 a set of movements you do to music: *I am learning a new dance.*

2 a party for dancing: *Are you going to the dance?*

danc·er /'dænsɚ/ *noun*
a person who is dancing, or who dances as a job

dan·de·li·on /'dændəˌlaɪən/ *noun*
a small yellow flower which grows wild

dan·druff /'dændrəf/ *noun* [U]
very small, white pieces of dead skin in a person's hair

dan·ger /'deɪndʒɚ/ *noun*
1 [U] the chance of harm: *You are not in any danger here.* (=there is no danger)
2 something that can cause harm: *Do you know the dangers of smoking?*

dan·ger·ous /'deɪndʒərəs/ *adjective*
likely to harm people: *He is a dangerous driver.*
—**dangerously** *adverb*

dare /dɛr/ *verb (***daring, dared***)*
1 to be brave enough to do something: *He wouldn't dare say anything to your boss!*
2 **dare someone to do something** to try to make someone do something to prove they are not afraid: *I dare you to jump off this chair.*
3 **don't you dare** used when telling someone not to do something: *Don't you dare touch that!*
4 **how dare you** used when saying you are angry about what someone has done or said: *How dare you speak to me like that!*

dark¹ /dɑrk/ *adjective*
1 like night; not light or bright: *It was getting dark, so we hurried home.* ≫ compare LIGHT²
2 of a deep color, nearer black than white: *She has dark hair.* | *He wore a dark suit.* ≫ compare FAIR¹, PALE

dark² *noun* [U]
the lack of light: *We could not see in the dark.* | *Make sure you are home before dark.* (=before it is night)

dark·ness /'dɑrknɪs/ *noun* [U]
lack of light: *The whole room was in darkness.* (=was dark)

dar·ling /'dɑrlɪŋ/
a name you call someone you love: *Come on darling, or we'll be late.*

dart /dɑrt/ *verb*
to move suddenly and quickly: *A mouse darted across the floor.*

darts /dɑrts/ *plural noun* [U]

a game in which you throw small objects with sharp points at a board with numbers on it

dash¹ /dæʃ/ *verb*

to run quickly: *She dashed out of the room.*

dash² *noun* [*plural* **dashes**]

the sign (–) used in writing to separate two parts of a sentence

da·ta /'deɪtə, 'dætə/ *plural noun* [U]

facts and information

da·ta pro·cess·ing /'deɪtə ˌprɑsɛsɪŋ, 'dætə-/ *noun* [U]

the use of computers to store and change information, especially in a business

date¹ /deɪt/ *noun*

1 the day of the month or year: *"What date is your birthday?" "It's April 2nd."* | *Please write today's date.*

2 an arrangement to meet a boy- or girlfriend: *I've got a date tonight.*

3 someone you are dating: *Where's your date?*

4 a small sweet brown fruit

date² *verb* [**dating, dated**]

to have a romantic relationship with a boy- or girlfriend: *How long have you been dating Tina?*

daugh·ter /'dɔtɚ/ *noun*

your female child: *They have three daughters and one son.*

daughter-in-law /'.. . ˌ./ *noun* [*plural* **daughters-in-law**]

the wife of your son

dawn /dɔn/ *noun*

the start of the day when the sun rises ≫ compare DAYBREAK

day /deɪ/ *noun*

1 the time when it is light: *The days get longer in the summer.* ≫ compare NIGHT

2 24 hours: *Wait three days before calling.*

3 a period of work in a 24-hour period: *She works an eight-hour day.*

4 one day, some day at some time in the future: *Some day I'll be rich.*

5 the other day a few days ago: *I went to the movies the other day.*

6 these days at the present time: *Everyone seems so busy these days.*

day·break /'deɪbreɪk/ *noun* [U]

the start of the day when the light first appears ≫ compare DAWN

day·care /'deɪkɛr/ *noun* [U]

a place where children can go to play while their parents are at work

day·dream /'deɪdrim/ *verb*

to imagine nice things, especially things you would like to happen in the future

day·light /'deɪlaɪt/ *noun* [U]

the light of the day: *We want to travel in daylight.* [=before it goes dark]

day·time /'deɪtaɪm/ *noun* [U]

the time when it is light ≫ compare NIGHTTIME

dead¹ /dɛd/ *adjective*

1 not living: *My grandfather has been dead for ten years.* ≫ compare ALIVE, LIVING¹

2 not working: *I think the radio is dead.*

dead² *noun*

the dead dead people: *After the battle, they counted the dead.* ≫ compare LIVING²

dead·ly /'dɛdli/ *adjective* [**deadlier, deadliest**]

likely to cause death: *She drank a deadly poison.* ≫ compare FATAL

deaf /dɛf/ *adjective*

not able to hear: *I'm deaf in my right ear.* —**deafness** *noun* [U]

deal¹ /dil/ *noun*

1 a business arrangement: *We have a deal with them to build cars.*

2 a good deal, a great deal a lot: *There's a good deal of work to do.*

deal² *verb* [*past* **dealt** /dɛlt/]

1 deal with someone to do business with someone: *We have been dealing with them for years.*

2 deal with something to do what is necessary for something: *I will deal with any questions now.* [=answer them]

3 to buy or sell illegal drugs

deal·er /'dilɚ/ *noun*

a person who buys and sells a certain thing: *He works as a car dealer.*

dealt /dɛlt/

the PAST TENSE and PAST PARTICIPLE of the verb **deal**

dear¹ /dɪr/ *adjective*

1 much loved: *She is a very dear friend.*

2 used at the start of a letter to someone: *Dear Sue, Thank you for your gift.*

dear²
a word you say when you are surprised, annoyed or upset: *Oh, dear! I forgot to call my son.*

death /dɛθ/ *noun*
the state of being dead, or the act of dying: *The death of his father was very sad for us all.*

de·bate¹ /dɪ'beɪt/ *noun*
a public talk at which people give opinions about a subject

debate² *verb* (debating, debated)
to talk about something so you can make a decision: *We are debating about which person to choose.*

debt /dɛt/ *noun*
money that you owe: *I don't have enough money to pay my debts.*

dec·ade /'dɛkeɪd/ *noun*
a period of ten years

de·cay¹ /dɪ'keɪ/ *verb* (decaying, decayed)
to be destroyed slowly; to become bad ≫ compare ROT

decay² *noun* [U]
the state or process of decaying

de·ceit /dɪ'sit/ *noun* [U]
behavior that makes someone believe something that is not true

de·ceive /dɪ'siv/ *verb* (deceiving, deceived)
to make someone believe something that is not true: *He tried to deceive us all.*

De·cem·ber /dɪ'sɛmbə/ *noun*
the 12th month of the year

de·cent /'disənt/ *adjective*
good, or acceptable: *Make sure you eat a decent breakfast.* —decently *adverb*

de·cide /dɪ'saɪd/ *verb* (deciding, decided)
to choose what to do: *I decided to go home.* | *She could not decide which dress to buy.*

dec·i·mal /'dɛsəməl/ *noun*
a number less than one that is shown by a point (.) followed by numbers, such as 0.1237

de·ci·sion /dɪ'sɪʒən/ *noun*
a choice: *We have to make a decision by next week.*

deck /dɛk/ *noun*
1 a part of a ship where you can sit or stand
2 a set of cards that you play games with
3 a flat wooden area next to a house where you can sit outdoors

dec·la·ra·tion /ˌdɛklə'reɪʃən/ *noun*
an official statement: *The country made a declaration of war.*

de·clare /dɪ'klɛr/ *verb* (declaring, declared)
to say in public what you think or decide: *The judge declared him to be not guilty.*

de·cline¹ /dɪ'klaɪn/ *verb* (declining, declined)
to become less in number or quality: *House sales are declining this year.*

decline² *noun*
a decrease in the number or quality of something

decorate

dec·o·rate /'dɛkəˌreɪt/ *verb* (decorating, decorated)
to make something look more attractive by adding things to it: *I need to decorate the cake.*

dec·o·ra·tion /ˌdɛkə'reɪʃən/ *noun*
an attractive thing that is added to something to improve its appearance

dec·o·ra·tor /'dɛkəˌreɪtə/ *noun*
a person whose job is to choose furniture, paint etc. for a place

de·crease¹ /dɪ'kris/ *verb* (decreasing, decreased)
to become less or fewer: *The number of students in the school has decreased this year.* ≫ opposite INCREASE¹

decrease² /'dikris/ *noun*
the process of having less or fewer of something ≫ opposite INCREASE²

deed /did/ *noun*
an action: *Did you do a good deed?* [=do something to help someone]

deep /dip/ *adjective*
1 going down a long way: *How deep is the river?* | *He has a deep cut on his leg.*

2 having a low sound: *John has a deep voice.*

3 strong or dark in color: *I love her deep blue eyes.*

4 felt strongly: *She feels a deep love for her son.*

deep freeze /ˌ. './ *noun*

a FREEZER

deep·ly /'dipli/ *adverb*

very strongly: *I am deeply in love with her.*

deer /dɪr/ *noun* (*plural* **deer**)

a wild animal that can run fast. The male usually has horns.

de·feat¹ /dɪ'fit/ *verb*

to beat an opponent in a war, game etc.

defeat² *noun*

an experience or event in which you do not win or succeed: *The football team suffered a defeat.* ≫ opposite VICTORY

de·fend /dɪ'fɛnd/ *verb*

to protect someone or something from an attack: *You should learn to defend yourself.* ≫ compare ATTACK¹

de·fense /dɪ'fɛns/ *noun* [U]

protecting someone or something from an attack: *The weapons are for the defense of our country.*

de·fi·ant /dɪ'faɪənt/ *adjective*

not obeying someone, and showing him or her no respect

def·i·nite /'dɛfənɪt/ *adjective*

clear; sure: *Let's choose a definite time for the next meeting.*

definite ar·ti·cle /ˌ... '.../ *noun*

the word **the**

def·i·nite·ly /'dɛfənɪtli/ *adverb*

certainly; without any doubt: *I'm definitely going to come.*

def·i·ni·tion /ˌdɛfə'nɪʃən/ *noun*

an explanation of what a word means, which you find in a dictionary

de·fy /dɪ'faɪ/ *verb* (**defying, defied**)

to refuse to obey someone and show no respect for him or her: *He defied his parents' wishes and went to the party anyway.*

de·gree /dɪ'gri/ *noun*

1 a measurement used for temperatures or angles: *The temperature is 45 degrees.* (=45°)

2 an official piece of paper that says someone has completed their studies at a university: *I have a degree in history.*

de·lay¹ /dɪ'leɪ/ *noun* (*plural* **delays**)

a time of waiting before something happens: *We are sorry for the delay.*

delay² *verb* (**delaying, delayed**)

1 to wait until later to do something: *Don't delay; call her now!*

2 to make something late: *The plane has been delayed by bad weather.*

de·lete /dɪ'lit/ *verb* (**deleting, deleted**)

to remove a piece of information from a computer

de·lib·er·ate /dɪ'lɪbrɪt, -bərɪt/ *adjective*

planned or done on purpose

de·lib·er·ate·ly /dɪ'lɪbrɪt⌐li/ *adverb*

on purpose: *I didn't do it deliberately – it was an accident.*

del·i·cate /'dɛlɪkɪt/ *adjective*

easily harmed, damaged, or broken: *Be careful with the glass. It is delicate.*

del·i·ca·tes·sen /ˌdɛlɪkə'tɛsən/ *noun*

a small store that sells cheese, meats, breads etc. —see color picture on page 193

de·li·cious /dɪ'lɪʃəs/ *adjective*

good to eat: *The cake is delicious.*

de·light¹ /dɪ'laɪt/ *noun* [U]

great happiness or pleasure: *She laughed with delight.*

delight² *verb*

to give someone a feeling of happiness

de·light·ed /dɪ'laɪt̬ɪd/ *adjective*

very pleased or happy: *We are delighted to hear the good news.*

de·light·ful /dɪ'laɪt⌐fəl/ *adjective*

very nice or attractive: *We had a delightful day in the park.*

de·liv·er /dɪ'lɪvɚ/ *verb*

1 to take something to a particular place: *Have you delivered the package yet?*

2 **deliver a baby** to help a baby come out of its mother's body

de·liv·er·y /dɪ'lɪvəri/ *noun* (*plural* **deliveries**)

the act of taking something to a particular place

de·mand¹ /dɪ'mænd/ *verb*

to ask for something in a way that is very strong

and firm: *"Give me the book right now,"* she demanded.

demand[2] *noun*
1 a very strong request: *The workers made a demand for more money.*
2 **in demand** wanted by a lot of people

de·moc·ra·cy /dɪ'mɑkrəsi/ *noun* (*plural* democracies)
a government or country where everyone has an equal right to vote and choose the leaders —**democratic** *adjective*

de·mol·ish /dɪ'mɑlɪʃ/ *verb*
to destroy something completely: *The houses were demolished in a few days.*

dem·o·li·tion /ˌdɛmə'lɪʃən/ *noun* [U]
the act of destroying a building completely

dem·on·strate /'dɛmənˌstreɪt/ *verb* (demonstrating, demonstrated)
1 to show how to do something: *He demonstrated how the new machine works.*
2 to meet with other people in public to support or show you are angry about something

dem·on·stra·tion /ˌdɛmən'streɪʃən/ *noun*
1 the act of showing how to do something: *She gave a demonstration to our class.*
2 an event in which people meet in public to support or show that they are angry about something

den /dɛn/ *noun*
a place in which a wild animal lives

den·im /'dɛnəm/ *noun* [U]
a strong cloth, usually blue in color, which is used to make JEANS

dense /dɛns/ *adjective*
thick, or very close together: *She was found in a dense forest.* (=a lot of trees) —**densely** *adverb*: *a densely populated area* (=with a lot of people)

den·tist /'dɛntɪst/ *noun*
a person whose job is to clean and fix people's teeth

den·tures /'dɛntʃɚz/ *plural noun*
false teeth worn by people who have lost their real teeth

de·ny /dɪ'naɪ/ *verb* (denying, denied)
to say that something someone has said about you is not true » opposite ADMIT

de·o·dor·ant /di'oʊdərənt/ *noun*
a substance that people put under their arms, to stop their body from smelling bad

de·part /dɪ'pɑrt/ *verb*
to leave; to go away: *When does the next flight to Boston depart?* » opposite ARRIVE

de·part·ment /dɪ'pɑrtᵊmənt/ *noun*
a part of a business, college, government etc.

department store /.'.. ,./ *noun*
a large store that sells many different kinds of goods —see color picture on page 193

de·par·ture /dɪ'pɑrtʃɚ/ *noun*
an act of leaving a place: *Try to be here an hour before your departure.* » opposite ARRIVAL

de·pend /dɪ'pɛnd/ *verb*
1 **it depends** said when you are not sure about something, or you cannot decide: *"How long will the trip take?" "I don't know – it depends."*
2 **depend on** to need the help of someone or something

de·pend·ent[1] /dɪ'pɛndənt/ *adjective*
needing someone or something to help or support you » opposite INDEPENDENT

dependent[2] *noun*
a person, especially a child, who depends on someone for money, food etc.

de·pos·it[1] /dɪ'pɑzɪt/ *verb*
to put money into a bank account

deposit[2] *noun*
1 part of the cost of something that you pay at once so that it will not be sold to someone else
2 money that is added to a bank account

de·press /dɪ'prɛs/ *verb*
to make someone feel sad

de·pressed /dɪ'prɛst/ *adjective*
very sad: *She feels depressed.*

de·press·ing /dɪ'prɛsɪŋ/ *adjective*
making you feel sad: *I heard some depressing news.*

de·pres·sion /dɪ'prɛʃən/ *noun* [U]
a feeling of great sadness

depth /dɛpθ/ *noun*
the distance from the top to the bottom of something: *The river has a depth of 50 feet.*

dep·u·ty /'dɛpyəti/ *noun* (*plural* deputies)
a person who is second in importance in a business, the police etc.

de·scend /dɪ'sɛnd/ *verb*

to go down

de·scend·ant /dɪ'sɛndənt/ *noun*

someone who is related to a person who lived a long time ago ≫ compare ANCESTOR

de·scribe /dɪ'skraɪb/ *verb* (describing, described)

to say what someone or something is like: *Can you describe the man?*

de·scrip·tion /dɪ'skrɪpʃən/ *noun*

an account of what someone or something is like

des·ert /'dɛzət/ *noun*

a large empty area of land where it is hot and dry

de·sert·ed /dɪ'zətɪd/ *adjective*

empty of people: *At night the streets are deserted.*

de·serve /dɪ'zəv/ *verb* (deserving, deserved)

to be worthy of something: *You deserve a rest after all your hard work.*

de·sign¹ /dɪ'zaɪn/ *noun*

1 a pattern: *The chair has a design of blue flowers.*

2 a drawing of how to make something: *Have you seen the designs for the new house?*

design² *verb*

to make a drawing as a plan for something: *He is trying to design a new car.*

de·sign·er /dɪ'zaɪnə/ *noun*

a person whose job is to think of ideas for making things and then draw them

de·sire¹ /dɪ'zaɪə/ *noun*

a strong wish: *He has a strong desire to succeed.*

desire² *verb* (desiring, desired)

to want something very much —**desirable** *adjective*

desk /dɛsk/ *noun*

a table that you can sit at to write and work

de·spair¹ /dɪ'spɛr/ *noun* [U]

a feeling of being very sad and having no hope

despair² *verb*

to feel that there is no hope

des·per·ate /'dɛsprɪt, -pərɪt/ *adjective*

wanting or needing something very much: *I was desperate for a job.*

de·spise /dɪ'spaɪz/ *verb* (despising, despised)

to hate someone or something very much

de·spite /dɪ'spaɪt/ *preposition*

although something is true: *Despite the bad weather, we enjoyed our trip.*

des·sert /dɪ'zət/ *noun*

a sweet food that you eat at the end of a meal

des·ti·na·tion /ˌdɛstə'neɪʃən/ *noun*

the place you are going to: *What is your destination?*

de·stroy /dɪ'strɔɪ/ *verb* (destroying, destroyed)

to break or damage something completely: *The building was destroyed by fire.*

de·struc·tion /dɪ'strʌkʃən/ *noun* [U]

the act of breaking or damaging something completely

de·tail /'diteɪl, dɪ'teɪl/ *noun*

1 one fact or piece of information about something: *Tell me the details of the plan.*

2 **in detail** thoroughly; using a lot of facts: *We talked about the problem in detail.*

de·tect /dɪ'tɛkt/ *verb*

to discover or notice something

de·tec·tive /dɪ'tɛktɪv/ *noun*

a special police officer who tries to discover who has done a crime

de·ter·gent /dɪ'tədʒənt/ *noun*

soap in the form of powder or liquid for washing clothes, dishes etc.

de·te·ri·o·rate /dɪ'tɪriəˌreɪt/ *verb* (deteriorating, deteriorated)

to become worse: *Her health is deteriorating quickly.*

de·ter·mi·na·tion /dɪˌtəmə'neɪʃən/ *noun* [U]

a strong desire to succeed even when it is difficult

de·ter·mined /dɪ'təmɪnd/ *adjective*

having a strong desire to do something even if it is difficult: *She is a very determined woman.*

de·test /dɪ'tɛst/ *verb*

to hate someone or something very much

de·vel·op /dɪ'vɛləp/ *verb*

1 to grow or change into something: *The fighting could develop into a war.* | *This insect develops wings.*

2 to make something successful by working on it: *We have plans to develop industry in the area.*

3 to begin to happen or exist: *Clouds are developing in the distance.*

4 to make pictures out of the film in a camera

de·vel·oped /dɪ'vɛləpt/ *adjective*

1 larger, stronger, or more improved: *He has well developed muscles.*

2 developed country a rich country that has a lot of industry

de·vel·op·ment /dɪ'vɛləpmənt/ *noun*

1 a new event or change that makes something different or better

2 [U] growth: *Good food is necessary for a child's development.*

de·vice /dɪ'vaɪs/ *noun*

a thing that you use for a particular purpose: *He made a device for opening wine bottles.*

dev·il /'dɛvəl/ *noun*

an evil spirit who some people believe causes bad things in the world

de·vote /dɪ'voʊt/ *verb* (**devoting, devoted**)

devote yourself to something to do all you can do to achieve something: *She devoted herself to helping others.*

dew /du/ *noun* [U]

small drops of water that form on the ground or on plants during the night

di·ag·o·nal /daɪ'æɡənəl/ *noun*

a line that goes from one corner of a square to the opposite corner, dividing it into two parts

di·a·gram /'daɪə,ɡræm/ *noun*

a plan or picture drawn to explain an idea, or to show how something works

di·al¹ /'daɪəl/ *noun*

a round part of a machine or instrument, often with numbers on it

dial² *verb*

to turn the DIAL¹ or press the numbers of a telephone to make a call: *Dial this number if you need me.*

di·a·lect /'daɪə,lɛkt/ *noun*

a form of one language that is spoken in one area in a different way than it is in another area

≫ compare ACCENT

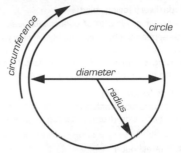

diameter

circumference

circle

diameter

radius

di·am·e·ter /daɪ'æmətə/ *noun*

a straight line that divides a circle in half

di·a·mond /'daɪmənd, 'daɪə-/ *noun*

a very hard, bright, clear stone that is worth a lot of money and is used in jewelry

di·a·per /'daɪpə, -'daɪə/ *noun*

a piece of cloth that is put between a baby's legs and fastened at the waist

di·ar·rhe·a /,daɪə'riə/ *noun* [U]

an illness in which a person's waste is like water and comes out often

di·a·ry /'daɪəri/ *noun* (*plural* **diaries**)

a book in which you write about the things that happen to you each day

dice /daɪs/

the plural of DIE²

dic·tate /'dɪkteɪt, dɪk'teɪt/ *verb* (**dictating, dictated**)

to say words for someone else to write down: *I dictated a letter to my secretary.*

dic·ta·tion /dɪk'teɪʃən/ *noun*

words that a teacher says, that you must write without making mistakes

dic·ta·tor /'dɪkteɪtə/ *noun*

a strong leader who is not fair and often uses soldiers to control people

dic·tion·ar·y /'dɪkʃə,nɛri/ *noun* (*plural* **dictionaries**)

a book that tells you what words mean and how to spell them

did /dɪd, d; *strong* dɪd/

the PAST TENSE of the verb **do**: *"Did you go there?" "Yes, I did."*

did·n't /ˈdɪdnt/

did not: *I didn't enjoy the movie. Did you?*

die¹ /daɪ/ *verb* (**dying, died**)

1 to stop living: *He died of cancer last year.*

2 to disappear or stop existing: *My love for you will never die.*

3 **be dying to do something** to want to do something very much: *I'm dying to meet her.*

die² *noun* (*plural* **dice**)

a small square block with a different number of spots on each side (from 1 through 6), which is used in games

di·et /ˈdaɪət/ *noun*

1 the food that you eat: *She has a healthy diet.* (=she usually eats good food)

2 a plan to eat less food or a particular type of food: *Are you on a diet?* (=trying to eat less food)

dif·fer·ence /ˈdɪfrəns/ *noun*

1 a way in which things are not the same: *There is not much difference in price between the two books.* ≫ compare SIMILARITY

2 **make a difference** to have a good effect on something or someone: *Exercise can make a big difference in how you feel.*

3 **make no difference** to have no importance or effect: *It makes no difference to me what you do.*

dif·fer·ent /ˈdɪfrənt/ *adjective*

not the same: *I don't like that dress. I want a different one.* ≫ compare SAME

dif·fi·cult /ˈdɪfəˌkʌlt/ *adjective*

not easy to do or understand: *He asked a difficult question.* ≫ compare EASY

dif·fi·cul·ty /ˈdɪfɪˌkʌlti/ *noun* (*plural* **difficulties**)

a problem: *He is having difficulty finding a new job.*

dig /dɪg/ *verb* (**digging, dug** /dʌg/)

to make a hole in the ground by moving earth: *She likes digging in the sand.*

di·gest /daɪˈdʒɛst, dɪ-/ *verb*

to change food in your stomach so that your body can use it —**digestion** *noun* [U] —**digestive** *adjective*: *the digestive system*

dig·i·tal /ˈdɪdʒɪt̬l/ *adjective*

giving information in the form of numbers

dig·ni·fied /ˈdɪgnəˌfaɪd/ *adjective*

calm, serious, and proud

dig·ni·ty /ˈdɪgnət̬i/ *noun* [U]

calm serious behavior that makes people respect you

dim /dɪm/ *adjective*

not very bright: *The room was very dim.* —**dimly** *adverb*

dime /daɪm/ *noun*

a coin that is worth ten cents

din /dɪn/ *noun* [U]

loud continuous noise

din·er /ˈdaɪnɚ/ *noun*

1 a small restaurant that serves inexpensive meals

2 someone who is eating in a restaurant

di·ning room /ˈ.. ˌ./ *noun*

a room with a table where you eat meals

din·ner /ˈdɪnɚ/ *noun*

the main meal of the day, usually eaten in the evening ≫ compare LUNCH

di·no·saur /ˈdaɪnəˌsɔr/ *noun*

an animal that lived a long time ago and no longer exists

dip /dɪp/ *verb* (**dipping, dipped**)

to put something into a liquid and then take it out again: *She dipped her foot in the water.*

di·plo·ma /dɪˈploʊmə/ *noun*

a piece of paper given to someone to show that he or she has completed a course of study

di·rect¹ /dəˈrɛkt, daɪ-/ *adjective*

1 going straight from one place to another: *We took a direct flight to Paris.*

2 saying exactly what you mean in an honest way: *It is better to be direct with people if you can.*

direct² *verb*

to tell someone the way to go or what to do: *I directed him to the hotel.*

di·rec·tion /dəˈrɛkʃən, daɪ-/ *noun*

1 the way that someone or something is moving or pointing: *Which direction are you going, north or south?*

2 control or advice: *She followed the directions on the package to bake the cake.* | *The company has done well under his direction.*

di·rect·ly /dəˈrɛktli, daɪ-/ *adverb*

1 involving only the people or action necessary: *You must speak to her directly.*

2 straight from one place to another: *We are going directly to New York.*

di·rec·tor /də'rɛktə, daɪ-/ *noun*

a person who makes movies and tells the actors and other people what to do

di·rec·to·ry /də'rɛktəri, daɪ-/ *noun* (*plural* **directories**)

a book or list that tells you the names of people, events etc.

dirt /dət/ *noun* [U]

anything such as dust or soil that makes things not clean: *He had dirt all over his face.*

dirt·y /'dəti/ *adjective* (**dirtier, dirtiest**)

not clean: *My shoes are dirty.* ≫ compare CLEAN[1]

dis·a·bled /dɪs'eɪbəld/ *adjective*

not being able to move or use a part of your body well

dis·ad·van·tage /,dɪsəd'væntɪdʒ/ *noun*

something that makes things more difficult for you: *It is a disadvantage not having a car.* ≫ opposite ADVANTAGE

dis·a·gree /,dɪsə'gri/ *verb* (*past* **disagreed**)

not to agree with someone; to have different opinions: *I'm afraid I disagree **with** you.* ≫ opposite AGREE

dis·a·gree·ment /,dɪsə'grimənt/ *noun*

an argument, or having a different opinion from someone: *We had a disagreement **over** money.* ≫ opposite AGREEMENT

dis·ap·pear /,dɪsə'pɪr/ *verb*

to go out of sight suddenly: *The boy disappeared around the corner.* ≫ opposite APPEAR
—**disappearance** *noun*

dis·ap·point /,dɪsə'pɔɪnt/ *verb*

to be less interesting or not as good as you expected, and so make you sad

dis·ap·point·ed /,dɪsə'pɔɪntɪd/ *adjective*

sad because something is not as good as you expected: *We were disappointed **with** the meal.*

dis·ap·point·ing /,dɪsə'pɔɪntɪŋ/ *adjective*

not as good as you expected: *I had a disappointing score on the test.*

dis·ap·point·ment /,dɪsə'pɔɪnt¬mənt/ *noun*

a feeling of sadness because something is not as good as you expected

dis·ap·prov·al /,dɪsə'pruvəl/ *noun* [U]

the feeling or opinion that someone or something is bad or wrong ≫ opposite APPROVAL

dis·ap·prove /,dɪsə'pruv/ *verb* (**disapproving, disapproved**)

to think that someone or something is bad or wrong: *My mother disapproves **of** my friends.* ≫ opposite APPROVE

dis·as·ter /dɪ'zæstə/ *noun*

a sudden event that happens to a lot of people and causes much damage or harm

dis·ci·pline /'dɪsəplɪn/ *noun* [U]

a way of training your body and mind so that you control your actions and thoughts: *Soldiers have to learn discipline in the army.*

dis·count /'dɪskaʊnt/ *noun*

an amount of money taken away from the price of something: *I got a $5 discount on the tickets.*

dis·cour·age /dɪ'skəɪdʒ -'skʌr-/ *verb* (**discouraging, discouraged**)

to try to stop someone doing something: *His father tried to discourage him from buying the car.* ≫ opposite ENCOURAGE

dis·cov·er /dɪ'skʌvə/ *verb*

to find something that was hidden, or to learn about something for the first time: *They discovered gold in the mountains.*

dis·cov·er·y /dɪ'skʌvri, -vəri/ *noun* (*plural* **discoveries**)

a fact or answer to a question that someone finds or learns about: *Is this a new discovery in medical science?*

dis·crim·i·na·tion /dɪ,skrɪmə'neɪʃən/ *noun* [U]

unfair treatment of some people because of the color of their skin, where they come from etc.

dis·cuss /dɪ'skʌs/ *verb*

to talk about something: *I want to discuss your work **with** you.*

dis·cus·sion /dɪ'skʌʃən/ *noun*

a talk about something: *We had a discussion **about** sex.*

dis·ease /dɪ'ziz/ *noun*

an illness or unhealthy condition: *The doctor said he has heart disease.*

dis·grace /dɪs'greɪs, dɪ'skreɪs/ *noun* [U]

something that makes people feel ashamed or lose their good opinion of you

dis·grace·ful /dɪsˈgreɪsfəl/ *adjective*
very bad and wrong: *Your attitude is disgraceful!*

dis·guise¹ /dɪsˈgaɪz, dɪˈskaɪz/ *verb* (**disguising, disguised**)
to make yourself look like someone else so that people do not know who you are

disguise² *noun*
something that you wear to make you look like someone else so that people do not know who you are

dis·gust¹ /dɪsˈgʌst, dɪˈskʌst/ *verb*
to make you feel that something is very bad or unpleasant: *The smell disgusted me.*

disgust² *noun* [U]
a strong feeling of not liking something or finding it unpleasant

dis·gust·ing /dɪsˈgʌstɪŋ/ *adjective*
very bad and unpleasant: *The medicine tasted disgusting!*

dish /dɪʃ/ *noun* (*plural* **dishes**)
a container used for cooking or holding food: *Have you washed the dishes?*

dis·hon·est /dɪsˈɑnɪst/ *adjective*
not honest —**dishonestly** *adverb*

dish·tow·el /ˈdɪʃtaʊəl/ *noun*
a cloth used for drying dishes

dish·wash·er /ˈdɪʃˌwɑʃɚ/ *noun*
1 a machine that washes dirty dishes
2 someone whose job is to wash dirty dishes in a restaurant

dis·in·fect·ant /ˌdɪsɪnˈfɛktənt/ *noun*
a chemical that cleans things thoroughly

disk /dɪsk/
1 a flat piece of plastic used for storing information on a computer
2 a round flat object in the shape of a circle

disk

disk drive /ˈ. ./ *noun*
a piece of equipment in a computer that stores or gets information from a disk

disk jock·ey /ˈ. ˌ../ *noun*
(*also* **DJ**; *plural* **disk jockeys**) a person whose job is to play music on the radio or at a party

dis·like¹ /dɪsˈlaɪk/ *verb* (**disliking, disliked**)
not to like someone or something

> NOTE: The verb **dislike** is not often used in ordinary conversation because it is fairly formal. People usually say that they **don't like** something, rather than saying that they **dislike** it, e.g. *I don't like her.* | *He doesn't like swimming.*

dis·like² *noun*
a feeling of not liking someone or something

dis·loy·al /dɪsˈlɔɪəl/ *adjective*
not faithful or true to someone » opposite LOYAL

dis·may /dɪsˈmeɪ/ *noun* [U]
a feeling of being disappointed and not happy

dis·miss /dɪsˈmɪs/ *verb*
1 to send someone away: *Class is dismissed.*
2 to refuse to think about someone's idea or opinion
3 to remove someone from their job

dis·o·be·di·ence /ˌdɪsəˈbidiəns/ *noun* [U]
the act of refusing to obey someone » opposite OBEDIENCE

dis·o·be·di·ent /ˌdɪsəˈbidiənt/ *adjective*
not willing to obey someone: *He is a disobedient child.* » opposite OBEDIENT

dis·o·bey /ˌdɪsəˈbeɪ/ *verb* (**disobeying, disobeyed**)
not to do what someone tells you to do: *You should never disobey your parents.* » opposite OBEY

dis·or·ga·nized /dɪsˈɔrgəˌnaɪzd/ *adjective*
not planned or arranged well » opposite ORGANIZED

dis·play¹ /dɪˈspleɪ/ *verb* (**displaying, displayed**)
to show something so that many people can see it: *The children's pictures are displayed on the wall.*

display² *noun* (*plural* **displays**)
1 a show or performance for people: *We saw a display of students' paintings.*
2 **on display** in a public place for many people to see

dis·pos·al /dɪˈspoʊzəl/ *noun* [U]
the act of getting rid of something

dis·pose /dɪ'spouz/ *verb*

dispose of something to get rid of something: *How did he dispose of the body?*

dis·pute /dɪ'spyut/ *noun*

an argument or disagreement: *They are having a legal dispute.* (=an argument about the law)

dis·sat·is·fied /dɪ'sætɪsˌfaɪd/ *adjective*

not content or pleased with something: *We were very dissatisfied **with** the food at the restaurant.* ≫ opposite SATISFIED

dissolve

dis·solve /dɪ'zɑlv/ *verb* (**dissolving, dissolved**)

to mix completely with a liquid: *Sugar dissolves in water.*

dis·tance /'dɪstəns/ *noun*

1 the amount of space between two places: *What's the distance between Boston and New York?*

2 **in the distance** far away: *That is my house in the distance.*

dis·tant /'dɪstənt/ *adjective*

far away. *She traveled to a distant country.*

dis·tinct /dɪ'stɪŋkt/ *adjective*

1 different; separate: *There are several distinct languages in the country.*

2 easy to see, hear, or understand; clear: *This apple has a distinct taste.*

dis·tinct·ly /dɪ'stɪŋktli/ *adverb*

very clearly: *I distinctly remember telling you to go to the store.*

dis·tin·guish /dɪ'stɪŋgwɪʃ/ *verb*

1 to see the difference between two things: *You are old enough to distinguish **between** good and bad.*

2 to be able to see, hear, or taste something even if it is difficult: *It was dark, but I could just distinguish their faces.*

dis·tin·guished /dɪ'stɪŋgwɪʃt/ *adjective*

famous and respected by many people: *Her mother is a distinguished scientist.*

dis·tress¹ /dɪ'strɛs/ *noun* [U]

a feeling of sadness, pain, or worry

distress² *verb*

to make someone sad or upset

dis·tress·ing /dɪ'strɛsɪŋ/ *adjective*

making you feel sad or upset

dis·trib·ute /dɪ'strɪbyət/ *verb* (**distributing, distributed**)

to give or send something to different people or places: *They are distributing food to the people.* —**distribution** *noun* [U]

dis·trict /'dɪstrɪkt/ *noun*

a part of a county, city etc.

dis·turb /dɪ'stɚb/ *verb*

1 to interrupt someone by making a noise, asking a question etc.: *Please don't disturb me while I'm working.*

2 to make someone feel worried or upset: *We were very disturbed by the news.*

dis·turb·ance /dɪ'stɚbəns/ *noun*

1 something that interrupts you and stops you from working: *I can't think with all these disturbances.*

2 a situation in which people fight or cause trouble: *There has been a disturbance in the street.*

ditch /dɪtʃ/ *noun* (*plural* **ditches**)

a long narrow place for water to go along, especially at the side of a road or field

dive /daɪv/ *verb* (**diving, dived** *or* **dove**)

to jump into water with your head and arms going in first: *He dived **into** the pool.*

div·er /'daɪvɚ/ *noun*

a person who swims under water and wears special equipment to help him or her breathe

di·vide /də'vaɪd/ *verb* (**dividing, divided**)

1 to separate into pieces or parts: *The class divided into groups.*

2 to share something: *We divided up the money **between** us.*

3 to find how many times a number will go into a bigger number: *10 divided **by** 5 is 2.*

di·vine /də'vaɪn/ *adjective*
from a god, or like a god

div·ing board /'.. ,./ *noun*
a board that you stand on before jumping into the water

di·vi·sion /də'vɪʒən/ *noun*
1 [U] the process of finding how many times a number will go into a bigger number
2 a part of something: *Which division of the company do you work for?*

di·vorce¹ /də'vɔrs/ *verb* (**divorcing, divorced**)
to arrange by law for a marriage to end: *They are getting divorced.*

divorce² *noun*
the ending of a marriage according to the law

diz·zy /'dɪzi/ *adjective* (**dizzier, dizziest**)
feeling as if you are going to fall and as if things are moving when they are not: *I feel dizzy when I look out of a high window.*

DJ /'di dʒeɪ/ *noun*
a DISK JOCKEY

---

do¹ /də; *strong* du/ *verb*
present tense

singular	plural
I **do**	We **do**
You **do**	You **do**
He/She/It **does**	They **do**

past tense

singular	plural
I **did**	We **did**
You **did**	You **did**
He/She/It **did**	They **did**

present participle	**doing**
past participle	**done**
negative short forms	**don't, doesn't**
	didn't

(You can find each of these words in its own place in the dictionary)

1 to perform an action or job: *I have to do some work.* | *What are you doing?* | *Have you done your homework?*
2 **do well** to be a success: *He has done well in school this year.*
3 **do someone good** to make someone feel better or more healthy: *Some exercise will do you good.*

4 **do away with something** to get rid of something: *Some people want to do away with the program.*
5 **could do with** to want or need something: *I could do with some sleep.*
6 **have to do with something** to be about or concerning someone or something: *The book has to do with studying the stars.*
7 **How do you do?** said as a polite greeting when you meet someone for the first time
8 **What do you do?** What is your job?
9 **do something over** to do something again, especially because you did it wrong the first time: *If there are mistakes, the teacher makes you do it over.*
10 **do without (something)** to live or continue without a particular thing: *With no money for shoes, we had to do without.*
11 **What did you do with ...** said when asking where someone has put something: *What did you do with my socks?*
12 **do as you are told** to do what someone, especially a parent, tells you to do

---

NOTE: Compare the verbs **do** and **make**. Use **do** when you are talking about an action or activity, e.g. *to do some work, to do the grocery shopping.* Use **make** when you are talking about producing something or causing a result, e.g. *to make a cake, to make a noise*, or when you are talking about plans or decisions: *to make a plan, to make a choice, to make an appointment.*

---

do² *verb*
1 used with NOT before another verb to say that something is not so: *I do not agree with you.* | *He doesn't* (=does not) *have a car.*
2 used with another verb, to ask a question: *Do you like dancing? Did you find the answer?*
3 used with **not**, to tell someone not to do something: *Do not lean out of the window.* | *Don't* (=do not) *do that!*
4 used to make the meaning of another verb stronger: *You do believe me, don't you?*

dock¹ /dak/ noun
a place where a boat or ship can stop and people can go on and off

dock² verb
to come into a dock, used about a ship

doc·tor /'daktɚ/ noun
a person whose job is to take care of people who are sick

doc·u·ment /'dakyəmənt/ noun
a piece of paper with official information on it

doc·u·men·ta·ry /,dakyə'mɛntri, -'mɛntəri/ noun (plural documentaries)
a movie giving information and facts about something

dodge /dadʒ/ verb (dodging, dodged)
1 to move quickly to one side to avoid something
2 to avoid doing something that you should do: He tried to dodge the question. (=not answer it)

does /dəz, z, s; strong dʌz/ verb
the part of the verb do that is used with he, she and it: Does she have a job?

does·n't /'dʌzənt/
does not: She doesn't like school.

dog /dɔg/ noun
an animal with four legs and a tail, that is often kept as a pet and used for protecting buildings

doll /dal/ noun
a toy that looks like a small person

dol·lar /'dalɚ/ noun
the money used in the U.S. and some other countries

dol·phin /'dalfin, 'dɔl-/ noun
a gray sea animal with a long pointed nose

dome /doum/ noun
a round curved roof on a room or building

do·mes·tic /də'mɛstɪk/ adjective
1 in one country and not involving other countries
2 in the home or about the home

dom·i·nate /'damə,neɪt/ verb (dominating, dominated)
to have power and control over someone or something

dom·i·noes /'damə,nouz/ plural noun
a game played with small flat pieces of wood with different numbers of spots on them

do·nate /'douneɪt, dou'neɪt/ verb (donating, donated)
to give something to a person or organization that needs help: We want to donate money to the hospital.

do·na·tion /dou'neɪʃən/ noun
a gift made to a person or organization that needs help: Please make a donation today.

done¹ /dʌn/
the PAST PARTICIPLE of the verb do

done² adjective
finished: The work is almost done.

don·key /'daŋki, 'dʌŋ-, 'dɔŋ-/ noun (plural donkeys)
an animal like a small horse with long ears

do·nor /'dounɚ/ noun
someone who gives something: She is a blood donor. (=she gives her blood to be used in a hospital)

don't /dount/
do not: I don't want to go. | Don't touch that!

do·nut /'dounʌt/ noun
a DOUGHNUT

door /dɔr/ noun
1 the flat piece of wood or metal that you push or pull to go into a room: Please open the door for me.
2 the entrance to a building or room: You go through this door and turn to the left.
3 answer the door to open the door to see who is there
4 door to door going from one house or building to another: I sold candy door to door.
5 next door to in the building or room next to a place: He lives next door to my parents. (=in the house next to theirs)
6 at the door waiting at the door for someone to open it: Is someone at the door?

door·bell /'dɔrbɛl/ noun
a button by a door that you push to make a sound so that someone inside knows you are there

door·knob /'dɔrnab/ noun
a handle on a door that you turn to open it

door·mat /'dɔrmæt/ *noun*
a thick piece of material outside a door for you to clean your shoes on

door·step /'dɔrstɛp/ *noun*
1 a step in front of the door of a house
2 on your doorstep very near to where you live

door·way /'dɔrweɪ/ *noun* [*plural* doorways]
an opening where there is a door: *He stood in the doorway.*

dorm *noun*
a large building where students live

dor·mi·to·ry /'dɔrmə,tɔri/ *noun* [*plural* dormitories]
a DORM

dose /doʊs/ *noun*
an amount of a medicine that you take at one time: *The dose is two spoonfuls every four hours.*

dot /dɑt/ *noun*
a small round mark: *On the map, towns were marked by a red dot.*

dou·ble¹ /'dʌbəl/ *adjective, adverb*
1 twice as much: *I'll pay you double if you finish the work quickly.*
2 made for two people: *Our room has a double bed.* —see picture at BED
3 having two parts that are the same: *We went through the double doors into the room.*
4 on the double very quickly: *I need that report on the double!*

double² *verb* [doubling, doubled]
1 to become twice as big or twice as much: *The value of our house has almost doubled.*
2 to make something twice as big or twice as much as before: *My new job will double my pay.*

doubt¹ /daʊt/ *verb*
to think that something may not be true or may not happen: *I doubt that she will pass the test.*

doubt² *noun*
1 the feeling of not being sure about something: *I have doubts about whether he is the best man for the job.*
2 no doubt almost certainly: *He is no doubt guilty.*

doubt·ful /'daʊtˀfəl/ *adjective*
not likely: *It's doubtful whether she'll succeed.*

doubt·less /'daʊtˀlɪs/ *adverb*
certainly; without a doubt: *He will doubtless try to change her mind.*

dough /doʊ/ *noun* [U]
a soft mixture of flour, water, and fat that is cooked to make bread, cookies etc.

dough·nut /'doʊnʌt/ *noun*
a small round sweet cake

dove¹ /dʌv/ *noun*
a small white bird, often used as a sign of peace

dove² /doʊv/
a PAST TENSE and PAST PARTICIPLE of the verb **dive**

down¹ /daʊn/ *adverb, preposition*
1 in or to a lower place: *Sit down, please.* | *The children ran down the hill.* ≫ opposite UP —see color picture on page 194
2 to a lower level or number: *Our sales are down this year.* ≫ opposite UP
3 written on paper: *Write this down so you don't forget.*
4 along or toward the far end of something: *We walked down the beach.*
5 in or toward the south: *We drove down to Texas.*

down² *adjective*
1 sad: *Why are you so down?*
2 not working properly: *The computers are still down.*

down·hill /,daʊn'hɪl/ *adjective, adverb*
toward the bottom of a hill: *The ball rolled downhill.* ≫ opposite UPHILL

down·stairs /,daʊn'stɛrz/ *adjective, adverb*
on or toward a lower part of a house: *The bathroom is downstairs.* ≫ opposite UPSTAIRS

down·town /,daʊn'taʊn/ *adverb*
in or to the center of a town or city, where there are many businesses: *We went downtown to do some shopping.*

down·ward /'daʊnwərd/ *adverb*
from a higher place or level to a lower one ≫ opposite UPWARD

doze /doʊz/ *verb* [dozing, dozed]
1 to sleep for a short time
2 doze off to go to sleep when you do not intend to: *I dozed off in front of the television.*

doz·en /'dʌzən/ noun

1 twelve: *I need a dozen eggs.*

2 dozens very many: *There were dozens of people there.*

Dr /'dɑktər/

the short way of writing the word "doctor" when you are writing someone's name

draft /dræft/ noun

air blowing into a room: *I felt a cold draft under the door.*

drag /dræg/ verb **(dragging, dragged)**

to pull something heavy along behind you

drag·on
/'drægən/ noun
a fierce animal in stories that has wings and can breathe out fire

drain¹ /dreɪn/
noun

a hole in something such as a bathtub, connected to a pipe that takes dirty water away

drain² verb

to flow away, or to make water flow away: *The water drained away slowly.*

dra·ma /'drɑmə, 'dræmə/ noun [U]

1 acting and plays: *She's studying drama.*

2 excitement: *I like the drama of a big game.*

dra·mat·ic /drə'mætɪk/ adjective

1 sudden and noticeable: *There was a dramatic change in the temperature.*

2 exciting: *He told a dramatic story.* —**dramatically** adverb

drank /dræŋk/

the PAST TENSE of the verb **drink**

draw /drɔ/ verb **(past tense drew, past participle drawn)**

1 to make a picture using a pencil or pen: *I like drawing. | Can you draw a dog?*

2 to take something from its place: *He drew a gun from his bag.*

3 draw back to move away from someone or something

4 draw a conclusion to decide that something is true or false after thinking about it

5 to attract or interest people: *The movie is drawing big crowds.*

6 draw up to prepare a written document: *Draw up an agreement, and I will sign it.*

7 draw the curtains to open or close the curtains on a window

drawer /drɔr/ noun

a part of a piece of furniture, used for keeping things in, which can be pulled out or pushed in

draw·ing /'drɔ-ɪŋ/ noun

1 [U] the making of pictures with a pencil or pen: *Are you good at drawing?*

2 a picture you make with a pen or pencil: *She showed me a drawing of her mother.*

drawn /drɔn/

the PAST PARTICIPLE of the verb **draw**

dream¹ /drim/ verb **(dreaming, past dreamed or dreamt /drɛmt/)**

1 to imagine things while you are asleep: *I dreamed about you last night.*

2 to think about something nice that you want to do: *He dreamed of becoming rich and famous.*

dream² noun

1 something that you imagine while you are asleep: *I had a strange dream last night.*

2 something nice that you have wanted to do: *It is her dream to visit Australia.*

dreamt /drɛmt/

a PAST TENSE and PAST PARTICIPLE of the verb **dream**

drear·y /'drɪri/ adjective **(drearier, dreariest)**

very dull, and making you feel sad: *It was a long and dreary day.*

drench /drɛntʃ/ verb

to make someone or something completely wet: *I was drenched in the storm.*

dress¹ /drɛs/ verb

1 to put clothes on someone or on yourself: *She got up, dressed quickly, and went to work.*

2 to wear a particular type of clothes: *Dress warmly – it is cold outside!*

3 be dressed to be wearing clothes: *They arrived before I was dressed.*

4 get dressed to put on clothes: *Hurry up and get dressed.*

5 dress up **(a)** to put on special clothes for an important occasion **(b)** to wear special clothes, shoes etc. for fun or as a game

dress² *noun*

1 [*plural* **dresses**] a piece of clothing covering the body and legs of a woman or girl: *Do you like my new dress?* —see color picture on page 190

2 [U] clothes of a particular type or for a particular purpose: *You must wear formal dress to the party.*

dresser

dress·er /ˈdrɛsɚ/ *noun*

a piece of furniture with drawers in which you keep clothes

dress·ing /ˈdrɛsɪŋ/ *noun* [U]

a liquid made with oil that you pour over food

dress·mak·er /ˈdrɛsˌmeɪkɚ/ *noun*

a person whose job is to make clothes for women

drew /dru/

the PAST TENSE of the verb **draw**

dried /draɪd/

the PAST TENSE and PAST PARTICIPLE of the verb **dry**

drift /drɪft/ *verb*

to move slowly on water or through the air: *I saw a boat drifting down the river.*

drill¹ /drɪl/ *verb*

to make a hole in something with a drill: *I drilled a hole in the wall to put up the shelf.*

drill² *noun*

a machine for making holes

drink¹ /drɪŋk/ *verb* (**drinking, drank** /dræŋk/, *past participle* **drunk**)

1 to pour liquid into your mouth and swallow it: *Would you like something to drink?* | *He drinks too much coffee.*

2 to drink alcohol, especially too much: *You should never drink and drive.*

drink² *noun*

a liquid that you can swallow: *Can I have a drink of water?*

drip /drɪp/ *verb* (**dripping, dripped**)

1 to fall in small drops: *Sweat was dripping from his face.*

2 to produce small drops of liquid: *Is the pipe still dripping?*

faucet

drip

drive¹ /draɪv/ *verb* (**driving, drove** /droʊv/, *past participle* **driven**)

to make a vehicle move in the direction you want: *Can you drive?* | *I drove to town yesterday.*

drive² *noun*

a trip in a car: *It is a short drive to the city.*

driv·en /ˈdrɪvən/

the PAST PARTICIPLE of the verb **drive**

driv·er /ˈdraɪvɚ/ *noun*

a person who drives, sometimes as a job

driver's li·cense /ˈ.. ˌ../ *noun*

an official piece of paper that shows you are allowed to drive a car

drive-through /ˈ. ./ *adjective*

able to be used without getting out of your car: *We got our food at the drive-through window.*

drive·way /ˈdraɪvweɪ/ *noun* (*plural* **driveways**)

a short road that leads to one house only: *The car is parked in the driveway.*

droop /drup/ *verb*

to hang or bend down: *The flowers are starting to droop.*

drop¹ /drɑp/ *verb* (**dropping, dropped**)

1 to fall or let something fall: *She dropped the plate.* —see color picture on page 189

2 to go down in level or amount: *The price of gas is dropping.*

3 drop in on someone to visit someone when he or she is not expecting you

drop² *noun*

a small amount of liquid: *Drops of rain ran down the window.*

drought /draʊt/ *noun*

a time when no rain falls and the land becomes very dry

drove /droʊv/

the PAST TENSE of the verb **drive**

drown /draʊn/ *verb*

to die under water because you cannot breathe

drows·y /'draʊzi/ *adjective* (**drowsier, drowsiest**)

tired and wanting to sleep: *The medicine made me feel drowsy*

drug /drʌg/ *noun*

1 something that people take to change the way they feel or behave. Many drugs are not allowed: *Do you think he is on drugs?*
2 a medicine

drug·store /'drʌgstɔr/ *noun*

a store where you can buy medicines and some small things for the house

drum

drum¹ /drʌm/ *noun*

1 a musical instrument made of a round hollow box with a skin stretched over it which you hit to make a sound
2 a large metal container for oil, gas etc.

drum² *verb* (**drumming, drummed**)

to hit the surface of something again and again

drunk¹ /drʌŋk/ *adjective*

having had too much alcohol so you do not control your behavior: *I think he's drunk!*

drunk²

the PAST PARTICIPLE of the verb **drink**

drunk·en /'drʌŋkən/ *adjective*

caused by too much alcohol

dry¹ /draɪ/ *adjective* (**drier, driest**)

1 having no water in or on it; not wet: *This coat will keep you dry in the rain.*
2 without any rain: *It has been a very dry summer.* » opposite WET¹

dry² *verb* (**drying,** *past* **dried**)

1 to become dry: *The clothes dried quickly outside.*
2 **dry out** to dry completely
3 **dry up** to have no water in it

dry clean·ers /ˌ. '.., '. ˌ../ *noun*

a place that cleans clothes in a special way without using water

duck

duck   duckling

duck¹ /dʌk/ *noun*

a bird that swims on water and is used for its eggs, meat, and feathers

duck² *verb*

to suddenly move your head or body down so you are not hit by something or seen by someone

duck·ling /'dʌklɪŋ/ *noun*

a young duck

due /du/ *adjective*

1 **be due** to be expected to happen or arrive at a particular time: *The flight is due at 5 o'clock.* | *When is the baby due?* (=expected to be born)
2 needing to be paid: *The rent is due at the end of the month.*
3 owed to someone, or deserved by someone: *She never gets the credit she is due.*
4 **due to** because of: *His success is due to hard work.*
5 **in due course** at a more suitable time in the future

du·et /du'ɛt/ *noun*

a song or piece of music for two people

dug /dʌg/

the PAST TENSE and PAST PARTICIPLE of the verb **dig**

dull /dʌl/ *adjective*

1 not bright or light: *It was a dull, cloudy day.*
2 not interesting or exciting: *What a dull party!*
3 not sharp: *This knife is too dull.*

dumb /dʌm/ *adjective*
stupid: *That was a dumb thing to say.*

dump[1] /dʌmp/ *verb*
to drop or put something somewhere: *We dumped our bags on the floor.*

dump[2] *noun*
a place where waste can be taken and left

dune /dun/ *noun*
a hill of sand

dun·geon /'dʌndʒən/ *noun*
a dark PRISON under a castle

dur·ing /'dʊrɪŋ/ *preposition*
1 all the time that something is happening: *They swim every day during the summer.*
2 at some time while something else is happening: *He died during the night.*

dusk /dʌsk/ *noun* [U]
the time in the evening when the sun has just gone down

dust[1] /dʌst/ *noun* [U]
very small pieces of dirt like a dry powder

dust[2] *verb*
to clean dust from something: *She dusted the table.*

dust·pan /'dʌstpæn/ *noun*
a flat container for taking away the dust after you sweep the floor

dust·y /'dʌsti/ *adjective* (**dustier, dustiest**)
covered in dust

du·ty /'duti/ *noun* (*plural* **duties**)
1 something you must do because it is right or part of your job: *You have a duty to look after your family.*
2 **off duty** not working, or not at your job: *The nurses are off duty.*
3 **on duty** working, or at your job

dwarf /dwɔrf/ *noun* (*plural* **dwarves** *or* **dwarfs**)
a person, plant, or animal that is much smaller than usual

dye[1] /daɪ/ *verb* (**dyeing, dyed**)
to give a different color to something: *She dyed her hair black.*

dye[2] *noun*
a liquid or powder that is used to change the color of something

dy·na·mite /'daɪnə,maɪt/ *noun* [U]
a substance used to make explosions

each /itʃ/
1 every single one: *Each child has an exercise book.* | *The tickets are $10 each.*
2 **each other** used for showing that each of two people do something to the other person: *Karen and Mark kissed each other.*

ea·ger /'igɚ/ *adjective*
having a strong desire to do something: *The girl was eager to show me her photographs.*
—**eagerly** *adverb*

ea·gle /'igəl/ *noun*
a large bird that lives in mountain areas and eats small animals

ear /ɪr/ *noun*
1 one of the parts of your body with which you hear —see picture at HEAD¹
2 the part of a plant where the seed is: *I ate an ear of corn.*

ear·ache /'ɪreɪk/ *noun*
a pain inside your ear

ear·ly /'ɚli/ *adjective, adverb* (**earlier, earliest**)
1 before the usual or expected time: *The plane landed ten minutes early.*
2 near the beginning of the day or a period of time: *It often rains in the early morning.* | *Do you get up early?* ≫ compare LATE

earn /ɚn/ *verb*
1 to get money for work you do: *She earns a lot of money on her job.*
2 to get something that you deserve by working hard: *You've earned a good rest.*

ear·ring /'ɪrɪŋ/ *noun*
a piece of jewelry you wear on your ear —see picture at JEWELRY

earth /ɚθ/ *noun* [U]
1 the world in which we live: *The Earth goes around the sun once a year.* —see color picture on page 192

2 the substance on the ground in which plants can grow; dirt: *She planted the seeds in the wet earth.*

earth·quake /'ɚθkweɪk/ *noun*
a strong and sudden shaking of the ground

ease¹ /iz/ *noun* [U]
1 **with ease** very easy for you to do: *He passed the test with ease.*
2 **at ease** feeling comfortable and sure of yourself: *He was very friendly and made her feel at ease.*

ease² *verb* (**easing, eased**)
1 to make something better: *The medicine eased the pain.*
2 to move very slowly and with care: *She eased herself out of bed.*

ea·sel /'izəl/ *noun*
a frame to hold a picture that is being painted —see color picture on page 185

eas·i·ly /'izəli/ *adverb*
without difficulty: *I can easily be there by tomorrow.*

east /ist/ *noun, adjective, adverb*
the direction from which the sun comes up in the morning: *Our house faces east.* ≫ compare WEST

Eas·ter /'istɚ/ *noun*
a special Sunday in March or April when Christians remember Christ's death and his return to life

Easter egg /'.. ,./ *noun*
an egg that is colored for Easter, and hidden as a game for children

east·ern /'istɚn/ *adjective*
in or from the east

east·ward /'istwɚd/ *adverb*
toward the east

eas·y /'izi/ *adjective* (**easier, easiest**)
not difficult; done with no trouble: *I need a book that is easy to read.* ≫ opposite DIFFICULT, HARD¹

eat /it/ *verb* (*past tense* **ate**, *past participle* **eaten**)
1 to put food into your mouth and swallow it: *Have you eaten breakfast yet?*
2 to have a meal: *What time do you eat?*

eat·en /'itⁿn/
the PAST PARTICIPLE of the verb **eat**

ech·o¹ /'ɛkoʊ/ *verb*
if a sound echoes, you hear it again: *Our voices echoed in the empty room.*

echo² *noun* [*plural* **echoes**]
a sound that you hear again

e·clipse /ɪ'klɪps/ *noun*
a short time when you cannot see the sun or moon because it is blocked by the moon or Earth —see color picture on page 192

ec·o·nom·ic /ˌɛkə'nɑmɪk, ˌi-/ *adjective*
relating to industry and business: *The country's economic problems can be solved.*

ec·o·nom·i·cal /ˌɛkə'nɑmɪkəl, ˌi-/ *adjective*
using time, money etc. without wasting any; cheap: *We want an economical way to produce energy.*

e·con·o·my /ɪ'kɑnəmi/ *noun* [*plural* **economies**]
the system by which a country's industry and money is organized: *The new tax laws will help the economy.*

edge /ɛdʒ/ *noun*
1 the outside end of something; the part which is farthest from the center: *The edge of the plate is painted red.*
2 the sharp cutting part of a knife or tool
3 on edge nervous and worried

e·di·tion /ɪ'dɪʃən/ *noun*
a book or newspaper brought out at a particular time

ed·i·tor /'ɛdəṭɚ/ *noun*
a person who prepares books or newspapers for printing

ed·u·cate /'ɛdʒə,keɪt/ *verb* [**educating, educated**]
to teach someone, especially in a school or a college: *Every child deserves the chance to be educated.*

ed·u·cat·ed /'ɛdʒə,keɪṭəd/ *adjective*
knowing a lot of information after studying and learning

ed·u·ca·tion /ˌɛdʒə'keɪʃən/ *noun*
teaching and learning: *It is important to get a good education.*

ed·u·ca·tion·al /ˌɛdʒə'keɪʃənəl/ *adjective*
1 relating to teaching or learning
2 helping you to learn: *He has a new educational toy.*

eel /il/ *noun*
a long fish that looks like a snake

ef·fect /ɪ'fɛkt/ *noun*
a result: *Eating too much candy can have a bad effect **on** your health.* ≫ compare AFFECT

ef·fec·tive /ɪ'fɛktɪv/ *adjective*
getting the result you want: *These pills are an effective cure for a headache.*

ef·fi·cient /ɪ'fɪʃənt/ *adjective*
working well, quickly, and without waste: *She is a very efficient worker.*

ef·fort /'ɛfɚt/ *noun*
the physical or mental energy needed to do something: *With great effort, he pushed open the door.*

EFL /ˌi ɛf 'ɛl/ *noun* [U]
English as a Foreign Language; English classes for people who live in a country where most people do not speak English

e.g. /ˌi 'dʒi/
a short way of writing or saying "for example": *You can try many different sports here, e.g. sailing, tennis, and swimming.*

egg · yolk · white

egg /ɛg/ *noun*
a round object with a hard shell that contains a baby bird, snake, fish, or insect; eggs are often used as food: *We had eggs for breakfast.* —see picture at NEST

egg·plant /'ɛgplænt/ *noun*
a large vegetable with a dark purple skin

eight /eɪt/ *adjective, noun*
the number 8

eight·een /ˌeɪ'tin◂/ *adjective, noun*
the number 18

eighth /eɪtθ/ *adjective, noun*
8th

eight·y /'eɪṭi/ *adjective, noun*
the number 80

ei·ther /'iðɚ, 'aɪ-/

1 one or the other of two people or things: *You can have either tea or coffee.*

2 used in sentences with "not," to say that something else is also true: *I haven't been to Canada, or to Mexico either.* ≫ compare NEITHER

e·lab·o·rate /ɪ'læbrɪt/ *adjective*

having a lot of details, or a large number of parts

e·las·tic /ɪ'læstɪk/ *adjective*

able to be stretched and then go back to its usual shape: *Rubber is an elastic substance.*

el·bow /'ɛlboʊ/ *noun*

the middle part of your arm which bends

el·der·ly /'ɛldɚli/ *adjective*

old: *I spoke with an elderly woman with white hair.*

e·lect /ɪ'lɛkt/ *verb*

to choose someone for an official position, usually by voting: *Clinton was elected President in 1996.*

e·lec·tion /ɪ'lɛkʃən/ *noun*

a time when you vote to choose someone for an official position: *When is the next election?*

e·lec·tric /ɪ'lɛktrɪk/ *adjective*

needing electricity to work: *I forgot my electric razor.*

e·lec·tri·cal /ɪ'lɛktrɪkəl/ *adjective*

relating to or using electricity

e·lec·tri·cian /ɪˌlɛk'trɪʃən, i-/ *noun*

a person whose job is to connect and repair electrical equipment

e·lec·tric·i·ty /ɪˌlɛk'trɪsəţi, i-/ *noun* [U]

power that is sent through wires and is used for lighting, heating, and making machines work

e·lec·tron·ics /ɪˌlɛk'trɑnɪks/ *noun* [U]

the study of making equipment that uses electricity, such as televisions and computers
—**electronic** *adjective*

el·e·gant /'ɛləgənt/ *adjective*

very beautiful and graceful: *She is a tall, elegant woman in a black dress.*

el·e·ment /'ɛləmənt/ *noun*

1 a simple substance from which everything is made: *Gold and oxygen are elements.*

2 one part of a whole: *Being honest is an important element of the job.*

el·e·men·ta·ry /ˌɛlə'mɛntri, -'mɛntəri/ *adjective*

simple and easy: *Here is a book of elementary exercises for math.*

elementary school *noun*

a school for children who are about 6 to 12 years old

el·e·phant /'ɛləfənt/ *noun*

a very large gray animal with a long nose and big ears, which lives in hot countries

el·e·va·tor /'ɛləˌveɪţɚ/ *noun*

a machine in a building that takes people from one level to another

e·lev·en /ɪ'lɛvən/ *adjective, noun*

the number 11

elf /ɛlf/ *noun*

(*plural* **elves** /ɛlvz/)

a small imaginary person with pointed ears

else /ɛls/ *adverb*

1 other; different; instead: *If you don't like eggs, I can cook something else.* | *She was wearing someone else's coat.*

2 more; also: *Is there anything else I can get for you?*

3 **or else** used when saying what the result will be if you do not do something: *He has to pay, or else he will be in trouble.*

else·where /'ɛlswɛr/ *adverb*

in or to some other place: *They left the restaurant and went elsewhere.*

elves /ɛlvz/ *noun*

the plural of **elf**

e-mail /'i meɪl/ *noun*

a system for sending letters from one computer to another, or a letter that is sent from one computer to another: *I sent Jill an e-mail yesterday.* —**e-mail** *verb*

em·bar·rass /ɪm'bærəs/ *verb*

to make someone feel nervous or uncomfortable in front of other people: *I'm sorry, I didn't mean to embarrass you.*

em·bar·rassed /ɪm'bærəst/ *adjective*

nervous or uncomfortable in front of other people: *I feel so embarrassed when I think about what I said.* ≫ compare ASHAMED

NOTE: **1** People feel **embarrassed** about small things that they have done which make them appear silly to other people, such as forgetting someone's name, or going to a party in the wrong type of clothes. If someone is sorry because they have done something very bad and important, they feel **ashamed**, not **embarrassed**. **2** Do not confuse **embarrassed** (=feeling uncomfortable and nervous) and **embarrassing** (=making someone feel like this): *It was an embarrassing mistake. We all felt very embarrassed.*

em·bar·ras·sing /ɪm'bærəsɪŋ/
adjective
making you feel nervous or uncomfortable: *He asked a lot of embarrassing questions.*

em·bar·rass·ment /ɪm'bærəsmənt/
noun [U]
the feeling of being nervous or uncomfortable in front of other people

em·bas·sy /'ɛmbəsi/ *noun* (*plural* embassies)
a place where people work for their government to represent their own country in another country

em·brace¹ /ɪm'breɪs/ *verb* (**embracing, embraced**)
to put your arms around someone to show that you love him or her: *The couple reached out to embrace each other.*

embrace² *noun*
the act of holding someone in your arms as a sign of love

embroidery

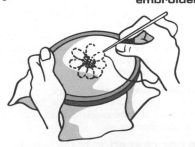

em·broi·der·y /ɪm'brɔɪdri, -dəri/ *noun* [U]
beautiful patterns that you sew on cloth: *She has a dress covered with embroidery.*

em·er·ald /'ɛmərəld/ *noun*
a valuable bright green stone

e·merge /ɪ'mɝdʒ/ *verb* (**emerging, emerged**)
to appear from somewhere after being hidden: *The baby birds emerged **from** their eggs.*

e·mer·gen·cy /ɪ'mɝdʒənsi/ *noun* (*plural* emergencies)
an unexpected and dangerous situation that you must deal with immediately: *Call an ambulance! This is an emergency!* —**emergency** *adjective*: *an emergency exit*

emergency room /.'... ,./ *noun*
a part of a hospital where people with very serious injuries or illnesses can be helped quickly

em·i·grant /'ɛməgrənt/ *noun*
a person who leaves their own country to live in another country ≫ compare IMMIGRANT

em·i·grate /'ɛmə,greɪt/ *verb* (**emigrating, emigrated**)
to leave your own country to go and live in another country: *Her family emigrated to Australia.* ≫ compare IMMIGRATE

em·i·gra·tion /,ɛmə'greɪʃən/ *noun* [U]
the act of leaving your own country to go and live in another country ≫ compare IMMIGRATION

e·mo·tion /ɪ'moʊʃən/ *noun*
a strong feeling: *Anger and love are emotions.*

e·mo·tion·al /ɪ'moʊʃənəl/ *adjective*
having strong feelings that you show, sometimes by crying

em·per·or /'ɛmpərɚ/ *noun*
a ruler of a big country or several countries

em·pha·size /'ɛmfə,saɪz/ *verb* (**emphasizing, emphasized**)
to show that something is important: *He emphasized the need for hard work.* ≫ compare STRESS²

em·pire /'ɛmpaɪɚ/ *noun*
a group of countries ruled by one government

em·ploy /ɪm'plɔɪ/ *verb* (**employing, employed**)
to pay someone to work for you: *The business employs hundreds of people.*

em·ploy·ee /ɪm'plɔɪ-i, ,ɪmplɔɪ'i, ,ɛm-/ *noun*
a person who works for someone else: *There are ten employees in his firm.*

em·ploy·er /ɪmˈplɔɪɚ/ *noun*
a person or group that pays people to work for them

em·ploy·ment /ɪmˈplɔɪmənt/ *noun* [U]
work that you do to get money: *She's looking for employment.* ≫ opposite UNEMPLOYMENT

em·press /ˈɛmprɪs/ *noun*
a female ruler of a country or several countries; the wife of an EMPEROR

empty

full   *empty*

emp·ty¹ /ˈɛmpti/ *adjective*
having nothing inside: *The cup is empty.* ≫ compare FULL

empty² *verb* (**emptying, emptied**)
to take everything out of something: *He emptied the bottle.* ≫ compare FILL

en·a·ble /ɪˈneɪbəl/ *verb* (**enabling, enabled**)
to make someone able to do something: *The new machines enable us to work very fast.*

en·close /ɪnˈkloʊz/ *verb* (**enclosing, enclosed**)
1 to put something in an envelope with a letter: *I enclosed a picture of the baby with my letter.*
2 to surround something completely: *The football field is enclosed by a fence.*

en·cour·age /ɪnˈkɚɪdʒ, -ˈkʌr-/ *verb* (**encouraging, encouraged**)
to give praise and support to someone so that he or she will do something: *I encouraged her to start playing tennis.* ≫ opposite DISCOURAGE

en·cour·age·ment /ɪnˈkɚɪdʒmənt, -ˈkʌr-/ *noun* [U]
praise and support given to someone so that he or she will do something: *Her parents gave her lots of encouragement.*

en·cour·ag·ing /ɪnˈkɚɪdʒɪŋ/ *adjective*
making you feel hopeful and confident: *The doctor gave us some encouraging news.*

en·cy·clo·pe·di·a /ɪnˌsaɪkləˈpidiə/ *noun*
a book that has a lot of facts about many subjects

end¹ /ɛnd/ *noun*
1 the point where something finishes: *When you get to the end of this street, turn right.* | *We had to wait until the end of August.* ≫ compare BEGINNING
2 **in the end** at last: *We walked for hours, but in the end we found the house.*

end² *verb*
1 to finish: *The party ended at midnight.* ≫ compare BEGIN
2 **end up** to be in a particular situation that you did not expect or intend: *Our car didn't start, so we ended up taking the bus.*

end·ing /ˈɛndɪŋ/ *noun*
the end of a story, movie, or play: *The movie has a happy ending.*

end·less /ˈɛndlɪs/ *adjective*
continuing for a long time, seeming never to end: *With children in the house, the work is endless.*

en·e·my /ˈɛnəmi/ *noun* (*plural* **enemies**)
a person or country that is not friendly to you or wants to harm or fight you: *He's made a lot of enemies at work.*

en·er·get·ic /ˌɛnɚˈdʒɛtɪk/ *adjective*
very active: *My kids are very energetic.*

en·er·gy /ˈɛnɚdʒi/ *noun* [U]
1 the ability to be active and to do a lot without feeling tired: *I have no energy left after working all day.*
2 the power that makes machines work or gives heat: *Coal provides energy for the city.*

en·gaged /ɪnˈgeɪdʒd/ *adjective*
having promised to marry someone: *My brother is engaged **to** Anne. They will get married next year.*

en·gage·ment /ɪnˈgeɪdʒmənt/ *noun*
1 an agreement to marry someone: *William told everyone about his engagement to Linda.*
2 an arrangement to meet someone: *I'm not able to come this evening. I have another engagement.*

en·gine /ˈɛndʒɪn/ *noun*
a machine that uses oil, gas, electricity, or steam and makes things work or move: *The car has a problem with its engine.* —see picture at AIRPLANE

en·gi·neer /ˌɛndʒəˈnɪr/ *noun*
1 a person who plans the way machines, roads etc. are built
2 a person who drives a train

en·gi·neer·ing /ˌɛndʒəˈnɪrɪŋ/ *noun* [U]
the science or job of an engineer

En·glish /ˈɪŋglɪʃ/ *noun*
1 [U] the language that is spoken in the U.S., Canada, Great Britain, and many other countries: *Carlos is learning English.* | *Do you speak English?*
2 **the English** [*plural*] the people of England
—**English** *adjective*

en·joy /ɪnˈdʒɔɪ/ *verb* (**enjoying, enjoyed**)
1 to get pleasure and happiness from something: *I enjoy listening to music.*
2 **enjoy yourself** to have a good time: *Did you enjoy yourself at the wedding?*

en·joy·a·ble /ɪnˈdʒɔɪəbəl/ *adjective*
giving pleasure or happiness: *We had an enjoyable weekend at the beach.*

en·joy·ment /ɪnˈdʒɔɪmənt/ *noun* [U]
pleasure: *I get a lot of enjoyment from my job.*

en·large /ɪnˈlɑrdʒ/ *verb* (**enlarging, enlarged**)
to make something bigger: *I want to enlarge this photograph.*

e·nor·mous /ɪˈnɔrməs/ *adjective*
very large: *Their house is enormous!* ≫ compare GIGANTIC, HUGE, IMMENSE

e·nor·mous·ly /ɪˈnɔrməsli/ *adverb*
very much: *The movie was enormously popular.*

enough

e·nough /ɪˈnʌf/ *adjective, adverb*
as much as is needed: *There is enough food for three people.* | *This bag isn't big enough for my books.*

en·ter /ˈɛntɚ/ *verb*
1 to go or come in to a particular place: *He entered the room quietly.*
2 to become part of a profession or organization: *He decided to enter college.*
3 to start to take part in an activity: *She entered the race and won.*
4 to write down information or put it into a computer: *Please enter your name on the first line.*

en·ter·tain /ˌɛntɚˈteɪn/ *verb*
1 to do something to amuse or interest people: *He entertained us with stories about life in France.*
2 to give food and drink to guests

en·ter·tain·er /ˌɛntɚˈteɪnɚ/ *noun*
someone whose job is to amuse people, for example by telling jokes

en·ter·tain·ing /ˌɛntɚˈteɪnɪŋ/ *adjective*
amusing and interesting

en·ter·tain·ment /ˌɛntɚˈteɪnmənt/ *noun* [U]
activities which amuse or interest people: *For entertainment, we usually watch television.*

en·thu·si·as·m /ɪnˈθuziˌæzəm/ *noun* [U]
a strong feeling of being interested in something or wanting to do something: *He is full of enthusiasm for his job.*

en·thu·si·as·tic /ɪnˌθuziˈæstɪk/ *adjective*
showing a lot of interest or excitement about something

en·tire /ɪnˈtaɪɚ/ *adjective*
whole; complete: *The entire class will be there.*

en·tire·ly /ɪnˈtaɪɚli/ *adverb*
completely: *I agree with you entirely.*

en·trance /ˈɛntrəns/ *noun*
1 a place where you go in to a building: *Where's the entrance **to** the hospital?*
2 the arrival of a person, or the right to enter a place: *The music played for the entrance of the dancers.*

en·try /ˈɛntri/ *noun* (*plural* **entries**)
1 [U] the right to enter a building or country: *They were not allowed entry to the U.S.*
2 a person or thing in a race or competition: *The winning entry was a beautiful picture.*

envelope

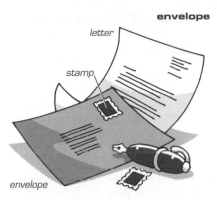

letter

stamp

envelope

en·ve·lope /ˈɛnvə,loʊp, ˈɑn-/ *noun*
the paper cover in which you put a letter

en·vi·ous /ˈɛnviəs/ *adjective*
wishing you had something that belongs to someone else: *He was envious **of** my success.*
≫ compare JEALOUS

en·vi·ron·ment /ɪnˈvaɪənmənt/ *noun*
1 the world of land, sea, and air that you live in: *Cutting down too many trees harms the environment.*
2 the conditions of the society around you: *Children need a happy home environment.*

en·vy¹ /ˈɛnvi/ *noun* [U]
the feeling of wanting something that someone else has: *She looked with envy at his new car.*
≫ compare JEALOUSY

envy² *verb* (envying, envied)
to want what someone else has: *I envy John – he seems so happy.*

ep·i·dem·ic /ˌɛpəˈdɛmɪk/ *noun*
an illness that spreads quickly to a lot of people

e·qual¹ /ˈikwəl/ *adjective*
the same in size, number, or value: *Divide the cake into four equal parts.* | *Women want equal pay with men.*

equal² *verb* (equalling, equalled)
1 to be the same as something else in number or amount: *Three plus five equals eight.* $(3 + 5 = 8)$
2 to be as good as someone or something else

equal³ *noun*
a person who has the same ability and rights as someone else: *All people should be treated as equals by the law.*

e·qual·i·ty /ɪˈkwɑləti/ *noun* [U]
having the same ability and rights: *Women want equality with men.*

e·qua·tor /ɪˈkweɪtə/ *noun*
an imaginary line around the middle of the Earth

e·quip /ɪˈkwɪp/ *verb* (equipping, equipped)
to give someone things that are needed for doing something: *Our school is equipped **with** new computers.*

e·quip·ment /ɪˈkwɪpmənt/ *noun* [U]
the things that you need for a particular activity: *I want to buy some camera equipment.*

e·rase /ɪˈreɪs/ *verb* (erasing, erased)
to remove something that is written or recorded so it cannot be seen or heard: *Erase any words that are not spelled correctly.*

erase

eraser

e·ras·er /ɪˈreɪsə/ *noun*
a piece of rubber used for getting rid of pencil marks

e·rect¹ /ɪˈrɛkt/ *adjective*
standing straight; upright: *All the soldiers are standing erect.*

erect² *verb*
to put something together and make it stand up: *They erected the tent quickly.*

er·rand /ˈɛrənd/ *noun*
a short trip you make to do or to buy something

er·ror /ˈɛrə/ *noun*
a mistake: *The doctor said that he made an error.*

e·rupt /ɪˈrʌpt/ *verb*
to explode and send out fire and smoke, used about a VOLCANO

escalator

es·ca·la·tor /ˈɛskəˌleɪtə/ *noun*
a set of moving stairs that can take you up or down so that you do not have to walk

es·cape¹ /ɪˈskeɪp/ *verb* (escaping, escaped)
to get out of a place, especially when someone is trying to stop you: *He escaped **from** prison.*

escape² *noun*
the act of escaping: *The prisoner made his escape at night.*

es·cort¹ /ɪˈskɔrt, ˈɛskɔrt/ *verb*
to go with someone, especially to protect him or her: *Soldiers escorted the President.*

escort² /ˈɛskɔrt/ *noun*
people, cars, planes etc. that travel with someone, especially for protection: *She traveled with a police escort.*

ESL /ˌi ɛs ˈɛl/ *noun* [U]
English as a Second Language; English classes for people who live in a country where most do not speak English

es·pe·cial·ly /ɪˈspɛʃəli/ *adverb*
1 very; more than usual: *She is especially good at science.*
2 most of all: *Everyone is excited about our trip, especially Sam.*

es·say /ˈɛseɪ/ *noun* (plural essays)
a short piece of writing on a subject: *She wrote an essay on "My Family."*

es·sen·tial /ɪˈsɛnʃəl/ *adjective*
necessary; very important: *Good food is essential for good health.*

es·tab·lish /ɪˈstæblɪʃ/ *verb*
to start a company, system, situation, etc.: *The company was established in 1985.* | *We have established **contact with** another school in France.*

es·tate /ɪˈsteɪt/ *noun*
a large piece of land, usually with a large house on it

es·ti·mate¹ /ˈɛstəˌmeɪt/ *verb* (estimating, estimated)
to make a guess about the size or amount of something: *They estimated that the house cost $2 million.*

estimate² /ˈɛstəmɪt/ *noun*
a guess about the size or amount of something

etc /ɛt ˈsɛtrə, -ˌtərə/
and so on: *There are lots of things to buy – milk, sugar, bread etc.*

Eu·ro·pe·an¹ /ˌyʊrəˈpiən/ *adjective*
coming from or related to a country in Europe

European² *noun*
a person from a country in Europe

e·vac·u·ate /ɪˈvækyuˌeɪt/ *verb* (evacuating, evacuated)
to move people from a dangerous place to a safer place

eve /iv/ *noun*
the night or day before a religious day or holiday: *Where will you be on Christmas Eve?*

e·ven¹ /ˈivən/ *adjective*
1 flat, level, or smooth: *The table has an even surface.* ≫ opposite UNEVEN
2 not changing much: *Try to keep the oven at an even temperature.*
3 **even number** a number that can be divided by two, for example 2, 4, and 6 ≫ compare ODD
4 **be even** to no longer owe someone money: *Here's your $10 – now we're even.*

even² *adverb*
1 used for showing when something is surprising or unusual: *Even Peter helped us, and he usually never helps!*
2 used when you are comparing two things, to make the second seem more important: *Yesterday it rained hard, and today it's raining even harder.*

even³ *verb*
even out/even up to become equal or the same as something else

eve·ning /ˈivnɪŋ/ *noun*
the end of the day and the early part of the night: *I have a class on Monday evening.*

even·ly /ˈivənli/ *adverb*
equally: *Divide the money evenly among the men.* (=give the same amount to each man)

e·vent /ɪˈvɛnt/ *noun*
something that happens, often something important or unusual: *What events do you remember from the last ten years?*

e·ven·tu·al·ly /ɪˈvɛntʃəli, -tʃuəli/ *adverb*
at last; after a long time: *I looked everywhere for my glasses, and eventually, I found them under my chair.*

ev·er /ˈɛvə/ *adverb*
1 at any time: *Have you ever been to the Bahamas?* | *Nothing ever makes Carol angry.*
2 **ever since** since a particular time: *I have lived here ever since I was a child.*

ev·ery /'ɛvri/
1 each one: *I have read every book he has written.*
2 used for showing how often something happens: *We go to Florida every year or so.*

ev·ery·bod·y /'ɛvri,bɑdi, -,bʌdi/
every person: *Everybody wants to watch the movie.* | *She likes everybody in her class.*

NOTE: Remember that **everybody** and **everyone** are singular words, like **he** or **she**, so you must use them with a singular verb ending: *Everyone knows that sugar is bad for your teeth.*

ev·ery·day /'ɛvri,deɪ/ *adjective*
usual or ordinary: *Problems are a part of everyday life.*

ev·ery·one /'ɛvri,wʌn/
every person: *Everyone is welcome to the party.*

ev·ery·thing /'ɛvri,θɪŋ/
1 all things, or each thing: *I got everything I needed at the store.*
2 used when you are talking about something in general: *So, how is everything with you?*

ev·ery·where /'ɛvri,wɛr/ *adverb*
in or to every place: *I looked everywhere for my watch, but I couldn't find it.* ≫ compare NOWHERE

ev·i·dence /'ɛvədəns/ *noun* [U]
words or facts that prove something: *Police have evidence that the killer is a woman.*

ev·i·dent /'ɛvədənt/ *adjective*
easy to notice or understand: *It was evident that she was not telling the truth.*

e·vil /'ivəl/ *adjective*
very cruel and causing harm: *In the story, the good queen saves her from an evil man.*

ex·act /ɪg'zækt/ *adjective*
completely correct: *Can you tell me the exact time?*

ex·act·ly /ɪg'zæktli/ *adverb*
1 with complete correctness: *Where exactly do you live?*
2 said when you agree with someone: *"So you think we should wait until later?" "Exactly."*

ex·ag·ger·ate /ɪg'zædʒə,reɪt/ *verb*
(exaggerating, exaggerated)
to make something seem bigger, better, worse etc. than it really is: *He exaggerated when he said the dog was the size of a horse.*

ex·am /ɪg'zæm/ *noun*
an official test of knowledge in a subject, usually at the end of a course: *When do you take your history exam?*

ex·am·i·na·tion /ɪg,zæmə'neɪʃən/ *noun*
a careful look at someone or something: *An examination of the metal proved that it was gold.*

ex·am·ine /ɪg'zæmɪn/ *verb* **(examining, examined)**
1 to look at someone or something closely and carefully: *The doctor examined my ears.*
2 to ask someone questions to test his or her knowledge

ex·am·ple /ɪg'zæmpəl/ *noun*
1 one thing that you mention to show what other things are like. *Can anyone give me an example of a verb?* | *This painting is a good example of African art.*
2 **for example** used for giving an example of something which makes what you say easier to understand: *Prices are going up. For example, gas costs a lot more now.*

ex·as·per·ate /ɪg'zæspə,reɪt/ *verb*
(exasperating, exasperated)
to annoy someone or to make him or her angry

ex·ceed /ɪk'sid/ *verb*
to be more than a particular amount: *The total cost should not exceed $100.*

ex·cel·lent /'ɛksələnt/ *adjective*
very good: *This is excellent work, Peter.*

ex·cept /ɪk'sɛpt/
not including; apart from: *I have washed all the clothes except your shirt.*

ex·cep·tion /ɪk'sɛpʃən/ *noun*
1 someone or something that is different, or is not included in something: *It has been cold, but today is an exception.* [=today it is not cold]
2 **with the exception of** not including; apart from: *They'd all been there before with the exception of Jim.*

ex·cep·tion·al /ɪk'sɛpʃənəl/ *adjective*
1 unusually good: *She is an exceptional student.*
2 unusual and not happening often: *We've had an exceptional number of rainy days this month.*

ex·cep·tion·al·ly /ɪk'sɛpʃənəli/ *adverb*
unusually or especially: *This has been an exceptionally cold winter.*

ex·cess /ˈɛksɛs, ɪkˈsɛs/ *noun, adjective*
(*plural* **excesses**)
more than is usual or allowed: *You have to pay extra for excess luggage.*

ex·change¹ /ɪksˈtʃeɪndʒ/ *verb*
(**exchanging, exchanged**)
to give something to someone who gives you something else: *This skirt is too small. Can I exchange it for a larger one?*

exchange² *noun*
1 the act of giving something to someone who gives you something else: *The two countries are planning an exchange of prisoners.*
2 **in exchange for** in the place of something that you give to someone: *I gave him the book in exchange for a CD.*

exchange rate /.ˈ. ˌ./ *noun*
the value of the money of one country compared to that of another country

ex·cite /ɪkˈsaɪt/ *verb* (**exciting, excited**)
to make someone feel happy or eager to do something: *The games excited the children and made them laugh.*

ex·cit·ed /ɪkˈsaɪtɪd/ *adjective*
having strong feelings of happiness or pleasure; not calm: *Everyone is excited about our trip to New York.*

ex·cite·ment /ɪkˈsaɪtˉmənt/ *noun* [U]
the feeling of being excited: *The excitement of the crowd grew when the singers arrived.*

ex·cit·ing /ɪkˈsaɪtɪŋ/ *adjective*
making you feel very happy or interested: *I heard the exciting news about your baby.*

ex·claim /ɪkˈskleɪm/ *verb*
to say something loudly and suddenly because you are surprised: *"Look – Sarah is on TV,"* *exclaimed Peter.*

ex·cla·ma·tion /ˌɛkskləˈmeɪʃən/ *noun*
words showing a sudden, strong feeling

exclamation mark /..ˈ.. ˌ./ *noun*
the sign "!" used in writing to show a strong feeling like surprise, or when calling someone: *Come here!* | *I don't believe it!*

ex·clude /ɪkˈsklud/ *verb* (**excluding, excluded**)
1 to stop someone or something from doing something, or from entering a place: *Women were excluded from the meeting.*
2 to not include someone or something: *Some test scores are excluded from the total.*
≫ opposite INCLUDE

ex·clud·ing /ɪkˈskludɪŋ/ *preposition*
not including: *The store is open every day, excluding Sundays.* ≫ opposite INCLUDING

ex·cur·sion /ɪkˈskɚʒən/ *noun*
a short trip made for pleasure: *We went on an excursion down the Nile river.*

ex·cuse¹ /ɪkˈskyuz/ *verb* (**excusing, excused**)
1 **excuse me** said to get someone's attention, to leave a group of people, or to say you are sorry for doing something rude: *Excuse me, but do you know what time it is?* | *Oh, excuse me. I didn't mean to step on your foot.*
2 to forgive someone: *Please excuse this messy house.*
3 to give someone permission not to do something or to leave a place: *The teacher excused her from class.*

excuse² /ɪkˈskyus/ *noun*
a reason that you give to say why you did something bad or wrong: *What was his excuse for being late?*

ex·e·cute /ˈɛksɪˌkyut/ *verb* (**executing, executed**)
to kill someone as a punishment decided by law

ex·e·cu·tion /ˌɛksɪˈkyuʃən/ *noun*
a killing which is a punishment decided by law

ex·er·cise¹ /ˈɛksɚˌsaɪz/ *noun*
1 activity for your body which you do again and again to stay strong and healthy: *Running is good exercise.* | *Have you done your leg exercises yet?*
2 a set of questions to test your knowledge or ability: *Please do exercises 3 and 4.*

exercise² *verb* (**exercising, exercised**)
to do activity for your body again and again to stay strong and healthy: *The doctor told him to exercise more.*

ex·haust¹ /ɪgˈzɔst/ *verb*
to make someone very tired: *The long walk exhausted her.*

exhaust² *noun*
1 [U] gas that is made when a machine works
2 a pipe that lets waste gas come out the back of a car

ex·haust·ed /ɪgˈzɔstɪd/ *adjective*
very tired: *I'm exhausted from not getting enough sleep.*

ex·haust·ing /ɪgˈzɔstɪŋ/ *adjective*
making you feel very tired: *Taking care of babies can be exhausting.*

ex·hib·it¹ /ɪgˈzɪbɪt/ *verb*
to show things in public: *She exhibited her paintings at our school.*

ex·hib·it² *noun*
a public show of objects such as paintings, photographs etc.: *We went to an art exhibit.*

ex·ile¹ /ˈɛgzaɪl, ˈɛksaɪl/ *noun*
1 in exile away from your own country as a punishment: *After the revolution, they had to live in exile in Europe.*
2 a person who is not allowed to live in his or her own country as a punishment, often for political reasons

exile² *verb* (exiling, exiled)
to send a person away from their own country as a punishment

ex·ist /ɪgˈzɪst/ *verb*
to be real or alive: *Do you believe that God exists?*

ex·ist·ence /ɪgˈzɪstəns/ *noun* [U]
the state of being real or alive: *The elephant is the largest land animal in existence.*

ex·it /ˈɛgzɪt, ˈɛksɪt/ *noun*
the way out of a place: *Where is the exit?*

ex·pand /ɪkˈspænd/ *verb*
to become larger or make something larger: *The business has expanded from one office to four.*

ex·pan·sion /ɪkˈspænʃən/ *noun* [U]
an increase in size, number, or amount

ex·pect /ɪkˈspɛkt/ *verb*
1 to think that something will happen: *Do you expect to win the race? | The car cost more than I expected.*
2 **be expecting someone or something** to feel sure that someone or something will arrive, often because you have arranged it: *We're expecting the Johnsons for lunch.*
3 to ask strongly for someone to do a particular thing: *Visitors to the hospital are expected not to smoke.*
4 **be expecting (a baby)** to be going to have a baby

ex·pe·di·tion /ˌɛkspəˈdɪʃən/ *noun*
a long difficult trip, especially to a dangerous place: *They are planning an expedition to the North Pole.*

ex·pel /ɪkˈspɛl/ *verb* (expelling, expelled)
to force someone to leave a school, group, or country: *The students were expelled for stealing.*

ex·pense /ɪkˈspɛns/ *noun*
the amount of money you spend on something: *We built the house at our own expense.*

ex·pen·sive /ɪkˈspɛnsɪv/ *adjective*
costing a lot of money: *It is expensive to travel by plane.* ≫ compare CHEAP

ex·pe·ri·ence¹ /ɪkˈspɪriəns/ *noun*
1 something that happens to you: *The accident was an experience she will never forget.*
2 [U] knowledge or skill that you get from doing a job: *She is a teacher with 5 years of experience.*

experience² *verb* (experiencing, experienced)
to be influenced or affected by something that happens to you: *We are experiencing some problems with our computers.*

ex·pe·ri·enced /ɪkˈspɪriənst/ *adjective*
good at something because you have done it before: *He is an experienced heart doctor.*

ex·per·i·ment¹ /ɪkˈspɛrəmənt/ *noun*
a careful test you do to see whether something is true: *He did a scientific experiment for the class.* —**experimental** *adjective*

experiment² *verb*
to do a careful test to see if something is true: *We will not experiment on animals in testing these products.*

ex·pert¹ /ˈɛkspɚt/ *noun*
a person with special skill or knowledge in a subject: *Paul is an expert in modern art.*

expert² *adjective*
having special skill or knowledge of something: *I need some expert advice.*

ex·plain /ɪkˈspleɪn/ *verb*
to make something easy to understand, or to give the reason for something: *Can you explain what this word means? | I explained to him why I was mad.*

ex·pla·na·tion /ˌɛkspləˈneɪʃən/ *noun*
something that makes something easy to understand, or gives the reason for it: *I don't know why he did it, but he had better have a good explanation.*

ex·plode /ɪkˈsploʊd/ *verb* (exploding, exploded)
to burst into small pieces with a loud noise and a lot of force: *A bomb exploded there last night.*

ex·plo·ra·tion /ˌɛkspləˈreɪʃən/ *noun*
a trip to a place to learn about it: *I read a book about space exploration.*

ex·plore /ɪk'splɔr/ *verb* [exploring, explored]
1 to find out about a place by traveling through it
2 to study or examine something carefully

ex·plor·er /ɪk'splɔrə/ *noun*
someone who travels into an unknown area to find out about it

ex·plo·sion /ɪk'splouʒən/ *noun*
a sudden loud noise caused, for example, by a bomb: *The explosion damaged three houses.*

ex·plo·sive /ɪk'splouzɪv/ *adjective*
that can burst with a loud noise and a lot of force like a bomb

ex·port¹ /ɪk'spɔrt, 'ɛkspɔrt/ *verb*
to send goods out of the country to be sold abroad: *Japan exports cars.* ≫ compare IMPORT¹

export² /'ɛkspɔrt/ *noun*
something that is sold and sent to another country: *Fruit is one of our main exports.* ≫ compare IMPORT²

ex·pose /ɪk'spouz/ *verb* [exposing, exposed]
to show something that is usually covered: *You should not expose your skin to the sun.*

ex·press¹ /ɪk'sprɛs/ *verb*
to say or do something to let other people know what you think or feel: *It can be difficult to express how you feel about someone.*

express² *adjective*
going or sent quickly: *We are taking the express train from Boston to Chicago.*

ex·pres·sion /ɪk'sprɛʃən/ *noun*
1 a word or words with a particular meaning: *You should not use that expression – it's not polite.*
2 the look on someone's face: *She had a sad expression.*

ex·quis·ite /ɪk'skwɪzɪt, 'ɛkskwɪ-/ *adjective*
very beautiful or delicate: *Mary wore an exquisite piece of jewelry.*

ex·tend /ɪk'stɛnd/ *verb*
1 to reach or stretch over an area: *The yard extends all the way to the fence.*
2 to make something larger or longer: *They extended their visit for two more days.*

ex·ten·sion /ɪk'stɛnʃən/ *noun*
1 a part that is added to something to make it longer or bigger: *They're building an extension to the subway line.*

2 one of many telephone lines in a large company: *What's your extension number?*

ex·ten·sive /ɪk'stɛnsɪv/ *adjective*
1 very large in size or amount: *The fire spread over an extensive area.*
2 having a lot of details, facts etc.: *He did an extensive study on the disease.*

ex·tent /ɪk'stɛnt/ *noun*
the size or limit of something: *What is the extent of the damage?*

ex·te·ri·or¹ /ɪk'stɪriə/ *adjective*
on the outside of something: *We painted the exterior walls of the house.* ≫ opposite INTERIOR²

exterior² *noun*
the outside part of something: *The exterior of the building is glass.* ≫ compare INTERIOR¹

ex·ter·nal /ɪk'stənl/ *adjective*
outside a place, person, or thing: *He had no external signs of injury.* ≫ opposite INTERNAL

ex·tin·guish /ɪk'stɪŋgwɪʃ/ *verb*
to make a fire stop burning

ex·tin·guish·er /ɪk'stɪŋgwɪʃə/ *noun*
a FIRE EXTINGUISHER

ex·tra¹ /'ɛkstrə/ *adjective, adverb*
more than usual, necessary, or expected: *I want a large pizza with extra cheese.* | *The car costs extra if you want air conditioning.*

extra² *noun*
something that is added to a product and usually costs more: *The computer was very expensive with all these extras.*

ex·traor·di·nar·y /ɪk'strɔrdn,ɛri/ *adjective*
very unusual or strange: *I heard an extraordinary story the other day.*

ex·trav·a·gance /ɪk'strævəgəns/ *noun*
the act of spending too much money

ex·trav·a·gant /ɪk'strævəgənt/ *adjective*
spending too much money on things: *She's very extravagant – she spends all her money on clothes.*

ex·treme /ɪk'strim/ *adjective*
1 very great: *Sometimes the police are in extreme danger on their job.*
2 extreme actions, opinions etc. are not acceptable because they are unusual or not reasonable

ex·treme·ly /ɪk'strimli/ *adverb*
very: *I am extremely grateful for your help.*

eye /aɪ/ *noun*
1 the part of your head with which you see: *I have green eyes.* —see picture at HEAD[1]
2 keep an eye on to watch people or things to make sure that they are safe: *Can you keep an eye on my house while I'm gone?*
3 in someone's eyes in someone's opinion: *In her eyes, he's perfect.*
4 see eye to eye to agree with someone completely: *My father and I have never seen eye to eye.*
5 a small hole in a needle through which you put thread

eye·brow /'aɪbraʊ/ *noun*
the line of short hairs above your eye —see picture at HEAD[1]

eye·lash /'aɪlæʃ/ *noun*
one of the small hairs that grow on your eyelid —see picture at HEAD[1]

eye·lid /'aɪˌlɪd/ *noun*
a piece of skin which covers your eye when it is closed —see picture at HEAD[1]

eye·sight /'aɪsaɪt/ *noun* [U]
your ability to see: *I think she is losing her eyesight.*

F /ɛf/

another way of writing FAHRENHEIT: *It is 32°F.* (=32 degrees Fahrenheit)

fa·ble /ˈfeɪbəl/ *noun*

a story that teaches a lesson about how to behave

fab·ric /ˈfæbrɪk/ *noun*

cloth used for making clothes etc. ≫ compare MATERIAL

fab·u·lous /ˈfæbyələs/ *adjective*

very good or nice: *You look fabulous tonight.* ≫ compare WONDERFUL

face¹ /feɪs/ *noun*

1 the front part of your head, with your eyes, nose, and mouth —see picture at HEAD¹

2 the part of a clock or watch that has numbers on it

face² *verb* **(facing, faced)**

1 to be turned toward or to look toward something: *Our house faces the park.* | *He turned to face me.*

2 to deal with a difficult situation, or someone you want to avoid: *I could not face him.* | *You must face **the fact that** you are sick.*

fa·cil·i·ties /fəˈsɪlətiz/ *plural noun*

rooms, equipment etc. used for a particular purpose: *The university has very good sports facilities.* (=places and equipment for sports)

fact /fækt/ *noun*

1 something that you know is true, or something that you know has happened: *The book contains a lot of facts about plants.*

2 in fact used when you add information to something you have said, or to emphasize that something is true: *I don't know him very well. In fact, I've only met him once.*

fac·to·ry /ˈfæktəri/ *noun* (*plural* **factories**)

a place where goods are made: *Harry works in a car factory.* (=a place where cars are made)

fade /feɪd/ *verb* **(fading, faded)**

to become less bright or to have less color: *If you leave that dress in the sun, it will fade.*

Fahr·en·heit /ˈfærən,haɪt/ *noun* [U]

a way to measure temperature (=how hot something is): *Water freezes at 32 degrees Fahrenheit.* (=32 °F)

fail /feɪl/ *verb*

1 not to succeed, or not to do what is expected: *The crops have failed because of lack of rain.* | *I failed my math test.* | *Our flight failed **to** arrive on time.*

2 if a bank or company fails, it stops working because it has no money ≫ compare SUCCEED

fail·ure /ˈfeɪlyɚ/ *noun*

someone or something that does not succeed: *The plan was a failure.* ≫ compare SUCCESS

faint¹ /feɪnt/ *adjective*

not strong or not easy to see, hear, or smell: *I heard a faint sound from the room.* | *There is a faint hope that she is still alive.*

faint² *verb*

to suddenly become unconscious for a short time

fair¹ /fɛr/ *adjective*

1 equal for everyone: *I try to be fair **to** all my children.* | *It's not fair – I want one too!* ≫ opposite UNFAIR

2 played or done according to the rules: *Everyone wants to have a fair election.*

3 good, but not very good; average: *His writing is very good, but his reading is only fair.*

4 light in color; pale: *She had blue eyes and fair hair.* ≫ compare DARK¹

fair² *noun*

a place where people, especially children, ride on special machines and play games to win prizes

fair·ly /ˈfɛrli/ *adverb*

1 a little bit, but not very: *He speaks French fairly well.*

2 in a way that is honest and reasonable: *I expect to be treated fairly.*

fair·y /ˈfɛri/ *noun* (*plural* **fairies**)

a small imaginary person with wings who can do magic things in stories

fairy tale /ˈ.. ,./ *noun*

a story for children about magic people or events

faith /feɪθ/ *noun*

1 [U] a strong belief in something or someone: *I have faith **in** your judgment.*

2 [U] belief and trust in God

3 a religion: *He is a member of the Jewish faith.*

faith·ful /'feɪθfəl/ *adjective*
able to be trusted, showing loyalty: *He is a faithful friend. I would trust him with anything.*

fake /feɪk/ *adjective*
not real, but made to look like a real object in order to deceive people

fall¹ /fɔl/ *verb*
(*past tense* **fell** /fɛl/, *past participle* **fallen** /'fɔlən/)
1 to move or drop to the ground: *The leaves are falling from the trees. | Rain was falling. | She fell down the stairs. | Be careful, or you will fall off the ladder* —see color picture on page 189

2 to become less in amount; to decrease: *House prices are falling. | The temperature could fall below zero tonight.*
3 fall apart to break into pieces: *These old shoes are falling apart.*
4 fall asleep to start to sleep: *I fell asleep in front of the fire.*
5 fall in love to begin to love someone: *We fell in love in Paris.*
6 to happen, especially at a particular time: *Christmas falls on a Monday this year.*
7 fall out if a tooth or your hair falls out, it drops from the place where it was
8 fall for something to be tricked into thinking that something is true: *I can't believe she fell for that old story.*
9 to be a part of a particular group: *The examples fall into two different groups.*

fall² *noun*
1 the act of falling to the ground: *He had a bad fall and hurt himself.*
2 the season before winter, when the leaves fall off the trees in cool countries
3 a decrease in the level, price etc. of something: *There was a sudden fall in house prices.*

fall·en /'fɔlən/
the PAST PARTICIPLE of the verb **fall**

false /fɔls/ *adjective*
1 not true or correct: *Is this statement true or false?* ≫ compare TRUE
2 not real: *He has a set of false teeth.*

fame /feɪm/ *noun* [U]
the state of being known and admired by a lot of people

fa·mil·iar /fə'mɪlyər/ *adjective*
1 easy for you to recognize because you have seen or heard it before: *This song sounds familiar.*
2 be familiar with to know something well: *Are you familiar with this story?*

fam·i·ly /'fæmli, -məli/ *noun* (*plural* **families**)
a group of people who are related to each other, especially a father, mother, and their children: *I come from a family of four.* (=with four people in it)

family tree /,.. './ *noun*
a drawing that shows how all the people in a family are related to each other

fam·ine /'fæmɪn/ *noun*
a time when there is not enough food for people to eat

fa·mous /'feɪməs/ *adjective*
known about and admired by a lot of people: *This town is famous for its wine. | She is a famous writer.*

fan¹ /fæn/ *noun*
1 an instrument for moving the air around you to make you cooler
2 someone who likes a particular person or thing very much: *I'm a big fan of his music.*

fan² *verb* (**fanning, fanned**)
to make the air around you move: *She fanned herself with a newspaper to cool her face.*

fan·cy /'fænsi/ *adjective*
not ordinary, plain, or simple: *We stayed in a fancy hotel.*

fan·tas·tic /fæn'tæstɪk/ *adjective*
very good or attractive: *You look fantastic in that dress. | That is a fantastic idea.*

fan·ta·sy /'fæntəsi, -zi/ *noun*
an imagined situation that is not real

far¹ /fɑr/ *adverb* (**farther, farthest** or **further, furthest**)
1 a long distance from a place: *How far away is your house from here? | I don't want to drive too far. | Let's see who can jump the farthest.* ≫ compare NEAR
2 very much: *I'm far too tired to go out. | I saw a plane flying far above the clouds.*
3 go too far to do something too much so that you annoy or upset someone: *I know he likes jokes, but this time he has gone too far!*
4 so far until now: *We have not had any problems so far.*

5 so far, so good said when things have been successful until now: *"How is your new job?" "So far, so good."*

NOTE: Use **far** in questions, in NEGATIVE sentences and after **too**, **as** and **so**: *How far is it to your house? It isn't far. It's too far to walk. We drove as far as the next town. We didn't want to walk so far.* In other types of sentence, use **a long way**: *We walked a long way. It's a long way from the school to my house.*

far² *adjective*
not near; distant: *I left the car on the far side of the parking lot.* ≫ compare NEAR

fare /fɛr/ *noun*
the money that you pay to travel on a bus, train, plane etc.

farm /farm/ *noun*
land on which people grow food or keep animals

farm·er /'farmɚ/ *noun*
a person who owns or works on a farm

farm·house /'farmhaʊs/ *noun*
the house on a farm where the farmer lives

farm·ing /'farmɪŋ/ *noun* [U]
the job of growing food or keeping animals ≫ compare AGRICULTURE

farm·yard /'farmyard/ *noun*
the area next to farm buildings

far·ther /'farðɚ/
the comparative of **far**

far·thest /'farðɪst/
the superlative of **far**

fas·ci·nate /'fæsə,neɪt/ *verb* (**fascinating, fascinated**)
to interest someone very much

fas·ci·na·tion /,fæsə'neɪʃən/ *noun* [U]
very strong interest in something

fash·ion /'fæʃən/ *noun*
1 the way of dressing or doing something that is liked by a lot of people at a particular time: *She always buys the newest fashions.*
2 in fashion liked by many people now: *Short skirts are in fashion this year.*
3 out of fashion no longer liked by many people

fash·ion·a·ble /'fæʃənəbəl/ *adjective*
liked by many people at a particular time: *fashionable suits* ≫ opposite UNFASHIONABLE

fast¹ /fæst/ *adjective*
1 quick; not slow: *He is a fast runner.* | *What is the fastest way to get to the airport?*
2 showing a time that is later than the real time: *I think my watch is fast.* ≫ compare SLOW

fast² *adverb*
1 quickly: *He likes driving fast.*
2 in a short time: *You are learning fast.*
3 fast asleep sleeping very well
4 firmly; tightly: *The boat is stuck fast in the mud.*

fast³ *verb*
to eat no food, usually for religious reasons ≫ compare STARVE

fas·ten /'fæsən/ *verb*
to join or tie together two sides of something so that it is closed: *Fasten your seat belt when you get into the car.*

fastener

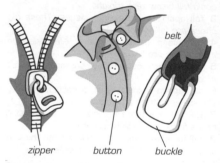

zipper   button   buckle

fas·ten·er /'fæsənɚ/ *noun*
something used to join or tie things together

fast food /ˌ. './ *noun* [U]
food, such as HAMBURGERs, that is made and served quickly

fat¹ /fæt/ *adjective*
1 weighing too much: *She worries a lot about getting fat.*
2 thick or wide: *I had to read a big fat book for his class.* ≫ opposite THIN

fat² *noun*
1 an oily substance in some foods: *I buy meat that is low in fat.*
2 a substance that is under the skin of people and animals

fa·tal /'feɪtl/ *adjective*
causing someone to die: *She was involved in a fatal car accident.* ≫ compare DEADLY —**fatally** *adverb*: *He was fatally injured.*

fate /feɪt/ *noun*
1 [U] a power which some people believe controls what happens to you during your life: *I believe fate brought us together.*
2 the things that happen to someone: *The fate of the children is unknown.*

fa·ther /'fɑðɚ/ *noun*
your male parent

father-in-law /'.. . ,./ *noun* (plural fathers-in-law)
the father of your wife or husband

fau·cet /'fɔsɪt/ *noun*
a piece of equipment that you turn on and off to control the flow of water from a pipe —see picture at DRIP

fault /fɔlt/ *noun*
1 responsibility for a mistake: *I'm sorry – it's all my fault.*
2 a problem with something that stops it from working: *There is a fault in the engine.*

fault·less /'fɔltlɪs/ *adjective*
having no faults; perfect: *He gave a faultless performance.*

fault·y /'fɔlti/ *adjective*
not working correctly: *We have a faulty wire in the telephone.*

fa·vor /'feɪvɚ/ *noun*
1 something you do for someone to help or be kind to him or her: *Can I ask you a favor?* | *Will you do me a favor and help me lift this?*
2 **be in favor of** to choose one plan or idea instead of another: *Are you in favor of changing the law?*

fa·vor·a·ble /'feɪvərəbəl/ *adjective*
1 making people like or approve of someone or something: *I've heard some favorable reports about your work.*
2 good and likely to help something succeed: *We need favorable weather to take the boat out.* —**favorably** *adverb*

fa·vor·ite[1] /'feɪvrɪt, -vərɪt/ *adjective*
liked more than others: *Orange is my favorite color.*

favorite[2] *noun*
someone or something that you like more than any others: *Which book is your favorite?*

fax /fæks/ *noun*
a machine, joined to a telephone, with which you can send a copy of a letter or a picture to another place

fear[1] /fɪr/ *noun*
1 the feeling of being afraid: *He was shaking with fear.* | *I have a fear of snakes.*
2 [U] the feeling of being worried because you think something bad will happen: *You cannot live in fear.*

fear[2] *verb*
1 to be afraid of someone or something: *What do you fear most of all?*
2 to worry because you think that something bad will happen: *Many parents fear for their children's safety.*

fear·ful /'fɪrfəl/ *adjective*
causing fear; afraid: *Everyone is fearful of getting the disease.*

fear·less /'fɪrlɪs/ *adjective*
not afraid of anything: *He is a fearless soldier.* >> compare BRAVE

feast[1] /fist/ *noun*
a large meal for a lot of people for a special reason

feast[2] *verb*
to eat and drink a lot to celebrate something

feath·er /'fɛðɚ/ *noun*
one of the soft things that cover a bird's body

fea·ture /'fitʃɚ/ *noun*
1 one part of something that you notice because it is important or interesting
2 a part of your face, especially your eyes, nose, or mouth

Feb·ru·ar·y /'fɛbyu,ɛri, 'fɛbru,ɛri/ *noun*
the second month of the year

fed /fɛd/
the PAST TENSE and PAST PARTICIPLE of the verb feed

fed·er·al /'fɛdərəl/ *adjective*
relating to the central government of a country that controls a group of states

fed up /,. './ *adjective*
annoyed or bored and wanting something to change: *I'm fed up with staying at home all day.*

fee /fi/ *noun*
money that you pay for a service or to do something

fee·ble /'fibəl/ *adjective*
very weak: *His voice sounded feeble.*

feed /fid/ *verb* (feeding, fed /fɛd/)
to give food to a person or an animal: *Have you fed the cat?*

feel /fil/ *verb* [**feeling, felt** /fɛlt/]
1 to have a particular feeling or emotion: *I feel very happy for you.* | *Do you feel cold?*
2 to touch something with your fingers to see what it is like: *Feel this cloth – it's so smooth.*
3 to notice something touching you: *I felt a bug on my arm.*
4 to have an opinion because of your feelings rather than facts: *I feel sure that she will agree.*
5 **feel like** to want something: *I feel like getting something to eat.*
6 **feel for someone** to have sympathy for someone: *She is very unhappy, and I feel for her.*

feel·ing /'filɪŋ/ *noun*
1 something that you feel in your mind or body: *You have to deal with your feelings **of** anger.*
2 a belief or opinion about something: *I **have a** feeling she is not being honest with me.*
3 **hurt someone's feelings** to upset someone

feet /fit/
1 the plural of **foot**
2 **on your feet** standing up: *I've been on my feet all day.*
3 **put your feet up** to rest and relax

fell /fɛl/
the PAST TENSE of the verb **fall**

fel·low¹ /'fɛlou/ *noun*
a man

fellow² *adjective*
like you or from the same place as you: *He likes his fellow students.*

felt /fɛlt/
the PAST TENSE and PAST PARTICIPLE of the verb **feel**

felt tip pen /ˌ. . '. / *noun*
a thick colored pen

fe·male¹ /'fimeɪl/ *adjective*
belonging to the sex that gives birth to babies ≫ compare MALE¹

female² *noun*
a girl or woman; an animal of the sex that gives birth to babies ≫ compare MALE²

fem·i·nine /'fɛmənɪn/ *adjective*
like a woman or typical of a woman ≫ compare MASCULINE

fem·i·nis·m /'fɛməˌnɪzəm/ *noun* [U]
the belief that women should have the same rights and opportunities as men

fence /fɛns/ *noun*
a wooden or metal wall around a piece of land —see color picture on page 188

fend·er /'fɛndɚ/ *noun*
1 the part of a car that covers the wheels
2 a curved piece of metal that covers the wheel on a bicycle

fern /fɚn/ *noun*
a green plant that has no flowers

fe·ro·cious /fəˈrouʃəs/ *adjective*
very fierce or violent: *He had a ferocious dog in the back yard.*

fer·ry /'fɛri/ *noun* (*plural* **ferries**)
a boat that takes people or things across a narrow area of water

fer·tile /'fɚtl/ *adjective*
able to grow a lot of plants very well: *His farm is on fertile land.*

fer·til·iz·er /'fɚtlˌaɪzɚ/ *noun*
a substance put on soil to help crops grow

fes·ti·val /'fɛstəvəl/ *noun*
1 a set of special events of a particular type: *We went to a music festival.*
2 a time of public celebration, especially for a religious event

fetch /fɛtʃ/ *verb*
to go and get something and bring it back with you: *The dog fetched the stick that I threw.*

fete /feɪt/ *noun*
an event to celebrate something

fe·ver /'fivɚ/ *noun*
an illness which causes an increase in how hot your body is: *I am sick and have a fever.*

few /fyu/
1 **a few** a small number of: *Can I ask you a few questions?* | *We'll wait a few more minutes.*
2 not many: *He has few friends.* | *Few people would agree with you.* ≫ compare MANY
3 **quite a few** a large number of: *There were quite a few people at the party.*

fi·an·cé /ˌfianˈseɪ, fiˈanseɪ/ *noun*
a man who is to marry a particular woman

fi·an·cée /ˌfianˈseɪ, fiˈanseɪ/ *noun*
a woman who is to marry a particular man

fib /fɪb/ *noun*
a lie; not the truth: *Are you **telling** a fib?*

fi·ber /'faɪbɚ/ *noun*
a thin thread used for making cloth

fic·tion /'fɪkʃən/ noun [U]
books and stories about imaginary people and
events —**fictional** adjective: They're just fictional characters.

field /fild/ noun
a piece of ground used for a particular purpose:
I see a field of wheat. | Meet me at the football
field. —see colour picture on page188

fierce /fɪrs/ adjective
very angry, violent, or ready to attack: Some
fierce dogs guarded the house.

fif·teen /ˌfɪf'tin/ adjective, noun
the number 15

fifth /fɪfθ/ adjective, noun
1 5th
2 one of five equal parts

fif·ty /'fɪfti/ adjective, noun
the number 50

fig /fɪg/ noun
a sweet fruit which is full of small seeds —see
picture at FRUIT

fight¹ /faɪt/ verb (fighting, fought)
1 to use weapons, guns etc. to try to hurt or
kill someone: He fought in the war.
2 to argue with someone: The kids are fighting
again.

fight² noun
1 an act of fighting; argument: The two boys
had a fight.
2 a battle between two armies

fig·ure /'fɪgyɚ/ noun
a shape, especially the shape of a human body:
I saw a tall figure near the door. | She has a
great figure. (=her body is very attractive).

file¹ /faɪl/ noun
1 a box or paper cover for keeping papers
organized
2 a collection of information in a computer that
is kept in a particular place
3 a tool with a rough edge that you use for
making things smooth

file² verb (filing, filed)
1 to put papers into a file: Can you file these
reports, please?
2 make something smooth using a special tool
3 to walk in a line of people, one behind the
other: The children filed into the classroom.

file cab·i·net /'. ˌ.../ noun
a tall, narrow piece of furniture with drawers
where you put important papers

fill /fɪl/ verb
1 to become full, or make something full: I
filled the glass with water. | The room was filled
with smoke.
2 **fill something in** to write information on an
official piece of paper: Fill in the answers to
these questions.
3 **fill something up** to put enough of something in a container to make it full: Did you fill
up the car with gas?
4 to put something in a hole or crack to make
a smooth surface ≫ compare EMPTY²

fill·ing /'fɪlɪŋ/ noun
a substance that is put in a hole in your tooth
to preserve the tooth

film¹ /fɪlm/ noun
1 the object you put in a camera which makes
photographs
2 a movie

film² verb
to use a camera to make a movie: The movie
was filmed in Mexico.

fil·ter¹ /'fɪltɚ/ noun
something that gas or liquid is put through to
remove unwanted substances: a water filter

filter² verb
1 to clean a liquid or gas using a FILTER:
filtered drinking water
2 If people filter somewhere, they gradually
move in that direction through a door, hall etc.:
The audience began to **filter into** the hall.
3 if information filters somewhere, people
gradually hear about it: The news slowly **filtered
through to** everyone in the office.
4 if light or sound filters into a place, it can be
seen or heard only slightly: Sunshine **filtered
through** the curtains.

filth·y /'fɪlθi/ adjective (filthier, filthiest)
very dirty: His clothes are filthy.

fin /fɪn/ noun
a thin body part on a fish that helps it to swim
—see picture at FISH¹

fi·nal¹ /'faɪnl/ adjective
1 coming at the end; last: Did you read the
final part of the story?
2 not able to be changed: That is my decision,
and it is final!

final² noun
the last and most important game in a competition

fi·nal·ly /ˈfaɪnl-i/ *adverb*
1 after a long time: *We finally left after waiting for two hours.*
2 a word you use when you come to the last thing you want to say about something: *Finally, I want to thank Betty for all her help.*

fi·nance¹ /fəˈnæns, ˈfaɪnæns/ *noun* [U]
the controlling of large amounts of money, especially by a bank, company, or government

finance² *verb* (financing, financed)
to give money for something: *The government will finance the building of the new roads.*

fi·nan·cial /fəˈnænʃəl, faɪ-/ *adjective*
related to money: *Do you need any financial advice?* —**financially** *adverb*

find /faɪnd/ *verb* (past **found** /faʊnd/)
1 to see or get something after you have been looking for it: *I can't find my keys.* | *Have you found a job yet?* ≫ compare LOSE
2 to learn or discover something: *I want to find the answer to her question.*
3 **find someone guilty** to say that someone is guilty of a crime: *The court found him guilty of murder.*
4 **find something out** to discover the facts about something: *She will find out the truth sooner or later.*
5 **be found** to live or exist somewhere: *This type of bear is found only in China.*

fine¹ /faɪn/ *adjective*
1 very nice or of high quality: *He owns a store that sells fine wines.*
2 good enough; all right: *"How is your meal?" "Fine, thanks."*
3 very well, happy, or healthy: *"How do you feel?" "Fine."*
4 very thin: *The painting has fine lines of blue in it.*

fine² *noun*
money that you pay as a punishment for doing something wrong

fine³ *verb* (fining, fined)
to make someone pay money as a punishment: *Robert was fined $50 for driving too fast.*

fin·ger /ˈfɪŋɡɚ/ *noun*
one of the five long parts on your hand

fin·ger·nail /ˈfɪŋɡɚˌneɪl/ *noun*
one of the hard, flat parts that covers the top end of your finger

fin·ger·print /ˈfɪŋɡɚˌprɪnt/ *noun*
mark made by the lines on the end of your fingers

fin·ger·tip /ˈfɪŋɡɚˌtɪp/ *noun*
the end of a finger

fin·ish¹ /ˈfɪnɪʃ/ *noun*
the end of something ≫ compare START²

finish² *verb*
1 to end or to be complete: *The game finished at four o'clock.*
2 to eat or drink the rest of something: *Finish your dinner, and then you can watch television.*
3 **finish something off** to use or eat all of something: *I'm just finishing off the last of the cake.*

fin·ished /ˈfɪnɪʃt/ *adjective*
be finished to not be doing or using something any more, because it is complete or because you do not need it any more: *Are you finished with the scissors?*

fir /fɚ/ *noun*
a tree with leaves shaped like needles that do not fall off in winter

fire¹ /faɪɚ/ *noun*
1 [U] heat and flames made when something burns: *The fire destroyed our house.*
2 burning wood or coal that provides heat: *I like to sit in front of the fire.*
3 **catch fire** to begin to burn
4 **on fire** burning: *The house is on fire.*
5 **set fire to something** to make something burn
6 [U] shooting by guns: *The soldiers came under fire.* [=were being shot at]

fire² *verb*
1 to shoot with a gun
2 to make someone leave his or her job: *Four people were fired last week.*

fire a·larm /ˈ. .,./ *noun*
a bell that makes a loud noise to warn you when a building starts to burn

fire de·part·ment /ˈ. .,../ *noun*
a group of people whose job is to stop dangerous fires

fire en·gine /ˈ. ,../ *noun*
a large vehicle which has water and special equipment for stopping fires from burning —see color picture on page 187

fire es·cape /ˈ. .,./ *noun*
a set of stairs on the outside of a building, that you can use in getting away from a fire

fire ex·tin·guish·er /ˈ. .,.../ *noun*
a metal container with water or chemicals in it, used for stopping fires

fire·fight·er /ˈfaɪəˌfaɪtə/ *noun*
someone whose job is to stop dangerous fires

fire·man /ˈfaɪəmən/ *noun* (*plural* firemen /-mɛn/)
a man whose job is to stop dangerous fires

fire·place /ˈfaɪəpleɪs/ *noun*
an open place in a wall of a room where you have a fire

fire sta·tion /ˈ. ˌ../ *noun*
the building where people and equipment stay until they are needed to stop a fire

fire·wood /ˈfaɪəwʊd/ *noun* [U]
wood that you burn in a fire

fireworks

fire·works /ˈfaɪəwɜːks/ *plural noun*
explosives which make a lot of bright light and color in the air and are burned to celebrate a special day

firm¹ /fɜːm/ *adjective*
1 not soft: *I need a firm bed to sleep on.*
2 having strong control; not weak: *The government kept firm control over the military.*
3 **a firm grip, a firm hold** a tight strong hold on something

firm² *noun*
a group of people who work together in a business; a small company: *a law firm*

firm·ly /ˈfɜːmli/ *adverb*
in a way that shows strong control: *She told him firmly that he must wait.*

first /fɜːst/
1 coming before anyone or anything else: *It's his first year at school. | Who wants to go first?* ≫ compare LAST¹
2 **first of all** (**a**) before doing anything else: *First of all, can you tell me your name?* (**b**) used when telling the first or most important thing in a list: *First of all we had dinner, then we went to a movie, and then we went home.*

3 **at first** at the start of something: *At first I didn't enjoy my job, but now I like it.*

first aid /ˌ. ˈ./ *noun* [U]
simple help that you give to someone who is sick or injured before the doctor comes

first aid kit /ˌ. ˈ. ./ *noun*
a box containing medicines to give to someone who is sick or injured

first-class /ˌfɜːstˈklæs◄/ *adjective*
using the best or most expensive type: *He bought a first-class plane ticket.*

first·ly /ˈfɜːstli/ *adverb*
used when telling someone the first or most important thing: *Firstly, let me thank everyone for coming here this evening.* ≫ compare LASTLY

> NOTE: **Firstly** does NOT mean "in the beginning." Use **at first** instead: *At first I didn't like my new job, but then I started to enjoy it.*

first name /ˈ. ./ *noun*
the name or names that come before your family name: *"What is your first name, Mrs. Jones?" "It's Anne. I'm Mrs. Anne Jones."* ≫ compare LAST NAME

fish¹ /fɪʃ/ *noun*
(*plural* **fish** or **fishes**)
an animal that lives in water and can swim, and which people eat as food

fins

gills

fish² *verb*
1 to try to catch a fish
2 **go fishing** to go to a place to try and catch a fish

fish·er·man /ˈfɪʃəmən/ *noun* (*plural* fishermen /-mɛn/)
a person who catches fish for sport or as a job

fish·ing /ˈfɪʃɪŋ/ *noun* [U]
the sport or job of catching fish: *We went fishing on Saturday.*

fishing rod /ˈ.. ˌ./ *noun*
a long stick with a long string at the end used for catching fish

fist /fɪst/ *noun*
a hand with the fingers closed tightly together: *He hit me with his fist.*

fit¹ /fɪt/ *verb* [fitting, fit]

1 to be the right size or shape for someone or something: *The pants don't fit him – they are too small.*

2 to find space to put someone or something: *We can't fit any more people in the car.*

3 fit in to be accepted by other people in a group: *The new students had a difficult time fitting in.*

fit² *adjective*

1 not sick; healthy and strong: *I want to get physically fit.*

2 good enough, or suitable for something: *This food is not fit for people.*

fit³ *noun*

have a fit, throw a fit to become very angry and shout a lot

five /faɪv/ *adjective, noun*
the number 5

fix /fɪks/ *verb*

1 to repair something: *Can you fix my bicycle?*

2 to prepare a meal or drinks: *I will fix dinner for us tonight.*

3 to arrange something: *We have fixed a date for the meeting.*

4 fix up to make a place look better by doing repairs, decorating it etc.

fizz /fɪz/ *noun* [U]
the BUBBLEs of gas in some types of drink, or the sound they make: *The soda in the fridge has lost its fizz.* —**fizz** *verb* —**fizzy** *adjective*

flag /flæg/ *noun*
a piece of cloth with a special pattern on it, used as the sign of a country or organization

flag·pole /ˈflæɡpoʊl/ *noun*
a tall pole at the top of which you put a flag

flake /fleɪk/ *noun*
a small thin piece of something that has broken off a larger piece

flame /fleɪm/ *noun*

1 a bright piece of burning gas that you see in a fire

2 in flames burning: *The house was in flames.*

flap¹ /flæp/ *verb* [flapping, flapped]
to move up and down: *The bird flapped its wings.*

flap² *noun*
a piece of something that hangs down and covers an opening: *I tore the flap on my shirt pocket.*

flash¹ /flæʃ/ *noun*

1 a sudden bright light: *We saw a flash of lightning.*

2 a light on a camera that you use when you take a photograph where it is dark

3 in a flash very quickly: *We'll be there in a flash.*

flash² *verb*
to shine brightly for a moment

flash·light /ˈflæʃlaɪt/ *noun*
a small electric light that you carry in your hand
—see picture at LAMP

flat¹ /flæt/ *adjective*

1 smooth and level; without any raised places: *The house has a flat roof.*

2 not having enough air inside: *We have a flat tire.*

flat² *adverb*
in a straight position; not raised: *I have to lie flat on my back to sleep.*

flat·ten /ˈflætn/ *verb*
to make something flat: *The heavy rain flattened the corn.*

flat·ter /ˈflætɚ/ *verb*
to say nice things to someone because you are trying to please him or her

flat·ter·y /ˈflætəri/ *noun* [U]
nice things that you say to someone because you are trying to please him or her

fla·vor /ˈfleɪvɚ/ *noun*
a taste of a food or drink: *They have 39 flavors of ice cream!*

flea /fli/ *noun*
a very small jumping insect that drinks blood from animals and people

flee /fli/ *verb* [fleeing, fled]
to run away quickly; to escape

fleece /flis/ *noun*
the wool of a sheep

fleet /flit/ *noun*
a lot of ships or boats together: *A fleet of ships sailed into the sea.*

flesh /flɛʃ/ *noun* [U]
the soft part of your body that covers your bones ≫ compare SKIN

flew /flu/
the PAST TENSE of the verb **fly**

flight /flaɪt/ *noun*
1 a trip on a plane: *When is the next flight to New York?*
2 a flight of stairs a set of stairs from one level to another

flight at·tend·ant /'. .,../ *noun*
a person whose job is to take care of the passengers on a plane and give them food and drinks

fling /flɪŋ/ *verb*
to throw or move something with force: *She flung her arms around his neck.*

flip /flɪp/ *verb*
(flipping, flipped)
1 to turn something over or put it in a different position with a quick movement: *Can you flip that switch for me?*
2 to throw something flat like a coin so that it turns over in the air

flip·per /'flɪpɚ/ *noun*
1 a flat part on the body of some sea animals which helps them to swim
2 a large flat plastic shoe that you wear to help you swim faster

flirt /flɚt/ *verb*
to behave as if you are attracted to someone in a sexual way: *He flirts **with** all the women.*

float /floʊt/ *verb*
to stay on the surface of a liquid: *A boat floats on water.* ≫ compare SINK[1]

flock /flɑk/ *noun*
a group of sheep, goats, or birds ≫ compare HERD[1]

flood[1] /flʌd/ *noun*
a great amount of water that covers a place that is usually dry: *The floods destroyed many homes.*

flood[2] *verb*
to cover or fill a place with water: *The river flooded the fields.*

flood·light /'flʌdlaɪt/ *noun*
a very bright light used at night to light the outside of buildings, or at sports events

floor /flɔr/ *noun*
1 the flat part of a room on which you walk: *The room has a lovely wooden floor.*
2 all the rooms on the same level of a building: *We live on the third floor.* (=above the ground)

floor·board /'flɔrbɔrd/ *noun*
a long, narrow piece of wood used to make floors

flop·py disk /,.. './ *noun*
a piece of plastic that you can put into a computer and on which information can be stored ≫ compare HARD DISK

flo·rist /'flɔrɪst, 'flɑr-/ *noun*
a person who sells flowers in a store

flour /flaʊɚ/ *noun* [U]
fine powder made from wheat, used for making bread, cake etc.

flour·ish /'flɚɪʃ, 'flʌrɪʃ/ *verb*
to grow well: *The plant is flourishing in the warm sun.*

flow[1] /floʊ/ *verb*
if a liquid flows, it moves slowly along: *The river flows by our hotel.*

flow[2] *noun* [U]
a smooth continuous movement: *The flow of cars through the city never stops.*

flow·er /'flaʊɚ/ *noun*
the part of a plant which has the seeds and is brightly colored —see picture at ROSE[2] and see color picture on page 188

flow·er·bed /'flaʊɚ,bed/ *noun*
an area of earth with flowers growing in it

flow·er·pot /'flaʊɚ,pɑt/ *noun*
a container in which you grow plants

flown /floʊn/
the PAST PARTICIPLE of the verb **fly**

flu /flu/ *noun*
the flu a disease like a bad cold but more serious

flu·ent /'fluənt/ *adjective*
able to speak or write a language very well: *He speaks fluent English.*

fluff /flʌf/ *noun* [U]
soft light pieces that come off wool, fur, feathers etc.

flu·id[1] /'fluɪd/ *noun*
a liquid

fluid² *adjective*
able to flow or move like a liquid

flush /flʌʃ/ *verb*
1 to clean a toilet by making water go down it
2 to become red in the face because you are embarrassed or angry: *His face flushed with anger.*

flute /fluːt/ *noun*
a musical instrument like a pipe that you hold across your lips and blow

flut·ter /ˈflʌtɚ/ *verb*
to move or wave in the air quickly: *I saw the flag fluttering in the wind.*

fly¹ /flaɪ/ *verb* (**flying, flew** /fluː/; *past participle* **flown**)
1 to move through the air: *Birds were flying above the trees. | The plane flew from Paris to Rome.*
2 to move quickly: *She flew (=ran) out of the house.*
3 to be the pilot of a plane: *Kathy is learning to fly.*

fly² *noun* (*plural* **flies**)
a small flying insect

fly·ing sau·cer /ˌ..ˈ../ *noun*
a space vehicle which some people think carries creatures from another world

foal /foʊl/ *noun*
a very young horse

foam /foʊm/ *noun* [U]
the white substance that you sometimes see on top of water

fog /fɑg, fɔg/ *noun* [U]
thick cloud close to the ground that is difficult for you to see through »compare MIST

fog·gy /ˈfɑgi, ˈfɔgi/ *adjective* (**foggier, foggiest**)
not easy to see through because of FOG: *It's a very foggy morning.* »compare MISTY

fold¹ /foʊld/ *verb*
1 to bend a piece of paper or cloth so that one part covers another: *She folded her shirts and put them away.*
2 **fold your arms** to bend your arms so they are resting across your chest
3 to make something smaller by bending or closing it: *Fold up the ironing board when you are finished.*

fold² *noun*
a line made in paper or cloth when you bend one part of it over another

fold·er /ˈfoʊldɚ/ *noun*
a large piece of hard paper that is folded so you can keep papers in it

folk /foʊk/ *adjective*
typical of the ordinary people of a particular country or area: *I like folk music.*

folks /foʊks/ *plural noun*
your parents or family: *Have you met my folks?*

fol·low /ˈfɑloʊ/ *verb*
1 to come or go after someone or something: *He left the room and I followed. | Follow me. I will show you where she is.*
2 to go in the same direction as a road, river etc.: *Follow the road as far as the church.*
3 to go behind someone to watch or find out where he or she is going: *I think I am being followed.*
4 to happen immediately after something else: *I heard a shout followed by a loud crash.*
5 to understand something: *I'm sorry, I don't follow you.*
6 to do what someone tells you to do: *Did you follow the instructions on the box?*
7 **follow in someone's footsteps** to do something that someone else did before you: *He followed in his father's footsteps and became a doctor.*

fol·low·ing /ˈfɑloʊɪŋ/ *adjective*
the following day, week, year etc. the next day, week, year etc.: *We leave on Friday and return the following Monday.*

fond /fɑnd/ *adjective*
be fond of to like someone or something: *I'm very fond of you.*

food /fud/ *noun* [U]
things that you eat: *He had no food for two days.*

fool¹ /ful/ *noun*
1 a stupid person »compare IDIOT
2 **make a fool of yourself** to do something embarrassing in front of other people

fool² *verb*
1 to trick or deceive someone: *He fooled me into giving him money.*
2 **fool around** (a) to behave in a silly way: *Stop fooling around!* (b) to do something you enjoy: *Today I fooled around at the beach.*

fool·ish /ˈfulɪʃ/ *adjective*
not reasonable or wise; stupid —**foolishly** *adverb*

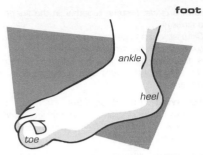

foot

ankle

heel

toe

foot /fʊt/ *noun* (*plural* **feet** /fiːt/)
1 the part of your body that you stand on
2 the bottom of something: *We waited at the foot of the hill.*
3 a measure of length equal to 12 inches: *Mike is six feet tall.*
4 on foot walking: *They made their way into town on foot.*

foot·ball /'fʊt‚bɔl/ *noun*
1 [U] a game in which two teams carry, kick, or throw a ball into an area at the end of the field to win points —see color picture on page 184
2 a ball used in this game

foot·print /'fʊt‚prɪnt/ *noun*
the mark left by a person's foot: *I saw a cat's footprints in the snow.*

foot·step /'fʊtstɛp/ *noun*
the sound of someone walking: *I heard footsteps behind me.*

for /fɚ; *strong* fɔr/
1 meant to be given to or used by someone or something: *Here's a letter for you.* | *I'm making some curtains for the bedroom.* | *She goes to a school for girls.*
2 meant to be used in this way: *Do you have a knife for cutting bread?*
3 showing how far or how long: *She has lived here for many years.* | *I waited for three hours.* ≫ compare SINCE
4 toward a place: *I was leaving for church when you called.*
5 at a price of: *She bought the dress for $50.*
6 with the meaning of: *What is the word for "tree" in Korean?*
7 in favor of someone or something; agreeing with: *The government is for the plan.*
8 by or at a particular time: *We'll be home for Christmas.*
9 because of; showing the reason: *He won a prize for singing.* | *They were punished for their bad behavior.*

10 in order to help someone: *She did some work for her father.*
11 used for showing who a feeling is about: *I'm very happy for you.*

for·bid /fɚ'bɪd/ *verb* (**forbidding,** **forbade**/fɚ'beɪd/, *past participle* **forbidden**)
to tell someone they must not do something: *I forbid you to go there again!* ≫ compare ALLOW, BAN[1]

force[1] /fɔrs/ *verb* (**forcing, forced**)
1 to make someone do something he or she does not want to do: *Bad health forced me to quit my job.*
2 to use your strength to make something move: *He had to force the door open.* (=make it open by pushing or pulling)

force[2] *noun*
1 [U] power or strength: *The force of the explosion threw me to the ground.*
2 a group of people like the army or police who are trained to fight together: *Both of her sons are in the police force.*
3 [U] violent physical action used for getting what you want

fore·cast /'fɔrkæst/ *noun*
something that says what is likely to happen in the future: *Did you see the weather forecast?*

fore·head /'fɔrhɛd, 'fɔrɪd, 'farɪd/ *noun*
the top part of your face, above your eyes and below your hair —see picture at HEAD[1]

for·eign /'farɪn, 'fɔrɪn/ *adjective*
from a country that is not your country: *Can you speak a foreign language?* | *I like foreign cars.*

for·eign·er /'farənɚ, 'fɔr-/ *noun*
a person who comes from a country that is not your country

fore·man /'fɔrmən/ *noun* (*plural* **foremen**)
a man who is the leader of a group of workers

for·est /'fɔrɪst, 'far-/ *noun*
an area where there is a lot of trees —see color picture on page 188

for·ev·er /fə'rɛvɚ, fɔ-/ *adverb*
always; for all time in the future: *I will love you forever.*

for·gave /fɚ'geɪv/
the PAST TENSE of the verb **forgive**

forge /fɔrdʒ/ *verb* (**forging, forged**)
to make a copy of something in order to make people think it is real: *The police think the money is forged.*

for·ger·y /ˈfɔrdʒəri/ *noun*
1 [U] the crime of making a copy of something in a way that is not legal: *She went to prison for forgery.*
2 (*plural* **forgeries**) a copy which is intended to make people think it is real

for·get /fəˈgɛt/ *verb* (**forgetting, forgot** /fəˈgɑt/, *past participle* **forgotten** /fəˈgɑtˈn/)
1 not to remember something: *I have forgotten her name.* | *Don't forget that Chuck's birthday is Friday.* ≫ compare REMEMBER
2 to stop thinking or worrying about someone or something: *You have to forget **about** your problems for a while.*

NOTE: If you want to say **where** you have left something, use **leave**, not **forget** e.g. *Oh, no – I forgot my bag!* compared with *I left my bag on the bus.*

for·get·ful /fəˈgɛtfəl/ *adjective*
often forgetting things: *Bill is getting forgetful in his old age.*

for·give /fəˈgɪv/ *verb* (**forgiving, forgave,** *past participle* **forgiven**)
to not be angry at someone, even though he or she has done something wrong: *Please forgive me – I didn't mean to do it.*

for·got /fəˈgɑt/
the PAST TENSE of the verb **forget**

for·got·ten /fəˈgɑtˈn/
the PAST PARTICIPLE of the verb **forget**

fork¹ /fɔrk/ *noun*
1 an instrument with a handle and two or more points at one end, used for picking up food to eat
2 a place where a road or a river divides into two parts: *Turn left at the fork **in** the road.*

fork² *verb*
if a road or river forks, it divides into two parts

form¹ /fɔrm/ *noun*
1 a type of something: *The country has a new form **of** government.*
2 a shape: *She had a birthday cake in the form of the number 18.*
3 an official piece of paper with spaces where you write information

form² *verb*
1 to start to appear or exist; develop: *Ice was forming on the roads.*
2 to make a particular shape: *Now children,* form a circle. (=stand together in the shape of a circle)
3 to start an organization or group: *We want to form a computer club at school.*
4 to make or produce something: *You form the adverb of the word "quick" by adding "-ly" to the end.*

for·mal /ˈfɔrməl/ *adjective*
suitable for an official or important occasion: *I received a formal letter from her office.* ≫ opposite INFORMAL

for·mer¹ /ˈfɔrmɚ/ *noun*
the former the first of two people or things that you are mentioning: *Our company has agreements with both Acme and General, but its agreement with the former* (=Acme) *will end soon.* ≫ compare LATTER

former² *adjective*
at an earlier time but not any more: *The former U.S. President was at the meeting.*

for·mer·ly /ˈfɔrmɚli/ *adverb*
in the past: *The house was formerly owned by his family.*

for·mu·la /ˈfɔrmyələ/ *noun* (*plural* **formulas** or **formulae** /ˈfɔrmyuli/)
a list of the substances used to make something: *He developed a new formula for the drug.*

fort /fɔrt/ *noun*
a strong building used by soldiers to defend an important place

for·tu·nate /ˈfɔrtʃənɪt/ *adjective*
lucky ≫ opposite UNFORTUNATE

for·tu·nate·ly /ˈfɔrtʃənɪtli/ *adverb*
happening because of good luck: *Fortunately, we arrived in time to help.* ≫ opposite UNFORTUNATELY

for·tune /ˈfɔrtʃən/ *noun*
1 [U] luck: *I had the good fortune* (=I was lucky) *to get a job.*
2 a very large amount of money: *He made a fortune by selling houses.*
3 **tell someone's fortune** to tell someone what is going to happen to them in the future

for·ty /ˈfɔrt̬i/ *adjective, noun*
the number 40

for·ward¹ /ˈfɔrwɚd/ *adverb* (*also* **forwards**)
1 in the direction that is in front of you: *I leaned forward to hear what she was saying.* ≫ compare BACKWARD¹

2 toward the future: *I am looking forward to meeting your parents.* (=I am excited that I will meet them)

forward² /ˈfɔːrwərd/ *adjective*
in the direction that is in front of you: *We sat in the forward part of the plane.* ≫ compare BACKWARD²

fought /fɔt/
the PAST TENSE and PAST PARTICIPLE of the verb **fight**

foul /faʊl/ *adjective*
very dirty and unpleasant: *A foul smell was coming from the room.*

found¹ /faʊnd/
the PAST TENSE and PAST PARTICIPLE of the verb **find**

found² *verb*
to start: *The school was founded in 1884.*

foun·da·tion /faʊnˈdeɪʃən/ *noun*
the solid base that is under the ground and supports a building

foun·tain
/ˈfaʊntɪn/ *noun*
a structure that sends water high into the air, built for decoration

four /fɔr/ *adjective, noun*
the number 4

four·teen
/ˌfɔrˈtin/ *adjective, noun*
the number 14

fourth /fɔrθ/ *adjective, noun*
4th

fowl /faʊl/ *noun*
a bird, especially one that is kept for food

fox /faks/ *noun* (*plural* **foxes**)
a wild animal like a dog, with dark red fur and a thick tail

frac·tion /ˈfrækʃən/ *noun*
a division or part of a number such as ¼, ½

frac·ture¹ /ˈfræktʃər/ *verb* (**fracturing, fractured**)
to crack or break something hard: *I fractured my leg skating.*

fracture² *noun*
a crack or break in something hard

frag·ile /ˈfrædʒəl/ *adjective*
easy to break or damage

frag·ment /ˈfrægmənt/ *noun*
a small piece that has broken off something: *Fragments of glass lay on the floor.*

fra·grance /ˈfreɪgrəns/ *noun*
a sweet or pleasant smell: *The fragrance of flowers filled the air.*

fra·grant /ˈfreɪgrənt/ *adjective*
having a pleasant smell

frail /ˈfreɪl/ *adjective*
thin and weak; not healthy

frame¹ /freɪm/
noun
1 the bars around which a building, car etc. is made: *My bicycle frame was damaged in the accident.*

2 a piece of wood or metal around the edges of a picture, window etc.
3 (*plural*) the part of a pair of glasses which holds the glass —see picture at GLASSES

frame² *verb* (**framing, framed**)
to put a wood or metal frame around the edges of a picture

frank /fræŋk/ *adjective*
honest and not afraid to say what you think: *Mark and I have always been frank with each other.*

frank·ly /ˈfræŋkli/ *adverb*
1 used when saying what you really think about something: *Frankly, I think you are wasting your time.*
2 in an honest way: *They talked frankly about their problems.*

fraud /frɔd/ *noun*
the crime of deceiving people in order to get money

fray /freɪ/ *verb* (**fraying, frayed**)
if a cloth or rope frays, its threads become loose at the edges

freak /frik/ *noun*
a person or animal that is very strange

freck·le /ˈfrɛkəl/ *noun*
a small brown spot on someone's skin —see color picture on page 191

free¹ /fri/ *adjective*
1 able to do what you like: *You are free to leave at any time.*
2 not costing any money: *I have a free ticket to the play.*
3 not working or busy: *Are you free this evening?*
4 not being used at this time: *Excuse me. Is this seat free?*
5 **feel free** used when telling someone that he or she is allowed to do something: *Feel free to ask any questions after class.*
6 **set someone free** to allow someone to leave a prison

free² *verb* (*past* **freed**)
to let a person or an animal leave a place where they have been kept as a prisoner: *They freed the birds from the cages.*

free³ *adverb*
1 without having to pay any money: *You can visit the museum for free.*
2 not controlled by someone or held in a particular position: *He held my arm, but I pulled free.*

free·dom /'fridəm/ *noun* [U]
the state of being free and able to do what you want

freeze /friz/ *verb* (**freezing, froze,** *past participle* **frozen**)
1 to become very cold and change from a liquid into a solid: *Water freezes to become ice.*
2 **be freezing** to feel very cold: *It's freezing outside!*

freez·er /'frizɚ/ *noun*
a machine that keeps food very cold, so you can keep it for a long time

French fries /'frɛntʃ fraɪz/ *plural noun*
long thin pieces of potato cooked in oil

fre·quent /'frikwənt/ *adjective*
happening often: *They make frequent trips to New York.* —**frequently** *adverb*

fresh /frɛʃ/ *adjective*
1 in good condition because of being picked, prepared etc. a short time ago: *I bought some fresh fish at the store.*
2 adding to or replacing what was there before: *Would you like a fresh cup of coffee?*
3 **fresh air** pleasant, cool air from outside, not in a building: *I'm going for a walk to get some fresh air.*
4 a new way of doing something: *He has some fresh ideas for the business.*

fresh·man /'frɛʃmən/ *noun* (*plural* **freshmen**)
a student in the first year of high school or college

Fri·day /'fraɪdi, -deɪ/ *noun*
the sixth day of the week

fridge /frɪdʒ/ *noun*
a REFRIGERATOR

fried¹ /fraɪd/
the PAST TENSE of the verb **fry**

fried² *adjective*
cooked in hot oil or fat: *We had fried eggs for breakfast.*

friend /frɛnd/ *noun*
1 a person who you like and trust very much: *He is a friend of mine.* | *Lee and I are* **best friends.**
2 **make friends with** to start to know someone as a friend

friend·ly /'frɛndli/ *adjective* (**friendlier, friendliest**)
behaving in a nice way like a friend » opposite UNFRIENDLY

friend·ship /'frɛndʃɪp/ *noun*
the state of being friends: *Our friendship began in college.*

fries /fraɪz/ *plural noun*
potatoes cut into thin long pieces and cooked in hot oil: *Do you want fries with that?*

fright /fraɪt/ *noun* [U]
a feeling of fear

fright·en /'fraɪtⁿn/ *verb*
to make someone feel afraid: *The noise frightened me.*

fright·ened /'fraɪtⁿnd/ *adjective*
feeling afraid: *I was* **too** *frightened* **to** *sleep.*

fright·en·ing /'fraɪtⁿnɪŋ/ *adjective*
making you feel afraid: *We had a frightening experience last night.*

fro /froʊ/ *adverb*
to and fro moving in one direction and then back again: *He was walking to and fro in front of the house.*

frog /frɔg, frɑg/ *noun*
a small brown or green animal that lives in water and has long legs for jumping

frog

from /frəm; strong frʌm/ preposition
1 starting at or coming out of a place: *He is from Spain.* | *I drove all the way from California.*
2 given or sent by someone: *This letter is from my uncle.*
3 used to show how far away something is: *The town is 10 miles from here.*
4 **from now on** starting now and going on into the future: *From now on, you will do as you are told!*
5 used for showing that someone or something is moved, separated, or taken away: *Her children were taken from her.*
6 made of something: *Bread is made from flour.*
7 because of something: *She was crying from the pain.*

front

front¹ /frʌnt/ noun
1 the side opposite the back of something: *I am sitting at the front of the class.* ≫ compare BACK¹, REAR²
2 **in front of something** near something in the direction that it faces or moves: *I'll meet you in front of the theater.* —see color picture on page 194
3 **in front of someone** ahead of someone: *How many people are in front of us?* ≫ compare BEHIND

front² adjective
at or in the front of something: *He got in the front seat of the car.* | *She ran out the front door.* ≫ compare BACK²

fron·tier /frʌnˈtɪr/ noun
an area of land where people are just beginning to live

frost /frɔst/ noun [U]
ice that covers things that are outside when it is very cold: *The trees were white with frost.*

frost·ing /ˈfrɔstɪŋ/ noun [U]
a mixture of sugar and butter that you put on cakes

frown /fraʊn/ verb
to look as if you are angry or unhappy by moving your EYEBROWS together so that lines appear at the top of your face

froze /froʊz/
the PAST TENSE of the verb **freeze**

fro·zen¹ /ˈfroʊzən/
the PAST PARTICIPLE of the verb **freeze**

frozen² adjective
1 preserved by being kept very cold: *Buy a bag of frozen peas.*
2 turned into ice because of the cold: *The lake is frozen.*

fruit

fruit /frut/ noun
the part of a plant that has the seeds and is often sweet and good to eat: *Apples are my favorite fruit.*

fry /fraɪ/ verb (**frying, fried**)
to cook something in hot oil: *Can you fry an egg?*

fry·ing pan /'.. ,./ *noun*
a wide, flat pan used for cooking food in hot oil or fat —see picture at PAN

ft
another way of writing **foot** or **feet**, used as a measurement: *He's 6ft.* [=6 feet] *tall.*

fu·el /'fyuəl, fyul/ *noun*
a substance that burns to give heat, light, or power: *Gas and coal are fuels.*

ful·fill /fʊl'fɪl/ *verb*
to do what you have promised, or what is expected: *He wants to fulfill his promise to cut taxes.*

full /fʊl/ *adjective*
1 containing as much as possible: *My cup is full.* ≫ compare EMPTY¹ —see picture at EMPTY¹
2 having had as much as you want to eat: *I couldn't eat any more. I'm full.*
3 complete or whole: *What is your full name and address?* | *Do I have your full support?*
4 be full of something to contain a lot of something: *The streets were full of people.*
5 as large, fast, strong etc. as possible: *He is running at full speed.*

full-time /'fʊl taɪm/ *adjective*
lasting for the whole day: *She has a full-time job.* —**full-time** *adverb*: *He works full-time.*

fun¹ /fʌn/ *noun* [U]
1 amusement, enjoyment, or pleasure: *Did you have fun* [=enjoy yourself] *at the party?*
2 make fun of someone to laugh at someone in a cruel way, or to make others do this

fun² *adjective*
enjoyable: *Swimming is a fun thing to do.*

func·tion¹ /'fʌŋkʃən/ *noun*
the purpose of something, or the job that some-one does

function² *verb*
to work: *How does the new system function?*

fund /fʌnd/ *noun*
an amount of money collected for a particular purpose: *We have a fund to build the new church.*

fu·ner·al /'fyunərəl/ *noun*
a ceremony in which the body of a dead person is burned or put into the ground

fun·gus /'fʌŋgəs/ *noun* (*plural* fungi /'fʌŋgaɪ, -dʒaɪ/ *or* funguses)
a plant such as a MUSHROOM which has no leaves and grows in wet places

fun·nel /'fʌnl/ *noun*
a tube with a wide top and a narrow bottom, used for pouring things into a container

fun·ny /'fʌni/ *adjective* (funnier, funniest)
1 making you laugh: *I heard a funny joke.* | *What's so funny?* ≫ compare AMUSING
2 strange; unusual: *I smell something funny.*

fur /fɚ/ *noun* [U]
the soft hair on some animals such as cats and rabbits, sometimes used to make clothes

fu·ri·ous /'fyʊriəs/ *adjective*
very angry: *Dad will be furious with us if we are late.*

fur·nace /'fɚnɪs/ *noun*
a large container with a hot fire inside for heating metals or producing heat in a house or building

fur·nish /'fɚnɪʃ/ *verb*
to put furniture in a place: *It costs a lot of money to furnish a house.*

fur·ni·ture /'fɚnɪtʃɚ/ *noun* [U]
things used in a house such as beds, tables, and chairs

fur·ry /'fɚi/ *adjective* (furrier, furriest)
covered with fur: *She had a furry little rabbit.* ≫ compare HAIRY

fur·ther¹ /'fɚðɚ/
1 the comparative of **far¹**
2 more than before: *Do you have anything fur-ther to say?*
3 a longer way in space or time: *My house is further down this road.*

further² *adjective*
additional: *Are there any further questions?*

fur·thest /'fɚðɪst/
the superlative of **far¹**

fu·ry /'fyʊri/ *noun* [U]
very great anger

fuss¹ /fʌs/ *noun* [U]
1 worry or excitement that makes something seem more important than it is: *What's all the fuss about?* [=why is everyone so excited, upset etc.]
2 make a fuss to complain or become angry about something
3 make a fuss over someone to give too much attention to someone

fuss² *verb*
1 to complain or become upset

2 fuss over to give too much attention to someone or something

fuss·y /ˈfʌsi/ *adjective* (**fussier, fussiest**)
thinking or worrying too much about things that are not important

fu·ture /ˈfyutʃɚ/ *noun* [U]
1 the future time that will come; things that have not happened yet: *What are your plans for the future?*
2 in the future after now: *We hope to go to Europe in the near future.* (=very soon) ≫ compare PAST[1]

future tense /ˌ.. ˈ./ *noun*
the form of a verb that you use when you are talking about the future; in English "I will go" is in the future tense

fuzz·y /ˈfʌzi/ *adjective* (**fuzzier, fuzziest**)
1 having a lot of soft thin hairs
2 not having very clear details: *Some of the photographs are a little fuzzy.*

g
a short way of writing the word **gram** or **grams**

gadg·et /'gædʒɪt/ *noun*
a machine or tool that is small but useful: *Here is an interesting gadget for cleaning glass.*

gain /geɪn/ *verb*
1 to get something important or useful: *What did you gain from your computer course? | She is gaining good experience in her job.*
2 gain weight to increase in weight: *The baby is gaining weight quickly.* ≫ compare LOSE

gale /geɪl/ *noun*
a very strong wind

gal·ler·y /'gæləri/ *noun (plural* **galleries***)*
a building or a large long room where people can look at paintings, photographs etc.: *I went to the art gallery today.*

gal·lon /'gælən/ *noun*
a measure of liquid equal to eight PINTs

gal·lop¹ /'gæləp/ *verb*
if a horse gallops, it runs very fast

gallop² *noun* [U]
the fastest speed that a horse can run

gam·ble¹ /'gæmbəl/ *verb (***gambling, gambled***)*
1 to try to win money on card games, horse races etc.: *He lost a lot of money by gambling.* ≫ compare BET¹
2 to take a risk because you hope to get something

gamble² *noun*
an action or plan in which you take a risk because you hope to get something: *The doctors say the operation is a gamble, but it may succeed.*

gam·bler /'gæmblɚ/ *noun*
a person who tries to win money on card games, horse races etc.

game /geɪm/ *noun*
1 an activity or sport that you play for fun or to defeat another person or team: *Football is a team game. | Do you like card games?*

2 one of the parts of a competition such as tennis: *He is ahead five games to four.*
3 play games to behave in a way that is not honest so you can trick someone
4 games [*plural*] sports played at a large event: *The Olympic Games are very exciting.*
5 [U] wild animals or birds that people hunt for food or sport

game show /'. ./ *noun*
a television program on which people play games to win things or money

gang¹ /gæŋ/ *noun*
1 a group of young people who cause trouble and fight other groups: *Two members of the gang were killed.*
2 a group of people such as prisoners who work together

gang² *verb*
gang up on someone to join a group to criticize or attack someone: *The older children ganged up on him.*

gap /gæp/ *n*
1 an empty space between two things or two parts of something: *Diana has a really big **gap between** her two front teeth. | a **gap in** the fence*
2 a difference between two situations, groups, amounts etc.: *a group trying to **bridge the gap between** college students and the local citizens* [=reduce the importance of the differences between them] *| a large **age gap between** Jorge and his sister*
3 something that is missing that stops something else from being good or complete: *No new producers have yet **filled the gap** in the market. | His death left a **gap in** my life. | a **gap in** her memory*
4 a period of time in which nothing happens or nothing is said: *an uncomfortable **gap in** the conversation*
5 a low place between two higher parts of a mountain

ga·rage /gə'rɑʒ, gə'rɑdʒ/ *noun*
1 a place where a car, bus etc. is kept —see color picture on page 186
2 a place where a car is repaired

gar·bage /'gɑrbɪdʒ/ *noun*
[U] waste material such as old food, dirty paper etc., or the container in which you put this

garbage can /'.. ./ *noun*
a large container in which you put waste, usually kept outside

garbage man /'.. ,./ noun [plural garbage men]
a man whose job is to take away the things inside garbage cans

garbage truck /'.. ,./ noun
a large vehicle that carries away GARBAGE

gar·den /'gɑrdn/ noun
a piece of land where flowers or vegetables are grown around a house or in a public place

gar·den·er /'gɑrdnə/ noun
a person whose job is to work in a garden

gar·den·ing /'gɑrdn-ɪŋ/ noun [U]
work in a garden: *He enjoys gardening.*

gar·lic /'gɑrlɪk/ noun [U]
a plant like an onion used in cooking to give a strong taste —see picture at VEGETABLE

gar·ment /'gɑrmənt/ noun
a piece of clothing: *This garment should be washed by hand.*

gas /gæs/ noun [U]
1 (*also* **gasoline**) a liquid that you put in a car, bus etc. to make it go
2 a clear substance like air that is burned for heating and cooking: *She cooks with gas.*

gas·o·line /ˌgæsəˈlin/ noun [U]
a liquid that you put in a car, bus etc. to make it go

gasp[1] /gæsp/ verb
to take quick, short breaths: *I climbed out of the water, gasping for air.*

gasp[2] noun
the sound of a quick, short breath

gas sta·tion /'. ,../ noun
a place where you buy gas for your car

gate /geɪt/ noun
1 the part of a wall or fence that you can open like a door
2 the part of an airport that you walk through to get on a plane

gath·er /'gæðə/ verb
1 to come together in a group: *A crowd soon gathered around to see what had happened.*
2 to collect things into one place or pile: *The animals were gathering nuts to eat.*

gath·er·ing /'gæðərɪŋ/ noun
a meeting or group of people who are together for a particular purpose

gauge /geɪdʒ/ noun
an instrument that measures the amount of something: *A gas gauge shows you how much gas is left in the car.*

gave /geɪv/
the PAST TENSE of the verb **give**

gay /geɪ/ adjective
1 sexually attracted to people of the same sex; HOMOSEXUAL
2 bright and attractive

gaze /geɪz/ verb (gazing, gazed)
to look at someone or something for a long time: *The child gazed at the toys in the store window.*

gear /gɪr/ noun
1 the equipment in a vehicle that turns power from the engine into movement
2 [U] the special clothes or things you need for a particular activity: *We are getting some new camping gear.*

gee /dʒi/
something you say when you feel surprised or excited: *Gee, what a nice car!*

geese /gis/
the plural of **goose**

gel /dʒɛl/ noun
a thick liquid that you can put into your hair or on your body

gem /dʒɛm/ noun
a jewel that is cut into a particular shape

gen·der /'dʒɛndə/ noun
the fact of being male or female

gene /dʒin/ noun
a part of a cell that controls the development of a quality that is passed to a living thing from its parents

gen·er·al[1] /'dʒɛnərəl/ adjective
1 concerning the whole of something, rather than its parts or details: *The general condition of the car is good, but it needs to be painted.* | *We had a general introduction to computers.*
2 **in general** in most cases; usually: *In general, I like the people I work with.*
3 concerning most people or places: *This drug is available for general use.* (=most people can use it)

4 the general public the ordinary people in a society

general² *noun*
a very important officer in the army

gen·er·al·ly /ˈdʒɛnərəli/ *adverb*
1 usually: *Children generally start school when they are five or six.*
2 considering something as a whole: *Generally, his homework is very good.*

gen·er·ate /ˈdʒɛnəˌreɪt/ *verb* (generating, generated)
to produce or make something such as heat or power: *Coal is used for generating electricity.*

gen·er·a·tion /ˌdʒɛnəˈreɪʃən/ *noun* ⎯
all the people who are about the same age: *My parents and I belong to different generations.*

gen·er·a·tor /ˈdʒɛnəˌreɪtə/ *noun*
a machine that makes electricity

gen·er·os·i·ty /ˌdʒɛnəˈrɑsəti/ *noun* [U]
the willingness to give money, help, or time to someone: *Thank you for your generosity.*

gen·er·ous /ˈdʒɛnərəs/ *adjective*
willing to give money, help, or time to someone: *It is very generous of you to offer to help.*

ge·nius /ˈdʒinyəs/ *noun* (plural geniuses)
someone who has a lot of intelligence or ability

gen·tle /ˈdʒɛntəl/ *adjective*
1 careful in the way you behave; kind and calm: *Be gentle with the baby.*
2 not rough, loud, or forceful: *She has a gentle voice.*

gen·tle·man /ˈdʒɛntəlmən/ *noun* (plural gentlemen /-mɛn/)
1 a man who is polite and behaves well toward other people
2 a polite word for a man whose name you do not know: *Show this gentleman to his seat.*

gen·tly /ˈdʒɛntli/ *adverb*
in a kind, calm way, without being loud or rough: *She gently lifted the child.*

gen·u·ine /ˈdʒɛnyuɪn/ *adjective*
real and true: *He has a genuine concern for other people.* —**genuinely** *adverb*: *She genuinely loves him.*

ge·og·ra·phy /dʒiˈɑgrəfi/ *noun* [U]
the study of the countries of the world and things like oceans, mountains, and weather —**geographical** *adjective*

ge·ol·o·gy /dʒiˈɑlədʒi/ *noun* [U]
the study of rocks and how they were made —**geological** *adjective*

ge·om·e·try /dʒiˈɑmətri/ *noun* [U]
the study of the form of shapes, lines, curves etc. —**geometric** *adjective*

germ /dʒəm/ *noun*
a very small living thing that grows in dirty places and can make you sick

ges·ture¹ /ˈdʒɛstʃə, ˈdʒɛʃtʃə/ *noun*
a movement of your hands, head, or arms that shows what you mean or how you feel

gesture² *verb* (gesturing, gestured)
to tell someone something by moving your head, hands, or arms: *He gestured for me to come over.*

get /gɛt/ *verb* (getting, got /gɑt/, past participle gotten /ˈgɑtⁿn/)
1 to obtain or buy something: *I have to get a birthday present for my mother.* | *Can I get four bananas for a dollar?*
2 to receive or be given something: *The boy got a bicycle from his aunt.* | *Did you get any mail?*
3 to become: *She got really mad at me.* | *The weather is getting colder.*
4 to bring someone something, or take something from a place: *She went to get the kids from school.* | *Can I get you a drink?*
5 to reach a particular place or position: *Did you ever get to the end of the book?*
6 get away to leave a place, or escape: *Four prisoners got away.*
7 get back to return: *When did you get back from your trip?*
8 get along with someone to have a friendly relationship with someone: *I get along well with Thomas.*
9 get off to finish working: *What time do you get off?*
10 get away with something to not be seen or punished for doing something wrong: *He lied to me – and he thinks he is going to get away with it!*
11 get up to rise from a lying or sitting position, especially from your bed after sleeping: *What time do you get up on Sundays?*
12 get through something to deal with a bad experience until it ends: *It will be hard to get through the funeral.*
13 get by to have just enough money to buy the things you need, but not more: *Some families don't have enough to get by.*

ghet·to /ˈgɛtoʊ/ *noun*
a part of a city that is very poor and has a lot of people

ghost /goʊst/
noun
the spirit of a dead person, that some people believe can be seen

gi·ant¹ /ˈdʒaɪənt/
noun
a very tall strong man in children's stories

giant² *adjective*
very large

gift /gɪft/ *noun*
1 something that you give to someone you like or want to thank
2 a special ability to do something: *He has a gift for learning languages.*

gi·gan·tic /dʒaɪˈgæntɪk/ *adjective*
very big ≫ compare ENORMOUS

gig·gle /ˈgɪgəl/ *verb* (**giggling, giggled**)
to laugh in a quiet way: *The girls were giggling in class.* —**giggle** *noun*

gills /gɪlz/ *plural noun*
the part of a fish, near its head, through which it breathes —see picture at FISH¹

gin·ger /ˈdʒɪndʒɚ/ *noun* [U]
a plant with a root that can be used in cooking

gi·raffe /dʒəˈræf/ *noun* (*plural* **giraffe** *or* **giraffes**)
a tall animal with a very long neck and large brown spots on its fur, that lives in Africa —see color picture on page 183

girl /gɚl/ *noun*
a female child: *She has two children, a girl and a boy.*

girl·friend /ˈgɚlfrɛnd/ *noun*
1 a girl or woman with whom you have a romantic relationship ≫ compare BOYFRIEND
2 a girl or woman who is the friend of another girl or woman

Girl Scouts /ˈgɚl skaʊts/ *plural noun*
an organization for girls that teaches them practical skills —**Girl Scout** *noun*

give /gɪv/ *verb* (**giving, gave** /geɪv/, *past participle* **given** /ˈgɪvən/)
1 to put something in someone's hand: *I gave the book to her.* | *Give me your coat and I will put it away.*
2 to provide someone with something, or to let someone do something: *Who did they give the job to?* | *He gave me a bicycle for Christmas.*
3 to perform an action: *Sharon gave her grandmother a big kiss.* | *Give me a call* (=telephone me) *when you can.*
4 to tell someone something: *Will you give her a message from me?* | *Let me give you some advice.*
5 **give something away** to let someone have something of yours, instead of selling it: *I'm giving away all my clothes that are too small.*
6 **give something back** to return something to someone who owns it: *I'll give your book back next week.*
7 **give in** to agree to do something that you were not willing to do before: *He kept asking her for money, and she finally gave in.*
8 **give something out** to give something to each of several people: *The teacher gave out copies of the paper.*
9 **give something up** to stop doing or having something: *She's trying to give up smoking.*
10 **give something off** to produce a smell, heat etc.: *The factory smoke gives off a bad smell.*

giv·en¹ /ˈgɪvən/ *adjective*
1 **any/a given ...** any particular time, idea, or thing that is being used as an example: *In any given year, over half of all accidents happen in the home.*
2 a given time, date etc. is one that has been fixed or agreed on: *How much electricity is used in any given period?*

given² *preposition*
if you consider: *Given the number of people we invited, I'm surprised that so few came.*

given³ *verb*
the PAST PARTICIPLE of the verb **give**

given⁴ *noun*
a given a basic fact that you accept as the truth

gla·cier /ˈgleɪʃɚ/ *noun*
a very large area of ice that moves slowly over the ground

glad /glæd/ *adjective*
pleased and happy: *I am glad to see you.*

glad·ly /ˈglædli/ *adverb*
willingly: *I gladly accepted his offer.*

glance¹ /glæns/ *verb* (**glancing, glanced**)
to look quickly at someone or something: *She glanced at her watch.*

glance² *noun*
a quick short look

glare¹ /glɛr/ *verb* (glaring, glared)
1 to shine with a very bright light so that it hurts your eyes: *The sun glared down on them.*
2 to look at someone in an angry way: *She glared at me and then walked away.*

glare² *noun*
1 a very bright light: *The glare of the sun made her eyes hurt.*
2 an angry look

glass

glass /glæs/ *noun*
1 [U] a clear hard substance used for making windows and bottles
2 (*plural* **glasses**) a cup made of glass, without a handle

glasses

lens
frame

glass·es /ˈglæsɪz/ *plural noun*
two round pieces of glass that you wear in front of your eyes to help you see better —see color picture on page 191

gleam /glim/ *verb*
to shine: *The river gleamed in the moonlight.*

glide /glaɪd/ *verb* (gliding, glided)
to move forward smoothly and quietly

glim·mer /ˈglɪmɚ/ *verb*
to shine with a light that is not very bright
—**glimmer** *noun*

glimpse¹ /glɪmps/ *noun*
a very quick look: *I only caught a glimpse of the man's face.*

glimpse² *verb* (glimpsing, glimpsed)
to look at someone or something quickly

glis·ten /ˈglɪsən/ *verb*
to shine as if wet: *Her eyes glistened with tears.*

globe /gloʊb/ *noun*
1 **the globe** the world: *She's traveled all over the globe.*
2 a ball with a map of the world on it

gloom·y /ˈglumi/ *adjective* (gloomier, gloomiest)
1 dark: *It was cold and gloomy all day.*
2 sad and not having a lot of hope: *He had a gloomy expression on his face.*

glo·ri·ous /ˈglɔriəs/ *adjective*
1 deserving praise and honor
2 very pleasant or nice

glo·ry /ˈglɔri/ *noun* [U]
fame and respect that is given to someone who has done something great

gloss /glɔs/ *noun* [U]
a shiny surface on something

glove /glʌv/ *noun*
a piece of clothing that you wear on your hand, with separate parts for all your fingers —see color picture on page 190

glow¹ /gloʊ/ *verb*
to shine with a steady light: *The fire glowed in the dark.*

glow² *noun*
a soft steady light: *An orange glow filled the sky.*

glue¹ /glu/ *noun* [U]
a substance used for sticking two things together: *She stuck the handle onto the cup with glue.*

glue² *verb* (gluing, glued)
to stick two things together using glue: *She glued the pieces together.*

gnaw /nɔ/ *verb*
to continue biting something for a long time: *The dog is gnawing on a bone.*

go¹ /goʊ/ *verb* (*past tense* **went**, *past participle* **gone**)
1 to move toward a place, or for a particular distance: *She went into the kitchen.* | *Where are you going?*
2 to leave a place: *I wanted to go, but she wanted to stay.* | *She has gone away for a while.* | *Are you going out tonight?*
3 to visit a place, then leave it: *We are going to Florida this summer.*

4 to become: *His hair is going gray.*

5 to happen in a particular way: *Everything went wrong from the start.*

6 to work in the right way: *The car won't go.*

7 be going to do something used for saying that something will happen in the future: *I think it's going to snow. | I'm going to buy that bicycle.*

8 go off to explode: *The bomb went off suddenly.*

9 go up to increase: *Prices have really gone up this year.*

10 go by to pass: *Several days went by before he called.*

11 go on to continue without changing: *We cannot go on fighting like this!*

**go² ** *noun*

1 on the go very busy all the time. *Steve is always on the go!*

2 make a go of to try and make something a success

goal /goul/ *noun*

1 something you want to do in the future: *My goal is to go to college.*

2 a point that you win in a sport when the ball goes into a special area: *Our team won by three goals to one.*

3 the area into which you try to put the ball to win a point

goal·ie /'gouli/ *noun*
a GOALKEEPER

goal·keep·er /'goul,kipər/ *noun*
the player on a sports team who tries to stop the ball before it goes into the GOAL

goat /gout/ *noun*
a farm animal with horns and long hair under its chin

god /gad/ *noun*

1 [U] the being who you pray to, especially in the Christian, Muslim, and Jewish religions

2 a male being who is believed to control the world, or part of it

god·dess /'gadıs/ *noun*
a female god

gog·gles /'gagəlz/ *plural noun*
a piece of equipment with two large round pieces of glass with an edge that fits against your skin to keep your eyes safe

gold /gould/ *noun* [U]

1 a yellow metal used for making jewelry, coins etc.

2 the color of this metal

gold·en /'gouldən/ *adjective*
like gold or made of gold: *The little girl had golden hair.*

gold·fish /'gould,fıʃ/ *noun* (plural **goldfish**)
a small orange fish often kept as a pet

golf /galf, gɔlf/ *noun* [U]
a game in which you hit a small hard ball into a hole in the ground using a special stick —see color picture on page 184

gone /gɔn, gɑn/
the PAST PARTICIPLE of the verb **go**

NOTE: Look at the difference between **been** and **gone**. If you have **been** to a place, you have traveled there and returned. If you have **gone** to a place, you have traveled there and have not yet returned: *Liz has gone to Spain.* (–she is in Spain now) *Liz has been to Spain.* (=she went there and now she has returned)

---

good¹ /gud/ *adjective*

1 of a high standard or quality: *You did a good job. | She has a very good memory.* ≫ compare BAD, BETTER¹, BEST¹

2 pleasant, or enjoyable: *Have a good time | It's good to see you again!*

3 smart or successful at something: *She's very good at languages. | He's good with babies.*

4 useful or suitable for a particular purpose: *This music is good **for** dancing.*

5 behaving in a way that is acceptable: *Sit here and be a good girl.*

6 kind and helpful: *He's been very good **to** me.*

7 healthy: *Too much candy is not good for you.*

8 as good as almost: *The job is as good as done.*

9 good luck said when you hope someone is successful

10 Good for you! said when you are pleased with what someone has done

good² *noun* [U]

1 something that improves a situation, or gives you an advantage: *What's the good of having a car if you can't drive?*

2 for good always; for a very long time: *She has left her job for good.*

3 do no good to not be of any use, or to have no effect on something: *You can talk to her, but it will not do any good.*

good af·ter·noon /. ,..'./
used for saying hello to someone in the afternoon

good·bye /gʊdˈbaɪ, gədˈbaɪ/
said when you leave someone or someone leaves you ≫ compare HELLO

good eve·ning /. ˈ../
used for saying hello to someone in the evening

Good Fri·day /ˌ. ˈ../ noun
the Friday before EASTER, a Christian religious holiday

good-look·ing /ˌ. ˈ..‹/ adjective
attractive, used about a person: *He's very good-looking.*

good morn·ing /. ˈ../
used for saying hello to someone in the morning

good·ness /ˈgʊdnɪs/ noun
1 said when you are surprised or annoyed: *My goodness, you look tired!*
2 [U] kindness, the quality of being good

good night /. ˈ./
said when you are going home at night, or to someone who is leaving you at night

goods /gʊdz/ plural noun
things like food or clothes that are bought and sold

goose /gus/ noun [plural **geese** /giːs/]
a large white bird that looks like a duck and makes a loud noise

gor·geous /ˈgɔrdʒəs/ adjective
very beautiful or pleasant: *Linda looks gorgeous in that dress.*

go·ril·la /gəˈrɪlə/ noun
a very large strong animal that looks like a monkey —see color picture on page 183

gosh /gɑʃ/
said when you are surprised: *Gosh! What are you doing here?*

gos·pel /ˈgɑspəl/ noun
1 one of the stories about Christ's life in the Bible
2 [U] a type of Christian religious music, that people sing loudly

gos·sip¹ /ˈgɑsəp/ noun
1 [U] talk about someone's private life that is not nice: *You should not listen to gossip.*
2 someone who likes to talk about other people's private lives

gossip² verb
to talk about other people's private lives in a way that is not nice

got /gɑt/
the PAST TENSE of the verb **get** ≫ compare HAVE

got·ten /ˈgɑt̚n/
the PAST PARTICIPLE of the verb **get**

gov·ern /ˈgʌvən/ verb
to control and rule a country and its people: *The army governed the country for five years.*

gov·ern·ment /ˈgʌvəmənt, ˈgʌvənmənt/ noun
the people who control what happens in a country

gov·er·nor /ˈgʌvənə, -və-/ noun
the person who controls a U.S. state

gown /gaʊn/ noun
a long dress for a woman: *She wore a beautiful evening gown.*

grab /græb/ verb (**grabbing, grabbed**)
to take hold of something quickly and roughly: *The man grabbed my bag and ran.*

grace /greɪs/ noun [U]
1 an attractive way of moving: *She dances with such grace.*
2 a short prayer before a meal: *Who is going to say grace?*

grace·ful /ˈgreɪsfəl/ adjective
moving in an attractive and smooth way

grade¹ /greɪd/ noun
1 one of the 12 years you are in school in the U.S.: *Our son goes into the fourth grade this year.*
2 a letter or number that shows how well you did in school: *My grades were mostly B's and C's.*
3 a level, size, or quality that a product has: *We always buy Grade A eggs.*

grade² verb (**grading, graded**)
1 to decide how good a piece of school work is: *I grade papers all day.*
2 to put things into groups according to size, quality etc.: *The farmers graded the apples into two sizes.*

grad·u·al /ˈgrædʒuəl/ adjective
happening or changing slowly: *I have seen a gradual improvement in his work.* —**gradually** adverb

grad·u·ate¹ /ˈgrædʒueɪt/ verb (**graduating, graduated**)
to finish your education and receive your degree: *She graduated **from** Yale.*

graduate² /'grædʒuɪt/ *noun*
someone who has finished their studies at a school or university

grain /greɪn/ *noun*
1 [U] the seeds of a crop such as wheat, rice, or corn used as food: *Grain is used for making flour.*
2 a very small piece of something such as salt or sand

gram /græm/ *noun*
a measure of weight; there are 1,000 grams in a kilogram

gram·mar /'græmər/ *noun* [U]
the rules of a language: *We are learning English grammar.*

gram·mat·i·cal /grə'mætɪkəl/ *adjective*
correct according to the rules of language: *Saying "I are not" is not grammatical.* —**grammatically** *adverb*

grand /grænd/ *adjective*
better or higher in rank than others: *I won the grand prize!*

grand·child /'græntʃaɪld/ *noun* [plural **grandchildren** /'græntʃɪldrən/]
the child of your son or daughter

grand·daugh·ter /'græn,dɔtər/ *noun*
the daughter of your son or daughter

grand·fa·ther /'grænd,fɑðər/ *noun*
the father of one of your parents

grand·ma /'grændmɑ, 'græmɑ/ *noun*
your grandmother

grand·moth·er /'grænd,mʌðər/ *noun*
the mother of one of your parents

grand·pa /'grændpɑ 'græmpɑ/ *noun*
your grandfather

grand·par·ent /'græn,pɛrənt. -,pær-/ *noun*
the parent of your mother or father

grand·son /'grændsʌn/ *noun*
the son of your son or daughter .

grant¹ /grænt/ *verb*
1 take something for granted to think that something is true without making sure: *I took it for granted that she would be successful.*
2 to give or allow someone something, especially in an official way: *She was granted permission to enter the country.*

grant² *noun*
an amount of money given to someone for a particular purpose: *The government gave us a grant to study the disease.*

grape /greɪp/ *noun*
a small round green or red fruit that is used for making wine —see picture at FRUIT

grape·fruit /'greɪpfrut/ *noun*
a large round yellow fruit with thick skin like an orange, but not as sweet

graph

graph /græf/ *noun*
a picture or drawing that shows information: *The graph shows how the population changed over ten years.*

graph·ics /'græfɪks/ *plural noun*
the activity of drawing pictures, or the pictures themselves

grasp /græsp/ *verb*
1 to take and hold something firmly: *He grasped the rope and pulled himself up.*
2 to understand something: *I could not grasp what the teacher said.*

grass /græs/ *noun* [U]
a common plant with thin green leaves that covers fields and yards: *We sat on the grass and read our books.* —see color picture on page 188

grass·hop·per /'græs,hɑpər/ *noun*
an insect that jumps with its long back legs and makes loud noises —see color picture on page 183

gras·sy /'græsi/ *adjective* [**grassier, grassiest**]
covered with grass

grate¹ /greɪt/ *noun*
a metal frame over a hole in the street or in front of a window

grate² *verb* [**grating, grated**]
to rub food such as cheese against a rough surface to break it into small pieces

grate·ful /ˈgreɪtfəl/ *adjective*
feeling that you want to thank someone: *I am grateful to you for helping me.*

grat·i·tude /ˈgrætəˌtud/ *noun* [U]
the feeling of wanting to thank someone: *He expressed his gratitude to all the workers.*

grave¹ /greɪv/ *noun*
a hole in the ground where a dead body is buried

grave² *adjective*
very serious or worrying: *She had grave doubts whether we would succeed.*

grav·el /ˈgrævəl/ *noun* [U]
small stones and sand used for making the surfaces of roads

grave·stone /ˈgreɪvstoʊn/ *noun*
a stone on a grave with the name of the dead person and the dates of his or her birth and death

grav·i·ty /ˈgrævəti/ *noun* [U]
the force that makes things fall to the ground when they are dropped

gra·vy /ˈgreɪvi/ *noun* [U]
a food that is made from meat juice, flour, and milk

gray /greɪ/ *adjective, noun*
the color of rain clouds; a mixture of black and white: *She wore a gray dress.*

graze /greɪz/ *verb* (**grazing, grazed**)
1 to eat grass: *Cattle were grazing in the field.*
2 to touch something while passing it, often causing damage: *The bullet grazed his arm.*

grease¹ /gris/ *noun* [U]
oil or fat: *Put some grease on the engine and it will run smoother.*

grease² *verb* (**greasing, greased**)
to put oil or fat on something

greas·y /ˈgrisi, -zi/ *adjective* (**greasier, greasiest**)
covered with oil or fat

great /greɪt/ *adjective*
1 very good: *It was a great party. | I feel great.*
2 useful or suitable for something: *This soap is great for removing stains.*
3 large in size or amount: *He has a great big dog.*
4 important or famous: *Browning is one of our greatest poets.*
5 **great-granddaughter, great-grandson** the daughter or son of your GRANDCHILD

6 **great-grandfather, great-grandmother** the father or mother of one of your GRANDPARENTs

great·ly /ˈgreɪtli/ *adverb*
very much: *She greatly admired his courage.*

greed /grid/ *noun* [U]
a strong desire to have more food, money, or power than you need

greed·y /ˈgridi/ *adjective* (**greedier, greediest**)
wanting too much of something: *That greedy boy ate all the cake.*

green¹ /grin/ *adjective*
1 the color of grass: *She has green eyes.*
2 covered with grass and trees: *Cities need more green areas.*

green² *noun* [U]
the color of grass: *She was dressed in green.*

green card /ˈ. ./ *noun*
a special card with your name and picture on it, that allows you to live and work in the U.S.

green·house /ˈgrinhaʊs/ *noun*
a glass building in which you grow plants

greet /grit/ *verb*
to say hello to someone or welcome him or her: *He greeted her with a smile.*

greet·ing /ˈgritɪŋ/ *noun*
something you say or do when you meet someone, or send him or her a message

grew /gru/
the PAST TENSE of the verb **grow**

grey /greɪ/ *adjective, noun* [U]
gray

grief /grif/ *noun* [U]
great sadness: *The death of her son caused her much grief.*

grieve /griv/ *verb*
to feel very sad, because someone you love has died

grill¹ /grɪl/ *verb*
to cook meat, fish etc. over a fire

grill² *noun*
a metal frame over a fire so you can cook things on it

grim /grɪm/ *adjective* (**grimmer, grimmest**)
1 making you feel sad or unhappy: *The news of her death was grim.*
2 not pleasant or attractive, used about a place

grin¹ /grɪn/ *verb* (grinning, grinned)
to smile, showing your teeth: *He grinned at me from across the room.*

grin² *noun*
a big smile: *She had a grin on her face.*

grind /graɪnd/ *verb* (past **ground** /graʊnd/)
to crush something into small pieces or powder: *First, we grind the coffee beans.*

grip¹ /grɪp/ *verb* (gripping, gripped)
to hold something very tightly: *She gripped his hand in fear.*

grip² *noun*
a tight hold on something: *She kept a firm grip on the rope.*

groan /groʊn/ *verb*
to make a long deep noise because you are in pain or are not happy: *He groaned with pain.* —**groan** *noun* ≫ compare MOAN

gro·cer·ies /ˈgroʊsəriz, ˈgroʊʃriz/ *plural noun*
foods like sugar, coffee, and rice which you can buy in a GROCERY STORE

gro·cer·y store /ˈgroʊsri ˌstɔr, -ˌʃri/ *noun*
a store where you can buy foods like sugar, coffee, and rice

groom /grum/ *noun*
a man who is getting married: *The groom wore a dark blue suit.* ≫ compare BRIDE

grope /groʊp/ *verb* (groping, groped)
to try to find something that you cannot see using your hands: *He groped for his matches in the dark.*

ground¹ /graʊnd/ *noun*
1 [U] the surface of the earth: *An apple fell to the ground.*
2 [U] soil or land: *The ground is too hard to plant crops now.*

ground²
the PAST TENSE and PAST PARTICIPLE of the verb **grind**

ground beef /ˌ. ˈ./ *noun* [U]
meat that is used to make HAMBURGERs

ground floor /ˌ. ˈ./ *noun*
the part of a building on the same level as the ground

grounds /graʊndz/ *plural noun*
the land around a large building

group /grup/ *noun*
1 a number of things or people together: *A group of girls waited by the school.*
2 a small number of people who sing and play popular music together

grow /groʊ/ *verb* (past tense **grew** /gru:/, past participle **grown**)
1 to get bigger, taller, longer etc.; develop: *My son has grown two inches this year.* | *Are you growing a beard?*
2 to care for plants and help them to grow: *The farmer is growing potatoes.*
3 to increase in size, amount, or degree: *We have a growing business.*
4 to become: *My uncle is growing old.*
5 **grow out of something** to become too big or too old for something: *My daughter has grown out of all her dresses.*
6 **grow up** to change from being a child to being a man or a woman: *He grew up in China.*

growl /graʊl/ *verb*
to make a low angry sound: *The dog growled at me.* —**growl** *noun*

grown /groʊn/
the PAST PARTICIPLE of the verb **grow**

grown·up /ˈ. ./ *noun*
an adult, not a child

grown-up /ˌ. ˈ./ *adjective*
old enough to be an adult, not a child: *Her children are all grown-up now.*

growth /groʊθ/ *noun* [U]
an increase in size, quality, amount, or importance: *The growth of the company is impressive.* | *We are studying population growth.*

grum·ble /ˈgrʌmbəl/ *verb* (grumbling, grumbled)
to complain in a quiet, but slightly angry way: *She grumbled about having to wait for so long.*

grump·y /ˈgrʌmpi/ *adjective* (grumpier, grumpiest)
having a bad temper and wanting to complain

grunt /grʌnt/ *verb*
to make a short low sound like a pig makes —**grunt** *noun*

guar·an·tee¹ /ˌgærənˈti/ *noun*
1 a promise that something will happen or be done: *There is no guarantee that your car will be ready today.*
2 a written promise to repair a product if the one you buy has a problem: *The watch has a two-year guarantee.*

guarantee² *verb* [*past* **guaranteed**]
1 to promise that something will happen or be done: *He guaranteed that he would do it today.*
2 to promise to repair a product if the one you buy has a problem: *My radio is guaranteed for three years.*

guard¹ /gɑrd/ *verb*
1 to keep someone or something safe from danger by watching it carefully: *A dog guards their house.*
2 to watch a prisoner so that he or she does not escape

guard² *noun*
1 someone who watches over someone or something to prevent danger or escape: *He works as a prison guard.*
2 **be on guard, stand guard** to be ready to protect someone or something: *Two police officers were on guard outside.*

guard·i·an /'gɑrdiən/ *noun*
a person who takes care of someone or something, especially a child

guer·ril·la /gə'rɪlə/ *noun*
a person who fights against a government or an army, and often makes surprise attacks

guess¹ /gɛs/ *verb*
1 to give an answer that you think may be right although you do not know the facts: *I didn't know where she lived, but I could guess. | Can you guess my age?*
2 **I guess** said when you think something may be true or likely: *He's not here. I guess he went on without us.*

guess² *noun* [*plural* **guesses**]
an answer that you think is right, although you do not know for sure: *If you don't know the answer,* **take a guess.**

guest /gɛst/ *noun*
1 someone who is visiting someone else's house: *We have three guests for dinner.*
2 a person who pays to stay in a hotel

guid·ance /'gaɪdns/ *noun* [U]
help and advice: *With my teacher's guidance, I finished the work.*

guide¹ /gaɪd/ *verb* [**guiding, guided**]
to lead or show someone the way to a place: *He guided us around the city.*

guide² *noun*
1 someone who shows you the way to a place, sometimes as a job: *How much does it cost to have a guide?*

2 a book that teaches you about something: *She gave me a guide for new parents.*

guide·book /'gaɪdbʊk/ *noun*
a book that gives information about a place and its history

guilt /gɪlt/ *noun* [U]
1 the feeling of shame and sadness you have when you have done something wrong: *I felt a sense of guilt for not being honest with her.*
2 the fact of having broken the law: *The court was sure of his guilt.* » compare INNOCENCE

guilt·y /'gɪlti/ *adjective*
1 feeling shame or sadness because you have done something wrong: *Do you feel guilty about not returning the money?*
2 having broken a law: *He was guilty of stealing the car.* » compare INNOCENT

guin·ea pig /'gɪni ˌpɪg/ *noun*
a small animal like a rat with fur and no tail, often kept as a pet

gui·tar /gɪ'tɑr/ *noun*
a musical instrument with six strings, a long neck, and a wooden or plastic body —see color picture on page 185

gulf /gʌlf/ *noun*
an area of ocean with land on three sides of it: *We sailed into the Persian Gulf.*

gulp¹ /gʌlp/ *verb*
1 [*also* **gulp down**] to swallow food or drink quickly: *He gulped down the water.*
2 [*also* **gulp in**] to breathe in air quickly

gulp² *noun*
an act of swallowing something quickly: *He drank the milk in one gulp.*

gum /gʌm/ *noun*
1 [U] a sweet candy that you put in your mouth and bite with your teeth but do not swallow
2 **gums** [*plural*] the pink part of your mouth that holds your teeth

gun /gʌn/ *noun*
a weapon that sends out bullets and is used for hurting or killing animals or people: *Soldiers carry guns.*

gun·man /'gʌnmən/ *noun* [*plural* **gunmen** /-mɛn/]
a criminal who uses a gun

gun·pow·der /'gʌnˌpaʊdər/ *noun* [U]
a substance that explodes easily and is used in bullets

gun·shot /'gʌnʃɑt/ *noun*
the sound that is made when someone uses a gun: *I heard three gunshots.*

gush /gʌʃ/ *verb*
to flow quickly in large quantities: *Blood gushed from the cut in his leg.*

gust /gʌst/ *noun*
a sudden strong wind: *A gust of wind blew the tent down.*

gut·ter /'gʌtɚ/ *noun*
an open pipe along the edge of a roof, or a low place on the side of the road which carries away rain water

guy /gaɪ/ *noun* (*plural* **guys**)
1 a man: *What a nice guy!*
2 **you guys** you people, used for men or women: *What do you guys want to do today?*

gym /dʒɪm/ *noun*
1 a large room where you do exercises or training
2 [U] exercises done indoors, especially in school: *Do you like gym class?*

gym·nast /'dʒɪmnæst, -nəst/ *noun*
someone who does GYMNASTICS as a sport

gym·nas·tics /dʒɪm'næstɪks/ *plural noun*
a sport doing exercises for your body using skill and control —see color picture on page 184

hairstyle

bun

ponytail

bangs

pigtails

braid

hab·it /'hæbɪt/ *noun*
something that you always do, often without thinking about it: *She has a habit of always being late.* | *Don't play with your hair – that's a bad habit.*

had /d, əd, həd; *strong* hæd/
the PAST TENSE and PAST PARTICIPLE of the verb **have**

had·n't /'hædnt/
had not: *I hadn't finished making dinner when everyone arrived.*

hail¹ /heɪl/ *noun* [U]
drops of hard frozen rain: *We had a hail storm yesterday.*

hail² *verb*
1 to rain with hard frozen drops
2 to call out to someone to get his or her attention

hair /hɛr/ *noun*
1 one of the thin threads that grow on the head and skin of people and animals: *There's a hair in my soup!*
2 [U] the things like thin threads that grow on your head: *I need to get my hair cut.* —see picture at HEAD¹

hair·brush /'hɛrbrʌʃ/ *noun* (*plural* **hairbrushes**)
a brush you use to keep your hair neat —see picture at BRUSH¹

hair·cut /'hɛrkʌt/ *noun*
1 the act of having your hair cut: *I am getting a haircut today.*
2 the style in which your hair is cut: *I like your new haircut.*

hair·dress·er /'hɛr,drɛsɚ/ *noun*
someone whose job is to wash, cut, and arrange your hair

hair·dryer /'hɛr,draɪɚ/ *noun*
a machine that you use to dry your hair

hair·spray /'../ *noun*
a liquid that you put on your hair to make it keep its shape

hair·style /'hɛrstaɪl/ *noun*
the style in which your hair is cut or arranged: *Is that a new hairstyle?* —see color picture on page 191

hair·y /'hɛri/ *adjective* (**hairier, hairiest**)
having a lot of hair: *His arms are very hairy.*
≫ compare FURRY

half¹ /hæf/ *noun* (*plural* **halves** /hævz/)
1 one of the two equal parts of something: *I had half the apple and my brother had the other half.*
2 **in half** into two equal pieces: *I cut the pie in half.*
3 **half an hour** 30 minutes: *I will be there in half an hour.*
4 **half a dozen** six

half² *adverb*
1 partly but not completely: *There were two half empty cups of tea on the table.*
2 **not half bad** said when something you expected to be bad is good instead: *This food isn't half bad.*

half-broth·er /'. ,../ *noun*
a brother who is the child of only one of your parents

half-sis·ter /'. ,../ *noun*
a sister who is the child of only one of your parents

half·time /'. ./ *noun* [U]
a time of rest between two parts of a game

half·way /,hæf'weɪ◂/ *adverb*
1 in the middle between two places or things: *He threw the ball halfway across the field.*
2 in the middle of a period of time or an event: *I fell asleep halfway through the movie.*

hall /hɔl/ *noun*
1 a passage in a house that goes to other rooms
2 a large room or public building used for important events

Hal·low·een /ˌhælə'win, ˌhɑ-/ *noun*
a holiday on October 31, when children dress in special clothes and visit people's houses to ask for candy

hall·way /'hɔlweɪ/ *noun*
a passage in a building that goes to other rooms —see color picture on page 186

halt¹ /hɔlt/ *verb*
to stop: *The police halted all the traffic.*

halt² *noun*
a stop: *All the cars came to a halt.*

ham /hæm/ *noun* [U]
meat from a pig's leg that has had salt added to keep it fresh ≫ compare BACON

ham·burg·er /'hæmˌbɚgɚ/ *noun*
1 a flat round piece of cooked meat eaten between two pieces of bread
2 [U] meat that is used to make hamburgers

ham·mer¹ /'hæmɚ/ *noun*
a tool with a metal head and a wooden handle, used for hitting nails into wood

hammer² *verb*
to hit something with a hammer

ham·ster /'hæmstɚ/ *noun*
a small animal like a mouse with soft fur and no tail, often kept as a pet

hand

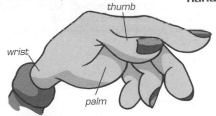

thumb
wrist
palm

hand¹ /hænd/ *noun*
1 the part of your body at the end of your arm, with which you hold things
2 **by hand** by a person, not by machine: *This toy was made by hand.*
3 **a hand** help: *Will you give me a hand with this box?* | *Do you need a hand with the cooking?*
4 **hand in hand** holding each other by the hand: *They were walking hand in hand.*

5 **on hand** close and ready to be used: *We always keep some glue on hand.*
6 **get out of hand** to not be possible to control: *The party was beginning to get out of hand.*
7 the part of a clock that moves to show the time

hand² *verb*
1 to give something to someone using your hands: *Hand me that plate.* | *She handed the letter to John.*
2 **hand something in** to give something to someone in authority such as a teacher: *You can hand in your papers now.*
3 **hand something out** to give something to each person in a group: *Please hand out the pencils.*

hand·cuffs /'hændkʌfs/ *plural noun*
two metal rings joined by a chain, used for holding a prisoner's wrists together

hand·ful /'hændfʊl/ *noun*
1 **a handful of something** a small number or amount of something: *Only a handful of people came to the meeting.*
2 an amount that you can hold in your hand: *He took a handful of candy.*

hand·gun /'hændgʌn/ *noun*
a small gun that you can hold in one hand

hand·i·cap /'hændiˌkæp/ *noun*
something that makes you unable to use a part of your body or mind because it is damaged

hand·i·capped /'hændiˌkæpt/ *adjective*
not able to use a part of your body or mind because it is damaged: *He goes to a school for physically handicapped children.*

hand·ker·chief /'hæŋkɚtʃɪf, ˌtʃif/ *noun*
a square piece of cloth for drying your nose or eyes

handle

handle

han·dle¹ /'hændl/ *noun*
the part of a tool or instrument that you hold in your hand

handle² *verb* **(handling, handled)**
1 to hold or touch something: *Handle the package with care.*
2 to control or deal with someone or something: *I can't handle the children by myself.*

han·dle·bars /'hændlˌbɑrz/ *plural noun*
the parts of a bicycle that you hold when you ride it

hand·some /'hænsəm/ *adjective*
attractive, usually used about a man ≫ compare BEAUTIFUL

hand·writ·ing /'hændˌraɪtɪŋ/ *noun* [U]
the way someone writes with his or her hand: *He has very neat handwriting.*

hand·y /'hændi/ *adjective* **(handier, handiest)**
1 useful: *A second car comes in handy sometimes.*
2 near: *Keep the medicine handy in case we need it.*

hang

He hung the clothes out to dry.

hang /hæŋ/ *verb*
1 (*past* **hung** /hʌŋ/) to fasten something at the top so that the bottom part is free to move: *I hung up my coat in the closet.*
2 (*past* **hanged**) to kill someone by holding him or her above the ground with a rope around his or her neck
3 **hang around** to stay in one place and do nothing, or to wait around for someone: *He was hanging around outside my house.*
4 **hang on** to hold something tightly: *Hang on to your hat, it's very windy.*
5 **hang out** to stay in one place and not do very much: *We usually hang out at Jill's house after school.*
6 **hang up** to finish speaking to someone on the telephone by putting the telephone down

hang·er /'hæŋɚ/ *noun*
a curved piece of wire or wood that you hang clothes on

hap·pen /'hæpən/ *verb*
1 to start or continue, usually without being planned: *The accident happened outside my house.*

2 **happen to do something** to do something by chance: *If you happen to see Susan, give her this message.*

> NOTE: If an event **occurs** or **happens**, it is not planned: *The explosion happened Friday evening.* If an event **takes place**, it is the result of a plan or arrangement: *The wedding will take place on June 6th.*

hap·pen·ing /'hæpənɪŋ/ *noun*
an event

hap·pi·ly /'hæpəli/ *adverb*
in a happy way: *They were laughing happily.*

hap·pi·ness /'hæpɪnɪs/ *noun* [U]
the state of being happy or pleased: *They've had years of happiness together.*

hap·py /'hæpi/ *adjective* **(happier, happiest)**
1 feeling very pleased: *I am happy to see you again.* ≫ opposite UNHAPPY
2 Happy Birthday!, **Happy New Year!** said to someone to wish him or her good luck on a special occasion

har·ass /hə'ræs, 'hærəs/ *verb*
to annoy someone by treating him or her in a way that is not nice —**harassment** *noun* [U]

har·bor /'hɑrbɚ/ *noun*
an area of water next to land where it is safe to leave ships

hard¹ /hɑrd/ *adjective*
1 firm and stiff; difficult to break or cut: *The ground is too hard to dig into.* ≫ compare SOFT
2 difficult to do or understand: *Math is the hardest class I have.* ≫ compare EASY
3 involving a lot of effort or work: *I had a hard day on the job.*

hard² *adverb*
using a lot of effort or force; very much: *It's raining hard.* | *Are you working hard?*

hard disk /ˌ. './ *noun*
a part of a computer on which you can store information permanently ≫ compare FLOPPY DISK

hard·en /'hɑrdn/ *verb*
to become firm or stiff

hard·ly /'hɑrdli/ *adverb*
almost not at all: *It was so dark that I could hardly see.* | *He hardly ever* [=almost never] *eats meat.* ≫ compare BARELY

hard·ware /'hɑrdwɛr/ *noun* [U]
1 tools that you use to build and repair things

2 computer machinery and equipment
≫ compare SOFTWARE

hare /hɛr/ *noun*
an animal like a large rabbit but with longer ears and longer back legs

harm¹ /harm/ *noun* [U]
1 damage or injury
2 **there's no harm in doing something** said when it may be useful or helpful to do something: *There's no harm in asking him for a job.*

harm² *verb*
to hurt someone or something: *Too much sun can harm your skin.*

harm·ful /'harmfəl/ *adjective*
dangerous or causing harm: *Smoking is harmful to your health.*

harm·less /'harmlıs/ *adjective*
not dangerous and not likely to cause harm: *Don't worry, the dog is harmless.*

harsh /harʃ/ *adjective*
very unpleasant; cruel: *He said some harsh things to her.*

har·vest¹ /'harvıst/ *noun*
1 the time when crops are gathered from the fields
2 the size or quality of the crops: *The corn harvest was good this year.*

harvest² *verb*
to gather crops from the fields

has /z, s, əz, həz; *strong* hæz/
the part of the verb **have** that we use with **he**, **she** and **it**: *She has three children.*

has·n't /'hæzənt/
has not: *I haven't been here before?*

has·sle /'hæsəl/ *noun* [U]
something that annoys you because it is difficult or causes problems: *Driving in the city is such a hassle!*

haste /heıst/ *noun* [U]
quick movement or action: *In my haste I forgot my coat.*

hast·y /'heısti/ *adjective* (**hastier, hastiest**)
done in a hurry: *I made a hasty decision.*

hat /hæt/ *noun*
a piece of clothing that you wear on your head
—see color picture on page 190

hatch /hætʃ/ *verb*
to come out of an egg: *The chickens hatched this morning.*

hate¹ /heıt/ *verb* (**hating, hated**)
not to like someone or something at all: *I hate snakes.* ≫ compare LOVE¹

hate² *noun* [U]
an angry feeling of wanting to hurt someone you do not like ≫ compare LOVE²

ha·tred /'heıtrıd/ *noun* [U]
hate ≫ compare LOVE²

haul /hɔl/ *verb*
to carry or pull something heavy: *They hauled the boat up onto the shore.*

haunt /hɔnt, hant/ *verb*
if the spirit of a dead person haunts a place, it appears there: *People say that the old house is haunted.*

---

have /v, əv, həv; *strong* hæv/ *verb*
present tense

singular	plural
I **have** (I**'ve**)	We **have**
(We**'ve**)	
You **have** (You**'ve**)	You **have**
(You**'ve**)	
He/She/It **has**	They **have**
(He**'s**/She**'s**/It**'s**)	(They**'ve**)

past tense

singular	plural
I **had** (I**'d**)	We **had** (We**'d**)
You **had** (You**'d**)	You **had** (You**'d**)
He/She/It **had**	They **had**
(They**'d**)	
(He**'d**/She**'d**/It**'d**)	

present participle	**having**
past participle	**had**
negative short	**haven't, hasn't**
forms	**hadn't**

For the pronunciation of all these words, find them at their place in the dictionary
1 a word that helps another word to say that something happened in the past: *We have been to the store.* | *When I arrived, she had already gone away.*
2 used for saying what someone or something is like: *He has red hair.* | *Japan has a large population.*
3 to own or be able to use something: *Do you have a car?* | *I do not have any money.*
4 to do something: *I have my breakfast at 8 o'clock.* | *We had fun at the party.*
5 to put or keep something in a particular place: *He has his eyes closed.*

6 to become sick or injured: *She has a headache.*
7 to receive something: *You have a telephone call.*

have·n't /'hævənt/
have not: *I haven't seen that film.*

have to /'hævtə/ *verb* (also **have got to**)
must: *We have to leave now, so we can catch the bus.* | *I have got to talk to him.*

hawk /hɔk/ *noun*
a large bird that eats small animals and birds

hay /heɪ/ *noun* [U]
dry grass that is fed to cattle

haz·ard /'hæzəd/ *noun*
a danger or problem: *Drinking this water may be a health hazard.*

haz·ard·ous /'hæzədəs/ *adjective*
dangerous

haze /heɪz/ *noun* [U]
smoke or dust in the air which is difficult to see through

ha·zel·nut /'heɪzəl,nʌt/ *noun*
a sweet round nut

haz·y /heɪzi/ *adjective* (hazier, haziest)
not clear: *On a hazy day you cannot see the mountains.*

he /i; *strong* hi/
the male person or animal that the sentence is about: *I remember John. He lives in New York.* | *Watch out for that dog. He bites.*

head¹ /hɛd/ *noun*
1 the top part of your body where your mouth, eyes, and ears are

head

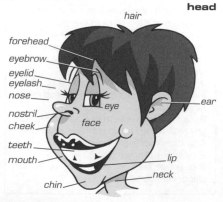

forehead
eyebrow
eyelid
eyelash
nose
nostril
cheek
teeth
mouth
chin
hair
eye
face
ear
lip
neck

2 your mind: *His head is full of ideas.*
3 the most important part of something: *She sat at the head of the table.*
4 someone who is in charge of a group of people: *He is the head of a large company.*
5 the top or the front of something: *We stood at the head of the line.*
6 use your head to think about something in a careful way so you can do it
7 keep your head to stay calm in a difficult situation
8 lose your head to do things without thinking, or to become angry in a difficult situation

head² *verb*
1 to go in a particular direction: *Where are you heading?* | *The car was headed for a wall.*
2 to be in charge of a group, government etc.
3 to be at the top or front of something

head·ache /'hɛdeɪk/ *noun*
a pain in your head: *I have a headache.*

head·ing /'hɛdɪŋ/ *noun*
something written at the top of a piece of writing

head·light /'hɛdlaɪt/ *noun*
one of the large lights at the front of a car

head·line /'hɛdlaɪn/ *noun*
words printed in large letters at the top of a newspaper story

head·phones /'hɛdfoʊnz/ *plural noun*
a piece of equipment you wear over your ears to listen to music —see picture at HEAR

head·quar·ters /'hɛd,kwɔtəz/ *noun*
the main office of a business or other group

heal /hil/ *verb*
to make something healthy again or become healthy again: *The wound on my arm has healed.*

health /hɛlθ/ *noun* [U]
how well your body is: *You should take better care of your health.*

health·y /'hɛlθi/ *adjective* (healthier, healthiest)
1 strong and well in your body: *She had a healthy baby girl.*
2 good for your body or mind: *It is healthy to eat a lot of fruit.* ≫ opposite UNHEALTHY

heap¹ /hip/ *noun*
a large messy pile of things: *A heap of old clothes was on the floor.*

heap² *verb*
to put a lot of things on top of each other: *He heaped his plate with food.*

Her music was so loud that she couldn't hear the phone.

headphones

hear

hear /hɪr/ *verb* (*past* **heard** /hɚd/)
1 to listen to sounds using your ears: *I heard the rain on the roof.* | *Did you hear their new song?*
2 to be given information about something: *I heard that he was sick.*
3 **hear from someone** to get news or information from someone: *Have you heard from John lately?*
4 **have heard of someone/something** to know about someone or something: *I've never heard of her.*

hear·ing /'hɪrɪŋ/ *noun* [U]
your ability to hear: *My hearing is not very good.*

heart /hɑrt/ *noun*
1 the part of your body in your chest that pumps blood around your body
2 the part of you that feels strong emotions: *I know in my heart that I love her.*
3 a shape like a heart representing love
4 **the heart of something** (a) the middle of something: *Our hotel was in the heart of the city.* (b) the most important part of something: *We need to get to the heart of the problem.*
5 **break someone's heart** to make someone very unhappy
6 **by heart** so well that you can remember it easily: *I know this song by heart.*
7 **lose heart** to have less courage and hope: *We are losing heart that they are still alive.*
8 **take heart** to be encouraged and more hopeful about something
9 **at heart** what someone is really like: *He seems serious, but he is a boy at heart.*
10 **with a heavy heart** sadly

heart·beat /'hɑrtbit/ *noun*
the movement or sound of someone's heart

heart·bro·ken /'hɑrt,broʊkən/ *adjective*
very sad

heart·less /'hɑrtlɪs/ *adjective*
not kind; cruel

heat¹ /hit/ *noun*
1 [U] hotness or warmth: *Heat from the sun is used for making energy.* ≫ compare COLD²
2 **the heat** (a) hot weather: *I hate the heat.* (b) a system that keeps a place warm: *Can you turn the heat off?*
3 a part of a competition in which those who win go on to the next part

heat² *verb*
to make something warm or hot: *We could heat up some soup to eat.*

heat·er /'hitɚ/ *noun*
a machine that heats air or water

heave /hiv/ *verb* (**heaving, heaved**)
to lift or pull something with a lot of effort: *I heaved the boxes onto the truck.*

heav·en /'hɛvən/ *noun* [U]
a place where people think God or the gods live, and where good people will go after they die ≫ compare HELL

heav·y /'hɛvi/ *adjective* (**heavier, heaviest**)
1 weighing a lot: *This bag is too heavy to carry.*
2 large in amount: *We had a heavy rain today.* | *Traffic is heavy on Fridays.*
3 **a heavy sleeper** someone who does not wake up easily
4 **a heavy smoker, a heavy drinker** someone who smokes a lot, or drinks too much alcohol

heavy met·al /,.. '../ *noun* [U]
a type of loud music played on electric instruments and drums

he'd /id; *strong* hid/
1 he had: *He'd met her before.*
2 he would: *He said he'd tell me tomorrow.*

hedge /hɛdʒ/ *noun*
a row of bushes around a yard or between yards

heel /hil/ *noun*
1 the back part of your foot —see picture at FOOT
2 the part of a shoe or sock under your heel

height /haɪt/ *noun*
how tall or far from the ground something is: *The boys are about the same height.* —see picture at LENGTH and see color picture on page 191

heir /ɛr/ *noun*
a person who gets money or goods when someone dies

held /hɛld/
the PAST TENSE and PAST PARTICIPLE of the verb **hold**

hel·i·cop·ter /ˈhɛlɪˌkɑptɚ/ noun
an aircraft with blades on top of it which spin very fast —see color picture on page 187

he'll /ɪl, il, hɪl; strong hil/
he will: He'll be here soon.

hell /hɛl/ noun [U]
a place where some people think bad people will go after they die ≫ compare HEAVEN

hel·lo /hə'lou, hɛ'lou, 'hɛlou/
said when you meet someone or talk on the telephone: Hello, is Jane there? ≫ compare GOODBYE

hel·met /ˈhɛlmɪt/ noun
a hard hat that covers and protects your head

help¹ /hɛlp/ verb
1 to do something for someone: Could you help me move this table?
2 can't help, couldn't help said when you are not able to stop doing something: I couldn't help laughing when I saw his hat.
3 help yourself take as much as you want: Help yourself **to** some milk.
4 help! said when you are in danger, especially to get someone's attention

help² noun [U]
the action of helping someone: If you want any help, just ask.

help·ful /ˈhɛlpfəl/ adjective
1 useful: This map is not very helpful.
2 willing to help: She's so kind and helpful.
—**helpfully** adverb

help·ing /ˈhɛlpɪŋ/ noun
the amount of food on a plate: Would you like another helping **of** pie?

help·less /ˈhɛlplɪs/ adjective
not able to take care of or protect yourself
—**helplessness** noun [U]

hem /hɛm/ noun
the bottom edge of a skirt, shirt etc.

hen /hɛn/ noun
a female chicken

her /ɚ, hɚ; strong hɚ/
1 a woman or girl: Give her the book. | I had a letter from her.
2 belonging to a woman or girl: Her baby is sleeping in her arms.

herb /ɚb/ noun
a plant used for medicine or for giving more taste to food

herd¹ /hɚd/ noun
a group of animals of the same kind: He owns a herd **of** cattle. ≫ compare FLOCK

herd² verb
to make a number of people or animals move together as a group

here /hɪr/ adverb
1 in or to this place: Come here and sit by me. | How far is your house from here? ≫ compare THERE¹
2 here you are said when you are giving someone something that he or she wants
3 here and there in different places: There were a lot of boats here and there on the water.

he·ro /ˈhɪrou/ noun [plural **heroes**]
1 someone who you admire very much for doing something good
2 a man who is a character in a book or movie

he·ro·ic /hɪ'rouɪk/ adjective
very brave

her·o·ine /ˈhɛrouɪn/ noun
a woman who is a character in a book or movie

hers /hɚz/
something belonging to a woman or girl: My hand touched hers.

her·self /ɚ'sɛlf; strong hɚ'sɛlf/ [plural **themselves**]
1 the same girl or woman as the subject of a sentence: She made herself a cup of coffee.
2 used for giving the word "she" a stronger meaning: She gave me the money herself.
3 by herself alone; without help: She went for a walk by herself. | She made dinner all by herself.

he's /iz; strong hiz/
1 he is: He's a doctor.
2 he has: He's lost his keys again.

hes·i·tate /ˈhɛzəˌteɪt/ verb [**hesitating, hesitated**]
to pause before you do or say something because you are not sure what to do: He hesitated before answering the question.

hes·i·ta·tion /ˌhɛzə'teɪʃən/ noun [U]
a pause before you do or say something because you are not sure what to do

hi /haɪ/
a friendly way of saying "hello"

hic·cups /ˈhɪkʌps/ *plural noun*
sudden loud sounds in your throat caused by eating or drinking too fast

hide¹ /haɪd/ *verb* [hiding, hid /hɪd/, *past participle* hidden /ˈhɪdn/]
1 to put something in a place where no one can see it or find it: *Where did you hide the money?*
2 to go to a place where no one can see or find you: *I hid behind the door.*
3 to not show your feelings or tell someone about something: *She hid her feelings from her family.*

hide² *noun*
the skin of an animal

hide-and-seek /ˌ . . ˈ./ *noun* [U]
a children's game in which one child shuts his or her eyes while other children hide, then the one child tries to find them

high /haɪ/ *adjective*
1 tall, or far from the ground: *The highest mountain in Asia is Mount Everest.* ≫ compare TALL, LOW
2 a high number, amount, or level is greater than usual: *The clothes are selling at high prices.* | *High winds knocked down the trees.* ≫ compare: LOW
3 having an important position or job: *She has a high position in the government.*
4 very good: *The teacher has a high opinion of my work.*
5 near the top of a range of sounds that you can hear: *You need a high voice to sing this song.*

high·lands /ˈhaɪləndz/ *plural noun*
an area with a lot of hills or mountains

high·ly /ˈhaɪli/ *adverb*
1 very: *We had a highly successful meeting.*
2 to a high level or amount

High·ness /ˈhaɪnɪs/ *noun*
a title for certain royal people

high school /ˈ. ./ *noun*
a school in the U.S. for students over the age of 14

high-tech /ˌ. ˈ.◂/ *adjective*
using the most modern information, machines etc.: *I bought a new high-tech camera.*

high tide /ˌ. ˈ./ *noun*
the time when the sea is at its highest level ≫ compare LOW TIDE

high·way /ˈhaɪweɪ/ *noun*
a wide fast road between cities

hi·jack /ˈhaɪdʒæk/ *verb*
to take control of a plane etc. illegally

hi·jack·er /ˈhaɪdʒækɚ/ *noun*
someone who takes control of a plane etc. illegally

hike /ˈhaɪk/ *verb* [*present participle* **hiking** *past* **hiked**]
to take a long walk in the country or in the mountains

hill /hɪl/ *noun*
an area of high land; a small mountain —see picture at MOUNTAIN and see color picture on page 188

him /ɪm; *strong* hɪm/
a man or boy: *Give him the book.* | *I had a letter from him.*

him·self /ɪmˈsɛlf; *strong* hɪmˈsɛlf/ (*plural* **themselves**)
1 the same man or boy as the subject of the sentence: *Peter bought himself a new car.*
2 used for giving the word "he" a stronger meaning: *He told me so himself.*
3 by himself alone; without help: *He stayed at home by himself.* | *He repaired the roof all by himself.*

hin·der /ˈhɪndɚ/ *verb*
to make it difficult for someone to do something

Hin·du·ism /ˈhɪnduˌɪzəm/ *noun* [U]
the main religion in India —**Hindu** *adjective, noun*

hinge /hɪndʒ/ *noun*
a piece of metal that joins two things together so that one of them can swing open and shut: *We need a new hinge for the door.*

hint¹ /hɪnt/ *verb*
to say something that helps someone guess what you want: *He hinted that he wants a bicycle.*

hint² *noun*
1 something that you say that helps someone guess what you want: *She said she was tired, but it was a hint for us to go.*
2 a piece of useful advice: *I have a book full of decorating hints.*

hip /hɪp/ *noun*
the part of your body where your legs join your body

hip·po·pot·a·mus /ˌhɪpəˈpɑtəməs/ *noun* (*plural* **hippopotamuses** *or* **hippopotami**)
a large animal in Africa with short legs, a fat body, and thick hairless skin, that lives near rivers

hire /haɪɚ/ *verb* (**hiring, hired**)
to pay someone to work for you: *I got hired by the new company.*

his /ɪz; *strong* hɪz/
1 belonging to a man or boy: *He sat drinking his coffee.*
2 something belonging to a man or boy: *My hand touched his.*

His·pan·ic /hɪˈspænɪk/ *adjective*
from or relating to a country where people speak Spanish —**Hispanic** *noun*

hiss¹ /hɪs/ *verb*
to make a sound like "ssss": *Steam was hissing from the pipe.*

hiss² *noun* (*plural* **hisses**)
a sound like "ssss"

his·tor·ic /hɪˈstɔrɪk, -ˈstɑr-/ *adjective*
important as a part of history: *It was a historic meeting between the two leaders.*

his·tor·i·cal /hɪˈstɔrɪkəl, -ˈstɑr-/ *adjective*
relating to the past: *I found some historical documents relating to the war.*

his·to·ry /ˈhɪstəri/ *noun* [U]
1 all the things that happened in the past
2 the study of things that happened in the past: *Our class is on the history of Rome.*

hit¹ /hɪt/ *verb* (**hitting, hit**)
to touch something suddenly and with a lot of force: *He hit me **on** the face.* | *The car hit a wall.* | *She was hit in the arm by a bullet.* —see color picture on page 189

hit² *noun*
1 a song or movie that is popular and successful: *That song is a big hit.*
2 an act of touching something suddenly and with a lot of force

hitch·hike /ˈhɪtʃhaɪk/ *verb* (**hitchhiking, hitchhiked**)
to travel by asking for free rides in other people's cars

HIV /ˌeɪtʃ aɪ ˈvi/ *noun* [U]
a type of infection that enters the body through the blood or sexual activity, and can cause AIDS

hive /haɪv/ *noun*
(*also* **beehive**) a place where BEEs live

hoard¹ /hɔrd/ *verb*
to collect things in large amounts and hide them to keep them safe: *The people were hoarding food and water because of the war.*

hoard² *noun*
a large amount of something that is hidden to keep it safe

hoarse /hɔrs/ *adjective*
having a voice that sounds rough because your throat is sore and dry: *He was hoarse after talking for an hour.*

hob·ble /ˈhɑbəl/ *verb* (**hobbling, hobbled**)
to walk slowly and with difficulty, usually because you are injured

hob·by /ˈhɑbi/ *noun* (*plural* **hobbies**)
an activity that you enjoy doing in your free time: *I collect old coins as a hobby.*

hock·ey /ˈhɑki/ *noun* [U]
a sport played on ice by two teams who use curved sticks to hit a flat hard object into a GOAL —see color picture on page 184

hoe /hoʊ/ *noun*
a tool with a long handle, used for making the soil loose

hoist /hɔɪst/ *verb*
to lift or raise something using ropes or a special machine

hold¹ /hoʊld/ *verb* (*past* **held** /held/)
1 to have something in your hand or arms: *The little girl held the doll.* | *I held her in my arms.*
2 to keep something in a particular position: *Can you hold the picture up for us?*
3 to have space for an amount of something: *The bottle holds one gallon.*
4 to arrange and make something happen: *The meeting will be held on Tuesday.*
5 to keep or contain something: *All the information is held in our computer.*
6 to have a particular position or job: *He holds an important position at the bank.*
7 to wait for a short time until the person you telephone is ready to talk with you: *I have another call. Can you hold?*
8 hold back to control something or make it stay in one place: *The police tried to hold the crowd back.*
9 hold a conversation to talk to someone
10 hold your breath to breathe in, close your mouth, and keep the air in your lungs: *You have to hold your breath under water.*
11 hold on said when you want someone to wait or stop talking: *Can you hold on? I'll see if he's in.*

hold² *noun*
1 the action of taking something in your hand and holding it: ***Take** hold **of** the rope and we will pull you up.*

2 the place on a ship where goods are stored
3 **get hold of** to find someone or something:
I wanted to get hold of Mark before he left.
4 **on hold** waiting on a telephone to speak to
someone: *They have put me on hold.*

hold·up /'houldʌp/ *noun*
1 a delay: *Sorry I'm late. There was a holdup
near the bridge.*
2 an attempt to rob someone, especially using
a gun

hole /houl/ *noun*
an empty space or opening in something: *The
dog is digging a hole in the yard.*

hol·i·day /'hɑlə,deɪ/ *noun*
a day when you do not have to go to school or
work: *Next Friday is a holiday.*

hol·low /'hɑloʊ/ *adjective*
having an empty space inside: *The old tree is
hollow on the inside.* ≫ compare SOLID¹

hol·ly /'hɑli/ *noun* [U]
a small tree with dark green pointed leaves and
small red fruits

ho·ly /'houli/ *adjective* (holier, holiest)
1 relating to God or religion: *I visited the holy
city of Mecca.*
2 very good and pure; religious: *a holy man*

home¹ /houm/ *noun*
1 the place where you live: *She is not at home
now.*
2 a place where a particular group of people
are cared for: *He lives in a children's home.*

home² *adjective*
1 relating to or belonging to your home or
family: *What is your home address?*
2 playing on your own sports field rather than
another one: *The home team won the game!*

home³ *adverb*
to or at your own house: *Let's go home.* | *Hello,
I'm home.*

home·less /'houmlɪs/ *adjective*
not having a place to live

home·made /ˌhoʊm'eɪd⊲/ *adjective*
made at home, not in a store: *homemade bread*

home page /'. ./ *noun*
a place on the INTERNET where you can find
information about a person, company etc.

home·sick /'houm,sɪk/ *adjective*
feeling sad because you are away from home:
I felt homesick living in Paris by myself.

home·work /'houmwɚk/ *noun*
work for school that you do at home: *We have
to do a lot of homework every night.*

ho·mo·sex·u·al /ˌhoʊmə'sɛkʃuəl/
adjective
sexually attracted to people of the same sex

hon·est /'ɑnɪst/ *adjective*
not likely to lie, steal, or cheat; truthful ≫ opposite DISHONEST

hon·est·ly /'ɑnɪstli/ *adverb*
1 without telling lies, stealing, or cheating: *If I
can't get the money honestly, I'll have to do
something else.*
2 said when you want to make someone
believe what you are saying: *I honestly don't
mind working late tonight.*

hon·es·ty /'ɑnəsti/ *noun* [U]
behavior in which you tell the truth, and do not
lie, steal, or cheat: *He was praised for his honesty when he returned the money.*

hon·ey /'hʌni/ *noun* [U]
sweet, sticky liquid that is made by BEEs, used
for food

hon·ey·moon /'hʌni,mun/ *noun*
a vacation taken by two people who have just
been married

hon·or /'ɑnɚ/ *noun* [U]
1 great respect
2 **in honor of** done to show respect for someone: *There is a ceremony in honor of those who
died.*

hood /hʊd/ *noun*
1 the part of a coat that you can pull up to
cover your head
2 the metal cover over the engine on a car

hoof /hʊf/ *noun* (*plural* **hooves** /huːvz/ or
hoofs)
the foot of a horse, cow, sheep, or goat

hook /hʊk/ *noun*
1 a curved object for hanging something on:
You can hang your coat on the hook.
2 a curved piece of metal with a sharp point
used for catching fish
3 **off the hook** having the part of the telephone
you speak into lifted so that the telephone will
not ring

hoop /hup/ *noun*
a round piece of wood, plastic, or metal —see
picture at NET

hoo·ray /huˈreɪ/
a shout of joy or approval: *Hooray! We've won!*

hoot¹ /hut/ *verb*
to make a loud noise like a car's horn or an OWL

hoot² *noun*
the sound made by a car's horn or an OWL

hooves /huvz, hʊvz/ *noun*
the plural of **hoof**

hop¹ /hɑp/ *verb* (**hopping, hopped**)
1 to move by making short quick jumps: *I saw a rabbit hopping across the yard.* —see color picture on page 189
2 to get into or out of a vehicle: *Hop in and I'll give you a ride.*

hop² *noun*
1 a short jump
2 a short trip by plane: *It is a short hop from Chicago to Detroit.*

hope¹ /hoʊp/ *verb* (**hoping, hoped**)
to want something to happen or be true: *I hope to go to college next year.* | *"Will you be at the party?" " I hope so!"*

hope² *noun*
1 [U] the feeling that something good will happen: *You must never lose hope.* [=stop hoping] | *The new medicine will give hope to many people.*
2 something that you hope will happen: *I had hopes of finishing early and going home.*

hope·ful /ˈhoʊpfəl/ *adjective*
believing that what you want is likely to happen: *I am hopeful that she will get better soon.* —**hopefulness** *noun* [U]

hope·ful·ly /ˈhoʊpfəli/ *adverb*
1 in a hopeful way: *"Can we go to the movies?" he said hopefully.*
2 used for saying what you hope will happen: *Hopefully, we'll be there by dinnertime.*

hope·less /ˈhoʊp-lɪs/ *adjective*
1 without any chance of success: *The country is in a hopeless situation.*
2 very bad, or unable to do something: *I am hopeless at science.* —**hopelessly** *adverb*

ho·ri·zon /həˈraɪzən/ *noun*
the line between the land or sea and the sky: *I can see a ship on the horizon.*

hor·i·zon·tal /ˌhɔrəˈzɑntəl, ˌhɑr-/ *adjective*
flat and level to the ground ≫ compare VERTICAL —**horizontally** *adverb*

horn /hɔrn/ *noun*
1 a hard pointed part that grows from the heads of some animals
2 an instrument on a car, bus etc. that gives a short, loud sound as a warning: *The taxi blew its horn.*
3 a musical instrument that you blow into

hor·ri·ble /ˈhɔrəbəl, ˈhɑr-/ *adjective*
very unpleasant: *I saw a horrible accident yesterday.* ≫ compare TERRIBLE —**horribly** *adverb*

hor·ri·fied /ˈhɔrəˌfaɪd, ˈhɑr-/ *adjective*
feeling very shocked or upset: *I was horrified by the news.*

hor·ror /ˈhɔrɚ, ˈhɑrɚ/ *noun* [U]
great fear and shock: *I watched in horror as the cars crashed into each other.*

horse /hɔrs/ *noun*
a large animal that people ride on and use for pulling heavy things —see color picture on page 183

horse·back /ˈhɔrsbæk/ *noun*
on horseback riding on a horse

horse·back rid·ing /ˈhɔrsbæk ˌraɪdɪŋ/ *noun* [U]
the activity of riding horses

horse·shoe /ˈhɔrʃ-ʃu, ˈhɔrs-/ *noun*
a curved piece of iron which is put on the bottom of a horse's foot to protect it

hose /hoʊz/ *noun*
a long tube that bends easily, used for getting water, air etc. from one place to another

hos·pi·tal /ˈhɑspɪtl/ *noun*
a building where people who are sick or injured are cared for: *Amy is in the hospital.*

hos·pi·tal·i·ty /ˌhɑspəˈtæləti/ *noun* [U]
nice attention given to visitors: *Thank you for your hospitality.*

host /hoʊst/ *noun*
the person who invites other people to his or her house

hos·tage /ˈhɑstɪdʒ/ *noun*
someone who is taken and kept as a prisoner by an enemy so other people will do what the enemy wants

host·ess /ˈhoʊstɪs/ *noun*
a woman who invites people to her house

hos·tile /ˈhɑstl, ˈhɑstaɪl/ *adjective*
angry and ready to attack; not friendly: *The hostile crowd began to throw rocks.*

hot /hɑt/ *adjective*
1 having a lot of heat: *The sun is very hot.* | *Here is some hot coffee for you.* ≫ compare COLD[1]
2 having a burning taste: *Pepper makes food taste hot.* ≫ compare MILD

hot dog
/ˈ. ./ *noun*
a long piece of cooked meat like a tube, eaten in a long piece of bread

ho·tel
/hoʊˈtɛl/ *noun*
a building where people pay to stay for a short time: *We stayed in a hotel near the airport.*

hound /haʊnd/ *noun*
a dog used for hunting

hour /aʊər/ *noun*
1 a measure of time; 60 minutes: *There are 24 hours in one day.* | *I'll be home in an hour.*
2 a particular time of day or night: *The subway doesn't run at this hour of the night.*
3 a time when you usually do a particular thing: *We are open between the hours of 9 and 5.*
4 for hours for a long time: *I've been waiting here for hours.*
5 on the hour exactly at one o'clock, two o'clock etc.: *The buses leave on the hour.*
6 after hours when a place is closed: *No one is allowed in after hours.*

hour·ly /ˈaʊərli/ *adverb, adjective*
happening or done every hour, or once an hour: *The planes arrive hourly.*

house /haʊs/ *noun*
1 a building that you live in, especially with a family
2 all the people who live in a house: *Be quiet or you will wake the whole house.*

house·hold /ˈhaʊshoʊld, ˈhaʊsoʊld/ *noun*
all the people who live in a house together

house·keep·er /ˈhaʊsˌkipər/ *noun*
someone whose job is to clean, cook etc. in a house or hotel

house·wife /ˈhaʊswaɪf/ *noun* (*plural* **housewives**)
a married woman who works at home for her family

house·work /ˈhaʊswərk/ *noun* [U]
the work you do to take care of a house

hov·er /ˈhʌvər/ *verb*
to stay in the air in one place: *The large bird hovered in the air.*

how /haʊ/ *adverb*
1 used for asking about something, or explaining how to do something: *How do you open this box?* | *How do you spell your name?*
2 used in questions about time, amount, or size: *How much money did you pay?* | *How many children do you have?* | *How old are you?*
3 used for asking about someone's health: *How is your mother?* | *How are you?*
4 used to make something you say stronger: *I can't tell you how boring the movie was!*
5 How do you do? said when you meet someone for the first time
6 how about? used when making a suggestion about what to do: *I can't come today. How about tomorrow instead?*

how·ev·er /haʊˈɛvər/ *adverb*
1 but: *I don't think we can do it; however, we will try.*
2 in whatever way; it does not matter: *She goes swimming every day, however cold it is.* | *I want that car, however much it costs.*

howl /haʊl/ *verb*
to make a long, loud crying sound like a dog: *My dog is howling at the moon.* —**howl** *noun*

hud·dle /ˈhʌdl/ *verb* (**huddling, huddled**)
to move close to the other people in a small group: *We huddled around the fire to keep warm.*

hug¹ /hʌg/ *verb* (**hugging, hugged**)
to put your arms around someone and hold him or her to show love or friendship: *He hugged his daughter.*

hug² *noun*
an act of holding someone close to you in your arms: *He gave her a big hug.*

huge /hyudʒ/ *adjective*
very large: *He ate a huge amount of food.* ≫ compare ENORMOUS

hum /hʌm/ *verb* (**humming, hummed**)
1 to make a low steady noise like a BEE
2 to sing with your lips closed

hu·man /ˈhyumən/ *adjective*
belonging to or relating to people: *This computer records the human voice.* —**human** *noun*

human be·ing /ˌ.. ˈ../ *noun*
a man, woman, or child; not an animal

hum·ble /ˈhʌmbəl/ *adjective*
1 thinking that you are not better or more important than other people; not proud: *He is a humble man with many friends.*
2 simple or poor: *She came from a humble family.*

hu·mid /ˈhyumɪd/ *adjective*
air that is humid feels warm and wet

hu·mor /ˈhyumɚ/ *noun* [U]
the ability to laugh at things or to make others laugh: *He doesn't have a sense of humor.* [=does not know when something is funny]

hu·mor·ous /ˈhyumərəs/ *adjective*
funny; making you laugh: *I read a humorous book about his life.*

hump /hʌmp/ *noun*
1 a round shape that rises above a surface
2 a raised part on the back of an animal or person

hun·dred /ˈhʌndrɪd/ *noun*
1 (*plural* **hundred**) the number 100: *The school was built one hundred years ago.* | *Three hundred people were killed in the flood.*
2 **hundreds of** a very large number of something: *We receive hundreds of letters each week.*

hun·dredth /ˈhʌndrɪdθ/ *adjective, noun*
100th

hung /hʌŋ/
the PAST TENSE and PAST PARTICIPLE of the verb **hang**

hun·ger /ˈhʌŋgɚ/ *noun* [U]
the feeling that you want or need to eat ≫ compare THIRST

hun·gry /ˈhʌŋgri/ *adjective* (**hungrier, hungriest**)
wanting or needing to eat: *I'm hungry, when are we going to eat?* ≫ compare THIRSTY

hunt /hʌnt/ *verb*
1 to chase and kill animals for food or sport
2 to look for something or someone very carefully: *I hunted everywhere for that book.*

hunt·er /ˈhʌntɚ/ *noun*
a person or animal who chases and kills animals, usually for food

hurl /hɚl/ *verb*
to throw something with force: *He hurled the brick through the window.*

hur·ri·cane /ˈhɚɪˌkeɪn, ˈhʌr-/ *noun*
a storm with very strong fast winds

hur·ry¹ /ˈhɚi, ˈhʌri/ *verb* (**hurrying, hurried**)
1 to move or do something quickly: *We have to hurry or we will be late!*
2 **hurry up** to do something more quickly: *I wish you would hurry up and get dressed!*

hurry² *noun*
be in a hurry to try to do things quickly because you do not have much time: *I can't talk now. I'm in a hurry.*

hurt¹ /hɚt/ *verb* (*past* **hurt**)
1 to injure yourself or someone else: *I fell over and hurt my knee.*
2 to feel pain or cause pain: *My feet hurt after all that walking.*
3 to make someone feel unhappy or upset: *I didn't mean to hurt your feelings.* ≫ compare INJURE

hurt² *adjective*
1 injured or feeling pain: *No one was hurt in the accident.*
2 unhappy or upset: *She is hurt because of what you said.*

hus·band /ˈhʌzbənd/ *noun*
the man to whom a woman is married ≫ compare WIFE

hush¹ /hʌʃ/ *verb*
said when telling someone to be quiet or to stop crying

hush² *noun* [U]
a peaceful silence

hut /hʌt/ *noun*
a small building with only one or two rooms

hy·e·na /haɪˈinə/ *noun*
a wild animal like a large dog that makes a sound like a loud laugh —see color picture on page 183

hymn /hɪm/ *noun*
a song of praise to God

hy·phen /ˈhaɪfən/ *noun*
the mark (-) used to join two words or parts of words: *We have a two-car garage.*

I /aɪ/
the person who is speaking: *I want to go home.* | *My friend and I went to the movies.* | *I'm (=I am) very glad to see you.* | *I've (=I have) been waiting a long time.* | *I'll (=I will) wait a little longer.* | *I thought I'd (=I had) missed the bus.*

ice

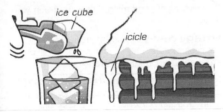

ice cube

icicle

ice /aɪs/ *noun* [U]
water that has frozen and become hard: *He put some ice in his drink.* | *There is ice on the roads.*

ice·berg
/'aɪsbɜg/ *noun*
a very large piece of ice floating in the sea

ice cream /'. ./
noun [U]
a sweet food made from frozen milk: *I want a bowl of chocolate ice cream.*

ice cube /'. ./ *noun*
a small square piece of ice that you put in a drink

ice skate¹ /'. ./ *noun*
a special shoe that you wear for moving on ice

ice skate² *verb* (ice skating, ice skated)
to move across ice wearing special shoes: *Do you want to go ice skating?* —see color picture on page 184

i·ci·cle /'aɪsɪkəl/ *noun*
a long thin piece of ice that hangs down from something: *There are icicles hanging from the roof.* —see picture at ICE

ic·ing /'aɪsɪŋ/ *noun* [U]
a mixture of sugar and water put on top of cakes

i·con /'aɪkɒn/ *noun*
a small picture on a computer screen that you can choose to make the computer do something

ic·y /'aɪsi/ *adjective* (icier, iciest)
1 very cold: *I felt an icy wind.*
2 covered with ice: *You can't drive on an icy road.*

I'd /aɪd/
1 I had: *I'd already left by the time she arrived.*
2 I would: *I'd like a cup of coffee, please.*

i·de·a /aɪ'dɪə/ *noun*
1 a thought or plan that you think of: *I've got an idea. Why don't we have a party?* | *What a good idea!*
2 **have no idea** not to know something: *I had no idea that you had a brother.*

i·de·al /aɪ'dɪəl/ *adjective*
the best that something can be: *This book is an ideal Christmas gift.*

i·den·ti·cal /aɪ'dentɪkəl, ɪ-/ *adjective*
exactly the same: *Your dress is identical to mine.*

i·den·ti·fi·ca·tion /aɪ,dentəfə'keɪʃən, ɪ-/ *noun* [U]
official documents that show who you are: *Do you have any identification with you?*

i·den·ti·fy /aɪ'dentə,faɪ, ɪ-/ *verb* (identifying, identified)
to say who someone is or what something is: *Can you identify the man in the picture?*

i·den·ti·ty /aɪ'dentəti, ɪ-/ *noun* (plural identities)
who someone is or what something is: *The identity of the dead man is still unknown.*

id·i·om /'ɪdiəm/ *noun*
a group of words which have a special meaning when they are used together: *To "have cold feet about something" is an English idiom which means to be worried or nervous about doing something.*

id·i·ot /'ɪdiət/ *noun*
a stupid person ≫ compare FOOL¹

i·dle /'aɪdl/ *adjective*
1 not working or being used: *The machines are sitting idle in the factory.*
2 lazy

i·dol /'aɪdl/ *noun*
1 a famous person who you admire very much
2 an image or object that people pray to as a god

i.e. /ˌaɪ 'i/
a short way to write that you want to explain what you mean by something: *The movie is for adults only, i.e. people over the age of 18.*

if /ɪf; *weak* əf/
1 used for saying what might happen: *If you want to catch the bus, you should go now.* | *If it snows, we will come tomorrow.*
2 whether: *I don't know if he will come or not.*
3 whenever: *I always visit them if I go to the city.*
4 **as if** used when you are describing something: *It looks as if it is going to rain.* | *He talks to me as if I'm stupid.*
5 **if I were you** said when you are giving advice to someone: *If I were you, I'd buy a bigger car.*
6 **do you mind if** a polite way of asking someone if you can do something: *Do you mind if I smoke?*

ig·no·rance /'ɪgnərəns/ *noun* [U]
the state of being without knowledge or education

ig·no·rant /'ɪgnərənt/ *adjective*
not knowing very much; not educated: *Students can be ignorant **about** other countries.*

ig·nore /ɪg'nɔr/ *verb* (**ignoring, ignored**)
to not pay any attention to someone or something: *She ignored me at the party.*

I'll /aɪl/
I will; I shall: *I'll come with you.*

ill /ɪl/ *adjective*
1 not feeling healthy; sick: *She can't go to work because she is ill.*
2 **ill at ease** nervous or embarrassed: *He seems to be ill at ease with me.*

il·le·gal /ɪ'ligəl/ *adjective*
not allowed by law: *It is illegal to steal things.*
≫ opposite LEGAL —**illegally** *adverb*

il·leg·i·ble /ɪ'lɛdʒəbəl/ *adjective*
not able to be read: *His writing is illegible.*
≫ opposite LEGIBLE

il·lit·er·ate /ɪ'lɪtərɪt/ *adjective*
not able to read or write

ill·ness /'ɪlnɪs/ *noun* (*plural* **illnesses**)
a disease of the body or mind: *He suffers from mental illness.*

il·lus·trate /'ɪlə,streɪt/ *verb* (**illustrating, illustrated**)
1 to explain something by giving an example
2 to add pictures to a book or magazine: *The book was illustrated with color drawings.*

il·lus·tra·tion /ˌɪlə'streɪʃən/ *noun*
a picture in a book or magazine

I'm /aɪm/
I am: *I'm very pleased to meet you.*

im·age /'ɪmɪdʒ/ *noun*
1 the way a person or organization appears to other people: *The company wants to change its image.*
2 a picture you see through a camera, on television, or in a mirror
3 a picture of something that you have in your mind

i·mag·i·nar·y /ɪ'mædʒə,nɛri/ *adjective*
not real; existing only in your mind: *He wrote a story about an imaginary world.*

i·mag·i·na·tion /ɪ,mædʒə'neɪʃən/ *noun* [U]
the ability to form pictures or ideas in your mind: *You didn't really see it. It was only your imagination.*

i·mag·ine /ɪ'mædʒɪn/ *verb* (**imagining, imagined**)
1 to form pictures and ideas in your mind: *Imagine what you would do if you had a lot of money.*
2 to have a false or wrong idea about something: *John thinks that we don't like him, but he is just imagining things.*

im·i·tate /'ɪmə,teɪt/ *verb* (**imitating, imitated**)
to do something in the same way as someone or something else: *He always tries to imitate Elvis.*

im·i·ta·tion /ˌɪmə'teɪʃən/ *noun*
a copy of something: *This isn't a real gun. It's an imitation.*

im·ma·ture /ˌɪmə'tʃʊr, -'tʊr/ *adjective*
not behaving in a way that is suitable for your age: *Don't be so immature!* ≫ opposite MATURE[1]

im·me·di·ate /ɪ'midiɪt/ *adjective*
happening or done at once: *Our immediate concern was to stop the fire.*

im·me·di·ate·ly /ɪ'midiɪtli/ *adverb*
now and with no delay: *I need to see you immediately.*

im·mense /ɪˈmɛns/ *adjective*
very large: *The size of the house was immense.*
≫ compare ENORMOUS

im·mense·ly /ɪˈmɛnsli/ *adverb*
very much: *I enjoyed the concert immensely.*

im·mi·grant /ˈɪməɡrənt/ *noun*
someone from another country who comes to
your country to live ≫ compare EMIGRANT

immigrate /ˈɪməɡreɪt/ *verb*
to come to live in another country: *Juan immi-
grated **to** the U.S. last year.* ≫ compare
EMIGRATE, MIGRATE

im·mi·gra·tion /ˌɪməˈɡreɪʃən/ *noun* [U]
the act of going to live in another country: *The
government wants to control immigration.*
≫ compare EMIGRATION

im·mor·al /ɪˈmɔrəl, ɪˈmɑr-/ *adjective*
bad or wicked and not acceptable to other people

im·mu·nize /ˈɪmyəˌnaɪz/ *verb*
(**immunizing, immunized**)
to protect someone from a disease by giving
him or her a weak form of the disease using a
special needle —**immunization** *noun* [U]

im·pa·tient /ɪmˈpeɪʃənt/ *adjective*
annoyed because you want something to happen now so you do not have to wait: *With the
delay, everyone was beginning to get impatient.*
≫ opposite PATIENT[1]

im·per·a·tive /ɪmˈpɛrət̮ɪv/ *noun, adjective*
the form of a verb that you use when you tell
someone to do something: *In the sentence
"Come here!", "come" is in the imperative.*

im·po·lite /ˌɪmpəˈlaɪt/ *adjective*
not polite; rude: *It would be impolite not to call
her back.* ≫ opposite POLITE

im·port[1] /ɪmˈpɔrt/ *verb*
to bring goods into a country to be sold or
used: *We import oil from other countries.*
≫ compare EXPORT[1]

import[2] /ˈɪmpɔrt/ *noun*
something that is brought into a country to be
sold or used: *Machinery is one of our main
imports.* ≫ compare EXPORT[2]

im·por·tance /ɪmˈpɔrt⌐ns, -ˈpɔrtn̩s/
noun [U]
great value or power: *I understand the importance **of** a good education.*

im·por·tant /ɪmˈpɔrt⌐nt, -ˈpɔrtn̩t/
adjective

1 very useful or valuable: *We had an important meeting today.*
2 having power or influence: *She is an important person in the company.* —**importantly**
adverb

im·pos·si·ble /ɪmˈpɑsəbəl/ *adjective*
not possible; not able to be done or happen: *It
is impossible to sleep with all the noise.*
≫ opposite POSSIBLE —**impossibly** *adverb*

im·press /ɪmˈprɛs/ *verb*
to make someone feel admiration and respect:
*I was very impressed **by** your work.*

im·pres·sion /ɪmˈprɛʃən/ *noun*
1 the opinion or feeling that you have about
someone or something: *It is important to **make**
a good impression on people.*
2 be under the impression that to think that
something is true when it is not: *I was under
the impression that he was from Germany.*

im·pres·sive /ɪmˈprɛsɪv/ *adjective*
very good and causing admiration: *He gave an
impressive performance.*

im·pris·on /ɪmˈprɪzən/ *verb*
to put someone in prison: *He was imprisoned
for two years.*

im·pris·on·ment /ɪmˈprɪzənmənt/
noun [U]
the state of being in prison: *He was given two
years' imprisonment.*

im·prove /ɪmˈpruv/ *verb* (**improving,
improved**)
to become better, or make something better:
My tennis is improving.

im·prove·ment /ɪmˈpruvmənt/ *noun*
1 a change which shows that something is
becoming better: *Her health is showing signs
of improvement.*
2 a change which makes something better:
We want to make some home improvements.

im·pulse /ˈɪmpʌls/ *noun*
a sudden desire to do something: *She had an
impulse to buy a new dress.*

im·pul·sive /ɪmˈpʌlsɪv/ *adjective*
doing things without thinking about the results:
I do not want to make an impulsive decision.

in /ɪn; *weak* ən, n/ *preposition*
1 for showing where someone or something is:
They were sitting in the kitchen. | *He once lived
in Mexico.* —see color picture on page 194
2 surrounded by something: *We took a walk in
the rain.* | *I dropped my keys in the water.*

3 using: *She spoke in a quiet voice.* | *The words were written in pencil.* | *They were speaking in French.*
4 during a period of time: *The house was built in the 1950s.* | *His birthday is in June.*
5 after a period of time: *I'll be ready in a few minutes.* | *She will be home in an hour.*
6 inside a building where you live or work: *Mrs. Jones is not in right now.*
7 working at a particular job: *She is in sales.*
8 wearing: *Who's the woman in the black dress?*
9 **in all** in total: *There were twenty of us in all.*

in·ac·cu·rate /ɪn'ækyərɪt/ *adjective*
not correct; having mistakes in it: *He gave us an inaccurate description of the car.* ≫ opposite ACCURATE

in·ad·e·quate /ɪn'ædəkwɪt/ *adjective*
not good enough for something: *The medical care we received was inadequate.* ≫ opposite ADEQUATE

in·ap·pro·pri·ate /ˌɪnə'proupriɪt/ *adjective*
not suitable or correct for a particular purpose: *Those clothes are inappropriate* **for** *work.* ≫ opposite APPROPRIATE

in·ca·pa·ble /ɪn'keɪpəbəl/ *adjective*
not able to do something: *Since the accident she has been incapable* **of** *moving her legs.* ≫ opposite CAPABLE

inch /ɪntʃ/ *noun* (*plural* **inches**)
a measure of length, equal to 2.45 centimeters: *There are 12 inches* (=12 in.) *in one foot.*

in·ci·dent /'ɪnsədənt/ *noun*
an event or something that happens

in·ci·den·tal·ly /ˌɪnsə'dɛntli/ *adverb*
used when you are giving more information, or when you begin talking about a new subject: *I saw Peter today. Incidentally, he wants us to come for lunch next week.*

in·clined /ɪn'klaɪnd/ *adjective*
to be inclined to do something to be likely to do something, or to want to do something: *He is inclined to get angry when someone does not agree with him.*

in·clude /ɪn'klud/ *verb* (**including, included**)
1 to have something as part of a whole: *The price of the trip includes food.* | *The group included several women.* ≫ opposite EXCLUDE
2 to make someone or something part of a larger group: *I included my uncle on my list of people to invite.*

in·clud·ing /ɪn'kludɪŋ/ *preposition*
used for showing that someone or something is part of a larger group: *The whole family is going, including the children.* [=they are going too] ≫ opposite EXCLUDING

in·come /'ɪnkʌm, 'ɪŋ-/ *noun*
all the money you earn: *What is your present income?*

income tax /'.. ˌ./ *noun*
money taken by the government from what you earn

in·com·plete /ˌɪnkəm'plit/ *adjective*
not finished; not having all its parts: *The work is incomplete.* | *He wrote an incomplete sentence.* ≫ opposite COMPLETE[1]

in·con·ven·ience[1] /ˌɪnkən'vinyəns/ *noun*
something that causes you problems or difficulty: *I hope the delay won't cause any inconvenience.*

inconvenience[2] *verb* (**inconveniencing, inconvenienced**)
to cause problems or difficulties for someone: *Am I inconveniencing you by staying here?*

in·con·ven·ient /ˌɪnkən'vinyənt/ *adjective*
causing problems or difficulty: *Is this an inconvenient time for me to visit?* ≫ opposite CONVENIENT

in·cor·rect /ˌɪnkə'rɛkt/ *adjective*
not right; wrong: *The answer is incorrect.* ≫ opposite CORRECT[1]

in·crease[1] /ɪn'kris/ *verb* (**increasing, increased**)
1 to become more in amount or number: *Prices have increased this year.*
2 to make something more in amount or number: *Smoking increases your chance of getting cancer.* ≫ opposite DECREASE[1]

increase[2] /'ɪŋkris/ *noun*
a rise in number or amount: *We have seen an increase* **in** *crime.* ≫ opposite DECREASE[2]

in·creas·ing·ly /ɪn'krisɪŋli/ *adverb*
more and more: *It's becoming increasingly difficult to find work.*

in·cred·i·ble /ɪn'krɛdəbəl/ *adjective*
1 very good: *The food here is incredible!*
2 very large in amount or impressive: *He won an incredible amount of money.*
3 very strange or difficult to believe: *She told us an incredible story.* —**incredibly** *adverb* ≫ compare AMAZING

in·deed /ɪnˈdid/ adverb
1 used for emphasizing a word, statement, or question: *"Did he really say that?" "He did indeed."* | *He claims that the payments have indeed been made.*
2 used for giving more information to what you have said: *I do not know where Sam is; indeed, I haven't seen him for weeks.*

in·def·i·nite /ɪnˈdɛfənɪt/ adjective
not clear or definite: *I will be away for an indefinite period of time.* [=I do not know how long I will be away]

in·de·pend·ence /ˌɪndɪˈpɛndəns/ noun [U]
1 the freedom to take care of yourself without needing other people: *Older people want to keep their independence.*
2 political freedom from the control of another country: *America declared its independence in 1776.*

Independence Day /ˌ..ˈ.. ˌ./ noun
a national holiday on July 4 in the U.S., when Americans celebrate their country's independence from Britain

in·de·pend·ent /ˌɪndɪˈpɛndənt/ adjective
1 able to take care of yourself without needing other people: *Although she is young, she is very independent.* ≫ opposite DEPENDENT[1]
2 free and not controlled by another country: *India became independent from Britain in 1947.* —independently adverb

in·dex /ˈɪndɛks/ noun (plural indexes or indices /ˈɪndɪsiz/)
a list at the end of a book which tells you what can be found in the book, and on what page

index fin·ger /ˈ.. ˌ./ noun
the finger next to your thumb

in·di·cate /ˈɪndəˌkeɪt/ verb (indicating, indicated)
1 to show that something is likely to be true: *Our studies indicate that men will buy the bigger model.*
2 to point at something: *Please indicate which one you have chosen.*

in·di·ca·tion /ˌɪndəˈkeɪʃən/ noun
a sign that something exists or may be true: *Did he give you any indication that he was unhappy?*

in·di·ces /ˈɪndəˌsiz/
the plural of **index**

indirect /ˌɪndəˈrɛkt, -daɪ-/ adjective
1 not directly relating to something: *The acci-*

dent was an indirect result of the heavy rain. | *She made some indirect criticism of students' work.*
2 not using the shortest or straightest way to get to a place: *We took an indirect route to avoid the traffic.* ≫ opposite DIRECT[1] —indirectly adverb

in·di·vid·u·al[1] /ˌɪndəˈvɪdʒuəl/ noun
a person, not a group: *The rights of the individual must be protected.*

individual[2] adjective
for one person: *The children had individual desks.* | *Students need individual attention.* —individually adverb

in·door /ˈɪndɔr/ adjective
inside a building: *The school has an indoor swimming pool.* ≫ opposite OUTDOOR

in·doors /ˌɪnˈdɔrz/ adverb
into or inside a building: *Let's stay indoors today.* ≫ opposite OUTDOORS

in·dus·tri·al /ɪnˈdʌstriəl/ adjective
relating to industry, or having a lot of industries: *We have a plan for getting rid of industrial waste.*

in·dus·try /ˈɪndəstri/ noun (plural industries)
the making of goods in factories: *What are the important industries in the town?*

in·fant /ˈɪnfənt/ noun
a baby

in·fect /ɪnˈfɛkt/ verb
to give someone a disease: *I spoke to a man who was infected with the disease.*

in·fec·tion /ɪnˈfɛkʃən/ noun
a disease or sickness: *My son has an ear infection.*

in·fec·tious /ɪnˈfɛkʃəs/ adjective
an infectious disease can be passed from one person to another

in·fe·ri·or /ɪnˈfɪriɚ/ adjective
worse than other things; very bad ≫ compare SUPERIOR

in·fi·nite /ˈɪnfənɪt/ adjective
very large or great and having no limits: *Some people believe the universe is infinite.*

in·fi·nite·ly /ˈɪnfənɪtli/ adverb
very much: *I feel infinitely better today.*

in·fin·i·tive /ɪnˈfɪnətɪv/ noun
the part of a verb which is used with the word **to**: *In the sentence "I want to go," "to go" is an infinitive.*

in·flate /ɪnˈfleɪt/ *verb* (inflating, inflated)
to fill something with air so that it becomes larger: *I need a pump to inflate the tire.*

in·flu·ence¹ /ˈɪnfluəns/ *noun*
1 the power to affect the way someone or something behaves, thinks, or develops: *Her parents have a strong influence on her.*
2 **be a bad influence, be a good influence** to make someone behave badly, or behave in a better way, because of how you behave ·
3 **be under the influence of something** to be drunk or feeling the effects of drugs

influence² *verb* (influencing, influenced)
to have an effect on the way someone or something behaves, thinks, or develops: *I do not want to influence your decision.*

in·flu·en·tial /ˌɪnfluˈɛnʃəl/ *adjective*
important and having the power to change someone or something: *She is an influential politician in this city.*

in·flu·en·za /ˌɪnfluˈɛnzə/ *noun* [U]
the FLU

in·form /ɪnˈfɔrm/ *verb*
to tell someone about something: *Our teacher informed us that the school will be closed on Monday.*

in·for·mal /ɪnˈfɔrməl/ *adjective*
easy, relaxed, and friendly: *We had an informal meeting at my house.* ≫ opposite FORMAL

in·for·ma·tion /ˌɪnfəˈmeɪʃən/ *noun* [U]
facts; knowledge: *Can you give me some information **about** this machine? | He told us an important piece of information about the plan.*

in·gre·di·ent /ɪnˈgridiənt/ *noun*
something that you add when you are making something, especially in cooking: *Flour, milk, and eggs are the main ingredients.*

in·hab·it /ɪnˈhæbɪt/ *verb*
to live in a place: *The country is inhabited by 20 million people.*

in·hab·it·ant /ɪnˈhæbətənt/ *noun*
someone who lives in a place: *The town has only 250 inhabitants.*

in·her·it /ɪnˈhɛrɪt/ *verb*
to receive something from someone when he or she dies: *He inherited the farm **from** his parents.*

in·her·i·tance /ɪnˈhɛrɪtəns/ *noun*
money or other things that you receive from someone after he or she has died

i·ni·tial¹ /ɪˈnɪʃəl/ *noun*
the first letter of a name, used to represent the name: *His name is John Smith, so his initials are J.S.*

initial² *adjective*
first; at the beginning: *The initial plan was to build a new hospital.*

in·i·tial·ly /ɪˈnɪʃəli/ *adverb*
at first: *Initially, my new job seemed strange.*

in·ject /ɪnˈdʒɛkt/ *verb*
to put a liquid medicine into your body using a special needle

in·jec·tion /ɪnˈdʒɛkʃən/ *noun*
an act of putting liquid medicine into your body using a special needle: *The nurse **gave** me **an** injection.*

in·jure /ˈɪndʒɚ/ *verb* (injuring, injured)
to harm or wound a person or animal: *Two people were injured in the accident. | I injured myself playing football.* ≫ compare HURT¹ —injured *adjective*

in·ju·ry /ˈɪndʒəri/ *noun* (plural injuries)
a wound: *The accident caused serious injuries.*

in·jus·tice /ɪnˈdʒʌstɪs/ *noun* [U]
a situation where you are not treated fairly: *He is determined to fight injustice in the government.* ≫ opposite JUSTICE

ink /ɪŋk/ *noun*
a colored liquid used for writing or printing

inn /ɪn/ *noun*
a small hotel, usually not in a city

in·ner /ˈɪnɚ/ *adjective*
on the inside, or in the middle: *I have a problem with my inner ear.* [=the part inside my head] ≫ compare OUTER

in·no·cence /ˈɪnəsəns/ *noun* [U]
the fact of not being guilty of a crime: *He had to prove his innocence.* ≫ compare GUILT

in·no·cent /ˈɪnəsənt/ *adjective*
not guilty of a crime: *No one believed that she was innocent.* ≫ compare GUILTY

in·quire /ɪnˈkwaɪɚ/ *verb* (inquiring, inquired)
to ask for information about something: *I am writing to inquire **about** the price of the house.*

in·quir·y /ɪnˈkwaɪəri, ˈɪŋkwəri/ *noun* (plural inquiries)
a question you ask for information: *People are making inquiries **about** the job.*

in·quis·i·tive /ɪnˈkwɪzətɪv/ *adjective*
interested in many different things and wanting to know more about them

in·sane /ɪnˈseɪn/ *adjective*
completely crazy, stupid or dangerous: *He must be insane to drive his car so fast.* ≫ opposite SANE

in·sect /ˈɪnsɛkt/ *noun*
a very small creature such as a fly, that has six legs

in·sert /ɪnˈsɜt/ *verb*
to put something into something else: *Insert the key in the lock and turn it to the right.*

in·side¹ /ˈɪnsaɪd/ *noun*
1 the inside the inner part of something: *The outside of an orange is bitter, but the inside is sweet.* | *Have you seen the inside of the house?* ≫ compare OUTSIDE¹
2 inside out with the inside part of something on the outside: *You have your shirt on inside out.*

inside² /ɪnˈsaɪd/ *adverb, preposition*
in or onto something: *Don't stand there in the rain – come on inside.* | *She put the money inside her bag.* ≫ compare OUTSIDE²

inside³ /ˈɪnsaɪd/ *adjective*
on the inside of something, or contained by something: *The inside walls of the house are painted white.* ≫ compare OUTSIDE³

in·sist /ɪnˈsɪst/ *verb*
1 to say firmly that something is true, especially when other people think it is not: *He insists that he is right.*
2 to say something that must happen or be done: *She insisted on seeing the manager.*

in·spect /ɪnˈspɛkt/ *verb*
to look at something carefully, to see if there is anything wrong: *Inspect the car before you buy it.*

in·spec·tion /ɪnˈspɛkʃən/ *noun*
a careful look to see if there is anything wrong with something

in·spec·tor /ɪnˈspɛktɚ/ *noun*
1 an official whose job is to visit places and see if there is anything wrong with them: *A health inspector visited our restaurant.*
2 a police officer

in·spire /ɪnˈspaɪɚ/ *verb* (**inspiring, inspired**)
to make someone want to do something: *He inspired us to think for ourselves.*

in·stall /ɪnˈstɔl/ *verb*
to put in new machinery so it can be used: *We installed a new computer system in the office.* —**installation** *noun* [U]

in·stall·ment /ɪnˈstɔlmənt/ *noun*
1 one of the regular payments that you make for something until you pay all the money that you owe: *She is paying for her car in installments.*
2 one of the parts of a long story in a magazine, newspaper etc.

in·stance /ˈɪnstəns/ *noun*
for instance for example: *She has a lot of friends. For instance, 30 people came to her party.*

in·stant¹ /ˈɪnstənt/ *adjective*
1 happening or working with no delay: *The new movie was an instant success.*
2 very quick to prepare: *I only have instant coffee.*

instant² *noun*
a moment: *He waited an instant before answering the question.*

in·stant·ly /ˈɪnstəntli/ *adverb*
with no delay; immediately: *He was killed instantly.*

in·stead /ɪnˈstɛd/ *adverb*
in place of someone or something else: *I don't have a pen, so I used a pencil instead.* | *Can you come on Saturday instead of Sunday?*

in·stinct /ˈɪnstɪŋkt/ *noun*
a natural ability to behave in a particular way without having to think about it or learn it: *Cats have the instinct to hunt for food.*

in·sti·tute /ˈɪnstətut/ *noun*
an organization that studies a particular thing such as science or education

in·sti·tu·tion /ˌɪnstəˈtuʃən/ *noun*
a large organization such as a school, hospital, or bank

in·struct /ɪnˈstrʌkt/ *verb*
1 to teach someone something
2 instruct someone to do something to tell someone that he or she must do something: *I've been instructed to wait here.*

in·struc·tion /ɪnˈstrʌkʃən/ *noun*
information or advice that tells you how to do something: *Read the instructions on the box.*

in·struc·tor /ɪnˈstrʌktɚ/ *noun*
someone who teaches a skill or an activity: *She is a swimming instructor.*

in·stru·ment /'ɪnstrəmənt/ *noun*
1 a tool for doing a particular thing: *Are these his medical instruments?*
2 an object used for making music: *A piano is a musical instrument.*

in·stru·men·tal /ˌɪnstrə'mɛntl/ *adjective*
1 **be instrumental in something** to be important in making something happen: *Her support was instrumental in passing the law.*
2 instrumental music only uses musical instruments with no human voices

in·sult[1] /ɪn'sʌlt/ *verb*
to be impolite to someone and offend him or her

insult[2] /'ɪnsʌlt/ *noun*
an impolite remark or action that offends someone: *He shouted insults at the police.* ≫ compare COMPLIMENT[1]

in·sur·ance /ɪn'ʃʊrəns/ *noun* [U]
money paid to a company that then agrees to pay an amount of money if something bad happens to you or your property: *Do you have car insurance?*

in·sure /ɪn'ʃʊr/ *verb* (insuring, insured)
to pay money for INSURANCE: *The house is insured against fire.*

in·tel·li·gence /ɪn'tɛlədʒəns/ *noun* [U]
the ability to learn and understand things: *She is a child of high intelligence.*

in·tel·li·gent /ɪn'tɛlədʒənt/ *adjective*
able to learn and understand things quickly

in·tend /ɪn'tɛnd/ *verb*
to plan to do something: *Do you intend to marry him?*

in·tense /ɪn'tɛns/ *adjective*
having a very strong or serious effect on someone: *His intense love for her caused the argument.*

in·ten·tion /ɪn'tɛnʃən/ *noun*
something that you plan to do: *I have no intention of going there.*

in·ter·ac·tive /ˌɪntə'ræktɪv/ *adjective*
involving communication between a computer or other machine and the person using it

in·ter·est[1] /'ɪntrɪst/ *noun*
1 [U] a desire to know more about something: *We both have an interest in music.*
2 something you do or study because you enjoy it: *What are her interests?*

interest[2] *verb*
to make someone want to know more about something: *Her story interested me.*

in·ter·est·ed /'ɪntrɪstɪd, 'ɪntəˌrɛstɪd/ *adjective*
wanting to do something or know more about something: *He is very interested in history.*

in·ter·est·ing /'ɪntrɪstɪŋ, 'ɪntəˌrɛstɪŋ/ *adjective*
unusual or exciting so that you pay attention: *That is an interesting idea.* ≫ compare BORING

in·ter·fere /ˌɪntə'fɪr/ *verb* (interfering, interfered)
1 to get involved in a situation when you are not wanted or needed: *Just go away and stop interfering!*
2 **interfere with** to prevent something from happening: *The rain interfered with our plans to go out.*

in·te·ri·or[1] /ɪn'tɪriə/ *noun*
the inside of something: *His car has a brown leather interior.* ≫ compare: EXTERIOR[2]

interior[2] *adjective*
on the inside of something: *The interior walls of the house were white.* ≫ compare EXTERIOR[2]

in·ter·me·di·ate /ˌɪntə'midiɪt/ *adjective*
on the middle level between two others: *I have a class in intermediate Spanish.*

in·ter·nal /ɪn'tɜnl/ *adjective*
of or on the inside: *She has an internal injury from the accident.* ≫ compare EXTERNAL

in·ter·na·tion·al /ˌɪntə'næʃənəl/ *adjective*
for or by many countries: *An international agreement was signed by the countries.* ≫ compare NATIONAL

In·ter·net /'ɪntəˌnɛt/ *noun* [also **the Net**]
the Internet a system in which computers around the world are connected and can exchange information: *Are you on the Internet?*

in·ter·pret /ɪn'tɜprɪt/ *verb*
to put the words spoken in one language into the words of another language: *He is able to interpret from French into English.* ≫ compare TRANSLATE

in·ter·pre·ta·tion /ɪnˌtɜprə'teɪʃən/ *noun*
an explanation for an event or what someone has done

in·ter·pret·er /ɪn'tɜprətə/ *noun*
someone whose job is to put the words spoken in one language into the words of another language

in·ter·ra·cial /ˌɪntəˈreɪʃəl◂/ *adjective*
between different races of people: *The program talked about interracial marriage.*

in·ter·rupt /ˌɪntəˈrʌpt/ *verb*
to say something when someone else is already speaking and cause him or her to stop: *I didn't mean to interrupt you.*

in·ter·rup·tion /ˌɪntəˈrʌpʃən/ *noun*
something that stops you from continuing what you are doing for a short time: *There are too many interruptions at work.*

in·ter·sec·tion /ˈɪntəˌsɛkʃən, ˌɪntəˈsɛkʃən/ *noun*
a place where two streets meet and cross each other

in·ter·state¹ /ˈɪntəˌsteɪt/ *noun*
a long road that goes between states

interstate² *adjective*
between or involving different states in the U.S.

in·ter·val /ˈɪntəvəl/ *noun*
1 a time or space between two events or activities: *The theater opened again after an interval of two years.*
2 **at intervals** with a particular amount of time or space between: *Water your plants at regular intervals.*

in·ter·view¹ /ˈɪntəˌvyu/ *noun*
1 a meeting to decide if someone is good enough for a job: *When is your job interview?*
2 an occasion when a famous person is asked questions about his or her life, opinions etc.

interview² *verb*
1 to ask someone questions to see if he or she is good enough for a job
2 to ask a famous person questions about his or her life, opinions etc.

in·to /ˈɪntə; *before vowels* ˈɪntʊ; *strong* ˈɪntu/ *preposition*
1 so as to be inside or in something: *They went into the house.* | *He fell into the water.* —see color picture on page 194
2 involved in an activity: *I want to go into business for myself.*
3 in a different form: *She made the material into a dress.* | *He rolled the dough into a ball.*
4 used when dividing one number by another number: *Five goes into twenty four times.*

in·tran·si·tive /ɪnˈtrænzətɪv/ *adjective, noun*
not having an object; where the action is not done to a person or thing: *In the sentence,*

"When he had finished, he sat down," "finished" and "sat down" are intransitive verbs. ➤ compare TRANSITIVE

in·tro·duce /ˌɪntrəˈdus/ *verb*
(introducing, introduced)
1 to cause two people to meet each other for the first time, and tell each person the name of the other person: *He introduced his friend to me.*
2 to make something happen for the first time: *The government is introducing a new law.*

in·tro·duc·tion /ˌɪntrəˈdʌkʃən/ *noun*
1 the act of making something happen for the first time: *The introduction of computers into the school is a good idea.*
2 a piece of writing at the beginning of a book that tells you what the rest of the book is about

in·vade /ɪnˈveɪd/ *verb* **(invading, invaded)**
to attack and enter a country or place with an army: *The army invaded the city.*

in·va·lid /ˈɪnvəlɪd/ *noun*
someone who needs to be taken care of because he or she is very old, sick, or injured

in·va·sion /ɪnˈveɪʒən/ *noun*
the act of an army attacking and entering a country or place

in·vent /ɪnˈvɛnt/ *verb*
to think of an idea, or to make something for the first time: *Who invented the telephone?*

in·ven·tion /ɪnˈvɛnʃən/ *noun*
1 the act of thinking of an idea, or of making something for the first time
2 something completely new that is made for the first time: *This machine is their latest invention.*

in·ven·tor /ɪnˈvɛntə/ *noun*
someone who thinks of and makes something completely new

in·vest /ɪnˈvɛst/ *verb*
to give money to a bank, business etc. so that you can get a profit later —**investment** *noun*

in·ves·ti·gate /ɪnˈvɛstəˌgeɪt/ *verb*
(investigating, investigated)
to search for information about something by looking, asking questions etc.: *The police are investigating the crime.*

in·ves·ti·ga·tion /ɪnˌvɛstəˈgeɪʃən/ *noun*
a search for information about something such as a crime or problem: *There will be an investigation into the cause of the accident.*

in·vis·i·ble /ɪn'vɪzəbəl/ *adjective*
not able to be seen: *Air is invisible.* ≫ opposite
VISIBLE

in·vi·ta·tion /ˌɪnvə'teɪʃən/ *noun*
an offer, in words or writing, of a chance to do
something or to go somewhere: *Did you get an
invitation to the party?*

in·vite /ɪn'vaɪt/ *verb* (**inviting, invited**)
to ask someone to come to a party, meal etc.:
She invited us to her house for lunch.

> NOTE: People do not use the verb **invite**
> when they are asking you if you want to go
> somewhere or do something. Instead they
> say things like, "Would you like to come to
> dinner at my house?" or, "Do you want to
> come to a party tonight?" (NOTE **never** say,
> "I invite you ...")

in·volve /ɪn'vɑlv/ *verb* (**involving, involved**)
1 to include or affect someone or something:
I saw an accident involving four cars.
2 to include something as a necessary part of
something else: *The job will involve a lot of hard
work.*

in·volved /ɪn'vɑlvd/ *adjective*
be involved in something to take part in something: *She is involved in politics.*

in·ward¹ /'ɪnwərd/ *adjective* (*also* **inwards**)
1 on or toward the inside of something
≫ compare OUTWARD¹
2 not shown to other people: *I had an inward
feeling of happiness.*

inward² *adverb*
toward the inside of something: *The door
swings inward.* ≫ compare OUTWARD²

IOU /ˌaɪ oʊ'yu/ *noun*
a short way to write "I owe you"; a piece of
paper that you sign to show that you owe someone money

IQ /ˌaɪ 'kyu/ *noun*
Intelligence, Quotient; the level of someone's
intelligence, with 100 being the average

i·ron¹ /'aɪərn/ *noun*
1 an object that is heated and pressed on
clothes to make them smooth
2 [U] a hard heavy metal used for making steel

iron² *verb*
to make your clothes smooth using a hot iron:
Do you want me to iron your shirt?

iron

iron

iron³ *adjective*
made of iron: *The gate has iron bars.*

i·ron·ing /'aɪərnɪŋ/ *noun* [U]
the activity of making clothes smooth using a
hot iron

ironing board /'... ,./ *noun*
a narrow board on which you make your clothes
smooth using a hot iron

ir·reg·u·lar /ɪ'rɛgyələ/ *adjective*
1 not happening or being repeated at the
same times: *He was in the hospital because of
an irregular heartbeat.*
2 an irregular noun or verb does not change
its form in the same way as most nouns or
verbs: *"Child" and "person" are irregular nouns*
≫ opposite REGULAR

ir·ri·gate /'ɪrə,geɪt/ *verb* (**irrigating,
irrigated**)
to make water flow to dry land or crops

ir·ri·ga·tion /ˌɪrə'geɪʃən/ *noun* [U]
the act of making water flow to dry land or
crops

ir·ri·tate /'ɪrə,teɪt/ *verb* (**irritating,
irritated**)
1 to make someone angry or annoyed: *The
noise of the children was irritating me.*
2 to make a part of your body painful: *The sun
irritates my eyes.*

IRS /ˌaɪ ɑr 'ɛs/ *noun*
the IRS Internal Revenue Service; the government organization in the U.S. that deals with
taxes

is /z, s, əz; *strong* ɪz/ *verb*
the part of the verb **be** that you use with **he,
she** and **it**: *She is Peter's sister.* | *He's* (=he is)
her brother. | *That boy's* (=boy is) *in my class.* |
She isn't (=is not) *very smart.*

Is·lam /ˈɪzlɑm, ɪzˈlɑm, ˈɪslɑm/ *noun*
the religion started by Muhammed

is·land /ˈaɪlənd/ *noun*
a piece of land surrounded by water

is·n't /ˈɪzənt/
is not: *She isn't coming.* | *It's a great day, isn't it?*

i·so·late /ˈaɪsəˌleɪt/ *verb* (isolating, isolated)
to make or keep one person or thing away from other people or things: *The sick man was isolated to stop the disease from spreading.*

i·so·lat·ed /ˈaɪsəˌleɪtɪd/ *adjective*
far away from other things: *He lives on an isolated farm.*

is·sue¹ /ˈɪʃu/ *verb* (issuing, issued)
1 to make an official statement: *The government issued a warning about the water.*
2 to supply something to someone: *The team was issued with new shoes.*

issue² *noun*
1 a subject or problem that people think is important: *We will raise the issue (=begin talking about it) with them.*
2 a magazine or newspaper that is printed on a particular day, month etc.: *Do you have the newest issue of Newsweek?*

it /ɪt/ *pronoun*
1 the thing, animal, or person that the sentence is about: *I lost my book, and I can't find it anywhere.* | *It was an interesting book.*
2 used when talking about the weather, time, and dates: *It is very hot today.* | *It's almost four o'clock.* | *It is Thursday.*
3 used when talking about a fact or something that happens: *It's a long way to town.* | *"What's that noise?" "It's a car."*
4 used when giving the name of a person or thing that is not already known: *"Who is it?" "It's me, Peter."* | *"What's that?" "It is a vegetable."*

itch¹ /ɪtʃ/ *verb*
to have an unpleasant feeling that makes you want to rub your skin: *The insect bite itched all night.*

itch² *noun*
an unpleasant feeling on your skin that makes you want to rub it: *I've got an itch on my back.*

itch·y /ˈɪtʃi/ *adjective* (itchier, itchiest)
having an unpleasant feeling on your skin that makes you want to rub it

it'd /ˈɪtəd/
1 it would: *It'd be lovely to see you.*
2 it had: *It'd taken us two hours to get there.*

i·tem /ˈaɪtəm/ *noun*
a single thing in a group: *On the desk there were two books, a pen, and some other items.*

it'll /ˈɪtl/
it will: *It'll soon be time to go.*

it's /ɪts/
1 it is: *It's raining outside.*
2 it has: *It's stopped raining.*

its /ɪts/ *adjective*
of it; belonging to it: *She gave the cat its food.* | *The tree has lost all its leaves.*

> NOTE: Do not confuse **its** (=belonging to it) with **it's** (=it is or it has) which is spelled with a '

it·self /ɪtˈsɛlf/ *pronoun* (plural **themselves**)
the same thing or animal as the one that the sentence is about: *Your body will try to defend itself against disease.*

I've /aɪv/
I have: *I've got two sisters.*

i·vo·ry /ˈaɪvəri/ *noun* [U]
the hard, white substance taken from the long tooth of an ELEPHANT

Jj

jab¹ /dʒæb/ *verb* (jabbing, jabbed)
to push something pointed into or toward something else: *I jabbed the needle into my arm.* | *He kept jabbing his finger into my back until I turned around.*

jab² *noun*
a short quick movement into or toward something else: *I hit him with a jab.*

jack

a car jack   *a phone jack*

jack /dʒæk/ *noun*
a piece of equipment used for lifting something heavy such as a car

jack·et /'dʒækɪt/ *noun*
a short light coat

jack-o'-lan·tern /'dʒæk ə ˌlæntən/ *noun*
a PUMPKIN with holes cut into it to make it look like a face, used as a decoration at HALLOWEEN

jag·ged /'dʒægɪd/ *adjective*
having a rough uneven edge with many sharp points: *He fell onto the jagged rocks.*

jag·uar /'dʒægwɑr/ *noun*
a large wild cat with black spots

jail /dʒeɪl/ *noun*
a prison: *The man was sent to jail.*

jam¹ /dʒæm/ *verb* (jamming, jammed)
1 to push someone or something together into a small space: *I jammed the letters into my pocket.*
2 to fill a place with people or things so nothing can move: *The streets were jammed with cars.*
3 to become stuck and unable to move: *The printer is jammed again.*

jam² *noun*
1 [U] a sweet food made of fruit and sugar, usually eaten on bread
2 a lot of people or things in a small space so nothing can move: *We were stuck in a **traffic jam.***

jan·gle /'dʒæŋgəl/ *verb* (jangling, jangled)
to make a noise like metal hitting metal: *She jangled her keys in her pocket.*

jan·i·tor /'dʒænətə/ *noun*
someone who cleans a building and repairs things in it

Jan·u·ar·y /'dʒænyuˌɛri/ *noun*
the first month of the year

jar /dʒɑr/ *noun*
a round glass container with a lid, used for storing food —see picture at CONTAINER

jav·e·lin /'dʒævəlɪn, -vlɪn/ *noun*
a long pointed stick which is thrown as a sport

jaw /dʒɔ/ *noun*
one of the two bones in your mouth that hold your teeth

jazz /dʒæz/ *noun* [U]
a type of music with a strong beat: *Do you like listening to jazz?*

jeal·ous /'dʒɛləs/ *adjective*
1 feeling unhappy or angry because you want what someone else has: *I was very jealous of Sarah's new shoes.* ≫ compare ENVIOUS
2 feeling angry because someone you love is paying too much attention to someone else: *Her husband gets jealous if she talks to other men.*

jeal·ous·y /'dʒɛləsi/ *noun* [U]
1 the feeling you have when you want something that someone else has ≫ compare ENVY¹
2 the feeling of being angry because someone you love is paying too much attention to someone else

jeans /dʒinz/ *plural noun*
a type of pants made of a strong cotton cloth, usually blue —see color picture on page 190

Jeep /dʒip/ *(trademark) noun*
a car that can travel over rough roads

jeer /dʒɪr/ *verb*
to laugh in a way that is not nice or shout at someone you do not like: *The crowd jeered at the speaker.*

jel·ly /'dʒɛli/ *noun* [U]
a sweet soft food made with fruit and sugar, usually eaten on bread

jel·ly·fish /'dʒɛli,fɪʃ/ *noun* (*plural* **jellyfish** or **jellyfishes**)
a soft sea creature that is almost transparent and has long things hanging down from its body

jerk¹ /dʒɝk/ *verb*
1 to pull something suddenly and quickly: *She jerked the door open.*
2 to move with a quick movement: *Her head jerked when she woke up.*

jerk² *noun*
1 a quick hard pull or sudden movement: *He pulled the cord with a jerk.*
2 a person who you think is not nice: *Jared's a real jerk.*

jer·sey /'dʒɝzi/ *noun* (*plural* **jerseys**)
a shirt worn as part of a sports uniform

Je·sus /'dʒizəs/ *noun* (*also* **Jesus Christ**)
the man on whose life and teachings Christianity is based

jet /dʒɛt/ *noun*
1 a narrow stream of gas, air, or liquid that comes out of a small hole: *Jets of steam came from the ground.*
2 a fast plane with a special engine

jew·el /'dʒuəl/ *noun*
a valuable stone that you wear as a decoration: *She had beautiful jewels around her neck.*

jewelry

earrings
necklace
ring
bracelet

jew·el·ry /'dʒuəlri/ *noun* [U]
things such as rings, gold etc. that you wear on your body for decoration

Jew·ish /'dʒuɪʃ/ *adjective*
belonging to a group of people whose religion is Judaism

jig·saw puz·zle /'dʒɪgsɔ ,pʌzəl/ *noun*
a picture cut into many small pieces that you put together

jin·gle /'dʒɪŋgəl/ *verb* (**jingling, jingled**)
to make a noise by shaking small metal objects together: *The coins jingled in his pocket.*

job /dʒɑb/ *noun*
1 work that you do to earn money: *"What is your job?" "I'm a teacher."* ⨠ compare WORK²
2 a piece of work or a duty that you do: *My job is to take the dog for a walk.*
3 on the job at work or doing work: *How long has he been on the job?*

jock·ey /'dʒɑki/ *noun* (*plural* **jockeys**)
someone who rides a horse in a race

jog¹ /dʒɑg/ *verb* (**jogging, jogged**)
to run slowly, usually for exercise: *She jogs every morning.*

jog² *noun* [U]
a slow, steady run, usually for exercise: *Let's go for a jog.*

jog·ger /'dʒɑgɚ/ *noun*
someone who runs slowly for exercise

join /dʒɔɪn/ *verb*
1 (*also* **join in**) to begin to take part in an activity or game that other people are doing: *I joined in the singing.* | *We are going to play. Do you want to join us?*
2 to connect together; meet: *The pipes join under the bathtub.*
3 to go and do something together with someone else: *Will you join me for dinner?*
4 to become a member of an organization or group: *He joined the army.*
5 join hands to hold each other's hands: *We all joined hands in a circle.*

joint¹ /dʒɔɪnt/ *noun*
1 a part of your body where two bones meet
2 a place where two things are joined together

joint² *adjective*
involving two or more people or groups: *They wrote it together; it was a joint effort.* | *We have a joint bank account.*

joke¹ /dʒouk/ *noun*
1 something funny that you say or do to make someone laugh: *My dad is always telling jokes.*
2 a situation that is so stupid or silly that you become annoyed: *The meeting was a complete joke!*

joke² *verb* (**joking, joked**)
to say things to make people laugh: *He knew that I was only joking.*

jol·ly /'dʒɑli/ *adjective* (**jollier, jolliest**)
happy and nice

jolt¹ /dʒoult/ *noun*
1 a sudden shake or movement: *The train started with a jolt.*

2 a sudden shock or surprise: *A jolt of electricity hit him.*

jolt² *verb*
to move suddenly or roughly: *The truck jolted to a stop.*

jot /dʒɑt/ *verb* (**jotting, jotted**)
jot something down to write something quickly: *I jotted down her address on my newspaper.*

jour·nal /'dʒɜ·nl/ *noun*
1 a newspaper or magazine for a particular subject: *A medical journal is missing from the library.*
2 a written record of the things you do each day

jour·nal·is·m /'dʒɜ·nl,ɪzəm/ *noun* [U]
the job of writing for a newspaper, magazine, television, or radio

jour·nal·ist /'dʒɜ·nl-ɪst/ *noun*
someone who writes for a newspaper, magazine, television, or radio

jour·ney /'dʒɜ·ni/ *noun* (*plural* **journeys**)
a trip, usually a long one: *He is on a journey across Africa.*

joy /dʒɔɪ/ *noun*
1 [U] great happiness or pleasure: *She was full of joy when the baby was born.*
2 (*plural* **joys**) something that gives great happiness: *Her child is a joy to her.*

joy·ful /'dʒɔɪfəl/ *adjective*
very happy: *Her birthday was a joyful occasion.*

joy·stick /'dʒɔɪ,stɪk/ *noun*
a handle that you use to control something in a computer game

Jr. *noun*
a short way to write the word JUNIOR

Ju·da·ism /'dʒudi,ɪzəm, -deɪ-, -də-/ *noun* [U]
the Jewish religion

judge¹ /dʒʌdʒ/ *noun*
1 the official person in a law court who decides how someone is punished: *The judge sent the man to prison for two years.*
2 someone who decides who is the winner of a competition

judge² *verb* (**judging, judged**)
1 to form an opinion about someone, especially after you have thought about it carefully: *How can you judge which dictionary to buy?*
2 to decide who or what is the winner of a

competition: *Who is judging the poetry competition?*

judg·ment /'dʒʌdʒmənt/ *noun*
1 an opinion that you have after thinking about something carefully: *You will have to make your own judgment about what to do.*
2 the official decision made by a judge in a court

ju·do /'dʒudoʊ/ *noun* [U]
a fighting sport in which you try to throw the other person to the ground —see color picture on page 184

jug /dʒʌg/ *noun*
a container with a small opening, for holding liquids

juggle

jug·gle /'dʒʌgəl/ *verb* (**juggling, juggled**)
to keep several things moving through the air by throwing and catching them quickly —**juggler** *noun*

juice /dʒus/ *noun*
the liquid that comes from fruit or vegetables: *Can I have a glass of orange juice?*

juic·y /'dʒusi/ *adjective* (**juicier, juiciest**)
having a lot of juice: *Here is a juicy orange.*

Ju·ly /dʒʊ'laɪ, dʒə-/ *noun*
the seventh month of the year

jum·ble¹ /'dʒʌmbəl/ *noun* [U]
a lot of things that are mixed together in a messy way: *There was a jumble of clothes on the floor.*

jumble² *verb* (**jumbling, jumbled**)
to mix things together in a messy way

jum·bo /'dʒʌmboʊ/ *adjective*
larger than others of the same type: *We flew on a jumbo jet.*

jump¹ /dʒʌmp/ *verb*
1 to push yourself up into the air or over something using your legs: *The children jumped up*

and down with excitement. | *The horse jumped over the fence.* —see color picture on page 189

2 to move suddenly because of fear or surprise: *The loud noise made me jump.*

3 to let yourself drop from a place above the ground: *She jumped out of the window to escape the fire.*

4 to increase suddenly in price or amount: *The price of gas jumped last week.*

jump² *noun*
the act of pushing yourself up into the air or over something using your legs: *He got over the fence in one jump.*

June /dʒuːn/ *noun*
the sixth month of the year

jun·gle /'dʒʌŋgəl/ *noun*
a thick forest with large plants that grow close together

Junior /'dʒuːnyɚ/ *adjective*
used after the name of a man who has the same name as his father ≫ compare SENIOR

jun·ior¹ *adjective*
1 lower in importance or position: *He is a junior member of the company.* ≫ compare SENIOR¹

2 younger: *He married a woman ten years his junior.*

junior² *noun*
a student in the third year of high school or college

junior high school /ˌ.. '. ˌ./
a school in the U.S. for children who are between 12 and 14 or 15 years old

junk /dʒʌŋk/ *noun* [U]
old things that you do not want or cannot use: *That room is full of junk.*

ju·ry /'dʒʊri/ *noun* (*plural* **juries**)
a group of people in a court who decide if someone is guilty or not: *The jury listened carefully to the case.*

just¹ /dʒʌst/ *adverb*
1 a very short time ago: *I just got home.* | *You just missed the bus.*

2 only: *I play tennis just for fun.* | *It happened just a few days ago.*

3 exactly: *You look just like your mother.* | *I have just enough money to buy a stamp.*

4 at the moment; now: *I am just making some coffee. Do you want some?*

5 just about almost: *She walks to school just about every day.* | *I am just about finished.*

6 just a minute, just a second said when asking someone to wait for a short time: *Just a minute, I can't find my keys.*

7 used for emphasizing something you are saying: *Just sit down and shut up!*

8 used for asking or telling someone something in a polite way: *Could you just lift your cup for a second?*

just² *adjective*
fair and right: *He received a just punishment.*

jus·tice /'dʒʌstɪs/ *noun* [U]
1 treatment of people which is fair and right: *She is fighting for freedom and justice.* ≫ opposite INJUSTICE

2 the system of law in a country

kan·ga·roo /ˌkæŋgəˈru/ *noun*
an animal in Australia that has large back legs for jumping and keeps its young in a special pocket of skin —see color picture on page 183

ka·ra·te /kəˈrɑṭi/ *noun* [U]
a fighting sport in which you use your hands and feet to hit and kick

keen /kin/ *adjective*
eager to do something; having a strong interest: *He was keen to do the job well.*

keep /kip/ *verb* (*past tense* **kept,** *past participle* **kept**)
1 to have something and not give it back to the person who had it before: *You can keep the book. I don't need it now.*
2 to continue to have something and not get rid of it: *I kept all her letters through the years.*
3 to make someone or something stay in a place or condition: *They kept her in the hospital for a week.* | *This blanket will keep you warm.*
4 keep doing something to continue doing something: *I keep making the same mistakes.*
5 to delay someone or stop someone from doing something: *What's keeping her?* | *Keep your dog out of my yard!*
6 keep a secret to not tell a secret
7 keep someone up to make someone stay awake: *The loud music is keeping me up.*
8 keep up to move as fast as someone else: *Slow down. I can't keep up!*
9 Keep out! used on signs to tell people that they are not allowed to go into a place

ken·nel /ˈkɛnl/ *noun*
a place where a dog is taken care of while its owner is away

kept /kɛpt/
the PAST TENSE and PAST PARTICIPLE of the verb **keep**

ketch·up /ˈkɛtʃəp, ˈkæ-/ *noun* [U]
a thick red liquid made from TOMATOes

ket·tle /ˈkɛṭl/ *noun*
a metal container used for boiling and pouring water

key¹ /ki/ *noun* (*plural* **keys**)
1 a shaped piece of metal that you put into a lock to open it: *Where are my car keys?*
2 a button on a computer or musical instrument that you press to make it work
3 the key the most important part of a plan or action: *Exercise is the key **to** a healthy body.*

key² *adjective*
very important and necessary for success: *Jobs are the key issue in the election.*

key·board /ˈkibɔrd/ *noun*
a row or several rows of keys on a computer or piano that you press to make it work

key·hole /ˈkihoʊl/ *noun*
the part of a lock that a key goes into

key ring /ˈ. ./ *noun*
a metal ring on which you keep keys

kg
a short way to write the word KILOGRAM

kha·ki /ˈkæki/ *adjective, noun* [U]
a green-brown color, or the cloth of this color

kick¹ /kɪk/ *verb*
1 to hit someone or something using your foot: *He kicked over the boxes.* —see color picture on page 189
2 to move your legs strongly: *The baby is kicking his legs.*
3 kick off to start, or make an event start
4 kick someone out to make someone leave a place: *They kicked Dan out of the club.*

kick² *noun*
1 the act of hitting someone or something using your foot: *If the door won't open, give it a kick.*
2 a feeling of pleasure or excitement: *I get a kick out of ice skating.*

kid¹ /kɪd/ *noun*
1 a child: *How many kids do you have?*
2 a young goat

kid² *verb* (**kidding, kidded**)
to say something to someone as a joke: *I didn't mean that. I was just kidding.*

kid·nap /ˈkɪdnæp/ *verb* (**kidnapping, kidnapped**)
to take someone away by force and ask for money for bringing him or her back safely

kid·nap·per /ˈkɪdnæpɚ/ *noun*
someone who KIDNAPs someone

kid·ney /ˈkɪdni/ *noun* (*plural* **kidneys**)
one of the two parts inside your body that removes waste liquid from your blood

kill /kɪl/ verb
to make a plant, animal, or person die: *Ten people were killed in the car crash.* | *The cat killed the bird.* ≫ compare MURDER¹

kill·er /'kɪlə/ noun
a person, animal, or thing that kills: *Police are searching for the killer.* ≫ compare MURDERER

ki·lo·byte /'kɪlə,baɪt/ noun
a unit for measuring computer information

kil·o·gram /'kɪlə,græm/ noun
a measure of weight, equal to 1,000 grams

ki·lo·me·ter /kɪ'lɑmətə, 'kɪlə,mitə/ noun
a measure of length, equal to 1,000 meters

kin /kɪn/ noun [U]
people in your family: *His next of kin (=his closest relative) was told about his death.*

kind¹ /kaɪnd/ noun
1 a type or sort of person or thing: ***What** kind of car does he have?* | *We sell all kinds of food.* ≫ compare TYPE¹
2 kind of slightly; in some way: *I am kind of sad that I didn't win.*

NOTE: Remember that if you use the singular of **kind¹** it must be followed by a singular noun, and the plural **kinds** must be followed by a plural noun, e.g. *this kind of car, these kinds of cars.*

kind² adjective
helpful, friendly, and nice to other people: *It's very kind of you to help me.* ≫ opposite UNKIND

kind·heart·ed /ˌ. '..◂/ adjective
caring and nice

kind·ly /'kaɪndli/ adverb
in a kind or generous way: *She kindly offered to drive me home.*

kind·ness /'kaɪndnɪs/ noun
kind behavior or a kind action: *Thank you very much for your kindness.*

king /kɪŋ/ noun
a male ruler of a country, especially one from a royal family: *I saw the King of Spain.* ≫ compare QUEEN

king·dom /'kɪŋdəm/ noun
a country ruled by a king or queen

kiss¹ /kɪs/ verb
to touch someone with your lips, as a sign of love or greeting: *He kissed his wife goodbye.*

kiss² noun (plural **kisses**)
the action of touching someone with your lips as a sign of love or greeting: *He gave his daughter a kiss.*

kit /kɪt/ noun
1 a set of tools or equipment used for a particular purpose: *Do you have a tool kit?*
2 a set of small pieces from which you make something: *We made a model plane from a kit.*

kitch·en /'kɪtʃən/ noun
a room where you prepare and cook food —see color picture on page 186

kite /kaɪt/ noun
a toy with a light frame covered with plastic or paper that you fly in the air on the end of a long string

kit·ten /'kɪt̚n/ noun
a young cat

kit·ty /'kɪt̬i/ noun (plural **kitties**)
a child's word for a young cat

Kleen·ex /'klinɛks/ (trademark) noun
a piece of soft thin paper, used especially for cleaning your nose

km
a short way to write the word KILOMETER

knead /nid/ verb
to press a mixture of flour and water with your hands so that it is ready to cook

knee /ni/ noun
the joint that bends in the middle of your leg

knee·cap /'nikæp/ noun
the bone at the front of your knee

knee-deep /ˌ. '.◂/ adjective
deep enough to reach your knees: *He was standing knee-deep in water.*

kneel /nil/ verb (past tense and past participle **knelt** /nɛlt/ or **kneeled**)
(also **kneel down**) to bend your legs and rest on your knees: *She knelt down to pray.* —see color picture on page 189

knew /nu/
the PAST TENSE of the verb **know**

knife /naɪf/ noun (plural **knives** /naɪvz/
a metal blade with a handle, used for cutting something or as a weapon

knight /naɪt/ *noun*
a soldier in the Middle Ages trained to fight on his horse

knit /nɪt/ *verb (past tense and past participle* **knit** *or* **knitted)**
to make clothes by joining wool or thick thread together using long needles: *She is knitting some clothes for the baby.* ≫ compare SEW

knit·ting /'nɪtɪŋ/ *noun* [U]
something that is being made, that you KNIT

knitting nee·dle /'.. ,../ *noun*
a long thin stick that you use to KNIT something
—see picture at NEEDLE

knob /nɑb/ *noun*
a round handle that you pull or turn to open a door, turn on a radio etc.

knock¹ /nɑk/ *verb*
1 to hit something hard and make a noise: *I knocked on the door.*
2 to hit something hard so that it moves or falls down: *He knocked the glass off the table. | The boy was knocked down by a car.*
3 knock someone out to make someone become unconscious, especially by hitting him or her
4 Knock it off! said when telling someone to stop doing something that is annoying you: *Hey, knock it off, I'm on the phone!*
5 knock something down, knock something off to reduce the price of something: *He knocked $50 off the price of the suit.*

knock² *noun*
the sound made by hitting something hard: *I heard a knock on the door.*

knock·out /'nɑk-aʊt/ *noun*
an act of hitting your opponent in BOXING so that he or she does not get up again

knot¹ /nɑt/ *noun*
1 a place where two ends of string or rope are tied together: *She tied the rope in a knot.*
2 a place where some of your hairs are twisted together: *My hair is full of knots.*
3 a measure of the speed of a ship, equal to 6,080 feet or 1,853 meters per hour

knot² *verb* **(knotting, knotted)**
to tie something with a knot

know /noʊ/ *verb (past tense* **knew** /nu/, *past participle* **known** /noʊn/)*
1 to have information or facts about something in your mind: *Do you know the answer? | I don't know your address.*
2 to be sure about something: *He knew she didn't like him. | I know that I am right.*
3 to understand something: *I know exactly how you feel. | You know what I am going through.*
4 to be familiar with a person or a place: *I have known Mary since she was a child. | How well do you know Denver?*
5 I know said when you agree with someone: *"It's a bad idea." "I know."*
6 you know said when you want to explain something more clearly: *That one is my car, you know, the red one.*
7 know better to be old enough or wise enough not to make a mistake: *He should have known better **than** to lie to me.*

NOTE: Compare **know**, **learn** and **teach**. If you **know** something, you already have the facts or information about it: *She knows a lot about computers.* If you **learn** something, you discover facts about something or discover how to do something, either on your own or with a teacher: *He's learning to drive. | The kids are learning math in school.* If you **teach** someone something, you make them learn something by giving them help and information: *He is teaching me to drive. | She teaches math to the kids in school.*

knowl·edge /'nɑlɪdʒ/ *noun* [U]
understanding or information that you have in your mind: *His knowledge **of** languages is excellent.*

knowl·edge·a·ble /'nɑlɪdʒəbəl/ *adjective*
having a lot of information or knowing a lot: *She is very knowledgeable **about** horses.*

known /noʊn/
the PAST PARTICIPLE of the verb **know**

knuck·le /'nʌkəl/ *noun*
one of the joints in your fingers

ko·a·la /koʊ'ɑlə/ *noun (also* **koala bear)**
an animal in Australia like a small bear

Ko·ran /kə'ræn, -'rɑn/
the holy book of the Muslim religion

lab /læb/ *noun*
a LABORATORY

label

label

la·bel¹ /ˈleɪbəl/ *noun*
a piece of paper attached to something, that has information on it. *Read the label on the wine bottle before you buy it.*

label² *verb*
to put a LABEL on something: *Label the boxes so we will remember what is in them.*

la·bor¹ /ˈleɪbər/ *noun* [U]
1 hard work that you do with your hands: *Many years of labor went into building the boat.*
2 the workers in a country or industry

labor² *verb*
to work very hard: *The farmers labored in the fields.*

lab·o·ra·to·ry /ˈlæbrəˌtɔri/ *noun* (*plural* **laboratories**)
(*also* **lab**) a room or building in which a scientist works

Labor Day /ˈ.. ˌ./ *noun*
a holiday in September that shows support for workers

la·bor·er /ˈleɪbərər/ *noun*
someone who does hard work with his or her hands ≫ compare WORKER

labor un·ion /ˈ.. ˌ../ *noun*
an organization that represents workers in a particular job

lace¹ /leɪs/ *noun* [U]
a type of cloth with many small holes in it, made from fine thread: *My dress has lace around the neck.*

lace² *verb* (**lacing, laced**)
lace something up to tie something with a lace: *Lace your boots up.*

lack¹ /læk/ *verb*
to not have enough of something: *He lacks the courage to tell her the truth.*

lack² *noun*
the state of not having something or not having enough of it: *The plan failed because of a lack of money.*

lad·der /ˈlædər/ *noun*
a piece of equipment with two long pieces of wood or metal connected by steps, used for climbing up to a high place: *I need a ladder to reach the roof.*

lad·en /ˈleɪdn/ *adjective*
carrying a lot of something: *The truck was laden with boxes of fruit.*

la·dies' room /ˈ.. ˌ./ *noun*
a room in a public place with toilets for women

la·dle /ˈleɪdl/ *noun*
a deep spoon with a long handle

la·dy /ˈleɪdi/ *noun* (*plural* **ladies**)
1 a polite word for a woman: *Good afternoon, ladies.*
2 said when speaking to a woman whose name you do not know, often in an impolite way: *Hey lady, hurry up!*

laid /leɪd/
the PAST TENSE and PAST PARTICIPLE of the verb **lay**

lain /leɪn/
the PAST PARTICIPLE of the verb **lie** ≫ compare LAY¹

lake /leɪk/ *noun*
a large area of water with land all around it ≫ compare POND —see color picture on page 188

lamb /læm/ *noun*
a young sheep

lame /leɪm/ *adjective* (**lamer, lamest**)
not able to walk easily because your leg or foot is injured: *My horse is lame so I can't ride her.*

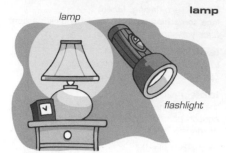

lamp

flashlight

lamp /læmp/ *noun*
an object that produces light using electricity, gas etc.: *I need a desk lamp.*

lamp·shade /'læmpʃeɪd/ *noun*
a cover put over a lamp to make the light less bright

land¹ /lænd/ *noun*
1 [U] ground that people own or that is used for farming: *Farmers own most of the land around here.*
2 [U] the dry part of the Earth not covered by water: *They reached land after six weeks.*
3 a country or place: *He wants to travel to foreign lands.*

land² *verb*
to arrive somewhere in a plane or boat: *We landed in Seattle at six in the evening.*

land·ing /'lændɪŋ/ *noun*
1 the floor at the top of a set of stairs
2 the action of a plane or boat arriving on land: *The plane made a safe landing.*

land·la·dy /'lænd,leɪdi/ *noun* (*plural* **landladies**)
a woman who owns a building and rents it to other people

land·lord /'lændlɔrd/ *noun*
someone who owns a building and rents it to other people

land·scape /'lændskeɪp/ *noun*
a view of an area of land: *The trees and mountains made a beautiful landscape.*

lane /leɪn/ *noun*
1 one of the parts that a main road is divided into by painted lines
2 a narrow road: *We drove along a country lane.*

lan·guage /'læŋgwɪdʒ/ *noun*
the words that people use in speaking and writing: *We are studying the English language.* | *Do you speak any foreign languages?*

lan·tern /'læntɚn/ *noun*
a lamp in a glass and metal frame with a handle so you can carry it

lap

The cat lapped up the milk.　　The cat was sleeping on her lap.

lap¹ /læp/ *noun*
1 the upper parts of your legs when you are sitting down: *Her little girl sat on her lap.*
2 the distance once around a track, or between two ends of a pool

lap² *verb* (**lapping, lapped**)
to drink liquid with the tongue, like a dog: *The dog lapped up the water.*

lapse /læps/ *noun*
a short period of time when you forget something, or do not do something that you should do

laptop

lap·top /'læptɑp/ *noun*
a small computer that you can carry with you

lard /lɑrd/ *noun* [U]
thick white fat from pigs, used in cooking

large /lɑrdʒ/ *adjective*
big: *I would like a large pizza.* | *What is the largest type of cat?* ≫ compare SMALL

large·ly /'lɑrdʒli/ *adverb*
mostly or mainly: *Our success was largely due to her good work.*

la·ser /'leɪzɚ/ *noun*
a very strong and narrow beam of light used in

some machines or in medical operations: *I have a laser printer.* | *He needs laser surgery on his eye.*

lash /læʃ/ *noun* (*plural* **lashes**)
an EYELASH

las·so /'læsoʊ/ *noun*
a rope with one end tied in a circle, used for catching cattle and horses

last¹ /læst/ *adjective*
1 at the end; after all others: *Mary is the last girl on the bus.* | *This is my last chance.* ≫ compare FIRST¹
2 happening just before this time; most recent: *I saw my friend last week.* | *The last time we played tennis, you won.*

last² *verb*
1 to continue to happen for a period of time: *Our vacation lasted for ten days.*
2 to stay in good condition or continue to be useful: *Good shoes last longer.* | *The batteries will last a long time*

last³ *adverb*
1 after everything or everyone else: *I am going to go last.*
2 most recently before now: *When I last saw him, he was just a boy.*

last·ing /'læstɪŋ/ *adjective*
continuing for a long time: *We want to have a lasting relationship.*

last·ly /'læstli/ *adverb*
said when telling someone the last thing you have to say: *Lastly, I would like to thank those who have made the school such a success.* ≫ compare FIRSTLY

last name /ˌ. './ *noun*
your family's name, which comes after your other names in English ≫ compare FIRST NAME

latch /lætʃ/ *noun* (*plural* **latches**)
a small metal object that fastens a door, gate, or window

late /leɪt/ *adjective, adverb*
1 after the usual or expected time: *She was late for school.* | *I may not be home until late.* ≫ compare EARLY
2 near the end of a period of time: *He began the work in late May.* | *The house was built in the late 19th century.*

late·ly /'leɪtli/ *adverb*
recently: *Have you seen him lately?* ≫ compare RECENTLY

lat·er¹ /'leɪtə/ *adverb*
1 after the present time: *I can't do it now. I'll do it later.* | *Can I talk to you later?*
2 later on after something else: *Your plan may cause more problems later on.*

later² *adjective*
1 continuing into the future; after something else: *A decision will be made at a later date.*
2 more recent: *The later models of this computer are much faster.*

lat·est /'leɪtɪst/ *adjective*
the most recent or newest: *Have you heard the latest news?*

Lat·in /'lætⁿn/ *noun* [U]
an old language, used in science and medicine: *Most doctors have to study Latin.*

lat·i·tude /'lætə,tud/ *noun*
the distance north or south of the middle of the Earth ≫ compare LONGITUDE

lat·ter /'lætə/ *noun*
the latter the second of two people or things that have been mentioned: *You can use glass or plastic, but the latter* (= plastic) *is cheaper.* ≫ compare FORMER¹

laugh¹ /læf/ *verb*
1 to make a sound that shows that you are happy or think something is funny: *It was so funny we couldn't stop laughing.*
2 laugh at someone or something to make unkind remarks about someone or something or to tell jokes about them: *All the kids at school are laughing at me!*

laugh² *noun*
the sound you make when you laugh: *We had a good laugh at his story.*

laugh·ter /'læftə/ *noun* [U]
the action or sound of laughing

launch /lɔntʃ, lantʃ/ *verb*
1 to start something new such as an activity or a product: *The company is launching a new perfume.*
2 to put a ship into the water, or to send a space vehicle into space

laun·dro·mat /'lɔndrə,mæt, 'lan-/ *noun*
a place where you pay to wash your clothes in a machine

laun·dry /'lɔndri, 'lan-/ *noun* [U]
clothes and sheets that need to be washed or have just been washed: *Did you **do the** laundry?*

la·va /ˈlɑvə, ˈlævə/ *noun* [U]
very hot liquid rock that comes out of the top of a mountain

lav·a·to·ry /ˈlævəˌtɔri/ *noun* (*plural* **lavatories**)
a room with a toilet, in a public building

law /lɔ/ *noun*
1 a rule made by the government that all people must obey: *There is a law **against** driving too fast.*
2 **the law** (a) the system of rules in a country: *Driving without a seat belt on is **against** the law.* (=not allowed by law) (b) the police: *Is he in trouble with the law?*

law·ful /ˈlɔfəl/ *adjective*
allowed by the law ≫ compare LEGAL

lawn /lɔn/ *noun*
an area of grass outside a house or in a park

lawn mow·er /ˈlɔn ˌmoʊər/ *noun*
a machine that you use to cut the grass

law·suit /ˈlɔsut/ *noun*
a problem that someone brings to a court of law to be settled

law·yer /ˈlɔyər/ *noun*
someone whose job is to advise people about the law, and speak for them in court

lay[1] /leɪ/ *verb* (**laying**, *past tense* **laid** /leɪd/, *past participle* **laid**)
1 to put someone or something in a particular place: *She laid her coat over a chair. | He laid the baby on the bed.* ≫ compare LIE[1]
2 to put or attach something in the correct place: *We are laying carpet in the living room.*
3 to make eggs come out of the body: *The hen laid an egg.*

NOTE: Do not confuse the verb **lay** (PAST TENSE and PAST PARTICIPLE **laid**) with the verb **lie** (PAST TENSE **lay**, PAST PARTICIPLE **lain**). **Lay**[1] means "to put something down" and is ALWAYS used with an object: *She laid the clothes on the bed.* **Lie** means "to have your body flat on something" and is NEVER used with an object: *She lay on her bed.* There is another verb **lie** (PAST TENSE and PAST PARTICIPLE **lied**) which means "to say something which is not true" and is also used without an object.

lay[2]
the PAST TENSE of the verb **lie**

lay·er /ˈleɪər/ *noun*
an amount of something that covers a surface: *There is a layer of dust on the furniture.*

la·zy /ˈleɪzi/ *adjective* (**lazier, laziest**)
not wanting to work: *He does not want a job. He's too lazy to work.*

lb.
(*plural* **lbs.**) a short way to write the word **pound**

lead[1] /lid/ *verb* (*past tense* **led** /led/, *past participle* **led**)
1 to show someone the way to a place, usually by going in front: *You lead, and we'll follow. | He led his horse to the barn.*
2 to go to a place: *This road leads to Springfield.*
3 to go in front of a group of people or vehicles: *He's going to lead the climb up Mount Everest.*
4 to be winning a game or competition: *We are leading 21-0 with ten minutes to play.*
5 to be more successful than others at something: *Our company leads the world in making cars.*
6 **lead to something** to make something happen: *The new factory has led to a lot of new jobs.*
7 **lead a ... life** to have a particular kind of life: *She led a very lonely life.*

lead[2] *noun*
1 a position in front of others: *The runner is still **in the** lead.*
2 the distance or number of points by which you are ahead of someone else: *We have a lead of ten points.*

lead[3] /lɛd/ *noun*
1 [U] a heavy soft gray metal: *The old house has lead pipes.*
2 the part inside a pencil that makes a mark when you write

lead·er /ˈlidər/ *noun*
someone who leads or controls other people: *The leaders of the world's richest nations are at the meeting.*

lead·er·ship /ˈlidərˌʃɪp/ *noun* [U]
1 the quality of being good at leading a team, organization etc.: *The company needs strong leadership.*
2 the position of being the leader

lead·ing /ˈlidɪŋ/ *adjective*
most important or most successful: *We are the world's leading producer of oil.*

leaf /lif/ *noun* (*plural* **leaves** /livz/)
one of the flat green parts of a plant or tree that grow out of branches or a stem: *It is beautiful when the leaves on the trees change colors.* —see picture at ROSE²

leaf·let /'liflɪt/ *noun*
a piece of paper with an advertisement or information printed on it

league /lig/ *noun*
1 a group of people or teams that play against each other in a competition: *How many teams are in the National Football League?*
2 a group of people or countries who have joined together to work for a special aim

leak¹ /lik/ *noun*
a hole or crack through which liquid or gas flows out. *The pipe has a leak.*

leak² *verb*
if a liquid or gas leaks, it goes through a hole or crack: *The roof is leaking.*

leak·y /'liki/ *adjective* (**leakier, leakiest**)
having a hole or crack so liquid or gas goes out of it

lean¹ /lin/ *verb*
1 to bend your body in a particular position: *She leaned forward to kiss him.*
2 to put something against something else to support it: *He leaned the ladder against the wall.*
3 to rest your body against something: *I saw him leaning against my car.*

lean² *adjective*
1 thin, in a healthy or attractive way: *His body was lean and muscular.*
2 not having a lot of fat: *I want to buy some lean meat.*

leap¹ /lip/ *verb* (*past tense and past participle* **leaped** *or* **leapt** /lɛpt/)
to jump into the air, or to jump over something: *The dog leaped **over** the fence.*

leap² *noun*
a big jump up into the air or over something: *With one leap, she crossed the stream.*

leap year /'. ./ *noun*
a year, once every four years, in which February has 29 days instead of 28 days

learn /lɚn/ *verb*
1 to get knowledge of something or the ability to do something: *Have you learned how to swim?* | *I am learning to speak German.*

2 to know something very well so it is easy to remember: *She learned the poem and said it in front of the class.* ≫ compare KNOW

learn·ing /'lɚnɪŋ/ *noun* [U]
knowledge you get through reading or studying

lease /lis/ *noun*
a legal agreement that allows you to live in a building for a particular period of time

leash /liʃ/ *noun*
a piece of rope, leather etc. used for controlling an animal: *Please keep your dog on a leash.*

least /list/ *pronoun, adverb*
1 less than anything or anyone else: *Which one is the least expensive?* | *They arrived when I least expected it.* (= when I did not expect them) ≫ compare MOST
2 at least (a) not less than: *He will be going away for at least a week.* (=a week or longer) (b) said when you want to change something you just said: *His name is Paul, at least I think it is.*
3 least of all especially not: *I don't like any of them, least of all John!*
4 not in the least not at all: *I'm not in the least interested in what she says.*
5 the smallest number or amount: *Even the least amount of poison can hurt you.*

leath·er /'lɛðɚ/ *noun* [U]
animal skins used for making things such as shoes and belts

leave¹ /liv/ *verb* (**leaving, left** /lɛft/)
1 to go away from a person or place: *The train leaves in five minutes.* | *He left his wife.*
2 to forget to take something with you when you go: *I think I left my books at home.*
3 to let something stay in a particular place or position: *Why did you leave the windows open?*
4 to put something in a place for someone: *Please leave a message for her.*
5 leave someone alone to stop worrying or annoying someone: *Go away and leave me alone!*
6 leave something alone used for telling someone to stop touching or moving something: *Leave those glasses alone or you will break them.*
7 leave someone or something out to not include someone or something in a group, list etc.: *Has anyone been left out?*
8 to give something to someone after you die: *My aunt left me some money.*
9 to remain after everything else is taken away: *Is there any coffee left?*

leave² *noun* [U]
a period of time away from your work: *He has taken one week's sick leave.*

leaves /livz/
the plural of **leaf**

lec·ture¹ /'lɛktʃɚ/ *noun*
a talk to a group of people about a particular subject: *I went to a lecture on modern art.*

lecture² *verb* (lecturing, lectured)
to talk to a group of people about a particular subject: *He lectures on American politics.*

led /lɛd/
the PAST TENSE and PAST PARTICIPLE of the verb **lead**

ledge /lɛdʒ/ *noun*
a narrow flat surface such as the one at the bottom of a window

left¹ /lɛft/
the PAST TENSE and PAST PARTICIPLE of the verb **leave**

left² *noun* [U]
the side opposite to the one with which most people write: *The school is on the left.* » compare RIGHT²

left³ *adjective*
on or toward the left side: *I hurt my left leg.* » compare RIGHT¹

left⁴ *adverb*
toward the left side: *Turn left here.* » compare RIGHT³

left·hand·ed /ˌ. '..ˌ/ *adjective*
using your left hand more than your right hand » compare RIGHT-HANDED

left·o·vers /'lɛft,oʊvɚz/ *plural noun*
food that remains at the end of a meal that you can keep and eat later

leg /lɛg/ *noun*
1 one of the two parts of your body on which you stand or walk: *Dogs have four legs.*
2 one of the parts on which a chair or table stands: *The chair has a broken leg.*

le·gal /'ligəl/ *adjective*
allowed by the law: *Voting is legal in the U.S. for those over the age of 18.* » opposite ILLEGAL

leg·end /'lɛdʒənd/ *noun*
1 an old story about people and the things they did in the past, which may not be true
2 a very famous person: *Elvis Presley was a legend in rock music.* —**legendary** *adjective*

leg·i·ble /'lɛdʒəbəl/ *adjective*
clear enough to read: *His writing is not very legible.* » opposite ILLEGIBLE

lei·sure /'liʒɚ/ *noun* [U]
the time when you are not working and can do things that you enjoy: *What do you do in your leisure time?*

lem·on /'lɛmən/ *noun*
a yellow fruit with a sour taste —see picture at FRUIT

lem·on·ade /ˌlɛmə'neɪd/ *noun* [U]
a sweet drink made from LEMONs

lend /lɛnd/ *verb* (past tense **lent** /lɛnt/, past participle **lent**)
1 to let someone use or have something for a time, after which he or she gives it back: *Can you lend me your book?* » compare BORROW
2 if a bank lends you money, you must pay the money back with an additional amount included

length /lɛŋkθ, lɛnθ/ *noun*
the distance from one end of something to the other; how long something is: *He caught a fish that was ten feet in length.*

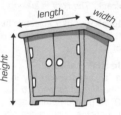

length·en /'lɛŋkθən/ *verb*
to make something longer: *I need to lengthen this dress.* » compare SHORTEN

length·y *adjective* (lengthier, lengthiest)
continuing for a long time: *He gave a lengthy speech.*

lens /lɛnz/ *noun* (plural **lenses**)
a curved piece of glass used for making things look bigger, smaller, or clearer —see picture at GLASSES

lent /lɛnt/
the PAST TENSE and PAST PARTICIPLE of the verb **lend**

len·til /'lɛntəl/ *noun*
a small round seed like a bean that you can cook and eat

leop·ard /'lɛpɚd/ *noun*
a large wild cat in Africa and Asia that has yellow fur with black spots

les·bi·an /'lɛzbiən/ *noun*
a woman who is sexually attracted to other women; HOMOSEXUAL

less /lɛs/ adverb
1 not so much; smaller: *I am trying to eat less.* | *There is a less expensive seat near the back.* | *He has less time to be with his family.* >> compare MORE
2 less and less continuing to become smaller in amount: *It seems like we have less and less money every week.*

less·en /'lɛsən/ verb
to become less, or make something become less: *Slowly the pain lessened.*

les·son /'lɛsən/ noun
a time when you learn something or how to do something: *I am taking piano lessons.*

let /lɛt/ verb (letting, past tense let, past participle let)
1 to allow someone to do something or to have something: *My mother wouldn't let me go to the movie.* | *I let her have $10.*
2 let's said when you ask someone to do something with you: *Let's go swimming.* | *I'm hungry. Let's eat!*
3 let go to stop holding something: *He let go of the dog and it ran away.*
4 let someone know to tell someone something: *Let me know what time you'll be arriving.*
5 let someone down to make someone feel disappointed when you do not do what you should do: *I thought she was coming, but she let me down.*
6 let someone go to allow someone to be free after keeping him or her somewhere: *The police let him go after asking him some questions.*

let·ter /'lɛtɚ/ noun
1 one of the signs that you use to write words: *A, B, and C are the first three letters in the English alphabet.*
2 a written message that you put into an envelope and send to someone: *I **wrote a letter** to my friend in Texas.* —see picture at ENVELOPE

let·tuce /'lɛtɪs/ noun
a round green vegetable with large thin leaves that you can eat —see picture at VEGETABLE

lev·el¹ /'lɛvəl/ adjective
1 flat; with no area that is higher or lower: *The floor of the house is not level.*
2 the same height as something else; equal

level² noun
1 the amount or number of something, compared to another amount or number: *There are high levels (= more than the usual amount) of lead in the water.*

2 the height or position of something: *Check the water level in the swimming pool.*

level³ verb
to make something flat: *The explosion leveled the building.*

lev·er /'lɛvɚ, 'li-/ noun
1 a metal stick that you use to lift something heavy by putting one end under the object and pushing down on the other end
2 a handle on a machine that you push or pull to make the machine work

li·a·ble /'laɪəbəl/ adjective
be liable to do something to be likely to do something: *He's liable to get angry if you do not agree with him.*

li·ar /'laɪɚ/ noun
someone who tells lies

lib·er·al /'lɪbrəl, -bərəl/ adjective
willing to understand and accept the different behavior or ideas of other people

lib·er·ty /'lɪbəti/ noun [U]
the freedom to do what you want without having to ask permission

li·brar·i·an /laɪ'brɛriən/ noun
someone who works in a library

li·brar·y /'laɪˌbrɛri/ noun (plural libraries)
a room or building that has books that you can read or borrow: *When does the library open?*

lice /laɪs/
the plural of LOUSE

li·cense¹ /'laɪsəns/ noun
an official piece of paper that allows you to own or do something: *He wants to see my driver's license.*

license² verb (licensing, licensed)
to give official permission for someone to own or do something: *He is licensed to carry a gun.*

license plate /'.. ,./ noun
a sign at the front and back of a car, truck etc. that has numbers and letters on it

lick /lɪk/ verb
to move your tongue across something: *She licked the stamp and put it on the envelope.*

lid /lɪd/ noun
a cover for a box, pot, or other container

lie¹ /laɪ/ verb (lying, past tense lay /leɪ/, past participle lain /leɪn/)
to have your body flat on something, or to get into this position: *He was lying on the bed.* | *She*

lay down on the floor. | Lie down and rest for a while. ≫ compare LAY¹

lie² verb (**lying**, past tense **lied**, past participle **lied**)
to tell someone something that is not true: *She lied to him about her age.*

lie³ noun (plural **lies**)
something you say that is not true: *Did he tell her a lie?*

lieu·ten·ant /lu'tɛnənt/ noun
an officer of middle rank in the army or the navy

life /laɪf/ noun (plural **lives**)
1 the period of time during which someone is alive: *She lived in Korea all her life.*
2 [U] all the experiences and activities someone has during his or her life: *Life in the city is exciting!*
3 [U] activity or movement: *There were no signs of life in the house.*
4 [U] living things such as people, animals, and plants: *No life was found on Mars.*

life·boat /'laɪfboʊt/ noun
a boat used for helping people who are in danger on the ocean

life·guard /'laɪfgɑrd/ noun
someone whose job is to help people who are in danger while swimming

life jack·et /'. ,../ noun
a special piece of equipment that you wear around your chest to make you float in water

life·less /'laɪflɪs/ adjective
1 dead, or seeming to be dead: *We pulled her lifeless body from the water.*
2 not exciting or interesting: *What a lifeless party!*

life·like /'laɪflaɪk/ adjective
very much like a real person: *It is a very lifelike sculpture.*

life sen·tence /,. '../ noun
the punishment of sending someone to prison for the rest of his or her life

life·style /'. ./ noun
the way in which you live, including your job, what you own, and what you do: *My lifestyle changed when I went to college.*

life·time /'laɪftaɪm/ noun
the time in which someone is alive: *I never thought that would happen in my lifetime.*

lift¹ /lɪft/ verb
to take something in your hands and raise it higher: *Can you lift the other end of the table? | "Lift me up so I can see," said the little girl.*
—see color picture on page 189

lift² noun
give someone a lift to take someone somewhere in a vehicle: *Sometimes he gives me a lift to school.*

lift·off /'. ./ noun
the moment when a space vehicle leaves the ground and rises up into the air

light¹ /laɪt/ noun
1 [U] the energy from the sun or a lamp, that allows you to see things: *There's more light near the window.*
2 a thing that produces light: *Turn off the lights when you go to bed.*
3 one of the red, yellow, or green lights used for telling cars when they can stop and go: *Turn left at the lights.*

light² adjective
1 not dark in color; pale: *She wore a light blue dress.* ≫ compare DARK¹
2 easy to lift; not heavy: *The box is very light.* ≫ compare HEAVY
3 not having much force or power: *I felt a light wind on my face.*
4 small in amount or degree: *Traffic is very light this evening.*

light³ verb (past tense and past participle **lit** /lɪt/ or **lighted**)
to make a lamp, fire, or cigarette burn or give out light: *Will you light the fire for me? | The room was lit by two small lamps.*

light bulb /'. ./ noun
the glass part of a lamp that gives out light

light·en /'laɪtⁿn/ verb
to make something less heavy, or less dark in color: *I took some boxes out of the car to lighten the load.*

light·er /'laɪtɚ/ noun
an object that makes a small flame so you can light a cigarette

light·house /'laɪthaʊs/ noun (plural **lighthouses**)
a tall building near the ocean with a powerful light at the top that warns ships of danger

light·ing /'laɪtɪŋ/ noun [U]
the system that gives light to a place: *We need more lighting in the office.*

light·ly /'laɪtli/ *adverb*
with only a small amount of weight or force:
She touched me lightly on the arm.

light·ning /'laɪtnɪŋ/ *noun* [U]
a bright flash of light in the sky that happens
during a storm

lik·a·ble /'laɪkəbəl/ *adjective*
nice and easy to like: *He is a likable sort of man.*

like¹ /laɪk/ *verb* (**liking, liked**)
1 to enjoy something, or think that someone or
something is pleasant: *I like bananas.* | *Do you
like to dance?* | *I never liked her brother.*
2 used when saying something in a polite way:
Would you like some more coffee? | *I would like
to know how to get to Main Street.*

like² *preposition*
1 the same or similar to something else: *The
bread was round like a ball.* | *He looks like his
brother.*
2 typical of a person or thing: *It is not like
Nancy to be late.* (= she is usually never late)
3 as if: *He acts like he's the most important
person here.*

like·ly /'laɪkli/ *adjective*
probably, or almost certainly: *It is likely to rain
tomorrow.* | *She is the one who is most likely to
win.* ≫ opposite UNLIKELY

like·wise /'laɪk-waɪz/ *adverb*
in the same way: *We respect his wishes, and
we hope you will do likewise.*

lik·ing /'laɪkɪŋ/ *noun*
have a liking for something to like or enjoy
something: *He has a liking for fast cars.*

li·lac /'laɪlɑk, -læk, -lək/ *noun*
1 a small tree with pale purple and white flowers
2 [U] a pale purple color —**lilac** *adjective*

lil·y /'lɪli/ *noun* (*plural* **lilies**)
a plant with large white flowers

limb /lɪm/ *noun*
1 a large branch of a tree
2 an arm or leg

lime /laɪm/ *noun*
1 a green fruit with a sour taste, or the tree
on which this grows
2 [U] a white substance used for making
CEMENT

lim·it¹ /'lɪmɪt/ *noun*
1 the greatest amount, number, or distance

that is allowed or is possible: *There is a 30 mile
per hour speed limit here.*
2 the edge or border of something: *The fence
marks the limits of the field.*

limit² *verb*
to stop a number, amount etc. from going
beyond a point or level: *The government limits
the amount of money you can take out of the
country.*

limp¹ /lɪmp/ *adjective*
not firm or stiff: *His body went limp as he fell
asleep.*

limp² *verb*
to walk with difficulty because one leg or foot is
hurt: *He limped off the football field.*

limp³ *noun*
a way of walking when one leg or foot is hurt:
With an injured knee, I walked with a limp.

line

line¹ /laɪn/ *noun*
1 a long thin mark on something: *Do not write
below this line.*
2 a group of people or things one after the
other; a row: *I stood in line for the tickets.*
3 a long piece of string or rope: *Did you put
the clothes on the line?*

line² *verb* (**lining, lined**)
1 to form a line or row: *People lined the
streets to see the President.* | *The class lined
up at the front of the room.*
2 to cover the inside of something with another material: *The box was lined with soft paper.*

lin·en /'lɪnən/ *noun* [U]
sheets and coverings for tables, or the cloth
used for making some of these

lin·er /'laɪnə/ *noun*
a large ship used for carrying many people

lin·ing /'laɪnɪŋ/ *noun*
the cloth covering the inside of a coat, box etc.:
The lining of my coat is red.

link¹ /lɪŋk/ *noun*
1 something that connects two events, people, or ideas: *There is a link **between** smoking and lung cancer.*
2 one of the rings in a chain

link² *verb*
to join two things or places together: *The two towns are linked by a highway.*

lint /lɪnt/ *noun* [U]
soft light pieces of thread or cloth that come off cotton and other material

li·on /'laɪən/ *noun*
a large wild animal in Africa and Asia like a big cat —see color picture on page 183

li·on·ess /'laɪənɪs/ *noun* (*plural* lionesses)
a female lion

lip /lɪp/ *noun*
one of the two edges of your mouth: *He kissed her on the lips.* —see picture at HEAD¹

lip·stick /'lɪp,stɪk/ *noun*
a colored substance that women put on their lips, or the tube containing this: *Do you use lipstick?*

liq·uid¹ /'lɪkwɪd/ *noun*
a substance like water that can be poured; not a solid or a gas

liquid² *adjective*
in the form of a liquid: *a bottle of liquid soap.*

liq·uor /'lɪkɚ/ *noun* [U]
strong alcoholic drink

list¹ /lɪst/ *noun*
a set of names or things to do that you write one below the other so you will remember them: *I have to make a shopping list.*

list² *verb*
to write or say things as a list: *I listed all the things I needed to buy.*

lis·ten /'lɪsən/ *verb*
to pay attention to what someone is saying; to hear: *Are you listening **to** me? | I told him not to do it, but he wouldn't listen.*

NOTE: Remember to use **to** after **listen**: *Listen to me! We were listening to the radio.*

lit¹ /lɪt/
the PAST TENSE and PAST PARTICIPLE of the verb **light**

lit² *adjective*
having light or burning: *He threw a lit cigarette into the garbage.*

li·ter /'litɚ/ *noun*
a measure of liquid: *The bottle holds two liters of Coke.*

lit·er·a·ture /'lɪtərətʃɚ, 'lɪtrə-/ *noun* [U]
good books and writing, including plays and poetry: *She's studying French literature in college.*

lit·ter /'lɪtɚ/ *noun* [U]
waste paper and other things that people leave on the ground in public: *There was litter everywhere on the streets of the town.*

lit·tle¹ /'lɪtl/ *adjective*
1 small: *It's only a little house. | The mother was carrying her little girl.* ≫ compare BIG
2 a little bit a small amount; not very much: *Can I have a little bit **of** sugar?*
3 short in time or distance: *I will wait a little while, and then call her again.*

little² (less, least)
1 only a small amount of something: *She eats very little. | I have very little money at the moment.*
2 a little some, but not much: *I feel a little better today. | She knows a little English.*

live¹ /lɪv/ *verb* (living, lived)
1 to be alive, or stay alive; to not be dead: *Is your grandmother still living?*
2 to have your home in a place: *I live in Detroit.*
3 to keep alive by eating a particular thing or by doing something: *Cows live **on** grass.*
4 live with someone to live with another person, especially in a sexual relationship without being married
5 live up to something to do something as well, or to be as good as someone expects: *She couldn't live up to her parents' expectations.*

live² /laɪv/ *adjective*
1 not dead: *The company does not test products on live animals.*
2 done or performed for people who are watching: *The restaurant has live music on Fridays.*
3 shown on television at the same time as it happens

live·ly /'laɪvli/ *adjective* (livelier, liveliest)
very active and exciting: *It was a lively party.*

liv·er /'lɪvɚ/ *noun*
1 a large part inside your body which cleans your blood

2 [U] a part from inside an animal's body, eaten as meat

lives /laɪvz/
the plural of **life**

liv·ing¹ /'lɪvɪŋ/ *adjective*
alive: *She has no living relatives* ≫ compare DEAD¹

living² *noun*
1 [U] the way that you earn money: *What does he do for a living?*
2 the living all the people who are alive

living room /'.. ,./ *noun*
the main room in a house where people sit, watch television etc. —see color picture on page 186

liz·ard /'lɪzɚd/ *noun*
an animal that has four short legs, a long tail, and skin like a snake

'll /l, əl/ *verb*
will: *She'll do it tomorrow.*

load¹ /loʊd/ *noun*
a large amount of something that is carried by a person or vehicle: *The truck is carrying a load of bananas.*

load² *verb*
1 to put things on or into a vehicle: *We loaded the car with boxes.*
2 to put bullets in a gun, or film into a camera

loaf /loʊf/ *noun* (*plural* **loaves** /loʊvz/)
a large piece of bread that can be cut into smaller pieces: *Please buy a loaf of bread at the store.* —see picture at BREAD

loan¹ /loʊn/ *noun*
an amount of money that you borrow from a person or bank: *I want to take out a loan for a new car.*

loan² *verb*
to lend someone something, especially money

loaves /loʊvz/
the plural of **loaf**

lob·by /'labi/ *noun* (*plural* **lobbies**)
a large room inside the entrance of a building: *Wait for me in the hotel lobby.*

lob·ster /'labstɚ/ *noun*
a sea animal with a shell, a tail, and eight legs, or the meat of this animal

lo·cal /'loʊkəl/ *adjective*
in the area near a place; near where you live: *My children go to the local school.* —**locally** *adverb*

located /'loʊkeɪtɪd/ *adjective*
be located to be in a particular place: *The hotel is located near the airport.*

lo·ca·tion /loʊ'keɪʃən/ *noun*
a particular place or position: *The map shows the location of the church.*

lock¹ /lak/ *noun*
an object that keeps a door, gate, or drawer shut, and that can only be opened with a key

lock² *verb*
1 to close a door, gate, or drawer using a lock: *Did you remember to lock the door?* ≫ opposite UNLOCK
2 lock up to make a building safe by closing all the doors with a lock: *Don't forget to lock up when you leave.*

lock·er /'lakɚ/ *noun*
a small cupboard, often with a lock, in which you keep things: *Everyone has a locker at school.*

lock·smith /'lak,smɪθ/ *noun*
someone who makes and repairs locks

lo·cust /'loʊkəst/ *noun*
an insect that flies in large groups and eats crops in fields

lodge /ladʒ/ *verb* (**lodging**, **lodged**)
to become stuck somewhere: *He has a bone lodged in his throat.*

loft /lɔft/ *noun*
a raised area above a room or inside a BARN

log¹ /lɔg, lag/ *noun*
a large piece of wood cut from a tree: *Put another log on the fire.*

log² *verb* (**logging**, **logged**)
1 log on, log in to start using a computer by writing a special word
2 log off, log out to stop using a computer by writing a special word

lol·li·pop /'lali,pap/ *noun*
a hard candy attached to a small stick

lone·ly /ˈloʊnli/ *adjective* (**lonelier, loneliest**) unhappy because you are alone: *He is lonely without his wife.* —**loneliness** *noun* [U]

long

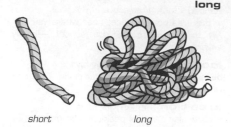

short   long

long¹ /lɔŋ/ *adjective*
measuring a great distance, length, or time: *Julie has long hair.* | *It takes a long time to walk to school.* | *There was a long line at the bank.* ≫ compare SHORT

long² *adverb*
1 for a long time: *Have you been waiting long?*
2 **long before, long after** a long time before or after a particular event: *He died long before you were born.*
3 **as long as, so long as** if: *You can go out as long as you are back by 9 o'clock.*

long³ *verb*
to want something very much: *She longed to go home.*

long·dis·tance /ˌ. ˈ..‹/ *adjective*
between places that are a long way from each other: *Can I make a long-distance phone call?*

long·ing /ˈlɔŋɪŋ/ *noun* [U]
a strong feeling of wanting something

lon·gi·tude /ˈlɑndʒəˌtud/ *noun*
a position on the Earth shown on maps as the distance east or west of a line that goes from the top of the Earth to the bottom ≫ compare LATITUDE

look¹ /lʊk/ *verb*
1 to turn your eyes toward something so that you can see it: *She looked at me angrily.* | *He sat and looked out of the window.* ≫ compare WATCH²
2 to seem to be something: *That dog looks dangerous.* | *You look like you are tired.*
3 **Look!** said when you are annoyed or want someone to notice something: *Look, I don't feel like arguing with you!*
4 **look as if, look like** to seem probable: *It looks as if we're going to miss the plane.*
5 **look after someone or something** to take care of someone or something: *She looked after our house while we were away.*
6 **look for someone or something** to try to find someone or something: *I'm looking for my keys.*
7 **look forward to something** to be happy or excited because you are going to do something: *We're looking forward to going to the party.*
8 **look ahead** to think about what will happen in the future: *It is time to look ahead to next year.*
9 **look something up** to find a piece of information in a book: *Did you look up that word in the dictionary?*
10 **look out** to pay attention to what is happening around you: *Look out! The ball almost hit you!*

look² *noun*
1 an act of looking at something: *Take a look at this book.*
2 the way something appears: *I don't like the look of the weather.* (=I think it is bad)
3 the expression on someone's face: *He gave me an angry look.*

looks /lʊks/ *plural noun*
how beautiful or attractive someone is: *She is always worried about her looks.*

loom /lum/ *noun*
a machine for weaving cloth

loop /lup/ *noun*
a shape like a curve or circle, or something that has this shape

loose /lus/ *adjective* (**looser, loosest**)
1 not firmly attached to something: *My shirt button is loose.*
2 loose clothes are big and do not fit tightly: *These pants are loose.*
3 free from control: *Don't let your dog run loose on the beach.*

loos·en /ˈlusən/ *verb*
to become less tight, or make something do this: *He loosened the tie around his neck.* ≫ compare TIGHTEN

Lord /lɔrd/ *noun*
the Lord God or Jesus Christ

lose /luz/ *verb* (**losing, lost** /lɔst/)
1 to not have something any more, or not know where it is: *I think I lost my watch.* | *He lost his job last week.* ≫ compare FIND
2 to not win a game, argument, war etc.: *Our team lost the match.* | *Did Harris lose the election?* ≫ compare WIN¹
3 to have less of something than before: *She has lost a lot of weight.* ≫ compare GAIN

4 lose your sight, lose your hearing etc. to stop being able to see, hear etc.
5 lose your temper to become angry

los·er /'luzər/ noun
someone who does not win

loss /lɔs/ noun (plural **losses**)
1 the act of losing something, or something that you have lost: *His death was a great loss to us.* | *The loss of her job was a shock.*
2 money that is lost by a company, person etc.: *The company had big losses this year.*

lost¹ /lɔst/
the PAST TENSE and PAST PARTICIPLE of the verb **lose**

lost² adjective
not knowing where you are: *I went for a walk and got lost.*

lost-and-found /ˌ. . '. / noun [U]
a place used for keeping things that people have lost, until they can get them again

lot /lɑt/ noun
1 a large amount or number: *I picked lots of flowers.* | *A lot of people do not like him.* ≫ compare MUCH
2 an area of land in a town or city: *There's an empty lot next to our house.*

lo·tion /'louʃən/ noun
a liquid that you put on your skin to make it soft, or protect it: *Put this lotion on to stop the sun from burning you.*

lot·ter·y /'lɑtəri/ noun (plural **lotteries**)
a game in which you buy a ticket to try and win money

loud /laʊd/ adjective
making a lot of noise: *Your music is too loud!* ≫ compare QUIET¹ —**loudly** adverb

loud·speak·er /'laʊdˌspikər/ noun
a piece of equipment that makes your voice sound louder: *The police spoke to him using a loudspeaker.*

lounge /laʊndʒ/ noun
a public room in an airport or hotel where you can sit and relax

louse /laʊs/ noun (plural **lice** /laɪs/)
a small insect that lives on the skin and hair of people and animals

lous·y /'laʊzi/ adjective (**lousier, lousiest**)
very bad: *What a lousy day!*

lov·a·ble /'lʌvəbəl/ adjective
very nice and easy to love

love¹ /lʌv/ verb (**loving, loved**)
1 to care very much for someone, or have a strong romantic feeling for someone: *Mothers love their children.* ≫ compare HATE¹
2 to like something very much: *Maria loves to read.*

love² noun
1 [U] a strong romantic feeling for someone: *Her love for her husband is real.* ≫ compare HATE², HATRED
2 something that you like very much: *Music is one of his great loves.*
3 **love** written at the end of a letter to a friend or someone in your family
4 fall in love to begin to love someone: *He fell in love with her.*

love af·fair /'. .ˌ./ noun
a romantic or sexual relationship between two people

love·ly /'lʌvli/ adjective
very nice or enjoyable: *I had a lovely evening!*

lov·er /'lʌvər/ noun
1 someone with whom you have a romantic or sexual relationship
2 someone who enjoys something: *He is an art lover.*

lov·ing /'lʌvɪŋ/ adjective
showing that you love someone: *He gave her a loving kiss.*

low /loʊ/ adjective
1 not high; near to the ground: *He threw the ball too low.* ≫ compare HIGH
2 small in number or amount: *Their prices are very low.*
3 bad, or not of good quality: *I have a low opinion of his work.*
4 not high in sound: *He has a low voice.*

low·er /'loʊər/ verb
1 to become less in amount or degree: *Can you lower your voice, please.* (=speak less loudly) ≫ compare RAISE¹
2 to move something down: *It is time to lower the flag.*

lower case /ˌ.. '. ◂/ noun [U]
letters written in their small form, such as a, b, d, g, j etc. ≫ compare UPPER CASE

low tide /ˌ. '. / noun
the time when the ocean is very low and far from the shore ≫ compare HIGH TIDE

loy·al /'lɔɪəl/ *adjective*
faithful; not changing your beliefs or opinions:
She is a loyal friend. >> opposite DISLOYAL

loy·al·ty /'lɔɪəlti/ *noun* [U]
the quality of being faithful: *His loyalty to his country is strong.*

LP /ˌel 'piː/ *noun*
a record that plays for about 25 minutes on each side

luck /lʌk/ *noun* [U]
the good and bad things that happen to you by chance: *Have you had any luck finding a job?* | *Good luck! I hope you win the game!*

luck·y /'lʌki/ *adjective* (luckier, luckiest)
having or bringing good luck: *He is lucky to still be alive.* >> opposite UNLUCKY

lug·gage /'lʌgɪdʒ/ *noun* [U]
the bags, containers, and other things you carry with you when you travel >> compare BAGGAGE

luke·warm /ˌluːk'wɔːm‹ / *adjective*
not very warm, but not cold

lum·ber /'lʌmbə/ *noun* [U]
wood that is used for building

lump /lʌmp/ *noun*
1 a piece of something that does not have a particular shape: *A lump of clay was on the table.*
2 a swelling on someone's body: *I've got a lump on my arm where I hit it.*

lump·y /'lʌmpi/ *adjective* (lumpier, lumpiest)
having LUMPs; not smooth: *The bed is lumpy.*

lu·na·tic /'luːnəˌtɪk/ *noun*
someone who behaves in a crazy or stupid way: *She must be a lunatic to drive her car so fast.*

lunch /lʌntʃ/ *noun* (*plural* lunches)
the meal that you eat in the middle of the day >> compare DINNER

lunch·time /'lʌntʃtaɪm/ *noun*
the time in the middle of the day when you eat

lung /lʌŋ/ *noun*
one of the two parts inside your body used for breathing

lust /lʌst/ *noun*
a strong feeling of sexual desire

lux·u·ri·ous /lʌg'ʒʊriəs, lʌk'ʃʊ-/ *adjective*
very comfortable and expensive

lux·u·ry /'lʌkʃəri, 'lʌgʒəri/ *noun* (*plural* luxuries)
something expensive that you want but do not really need: *A new car is a luxury we cannot afford.*

ly·ing /'laɪ-ɪŋ/
the PRESENT PARTICIPLE of the verb lie

lyr·ics /'lɪrɪks/ *plural noun*
the words of a popular song

'm /m/ *verb*
I am: *I'm hungry*

m
a short way to write the word **meter** or **meters**

ma'am /mæm/ *noun*
a polite way to speak to a woman whose name you do not know: *Can I help you, ma'am?*

ma·chine /mə'ʃin/ *noun*
a piece of equipment made up of many parts that uses power to do a job: *I have a new sewing machine.*

ma·chine gun /.'. ,./ *noun*
a gun that fires a lot of bullets very quickly

ma·chin·er·y /mə'ʃinəri/ *noun* [U]
machines, or the parts inside a machine: *The machinery is controlled by computers.*

mad /mæd/ *adjective*
1 very angry: *She was mad at me for being late.*
2 crazy; mentally ill: *We thought he might be going mad.*
3 **like mad** very hard or fast: *If you run like mad, you might catch the train.*
4 very stupid or dangerous: *You would have to be mad to try to climb that alone.*

mad·am /'mædəm/ *noun*
a polite way to write to a woman whose name you do not know

made¹ /meɪd/
the PAST TENSE and PAST PARTICIPLE of the verb **make**

made² *adjective*
be made of something to be built from or consist of: *My shirt is made of silk.*

mad·ly /'mædli/ *adverb*
1 in a wild or uncontrolled way: *She rushed madly from room to room.*
2 **madly in love** very much in love

mag·a·zine /,mægə'zin, 'mægə,zin/ *noun*
a thin book with a picture on the cover, that has stories and pictures in it, which you can buy weekly or monthly

mag·ic /'mædʒɪk/ *noun* [U]
1 a special power used for making strange things happen: *In the story he turned the thread into gold using magic.*
2 the skill of doing tricks done to amuse people

mag·i·cal /'mædʒɪkəl/ *adjective*
1 very enjoyable and exciting in a strange way: *It was a magical evening.*
2 done using magic: *He claimed to have magical powers.*

ma·gi·cian /mə'dʒɪʃən/ *noun*
someone who does strange tricks to amuse people

mag·net
/'mægnɪt/ *noun*
a piece of iron that makes other pieces of iron move toward it

mag·net·ic
/mæg'nɛtɪk/ *adjective*
having the power of a
MAGNET

mag·nif·i·cent
/mæg'nɪfəsənt/ *adjective*
very big or beautiful: *What a magnificent painting!*

mag·ni·fy /'mægnə,faɪ/ *verb* (**magnifying, magnified**)
to make something look larger than it really is

magnifying glass /'.... ,./ *noun*
a round piece of glass with a handle, that makes something appear larger than it really is

maid /meɪd/ *noun*
a female servant

maiden name /,.. './ *noun*
the family name of a woman before she marries and begins using her husband's name

mail¹ /meɪl/ *noun*
1 **the mail** the system of sending and receiving letters and packages: *I put the letters in the mail this morning.*
2 [U] the letters and packages that you send or receive using this system: *Is there any mail for me?*

mail² *verb*
to send a letter or package to someone: *I will mail this to you soon.*

mail·box /ˈmeɪlbɑks/ *noun* [*plural* mailboxes]
1 a special box near the street or a POST OFFICE where you put letters
2 a box outside your house where your letters are delivered

mail·man
/ˈmeɪlmæn, -mən/
noun
a man who delivers mail to people's houses

main /meɪn/
adjective
more important or bigger than something else: *I want to take the main road into town.*

main·ly /ˈmeɪnli/ *adverb*
mostly; true most of the time: *That hospital is mainly for older people.*

main·tain /meɪnˈteɪn/ *verb*
to keep something in good condition, or make it continue in the same way as before: *It is expensive to maintain a large house.* | *We want to maintain a good relationship with our workers.*

main·te·nance /ˈmeɪntˀn-əns/ *noun* [U]
the action of keeping something in good condition: *Car maintenance is important.*

ma·jes·tic /məˈdʒɛstɪk/ *adjective*
very big, important, or impressive: *We had a majestic view of the mountains.*

ma·jor¹ /ˈmeɪdʒɚ/ *adjective*
very large or important: *Our car needs major repairs.* ≫ compare MINOR¹

major² *noun*
1 the main subject that you study in a college or university
2 an officer who has a middle rank in the army

major³ *verb*
major in sth to study something as your main subject at a college or university: *I'm majoring in biology.*

ma·jor·i·ty /məˈdʒɔrəṭi, -ˈdʒɑr-/ *noun* [U]
most of the people or things in a group: *The majority of children in our class have dark hair.* ≫ compare MINORITY

make /meɪk/ *verb* (making, made /meɪd/)
1 to do something: *We need to make a decision.* | *I'll make some coffee.* | *Do you want to make a phone call?*
2 to produce or build something: *He made a model plane out of wood.* ≫ compare DO¹
3 to cause something to happen: *What he said made me mad!*
4 to force someone to do something: *I don't like milk, but she made me drink it.*
5 to earn: *I don't make enough money.*
6 to be a particular number or amount: *Two and two make four.*
7 **make it** to arrive somewhere: *We just made it to the hospital in time.*
8 **make the bed** to make a bed look neat by pulling the sheets and covers straight
9 **make sure** to be certain: *Make sure you lock the door.*
10 **make something out** to be able to see, hear, or understand something: *Can you make out what the sign says?*
11 **make something up** to think of and tell other people a story that is not true: *He made up an excuse about why he was late.*
12 **make up your mind** to decide something: *I've made up my mind to go to Spain this summer.*
13 **make of** to have an opinion of: *What do you make of his idea?*
14 **make believe** to pretend that something is true, especially as a game

make·up /ˈmeɪk-ʌp/ *noun* [U]
special powders and creams that people put on their faces

ma·lar·i·a /məˈlɛriə/ *noun* [U]
an illness in which someone has a high fever, caused by the bite of a MOSQUITO

male¹ /meɪl/ *adjective*
belonging to the sex that does not have babies: *The male bird is brightly-colored.* ≫ compare FEMALE¹

male² *noun*
a person or animal that does not have babies, such as a man or boy ≫ compare FEMALE²

mall /mɔl/ *noun*
a very large building with a lot of stores inside it

mam·mal /'mæməl/ *noun*
an animal that drinks its mother's milk when it is young, for example a cow, lion, or human

man /mæn/ *noun*
1 (*plural* **men**) a fully grown human male ≫ compare WOMAN
2 [U] all people: *Man uses animals in many ways.*

man·age /'mænɪdʒ/ *verb* (**managing, managed**)
1 to succeed in doing something: *He managed to avoid an accident.*
2 to control or direct a business or activity: *He manages the hotel.*

man·age·ment /'mænɪdʒmənt/ *noun* [U]
1 the control or organization of something such as a business or money: *I studied business management.*
2 the people who control a business: *We're meeting the management tomorrow.*

man·ag·er /'mænɪdʒə/ *noun*
someone who controls a business, store, sports team etc.

mane /meɪn/ *noun*
the long hair on the neck of a horse or lion

man·kind /ˌmæn'kaɪnd/ *noun* [U]
all humans

man-made /ˌ. '. ./ *adjective*
made by people, not grown or produced by the earth: *Plastic is a man-made material.*

man·ner /'mænə/ *noun*
the way in which something is done or happens: *The problem can be solved in this manner.*

manners /'mænəz/ *plural noun*
polite ways to behave or speak: *You must learn good manners.*

man·sion /'mænʃən/ *noun*
a very large house

man·tel /'mæntl/ *noun*
a shelf above a FIREPLACE

man·u·al¹ /'mænyuəl/ *adjective*
done with your hands, not with a machine: *He does manual work.* —**manually** *adverb*

manual² *noun*
a book that tells you how to do something such as use a machine: *Be sure to read the manual before you start.*

man·u·fac·ture¹ /ˌmænyə'fæktʃə/ *verb* (**manufacturing, manufactured**)
to use machines to make things in large numbers

manufacture² *noun* [U]
the making of goods in large numbers

man·y /'mɛni/ (**more, most**)
1 a lot; a large number of: *Many of the children cannot read.* | *I have eaten too many chocolates.* ≫ compare FEW
2 **how many** used for asking about the number of people or things: *How many people were there?*

map

map /mæp/ *noun*
a drawing of a country or an area: *Do you have a map of Florida?*

mar·ble /'marbəl/ *noun*
1 [U] a hard white rock that can be made smooth and shiny and is used in building things
2 a small glass ball used in a game: *Do you like to play marbles?*

March /martʃ/ *noun*
the third month of the year

march¹ /martʃ/ *verb*
1 to walk with regular steps like a soldier
2 to walk somewhere quickly: *She marched out of the room in anger.*

march² *noun* (*plural* **marches**)
an event in which many people walk together to protest about something

mar·ga·rine /'mardʒərɪn/ *noun* [U]
a soft yellow food like butter

mar·gin /'mardʒɪn/ *noun*
the empty space at each side of a page, without writing or printing

mark¹ /mark/ *noun*
1 a spot or dirty area that spoils the appearance of something: *You have a black mark on your shirt.*

2 a small area on someone or something that is damaged: *He had teeth marks on his arm.*

mark² verb
1 to put words or a sign on something to give information about it: *The door was marked "Private".*
2 to show where something is: *A bridge marks the place where the battle was fought.*
3 to put a spot or line on something which damages it: *His black shoes marked the floor.*
4 mark something down to make the price of something lower: *These shoes were marked down to $10.*

mar·ket /'mɑrkɪt/ *noun*
1 a place where people buy and sell goods
2 on the market for sale: *Their house has been on the market for months.*

mar·riage /'mærɪdʒ/ *noun*
1 the occasion when a man and a woman become husband and wife: *The marriage took place in church.* ≫ compare WEDDING
2 the relationship between two people who are married: *They have had a long and happy marriage.*

mar·ried /'mærid/ *adjective*
having a husband or wife: *He is a married man.*

mar·ry /'mæri/ *verb* (**marrying, married**)
1 to become someone's husband or wife: *I am going to marry John.* | *When are you going to get married?*
2 to perform the ceremony in which two people become husband and wife: *They were married by a priest.*

marsh /mɑrʃ/ *noun* (*plural* **marshes**)
an area of low, wet, soft ground

mar·vel·ous /'mɑrvələs/ *adjective*
very good or wonderful: *I read a marvelous book by him.* ≫ compare GREAT, FANTASTIC

mas·cu·line /'mæskyəlɪn/ *adjective*
like a man or typical of a man ≫ compare FEMININE

mash /mæʃ/ *verb*
to crush something to make it soft: *Mash the potatoes with a fork.*

mask /mæsk/ *noun*
something that covers all or part of your face: *The bank robbers both wore masks.*

Mass /mæs/ *noun*
a religious ceremony in the Roman Catholic church: *She goes to Mass every day.*

mass *noun* (*plural* **masses**)
a large amount or quantity of something: *Before the rain, the sky was a mass of clouds.*

mas·sa·cre /'mæsəkər/ *verb* (**massacring** /'mæsəkrɪn/, **massacred**)
to kill a lot of people in a violent and cruel way
—**massacre** *noun*

mas·sive /'mæsɪv/ *adjective*
very large, heavy, or powerful: *I saw a massive ship on the ocean.* ≫ compare HUGE, ENORMOUS

mass me·di·a /ˌ. '.../ *plural noun*
all the people that give news and information to the public

mast /mæst/ *noun*
a tall pole on which the sails of a ship are hung

mas·ter¹ /'mæstər/ *noun*
1 a man in control of people or animals: *The dog obeyed his master.*
2 someone who has a lot of skill or ability: *The painting is the work of a master.*

master² verb
to learn how to do something very well: *It takes a long time to master a new language.*

mat /mæt/ *noun*
a small piece of thick material that covers part of a floor ≫ compare CARPET, RUG

match¹ /mætʃ/ *noun* (*plural* **matches**)
1 a short stick of wood that produces a flame when you rub it against a rough surface: *I need a box of matches.*
2 a game or sports event: *We have a tennis match today.*

match² verb
to be like something else in size, shape, color etc.: *The shoes do not match my dress.*

mate¹ /meɪt/ *verb* [mating, mated]
if birds or animals mate, they have sex to produce babies: *Birds mate in the spring.*

mate² *noun*
one of a pair of animals or birds

ma·te·ri·al /mə'tɪriəl/ *noun*
1 anything from which something can be
made: *Building materials are expensive.*
2 cloth: *I used cotton material to make the
curtains.* ≫ compare FABRIC

math /mæθ/ *noun* [U]
the study or science of numbers and the measurement of shapes

math·e·mat·i·cal /mæθ'mætɪkəl/
adjective
relating to MATH

math·e·mat·ics /ˌmæθ'mætɪks,
ˌmæθə-/ *noun* [U]
MATH

mat·i·nee /ˌmætn'eɪ/ *noun*
a performance of a play or movie in the afternoon

mat·ter¹ /'mætər/ *noun*
1 an important event or subject that you must
talk about or think about: *I have an important
matter to discuss with you.*
2 what's the matter? used for asking someone why he or she is angry or upset: *What's
the matter with you? Why are you crying?*
3 [U] the material that things are made of,
which you can see and touch
4 no matter said when a situation will not
change: *We'll finish the job, no matter how long
it takes.* | *No matter how hard I pulled, the door
would not open.*
5 as a matter of fact in fact: *As a matter of
fact I'm only thirty-five, so don't say I'm old.*

matter² *verb*
to be important: *Money is all that matters to
him.*

mat·tress /'mætrɪs/ *noun* [plural
mattresses]
the large soft part of a bed on which you sleep

ma·ture¹ /mə'tʃʊr, mə'tʊr/ *adjective*
behaving in a responsible way like an adult:
She's a very mature girl. ≫ opposite IMMATURE

mature² *verb* [maturing, matured]
1 to become fully grown or developed
2 to begin to behave in a responsible way like
an adult

max·i·mum¹ /'mæksəməm/ *noun*
the largest amount, number, or size that is possible: *I can swim a maximum of 1 mile.* ≫ compare MINIMUM¹

maximum² *adjective*
biggest; largest: *What is the car's maximum
speed?* ≫ compare MINIMUM²

May /meɪ/ *noun*
the fifth month of the year

may /meɪ/ *verb*
1 used for saying that something is possible: *He
may come tonight, or he may come tomorrow.*
2 used for asking if you can do or have something: *May I use your pen?*
3 used in order to allow someone to do something: *You may begin writing now.*

may·be /'meɪbi/ *adverb*
used for saying something may be true or may
happen; perhaps: *"Are you coming?" "Maybe. I
don't know yet."*

mayor *noun*
someone who is elected to lead the government
of a city or town

me /mi/
1 the person who is speaking: *She handed the
book to me.* | *Can you see me?*
2 me too said when you agree with someone:
"I'm cold!" "Me too!"

meal /mil/ *noun*
the food that you eat at one time, or the time it
is eaten: *I always enjoy my evening meal.*

mean¹ /min/ *verb* [past meant /mɛnt/]
1 to have a particular meaning: *What does
this word mean in English?* | *The red light
means "stop."*
2 mean to do something to plan or want to do
something: *I meant to give you a book, but I forgot.*
3 mean a lot to someone to be very important
to someone: *His work means a lot to him.*

mean² *adjective*
not nice; cruel: *Don't be mean to your little sister.*

mean·ing /'minɪŋ/ *noun*
the information or idea that a word or sign has:
*If you don't understand the meaning of a word,
look it up in a dictionary.*

means /minz/ *plural noun*
1 a method, object etc. that is used for doing
something: *He climbed the tree by means of
(=using) a ladder.*

2 by all means certainly: *"May I borrow your pencil?" "By all means."*
3 the money that you have and can use: *His family does not have the means to help him.*
4 by no means not at all: *It is by no means certain that they will come.*

meant /mɛnt/
the PAST TENSE and PAST PARTICIPLE of the verb **mean**

mean·time /'mintaɪm/ *noun*
in the meantime in the time between two things happening, or while something is happening: *I'll call for a taxi. In the meantime you can pack.*

mean·while /'minwaɪl/ *adverb*
in the time between two things happening, or while something else is happening: *They will arrive soon. Meanwhile we can have a cup of coffee.*

meas·ure¹ /'mɛʒɚ/ *noun*
1 an official action for dealing with a problem: *Strong measures are needed to stop crime.*
2 an amount of something, or a way to measure size, weight etc.: *An inch is a measure of length.*

measure

measure² *verb* [measuring, measured]
to find out the size, weight, or amount of something: *He measured the width of the room.*

meas·ure·ment /'mɛʒɚmənt/ *noun*
the length, height, width, or amount of something

meat /mit/ *noun* [U]
the flesh of animals or birds, used as food: *I do not eat meat.*

me·chan·ic /mɪ'kænɪk/ *noun*
someone whose job is to repair vehicles or machines

me·chan·i·cal /mɪ'kænɪkəl/ *adjective*
relating to machines, or done by a machine

med·al /'mɛdl/ *noun*
a piece of metal given to someone as a prize or for doing something brave

med·i·cal /'mɛdɪkəl/ *adjective*
relating to medicine and to treating diseases and injuries: *He is a medical student.* —**medically** *adverb*

med·i·cine /'mɛdəsən/ *noun*
1 [U] the study and treatment of illnesses and injuries: *To become a doctor, you have to study medicine.*
2 something that you drink or eat when you are sick, to help you to get better

me·di·um /'midiəm/ *adjective*
of middle size or amount; not big or small: *She is of medium height.*

meet /mit/ *verb* [past **met**]
1 to come to the same place at the same time as someone else: *Let's meet at your house tonight.*
2 to see and talk to someone for the first time: *I would like you to meet my father.*

meet·ing /'mitɪŋ/ *noun*
a gathering of people to discuss something: *Many people came to the meeting.*

mel·o·dy /'mɛlədi/ *noun* [plural **melodies**]
a song or tune

mel·on /'mɛlən/ *noun*
a large juicy fruit with a thick skin—see picture at FRUIT

melt /mɛlt/ *verb*
to change from a solid to a liquid by heating: *The ice is melting in the sun.*

mem·ber /'mɛmbɚ/ *noun*
someone who has joined a group or organization: *Are you a member of the church?*

mem·ber·ship /'mɛmbɚˌʃɪp/ *noun* [U]
the fact of being a member of a group or organization, or all the people who are members: *Membership costs $20 a year.*

mem·o·ry /'mɛmri, -məri/ *noun* [plural **memories**]
1 the ability to remember things: *She has a good memory for faces.*
2 something that you remember about the past: *I have many happy memories of that summer.*

men /mɛn/
the plural of **man**

men·ace /'mɛnɪs/ *noun*
someone or something that causes danger or is annoying: *The insects are a menace this time of year.*

mend /mɛnd/ *verb*
to repair or fix a piece of clothing that is damaged: *Did you mend the hole in your shirt?*
≫ compare REPAIR¹

men·tal /ˈmɛntəl/ *adjective*
1 relating to the mind: *A lot of mental effort went into solving the problem.*
2 relating to an illness of the mind: *He is in a mental hospital.*

men·tion /ˈmɛnʃən/ *verb*
to speak or write about something in a few words: *He mentioned **to** me that he had been sick.*

men·u /ˈmɛnyu/ *noun*
1 a list of food that you can eat in a restaurant
2 a list of different choices shown on a computer

me·ow /miˈau/ *verb*
to make the sound that a cat makes —meow
noun

mer·cy /ˈmɔrsi/ *noun* [U]
kindness or pity shown to other people: *The man asked for mercy from the judge.*

mere·ly /ˈmɪrli/ *adverb*
only: *Don't get mad at me. I was merely making a suggestion.*

mer·it /ˈmɛrɪt/ *noun*
one of the good qualities of something

mer·maid /ˈmɔrmeɪd/ *noun*
a woman in children's stories who has a fish's tail instead of legs

mer·ry /ˈmɛri/ *adjective* (merrier, merriest)
happy, and having fun: *Have a merry Christmas!*

merry-go-round /ˈ.. . ,./ *noun*
a machine that turns around and around and has places where children can sit and ride

mess¹ /mɛs/ *noun*
1 a place or group of things that is not organized in a neat way: *Your room is in a mess.*
2 a situation in which there are a lot of problems: *My life is a real mess.*

mess² *verb*
1 **mess up** to make something dirty, or to make something go wrong: *I just cleaned the floor, and **now** you've messed it up again!*

2 **mess around** to play instead of working; to be silly: *Stop messing around and finish your work.*

mes·sage /ˈmɛsɪdʒ/ *noun*
a piece of information that you send to someone: *I have a message **for** you.*

mes·sen·ger /ˈmɛsəndʒɚ/ *noun*
someone who takes messages to other people

mess·y /ˈmɛsi/ *adjective* (messier, messiest)
1 dirty, or not arranged in a neat way: *What a messy room!* ≫ compare NEAT
2 unpleasant or difficult to deal with: *They had a messy divorce.*

met /mɛt/
the PAST TENSE and PAST PARTICIPLE of the verb meet

met·al /ˈmɛtl/ *noun*
a hard substance such as iron, gold, or steel

me·tal·lic /məˈtælɪk/ *adjective*
made of metal or like metal

meter /ˈmitɚ/ *noun*
1 a measure of length equal to 100 centimeters
2 a machine that measures the amount of something you use: *Where is your water meter?*

meth·od /ˈmɛθəd/ *noun*
a way of doing something: *What method **of** payment do you use?*

met·ric /ˈmɛtrɪk/ *adjective*
using the system of measuring based on meters, grams, and liters

mice /maɪs/
the plural of **mouse**

mi·cro·phone /ˈmaɪkrəˌfoun/ *noun*
a piece of equipment that makes your voice sound louder

mi·cro·scope /ˈmaɪkrəˌskoup/ *noun*
an instrument that helps you to see very small things by making them look much bigger: *She looked at the drop of water under a microscope.*

slide

mi·cro·wave /'maɪkrə,weɪv/ noun
a type of OVEN that cooks food very quickly

mid·day /'mɪd-deɪ/ noun [U]
the middle of the day, around 12 o'clock: She arrived just before midday. » compare NOON

mid·dle¹ /'mɪdl/ noun
the center of something: Please stand **in the middle of** the room. | I woke up in the middle of the night.

middle² adjective
in the center: I sat in the middle seat.

middle-aged /,mɪdl'eɪdʒd/ adjective
being between 40 and 60 years old —see color picture on page 191

middle school /'.. ,./ noun
a school for students between the ages of 11 and 14

mid·night /'mɪdnaɪt/ noun [U]
12 o'clock at night

might¹ /maɪt/ verb
1 the PAST TENSE of the verb **may**: I asked if I might borrow the book.
2 used for saying that something is possible: I might come and see you tomorrow.

might² noun [U]
strength and power: He tried with all his might to save her.

might·y /'maɪti/ adjective (mightier, mightiest)
strong and powerful: He gave the door a mighty push and it opened.

mi·grate /'maɪgreɪt/ verb (migrating, migrated)
1 to move from one place to another to live or find work » compare EMIGRATE
2 if birds or animals migrate, they travel at the same time every year from one part of the world to another

mi·gra·tion /maɪ'greɪʃən/ noun
the act of moving from one place to another: Many people study the migration of birds.

mild /maɪld/ adjective
1 not too severe or serious: I have a mild cold.
2 not tasting too hot or strong: This food is very mild. » compare HOT, SPICY
3 not too cold, wet, or hot: It's very mild today.
—**mildly** adverb

mile /maɪl/ noun
a measure of length equal to 1,760 yards or 1.6 kilometers

mil·i·tar·y¹ /'mɪlə,teri/ adjective
relating to soldiers or war: He is at a military hospital.

military² noun
the military the army, navy etc. of a country: My dad is in the military.

milk¹ /mɪlk/ noun [U]
the white liquid that comes from female animals and is used as food for their babies

milk² verb
to get milk from an animal: The farmer is going to milk the cows.

mill /mɪl/ noun
1 a large machine that crushes corn, grain etc. into powder
2 a building where things are made by machinery: She works in a cotton mill.

mil·len·ni·um /mə'leniəm/ noun
a period of time equal to 1,000 years, or the time when a new 1,000 year period begins

mil·li·me·ter /'mɪlə,mitɚ/ noun
a measure of length equal to 1/1000 of a meter

mil·lion /'mɪlyən/ noun
1 (plural million) the number 1,000,000
2 (also millions) a very large number: I have heard that song millions of times.

mil·lion·aire /,mɪlyə'nɛr/ noun
someone who is very rich

mime¹ /maɪm/ verb (miming, mimed)
to use actions and movements instead of words to entertain someone

mime² noun
an actor who uses actions and movements instead of words to entertain someone

mim·ic¹ /'mɪmɪk/ verb (mimicking, mimicked)
to copy the way someone speaks or moves in order to make people laugh: He mimicked the teacher's voice.

mimic² noun
someone who is good at copying the way someone speaks or moves

mince /mɪns/ verb (mincing, minced)
to cut food into very small pieces

mind¹ /maɪnd/ noun
1 your thoughts; your way of thinking: What's on your mind? (= what are you thinking about)
2 **change your mind** to change your opinion or

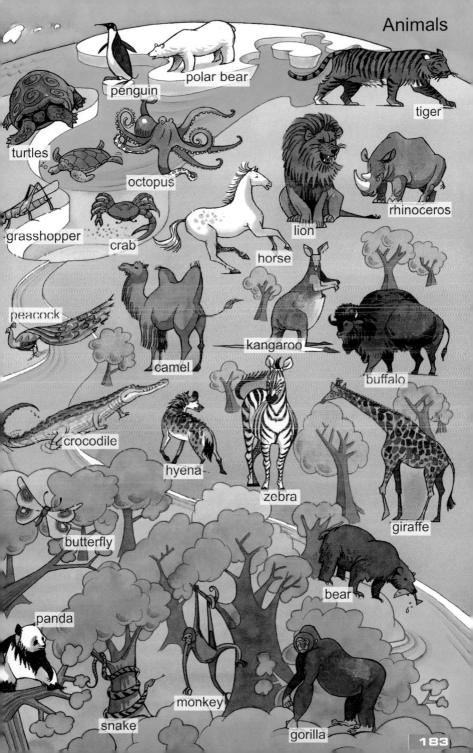

Animals

penguin

polar bear

tiger

turtles

octopus

rhinoceros

grasshopper

crab

horse

lion

peacock

camel

kangaroo

buffalo

crocodile

hyena

zebra

giraffe

butterfly

bear

panda

monkey

snake

gorilla

Sports

judo

snow-
boarding

football

basketball

hockey

skating

skiing

swimming

gymnastics

golf

baseball

track and field

tennis

soccer

ice
skating

Hobbies and Games

skateboard

books

guitar

posters

comic books

computer

joystick

CD player

camera

paint

Rollerblade™

photo album

easel

baseball bat, ball and glove

Walkman™

tennis racket

basketball

sport bag

185

The House

attic

bedroom

bathroom

hallway

living room

kitchen

garage

basement

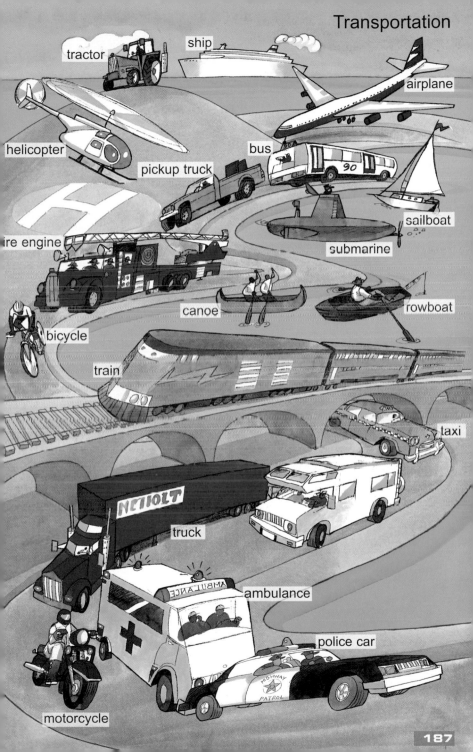

Transportation

tractor

ship

airplane

helicopter

bus

pickup truck

sailboat

submarine

fire engine

canoe

rowboat

bicycle

train

taxi

NETHOLT

truck

ambulance

police car

motorcycle

Camping

mountain

hill

valley

fence

forest

road

waterfall

woods

lake

bush

stream

tent

canoe

sleeping bag

backpack

field

stove

water bottle

fire

flowers

path

grass

river

188

Verbs of Movement

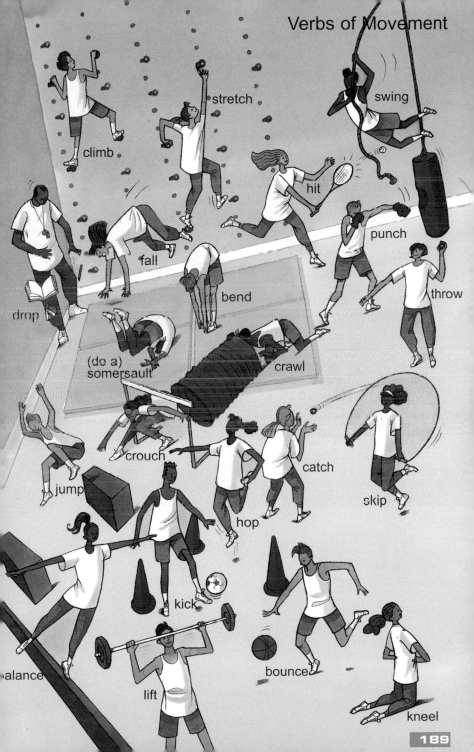

climb

stretch

swing

hit

punch

throw

fall

bend

drop

(do a) somersault

crawl

crouch

catch

skip

jump

hop

kick

bounce

balance

lift

kneel

Clothes

suit

sweats

sweater

overalls

T-shirt

shorts

sneaker

suspenders

scarf

cap

blouse

gloves

coa

skirt

jacket

raincoat

dress

jeans

pants

hat

shoes

mittens

shirt

boots

tie

socks

vest

Describing People

Movie THEATER

old slim
young
child
thin
overweight
teenager
baby
tall

beard
short
part
bangs
bald
bob
gray
braid
glasses
straight
light-brown
wrinkles
spiky
red
freckles
long
blond
receding
mustache
curly
black
ponytail
dark
wavy

191

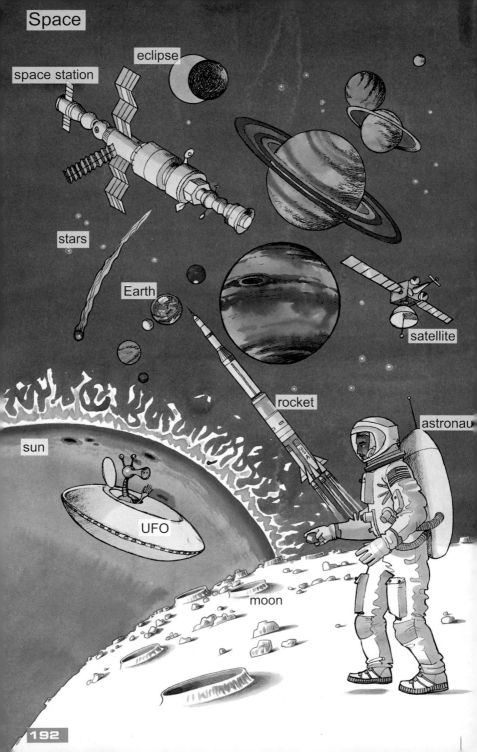

The Shopping Mall

bank — post office — delicatessen — bakery

NATIONAL BANK

POST OFFICE
US MAIL

Joe's Deli

Bob's BAKERY

toy store — bookstore — jewelry store — clothing store

TEDDY'S TOYS

J. C. BARRY BOOKS INC.

GOLD Jewelry

Jacob's CLOTHES

department store — shoe store — pet store — restrooms — CD store

MAYS CO

SHOE VIEW

Pets Corner

Pets Corner

CD STORE

phone booth

Phone Phone

193

Prepositions

decision about something: *I was going to go tomorrow, but I changed my mind.*
3 make up your mind to decide something: *I can't make up my mind which movie to see.*
4 take your mind off something to make you stop thinking about something: *I need a vacation to take my mind off all my problems.*
5 out of your mind crazy

mind² *verb*
1 to feel annoyed or angry about something: *Do you mind if I smoke?*
2 do you mind ..., would you mind ... a polite way of asking someone to do something: *Do you mind if I use the phone?* | *Would you mind moving your car?*
3 never mind said when telling someone that something is not important, or that you do not want to say something again: *"What did you say?" "Never mind."*
4 I wouldn't mind doing something said when you would like to do something: *I wouldn't mind moving to Arizona.*

mine¹ /maɪn/
something that belongs to the person speaking: *That bicycle is mine. I bought it yesterday.*

mine² *noun*
1 a deep hole in the ground from which coal, iron, gold etc. is dug
2 a kind of bomb that is put under the ground or in the ocean and explodes when it is touched

mine³ *verb* (mining, mined)
1 to dig into the ground for coal, iron, gold etc.: *They were mining for silver.*
2 to put bombs under the ground or in the ocean

min·er /ˈmaɪnɚ/ *noun*
someone who digs into the ground for coal, iron, gold etc.

min·er·al /ˈmɪnərəl/ *noun*
a natural substance like iron, coal, or salt that is found in the ground

mineral wa·ter /ˈ... ˌ../ *noun* [U]
water that comes from under the ground and has MINERALS in it

min·i·a·ture /ˈmɪniətʃɚ, ˈmɪnɪtʃɚ/ *adjective*
very small: *She has a miniature doll house.*

Prepositions

1. The child is sitting on a branch **above** her friend.

2. The boy is jumping **across** the stream.

3. There is a man leaning **against** a tree.

4. The children are running **around** the flowerbed.

5. The woman is walking **away from** the lake.

6. There is a boy hiding **behind** the tree.

7. There is a boy standing **below** the branch.

8. The man is standing **beside** his son.

9. The child is standing **between** its parents.

10. The mother is standing **by** the slide.

11. There is a child going **down** the slide.

12. The man is sitting **in** the car.

13. The man is standing **in front of** the bush.

14. The driver is getting **into** his car.

15. There is a woman standing **near** the parking lot.

16. The women are sitting **next to** each other.

17. The boy is jumping **off** the tree trunk.

18. There are lilies **on** the lake.

19. The men are climbing **onto** the pickup truck.

20. The children are standing **across from** each other.

21. The man is getting **out of** the car.

22. The girl is walking **over** the bridge.

23. The girl is skating **past** the tree.

24. The boy is running **through** the grass.

25. The child is running **toward** its mother.

26. The dog is sitting **under** the park bench.

27. The child is climbing **up** the slide.

min·i·mum¹ /ˈmɪnəməm/ *noun*
the smallest possible amount, number, or size: *You must pay a minimum of $40 every month.* ≫ compare MAXIMUM¹

minimum² *adjective*
smallest in amount that is possible or needed: *The minimum price he would accept was $1,000.* ≫ compare MAXIMUM²

min·is·ter /ˈmɪnəstɚ/ *noun*
a religious leader

min·is·try /ˈmɪnəstri/ *noun* [U]
the work done by a religious leader: *Her son joined the ministry.* (=became a minister)

mi·nor¹ /ˈmaɪnɚ/ *adjective*
smaller; not very important: *He has a minor illness.* ≫ compare MAJOR¹

minor² *verb*
minor in to study a second main subject as part of your college degree: *I'm minoring in African studies.*

mi·nor·i·ty /məˈnɔrəti, maɪ-, -ˈnɑr-/ *noun*
(*plural* **minorities**)
1 a group of people of a different race or religion than most people in a country: *Are you a member of a minority?*
2 [U] a small part of a larger group: *Only a minority of the children were noisy. Most were quiet.* ≫ compare MAJORITY

mint /mɪnt/ *noun*
1 a candy with a strong fresh taste
2 [U] a plant with a strong fresh taste, used in food and medicine

mi·nus /ˈmaɪnəs/ *preposition*
less: *10 minus 2 is 8.* [10 − 2 = 8] ≫ compare PLUS¹

min·ute¹ /ˈmɪnɪt/ *noun*
1 a measure of time equal to 60 seconds. There are 60 minutes in one hour: *The train arrives in ten minutes.*
2 in a minute very soon: *I'll be ready in a minute.*
3 just a minute wait for a short period of time: *Just a minute − I'll get some money.*
4 this minute now; immediately: *Come here this minute!*

mi·nute² /maɪˈnut/ *adjective*
very small: *His writing is minute.* ≫ compare TINY

mir·a·cle /ˈmɪrəkəl/ *noun*
1 something lucky that happens that you did not think was possible: *It was a miracle you weren't killed!*
2 an action or event that people believe is caused by God

mi·rac·u·lous /mɪˈrækyələs/ *adjective*
surprising and unexpected: *Her recovery from the illness was miraculous.*

mir·ror /ˈmɪrɚ/ *noun*
a flat piece of glass that you can look at and see yourself in: *She looked at her hair in the mirror.*

mis·be·have /ˌmɪsbɪˈheɪv/ *verb*
(**misbehaving, misbehaved**)
to behave badly: *I was angry because the children were misbehaving.*

mis·chief /ˈmɪstʃɪf/ *noun* [U]
bad behavior, especially by children: *He is always getting into mischief.*

mis·chie·vous /ˈmɪstʃəvəs/ *adjective*
wanting to do things which other people think are bad or silly

mis·er·a·ble /ˈmɪzərəbəl/ *adjective*
1 very unhappy: *I feel miserable about what happened.*
2 very bad in quality: *What miserable weather!*

mis·er·y /ˈmɪzəri/ *noun* [U]
great unhappiness: *He told us about the misery of life in prison.*

mis·for·tune /mɪsˈfɔrtʃən/ *noun*
bad luck; something bad that happens to you: *He had the misfortune of losing his job.*

miss¹ /mɪs/ *verb*
1 to not go somewhere or do something: *I will miss the meeting tomorrow.*
2 to arrive too late to get on a bus, train etc.: *Hurry or we'll miss the train.*
3 to feel sad when someone is not there: *We will miss you when you go away.*
4 to not hit or catch something: *He threw the ball to me, but I missed it.*
5 to not see, hear, or notice something: *Did you hear what he said? I missed it.*
6 miss out to not have the chance to do something that you enjoy: *You will miss out if you don't come to our party.*

miss² *noun*
1 Miss the title of a girl or a woman who is not married: *Have you seen Miss Johnson?* ≫ compare MRS., MS.
2 (*plural* **misses**) an action in which you try to hit or catch something, but do not

mis·sile /'mɪsəl/ *noun*
a weapon that can fly over a long distance and explode when it hits something

miss·ing /'mɪsɪŋ/ *adjective*
not in the correct place and not able to be found: *Police are searching for the missing child.*

mis·sion·ar·y /'mɪʃə,nɛri/ *noun (plural missionaries)*
someone who goes to another country to teach others about his or her religion

mist /mɪst/ *noun* [U]
a light cloud low over the ground: *We couldn't see through the mist.* ≫ compare FOG

mis·take¹ /mɪ'steɪk/ *noun*
1 something which is not correct: *You have made a mistake here; this 3 should be a 5.*
2 **by mistake** without intending to do something: *I took your pen by mistake.*

mistake² *verb* (**mistaking, mistook,** *past participle* **mistaken**)
1 to think that something is correct when it is not: *I was mistaken when I said she was a teacher. She is a doctor.*
2 **mistake someone for someone else** to think that someone is someone else: *I am sorry, I mistook you for someone I know.*

mist·y /'mɪsti/ *adjective*
having a lot of light cloud low over the ground: *It was a misty morning.* ≫ compare FOGGY

mit·ten /'mɪtⁿn/ *noun*
a piece of clothing that you wear on your hand, with one part for your four fingers together —see color picture on page 190

mix /mɪks/ *verb*
1 to put different things together to make something new; join together: *Mix the butter and flour together. | Oil and water don't mix.*
2 **mix someone up with** to think that someone is someone else: *It's easy to mix him up with his brother.*
3 **mix something up** to change the way things are arranged so that there is no order: *Someone mixed up my papers.* —**mixed** *adjective*

mix·ture /'mɪkstʃə/ *noun*
a substance made by mixing two or more different things together: *Pour the mixture into a pan.*

mm
the short way to write the word MILLIMETER or MILLIMETERs

moan /moʊn/ *verb*
to make a low sound of pain or sadness: *The child was moaning quietly.* —**moan** *noun*
≫ compare GROAN

mobile home /,moʊbəl 'hoʊm/ *noun*
a type of house made of metal that can be pulled by a vehicle and moved to another place

mock /mɑk/ *verb*
to laugh at someone in a way that is not nice: *You shouldn't mock the way he talks.*

mod·el¹ /'mɑdl/ *noun*
1 a small copy of something: *We built a model of the train.*
2 someone whose job is to wear new clothes at special shows so people will see them and want to buy the clothes

model² *verb*
1 to have a job in which you wear new clothes at special shows so people will see them and want to buy them
2 to make small objects from substances such as clay and wood

model³ *adjective*
a very small copy of something: *He is playing with a model car.*

mo·dem /'moʊdəm/ *noun*
a piece of electronic equipment that sends information from one computer along the telephone wire to another computer

mod·er·ate /'mɑdərɪt/ *adjective*
neither high nor low, fast nor slow, large nor small: *The train traveled at a moderate speed.*

mod·ern /'mɑdən/ *adjective*
new; belonging to the present time: *Do you like modern art?* ≫ compare OLD-FASHIONED

mod·est /'mɑdɪst/ *adjective*
not talking too much about your abilities or the things that you do well: *She is very modest about her success.* —**modesty** *noun* [U]

moist /mɔɪst/ *adjective*
a little wet; not dry: *His eyes were moist with tears.*

mois·ture /'mɔɪstʃə/ *noun* [U]
small drops of water: *I can see the moisture on the window.*

mold¹ /moʊld/ *verb*
to make something into a particular shape: *We molded the clay with our fingers.*

mold² *noun*
1 a hollow container that you pour a liquid into, so when it becomes solid it has the shape of the container
2 [U] a green substance that grows on old food and on things that are warm and wet

mold·y /'moʊldi/ *adjective* (**moldier, moldiest**)
covered with MOLD: *The bread is all moldy.*

mole /moʊl/ *noun*
1 a small animal that lives in holes in the ground
2 a small dark brown spot on someone's skin

mol·e·cule /'mɑlə,kyul/ *noun*
the smallest part into which a substance can be divided without changing its form

mom /mɑm/ *noun*
mother

mo·ment /'moʊmənt/ *noun*
1 a very short period of time: *I'll be back in a moment.*
2 a particular time: *He might come back at any moment.*
3 **at the moment** now: *At the moment, we are living in Tampa.*
4 **in a moment** very soon: *The doctor will see you in a moment.*
5 **for the moment** happening now but maybe not in the future: *The rain has stopped for the moment.*

mom·my /'mɑmi/ *noun* (*plural* **mommies**)
a word for mother, used by a child

mon·arch /'mɑnɚk, 'mɑnark/ *noun*
a king or queen

mon·ar·chy /'mɑnɚki/ *noun* (*plural* **monarchies**)
a country that is ruled by a king or queen

mon·as·ter·y /'mɑnəs,tɛri/ *noun* (*plural* **monasteries**)
a place where MONKs live

Mon·day /'mʌndi, -deɪ/ *noun*
the second day of the week

mon·ey /'mʌni/ *noun* [U]
1 coins and pieces of paper with their value printed on them: *How much money do you have?*

2 what you earn by working: *He **makes** a lot of money selling clothes.*
3 wealth: *Money isn't everything.*

monk /mʌŋk/ *noun*
one in a group of religious men who live together in a special building ≫ compare NUN

mon·key /'mʌŋki/ *noun* (*plural* **monkeys**)
an animal that has a long tail and uses its hands to climb trees —see color picture on page 183

mo·not·o·nous /mə'nɑtⁿn-əs/ *adjective*
boring because it is always the same: *My job is very monotonous.*

mon·soon /mɑn'sun/ *noun*
the heavy rain which falls at a particular time of year in parts of Asia

mon·ster /'mɑnstɚ/ *noun*
an imaginary creature that is frightening: *Do you believe in monsters?*

month /mʌnθ/ *noun*
one of the 12 periods of time into which a year is divided

month·ly /'mʌnθli/ *adjective, adverb*
happening every month or once a month: *We have a monthly meeting.*

mon·u·ment /'mɑnyəmənt/ *noun*
something that is built to help people to remember an important person or event

moo /mu/ *noun*
the sound that a cow makes —**moo** *verb*

mood /mud/ *noun*
the way you feel at any one time: *Why are you **in** such **a bad** mood?*

moon /mun/ *noun*
the large round object that shines in the sky at night ≫ compare SUN —see color picture on page 192

moon·light /'munlaɪt/ *noun* [U]
the light from the moon

mop¹ /mɑp/ *noun*
a long stick with thick threads on the end that you use to wash the floor

mop² *verb* (**mopping, mopped**)
to wash the floor using a wet MOP

mo·ped /'moʊpɛd/ *noun*
a vehicle with two wheels and a small engine

mor·al¹ /'mɔrəl, 'mɑrəl/ *adjective*
relating to the ideas of what is right and wrong:

I do not eat meat for moral reasons. —**morally** *adverb*

moral² *noun*
a lesson about what is right and wrong that you learn from a story or an event: *The moral of the story was that we should be honest.*

mor·als /'morəlz, 'mar-/ *plural noun*
the set of ideas about what is right and wrong that you use to decide how to live your life

more /mɔr/ *adverb*
1 a larger amount or number: *We spend more of our money on food these days.* ≫ compare LESS
2 in addition to what you have already, another thing or amount: *Would you like some more cake?*
3 more and more continuing to become greater in amount: *He got more and more angry.*
4 more or less about; almost: *The trip will cost us $500 more or less.*
5 once more again: *Read the sentence once more, please.*

morn·ing /'mɔrnɪŋ/ *noun*
the time from when the sun rises until the middle part of the day ≫ compare AFTERNOON

Morse code /ˌmɔrs 'koʊd/ *noun* [U]
a way of sending messages using short and long signals of light or sound

Mos·lem /'mazləm, 'mas-/ *noun*
a MUSLIM

mosque /mask/ *noun*
a building in which Muslims worship

mos·qui·to /məˈskiṭoʊ/ *noun* (*plural* mosquitoes)
a flying insect that drinks blood from people or animals and can spread disease from one person to another

moss /mɔs/ *noun* [U]
a flat green plant that grows on wet ground, trees, and rocks

most /moʊst/ *adverb*
1 the largest amount or number: *Most people travel in July and August.* ≫ compare LEAST
2 more than anything else: *Of course the coat I liked cost **the** most.*
3 at most, at the most not more than: *It will take an hour at the most.*
4 make the most of something to use something in the best way possible: *We only have two days here, so let's make the most of it!*

5 for the most part usually; most of the time: *Our students, for the most part, do very well.*

NOTE: Use **most** when you are talking about people or things in general: *Most kids like candy.* | *Most people have a TV.* Use **most of** when you are talking about a particular group of people or things: *Most of the people he works with are friendly.* | *I've read most of her books.*

most·ly /'moʊstli/ *adverb*
1 usually; most of the time: *When I go to the city, it's mostly on business.*
2 almost all: *The people at the party were mostly women.*

mo·tel /moʊˈtɛl/ *noun*
a hotel for people who travel by car, with a place for the car near the room

moth /mɔθ/ *noun*
an insect like a BUTTERFLY which flies at night

moth·er /'mʌðɚ/ *noun*
a female parent: *Her mother is a teacher.*

mother-in-law /'.. . ,./ *noun* (*plural* mothers-in-law)
the mother of your wife or husband

mo·tion /'moʊʃən/ *noun*
the process of moving, or the way something moves

mo·tion·less /'moʊʃənlɪs/ *adjective*
not moving: *The cat sat motionless.*

mo·tive /'moʊṭɪv/ *noun*
a reason for doing something: *Police think he had a motive for killing the man.*

mo·tor /'moʊṭɚ/ *noun*
an engine that makes things move or work

mo·tor·bike /'moʊṭɚˌbaɪk/ *noun*
a small MOTORCYCLE

motorcycle /'moʊṭɚˌsaɪkəl/ *noun*
a fast vehicle with two wheels and an engine —see color picture on page 187

mo·tor·ist /'moʊṭərɪst/ *noun*
someone who drives a car

mound /maʊnd/ *noun*
a small hill: *Your dog is digging in a mound of dirt.*

mount¹ /maʊnt/ *verb*
1 (*also* mount up) to become larger in size or amount

2 to get on a horse or bicycle

mount² *noun*

a mountain: *Mount Everest is the highest mountain in the world.*

mountain

mountain

hill

moun·tain /ˈmaʊntˀn/ *noun*

a very high hill: *Have you ever climbed a mountain?* —see color picture on page 188

mountain bike /ˈ.. ˌ./ *noun*

a strong bicycle with wide thick tires

mourn /mɔrn/ *verb*

to feel very sad because someone has died: *She mourned for her dead child.*

mourn·ing /ˈmɔrnɪŋ/ *noun* [U]

great sadness because someone has died: *She is in mourning (=feeling very sad) for her son.*

mouse /maʊs/ *noun*

1 (*plural* **mice**) a small animal with a long tail, which lives in buildings or fields ≫compare RAT

2 a small object connected to a computer that you can move and use to make the computer work

mouth /maʊθ/ *noun*

1 the part of your face that you put food into or use for speaking —see picture at HEAD¹

2 **keep your mouth shut** to not say anything: *I was very angry, but I kept my mouth shut.*

3 an opening, entrance, or a way out: *Our town is near the mouth of the river.*

mouth·ful /ˈmaʊθfʊl/ *noun*

the amount of food or drink that you put into your mouth at one time

move¹ /muv/ *verb* (**moving, moved**)

1 to go to a new place to live, work etc.: *I moved to New York.*

2 to change the position of something, or to take something from one place to another: *Can you move your car, please?* | *I can't move my legs.*

3 to make someone feel a strong emotion: *His story moved me.*

4 **move in** to start to live in a new home: *We should be able to move in next week.*

5 **move out** to leave the place where you are living and live somewhere else: *Mr. Smith moved out last week.*

move² *noun*

something you decide to do in order to achieve something: *Buying the house was a good move.*

move·ment /ˈmuvmənt/ *noun*

a change in position from one place to another: *I saw a movement behind the curtain.*

mov·ie /ˈmuvi/ *noun*

a story that is told using sound and moving pictures: *Do you want to go to the movies?* [=to the theater to see a movie]

movie star /ˈ.. ˌ./ *noun*

a famous movie actor or actress

mow /moʊ/ *verb* (**mowing, mowed,** *past participle* **mown**)

to cut grass with a machine

mow·er /ˈmoʊɚ/ *noun*

a machine that you use to cut the grass

Mr. /ˈmɪstɚ/ *noun*

a word put before a man's name: *This is Mr. Brown.*

Mrs. /ˈmɪsɪz/ *noun*

a word put before the name of a woman who is married: *This is Mrs. Brown.* ≫compare MISS², MS.

Ms. /mɪz/ *noun*

a word put before the name of a woman who does not want to call herself "Miss" or "Mrs."

much /mʌtʃ/

1 a lot; a large amount of: *Did you pay much for your bicycle?* | *Was there much traffic?* ≫compare LOT

2 **very much, so much** used for emphasizing something you are saying: *Thank you very much for your help.* | *I feel so much better today!*

3 **not much** (a) only a little or to a small degree: *She is not much older than I am.* (b) used for saying that something is not important or interesting: *"What have you been doing lately?" "Oh, not much."*

4 **how much** used for asking about the amount or cost of something: *How much milk is left?* | *I wonder how much that shirt costs.*

5 **too much** more than you need or want: *I have too much work to do.*

6 **as much as** the same amount as: *We don't have as much money as the Browns.*

NOTE: **Much** (1) is used in questions and in NEGATIVE sentences, e.g. *How much does it cost?* | *It doesn't cost much.* For other types of sentence, use **a lot of** instead: *It cost a lot of money.* | *He has a lot of work to do.*

mud /mʌd/ *noun* [U]
wet earth that is soft and sticky

mud·dy /ˈmʌdi/ *adjective* (**muddier, muddiest**)
covered with mud: *Take those muddy boots off!*

muf·fin /ˈmʌfən/ *noun*
a small sweet type of bread, often with fruit in it.

mug /mʌg/ *noun*
a large cup with straight sides and a handle
—see picture at CUP

mule /myul/ *noun*
an animal which is half horse and half DONKEY

mul·ti·ply /ˈmʌltə‚plaɪ/ *verb* (**multiplying, multiplied**)
to add a number to itself a particular number of times: *2 multiplied by 3 is 6 (2 x 3 = 6).*
≫ compare DIVIDE —**multiplication** *noun* [U]

mum·ble /ˈmʌmbəl/ *verb* (**mumbling, mumbled**)
to say something that is difficult for someone to hear or understand

mumps /mʌmps/ *noun* [U]
an illness that causes fever and swelling in your throat

mur·der[1] /ˈmɝdɚ/ *verb*
to kill someone on purpose and when it is against the law ≫ compare KILL, ASSASSINATE

murder[2] *noun*
the crime of killing someone on purpose

mur·der·er /ˈmɝdərɚ/ *noun*
someone who kills a person on purpose and when it is against the law ≫ compare KILLER

mur·mur[1] /ˈmɝmɚ/ *verb*
to say something in a soft quiet voice

murmur[2] *noun*
a soft quiet sound made by someone's voice: *I heard the murmur of voices in the hall.*

mus·cle /ˈmʌsəl/ *noun*
one of the parts of your body under your skin which make you strong and help you to move

mu·se·um /myuˈziəm/ *noun*
a building where you can see old, interesting, or beautiful things: *I went to the Museum of Modern Art.*

mush·room /ˈmʌʃrum/ *noun*
a plant with no leaves, a short stem, and a round top, some of which can be eaten

mu·sic /ˈmyuzɪk/ *noun* [U]
1 the pleasant sounds made by voices or by instruments: *What kind of music do you like?*
2 a set of written marks representing music: *I am looking for a sheet of music.*

mu·si·cal /ˈmyuzɪkəl/ *adjective*
1 relating to music or consisting of music: *The store sells musical instruments.*
2 good at playing or singing music: *She is very musical.*

mu·si·cian /myuˈzɪʃən/ *noun*
someone who plays a musical instrument very well or as a job

Mus·lim /ˈmʌzləm, ˈmʊz-, ˈmʊs-/ *noun*
someone whose religion is based on the Koran

must /məst; *strong* mʌst/ *verb*
1 used with another verb to show what is necessary or what has to be done: *I must go or I'll be late.*
2 used to show that you think something is very likely or certain: *It is very late, it must be nearly 12 o'clock.* | *I can't open the door. Someone must have locked it.*

mus·tache
/ˈmʌstæʃ, məˈstæʃ/
noun
hair that grows on a man's upper lip ≫ compare BEARD —see color picture on page 191

mustache

beard

mus·tard /ˈmʌstɚd/ *noun* [U]
a yellow powder made from the seeds of a plant, which is mixed with water to give a hot taste to food

must·n't /ˈmʌsənt/
must not: *You mustn't be late for school.*

must've /ˈmʌstəv/
must have: *Jane isn't here. She must've left.*

mut·ter /ˈmʌtɚ/ *verb*
to speak in a quiet voice which is difficult to hear: *He's always muttering to himself.*

mut·ton /ˈmʌtⁿn/ *noun* [U]
meat from a sheep eaten as food

my /maɪ/
belonging to the person speaking: *I hurt my knee when I fell off my bicycle.*

my·self /maɪˈsɛlf/
1 the same person as the one who is speaking: *I looked at myself in the mirror.*
2 used to give the word "I" a stronger meaning: *I made this shirt myself.*

mys·te·ri·ous /mɪˈstɪriəs/ *adjective*
very strange, and difficult to explain or understand: *He died suddenly of a mysterious illness.*

mys·ter·y /ˈmɪstəri/ *noun* [plural **mysteries**]
something that is difficult to explain or understand: *The location of the money remains a mystery.*

narrow   wide

nag /næg/ *verb* (**nagging, nagged**)
to complain to someone because you want him or her to do something: *Stop nagging me to fix the door!*

nail¹ /neɪl/ *noun*
1 a thin pointed piece of metal with one flat end that you push into a piece of wood using a hammer. ≫ compare SCREW¹
2 one of the hard flat parts at the end of your fingers and toes

nail² *verb*
to fasten something to something else using a nail: *Will you nail the sign on the door?*

na·ked /'neɪkɪd/ *adjective*
not wearing any clothes: *A naked body was found in the bushes.* ≫ compare NUDE

name¹ /neɪm/ *noun*
1 the word that you call someone or something: *My name is Jane Smith.* | *What is the name of this town?*
2 someone who is famous: *She is a big name in fashion.*

name² *verb* (**naming, named**)
to give a name to someone or something: *They named the baby Ann.*

name·ly /'neɪmli/ *adverb*
that is: *There is only one problem, namely, how to get more money.*

nan·ny /'næni/ *noun* (*plural* **nannies**)
a woman whose job is to take care of a family's children

nap /næp/ *noun*
a short sleep during the day: *He always takes a nap in the afternoon.*

nap·kin /'næpkɪn/ *noun*
a small piece of cloth or paper you use to keep your hands and mouth clean when you eat

nar·row /'næroʊ/ *adjective*
small in distance from one side to the other: *The gate is too narrow for cars to go through.* ≫ compare WIDE¹

nas·ty /'næsti/ *adjective* (**nastier, nastiest**)
1 not pleasant to see, taste, smell etc.: *The medicine has a nasty taste.*
2 not nice in behaviour: *Don't be so nasty to your sister!*

na·tion /'neɪʃən/ *noun*
all the people in one country and living under one government: *The whole nation supported the decision.*

na·tion·al /'næʃnl/ *adjective*
relating to a country: *Is today a national holiday?* ≫ compare INTERNATIONAL

national an·them /,... '../ *noun*
the official song of a nation, sung on special days and occasions

na·tion·al·i·ty /,næʃ'næləti/ *noun*
(*plural* **nationalities**)
the legal right of belonging to a particular country: *I have British nationality.*

na·tive¹ /'neɪtɪv/ *noun*
a native of something someone born in a particular place: *Mary is a native of Australia.*

native² *adjective*
relating to the place where you were born: *Her native language is Spanish.*

nat·u·ral /'nætʃərəl/ *adjective*
1 not made by people or machines: *Cotton is a natural material.*
2 usual or expected: *It's natural to feel nervous before your wedding.* ≫ compare NORMAL

nat·u·ral·ly /'nætʃrəli/ *adverb*
1 in a way that you would expect; usually: *You naturally make mistakes when speaking another language.*
2 not made or caused by anyone: *Her hair is naturally curly.*
3 of course: *"Are you excited to be home?" "Naturally."*

na·ture /'neɪtʃɚ/ noun [U]
1 the world and everything in it which people have not made, such as animals, weather, plants etc.: *These mountains are one of nature's most beautiful sights.*
2 the character of someone or something: *Peter is trusting by nature.*

naugh·ty /'nɔti/ adjective (**naughtier, naughtiest**)
a naughty child behaves badly and is not nice to people

na·val /'neɪvəl/ adjective
relating to the navy: *He wrote a book about naval battles.*

nav·i·gate /'nævə,geɪt/ verb (**navigating, navigated**)
to find the way to a place, especially using a map: *He navigated the ship across the ocean.*

nav·i·ga·tion /,nævə'geɪʃən/ noun [U]
the planning and directions about the way you get to a place: *Navigation on the river is difficult because of the rocks.*

nav·i·ga·tor /'nævə,geɪtɚ/ noun
someone on a ship or plane who plans the way it should go

na·vy /'neɪvi/ noun (**plural navies**)
the ships of a country used for fighting a war, and the people of these ships: *My son is in the navy.* ≫ compare ARMY, AIR FORCE

navy blue /,.. '.◄/ adjective, noun [U]
a very dark blue

near /nɪr/ adverb, preposition
1 not far; close, or only a short distance away: *My aunt lives near here.* ≫ compare FAR¹ —see picture on page 194
2 close in time to an event: *The work on the house is near completion.*

near·by /,nɪr'baɪ◄/ adjective, adverb
close, not far away: *We swim in a nearby river. | Is the school nearby?*

near·ly /'nɪrli/ adverb
1 almost: *We are nearly finished.*
2 not nearly   not at all: *I don't have nearly enough money to buy that book.*

neat /nit/ adjective
1 clean and well arranged: *She always keeps her room neat.* ≫ compare MESSY
2 very good or pleasant: *The movie was neat!* —**neatly** adverb —**neatness** noun [U]

nec·es·sar·y /'nesə,seri/ adjective
needed for you to do or have something: *Good food is necessary for your health.* ≫ opposite UNNECESSARY

ne·ces·si·ty /nə'sesəti/ noun (**plural necessities**)
something that you need to have or that must happen: *A car is a necessity for this job.*

neck /nɛk/ noun
1 the part of your body between your head and your shoulders —see picture at HEAD¹
2 the narrow part at the end of something: *The neck of the bottle is long and thin.*
3 be up to your neck in something   to be in a very difficult situation: *He is up to his neck in debt.*

neck·lace /'nɛk-lɪs/ noun
a piece of jewelry that you wear around your neck —see picture at JEWELRY

need¹ /nid/ noun
1 a situation in which something must be done to make the situation better: *There is a need to improve our schools.*
2 something that you want or must have: *The needs of a baby are simple.*
3 in need   not having enough food or money: *We're collecting money for children in need. | The country is in need of more doctors.*

need² verb
1 to want something that is necessary: *I need a hammer to take this nail out.*
2 need to do something   to have to do something: *You need to see a doctor as soon as you can.*

needle

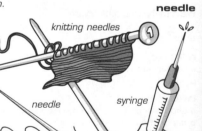

knitting needles

needle   syringe

nee·dle /'nidl/ noun
1 a thin piece of pointed metal with a hole at the end for thread, used for sewing
2 a thin, sharp, hollow piece of metal used for putting medicine directly into your body
3 a long, thin, pointed piece of plastic or metal you use to KNIT something

need·less /'nid-lɪs/ *adjective*
needless to say of course: *Needless to say, it rained the day we left.*

neg·a·tive¹ /'nɛgətɪv/ *adjective*
1 having a bad or harmful effect: *This decision will have a negative effect on the economy.*
2 saying or meaning "no": *He gave a negative answer.* (=he said "no")

negative² *noun*
a piece of film from which a photograph is made

ne·glect¹ /nɪ'glɛkt/ *verb*
to not pay enough attention to or to not take care of someone or something: *The animals were sick because they had been neglected.*

neglect² *noun* [U]
failure to take care of someone or something well: *His family suffered from neglect.*

ne·glect·ed /nɪ'glɛktɪd/ *adjective*
not well taken care of

neigh /neɪ/ *noun*
the loud sound that a horse makes

neigh·bor /'neɪbɚ/ *noun*
1 someone who lives near you: *He is my next door neighbor.*
2 someone who is sitting next to you: *Don't copy the answers from your neighbor's paper.*

neigh·bor·hood /'neɪbɚ,hʊd/ *noun*
the small area of a town and the people who live there: *There are several good restaurants in the neighborhood.*

neigh·bor·ing /'neɪbərɪŋ/ *adjective*
near to a place: *The flood affected the neighboring towns.*

nei·ther /'niðɚ, 'naɪ-/ *adjective*
1 not one and not the other of two people or things: *Neither boy could swim, but they both wanted to learn.* ≫ compare EITHER
2 used for agreeing with a negative statement: *"I don't like smoking." "Neither do I."*
3 neither ... nor ... used when two statements or facts are not true or possible: *Neither his father nor his mother is tall.*

neph·ew /'nɛfyu/ *noun*
the son of your brother or sister ≫ compare NIECE

nerd /nɚd/ *noun*
someone who is boring, wears stupid clothes, and does not know how to behave correctly

nerve /nɚv/ *noun*
1 the ability to stay calm in a dangerous or difficult situation: *It takes a lot of nerve to speak in front of people.*
2 a very small part of your body like a thread that controls your movements and carries messages to and from your brain

nerves /nɚvz/ *plural noun*
1 the feeling of being worried, nervous, or excited: *She is a bundle of nerves before a race.*
2 get on someone's nerves to annoy someone: *The loud music is beginning to get on my nerves.*

nerv·ous /'nɚvəs/ *adjective*
1 worried or afraid: *She is nervous about traveling alone.*
2 relating to the nerves in your body: *He has a disease of the nervous system.*

nest /nɛst/ *noun*
a place made by a bird, insect, or small animal to live in: *The bird laid three eggs in the nest.*

net /nɛt/ *noun*
1 material with open spaces between thread, string, or wire: *He hit the ball into the net.*
2 the INTERNET

net·tle /'nɛtl/ *noun*
a wild plant with rough leaves that sting you

net·work /ˈnɛtˀwɚk/ *noun*
1 a group of radio or television companies that show programs
2 a large group of lines, wires, roads etc. which cross or meet each other

nev·er /ˈnɛvɚ/ *adverb*
not at any time; not ever: *I've never been to Europe.* | *My brother never lets me ride his bicycle.* ⫸ compare ALWAYS

new /nu/ *adjective*
1 recently made, built, or bought: *We have a new car.* ⫸ compare OLD
2 not seen, used, known, or experienced before: *I'm learning a new language.*

new·com·er /ˈnuˌkʌmɚ/ *noun*
someone who has recently arrived or started a new activity: *He is a newcomer to the city.*

new·ly /ˈnuli/ *adverb*
very recently: *They are a newly married couple.*

news /nuz/ *noun* [U]
information about something that has just happened: *We watch the news on television.* | *Have you heard any news about Terry?*

news·pa·per /ˈnuzˌpeɪpɚ/ *noun*
a set of sheets of paper containing news and advertisements, which is sold every day or week: *I buy the local newspaper.*

news·stand /ˈnuzstænd/ *noun*
a place on a street where newspapers are sold

New Year's Day /ˌ. . ˈ./ *noun*
January 1

New Year's Eve /ˌ. . ˈ./ *noun*
December 31

next¹ /nɛkst/ *adjective*
1 coming or happening after the present one: *I'll see you next week.* | *When does the next flight leave?*
2 nearest: *Music is coming from the next room.*

next² *adverb*
1 just after something: *What did he do next?*
2 next to beside: *Come and sit next to me.*
—see color picture on page 194
3 next to nothing very little in amount: *I paid next to nothing for the shoes.*

next-door /ˌ. ˈ. ◂/ *adjective*
in the next room or building: *Did you meet the next-door neighbors?*

nib·ble /ˈnɪbəl/ *verb* (nibbling, nibbled)
to eat little bites of food: *She was nibbling on a piece of bread.*

nice /naɪs/ *adjective* (nicer, nicest)
1 pleasant, good, or attractive: *Have a nice time at the party.* | *You look nice!*
2 kind and friendly: *What a nice person!*

nick·el /ˈnɪkəl/ *noun*
a coin used in the U.S. that is worth 5 cents

nick·name /ˈnɪkneɪm/ *noun*
a name given to someone which is not their real name: *John's nickname is "Tiny" because he is very small.*

niece /nis/ *noun*
the daughter of your brother or sister ⫸ compare NEPHEW

night /naɪt/ *noun*
1 the time when it is dark and the sun cannot be seen: *It rained during the night.* | *Some nurses have to work at night.* ⫸ compare DAY
2 the evening: *We're going to a play Saturday night.*
3 the time when most people are sleeping: *The baby cries all night long.*
4 the other night a few nights ago
5 night and day all the time

night·gown /ˈnaɪtˀgaʊn/ *noun*
a piece of loose clothing that women wear in bed

night·in·gale /ˈnaɪtˀnˌgeɪl, ˈnaɪtɪŋ-/ *noun*
a bird that sings a beautiful song, especially at night

night·mare /ˈnaɪtˀmɛr/ *noun*
a dream which makes you very afraid

night·time /ˈnaɪt-taɪm/ *noun* [U]
the time during the night when the sky is dark ⫸ compare DAYTIME

nine /naɪn/ *adjective, noun*
the number 9

nine·teen /ˌnaɪnˈtin◂/ *adjective, noun*
the number 19

nine·ty /ˈnaɪnti/ *adjective, noun*
the number 90

ninth /naɪnθ/ *adjective, noun*
9th

nip /nɪp/ *verb* (nipping, nipped)
to bite someone with a small bite: *The dog nipped my leg.*

no /nou/ *adverb*
1 said to refuse something, to show that something is not true, or to not agree with something: *"Would you like some coffee?" "No, thanks."* | *I asked him for a dollar, but he said no.* ≫ compare YES
2 not any; not at all: *There are no children in the classroom.*
3 no way! a way of saying "no" very strongly: *"Are you going to help?" "No way!"*

no·ble /'noubəl/ *adjective* (**nobler, noblest**)
1 good or generous to others
2 belonging to one of the old important families in some countries

no·bod·y /'nou,bʌdi, -,badi/
(*also* **no one**) not anybody; no person: *I knocked on the door but nobody answered.* | *Nobody liked him.*

nod /nad/ *verb* (**nodding, nodded**)
to move your head up and down to show that you agree with someone, or to greet someone: *She nodded when I asked if she liked the movie.* —**nod** *noun*

noise /nɔɪz/ *noun*
a sound that is loud or unpleasant: *Planes make a lot of noise.* ≫ compare SOUND[1]

nois·y /'nɔɪzi/ *adjective* (**noisier, noisiest**)
making a lot of noise: *The class was filled with noisy children.* ≫ compare QUIET[1]

no·mad /'noumæd/ *noun*
someone who travels from place to place, especially as a member of a tribe —**nomadic** *adjective*

none /nʌn/
not one, not any: *None of my friends has a car.* | *I ate all the bread. There's none left.*

non·sense /'nansɛns, -səns/ *noun* [U]
1 ideas or opinions that are not true or seem stupid: *"I look fat in this dress." "Nonsense. You look fine."*
2 behavior that is stupid or annoying: *Stop that nonsense right now!*

non·stop /,nan'stap◂/ *adjective, adverb*
without stopping: *We went on a nonstop flight to Los Angeles.* | *We worked nonstop for two days.*

noon /nun/ *noun* [U]
the middle of the day; 12 o'clock: *At noon, the sun is high in the sky.* ≫ compare MIDDAY

no one /'. ./
(*also* **nobody**) nobody

nope /noup/ *adverb*
no: *"Are you hungry?" "Nope, not yet."*

nor /nɚ; *strong* nɔr/
a word used between two choices to show that neither is true: ***Neither** Anna nor Maria likes to cook.*

nor·mal /'nɔrməl/ *adjective*
usual or expected: *It's normal to feel tired after working hard.* ≫ compare NATURAL

nor·mal·ly /'nɔrməli/ *adverb*
usually: *Normally, I get up at seven o'clock.*

north /nɔrθ/ *noun, adjective, adverb*
the direction that is on the left when you look toward the rising sun: *The window faces north.* | *Which way is north?*

north·east /,nɔrθ'ist/ *noun, adjective, adverb*
the direction which is between north and east —**northeastern** *adjective*

north·ern /'nɔrðɚn/ *adjective*
in or from the north

North Pole /,. '. ./ *noun*
the North Pole the most northern point of the earth

north·ward /'nɔrθwɚd/ *adverb*
toward the north

north·west /,nɔrθ'wɛst/ *noun, adjective, adverb*
the direction which is between north and west —**northwestern** *adjective*

nose /nouz/ *noun*
1 the part of your face through which you breathe and with which you smell —see picture at HEAD[1]
2 turn up your nose at something to not accept something because you think it is not good enough for you
3 under someone's nose near to or in front of someone: *The pen I was looking for was under my nose the whole time!*

nos·tril /'nastrəl/ *noun*
one of the two holes in your nose through which you breathe —see picture at HEAD[1]

nos·y /'nouzi/ *adjective* (**nosier, nosiest**)
always trying to find out information about other people

not /nɑt/ *adverb*
a word that gives the opposite meaning to another word or a sentence: *I'm not going home now.* | *The flower is red, not pink.* | *Is the story true or not?*

note¹ /noʊt/ *noun*
1 a short written message: *I'll **write a note to** thank her for helping.*
2 something you write down to help you remember something: *Did you **make a note of** my new address?*
3 a particular sound in music, or the sign for this sound
4 take note of something to pay careful attention to something

note² *verb* [noting, noted]
to pay attention to something, or notice it: *Please note that the store is closed on Sunday.*

note·book /'noʊt‾bʊk/ *noun*
a book with plain pages in which you write your school work

note·pa·per /'noʊt‾ˌpeɪpɚ/ *noun* [U]
paper that you can write notes on

notes /noʊts/ *plural noun*
information that a student writes down from a class or book: *Did you **take** any notes?*

noth·ing /'nʌθɪŋ/
1 not anything; no thing: *There is nothing in this box.* | *She said nothing about the accident.*
2 for nothing (a) for no money: *Buy the table, and I'll give you the chairs for nothing.* **(b)** for no purpose, or for no good reason: *I did all that work for nothing.*

no·tice¹ /'noʊtɪs/ *noun*
a written or printed paper that gives information or is a warning to people: *The notice on the door said the library was closed.*

notice² *verb* [noticing, noticed]
to see, hear, or smell something: *Did you notice a strange smell in the room?*

no·tice·a·ble /'noʊtɪsəbəl/ *adjective*
easy to notice: *Your work is showing a noticeable improvement.*

no·to·ri·ous /noʊ'tɔriəs/ *adjective*
famous for doing something bad: *She is a notorious criminal.*

noun /naʊn/ *noun*
a word that is the name of a person, place, animal, or thing: *In the sentence, "The boy threw a stone at the dog," "boy," "stone," and "dog" are all nouns.*

nov·el /'nɑvəl/ *noun*
a book that tells a long story about someone or something

nov·el·ist /'nɑvəlɪst/ *noun*
someone who writes a NOVEL

No·vem·ber /noʊ'vɛmbɚ, nə-/ *noun*
the 11th month of the year

now /naʊ/ *adverb*
1 at this time: *Tokyo is now one of the largest cities in the world.* | *She should have been home by now.*
2 used for getting someone's attention, or to start talking about something else: *Now, children, open your books to page 6.*
3 for now for a short time: *Jim will be working here for now.*

no·where /'noʊwɛr/ *adverb*
not any place: *The birds on the island are found nowhere else.* ≫ compare EVERYWHERE

nu·cle·ar /'nukliɚ/ *adjective*
relating to or using the very great power made by dividing an atom or joining atoms: *Our electricity comes from nuclear power.*

nu·cle·us /'nukliəs/ *noun* [plural **nuclei** /'njuːklɪaɪ/]
the central part of an atom

nude /nud/ *adjective*
not wearing any clothes ≫ compare NAKED

nudge /nʌdʒ/ *verb* [nudging, nudged]
to push someone in a gentle way, using your elbow: *She nudged me when it was time to go.*
—**nudge** *noun*

nug·get /'nʌgɪt/ *noun*
a small rough piece of something such as metal: *a gold nugget*

nui·sance /'nusəns/ *noun*
someone or something that annoys you or causes problems: *Don't **make a** nuisance **of** yourself!*

numb /nʌm/ *adjective*
not able to feel anything: *My feet are numb from the cold.*

num·ber¹ /'nʌmbɚ/ *noun*
1 a figure such as 1, 2, 3 etc.
2 a set of numbers that you use to telephone someone: *Can you give me her number?* | *I dialed the wrong number.*

3 an amount of something that you can count: *A large number of tigers were in the cage.*
4 a sign that shows the position of something: *Look at question number four.* | *What is his room number?*

number² *verb*
to give a figure or number to something: *Number the pages from 1 to 100.*

nu·mer·al /ˈnumərəl, ˈnumrəl/ *noun*
a sign that represents a number: *3, 22, and 185 are numerals.*

num·er·ous /ˈnumərəs/ *adjective*
many: *We met on numerous occasions.*

nun /nʌn/ *noun*
one of a group of religious women who live together in a special building ≫compare MONK

nurse¹ /nɚs/ *noun*
someone who is trained to help doctors and take care of people who are sick or injured: *She works as a nurse in a hospital.*

nurse² *verb* (**nursing, nursed**)
to take care of people who are sick or injured: *She nursed her mother when she was sick.*

nurs·er·y /ˈnɚsəri/ *noun* (*plural* **nurseries**)
1 a place where plants and trees are grown and sold
2 a room for a very young child
3 a place where children are taken care of while their parents are at work or shopping

nursery rhyme /ˈ... ˌ./ *noun*
a short, well-known song for children

nursery school /ˈ... ˌ./ *noun*
a school for young children between three and five years old

nut /nʌt/ *noun*
1 a large seed that you can eat
2 someone who is crazy or behaves in a strange way
3 a small piece of metal with a hole in it which is used with a BOLT to fasten things together

nu·tri·tion /nuˈtrɪʃən/ *noun* [U]
the process of eating the right kinds of food in order to be healthy: *Exercise and good nutrition are important.*

ny·lon /ˈnaɪlɑn/ *noun* [U]
a strong material used for making plastic, cloth, rope etc.

o /oʊ/
used for saying the number zero: *She is in room 203.* [=two o three]

oak /oʊk/ *noun*
a large tree, or the hard wood of this tree

oar /ɔr/ *noun*
a long pole with a flat blade at the end, used for making a boat move through the water

o·a·sis /oʊˈeɪsɪs/ *noun* (*plural* **oases** /ɛʊreɪsiːz/)
a place in the desert with water and trees

oath /oʊθ/ *noun* (*plural* **oaths** /oʊðz, oʊθs/)
a very serious promise: *She took an oath to tell the truth in court.*

oat·meal /ˈoʊt⌐mil/ *noun* [U]
a hot breakfast food made by boiling grain in water until it is very soft

oats /oʊts/ *plural noun*
a grain that is used as food

o·be·di·ence /əˈbidiəns, oʊ-/ *noun* [U]
behavior in which you do what you are told to do: *He acted in obedience to the law.* ≫ opposite DISOBEDIENCE

o·be·di·ent /əˈbidiənt, oʊ-/ *adjective*
willing to do what someone tells you to do: *He is an obedient child.* ≫ opposite DISOBEDIENT

o·bey /əˈbeɪ, oʊ-/ *verb* (**obeying, obeyed**)
to do what someone tells you to do: *You should obey your teacher.* ≫ opposite DISOBEY

ob·ject¹ /ˈɑbdʒɪkt, ˈɑbdʒɛkt/ *noun*
1 a thing that you can see, hold, or touch: *What is that object there?*
2 the purpose of a plan or activity: *The object of this game is to roll the ball into the hole.*
3 a word used in grammar to describe the person or thing that is affected by the verb in a sentence: *In the sentence, "Jane bought the bread," "bread" is the object.*

ob·ject² /ɑbˈdʒɛkt/ *verb*
to say that you do not like or do not agree with something: *She objected to our plan.*

ob·jec·tion /əbˈdʒɛkʃən/ *noun*
a reason you give for not liking or agreeing with something: *She had strong objections to working on Sundays.*

ob·li·ga·tion /ˌɑbləˈgeɪʃən/ *noun*
something you must do because it is your duty

o·blige /əˈblaɪdʒ/ *verb* (**obliging, obliged**)
to make it necessary for someone to do something: *I felt obliged to tell her the truth.* ≫ compare FORCE¹

ob·long /ˈɑblɔŋ/ *adjective*
having a shape that is longer than it is wide ≫ compare RECTANGLE

ob·ser·va·tion /ˌɑbzɚˈveɪʃən, -sɚ-/ *noun*
1 [U] the act of carefully watching someone or something: *He is under observation in the hospital.*
2 a remark about something you have noticed: *She made several observations about the way people treated her.*

ob·serve /əbˈzɚv/ *verb* (**observing, observed**)
to watch someone or something carefully: *Children learn to do things by observing other people.*

ob·sta·cle /ˈɑbstɪkəl/ *noun*
something that makes it difficult for you to succeed

ob·struct /əbˈstrʌkt/ *verb*
to block a road, path, or someone's view: *The building obstructs our view of the beach.*

ob·struc·tion /əbˈstrʌkʃən/ *noun*
something that blocks the way: *The accident caused an obstruction in the road.*

ob·tain /əbˈteɪn/ *verb*
to get something: *Information about the disease is difficult to obtain.*

ob·vi·ous /ˈɑbviəs/ *adjective*
easy to see or understand: *It is obvious that she is lying.* ≫ compare APPARENT

oc·ca·sion /əˈkeɪʒən/ *noun*
1 a time when something happens: *I spoke to him on several occasions.*
2 a special event: *We are saving the wine for a special occasion.*

oc·ca·sion·al /əˈkeɪʒənl/ *adjective*
happening sometimes but not often —**occasionally** *adverb*: *We occasionally go to the movies.*

oc·cu·pa·tion /ˌɑkyə'peɪʃən/ *noun*
a job: *"What is your occupation?" "I am a doctor."*

oc·cu·py /'ɑkyə,paɪ/ *verb* (**occupying,
occupied**)
1 to live in a place: *Two families occupy the
house.*
2 to fill a particular position or space: *His pictures occupy the entire wall.*
3 to keep someone busy: *The game will keep
the kids occupied.*

oc·cur /ə'kɚ/ *verb* (**occurring, occurred**)
1 to happen: *The accident occurred at five
o'clock.*
2 occur to someone to suddenly come into
someone's mind: *The idea had never occurred
to me before.*

o·cean /'ouʃən/ *noun*
a very large area of water: *We sailed across
the Atlantic Ocean.*

o'clock /ə'klɑk/ *adverb*
a word used for saying what time it is: *It's four
o'clock.*

Oc·to·ber /ɑk'toubɚ/ *noun*
the 10th month of the year

oc·to·pus /'ɑktəpəs/ *noun* (*plural*
octopuses *or* **octopi**)
a soft sea creature with eight long arms —see
color picture on page 183

odd /ɑd/ *adjective*
1 strange or unusual: *It's odd that he hasn't
called me.*
2 odd number a number that cannot be divided by two: *3, 7, and 15 are odd numbers.*
>> compare EVEN[1]

odds /ɑdz/ *plural noun*
how likely it is that something will happen: *What
are the odds of our success?*

odds and ends /ˌ. . './ *plural noun*
various small things which are not very important or useful: *I have a box full of odds and
ends.*

o·dor /'oudɚ/ *noun*
a smell, especially a bad one: *Where is that
odor coming from?*

of /əv, ə; *strong* ʌv/ *preposition*
1 part of something; belonging to something:
The streets of New York are crowded.
2 used for showing a quality or relationship of
someone or something: *I like the color of her
hair.* | *The size of the building was huge!*

3 used for showing that someone or something is part of a larger group: *Here is one of
the books from his library.*
4 used for showing that one thing contains
something else: *I bought a carton of milk.*
5 used for showing an amount or measurement: *I want a cup of coffee.* | *The house has
plenty of space inside.*
6 used for giving the name of something: *I like
the game of chess.*
7 used for giving the reason or cause of something: *He is dying of cancer.*
8 used in dates: *He was born on the 12th of
June.*
9 used for showing direction or distance: *She
lives north of the city.*

off¹ /ɔf/ *adverb, preposition*
1 away from something: *Can you pull this lid
off?* | *One of my buttons fell off.* | *He got off the
bus.* >> compare ON[1] —see color picture on
page 194
2 not on something, not touching something:
Get your feet off the bed!
3 turn something off to make something stop
working: *Turn the lights off when you leave.*
4 far in distance or long in time: *I le drove off.* |
Summer is a long way off.
5 not working: *He's off for three days.*
6 lower in price: *Their computers are 25% off.*

off² *adjective*
1 removed or not connected: *The lights in the
house were all off.*
2 not happening: *Their wedding is off.*

of·fend /ə'fɛnd/ *verb*
to make someone angry or upset: *I offended
him by not answering his letter.* >> compare UP-
SET[1]

of·fense /ə'fɛns/ *noun*
1 something that is wrong; a crime: *It is an
offense to drink alcohol and drive a car.*
2 take offense to feel angry or upset about
something someone says to you: *She took
offense when I asked how old she was.*

of·fen·sive /ə'fɛnsɪv/ *adjective*
very impolite and likely to make people very
upset: *He made some offensive comments to
the waitress.*

of·fer¹ /'ɔfɚ, 'ɑfɚ/ *verb*
1 to show that you are willing to give something to someone: *I offered James some of my
candy.*
2 to say that you are willing to do something:
She offered to help me carry the boxes.

offer² *noun*

1 a statement that you are happy to help with something: *Thank you for your offer of help.*
2 the amount of money that you are willing to pay for something: *They **made** us **an** offer on the house.*

of·fice /ˈɔfɪs, ˈɑ-/ *noun*
a room or building where you do your work: *She works in an office.*

of·fi·cer /ˈɔfəsɚ, ˈɑ-/ *noun*
1 someone in the army, navy etc. who has a position of authority
2 someone who has an important position in an organization, the police etc.

of·fi·cial¹ /əˈfɪʃəl/ *adjective*
approved by someone in authority: *I received an official letter from the government.*

official² *noun*
someone who has an important job in the government or an organization

of·ten /ˈɔfən, ˈɔftən/ *adverb*
many times: *I often go to bed early.* | *How often does it rain here?*

oh /oʊ/
said when you are surprised, happy, annoyed etc.: *Oh, no! I missed the bus!*

oil¹ /ɔɪl/ *noun* [U]
thick dark liquid that comes from under the ground, used for cooking, burning, or making machines work smoothly: *The company is drilling for oil.*

oil² *verb*
to put oil on or into something

oil paint·ing /ˈ. ˌ../ *noun*
a picture painted with paint that has oil in it

oil rig /ˈɔɪl rɪg/ *noun*
a large piece of machinery used for digging in the ground or under the ocean to find oil

oil well /ˈ. ./ *noun*
a deep hole in the ground from which oil is taken

oil·y /ˈɔɪli/ *adjective* (**oilier, oiliest**)
covered with oil, or containing a lot of oil

oint·ment /ˈɔɪntˈmənt/ *noun*
a substance that you rub into your skin as a medical treatment

OK /ˌoʊˈkeɪ/ *adjective, adverb*
1 said when you agree with someone, or when saying that someone can do something: *"I'll go first." "OK."* | *Is it OK if I leave?*

2 not sick, injured, or unhappy: *"How is your mother?" "She's OK."*

o·kay /oʊˈkeɪ/
another way to write **OK**

old /oʊld/ *adjective*
1 having lived a long time: *My grandmother is very old.* ≫ compare YOUNG¹ —see color picture on page 191
2 having a particular age: *"How old are you?" "I am eleven years old."*
3 having been used for a long time: *What do you do with your old clothes?*
4 an old friend a friend you have known for a long time

old-fash·ioned /ˌ. ˈ..◂/ *adjective*
not modern or popular: *He has old-fashioned ideas about women.* ≫ compare MODERN, OUTDATED

ol·ive /ˈɑlɪv/ *noun*
a small green or black fruit eaten as food or used for making oil

O·lym·pic Games /əˌlɪmpɪk ˈgeɪmz, oʊ-/ *plural noun*
the Olympic Games (*also* **the Olympics**) an international sports competition which takes place every four years

ome·lette /ˈɑmlɪt/ *noun* (*also* **omelet**)
a mixture of eggs beaten together and cooked, often with other foods

o·mit /oʊˈmɪt, ə-/ *verb* (**omitting, omitted**)
to not include something; to leave something out: *My name was omitted **from** the list.*

on¹ /ɔn, ɑn/ *adverb, preposition*
1 touching or hanging from something: *The glass is on the shelf.* | *I have mud on my shoes.* ≫ compare OFF¹ —see color picture on page 194
2 in a particular place: *The picture is on page 40.* | *I grew up on a farm.*
3 continuing without stopping: *We drove on to the next city.*
4 at a particular time or date: *The party is on March 12th.*
5 being shown on television: *I saw the movie on television.*
6 forward or ahead: *We were tired, but we needed to move on.*
7 covering a part of your body: *Put your coat on.*
8 in a vehicle: *I saw Jane on the bus.*
9 used for saying what has been used for doing something: *I drew this on a computer.*

10 in a particular direction: *She sat on my right.*

on² *adjective*
1 being shown on television: *What's on tonight?*
2 working, or ready to use: *Is the oven on?*

once /wʌns/ *adverb*
1 one time: *I have been to America once.* | *We go shopping once a week.*
2 in the past, but not now: *My grandmother was a teacher once.*
3 from the time that something happens: *It is easy, once you learn how to do it.*
4 (every) once in a while sometimes, but not often: *We go fishing every once in a while.*
5 at once (a) at the same time: *You can't do two things at once.* (b) now; immediately: *We must go at once!*
6 once more one more time: *Try calling her once more.*
7 all at once suddenly: *All at once everyone stopped talking.*
8 once upon a time a phrase used at the beginning of children's stories, meaning "a long time ago"

one /wʌn/
1 the number 1
2 a single thing or person: *She only has one shoe on.*
3 one o'clock: *I have a meeting at one.*
4 a particular time in the past: *One week last December it snowed.*
5 a time in the future: *We should go to the movies one day.*
6 only: *My one goal is to do better in school.*
7 someone or something that has been mentioned or is known about: *"Which one do you want?" "That one."*

one-way /ˌ. '.◂/ *adjective*
moving or allowing movement only in one direction: *He lives on a one-way street.*

on·ion /ˈʌnyən/ *noun*
a round white vegetable with many layers and a strong taste —see picture at VEGETABLE

on-line /ˌ. '.◂/ *adjective*
connected to other computers that are on the INTERNET: *Is your school on-line?*

on·ly¹ /ˈoʊnli/ *adjective, adverb*
1 being the one person or thing of a particular kind: *She is the only girl in her family.*
2 and nothing more; and no one else: *You can only have one piece of cake.* | *This room is for teachers only.*

3 in one way or for one reason: *She is only doing this because she is angry.*
4 an only child a child with no brothers or sisters

only²
except that; but: *I want to come with you, only I have to stay home and help my mom.*

on·to /*before consonants* ˈɔntə, ˈɑn-; *before vowels and strong* ˈɔntu, ˈɑn-/ *preposition*
in or on a particular place: *He climbed onto the roof.* —see color picture on page 194

on·ward /ˈɔnwəd, ˈɑn-/ *adverb*
forward in time or space: *They hurried onward.* | *We studied history from 1900 onward.*

ooze /uz/ *verb* (**oozing, oozed**)
to move or flow slowly: *Blood oozed from his knee.*

o·pen¹ /ˈoʊpən/ *adjective*
1 not shut or closed: *Who left the window open?* | *I'm so tired I can't keep my eyes open.* ≫ compare CLOSED —see picture at AJAR
2 ready for business: *Is the bank open yet?* ≫ compare CLOSED
3 not surrounded or covered by other things: *We drove through open country.*
4 available to anyone: *Many jobs are open to women now.*
5 willing to listen to other people: *Are you open to suggestions?*

open² *verb*
1 to make something open, or become open: *Open your books to page three.* | *The door opened and I came in.*
2 to begin to do business: *When does the store open?*
3 to make something available to someone: *The building opened to the public this year.*

o·pen·er /ˈoʊpənə/ *noun*
an instrument for opening things: *Do you have a bottle opener?*

o·pen·ing /ˈoʊpənɪŋ/ *noun*
1 a hole or space in something: *I see an opening in the fence.*
2 a job that is available: *Are there any openings at the factory?*

op·er·a /ˈɑprə, ˈɑpərə/ *noun*
a play that has songs and music instead of spoken words

op·er·ate /'ɑpə,reɪt/ *verb* [operating, operated]
1 to work or to make something work: *Do you know how to operate this machine?*
2 to cut open someone's body to remove or repair a part that is damaged: *The doctors operated on her stomach.*

op·er·a·tion /,ɑpə'reɪʃən/ *noun*
the process of cutting open someone's body to remove or repair a part that is damaged: *He needs to have an operation on his back.*

op·er·a·tor /'ɑpə,reɪtə/ *noun*
1 someone who controls the telephone calls made to or from a place
2 someone who controls a machine or piece of equipment

o·pin·ion /ə'pɪnyən/ *noun*
your ideas or beliefs about something: *In my opinion* (=I think), *you're wrong.* | *What's your opinion on this subject?*

op·po·nent /ə'poʊnənt/ *noun*
someone who tries to defeat someone else in a game or competition

op·por·tu·ni·ty /,ɑpə'tunəti/ *noun* (*plural* opportunities)
a chance or time to do something: *I have an opportunity to travel to Asia.*

op·pose /ə'poʊz/ *verb* [opposing, opposed]
to not agree with something: *My mother opposes the idea of me getting married.* —**opposed** *adjective*

op·po·site¹ /'ɑpəzɪt, -sɪt/ *adjective, preposition*
1 as different as possible: *The buses went in opposite directions. One went south and the other went north.*
2 facing something or across from something: *The library is on the opposite side of the road from the school.*

opposite² *noun*
someone or something that is as different as possible from someone or something else: *Hot is the opposite of cold.*

op·ti·mist /'ɑptə,mɪst/ *noun*
someone who always believes that good things will happen ≫ compare PESSIMIST

op·ti·mis·tic /,ɑptə'mɪstɪk/ *adjective*
believing that good things will happen: *I'm optimistic that we'll win the game.* ≫ compare PESSIMISTIC

op·tion /'ɑpʃən/ *noun*
a choice; the power to choose: *What are our options?*

op·tion·al /'ɑpʃənl/ *adjective*
not needed by you, but able to be chosen or done if you want: *Red paint is optional on this car.*

op·tom·e·trist /ɑp'tɑmətrɪst/ *noun*
someone who tests your eyes and makes GLASSES

or /ə; *strong* ɔr/
1 used when giving a choice: *Do you want tea or coffee?*
2 not one thing and not the other: *I don't like lemons or oranges.*
3 used for giving a warning or the reason for something: *Hurry or you will be late!*

o·ral /'ɔrəl/ *adjective*
spoken, not written: *We had an oral test.*

or·ange /'ɔrɪndʒ, 'ɑr-/ *noun*
1 a round sweet juicy fruit with a thick skin —see picture at FRUIT
2 the color of this fruit —**orange** *adjective*

orbit

or·bit¹ /'ɔrbɪt/ *noun*
the path of one thing moving around another in space

orbit² *verb*
to move in a circle around something in space: *The space vehicle orbited the moon.*

or·chard /'ɔrtʃəd/ *noun*
a place where fruit trees are grown

or·ches·tra /'ɔrkɪstrə/ *noun*
a large group of people who play musical instruments together

or·der¹ /'ɔrdə/ *noun*
1 **in order to do something** so that something can happen, or someone can do something: *He stood on the chair in order to reach the light.*
2 the way that things are arranged or put on a list: *The words are in alphabetical order.* [=starting at A and finishing at Z]

3 a request for goods from a company, or the goods that are asked for: *Can I **take** your order?*
4 [U] a situation in which other people obey rules and authority: *Police want to keep **law and order** in the town.*
5 a command; something you must do: *Soldiers must obey orders.*
6 out of order not working: *The telephone is out of order.*

order² *verb*
1 to tell someone to do something: *He ordered the soldiers to attack.*
2 to ask for goods or services: *I ordered a new table for the office.* | *Who ordered the pie?*
3 to arrange something in a particular way: *Their society is ordered by family groups.*

or·di·nar·i·ly /ˌɔrdn'ɛrəli/ *adverb*
usually: *Ordinarily I would drive, but I don't feel well.*

or·di·nar·y /'ɔrdn,ɛri/ *adjective*
1 usual; not special or different: *It was just an ordinary day today.*
2 out of the ordinary very unusual or different: *Did you notice anything out of the ordinary at school today?*

ore /ɔr/ *noun*
rock or earth in which metal is found

or·gan /'ɔrgən/ *noun*
1 a part of an animal or a plant that has a special purpose: *The eyes are your organs of sight.*
2 a large musical instrument like a piano with long pipes that make sounds

or·gan·ic /ɔr'gænɪk/ *adjective*
grown without using dangerous chemicals: *organic fruit and vegetables*

or·ga·ni·za·tion /ˌɔrgənə'zeɪʃən/ *noun*
1 a group of people with a special purpose such as a club or business
2 [U] the way in which something is organized or planned: *Good organization makes your work easier.* —**organizational** *adjective*

or·ga·nize /'ɔrgə,naɪz/ *verb* (**organizing, organized**)
to plan or arrange something: *Did you organize the wedding by yourself?* | *I need to organize my business records.*

or·ga·nized /'ɔrgə,naɪzd/ *adjective*
1 planned or arranged carefully: *Her desk is always very organized.* ⟩⟩ opposite DISORGAN-IZED
2 arranged and done by many people: *The police think he is involved in organized **crime**.*

or·i·gin /'ɔrədʒɪn, 'ɑr-/ *noun*
the place or situation from which something comes: *What is the origin **of** the custom?*

o·rig·i·nal /ə'rɪdʒənl/ *adjective*
1 first; earliest: *Who was the original owner of the house?*
2 new and different: *He has an original idea for a new game.*
3 not copied: *This is the original painting.*

o·rig·i·nal·ly /ə'rɪdʒənl-i/ *adverb*
in the beginning: *My family originally came from Mexico.*

or·na·ment /'ɔrnəmənt/ *noun*
an object that is beautiful, but not useful and is used to decorate something: *We hung the ornaments on the Christmas tree.*

or·phan /'ɔrfən/ *noun*
a child whose mother and father are dead

or·phan·age /'ɔrfənɪdʒ/ *noun*
a home for children whose parents are dead

os·trich
/'ɑstrɪtʃ, 'ɔ-/ *noun*
(*plural* **ostriches**)
a very large bird with long legs which runs fast, but cannot fly

oth·er /'ʌðɚ/
1 not the same; a different one: *My brother sleeps in the other room.* ⟩⟩ compare ANOTHER
2 the remaining thing or person: *I can take Peter and Mary, but all the others will have to take the bus.* | *Where is my other sock?*
3 the other day on a recent day; not many days ago: *I saw John the other day.*
4 other than except: *I don't know much about him, other than he likes to fish.*

oth·er·wise /'ʌðɚ,waɪz/ *adverb*
1 if not: *You should buy the tickets now, otherwise you may not get any.*
2 except for what is mentioned: *It wasn't very sunny, otherwise the day was fine.*
3 differently: *We were going to buy the house, then we decided otherwise.* (= not to buy it)

ouch /aʊtʃ/
said when you feel sudden pain

ought to /'ɔtə; *strong* 'ɔtu/ *verb*
used for saying what you think someone should do: *She really ought to eat less.*

ounce /aʊns/ *noun*
a measure of weight equal to 28.35 grams; there are 16 ounces in one pound

our /ɑr; *strong* aʊɚ/ *adjective*
belonging to us: *We put our books in our bags.*

ours /aʊɚz, ɑrz/
something that belongs to us: *"Whose car is that?" "It's ours."*

our·selves /aʊɚˈsɛlvz, ɑr-/
1 the same people as we or us in a sentence: *We could see ourselves in the mirror.* | *We bought a lot of things for ourselves.*
2 **by ourselves** (a) without help from anyone: *We painted the bedroom by ourselves.* (b) alone, without anyone else: *Dad never lets us go to the store by ourselves.*

out /aʊt/ *adverb, adjective*
1 away from a place; not in a place: *Close the gate, or the dog will get out.*
2 not at home, or not at work: *My father is out right now.*
3 not on, or not working: *The lights were out and the house was dark.*
4 **out of** from a particular place or time: *She took the keys out of her bag.* —see color picture on page 194
5 not in a room or building; outside: *Why don't you go out and play?*
6 completely or carefully: *Clean out the car before you go.* | *I am worn out.* (=very tired)

out·dat·ed /ˌaʊtˈdeɪtɪd◂/ *adjective*
old; no longer useful: *No one can use outdated information.* ≫ compare OLD-FASHIONED

out·door /ˈaʊtdɔr/ *adjective*
happening outside; used outside: *We have an outdoor swimming pool.* ≫ compare INDOOR

out·doors /aʊtˈdɔrz/ *adverb*
(*also* **out of doors**) outside; not inside a building: *It's a nice day, let's play outdoors.* ≫ compare INDOORS

out·er /ˈaʊtɚ/ *adjective*
on the outside of something; far from the middle: *The outer walls of the house are made of brick.* ≫ compare INNER

out·fit /ˈaʊtˌfɪt/ *noun*
a set of clothes that you wear together: *Is that a new outfit?*

out·grow /aʊtˈɡroʊ/ *verb* [*past tense* **outgrew** /aʊtˈɡru/, *past participle* **outgrown** /aʊtˈɡroʊn/]
to grow too big for something: *Jack has outgrown his coat.*

out·ing /ˈaʊtɪŋ/ *noun*
a short trip for enjoyment: *We went on an outing to the beach.*

out·let /ˈaʊtlɛt, -lɪt/ *noun*
a place where electricity comes out of the wall

out·line /ˈaʊtlaɪn/ *noun*
1 a line around the edge of something that shows its shape: *He drew the outline of a house.*
2 the main facts or ideas about something

out·side¹ /ˌaʊtˈsaɪd, ˈaʊtsaɪd/ *noun*
the outer part or surface of something: *The outside of the house was painted white.* ≫ compare INSIDE¹

outside² *adverb*
out of a room or building: *He opened the door and went outside.* | *They were standing outside the school.* ≫ compare INSIDE²

outside³ *adjective*
on the outside of something, or containing something: *The outside walls are in bad condition.* ≫ compare INSIDE³

out·skirts /ˈaʊtskɚts/ *plural noun*
the parts of a town that are far away from the center: *We live on the outskirts of the town.*

out·stand·ing /aʊtˈstændɪŋ/ *adjective*
very good; excellent: *She is an outstanding student.*

out·ward¹ /ˈaʊtwɚd/ *adjective*
1 relating to how someone seems to be: *There were no outward signs that she was upset.*
2 going away from a place ≫ compare INWARD¹

outward² *adverb*
toward the outside; away from the middle: *The top of the box opens outward.* ≫ compare INWARD²

o·val /ˈoʊvəl/ *noun*
a shape like an egg —**oval** *adjective* —see picture at SHAPE¹

ov·en /ˈʌvən/ *noun*
a box that becomes hot so you can cook food inside it

o·ver¹ /ˈoʊvɚ/ *adverb*
1 down to a lying position: *He knocked the glass over and it broke.* | *She fell over.*

2 used for showing where someone or something is: *I'll sit over here, and you sit over there.* | *There is a chair over in the corner.*

3 to or in a particular place: *We went over to her house.*

4 again: *I made a mistake and had to start over.* | *She sings the same song over and over.*

5 **think something over** to think carefully about something: *Think it over and give me your decision tomorrow.*

6 so that another side is showing: *He rolled over and went to sleep.*

7 above: *It is very loud when the planes fly over.*

over² *preposition*

1 above or higher than something else: *The lamp is hanging over the table.* | *I leaned over the desk.* ☐☐☐ color picture on page 194

2 moving across the top; from one side to the other: *He jumped over the wall.*

3 covering something; on top of something: *Put this blanket over him.*

4 more than an amount or number: *Children over the age of 12 cannot come to this school.*

5 during: *I visited her over the summer.*

6 **all over** in every part, everywhere: *He has traveled all over the world.*

over³ *adjective*
finished: *The game is over.*

o·ver·all /ˌoʊvɚˈɔl/ *adverb, adjective*
including everything: *Overall, the situation is very good.*

o·ver·alls /ˈoʊvɚˌɔlz/ *plural noun*
heavy pants with a top part that you wear over your chest, held up by two pieces of cloth that go over your shoulders —see color picture on page 190

o·ver·board /ˈoʊvɚˌbɔrd/ *adverb*
over the side of a boat into the water: *He fell overboard.*

o·ver·coat /ˈoʊvɚˌkoʊt/ *noun*
a long thick warm coat

o·ver·dose /ˈoʊvɚˌdoʊs/ *noun*
too much of a drug taken at one time: *He died of a drug overdose.* —**overdose** *verb*

o·ver·flow /ˌoʊvɚˈfloʊ/ *verb*
to flow over the edge of something: *The river overflowed its sides.*

o·ver·head /ˌoʊvɚˈhɛd/ *adverb, adjective*
over or above your head: *The plane flew overhead.*

o·ver·hear /ˌoʊvɚˈhɪr/ *verb (past* **overheard** /ˌoʊvɚˈhɝd/)
to hear what other people are saying when they do not know you are listening: *I overheard them talking about me.*

o·ver·look /ˌoʊvɚˈlʊk/ *verb*

1 to not see or notice something: *You overlooked several mistakes in your writing.*

2 to have a view of something from above: *Our house overlooks the valley.*

o·ver·night /ˌoʊvɚˈnaɪt/ *adjective, adverb*
for the whole night: *We stayed overnight with my sister.*

o·ver·pass /ˈoʊvɚˌpæs/ *noun*
a part of a road that goes up and crosses over another road

o·ver·seas /ˌoʊvɚˈsiz/ *adverb, adjective*
to or in a place across the sea from your own country: *My brother lives overseas.*

o·ver·sleep /ˌoʊvɚˈslip/ *verb (past* **overslept** /ˌoʊvɚˈslɛpt/)
to sleep for longer than you wanted to: *I was late for school because I overslept.*

o·ver·weight /ˌoʊvɚˈweɪt/ *adjective*
too fat: *The doctor told her she was overweight.* —see color picture on page 191

owe /oʊ/ *verb* (**owing, owed**)

1 to have to give money to someone later because he or she has allowed you to borrow some: *I owe John $10 for my ticket.*

2 to feel grateful to someone for something: *Peter owes me a favor.*

owing to /ˈ.. ./ *preposition*
because of: *They arrived late, owing to the weather.*

owl /aʊl/ *noun*
a large bird that hunts at night and has large eyes

own¹ /oʊn/

1 belonging to a particular person: *I want my own room.* | *You must make your own decisions.*

2 **on your own** alone, with no one else helping you: *I was on my own all day.* | *Did you write this story on your own?*

own² *verb*
to have something that belongs to you: *Their family owns two restaurants.*

own·er /'ounə/ *noun*
someone who owns something: *Who is the owner of this car?*

ox /ɑks/ *noun*
a male cow that has had part of its sex organs removed

ox·y·gen /'ɑksɪdʒən/ *noun* [U]
a gas in the air that all plants and animals need in order to live

oys·ter /'ɔɪstər/ *noun*
a small ocean animal that has a hard shell and can produce a PEARL

oz.
a short way to write the word **ounce** or **ounces**

o·zone layer /'ouzoun,leɪə/ *noun* [U]
a layr of gases which protects the Earth from the bad effects of the sun

pace¹ /peɪs/ *noun* [U]
the speed at which you move forward, especially when walking: *They walk **at a** very **fast** pace.*

pace² *verb* (**pacing, paced**)
to walk in one direction and then the other, especially when you are waiting or worried about something

pac·i·fi·er /'pæsə,faɪɚ/ *noun*
a small rubber object that a baby sucks on so that he or she does not cry

pack¹ /pæk/ *verb*
1 (*also* **pack up**) to put things in a box, bag etc. to take them somewhere: *She packed her bags and left.*
2 if a crowd packs a place, there are a lot of people there so it is very full

pack² *noun*
1 a small container that holds a set of something: *Do you want a pack **of** cigarettes?* —see picture at CONTAINER
2 several things put or tied together to make them easy to sell, carry, or send: *I bought a six-pack of beer.* (=six beers)
3 a group of wild animals that hunt together
4 a BACKPACK

pack·age
/'pækɪdʒ/ *noun*
1 the bag or box that something is put into for selling: *I want to get a package **of** cookies.*
2 something wrapped in paper so that you can put it into the mail

pack

packed /pækt/ *adjective*
full of people or things

pack·et /'pækɪt/ *noun*
a small container for something: *I bought two packets **of** tomato seeds.*

pack·ing /'pækɪŋ/ *noun* [U]
the action of putting things into cases or boxes: *I **do** my packing the night before I leave.*

pact /pækt/ *noun*
an important agreement between two countries

pad¹ /pæd/ *noun*
1 a thick piece of soft material used for protecting a part of your body, or for making something more comfortable
2 a number of sheets of paper fastened together at one edge: *I need a writing pad.*

pad² *verb* (**padding, padded**)
to fill or cover something with soft material in order to protect it or make it more comfortable: *The jacket is padded at the shoulders.*

pad·dle¹ /'pædl/ *noun*
a piece of wood with a wide flat end used for moving a boat through water

paddle² *verb* (**paddling, paddled**)
to move a boat through water using a PADDLE

pad·dy /'pædi/ *noun*
(*also* **rice paddy**; *plural* **paddies**) a field for growing rice

pad·lock /'pædlɑk/ *noun*
a small lock that you can put on a door, bicycle etc.

page /peɪdʒ/ *noun*
one of the sheets of paper in a book or newspaper: *The book has 120 pages.* | *What story is on the front page?* (=first page)

pag·eant /'pædʒənt/ *noun*
a competition for women in which their beauty is judged

paid /peɪd/
the PAST TENSE and PAST PARTICIPLE of the verb **pay**

pail /peɪl/ *noun*
a BUCKET

pain /peɪn/ *noun*
1 the feeling have when a part of your body hurts: *I've got a pain in my leg.*

2 a pain, a pain in the neck a very annoying person or thing: *He's a real pain when he's tired.*
3 [U] suffering in your mind or your emotions: *Divorce causes great pain for children.*
4 take pains to do something make a special effort to do something

pain·ful /'peɪnfəl/ *adjective*
1 causing pain: *I have a painful cut on my leg.* ≫ opposite PAINLESS
2 making you feel unhappy: *I have painful memories of the war.*

pain·kill·er /'peɪnˌkɪlɚ/ *noun*
a medicine which helps to stop pain

pain·less /'peɪnlɪs/ *adjective*
causing no pain ≫ opposite PAINFUL

paint¹ /peɪnt/ *noun* [U]
a thick liquid that you put on a wall, house etc. to make it a particular color: *The wall needs another **coat** of paint.* (=another layer of paint)

paint² *verb*
1 to put paint on a surface: *They painted the house white.*
2 to make a picture of someone or something using paint: *She loves painting the mountains.*

paint·brush /'peɪntˌbrʌʃ/ *noun* (*plural* **paintbrushes**)
a special brush that you use for painting —see picture at BRUSH¹

paint·er /'peɪntɚ/ *noun*
1 someone who paints something as a job
2 someone who paints pictures ≫ compare ARTIST

paint·ing /'peɪntɪŋ/ *noun*
a painted picture: *I saw a painting **of** a boat.*

pair /pɛr/ *noun*
1 two things of the same kind that are used together: *I need a pair **of** socks.*
2 something made of two parts joined and used together: *Here is a pair of scissors.*
3 two people who are doing something together: *Everyone is dancing **in** pairs.*

paj·a·mas /pəˈdʒɑməz -ˈdʒæ/ *plural noun*
a loose shirt and pants that you wear in bed

pal /pæl/ *noun*
a friend

pal·ace /'pælɪs/ *noun*
a large beautiful building where a king or queen lives

pale /peɪl/ *adjective*
1 having a light color: *Her dress is pale green.*
2 lighter than the usual color: *She was very pale after her illness.* ≫ compare DARK¹

palm /pɑm/ *noun*
1 a tall tropical tree with pointed leaves, that grows near a beach
2 the flat part inside your hand: *He held the insect in the palm of his hand.* —see picture at HAND¹

pam·phlet /'pæmflɪt/ *noun*
a thin book with a paper cover, which gives information about something

pan

saucepan   frying pan

pan /pæn/ *noun*
a round metal container, usually with a long handle, in which you cook things

pan·cake /'pænkeɪk/ *noun*
a thin flat cake cooked in a pan

pan·da /'pændə/ *noun*
a large black and white animal like a bear that lives in China —see color picture on page 183

pane /peɪn/ *noun*
a single piece of glass in a window: *Who broke the pane of glass?*

pan·el /'pænl/ *noun*
1 a flat piece of wood used in a door or on a wall
2 a group of people who answer questions, discuss something, or decide something

pan·ic¹ /'pænɪk/ *noun* [U]
a sudden feeling of great fear that makes you do things quickly and without thinking: *There was panic when the fire started.*

panic² *verb* (**panicking, panicked**)
to feel a sudden fear which makes you do things quickly without thinking: *The crowd panicked at the sound of guns.*

panic-strick·en /'.. ˌ../ *adjective*
very afraid and not able to think clearly

pant /pænt/ *verb*
to breathe hard and quickly, especially after you

exercise or because it is very hot: *He was panting when he reached the top of the hill.*

pant·ies /'pæntiz/ *plural noun*
a piece of underwear for girls or women

pan·try /'pæntri/ *noun* (*plural* **pantries**)
a small room where food or dishes are kept

pants /pænts/ *plural noun*
a piece of clothing that covers your legs from your waist to your feet: *I need a new **pair of** pants.* —see color picture on page 190

pan·ty·hose /'pænti,hoʊz/ *plural noun*
a very thin, tight piece of clothing, which women wear to cover their feet, legs, and the lower part of their body

pa·per /'peɪpɚ/ *noun*
1 [U] thin sheets that you can write or draw on, or wrap things in: *I do not have any writing paper.*
2 a newspaper: *Here's today's paper.*
3 a piece of writing that you do for a class: *Have you finished your English paper?*

pa·per·back /'peɪpɚ,bæk/ *noun*
a book with a stiff paper cover

paper clip /'.. ,./ *noun*
a small curved piece of wire used for holding sheets of paper together

pa·pers /'peɪpɚz/ *plural noun*
official pieces of paper that give information about who you are and what you are allowed to do

par·a·chute
/'pærə,ʃut/ *noun*
a large piece of cloth that is attached to your back and allows you to fall through the air slowly when you jump from an aircraft

pa·rade¹
/pə'reɪd/ *noun*
a public celebration in which people walk or march in a long line down the street

parade² *verb* (**parading, paraded**)
to walk or march together to celebrate something: *The people paraded **through** the town.*

par·a·dise /'pærə,daɪs, -,daɪz/ *noun* [U]
1 a place that is beautiful and pleasant: *For me, paradise is lying on the beach all day.*
2 HEAVEN

par·a·graph /'pærə,græf/ *noun*
a group of several sentences that has one particular idea

par·al·lel /'pærə,lɛl/ *adjective*
two lines that are parallel are side by side, and are always the same distance apart: *The **sidewalk** runs parallel **to** the street.* —see picture at SHAPE¹

pa·ral·y·sis /pə'ræləsɪs/ *noun* [U]
not being able to move or feel a part of your body

par·a·lyze /'pærə,laɪz/ *verb* (**paralyzing, paralyzed**)
to make someone lose the ability to move or feel a part of his or her body: *He was paralyzed in a fall and couldn't walk.* —**paralyzed** *adjective*

par·don¹ /'pardn/ *noun* [U]
used for asking someone to say something again: *"It's four o'clock." "Pardon?" "I said it's four o'clock."*

pardon² *verb*
pardon me (a) excuse me; I am sorry: *Pardon me. I didn't mean to upset you.* (b) said for getting someone's attention: *Pardon me, what time is it?*

par·ent /'pɛrənt, 'pær-/ *noun*
a father or mother: *My parents live near here.*

pa·ren·the·ses /pə'rɛnθəsiz/ *plural noun*
the signs ( ). In the sentence "Do you want any (more) fruit?", (more) is in parentheses.

park¹ /park/ *noun*
a large area in a town with grass and trees, where you can walk, play games etc.

park² *verb*
to put a car in a particular place for a period of time: *She parked the car near the bank.*

park·ing /'parkɪŋ/ *noun* [U]
1 the act of putting a car in a particular place for a period of time
2 **No parking** a phrase used on a sign to show that you are not allowed to put your car there

parking lot /'.. ,./ *noun*
an open area where you can put your car

parking meter /'.. ,../ *noun*
a machine that you put money into so you can put your car next to it

par·lia·ment /'parləmənt/ *noun*
a group of people chosen by the people of a country to make laws

pa·ro·chi·al school /pə'roʊkiəl skul/
noun
a school that is run by or connected with a church

par·rot
/'pærət/ *noun*
a brightly-colored tropical bird with a curved beak

pars·ley
/'pɑrsli/ *noun* [U]
a small plant with strong-tasting leaves, often used in cooking

part¹ /pɑrt/ *noun*
1 a piece of an object, area etc., but not all of it: *Which part of the town do you live in?* | *The front part of the bus was damaged.*
2 one of the pieces that something is made of: *I need a new part for my car.*
3 the words and actions of a character in a play or movie: *James played the part of the soldier.*
4 **take part in something** to do an activity with other people: *He took part in the race.*
5 **in part** to some degree, but not completely: *Her success was due in part to good luck.*

part² *verb*
1 to pull two sides of something apart: *He parted the curtains and looked out the window.*
2 **part with something** to give away something although you do not want to: *She hates parting with her old clothes.*
3 to divide the hair on your head into two parts with a comb so that it makes a line

par·tial /'pɑrʃəl/ *adjective*
not complete: *The meeting was only a partial success.*

par·tial·ly /'pɑrʃəli/ *adverb*
not completely: *She is only partially to blame for the problem.*

par·tic·i·pant /pɑr'tɪsəpənt, pɚ-/ *noun*
someone who does an activity

par·tic·i·pate /pɑr'tɪsə,peɪt, pɚ-/ *verb*
(participating, participated)
to do a particular activity: *Most students participated in the program.*

par·ti·ci·ple /'pɑrtə,sɪpəl/ *noun*
one of two forms of a verb: *The past participle of "sing" is "sung" and the present participle is "singing."*

par·tic·u·lar /pɚ'tɪkyələ/ *adjective*
1 special or important: *Did you have a particular reason for choosing this book?*
2 this one and not any other: *On that particular day, I wasn't feeling well.*
3 **in particular** special or specific: *Is there anything in particular I can help you with?*

par·tic·u·lar·ly /pɚ'tɪkyələli, -'tɪkyəli/ *adverb*
especially: *It is particularly hot today.*

part·ly /'pɑrtli/ *adverb*
not completely: *The accident was partly my fault.*

part·ner /'pɑrt⌐nɚ/ *noun*
1 someone with whom you do an activity such as dancing, tennis etc.
2 one of the owners of a business
3 someone to whom you are married, or with whom you live

part-time /, '. ◂/ *adjective, adverb*
working or studying during only a part of the usual time: *I work part-time at the library.*

par·ty /'pɑrti/ *noun (plural parties)*
1 a meeting at which people enjoy themselves, eat, drink etc.: *Are you coming to my birthday party?*
2 a group of people with the same political opinions: *Are you a member of a political party?*

pass¹ /pæs/ *verb*
1 (*also* **pass by**) to go past someone or something: *She waved at me as she passed my house.*
2 to take something and put it in someone's hand: *Pass the salt, please.*
3 to kick, throw, or hit a ball to someone on your own team during a game
4 if time passes, it goes by: *Time passes very slowly when you're waiting.*
5 to succeed in a test or class: *Did you pass your driving test?*
6 to accept a law, especially by voting: *The law passed easily.*
7 **pass away** to die: *I was sorry to hear that Larry had passed away.*
8 **pass out** to suddenly become unconscious: *He passed out when he saw the blood.*
9 **pass something on** to tell someone information that someone told you: *I will pass the message on to her.*

pass² *noun (plural passes)*
1 the act of kicking, throwing, or hitting the ball to someone on your team in a game

2 an official piece of paper that allows you to go somewhere or do something

3 a road through a place that is difficult to travel through

pas·sage /'pæsɪdʒ/ *noun*

1 a narrow place in a building that connects one room to another: *The bathroom is at the end of the passage.*

2 a short piece of writing or music: *He read a passage from the book.*

pas·sen·ger /'pæsəndʒə/ *noun*

someone who travels in a car, bus, train etc. but does not drive it: *There are ten passengers on the bus.*

pass·er·by /ˌpæsə'baɪ/ *noun* (*plural* **passersby**)

someone who is walking past a place by chance: *A passerby stopped to help me.*

pass·ing /'pæsɪŋ/ *adjective*

going past: *Sometimes I watch the passing cars.*

pas·sion /'pæʃən/ *noun*

a very strong feeling such as love, hate, or anger: *She spoke with passion about feeding the poor.*

pas·sion·ate /'pæʃənɪt/ *adjective*

showing very strong feelings: *She is passionate about caring for animals.* **—passionately** *adverb*

pas·sive /'pæsɪv/ *adjective*

having the action done by someone else: *In the sentence "The ball was kicked by John," "was kicked" is a passive verb.* ≫ compare ACTIVE

pass·port /'pæspɔrt/ *noun*

a small book which has your photograph and facts about you, and which you must have to leave your country and go to another one

past¹ /pæst/ *noun* [U]

1 all the time that existed before now: *Traveling is much easier now than it was in the past.* ≫ compare FUTURE

2 someone's life before now: *I don't know anything about his past.*

3 the PAST TENSE

past² *adjective*

having happened or existed before now: *I've been sick for the past two weeks.* ≫ compare NEXT¹

past³ *adverb, preposition*

1 up to and beyond someone or something:

Do you drive past the school? | She walked past me and didn't say anything! —see color picture on page 194

2 after a particular time: *It's just past four o'clock.*

pas·ta /'pɑstə/ *noun* [U]

an Italian food made from flour and water, and often eaten with a SAUCE

paste¹ /peɪst/ *noun*

1 a thick glue used for sticking things together

2 a soft wet mixture that can be spread over something

paste² *verb* (**pasting, pasted**)

to stick something on to something else using PASTE

past par·ti·ci·ple /ˌ. '..../ *noun*

the form of a verb used for showing an action done or happening in the past: *"Done" and "walked" are the past participles of the verbs "do" and "walk".*

pas·try /'peɪstri/ *noun*

1 (*plural* **pastries**) a small sweet cake

2 [U] a mixture of flour, fat, and water which makes the outer part of a PIE

past tense /ˌ. './ *noun*

the form of a verb which shows past time: *The past tense of the verb "go" is "went."*

pas·ture /'pæstʃə/ *noun*

land covered with grass, used for cattle and sheep to feed on

pat /pæt/ *verb* (**patting, patted**)

to touch something lightly again and again with your hand: *She patted the dog on the head.* **—pat** *noun*

patch¹ /pætʃ/ *noun* (*plural* **patches**)

1 a piece of material used for covering a hole in something

2 a small area that looks different from the area around it: *I can see wet patches on the wall.*

patch² *verb*

to put a piece of material over a hole to cover it: *I patched the bicycle tire with a piece of rubber.*

path /pæθ/ *noun* (*plural* **paths** /pæðz/)

a narrow road you can walk on: *There is a narrow path through the forest.* —see color picture on page 188

pa·tience /'peɪʃəns/ *noun* [U]

the ability to deal with a problem, or wait for

something without getting angry or upset: *You need a lot of patience to be a teacher.*

pa·tient¹ /'peɪʃənt/ *adjective*
able to deal with a problem or wait for something without getting angry or upset: *Try to be patient **with** the children.* ≫opposite IMPATIENT

patient² *noun*
someone who is getting medical treatment: *There are 150 patients in the hospital.*

pat·i·o /'pæti,oʊ/ *noun*
an outside area with a hard surface near a house where you can sit, eat, relax etc.

pa·tri·ot·ic /,peɪtri'ɑtɪk/ *adjective*
showing great love for your country

pa·trol¹ /pə'troʊl/ *noun*
1 a small group of police or soldiers who are in an area to prevent problems or crime
2 on patrol moving around in an area to prevent problems or crime: *Four police were on patrol outside the building.*

patrol² *verb* (patrolling, patrolled)
to be in an area to prevent problems or crime: *Every hour the police patrol our street.*

pat·ter /'pætɚ/ *noun*
the sound of something light hitting a hard surface: *I heard the patter of rain on the roof.*

spotted

pattern

checked

striped

zigzag

pat·tern /'pætɚn/ *noun*
1 the regular way that something happens or is done: *There is a pattern to the crimes.*
2 an arrangement of shapes, lines, or colors: *The dress has a pattern of flowers on it.*
3 a shape that you copy onto cloth or paper to make something, especially clothing

pause¹ /pɔz/ *noun*
a short time when you stop doing something:

There was a pause in the conversation when Mary came in.

pause² *verb* (pausing, paused)
to stop doing something for a short time: *When he reached the top of the hill, he paused to rest.*

pave /peɪv/ *verb* (paving, paved)
to cover a road with a hard level surface such as CONCRETE

pave·ment /'peɪvmənt/ *noun* [U]
the hard surface of a road

paw /pɔ/ *noun*
the foot of an animal such as a dog or cat

pay¹ /peɪ/ *verb* (paying, paid /peɪd/)
1 to give money to someone so you can buy something, or for work that he or she has done for you: *She paid **for** the coffee and left. | He gets paid $10 an hour.*
2 pay attention to listen or watch something carefully: *Pay attention **to** the story, children.*
3 pay someone back to return the money you owe someone: *I'll pay you back next week.*
4 pay something off to pay all the money you owe for something: *We paid off our house this year!*

pay² *noun* [U]
the money that you receive for work that you have done: *You will get your pay on Friday.*

pay·check /'peɪtʃɛk/ *noun*
a small piece of paper that you receive as pay for work that you have done

pay·ment /'peɪmənt/ *noun*
1 [U] the act of paying: *This money is in payment for your work.*
2 an amount of money that you pay: *How much are your car payments?*

pay phone /'. ./ *noun*
a public telephone you can use by putting a coin or a card into it

pea /pi/ *noun*
a very small round green vegetable

peace /pis/ *noun* [U]
1 a time when there is no war or fighting: *We are working for world peace.*
2 quietness and calm: *Go away and leave me in peace.*

peace·ful /'pisfəl/ *adjective*
1 quiet and calm: *I had a peaceful day at the beach.*
2 not violent or fighting: *A peaceful crowd marched to the city.*

peach /pitʃ/ *noun* (*plural* **peaches**)
a juicy fruit with a large seed and a soft skin that feels FUZZY

pea·cock /'pikɑk/ *noun*
a large bird with long brightly-colored tail feathers that spread out —see color picture on page 183

peak /pik/ *noun*
1 the time when someone or something is the most successful, biggest etc.: *He is at the peak of his career.*
2 the pointed top of a hill or mountain

peal /pil/ *noun*
the long loud sound that a bell makes

pea·nut /'pinʌt/ *noun*
a small nut that you can eat, that has a soft brown shell

peanut but·ter /'.. ,../ *noun* [U]
a soft food made from PEANUTs, that you eat on bread

pear /pɛr/ *noun*
a sweet juicy fruit with a wide bottom and narrow top —see picture at FRUIT

pearl /pɚl/ *noun*
a small round white object, found in an OYSTER, used for making jewelry

peas·ant /'pɛzənt/ *noun*
someone who is poor and does farm work on a small piece of land

peb·ble /'pɛbəl/ *noun*
a small stone

pe·can /pə'kɑn, -'kæn/ *noun*
a long brown sweet nut

peck /pɛk/ *verb*
if a bird pecks something, it takes a quick bite of it

pe·cu·liar /pɪ'kyulyɚ/ *adjective*
strange or unusual: *A peculiar smell is coming from the room.* ≫ compare ODD

ped·al¹ /'pɛdl/ *noun*
a part of a machine that you move with your foot

pedal² *verb*
to move a bicycle by pushing the PEDALs with your feet

pe·des·tri·an /pə'dɛstriən/ *noun*
someone who is walking: *This bridge is for pedestrians only.*

peel

peel¹ /pil/ *noun* [U]
the outside part of a fruit or vegetable. *Apples have red or green peel.*

peel² *verb*
to take off the outside part of a vegetable or fruit: *Can you peel this banana?*

peep¹ /pip/ *verb*
to look at something quickly and secretly: *I peeped through the window to see if she was there.* ≫ compare GLANCE¹

peep² *noun*
a quick or secret look at something: *He took a peep in the back of the book to see how the story ends.*

peer /pɪr/ *verb*
to look very carefully at something, especially because you cannot see it well

peg /pɛg/ *noun*
a wooden or metal hook fastened to a wall, on which you can hang clothes

pen /pɛn/ *noun*
1 a long narrow object used for writing or drawing in ink ≫ compare PENCIL
2 a small area of land surrounded by a fence, in which farm animals are kept

pen·al·ty /'pɛnlti/ *noun* (*plural* **penalties**)
1 a punishment for not obeying a law or rule: *What is the penalty for speeding?*
2 a punishment given to a player or a team for not obeying the rules of a game or sport

pen·cil /'pɛnsəl/ *noun*
a long narrow object made of wood and filled with a black substance, used for writing or drawing ≫ compare PEN

pen·e·trate /ˈpɛnəˌtreɪt/ *verb*
(penetrating, penetrated)
to go into or through something, especially when that is difficult: *The sun penetrated through the thick clouds.*

pen·guin /ˈpɛŋgwɪn/ *noun*
a large black and white Antarctic sea bird, that cannot fly but uses its wings for swimming —see color picture on page 183

pen·knife /ˈpɛn-naɪf/ *noun* (plural penknives /-naɪvz/)
a POCKET KNIFE

pen·ny /ˈpɛni/ *noun* (plural pennies)
a coin worth one cent; there are 100 pennies in one dollar

pen pal /ˈ. ./ *noun*
someone in another country to whom you write letters, even though you may never meet him or her

pen·sion /ˈpɛnʃən/ *noun*
money given to someone regularly by a company when he or she has stopped working

peo·ple /ˈpipəl/ *noun*
the plural of **person**: *I like the people I work with.*

pep·per /ˈpɛpə/ *noun*
1 [U] a powder made from the seeds of a particular plant and used for giving a hot taste to food
2 a hollow red or green fruit that you can eat raw or use in cooking —see picture at VEGETABLE

pep·per·mint /ˈpɛpəˌmɪnt/ *noun*
1 [U] oil from a plant with a special strong taste used in candy, tea, medicine, or TOOTHPASTE
2 a candy with this taste

per /pə/ *preposition*
for each; during each: *How much do you earn per week?* | *The fruit costs 75 cents per pound.*

per·cent /pəˈsɛnt/ *noun*
an amount out of every hundred: *"Sixty per cent [=60%] of the students are boys"* means that out of every hundred students, sixty are boys.

perch /pətʃ/ *verb*
to sit on something: *Birds perched on the branch.*

per·fect¹ /ˈpəfɛkt/ *adjective*
1 of the best possible type: *They seem to have a perfect marriage.*

2 without any mistakes or problems: *She speaks perfect French.*
3 exactly right for a particular purpose: *This rug is perfect for the living room.*

perfect² /pəˈfɛkt/ *verb*
to make something very good or perfect: *They worked very hard to perfect their dancing.*

perfect³ *noun*
the PRESENT PERFECT form of a verb

per·fec·tion /pəˈfɛkʃən/ *noun* [U]
the quality of being perfect

per·fect·ly /ˈpəfɪktli/ *adverb*
1 completely or very: *She is perfectly happy now.*
2 without any mistakes or problems: *He is always perfectly dressed.*

per·form /pəˈfɔrm/ *verb*
1 to do something to amuse people: *They are performing a new play tonight.*
2 to work well: *The car performs well in wet weather.*

per·form·ance /pəˈfɔrməns/ *noun*
1 an act of doing something to amuse people: *I saw an excellent performance of the opera.*
2 [U] your ability to do something well: *Her performance on the test was very good.*

per·form·er /pəˈfɔrmə/ *noun*
an actor or singer who does something to amuse people

per·fume /ˈpəfyum, pəˈfyum/ *noun* [U]
1 a liquid with a strong pleasant smell that you put on your skin: *What perfume are you wearing?*
2 a sweet or pleasant smell

per·haps /pəˈhæps/ *adverb*
possibly: *Perhaps our team will win.* ⟫ compare MAYBE

pe·ri·od /ˈpɪriəd/ *noun*
1 a length of time: *There were long periods when we didn't hear from him.*
2 a particular time in history or in someone's life: *This is a difficult period of life for her.*
3 the mark (.) used in writing to show the end of a sentence, or after the short form of a word such as Mr., ft., or Dr.
4 a time when blood comes out of a woman's body once a month

per·ish /ˈpɛrɪʃ/ *verb*
to die: *The crops perished in the heat.*

per·ky /ˈpɔ˞ki/ *adjective* (perkier, perkiest)
very happy and having a lot of energy

perm /ˈpɔ˞m/ *noun*
a treatment with chemicals that puts curls in
your hair

per·ma·nent /ˈpɔ˞mənənt/ *adjective*
continuing for a long time or for all time: *She
has a permanent job.* ≫ compare TEMPORARY

per·mis·sion /pɔ˞ˈmɪʃən/ *noun* [U]
the act of allowing someone to do something:
Did you ask permission to use her computer?

per·mit¹ /pɔ˞ˈmɪt/ *verb* (permitting,
permitted)
to allow someone to do something, or something to happen: *You are not permitted to bring
food into the library.*

permit² /pɔ˞mɪt/ *noun*
an official piece of paper that allows you to do
something

per·son /ˈpɔ˞sən/ *noun* (plural people
/ˈpipəl/ or persons)
1 a human being; a man, woman, or child:
*She's a nice person. | You're just the person I
want to talk to.*
2 in person done when you are in a place, not
using a letter or the telephone: *I wanted to see
her in person.*

> NOTE: **1** The usual plural of **person** is
> **people. Persons** is very formal and is used
> only in official notices and ANNOUNCEMENTS,
> e.g. *The persons responsible for this crime
> must be caught.* **2** Do NOT say "all people."
> Use **everyone** or **everybody** instead.

per·son·al /ˈpɔ˞sənəl/ *adjective*
belonging to or relating to you: *These are my
personal letters.*

personal com·put·er /ˌ... .ˈ../ *noun*
(*also* **PC**)
a small computer which you use at work or at
home

per·son·al·i·ty /ˌpɔ˞səˈnæləti/ *noun* (plural personalities)
1 the character of someone and how he or
she behaves toward other people: *She has a
nice personality.*
2 someone who is well-known: *He is a television personality.*

per·son·al·ly /ˈpɔ˞sənəli/ *adverb*
used for giving your own opinion about some-

thing: *Personally I don't like him, but many people trust him.*

per·suade /pɔ˞ˈsweɪd/ *verb* (persuading,
persuaded)
to make someone decide to do something by
giving him or her good reasons: *He persuaded
her to agree with him.*

per·sua·sion /pɔ˞ˈsweɪʒən/ *noun* [U]
the act of persuading someone to do something: *After a lot of persuasion, she agreed to
go.*

pes·si·mist /ˈpɛsəmɪst/ *noun*
someone who always thinks that something bad
will happen ≫ compare OPTIMIST

pes·si·mis·tic /ˌpɛsəˈmɪstɪk/ *adjective*
always believing that something bad will happen
≫ compare OPTIMISTIC

pest /pɛst/ *noun*
1 an animal or insect that is harmful to crops
or is annoying
2 someone who annoys you or makes you
worry

pes·ter /ˈpɛstɔ˞/ *verb*
to annoy someone by asking him or her for
something again and again: *Stop pestering me,
I'll clean up my room tomorrow!*

pet¹ /pɛt/ *noun*
an animal that you take care of and keep at your
house: *She has two cats as pets.*

pet² *verb* (petting, petted)
to move your hand over an animal's fur to show
that you like it: *Can I pet your dog?*

pet·al /ˈpɛtl̩/ *noun*
one of the brightly-colored parts of a flower
—see picture at ROSE²

pe·ti·tion /pəˈtɪʃən/ *noun*
a piece of paper signed by a lot of people and
sent to someone in authority to ask for something or to complain about something

pe·tro·le·um /pəˈtroʊliəm/ *noun* [U]
oil from beneath the ground, used for making
GASOLINE

pet·ty /ˈpɛti/ *adjective*
not important or serious: *Don't bother me with
petty details!*

pew /pyu/ *noun*
a long wooden seat in a church

phan·tom /ˈfæntəm/ *noun*
a GHOST

phar·ma·cist /ˈfɑrməsɪst/ *noun*
someone who prepares and sells medicines

phar·ma·cy /ˈfɑrməsi/ *noun* (*plural* **pharmacies**)
a store that sells medicine

phase /feɪz/ *noun*
one part of the process by which something develops: *We are in the last phase of the project.*

phi·los·o·pher /fɪˈlɑsəfɚ/ *noun*
someone who studies PHILOSOPHY

phi·los·o·phy /fɪˈlɑsəfi/ *noun* [U]
the study of life and what it means, how we should live, or what knowledge is

phone¹ /foʊn/ *noun*
(*also* **telephone**) a piece of equipment you use to speak to someone in another place: *Can I use the phone?*

phone² *verb* (**phoning, phoned**)
(*also* **telephone**) to speak to someone using a telephone: *I phoned my parents to tell them the news.*

phone book /ˈ. ./ *noun*
a book that has the names, addresses, and telephone numbers of the people living in a particular area

phone booth /ˈ. ./ *noun*
a small structure that has a telephone that you can use —see color picture on page 193

phone number /ˈ. ˌ../ *noun*
a set of numbers that you press on a telephone when you call someone: *What's your phone number?*

pho·net·ic /fəˈnɛtɪk/ *adjective*
relating to the sounds you make when you speak: *This dictionary uses a phonetic alphabet to show you how to pronounce words.*

pho·net·ics /fəˈnɛtɪks/ *plural noun*
the study of the sounds you make when you speak

pho·ny /ˈfoʊni/ *adjective*
false or not real; FAKE: *He gave the police a phony address.*

pho·to /ˈfoʊtoʊ/ *noun*
a photograph: *She took a photo of the children.*

pho·to·cop·y¹ /ˈfoʊtəˌkɑpi/ *noun* (*plural* **photocopies**)
a copy of a piece of writing made on a special machine: *Here's a photocopy of the letter.*

photocopy² *verb* (**photocopying, photocopied**)
to make a copy of a piece of writing on a special machine

pho·to·graph¹ /ˈfoʊtəˌgræf/ *verb*
to make a picture of someone or something using a camera: *He has photographed many famous people.*

photograph² *noun*
a picture made using a camera

pho·tog·ra·pher /fəˈtɑgrəfɚ/ *noun*
someone who makes pictures using a camera, especially as a job

pho·tog·ra·phy /fəˈtɑgrəfi/ *noun* [U]
the art or business of making pictures using a camera: *She was enjoying her photography course.*

phras·al verb /ˌfreɪzəl ˈvɚb/ *noun*
a verb that contains more than one word and has a special meaning, such as "look something up" or "show off"

phrase /freɪz/ *noun*
a group of words that is not a complete sentence: *"Later that day" and "on the way home" are phrases.*

phys·i·cal /ˈfɪzɪkəl/ *adjective*
1 relating to the body, not the mind or soul: *I need to get more physical exercise.* ≫ compare MENTAL
2 relating to things that you can see, touch, smell, feel, or taste —**physically** *adverb*

phy·si·cian /fɪˈzɪʃən/ *noun*
a doctor

phys·ics /ˈfɪzɪks/ *plural noun*
the study of natural forces, such as heat, light, and movement

pi·an·ist /piˈænɪst, ˈpiənɪst/ *noun*
someone who plays the piano

pi·an·o /piˈænoʊ/ *noun*
a large musical instrument that you play by using your fingers to press small black and white BARs

pick¹ /pɪk/ *verb*
1 to choose something or someone: *The child picked the biggest toy.*
2 to pull a flower or a fruit from a plant or tree: *She picked an apple from the tree.*
3 **pick a fight** to begin an argument or a fight with someone

4 pick on someone to treat someone in an unfair or unkind way: *He's always picking on other children.*

5 pick something up to hold something and lift it up from a surface: *Pick up your toys and put them away.*

6 pick someone up to go somewhere and get someone: *I'll pick you up at the hotel.*

7 pick someone's pocket to steal something from someone's pocket

8 pick your nose to remove small pieces from inside your nose with your fingers

pick² *noun* [U]
choice: *You can **take your** pick (=choose one) of these cakes.*

pick·et /'pɪkɪt/ *noun* (*also* **picket line**)
a group of people who stand in front of a store or factory to protest something, or to stop people from going in to work

pick·le /'pɪkəl/ *noun*
a CUCUMBER (=vegetable) with a sour taste, or a piece of this

pick·pock·et /'pɪk,pɑkɪt/ *noun*
someone who steals something from someone's pocket

pick·up /'pɪkʌp/ *noun* (*also* **pickup truck**)
a vehicle with an open part at the back, used for carrying things —see color picture on page 187

pic·nic /'pɪknɪk/ *noun*
an occasion when you take food and eat it outdoors: *We had a picnic by the lake. | During the weekend the whole family set out for a picnic in the countryside.*

pic·ture¹ /'pɪktʃɚ/ *noun*
1 a drawing, painting, or photograph: *She drew a picture **of** me.*
2 take a picture to take a photograph of someone or something: *He took a picture of his girlfriend and put it in a frame.*

picture² *verb* (**picturing, pictured**)
to imagine something: *She pictured herself **as** a beautiful queen.*

pie /paɪ/ *noun*
a food made with fruit cooked and covered with PASTRY: *I love apple pie!*

piece /piːs/ *noun*
a part of something which has been separated or broken off from a larger object: *He took a piece **of** cake. | I need a piece of paper.*

piece
piece

pierce /pɪrs/ *verb* (**piercing, pierced**)
to make a hole in something: *She is having her ears pierced.*

pierc·ing /'pɪrsɪŋ/ *adjective*
very loud and unpleasant: *a piercing scream*

pig /pɪg/ *noun*
1 a fat pink farm animal kept for its meat
2 someone who eats too much or is very dirty

pi·geon /'pɪdʒən/ *noun*
a gray bird with short legs that is common in cities

pig·let /'pɪglɪt/ *noun*
a young pig

pig·pen /'pɪgpɛn/ *noun* (*also* **pigsty**)
a place on a farm where pigs are kept

pig·tails /'pɪgteɪlz/ *plural noun*
hair that is tied together at the sides of your head: *She wore her hair in pigtails.* —see picture at HAIRSTYLE

pile¹ /paɪl/ *noun*
1 a number of things put on top of each other: *A neat pile **of** books was on the floor.*
2 a large group of similar things that are together: *I saw a pile **of** papers on my desk.*

pile² *verb* (**piling, piled**)
(*also* **pile up**) to put things together in a pile: *She piled the boxes in the room.*

pill /pɪl/ *noun*
a small, hard piece of medicine that you swallow ≫ compare TABLET

pil·lar /'pɪlɚ/ *noun*
a strong solid post, used for supporting a building: *The roof of the church is supported by stone pillars.*

pil·low /ˈpɪloʊ/ *noun*
a cloth bag filled with soft material to put your head on when you sleep ≫ compare CUSHION

pil·low·case /ˈpɪloʊˌkeɪz/ *noun*
a cloth cover that you put on a pillow to keep it clean

pi·lot /ˈpaɪlət/ *noun*
someone who flies an aircraft

pim·ple /ˈpɪmpəl/ *noun*
a small raised red spot on your skin

pin¹ /pɪn/ *noun*
a short pointed piece of metal used for fastening pieces of cloth together

pin² *verb* (**pinning, pinned**)
to fasten or join things together with a pin: *Will you pin this notice to the board?*

pinch¹ /pɪntʃ/ *verb*
to take something between your thumb and finger and press it: *She pinched my arm.*

pinch² *noun* (*plural* **pinches**)
1 a very small amount: *Put a pinch of salt in the soup.*
2 an act of pressing something tightly between your thumb and finger

pine /paɪn/ *noun*
a tree that has thin leaves like needles

pine·ap·ple /ˈpaɪnˌæpəl/ *noun*
a large yellow tropical fruit with a hard skin and pointed leaves on top —see picture at FRUIT

ping-pong

ping-pong /ˈpɪŋpɑŋ, -pɔŋ/ *noun* [U]
a game in which two or four people hit a small ball over a net on a table

pink /pɪŋk/ *adjective, noun* [U]
the color made by mixing red and white —**pink** *adjective*

pint /paɪnt/ *noun*
a measure of liquid, equal to 0.47 litres; there are eight pints in one gallon

pi·o·neer /ˌpaɪəˈnɪr/ *noun*
someone who goes somewhere or does something before other people: *He was one of the pioneers who first came to this area.*

pipe¹ /paɪp/ *noun*
1 a tube for carrying water or gas
2 a small tube with a round bowl at one end used for smoking tobacco

pipe² *verb*
to send a liquid or gas through a pipe: *The oil is piped in from Alaska.*

pi·rate¹ /ˈpaɪrɪt/ *noun*
someone who sails on the ocean attacking and stealing from other ships

pirate² *verb*
to copy and sell other people's work in a way that is not legal

pis·tol /ˈpɪstl/ *noun*
a small gun

pit /pɪt/ *noun*
1 a deep hole in the ground
2 a large hard seed in some fruits

pitch¹ /pɪtʃ/ *verb*
1 to throw something somewhere: *He pitched the letters into the fire.*
2 **pitch a tent** to set up a tent: *We pitched our tent near the river.*

pitch² *noun* (*plural* **pitches**)
1 how high or low a sound is: *She has a high-pitched voice.*
2 a throw of the ball in a game such as baseball

pitch·er /ˈpɪtʃɚ/ *noun*
1 a container used for holding or pouring liquids
2 someone who throws the ball in baseball

pit·y¹ /ˈpɪti/ *noun* [U]
1 the sadness that you feel when someone else is hurt or unhappy: *I feel pity for people who have nowhere to live.*
2 **a pity** a sad or unfortunate situation: *What a pity you can't come with us!*

pity² *verb* (**pitying, pitied**)
to feel sadness for someone else because he or she is hurt or unhappy: *I pity anyone who has to work in such bad conditions.*

piz·za /ˈpitsə/ *noun*
a round, flat piece of bread covered with cheese and other foods and then baked

place¹ /pleɪs/ *noun*

1 a particular area, building, city, or country: *This is the place where I first saw her.* | *He traveled to places all over the world.*

2 the right or usual position for something: *Please put the book back in its place.*

3 the importance or position that someone or something has: *No one can ever take his place.* (=be as important as he was)

4 a seat: *Is this place taken?*

5 your house or home: *The party will be at Amy's place.*

6 take place to happen: *When will the ceremony take place?* ≫ compare HAPPEN

7 in place of instead of: *I am trying this in place of butter.*

place² *verb* (**placing, placed**)

1 to put something somewhere: *She placed her head on the pillow.*

2 to decide that someone or something is important or valuable: *He placed his trust in her.*

3 place an order to ask a store or business for some goods

plaid /plæd/ *n* [C,U]

a pattern of squares and lines, originally from Scotland and used especially on material for clothing —**plaid** *adj*: *a plaid work shirt*

plain¹ /pleɪn/ *adjective*

1 simple, without a pattern on it: *He wore a plain blue suit.*

2 easy to see, hear, or understand: *He made it plain that he did not like me.* ≫ compare CLEAR¹

plain² *noun*

a large area of flat land

plain·ly /'pleɪnli/ *adverb*

in a way that is easy to see, hear, or understand: *Let me speak plainly.*

plan¹ /plæn/ *noun*

1 something you have decided to do: *Do you have any plans for the weekend?*

2 a drawing showing all the parts of a building, machine, room etc.

plan² *verb* (**planning, planned**)

to think about something that you want to do and about how to do it: *We plan to build a bridge over the river.*

plane /pleɪn/ *noun*

a vehicle that flies using wings and an engine: *What time does the plane land?* (=arrive)

plan·et /'plænɪt/ *noun*

one of the large objects in space like the Earth that moves around a star such as the sun

plank /plæŋk/ *noun*

a long flat piece of wood used for building something

plant¹ /plænt/ *noun*

1 something living that is not an animal, but has leaves and roots: *Trees and vegetables are plants.*

2 a factory and all its equipment: *He works at the car plant.*

plant² *verb*

to put plants or seeds in the ground to grow: *Spring is the best time to plant flowers.*

plan·ta·tion /plæn'teɪʃən/ *noun*

a large farm on which tea, sugar, cotton etc. is grown

plas·ter¹ /'plæstər/ *noun* [U]

a soft white substance covering walls to make them smooth

plaster² *verb*

to cover a surface with something: *Papers were plastered all over the wall.*

plas·tic /'plæstɪk/ *noun*

a strong substance made from chemicals and used for making containers, toys etc.: *The blocks are made of plastic.* —**plastic** *adjective*. *She drank from a plastic cup.*

plate /pleɪt/ *noun*

a flat, usually round, dish from which you eat or serve food: *Here is a dinner plate for you.* ≫ compare BOWL

plat·form /'plætfɔrm/ *noun*

1 a raised structure on which you stand or work: *The teacher stood on a platform to speak to us.*

2 the part of a train station where you get on and off a train

play¹ /pleɪ/ *verb* (**playing, played**)

1 to do something you enjoy, especially using toys: *The little girl is playing with a doll.*

2 to take part in a game or sport: *He plays football every Sunday.*

3 to make sounds on a musical instrument: *She plays the drums.*

4 to act as a character in a play or movie: *Who does he play in the movie?*

5 play with something to continue to touch or move something: *Stop playing with that glass.*

play² *noun* (*plural* **plays**)
1 a story performed by people in a theater, on the radio etc.: *She is in a new play about a famous singer.*
2 the actions of someone in a game or sport: *He made a great play!*
3 [U] activity done for fun by children: *Children learn a lot through play.*

play·er /'pleɪɚ/ *noun*
someone who plays a game, sport, or musical instrument: *She is a tennis player.*

play·ful /'pleɪfəl/ *adjective*
fun, and not serious: *They had a playful little dog.*

play·ground /'pleɪgraʊnd/ *noun*
a small area of land where children can play

plead /plid/ *verb*
1 to ask for something that you want very much; BEG: *He pleaded **with** her to listen to him.*
2 to say officially in a court of law whether you are guilty of a crime: *The woman pleaded not guilty.*

pleas·ant /'plɛzənt/ *adjective*
nice or enjoyable: *We spent a pleasant day in the country.* —**pleasantly** *adverb* ≫ opposite UNPLEASANT

please¹ /pliz/
a word added to a question or request, to make it more polite: *Please bring your book to me.* | *Could I have a glass of water, please?*

please² *verb* (**pleasing, pleased**)
to make someone feel happy or satisfied: *You cannot please everyone.*

pleased /plizd/ *adjective*
happy or satisfied: *I'm so pleased to see you.*

pleas·ure /'plɛʒɚ/ *noun* [U]
the feeling of happiness, satisfaction, or enjoyment you get from doing something: *I like reading for pleasure.*

plen·ti·ful /'plɛntɪfəl/ *adjective*
more than enough in amount or number: *Fruit is plentiful this summer.*

plen·ty /'plɛnti/
a lot; a large amount: *We have plenty of time to get to the school.* | *There is plenty of bread.*

pli·ers /'plaɪɚz/ *plural noun*
a tool like a pair of strong scissors, used for cutting or bending wire

plot¹ /plɑt/ *noun*
1 the story of a book, movie, or play: *The movie had an exciting plot.*
2 a secret plan to do something wrong
3 a small piece of land

plot² *verb* (**plotting, plotted**)
to make a secret plan to do something wrong: *They are plotting to kill the king.*

plow¹ /plaʊ/ *noun*
1 a piece of farming equipment for cutting up the ground so seeds can be planted
2 a piece of equipment on a truck for moving snow off streets and roads

plow² *verb*
to break the ground with a PLOW: *The land must be plowed in the spring.*

pluck /plʌk/ *verb*
to pull something quickly to remove it from its place

plug¹ /plʌg/ *noun*
1 a small object at the end of an electrical wire, which you put into special holes in a wall to get electricity
2 a round piece of rubber used for blocking a hole in a bathtub or SINK²

plug² *verb*
(**plugging, plugged**)
1 to block or fill a hole with something
2 **plug something in** to connect an electrical machine to a supply of electricity: *You need to plug in the lamp.*

plum /plʌm/ *noun*
a sweet juicy red or purple fruit with a large seed —see picture at FRUIT

plumb·er /'plʌmɚ/ *noun*
someone whose job is to repair water pipes, toilets etc.

plumb·ing /'plʌmɪŋ/ *noun* [U]
all the water pipes in a house or building

plump /plʌmp/ *adjective*
round and fat: *The baby has plump little arms.*

plunge /plʌndʒ/ *verb* (**plunging, plunged**)
to fall down suddenly, or to push something down: *He plunged his hand into the water.*

plu·ral /'plʊrəl/ *adjective, noun*
more than one: *"Dogs" is the plural of "dog."*
≫ compare SINGULAR

plus¹ /plʌs/ *preposition*
added to; and: *Four plus two is six.* (4 + 2 = 6)

plus²
and also: *He works all week, plus he has two children at home.*

p.m. /ˌpi ˈɛm/
in the afternoon or evening: *It is 4 p.m.* ≫ compare A.M.

P.O. box /ˌpi ˈoʊ ˌbɑks/ *noun* [*plural* **P.O. boxes**]
a numbered box in a post office where you can receive mail, instead of at your home

pock·et /ˈpɑkɪt/ *noun*
a piece of material sewn onto clothes to make a little bag for you to keep things in: *He put his hands in his pockets.*

pock·et knife /ˈpɑkɪt ˌnaɪf/ *noun*
a small knife with a blade that you can fold into its handle

pod /pɑd/ *noun*
a long narrow part of some plants, in which seeds grow

po·em /ˈpoʊəm/ *noun*
a piece of writing that uses a pattern of lines and sounds to express ideas, emotions etc.: *I le wrote a poem about love.*

po·et /ˈpoʊɪt/ *noun*
someone who writes poems

po·et·ry /ˈpoʊətri/ *noun* [U]
poems: *She gave me a book of poetry.*

point¹ /pɔɪnt/ *noun*
1 the most important idea, fact, or opinion: *Stop talking so much and get to the point!* | *What is your point?*
2 a particular moment or time: *At the point when I left, the teacher was reading a story.*
3 an exact position or place: *The accident happened at the point where the two roads cross.*
4 [U] the aim or purpose of doing something: *I don't see **the** point **of** fixing a car this old.*
5 a number that you win in a game or sport: *Our team won by 15 points.*
6 a sign (.) used to separate a whole number from the DECIMALs that follow it: *Prices rose 5.5%.* [=five point five percent]
7 the sharp end of something: *I cut my finger on the point of a nail.*
8 up to a point partly, but not completely: *I believed what he said up to a point.*
9 point of view a belief or opinion about something: *Try to see it from my point of view.*

point² *verb*
to show someone something by holding your finger out toward it: *He pointed **to** the building and said, "That's where I work."*

point·ed /ˈpɔɪntɪd/ *adjective*
having a sharp point at the end

point·less /ˈpɔɪntlɪs/ *adjective*
with no purpose or meaning: *The meeting was completely pointless!*

poi·son¹ /ˈpɔɪzən/ *noun*
a substance that kills or harms you if it gets into your body

poison² *verb*
to kill or harm someone or an animal using poison: *The farmer poisoned the rats.*

poi·son·ous /ˈpɔɪzənəs/ *adjective*
containing poison: *This is a poisonous plant.*

poke /poʊk/ *verb* (**poking, poked**)
to push a pointed object such as your finger or a stick into someone or something: *He poked the fire with a stick.* —**poke** *noun*

pok·er /ˈpoʊkɚ/ *noun* [U]
a card game that you usually play for money

po·lar /ˈpoʊlɚ/ *adjective*
relating to the North Pole or the South Pole: *He is studying the polar winter.*

po·lar bear /ˈ.. ˌ./ *noun*
a large white bear that lives near the North Pole —see color picture on page 183

pole /poʊl/ *noun*
1 a long stick or post: *He has a new fishing pole.*
2 the most northern or southern area of the Earth

po·lice /pəˈlis/ *plural noun*
the group of people whose job is to protect people and property and to make sure that everyone obeys the law: *The police are searching for the thief.*

po·lice·man /pəˈlismən/ *noun* [*plural* **policemen** /-mɛn/]
a male police officer

police of·fi·cer /.ˈ. ˌ.../ *noun*
someone who works for the police

police sta·tion /.ˈ. ˌ../ *noun*
an office or building used by the police

po·lice·wom·an /pəˈlis ˌwʊmən/ *noun* [*plural* **policewomen** /-wɪmɪn/]
a female police officer

pol·i·cy /'pɑləsi/ *noun* (*plural* **policies**)
a plan that is agreed to by a political party, government, or company: *The policy of the government is to improve education.*

pol·ish¹ /'pɑlɪʃ/ *verb*
to rub something so that it shines: *I need to polish my shoes.*

polish² *noun* [U]
a liquid substance that you rub on something to make it shine

po·lite /pə'laɪt/ *adjective*
behaving or speaking in a nice and respectful way; not rude: *A polite person always says thank you.* ≫ compare IMPOLITE, RUDE

po·lit·i·cal /pə'lɪtɪkəl/ *adjective*
relating to the government or politics of a country: *How many political parties are there?* —**politically** *adverb*

pol·i·ti·cian /ˌpɑlə'tɪʃən/ *noun*
someone who works in the government or politics

pol·i·tics /'pɑləˌtɪks/ *noun* [U]
1 activities or opinions concerned with how power is used in the government of a country: *Are you interested in city politics?*
2 the job of being a politician: *He wants to go into politics.*

pol·lute /pə'lut/ *verb* (**polluting, polluted**)
to make the air, water, or soil dirty or dangerous by adding harmful substances: *The lake is polluted by chemicals.*

pol·lu·tion /pə'luʃən/ *noun* [U]
1 the process of making the air, water, or soil dirty and dangerous: *What are the causes of water pollution?*
2 a substance that makes the air, water, or soil dirty or dangerous: *The air in big cities is full of pollution.*

pond

pond /pɑnd/ *noun*
an area of water, smaller than a lake: *There's a small pond on our farm.* ≫ compare LAKE, PUDDLE

po·ny /'pouni/ *noun* (*plural* **ponies**)
a small horse

po·ny·tail /'pouniˌteɪl/ *noun*
hair tied together at the back of your head —see picture at HAIRSTLYLE

pool /pul/ *noun*
1 a structure that is filled with water for people to swim in: *I like swimming in the indoor pool.*
2 [U] an indoor game played on a table on which you hit balls into holes using a long stick
3 a small area of liquid on a surface: *He lay in a pool **of** blood.*

poor /por, pɔr/ *adjective*
1 not having very much money: *She comes from a poor family.* ≫ compare RICH, WEALTHY
2 not as good as it could be: *Your writing is poor.* | *He is in poor health.*
3 making you feel pity for someone or something: *The poor animal was in pain.*

poor·ly /'porli/ *adverb*
badly: *The room was poorly lit.*

pop¹ /pɑp/ *noun*
1 [U] modern music that many young people like and dance to
2 a sudden noise like a small explosion: *I heard the pop of a gun.*

pop² *verb* (**popping, popped**)
to burst something and make a sound like a small explosion: *He popped the balloon.*

pop·corn /'pɑpkɔrn/ *noun* [U]
a kind of corn that bursts open and becomes light and white when it is heated

Pope /poup/ *noun*
the leader of the Roman Catholic church

pop·u·lar /'pɑpyələ/ *adjective*
liked by many people: *She is popular at school.* | *This dance is popular **with** young people.* ≫ opposite UNPOPULAR

pop·u·lar·i·ty /ˌpɑpyə'lærəti/ *noun* [U]
the quality of being liked by a lot of people

pop·u·la·tion /ˌpɑpyə'leɪʃən/ *noun*
the number of people living in a place: *What is the population **of** this city?*

porch /pɔrtʃ/ *noun*
a structure with a floor and roof built outside a house's front or back door

pork /pɔrk/ *noun* [U]
meat from pigs

port /pɔrt/ *noun*
1 a place where ships can load or unload goods; HARBOR
2 a town or city with a HARBOR

port·a·ble /'pɔrtəbəl/ *adjective*
small, light, and easy to carry with you: *I want to buy a portable computer.*

por·ter /'pɔrtɚ/ *noun*
someone whose job is to carry things for people at airports, hotels etc.

port·hole /'pɔrthoʊl/ *noun*
a small window on the side of a ship or airplane

por·tion /'pɔrʃən/ *noun*
a part or share of something: *She only eats a small portion of her food.*

por·trait /'pɔrtrɪt/ *noun*
a painting, drawing, or photograph of someone: *He painted a portrait of his daughter.*

po·si·tion /pə'zɪʃən/ *noun*
1 the way someone sits, stands, or lies: *I could not find a comfortable position to sit in.*
2 the condition or situation that someone is in: *I have been in a difficult position since I lost my job.*
3 a job: *He has an important position at the bank.*
4 a place where someone or something is: *Our seats were in a good position to hear the music.*

pos·i·tive /'pazətɪv/ *adjective*
1 sure that something is true or right: *I am positive that I gave you his address.* ≫ compare CERTAIN
2 seeing the good qualities of a situation, person etc.: *She has a positive attitude toward work.*

pos·sess /pə'zɛs/ *verb*
to have or own something

pos·ses·sion /pə'zɛʃən/ *noun*
something that you own: *He lost most of his possessions in the fire.*

pos·si·bil·i·ty /,pasə'bɪləti/ *noun (plural possibilities)*
something that might happen or be true: *There's a possibility of rain today.*

pos·si·ble /'pasəbəl/ *adjective*
able to be done, happen, or exist: *Is it possible to get to the city by train?* ≫ opposite IMPOSSIBLE

pos·si·bly /'pasəbli/ *adverb*
used for saying something may be true or

likely; perhaps: *"Can you come tomorrow?" "Possibly."*

post¹ /poʊst/ *noun*
1 a thick piece of wood, metal, or stone fixed in the ground: *The fence is held up by wooden posts.*
2 an important job: *The new posts are all in Asia.*

post² *verb*
to put a notice about something on a wall, computer etc.

post·age /'poʊstɪdʒ/ *noun* [U]
the money that you pay to send something by mail

post·card /'poʊstkard/ *noun*
a card, often with a picture on the front, that you send in the mail without an envelope

post·er /'poʊstɚ/ *noun*
a large printed notice or picture, used for advertising something or as a decoration —see color picture on page 185

post of·fice /'. ,../ *noun*
a place where you can buy stamps, send letters etc. —see color picture on page 193

post of·fice box /'. .. ,./ *noun* (also P.O. box)
a numbered box in a post office where you can receive mail, instead of at your home

post·pone /poʊst'poʊn/ *verb* (postponing, postponed)
to change the time of an event to a later time: *The game was postponed because of rain.* ≫ compare DELAY²

pot /pat/ *noun*
a round container, used for cooking, pouring liquids etc.: *I've made a big pot of soup.* | *Where is the coffee pot?* | *The plant needs a bigger pot.*

po·ta·to /pə'teɪtoʊ, -tə/ *noun (plural potatoes)*
a round white vegetable that grows under the ground, that you can cook and eat —see picture at VEGETABLE

potato chip /.'.. ,./ *noun*
a thin hard piece of potato cooked in oil and sold in packages —see picture at CHIP¹

pot·ter·y /'patəri/ *noun* [U]
1 plates, cups, and other objects made from clay
2 the activity of making objects from clay

poul·try /'poʊltri/ *noun* [U]
birds kept on a farm for their eggs or meat

pounce /paʊns/ *verb* (**pouncing, pounced**)
to jump on something suddenly: *The cat pounced **on** the bird.*

pound¹ /paʊnd/ *noun*
a measure of weight equal to 16 OUNCEs or 454 grams: *I **lost** two pounds* (=I weigh two pounds less) *this week!*

pound² *verb*
to hit something hard many times: *He pounded on the door in anger.*

pour /pɔr/ *verb*
1 to make a liquid or other substance flow into or out of a container: *She poured some sugar into a bowl.* | *Will you pour me some more coffee?*
2 to rain hard and steadily: *It's been pouring all day.*

pov·er·ty /'pɑvɚt̬i/ *noun* [U]
the state of being poor: *She has lived in poverty all her life.*

pow·der /'paʊdɚ/ *noun*
a dry substance in the form of small grains, like dust: *I put some powder on the baby's bottom.*

pow·er /'paʊɚ/ *noun*
1 [U] control over people or events: *He works in politics because of his love for power.*
2 [U] energy that is used to make a machine work: *Our electricity is produced by nuclear power.*
3 the right or authority to do something: *Police have the power to arrest you.*

pow·er·ful /'paʊɚfəl/ *adjective*
very strong or having a lot of power: *The car has a powerful engine.*

pow·er·less /'paʊɚlɪs/ *adjective*
with no power or strength: *I was powerless to help her.*

power plant /'.. ,./ *noun*
a building where electricity is made

prac·ti·cal /'præktɪkəl/ *adjective*
1 relating to real things or events: *He has a lot of practical experience in fixing cars.*
2 sensible and likely to succeed or be effective: *We have to be practical and not spend too much money.*

practical joke /,... './ *noun*
a trick that surprises someone and makes other people laugh

prac·ti·cal·ly /'præktɪkli/ *adverb*
almost: *I'm practically finished; I'll be there in a minute.*

prac·tice¹ /'præktɪs/ *noun*
1 [U] a regular activity that you do to improve your skill or ability: *You need practice in order to play the piano well.*
2 something that you do in a particular way because it is usual; CUSTOM: *It is a practice in her country to kiss people when you meet them.*
3 **out of practice** not able to do something well because you have not done it for a long time

practice² *verb* (**practicing, practiced**)
to do something regularly to improve your skill or ability: *You have to practice to become a good singer.*

prai·rie /'prɛri/ *noun*
a large open area of land that is covered in wheat or long grass

praise¹ /preɪz/ *verb* (**praising, praised**)
to say that you admire someone or something: *She praised her daughter's hard work.*

praise² *noun* [U]
words that you say to praise someone: *Her new book received a lot of praise.*

prawn /prɔn/ *noun*
an ocean animal like a large SHRIMP, that is often eaten in restaurants

pray /preɪ/ *verb* (**praying, prayed**)
to speak to a god or gods to ask for help or to give thanks

prayer /prɛr/ *noun*
1 [U] the act of praying
2 words that you say when you pray: *They **said** a prayer for the soldiers in the war.*

preach /pritʃ/ *verb*
to give a speech about a religious subject, usually in a church

preach·er /'pritʃɚ/ *noun*
someone who gives a religious speech, usually in a church

pre·cau·tion /prɪ'kɔʃən/ *noun*
something that you do to stop something bad or

dangerous from happening: *He took the precaution of locking his door before leaving.*

pre·cious /'prɛʃəs/ *adjective*
1 very valuable or expensive: *Water is precious in the desert.*
2 very important or special to you: *I have precious memories of her birth.*

pre·cip·i·ta·tion /prɪˌsɪpə'teɪʃən/ *noun* [U]
rain or snow that falls to the ground

pre·cise /prɪ'saɪs/ *adjective*
exact and correct: *Your instructions need to be more precise.*

pre·cise·ly /prɪ'saɪsli/ *adverb*
1 exactly: *I don't remember precisely what happened.*
2 used for agreeing with what someone has said: *"So you think he was wrong?" "Precisely."*

pre·dict /prɪ'dɪkt/ *verb*
to say what is going to happen before it happens: *The newspapers are predicting a close election.*

pre·dic·tion /prɪ'dɪkʃən/ *noun*
a statement that something is going to happen before it happens: *Your prediction about the weather was wrong. It didn't rain at all!*

pre·fer /prɪ'fɚ/ *verb* (**preferring, preferred**)
to like one thing more than another: *Which of these two dresses do you prefer?*

pref·er·a·ble /'prɛfərəbəl/ *adjective*
better or more suitable: *We accept credit cards, but cash is preferable.*

pref·er·ence /'prɛfrəns, -fərəns/ *noun*
the state of liking one thing more than another: *We have a preference **for** flying rather than driving.*

pre·fix /'priˌfɪks/ *noun* (*plural* **prefixes**)
a group of letters added to the beginning of a word to make a new word: *If we add the prefix "un" to the word "happy", we make the word "unhappy."*

preg·nan·cy /'prɛgnənsi/ *noun* (*plural* **pregnancies**)
the condition of having a baby developing in your body: *You should not smoke during your pregnancy.*

preg·nant /'prɛgnənt/ *adjective*
having a baby developing in your body: *She is four months pregnant.* | *She wanted to get pregnant.*

prej·u·dice /'prɛdʒədɪs/ *noun*
an unfair opinion about someone that is not based on facts or reason: *You have a prejudice **against** women drivers.*

prej·u·diced /'prɛdʒədɪst/ *adjective*
having an unfair opinion about someone that is not based on facts or reason: *Why are you so prejudiced **against** people from other countries?*

prep·a·ra·tion /ˌprɛpə'reɪʃən/ *noun*
1 [U] the act of getting something ready: *Teachers have to do a lot of preparation before each class.*
2 preparations [*plural*] arrangements for something that is going to happen: *She's very busy with preparations **for** the wedding.*

pre·pare /prɪ'pɛr/ *verb* (**preparing, prepared**)
to make something ready: *I prepared the food for the party.* | *We're preparing to go on vacation.*

pre·pared /prɪ'pɛrd/ *adjective*
1 ready to do something; ready to be used: *Are you prepared **for** your new job?*
2 be prepared to do something to be willing to do something: *Are you prepared to accept our offer?*

prep·o·si·tion /ˌprɛpə'zɪʃən/ *noun*
a word such as *to, for, on, by,* etc. which is put in front of a noun to show where, when, or how: *In the sentences, "She sat by the fire" and "They went to town", "by" and "to" are prepositions.*

pre·scribe /prɪ'skraɪb/ *verb* (**prescribing, prescribed**)
to say what medicine or treatment someone should have

pre·scrip·tion /prɪ'skrɪpʃən/ *noun*
a piece of paper on which a doctor writes what medicine someone needs, or the medicine itself: *The doctor wrote me a prescription **for** the pills.*

pres·ence /'prɛzəns/ *noun*
1 [U] the state of being present in a particular place: *We are looking for the presence of chemical weapons.* ≫ compare ABSENCE
2 in someone's presence in the same place as someone: *Everyone was afraid to talk in her presence.*

pres·ent¹ /'prɛzənt/ *adjective*
1 be present to be in a particular place: *There are twenty children present.* ≫ opposite ABSENT
2 existing now: *What is your present job?*

present² *noun*
1 something that you give someone; GIFT: *He gave her a birthday present.*
2 at present at this time; now: *He's away at present.*

pre·sent³ /prɪˈzɛnt/ *verb*
to give something to someone, especially at an official ceremony: *He presented the gold cup **to** the winner.*

pres·en·ta·tion /ˌprɪzənˈteɪʃən, ˌprɛ-/ *noun*
the act of giving something to someone, especially at an official ceremony: *The presentation of the prizes is tonight.*

pres·ent·ly /ˈprɛzəntli/ *adverb*
at this time; now: *Presently he does not have a job.*

present par·ti·ci·ple /ˌ.. ˈ..../ *noun*
the form of a verb which ends in *-ing* and is used for showing continuous action, or as an adjective: *In the sentences, "The child is sleeping" and "I woke the sleeping child," "sleeping" is a present participle.*

present per·fect /ˌ.. ˈ../ *noun*
the form of a verb made by adding the verb "have" to the PAST PARTICIPLE of a verb: *In the sentence, "I have eaten the cake," "have eaten" is in the present perfect.*

pres·ent tense /ˌ.. ˈ./ *noun*
the tense of a verb that shows what exists or happens now

pres·er·va·tion /ˌprɛzɚˈveɪʃən/ *noun* [U]
the act of keeping something unharmed or unchanged: *We are working for the preservation **of** the forest.*

pre·serve /prɪˈzɚv/ *verb* [preserving, preserved]
to keep something from being harmed or damaged: *You can preserve fish in salt.*

pres·i·dent /ˈprɛzədənt/ *noun*
1 the leader of the government in a country that does not have a king or queen: *The President **of** the U.S. is coming to our country.*
2 the leader of a company, organization, college etc.

press¹ /prɛs/ *verb*
1 to push something with your finger: *He pressed the doorbell.*
2 to push against something firmly: *The children pressed their faces against the window.*

press² *noun*
the press [U] all newspapers and magazines, and the people who work for them: *Members of the press were waiting outside.*

press·ing /ˈprɛsɪŋ/ *adjective*
needing to be dealt with soon: *Crime is a pressing problem in our city.*

pres·sure /ˈprɛʃɚ/ *noun*
1 [U] an attempt to make someone do something by using influence, arguments etc.: *The company is **under** pressure to change its products.*
2 the conditions of your life that may cause problems for you: *The pressures of his job are great.*
3 the force caused by the weight of one thing being put on top of another

pre·tend /prɪˈtɛnd/ *verb*
to do something to make someone believe that something is true when it is not: *She pretended to be asleep.*

pret·ty¹ /ˈprɪti/ *adjective* [prettier, prettiest]
attractive and nice to look at: *She is a very pretty girl.* | *What a pretty dress!* ≫ compare BEAUTIFUL

pretty² *adverb*
fairly; very: *It was a pretty serious accident.* | *Dad was pretty mad at us.*

pret·zel /ˈprɛtsəl/ *noun*
a salty type of bread, baked in the shape of a loose knot —see picture at BREAD

pre·vent /prɪˈvɛnt/ *verb*
to stop something from happening, or someone from doing something: *He was trying to prevent a fight.* | *I wanted to prevent her **from** leaving.*

pre·ven·tion /prɪˈvɛnʃən/ *noun* [U]
the act of stopping something from happening: *The prevention of crime is an important issue for us.*

pre·vi·ous /ˈpriviəs/ *adjective*
happening before the present time: *In my previous job, I had to travel a lot.*

pre·vi·ous·ly /ˈpriviəsli/ *adverb*
before now: *Previously, I worked in a restaurant.*

prey /preɪ/ *noun* [U]
an animal that is hunted and eaten by another animal

price /praɪs/ *noun*
the money that you pay to buy something: *The price of the house is very high.*

price·less /'praɪslɪs/ *adjective*
very valuable: *He owns a priceless painting.*

prick /prɪk/ *verb*
to make a small hole in something with a sharp object: *I pricked my finger on a needle.*

pride /praɪd/ *noun* [U]
the feeling of pleasure and satisfaction that you have because of something good that you have: *She showed us her new home with great pride.*

priest /prist/ *noun*
someone whose job is to perform religious ceremonies and duties

pri·mar·y /'praɪˌmɛri, -məri/ *adjective*
most important; main

prime min·is·ter /ˌ. '.../ *noun*
the leader of a government in many countries

prim·i·tive /'prɪmətɪv/ *adjective*
early in human history: *Primitive people lived in caves.*

prince /prɪns/ *noun*
1 the son of a king or queen
2 the ruler of a country

prin·cess /'prɪnsɪs, -sɛs/ *noun*
the daughter of a king or queen, or the wife of a prince

prin·ci·pal¹ /'prɪnsəpəl/ *adjective*
most important; main: *What is your principal reason for taking the job?* —**principally** *adverb*

principal² *noun*
someone who is in charge of a school

prin·ci·ple /'prɪnsəpəl/ *noun*
a rule or idea that you believe is right and that makes you behave in a particular way: *It is a principle of mine to treat everyone equally.*

print¹ /prɪnt/ *verb*
1 to put words or pictures on paper or clothes using a machine: *The books are printed in Hong Kong.*
2 to write words without joining the letters together: *Please print your name clearly.*

print² *noun*
1 [U] words printed on a page: *The print is too small for me to read.*
2 a mark made on a surface or in something soft

print·er /'prɪntɚ/ *noun*
1 a machine connected to a computer that prints documents from the computer onto paper
2 someone whose job is to print books, magazines etc.

pris·on /'prɪzən/ *noun*
a large building where people are kept as a punishment for a crime: *He was sent to prison for ten years.* ≫ compare JAIL

pris·on·er /'prɪzənɚ/ *noun*
someone who is kept in a prison

pri·vate¹ /'praɪvɪt/ *adjective*
1 only for one particular person or group, not for everyone: *This is my private telephone.*
2 secret, not shared with other people: *I don't talk about my private life at work.*
3 quiet and without other people listening or seeing: *Is there a private place where we can talk?*

private² *noun* [U]
in private without other people listening or seeing: *I need to speak to you in private.*

private school /ˌ. '. / *noun*
a school that you must pay for ≫ compare PUBLIC SCHOOL

priv·i·lege /'prɪvlɪdʒ, -vəlɪdʒ/ *noun*
a special advantage given only to one person or group

prize /praɪz/ *noun*
something that you win in a game, race, or competition: *I won first prize in the race.*

prob·a·ble /'prɑbəbəl/ *adjective*
likely to happen or be true: *The probable cause of the accident may be the leaking gas.*

prob·a·bly /'prɑbəbli/ *adverb*
likely to happen or be true: *We will probably go to the show tomorrow.*

prob·lem /'prɑbləm/ *noun*
1 a difficult situation or person that you must deal with: *I have been **having** some problems **with** my car.*
2 **no problem** used for saying that you are willing to do something: *"Can you come over later?" "No problem."*

pro·ceed /prə'sid, prou-/ *verb*
to continue to do something that has already been started: *Our plans are proceeding smoothly.*

proc·ess /ˈprɑsɛs, ˈproʊ-/ noun (plural processes)
1 a series of actions that you do to get a particular result: *Learning to read is a slow process.*
2 a set of changes or developments that happen naturally: *She is studying the aging process in women.*

pro·ces·sion /prəˈsɛʃən/ noun
a line of people or vehicles following one another as part of a ceremony: *They watched the procession go past.*

pro·duce¹ /prəˈdus/ verb (producing, produced)
1 to make something happen or have a particular effect: *The drug produces bad effects in some people.*
2 to grow or make something naturally: *Trees produce oxygen.*
3 to make something using machines: *The factory produces 1,000 cars every week.*
4 to control the preparation of a play or movie, and show it to the public

produce² /ˈprɑdus, ˈproʊ-/ noun [U]
food that is grown, especially fruits and vegetables: *I only buy fresh produce.*

pro·duc·er /prəˈdusɚ/ noun
1 a person, company, or country that makes or grows food, goods, or material
2 someone who prepares a play or movie

prod·uct /ˈprɑdʌkt/ noun
something that is made in a factory: *The company makes plastic products.*

pro·duc·tion /prəˈdʌkʃən/ noun
1 [U] the process of making something, or the amount that is made
2 something made with skill, such as a play or movie

pro·fes·sion /prəˈfɛʃən/ noun
a job for which you need special education and training: *He is a doctor by profession.* [=as his job]

pro·fes·sion·al /prəˈfɛʃənl/ adjective
1 relating to a job for which you need special education and training: *Get some professional advice from your doctor.*
2 doing something for money, rather than for pleasure: *He is a professional football player.*
» compare AMATEUR

pro·fes·sor /prəˈfɛsɚ/ noun
a teacher at a university

prof·it /ˈprɑfɪt/ noun
money that you gain for selling something for more than you paid for it: *I sold the house for a $10,000 profit.*

prof·it·a·ble /ˈprɑfɪtəbəl/ adjective
making a profit: *The business is not very profitable.*

pro·gram¹ /ˈproʊgræm, -grəm/ noun
1 a set of instructions that a computer uses to do a particular job
2 a show on television or radio: *What's your favorite program?*
3 a printed description of what will happen at a play etc.: *Do you want to buy a program?*
4 a set of planned activities with a specific purpose

program² verb (programming, programmed)
to give a computer the instructions it needs to do a particular job

pro·gram·mer /ˈproʊˌgræmɚ, -grəmɚ/ noun
someone whose job is to write instructions that make a computer do a particular job

prog·ress¹ /ˈprɑgrəs, -grɛs/ noun [U]
1 continuous improvement in something: *You have made good progress with your English.*
2 movement toward a place

pro·gress² /prəˈgrɛs/ verb
1 to improve or develop over a period of time: *Work on the building is progressing slowly.*
2 to move forward

pro·hib·it /proʊˈhɪbɪt, prə-/ verb
to not allow something by law: *Smoking is prohibited in this building.* —**prohibition** /proʊəˈbɪʃən/ noun [U] » compare BAN¹

proj·ect /ˈprɑdʒɛkt, -dʒɪkt/ noun
a plan to do something: *There is a city project to build a new road.*

pro·jec·tor /prəˈdʒɛktɚ/ noun
a machine that can show a movie of pictures on a wall

prom·i·nent /ˈprɑmənənt/ adjective
1 large and easy to notice
2 important or famous: *She is a prominent politician.*

prom·ise¹ /ˈprɑmɪs/ verb (promising, promised)
to say that you will definitely do something: *She promised her brother she would write to him.*

promise² *noun*
something you have said that you will definitely do: *She made a promise to come and see him.*

pro·mote /prə'moʊt/ *verb* (promoting, promoted)
1 to help something develop and be successful: *The company is promoting its new products.*
2 to give someone a better position at work: *He was promoted to manager.*

pro·mo·tion /prə'moʊʃən/ *noun*
a move to a better position at work

prompt /prɑmpt/ *adjective*
done quickly and without delay: *He gave a prompt answer to a letter.*

pro·noun /'proʊnaʊn/ *noun*
a word like *he, she, it, they*, etc., which is used instead of using a noun again: *Instead of saying "Peter went to school," we can use a pronoun and say, "He went to school."*

pro·nounce /prə'naʊns/ *verb* (pronouncing, pronounced)
to make the sounds of a word: *How do you pronounce your name?*

pro·nun·ci·a·tion /prə,nʌnsi'eɪʃən/ *noun*
the way in which a word or language is spoken

proof /pruf/ *noun* [U]
facts that prove that something is true: *Do you have any proof that he took the money?*

prop /prɑp/ *verb* (propping, propped)
to support something or keep it in a particular position: *I propped my bicycle against the wall.*

pro·pel·ler /prə'pɛlɚ/ *noun*
a piece of equipment that has two or more blades that spin quickly to make a ship or aircraft move

prop·er /'prɑpɚ/ *adjective*
correct or suitable: *Put the book back in its proper place.* ≫ compare RIGHT¹

prop·er·ly /'prɑpɚli/ *adverb*
in a correct or suitable way: *You didn't do the job properly.*

prop·er·ty /'prɑpɚti/ *noun*
1 [U] something that someone owns: *Their job is to protect the property of the school.*
2 (*plural* **properties**) land or buildings: *This is private property.* (=not for the public)

proph·e·cy /'prɑfəsi/ *noun* (*plural* **prophecies**)
a statement that tells what will happen in the future

proph·et /'prɑfɪt/ *noun*
1 someone who says what will happen in the future
2 someone who teaches people about religion

pro·por·tion /prə'pɔrʃən/ *noun*
the amount of something compared to something else: *The proportion of girls to boys in the school is two to one.*

pro·pos·al /prə'poʊzəl/ *noun*
1 a plan or suggestion: *A proposal to build a new school is being considered.*
2 the act of asking someone to marry you

pro·pose /prə'poʊz/ *verb* (proposing, proposed)
1 to suggest that something be done: *He proposed that we build another factory.*
2 to ask someone to marry you: *He proposed to her, and she accepted.*

pros·per /'prɑspɚ/ *verb*
to be successful and become rich: *Her company is prospering.*

pros·per·i·ty /prɑ'spɛrəti/ *noun* [U]
success and wealth

pros·per·ous /'prɑspərəs/ *adjective*
rich and successful: *She has a prosperous business.*

pros·ti·tute /'prɑstə,tut/ *noun*
someone who has sex with people to earn money —**prostitution** *noun* [U]

pro·tect /prə'tɛkt/ *verb*
to prevent someone or something from being harmed or damaged: *The fence is to protect the farmer's cattle.*

pro·tec·tion /prə'tɛkʃən/ *noun* [U]
the act of keeping a person or thing safe from harm or damage: *Her thin coat gave her no protection against the cold.*

pro·test¹ /'proʊtɛst, prə'tɛst/ *verb*
to say strongly that you do not agree with something: *The group is protesting against the war.*

pro·test² /'proʊtɛst/ *noun*
a strong public complaint about something: *Many people joined the protest against government plans.*

Prot·es·tant /'prɑt̬əstənt/ *adjective*
relating to the Christian church that is not the Roman Catholic church

proud /praʊd/ *adjective*
1 feeling pleased about your actions, family, country etc. because you think they are very good: *He is proud of his daughter's success.*
2 thinking that you are better or more important than other people: *She is too proud to accept help from him.*

prove /pruv/ *verb* (**proving, proved**)
to show that something is definitely true: *Can you prove that he is guilty?*

prov·erb /'prɑvɚb/ *noun*
a short statement that most people know

pro·vide /prə'vaɪd/ *verb* (**providing, provided**)
to give something to someone: *We provide food for hungry children.*

pro·vid·ed /prə'vaɪdɪd/
if and only if: *I'll go to see her, provided you come too.*

prov·ince /'prɑvɪns/ *noun*
one of the large areas into which some countries are divided

pro·voke /prə'voʊk/ *verb* (**provoking, provoked**)
to annoy someone so that he or she becomes angry

prowl /praʊl/ *verb*
to move around quietly, especially to hunt

psalm /sɑm/ *noun*
a religious song or poem

pub·lic¹ /'pʌblɪk/ *adjective*
1 for anyone to use and see: *We have a new public library.*
2 relating to people in general: *Public opinion is now against the government.*

public² *noun* [U]
1 **the public** all the people in an area: *The pool is open to the public.*
2 **in public** in a place where anyone can see or hear

public school /ˌ.. './ *noun*
a school that all children can go to, without having to pay

pub·lish /'pʌblɪʃ/ *verb*
to print and sell a book, newspaper, or magazine: *The company publishes children's books.*

pub·lish·er /'pʌblɪʃɚ/ *noun*
a person or company that prints and sells books, newspapers, or magazines

pud·ding /'pʊdɪŋ/ *noun*
a thick sweet food that is eaten cold

pud·dle /'pʌdl/ *noun*
a small amount of water on the ground or road

puff¹ /pʌf/ *verb*
to breathe quickly, usually after physical activity: *I was puffing after climbing the stairs.*

puff² *noun*
a sudden short movement of air, smoke, or wind: *A puff of wind blew the papers off the table.*

pull¹ /pʊl/ *verb*
1 to move something or someone toward yourself: *He pulled the door open.* | *Stop pulling my hair!* ≫ compare PUSH¹
2 to make something move along behind you: *The horses are pulling a cart.* —see picture at PUSH¹
3 to remove something from its place, especially using force: *I had to have a tooth pulled.*

pull² *noun*
the act of pulling something: *He gave a pull on the rope.*

pulse /pʌls/ *noun*
the regular beat that you can feel as your heart moves blood in your body

pump¹ /pʌmp/ *noun*
a machine that makes liquid or gas go into or out of something

pump² *verb*
to make a liquid or gas move in a particular direction using a pump: *I need to pump up the tire.* (=fill it with air)

pump·kin /'pʌmpkɪn, 'pʌŋkɪn/ *noun*
a very large round orange fruit that grows on the ground

punch¹ /pʌntʃ/ *verb*
1 to hit someone or something with your closed hand: *I punched him in the nose.* ≫ compare SLAP¹—see color picture on page 189
2 to make a hole in something: *He punched a hole in the wall.*

punch² *noun*
1 (*plural* **punches**) a strong hit made with your closed hand

2 [U] a drink made from fruit juice, sugar, and water

punc·tu·ate /ˈpʌŋktʃu,eɪt/ *verb* (**punctuating, punctuated**)
to divide up a piece of writing into sentences, phrases etc. by using special marks like , ; . : and ?

punc·tu·a·tion /ˌpʌŋktʃuˈeɪʃən/ *noun* [U]
signs such as , ; . : and ? used for dividing a piece of writing into sentences, phrases etc.

punc·ture /ˈpʌŋktʃɚ/ *verb* (**puncturing, punctured**)
to make a small hole in something so that air or liquid can get out

pun·ish /ˈpʌnɪʃ/ *verb*
to make someone suffer because he or she has done something wrong: *Kelly was punished for telling a lie.*

pun·ish·ment /ˈpʌnɪʃmənt/ *noun*
the act of making someone suffer because he or she has done something wrong: *The punishment for their crime was severe.*

pu·pil /ˈpyupəl/ *noun*
a person being taught in a school

pup·pet /ˈpʌpɪt/ *noun*
a small figure of a person or animal that you can move by pulling the strings on it, or by putting your hand inside it

pup·py /ˈpʌpi/ *noun* (*plural* **puppies**)
a young dog

pur·chase¹ /ˈpɚtʃəs/ *noun*
1 the act of buying something: *She made several purchases.*
2 something you have bought

purchase² *verb* (**purchasing, purchased**)
to buy something

pure /pyʊr/ *adjective*
1 not mixed with anything else: *The ring is made of pure gold.*
2 clean, without anything harmful: *The water is pure, so you can drink it.*

pure·ly /ˈpyʊrli/ *adverb*
only: *She did it purely for selfish reasons.*

pur·ple /ˈpɚpəl/ *adjective, noun* [U]
the dark color made by mixing red and blue

pur·pose /ˈpɚpəs/ *noun*
1 a reason for doing something; aim: *The purpose of this activity is to improve your writing.*
2 **on purpose** deliberately; with the intention of doing what you do: *She broke the cup on purpose.*

pur·pose·ly /ˈpɚpəsli/ *adverb*
deliberately; with the intention of doing what you do

purr /pɚ/ *verb*
if a cat purrs, it makes a soft low sound in its throat

purse /pɚs/ *noun*
a small bag used by women to carry money and other things

pur·sue /pɚˈsu/ *verb* (**pursuing, pursued**)
to chase or follow someone to catch him or her

push

push   pull

push¹ /pʊʃ/ *verb*
1 to move someone or something away from you using your hands: *They pushed the door open and rushed in.* | *He pushed me off the chair.* ≫ compare PULL¹
2 to press a button to make a machine work: *Just push this button for the elevator.*

push² *noun*
the act of pushing something: *Give the door a hard push and it will open.*

put /pʊt/ *verb* (**putting, put**)
1 to place or move something into a particular position: *Put the books on the shelf.* | *Where did I put my keys?*
2 **put something off** to delay something, or to delay doing something: *The meeting has been put off until next week.*
3 **put something on** (a) to put clothes onto your body: *She put on her coat and went out.* (b) to make a piece of equipment begin working: *Why don't you put some music on?*
4 **put something out** (a) to stop a fire etc. from burning: *It took three hours to put the fire out.* (b) to produce something such as a book, movie etc.
5 **put something up** to build something such as a wall or building: *They plan to put up some houses over there.*

6 put up with something to accept a bad situation without complaining: *I don't know how she manages to put up with those children!*

puzzle

puz·zle¹ /ˈpʌzəl/ *noun*
1 a game or toy that is difficult to do or solve
2 something that is difficult to understand or explain

puzzle² *verb* (puzzling, puzzled)
to make someone feel confused or not able to understand something: *The computer puzzled me until Sarah showed me how it works.*

pyramid

pyr·a·mid /ˈpɪrəmɪd/ *noun*
a solid shape with a flat base and three sides that form a point at the top —see picture at SHAPE¹

quack /kwæk/ *verb*
to make the sound that a duck usually makes
—**quack** *noun*

quake /kweɪk/ *verb* (**quaking, quaked**)
to shake because you are afraid: *She was quaking with fear.*

qual·i·fi·ca·tion /ˌkwɑləfəˈkeɪʃən/ *noun*
a skill, experience etc. that makes you suitable to do a particular job

qual·i·fied /ˈkwɑləˌfaɪd/ *adjective*
having the right knowledge or skills to do something. *She is well-qualified **for** the job.*

qual·i·fy /ˈkwɑləˌfaɪ/ *verb* (**qualifying, qualified**)
to pass an examination or have the skills you need to do a particular job: *A high school diploma will qualify you **for** a lot of jobs.*

qual·i·ty /ˈkwɑləṭi/ *noun* (*plural* **qualities**)
1 how good something is: *We only sell cloth of the finest quality.*
2 the good parts of someone's character: *Her best qualities are courage and honesty.*

quan·ti·ty /ˈkwɑnṭəṭi/ *noun* (*plural* **quantities**)
an amount of something: *He ate a small quantity **of** rice.*

quar·rel¹ /ˈkwɔrəl, kwɑrəl/ *noun*
an angry argument: *We had a quarrel about money.*

quarrel² *verb*
to have an angry argument: *The children are always quarreling over something.*

quar·ry /ˈkwɔri, ˈkwɑri/ *noun* (*plural* **quarries**)
a large hole in the ground where stone or sand is dug out

quart /kwɔrt/ *noun*
a measure of liquid equal to 0.95 liters; there are two PINTs in one quart

quar·ter /ˈkwɔrtɚ/ *noun*
1 one of four equal parts of something; ¼: *We divided the pie into quarters and ate it.*

2 one of the four periods of 15 minutes into which one hour is divided: *Will you be ready in a quarter of an hour?* (=15 minutes) | *It is a quarter after five.* (=15 minutes after five o'clock)
3 a coin worth 25 cents, or ¼ of a dollar

quar·ter·ly /ˈkwɔrtɚli/ *adjective, adverb*
every three months, or four times a year: *Do you get a quarterly report card?*

quay /keɪ, ki/ *noun*
a place where boats can be tied up or loaded

queen /kwin/ *noun*
1 the female ruler of a country, especially the daughter of the former ruler ≫ compare KING
2 the wife of a king

quench /kwɛntʃ/ *verb*
quench your thirst to drink something so that you stop being thirsty

ques·tion¹ /ˈkwɛstʃən, ˈkwɛʃtʃən/ *noun*
1 something you ask someone: *You didn't answer my question.*
2 a problem to be talked about and dealt with: *The question of whether to cut taxes must be discussed.*

question² *verb*
1 to ask someone something: *Police questioned him about the crime.*
2 to start to have doubts about something: *Are you questioning my honesty?*

question mark /ˈ.. ˌ./ *noun*
the mark "?," used in writing at the end of a question: *Where are you going?*

quick /kwɪk/ *adjective*
done or happening in a short time: *We had a quick meal and returned to work.* | *This is the quickest way to get to school.* —**quickly** *adverb*
≫ compare SOON

qui·et¹ /ˈkwaɪət/ *adjective*
1 not making a lot of noise: *The streets are quiet at night.* | *He has a quiet voice.* ≫ compare LOUD, NOISY
2 not busy, without a lot of activity: *I had a quiet day at home.* —**quietly** *adverb*

quiet² *noun* [U]
the state of being quiet: *I love the peace and quiet of the morning.*

quilt /kwɪlt/ *noun*
a soft thick cover for a bed

quit /kwɪt/ *verb* (**quitting, quit**)
to stop doing something: *I quit smoking ciga-rettes last year.*

quite /kwaɪt/ *adverb*
1 very, but not extremely: *The instructions were quite clear.*
2 **not quite** not completely, or not exactly: *I am not quite sure how this works.*

quiv·er /'kwɪvər/ *verb*
to shake a little because you are angry, upset etc.: *The little girl quivered with fear.*

quiz /kwɪz/ *noun* (*plural* **quizzes**)
1 a small test

2 a competition in which you try to answer questions

quo·ta·tion /kwoʊˈteɪʃən/ *noun*
words from a book, speech etc. that you repeat in your own speech or writing

quotation marks /.'.. ,./ *plural noun*
the marks ("..."), used in writing to show what someone says

quote /kwoʊt/ *verb* (**quoting, quoted**)
to say or write exactly what someone else has said or written

rabbit

rab·bit /'ræbɪt/ *noun*
a small animal with long ears that lives in the ground

race¹ /reɪs/ *noun*
1 a competition to find who can run, drive, swim etc. the fastest: *Who won the race?*
2 a group of humans that is different from other groups in shape, skin color, size etc.

race² *verb* (racing, raced)
to compete in a race: *Paul raced John to the house.*

ra·cial /'reɪʃəl/ *adjective*
1 related to someone's race
2 between different races of people

rac·ism /'reɪsɪzəm/ *noun* [U]
1 the belief that some races of people are better than others
2 the unfair treatment of people because of their race

rac·ist /'reɪsɪst/ *noun*
someone who believes that some races of people are better than others

rack /ræk/ *noun*
a frame for holding things: *You can put that on the towel rack.*

rack·et /'rækɪt/ *noun*
1 loud noise: *Where's that racket coming from?*
2 an instrument used to hit the ball in games such as tennis

ra·dar /'reɪdɑr/ *noun* [U]
a way of finding the position and speed of ships and planes by using radio waves

radiation *noun* [U]
a form of energy that is very dangerous to living things if there is too much of it

ra·di·a·tor /'reɪdi,eɪtər/ *noun*
1 a flat metal object on a wall, which hot water passes through to heat a room
2 a part of a car that keeps the engine cool

ra·di·o /'reɪdioʊ/ *noun*
1 a piece of electrical equipment that you use to listen to music, news etc.: *I like listening to the radio.*
2 [U] the sending out or receiving of messages by electrical waves: *Ships send messages to each other by radio.*
3 [U] the activity of making programs that can be heard on the radio: *He wants to get a job in radio.*

ra·di·us /'reɪdiəs/ *noun* (plural **radii** /'reɪdiaɪ/)
the distance from the center of a circle to the edge —see picture at DIAMETER

raft /ræft/ *noun*
1 a large flat structure used as a boat
2 a small rubber boat filled with air

rag /ræg/ *noun*
1 a small piece of old cloth: *He cleaned the machine with an oily rag.*
2 **in rags** wearing torn old clothes: *The man was dressed in rags.*

rage /reɪdʒ/ *noun*
very strong anger: *My father flew into a rage and hit me.*

raid¹ /reɪd/ *noun*
a sudden attack on a place: *The city was damaged in an air raid.*

raid² *verb*
to attack a place: *The soldiers raided the village.*

rail /reɪl/ *noun*
1 a long piece of metal that is fixed along or around something to keep you from falling: *Do not lean on the rail.*
2 one of the two long metal bars on which a train moves

rail·ing /'reɪlɪŋ/ *noun*
a fence that keeps people from falling over an edge or helps support them going up stairs

rail·road /'reɪlroʊd/ *noun*
all the tracks, equipment etc. used by trains

rain¹ /reɪn/ *verb*
if it rains, drops of water fall from the sky: *It rained last night.*

rain² *noun* [U]
water that falls from the sky: *There was a lot of rain in the night.*

rain·bow
/'reɪnboʊ/ *noun*
a large curve of different colors in the sky that can appear after it rains

rain·coat
/'reɪnkoʊt/ *noun*
a coat that you wear to keep you dry in the rain —see color picture on page 190

rain·fall /'reɪnfɔl/ *noun*
that amount of rain that falls in a particular area

rain for·est /'. ,../ *noun*
a wet tropical area where trees grow very close together

rain·y /'reɪni/ *adjective* (**rainier, rainiest**)
having a lot of rain: *It has been a rainy day.*

raise¹ /reɪz/ *verb* (**raising, raised**)
1 to move or lift something up to a higher position: *He raised his arms above his head.* ≫ compare LOWER
2 to increase a number or amount: *There is a plan to raise taxes.*
3 to take care of children, animals, or crops: *She raised three sons on her own.*

raise² *noun*
an increase in the amount of money you received in your job: *She asked her boss for a raise.*

rai·sin /'reɪzən/ *noun*
a small dried GRAPE

rake¹ /reɪk/ *noun*
a tool that you use to gather leaves that are on the ground

rake² *verb* (**raking, raked**)
to pull a rake over a piece of ground

ram /ræm/ *verb* (**ramming, rammed**)
to run or drive into something using a lot of force

ramp /ræmp/ *noun*
1 a road that goes on or off a main road
2 a slope that connects two different levels

ran /ræn/
the PAST TENSE of the verb **run**

ranch /ræntʃ/ *noun*
a large farm where cattle, horses etc. are kept

rang /ræŋ/
the PAST TENSE of the verb **ring**

range /reɪndʒ/ *noun*
1 a group of things that are different but belong to the same general type: *They sell a **wide** range **of** shoes.*
2 the limits within which amounts, ages etc. can vary: *The house is out of our **price** range.* (=it is too expensive)
3 the distance that something can reach or travel: *The airplane has a range of 500 miles.*
4 a line of mountains or hills

rank¹ /ræŋk/ *noun*
the position or level someone has in a group or organization: *A general is an army officer with a very high rank.*

rank² *verb*
to put into a particular order: *The players are ranked in order of ability.*

ran·som /'rænsəm/ *noun*
money that is paid to free someone who is being held as a prisoner: *The rich man paid a high ransom for his daughter.*

rap /ræp/ *noun*
a type of popular music in which words are spoken in time with the music

rape¹ /reɪp/ *noun*
the crime of using violence to make someone have sex

rape² *verb*
to use violence to make someone have sex

rap·id /'ræpɪd/ *adjective*
quick, or done very quickly —**rapidly** *adverb*

rare /rɛr/ *adjective* (**rarer, rarest**)
not happening or seen very often: *That bird is very rare in this country.* ≫ compare COMMON¹

rare·ly /'rɛrli/ *adverb*
not very often: *She rarely goes out.*

rash¹ /ræʃ/ *adjective*
done too quickly without thinking carefully: *She made a rash decision.*

rash² *noun*
red spots on your skin: *With some illnesses you get a rash.*

rat /ræt/ *noun*
an animal like a large mouse with a long tail

rate /reɪt/ *noun*
1 the number of times something happens in a period of time: *The crime rate in this area is high.*
2 a charge or payment that is set according to a scale: *She is paid **at the rate of** $6 an hour.*
3 the speed at which something happens: *She reads at a fast rate.*

rath·er /'ræðɚ/
1 **rather than** instead of: *We decided to leave on Friday rather than Monday.*
2 **would rather do something** would prefer to do one thing more than another: *I think I would rather stay home tonight.*

rat·tle[1] /'rætl/ *verb* (**rattling, rattled**)
to shake something, making a knocking sound: *She rattled some coins in the box.*

rattle[2] *noun*
a toy that a baby shakes to make a noise

raw /rɔ/ *adjective*
not cooked: *The dog ate raw meat.*

ray /reɪ/ *noun*
a narrow beam of light: *The sun's rays warmed the water.*

razor

ra·zor /'reɪzɚ/ *noun*
a sharp instrument for removing hair from your body

razor blade /'.. ,./ *noun*
a thin flat piece of metal with a sharp edge, used in some razors

Rd.
a short way to write **road** in an address

're /ɚ/
are: *We're late.*

reach[1] /ritʃ/ *verb*
1 to arrive at a particular place: *It took several days for the letter to reach me.*
2 to stretch out your hand to touch or hold something: *I could not reach the top shelf.*

reach[2] *noun* [U]
the distance that you can stretch out your arm

to touch something: *The cup is **within easy reach**.* (=near enough to touch)

re·act /ri'ækt/ *verb*
to behave in a particular way because of what someone has said or done to you: *How did your mother react **to** the news?*

re·ac·tion /ri'ækʃən/ *noun*
the way you behave because of what someone has said or done to you: *What was his reaction **to** the question?*

read /rid/ *verb* (**reading, read** /rɛd/)
1 to look at words and understand them: *She read the newspaper.* | *I like to read.*
2 to say written words for other people to hear: *He read his son a story.*

read·i·ly /'rɛdl-i/ *adverb*
easily and quickly: *The information is readily available on the computer.*

read·y /'rɛdi/ *adjective*
1 prepared or able to do something: *Are you ready **to** go?* | *Breakfast will be ready soon.*
2 willing or likely to do something: *I'm always ready **to** help.*

re·al /ril/ *adjective*
1 not imaginary: *There is a real danger that the fire will spread.*
2 true and not pretended: *What is the real reason you were late?*

real es·tate /'. .,./ *noun* [U]
property such as houses or land: *Real estate prices are going up.*

real estate a·gent /'. .. ,../ *noun*
someone whose job is to sell houses and land

re·al·i·ty /ri'æləti/ *noun* [U]
what is true or actually happens

re·al·i·za·tion /,riələ'zeɪʃən/ *noun* [U]
the act of understanding or knowing something that you did not know before: *We **came to the** realization **that** the business was failing.*

re·al·ize /'riə,laɪz/ *verb* (**realizing, realized**)
to know or understand something that you did not know before: *I didn't realize that it was so late.*

real·ly /'rili/ *adverb*
1 in fact or very much: *I am really worried about my work.* | *He is a really nice guy.*
2 **really?** said when you are interested in or surprised by what someone has said: *"Ann is going to have a baby." "Really?"*
3 **not really** used for saying "no": *"Do you want to go out?" "Oh, not really."*

real·tor /'rɪltɚ/ *noun*
someone whose job is to sell houses and land

rear¹ /rɪr/ *noun*
the rear at the back: *The rear of the car is damaged.* » compare FRONT¹

rear² *adjective*
relating to the back of something: *We went in the rear entrance.* » compare FRONT¹

rea·son /'rizən/ *noun*
1 the cause why something is done or happens: *Did she give any reason for quitting?*
2 [U] the ability to think or understand something

rea·son·a·ble /'riznəbəl, -zən-/ *adjective*
1 fair and sensible: *He is asking a reasonable price for the car.*
2 having understanding or good sense: *The teacher is a very reasonable person.* » opposite UNREASONABLE

rea·son·a·bly /'riznəbli/ *adverb*
1 in a fair and sensible way: *He behaved reasonably.*
2 fairly but not completely: *I did reasonably well on the test.*

re·as·sure /ˌriə'ʃʊr/ *verb* (**reassuring, reassured**)
to make someone feel calm and less worried about something: *His mother reassured him.*

reb·el¹ /rɪ'bɛl/ *verb* (**rebelling, rebelled**)
to fight against a leader or government: *The soldiers rebelled **against** the government.*

rebel² /'rɛbəl/ *noun*
someone who fights against a leader or government

re·bel·lion /rɪ'bɛlyən/ *noun*
the act of fighting against a leader or government

re·call /rɪ'kɔl/ *verb*
to remember information or an event from the past: *I don't recall what she said.*

re·ceipt /rɪ'sit/ *noun*
a piece of paper that shows that you have paid money or bought goods

re·ceive /rɪ'siv/ *verb* (**receiving, received**)
to get something or be given something: *Did you receive my letter?*

re·ceiv·er /rɪ'sivɚ/ *noun*
the part of a telephone that you hold next to your mouth and ear

re·cent /'risənt/ *adjective*
happening a short time ago: *On a recent visit to the city, we saw a play.*

re·cent·ly /'risəntli/ *adverb*
not long ago: *I traveled to Japan recently.* » compare LATELY

re·cep·tion /rɪ'sɛpʃən/ *noun*
a large formal party: *I went to the wedding reception.*

rec·i·pe /'rɛsəpi/ *noun*
a set of instructions that tell you how to cook something: *Do you have a recipe for chocolate cake?*

reck·less /'rɛklɪs/ *adjective*
careless and dangerous: *His reckless driving caused an accident.* —**recklessly** *adverb* » compare CAREFUL

rec·og·ni·tion /ˌrɛkəg'nɪʃən/ *noun* [U]
the act of knowing someone or something when you see it: *She hoped to avoid recognition by wearing dark glasses.*

rec·og·nize /'rɛkəgˌnaɪz/ *verb* (**recognizing, recognized**)
to know someone or something when you see it: *I recognized Peter from his photograph.*

rec·om·mend /ˌrɛkə'mɛnd/ *verb*
to tell someone that someone or something is good for a particular purpose: *She recommended **that** I try the soup.*

rec·om·men·da·tion /ˌrɛkəmən'deɪʃən/ *noun*
the action of saying that someone or something is good for a particular purpose: *I went to the hotel on your recommendation.*

re·cord¹ /rɪ'kɔrd/ *verb*
1 to write information so that you can look at it later: *The statements are recorded on computer.*
2 to copy a television show so that you can watch it later
3 to store music or sounds so that you can listen to it later: *He recorded a CD this year.*

record² /'rɛkɚd/ *noun*
1 information that is written down so you can look at it later: *I need a copy of your medical records.*
2 something done faster, higher etc. than anyone has ever done it before: *He holds the world record **for** the high jump.*
3 a round flat piece of plastic on which music is stored

re·cord·ing /rɪˈkɔrdɪŋ/ *noun*
a piece of music or speech that has been recorded: *I heard the group's latest recording.*

record play·er /ˈ.. ˌ../ *noun*
a machine on which you play music records

re·cov·er /rɪˈkʌvəʳ/ *verb*
to get better again after an illness or injury: *Have you recovered **from** your cold?*

re·cov·er·y /rɪˈkʌvəri/ *noun* (plural **recoveries**)
the process of getting better after an illness or injury: *She made a quick recovery after her accident.*

rec·re·a·tion /ˌrɛkriˈeɪʃən/ *noun*
an activity that you do for pleasure or fun: *What do you do for recreation?*

re·cruit¹ /rɪˈkrut/ *noun*
someone who joins an organization, company etc.

recruit² *verb*
to find new people for an organization, company etc.: *We need to recruit new police officers.*

rec·tan·gle /ˈrɛkˌtæŋgəl/ *noun*
a flat shape with four straight sides two of which are longer than the other two » compare OBLONG —see picture at SHAPE¹

rec·tan·gu·lar /rɛkˈtæŋgyˈələʳ/ *adjective*
having a shape like a RECTANGLE

re·cy·cle /riˈsaɪkəl/ *verb* (**recycling, recycled**)
to use something again instead of throwing it away. *Glass bottles can be recycled.* —**recycled** *adjective*: *Many newspapers used recycled paper.*

red /rɛd/ *adjective, noun* [U]
having the color of blood

re·duce /rɪˈdus/ *verb* (**reducing, reduced**)
to make something smaller or less in size or amount: *The price is reduced from $50 to $35.*

re·duc·tion /rɪˈdʌkʃən/ *noun*
the act of making something smaller or less in size or amount

reed /rid/ *noun*
a tall plant like grass that grows in or near water

reef /rif/ *noun*
a line of sharp rocks or a raised area of sand near the surface of the ocean

reel /ril/ *noun*
a round object on which something such as film is wound

re·fer /rɪˈfəʳ/ *verb* (**referring, referred**)
refer to someone or something (a) to look at a book, map etc. to get information: *Refer to a dictionary if you don't know what the word means.* (b) to speak about someone or something: *He referred to Jack in his letter.*

ref·er·ee /ˌrɛfəˈri/ *noun*
someone who watches a game in sports to make sure that the rules are obeyed

ref·er·ence /ˈrɛfrəns/ *noun*
1 the act of looking at something for information: *I keep the dictionary on my desk for reference.*
2 a letter about your character and ability which is sent to someone who may give you a job

reference book /ˈ.. ˌ../ *noun*
a book such as a dictionary that you look at to find information

re·fill¹ /riˈfɪl/ *verb*
to fill something again: *Could you refill the glasses, please?* —**refillable** *adjective*

refill² /ˈrifɪl/ *noun*
1 a container filled with a particular substance that you use to REFILL something: *refills for an ink pen*
2 another drink to REFILL your glass: *Would you like a refill?*

re·flect /rɪˈflɛkt/ *verb*
1 to throw back light, heat, a picture etc.: *The mountains were reflected in the lake.*
2 to show or be a sign of a particular idea or feeling: *His attitude is reflected in his behavior.*
3 to think carefully

re·flec·tion /rɪˈflɛkʃən/ *noun*
reflection
1 careful thought: *The book is a collection of his reflections on American life.*
2 what you see in a mirror or water: *We looked at our reflections in the mirror.*

re·form¹ /rɪˈfɔrm/ *verb*
to improve an organization or system by making changes to it: *There are plans to reform the tax laws.*

reform² *noun*
a change that improves an organization or system

re·fresh /rɪ'frɛʃ/ *verb*
to make someone less hot or tired

re·freshed /rɪ'frɛʃt/ *adjective*
less hot or tired: *I feel refreshed after a hot shower.*

re·fresh·ing /rɪ'frɛʃɪŋ/ *adjective*
making you feel less hot or tired: *I had a refreshing drink.*

re·fresh·ments /rɪ'frɛʃmənts/ *plural noun*
food and drinks that are provided at an event, meeting etc.: *Refreshments will be served at seven o'clock.*

re·frig·er·a·tor /rɪ'frɪdʒə,reɪtə/ *noun*
(*also* **fridge**) a large piece of kitchen equipment used for keeping food cold and fresh: *Put the milk in the refrigerator.*

ref·uge /'rɛfyudʒ/ *noun*
a safe place

ref·u·gee /,rɛfyʊ'dʒi/ *noun*
someone who has to leave his or her own country, especially because of a war

re·fus·al /rɪ'fyuzəl/ *noun*
the act of not accepting something or saying that you will not do something: *Her refusal to help made me angry.*

re·fuse /rɪ'fyuz/ *verb* (**refusing, refused**)
to say that you will not do or accept something: *She refused **to** marry me.*

re·gard¹ /rɪ'gɑrd/ *verb*
to think about someone in a particular way: *We always regarded him **as** our friend.*

regard² *noun* [U]
respect for someone or something: *You **have no** regard **for** my feelings.*

re·gard·ing /rɪ'gɑrdɪŋ/ *preposition*
about: *I wrote you a letter regarding my daughter's illness.* ≫ compare CONCERNING

re·gard·less /rɪ'gɑrdlɪs/ *adverb*
in spite of: *He says whatever he wants, regardless **of** what other people think.*

re·gards /rɪ'gɑrdz/ *plural noun*
good wishes: ***Give my** regards **to** your parents.*

reg·gae /'rɛgeɪ/ *noun* [U]
a type of popular music from Jamaica

reg·i·ment /'rɛdʒəmənt/ *noun*
a large group of soldiers who are part of an army

re·gion /'ridʒən/ *noun*
a large area: *This is a farming region.* —**regional** *adjective*

reg·is·ter¹ /'rɛdʒəstə/ *noun*
a book containing an official list or record of something

register² *verb*
to have a name, details etc. put on an official list: *The car is registered in my sister's name.*

reg·is·tra·tion /,rɛdʒə'streɪʃən/ *noun* [U]
the act of having a name, details etc. put on an official list

re·gret¹ /rɪ'grɛt/ *verb* (**regretting, regretted**)
to be sorry about something: *I regret spending so much money on the car.*

regret² *noun*
a feeling of being sorry or sad

reg·u·lar /'rɛgyələ/ *adjective*
1 happening or being repeated at the same times: *His heartbeat is strong and regular.* | *We have a regular meeting every Monday.*
2 ordinary; usual: *Is he your regular doctor?*
3 a regular noun or verb changes its form in the same way as most nouns and verbs: *The verb "walk" is regular, but the verb "be" is not.*
≫ opposite IRREGULAR

reg·u·lar·i·ty /,rɛgyə'lærəti/ *noun* [U]
the state in which something happens or is repeated at the same times

reg·u·lar·ly /'rɛgyələli, 'rɛgyəli/ *adverb*
at the same time; often: *Take the medicine regularly three times a day.*

reg·u·la·tion /,rɛgyə'leɪʃən/ *noun*
an official rule

re·hears·al /rɪ'həsəl/ *noun*
a practice of a performance before it is shown to the public: *Anyone can come to the rehearsal.*

re·hearse /rɪ'həs/ *verb* (**rehearsing, rehearsed**)
to do or say something again and again, before showing it to the public: *He rehearsed his speech last night.*

reign¹ /reɪn/ *verb*
to be the king or queen of a country

reign² *noun*
the time when a king or queen rules a country: *during the reign of King George IV*

rein /reɪn/ *noun*
a long narrow piece of leather that you put around a horse's head to control it: *If you pull the reins, the horse will stop.*

re·ject /rɪˈdʒɛkt/ *verb*
to decide that you do not want something or someone: *We rejected his idea.*

re·jec·tion /rɪˈdʒɛkʃən/ *noun*
the act of not wanting or accepting someone or something

re·joice /rɪˈdʒɔɪs/ *verb* (**rejoicing, rejoiced**)
to feel or be very happy

re·late /rɪˈleɪt/ *verb* (**relating, related**)
1 to have or show a connection between two ideas or subjects: *The movie relates **to** what we read earlier.*
2 to tell a story

re·lat·ed /rɪˈleɪtɪd/ *adjective*
1 of the same family: *I'm related **to** him. He's my uncle.*
2 connected by similar ideas: *The book is about farming and related subjects.*

re·la·tion /rɪˈleɪʃən/ *noun*
1 in **relation to** used for comparing two things: *The land is small in relation to the population.*
2 a member of a family: *Some of my relations live in Canada.*

re·la·tions /rɪˈleɪʃənz/ *plural noun*
the way people, countries etc. behave toward each other: *Relations between the two countries are not good.*

re·la·tion·ship /rɪˈleɪʃənˌʃɪp/ *noun*
1 a situation in which two people have romantic or sexual feelings for each other: *She is involved in a relationship **with** an older man.*
2 the way in which people, countries etc. behave toward each other

rel·a·tive¹ /ˈrɛlətɪv/ *noun*
a member of your family

relative² *adjective*
having a particular quality when compared with something else: *The last few years have been a time of relative peace.*

rel·a·tive·ly /ˈrɛlətɪvli/ *adverb*
when compared with something else: *Traveling by train is relatively expensive.*

re·lax /rɪˈlæks/ *verb*
1 to become less worried or angry and more calm: *Don't worry about it. Just try to relax.*
2 to become less tight or stiff: *He relaxed his grip on the rope.*

re·lax·a·tion /ˌrilækˈseɪʃən/ *noun*
the state of being less worried, or less stiff in your body

re·laxed /rɪˈlækst/ *adjective*
calm and not worried ≫ compare TENSE¹

re·lease¹ /rɪˈlis/ *verb* (**releasing, released**)
to let someone or something go free: *I released the horse and it ran away.* | *Four prisoners were released.*

release² *noun*
the act of letting someone or something go free: *After their release, the men came home.*

re·li·a·ble /rɪˈlaɪəbəl/ *adjective*
able to be trusted: *He is a very reliable person, and he will do what he says.* ≫ opposite UNRELIABLE

re·lief /rɪˈlif/ *noun* [U]
a feeling of happiness because something bad did not happen or is finished: *It was a relief to know that she was safe.*

re·lieve /rɪˈliv/ *verb* (**relieving, relieved**)
to make pain or trouble less severe: *The medicine relieved his headache.*

re·lieved /rɪˈlivd/ *adjective*
happy because something bad did not happen or is finished: *Your mother will be relieved to hear that you are doing well.*

re·li·gion /rɪˈlɪdʒən/ *noun*
1 [U] belief in one or more gods: *Almost every country has some form of religion.*
2 a particular set of beliefs in one or more gods: *Hinduism and Buddhism are Eastern religions.*

re·li·gious /rɪˈlɪdʒəs/ *adjective*
1 relating to religion: *She has strong religious beliefs.*
2 showing a belief in religion and obeying its rules: *He comes from a very religious family.*

re·luc·tant /rɪˈlʌktənt/ *adjective*
not willing to do something: *The child was reluctant **to** ask for help.*

re·ly /rɪˈlaɪ/ *verb* (**relying, relied**)
to trust someone or something: *You can rely **on** me to help.*

re·main /rɪ'meɪn/ *verb*
1 to continue in the same state or condition:
We remained friends for years.
2 to stay in the same place: *I left, but my brother remained at home.*

re·main·der /rɪ'meɪndɚ/ *noun*
the rest of something: *I'll go with you; the remainder of the group can wait here.*

re·mains /rɪ'meɪnz/ *plural noun*
parts of something that are left: *We visited the remains of an ancient city.*

re·mark¹ /rɪ'mɑrk/ *noun*
something that you say: *He made a rude remark about the woman.*

remark² *verb*
to say something: *"That's where Jane lives,"* she remarked.*

re·mar·ka·ble /rɪ'mɑrkəbəl/ *adjective*
unusual, usually in a good way —**remarkably** *adverb*: *The food was remarkably good.*

rem·e·dy /'rɛmədi/ *noun* (*plural* **remedies**)
1 an answer to a problem
2 a medicine that cures pain or illness

re·mem·ber /rɪ'mɛmbɚ/ *verb*
to have something or someone in your mind:
Did you remember to feed the cat? | He suddenly remembered that he had left the lights on. » compare FORGET

re·mind /rɪ'maɪnd/ *verb*
1 to make someone remember something that he or she must do: *Remind me to write to my uncle. | That smell reminds me of the seaside.*
2 **remind you of someone** to be like someone else: *He reminds me of Charlie Chaplin.*

re·mote /rɪ'moʊt/ *adjective*
far away in distance: *They have a remote farm in the hills.*

remote con·trol /.,. .'./ *noun*
a piece of equipment that you use to control a television, radio etc. without touching it

re·mote·ly /rɪ'moʊtli/ *adverb*
not remotely not in any way: *He is not remotely like me.*

re·mov·al /rɪ'muvəl/ *noun*
the act of taking something away from a place

re·move /rɪ'muv/ *verb* (**removing, removed**)
to take something away from where it is:
Please remove your books from my desk.

re·new /rɪ'nu/ *verb*
1 to arrange for an official document to continue to be useful: *We need to renew our insurance.*
2 to begin to do something again: *The soldiers renewed their attack on the town.*

rent¹ /rɛnt/ *noun*
money that you pay for the use of a house, office etc. that belongs to someone else: *How much do you pay for rent?*

rent² *verb*
1 to pay money for the use of a house, office etc. that belongs to someone else: *I rent an office in the city.*
2 **rent something out** to let someone else live in a house, apartment, etc. that you own, for money: *She rents out the basement apartment to students.*

re·paid /ri'peɪd/
the PAST TENSE and PAST PARTICIPLE of the verb **repay**

re·pair¹ /rɪ'pɛr/ *verb*
to fix something that is broken or damaged: *Did you repair the chair yet?* » compare MEND

repair² *noun*
something that you do to fix something that is broken or damaged: *My car is in for repair.*

re·pay /ri'peɪ/ *verb* (**repaying, repaid** /ri'peɪd/)
to pay back money that you have borrowed: *Did you repay the loan?*

re·peat /rɪ'pit/ *verb*
to say or do something again: *Can you repeat the question?*

re·peat·ed /rɪ'pitɪd/ *adjective*
done again and again: *She made repeated attempts to escape.*

rep·e·ti·tion /,rɛpə'tɪʃən/ *noun* [U]
the act of saying or doing something again

re·place /rɪ'pleɪs/ *verb* (**replacing, replaced**)
1 to put something back in its place
2 to use a new or different thing instead of something else: *Can we afford to replace the television?*

re·place·ment /rɪ'pleɪsmənt/ *noun*
something new or different that is used instead of something else

re·play /'ripleɪ/ *noun* (*plural* **replays**)
an action in sports that you see on television that is immediately shown again

re·ply¹ /rɪ'plaɪ/ *verb* (**replying, replied**)
to give an answer to someone: *"I didn't do it," she replied.* | *Has anyone replied to your question?*

reply² *noun* (*plural* **replies**)
an answer: *Did you receive a reply **to** your letter?*

re·port¹ /rɪ'pɔrt/ *verb*
1 to tell people about something, especially in a newspaper or on television: *The accident was reported on the radio.*
2 to tell someone in authority that something has happened: *She reported the crime **to** the police.*

report² *noun*
facts about something that give people information: *We read a report of the accident.*

report card /.'. ,./ *noun*
a written document giving a student's grades

re·port·er /rɪ'pɔrtə/ *noun*
someone whose job is to write or tell about events in a newspaper, on television, or on radio

rep·re·sent /ˌrɛprɪ'zɛnt/ *verb*
1 to act officially for someone else: *I le represented his company at the meeting.*
2 to be a sign of something else: *The sign "&" represents the word "and".*

rep·re·sent·a·tive /ˌrɛprɪ'zɛntətɪv/ *noun*
someone who acts officially for someone else: *They sent a representative to the meeting.*

re·proach /rɪ'proʊtʃ/ *verb*
to say something to someone to try to make him or her sorry for doing something

re·pro·duce /ˌriprə'dus/ *verb*
(**reproducing, reproduced**)
1 to produce young plants or animals
2 to make a copy of something: *The paintings are all reproduced in the book.*

re·pro·duc·tion /ˌriprə'dʌkʃən/ *noun*
1 [U] the act of producing young plants or animals: *He wrote a book on human reproduction.*
2 a copy of something

rep·tile /'rɛptaɪl, 'rɛptl/ *noun*
an animal such as a snake whose blood changes temperature according to the temperature around it

re·pub·lic /rɪ'pʌblɪk/ *noun*
a country whose leader is a president, not a king

rep·u·ta·tion /ˌrɛpyə'teɪʃən/ *noun*
the opinion that people have about someone or something because of what has happened in the past: *This hotel has a good reputation.*

re·quest¹ /rɪ'kwɛst/ *verb*
to ask for something in a polite way: *We request that visitors remain quiet in the hospital.*

request² *noun*
the act of asking for something in a polite way: *She made a request **for** help.*

re·quire /rɪ'kwaɪə/ *verb* (**requiring, required**)
to need something: *Roses require a lot of light.*

re·quire·ment /rɪ'kwaɪəmənt/ *noun*
something that is needed: *The agreement meets all our requirements.*

rescue

res·cue¹ /'rɛskyu/ *verb* (**rescuing, rescued**)
to save someone from danger: *He rescued the boy **from** the river.*

rescue² *noun*
the act of saving someone from danger: *Another boat **came to our rescue**.*

re·search¹ /'risətʃ, rɪ'sətʃ/ *noun* [U]
careful study, especially to find out new facts about something: *She is **doing** medical research into the disease.*

research² *verb*
to study something to find out new facts about it

re·sem·blance /rɪ'zɛmbləns/ *noun*
a way in which two people or things look like each other: *There is no resemblance **between** the two brothers.*

re·sem·ble /rɪ'zɛmbəl/ *verb* (**resembling, resembled**)
to look like another person or thing: *She resembles her mother in many ways.*

re·sent /rɪˈzɛnt/ *verb*
to feel angry about something that someone has said or done to you: *He resents his father for leaving the family.*

re·sent·ment /rɪˈzɛntʰmənt/ *noun* [U]
the feeling of being angry about something that someone has said or done to you

res·er·va·tion /ˌrɛzəˈveɪʃən/ *noun*
1 an arrangement you make so that something is kept for you to use: *Did you make a reservation at the hotel?*
2 an area of land that is kept separate for Native Americans to live on

re·serve¹ /rɪˈzɚv/ *verb* (reserving, reserved)
to arrange for something to be kept for you to use: *I have reserved a table for us at the restaurant.*

reserve² *noun*
1 an amount of something that is kept to be used in the future: *We have large reserves of oil.*
2 an area of land where wild animals live and are protected: *Africa has many wildlife reserves.*

res·er·voir /ˈrɛzəˌvwɑr, -zɚ-, -ˌvwɔr/ *noun*
a place where a lot of water is stored

res·i·dence /ˈrɛzədəns/ *noun*
the place where you live: *Where is the President's official residence?*

res·i·dent /ˈrɛzədənt/ *noun*
someone who lives in a place: *Residents of this area are angry about the new prison.*

res·i·den·tial /ˌrɛzəˈdɛnʃəl/ *adjective*
relating to where people live instead of where they work: *The plane crashed in a residential area.*

re·sign /rɪˈzaɪn/ *verb*
to leave your job: *He resigned from the company.*

res·ig·na·tion /ˌrɛzɪgˈneɪʃən/ *noun*
1 the act of leaving your job, or a letter saying this: *I handed in my resignation last week.*
2 [U] the feeling of accepting something unpleasant that you cannot change

re·sist /rɪˈzɪst/ *verb*
1 to fight against someone or something: *They resisted the enemy attack.*
2 to not accept changes, or to try to stop a change from happening: *The government resisted all efforts to make peace.*

3 to try hard not to do something that you want to do: *I couldn't resist laughing at him.*
4 to not be changed or harmed by something: *Vitamins will help you resist disease.*

re·sist·ance /rɪˈzɪstəns/ *noun* [U]
the act of fighting against someone or something

res·o·lu·tion /ˌrɛzəˈluʃən/ *noun*
a promise that you make to yourself to do something: *Did you make any resolutions this year?*

re·solve /rɪˈzɑlv/ *verb* (resolving, resolved)
to decide to do something: *I resolved to try harder at school.*

re·sort /rɪˈzɔrt/ *noun*
a place where people go for a vacation: *We went to a beach resort.*

re·source /ˈrisɔrs, rɪˈsɔrs/ *noun*
something such as land, minerals, oil etc. that exists in a country

re·sour·ces /ˈriˌsɔrsɪz/ *plural noun*
all the money, skills etc. that you have available to use

re·spect¹ /rɪˈspɛkt/ *noun*
1 [U] a good opinion or admiration for someone: *He has great respect for his parents.*
2 in some respects in some ways: *In some respects, he is like his father.*

respect² *verb*
to admire someone's good qualities: *The children respect their teacher.*

re·spect·a·ble /rɪˈspɛktəbəl/ *adjective*
being good or honest so that people admire you: *He is a respectable young man.*

re·spond /rɪˈspɑnd/ *verb*
to answer: *How did she respond to your question?*

re·sponse /rɪˈspɑns/ *noun*
an answer: *I haven't had any response to my letter.*

re·spon·si·bil·i·ty /rɪˌspɑnsəˈbɪləṭi/ *noun* (plural responsibilities)
something that you have a duty to do or take care of: *My children are my responsibility.*

re·spon·si·ble /rɪˈspɑnsəbəl/ *adjective*
1 taking care of someone or something: *She is responsible for the children.*

rest¹ /rɛst/ noun

1 a period of time when you relax or sleep: *I had an hour's rest after work.*

2 the rest what is left after everything else has been used, eaten etc.: *We'll eat the rest of the cake tomorrow.*

rest² verb

1 to stop doing something and relax or sleep for a period of time: *I rested after work.*

2 to put something on or against something else: *I rested my elbows on the table.*

res·tau·rant /'rɛst͵rɑnt, 'rɛstə͵rɑnt, 'rɛstərənt/ noun

a place where you can buy and eat food

rest·ful /'rɛstfəl/ adjective

peaceful and quiet

rest·less /'rɛstlɪs/ adjective

not able to keep still: *The children are becoming restless.* —**restlessness** noun [U]

re·store /rɪ'stɔr/ verb (restoring, restored)

to make something as good as it was before: *He wants to restore the old car.*

re·strain /rɪ'streɪn/ verb

to stop or hold back something: *She couldn't restrain her tears.*

re·strict /rɪ'strɪkt/ verb

to keep something within a particular limit: *Swimming is restricted to this part of the river.*

re·stric·tion /rɪ'strɪkʃən/ noun

a limit: *There is a restriction on how many tickets you can buy.*

rest·room /'rɛstrum, -rʊm/ noun

a room in a public building with toilets in it —see color picture on page 193

re·sult¹ /rɪ'zʌlt/ noun

something that happens or exists because of something else: *As a result of the snow, school is closed today.*

result² verb

to happen or exist because of something else: *The accident resulted in three people being killed.*

re·sume /rɪ'zum/ verb (resuming, resumed)

to start doing something again: *We will resume our work soon.*

re·tire /rɪ'taɪɚ/ verb (retiring, retired)

to stop working because of old age: *He retired when he was 65.* —**retired** adjective

re·tire·ment /rɪ'taɪɚmənt/ noun

the period of time after someone has stopped working because of old age: *She plans to spend her retirement traveling.*

re·treat¹ /rɪ'trit/ verb

to go back or move away from something or someone: *The soldiers retreated as the enemy advanced.* ≫ compare ADVANCE¹

retreat² noun

a movement back or away from someone or something

re·turn¹ /rɪ'tɚn/ verb

1 to come back or go back to a place: *He returned to his own country.*

2 to give something back: *Will you return the books to the library?*

3 to be in a previous state or condition again: *Soon everything will return to normal.*

return² noun

1 the act of coming or going back to a place: *On my return, I saw that the door was open.*

2 the act of giving something back, or putting something back in its place

re·veal /rɪ'vil/ verb

to say or show something that was secret or hidden

re·venge /rɪ'vɛndʒ/ noun [U]

something bad that you do to someone who has done something bad to you: *The bombing was in revenge for an earlier attack.*

Rev·er·end /'rɛvrənd, -ərənd/ noun

a title for a Christian priest

re·verse /rɪ'vɚs/ verb (reversing, reversed)

to change something so that it is the opposite of what it was before: *The judge reversed his decision.*

re·view¹ /rɪ'vyu/ noun

a piece of writing that gives an opinion about a new book, movie etc.

review² verb

1 to prepare for a test by studying things again: *I'm reviewing for my math test.*

2 to look at a new book, movie etc. and say what you think about them

re·vise /rɪ'vaɪz/ *verb* (**revising, revised**)
to change your opinions, plans etc. because of new information or facts: *He revised the manuscript of his book before sending it to the publisher.*

re·vive /rɪ'vaɪv/ *verb* (**reviving, revived**)
to become conscious again or make someone do this: *She revived him with cold water.*

re·volt¹ /rɪ'voʊlt/ *verb*
to not obey a government, leader etc., often using violence: *The soldiers revolted **against** the government.*

revolt² *noun*
an event in which people fight against their leaders or government

re·volt·ing /rɪ'voʊltɪŋ/ *adjective*
very unpleasant: *What a revolting smell!* ≫ compare DISGUSTING

rev·o·lu·tion /ˌrɛvə'luʃən/ *noun*
a time of great change in a country, especially when violence is used for making the change

rev·o·lu·tion·ar·y /ˌrɛvə'luʃəˌnɛri/ *adjective*
1 relating to a political REVOLUTION
2 completely new and different: *Computers have had a revolutionary effect on business.*

re·volve /rɪ'vɑlv/ *verb* (**revolving, revolved**)
to spin around a central point: *The Earth revolves **around** the sun.*

re·volv·er /rɪ'vɑlvɚ/ *noun*
a small gun ≫ compare PISTOL

re·ward¹ /rɪ'wɔrd/ *noun*
something that is given for doing good work, giving information etc.: *The police offered a reward **for** information about the crime.*

reward² *verb*
to give something to someone for doing something good: *How can I reward you **for** all your help?*

rhi·noc·er·os /raɪ'nɑsərəs/ *noun* (*plural* **rhinoceroses**)
a large wild animal with a thick hard skin and one or two horns on its nose —see color picture on page 183

rhyme¹ /raɪm/ *noun*
1 a word that ends with the same sound as another word

2 a short poem or song that uses words that end with the same sound

rhyme² *verb* (**rhyming, rhymed**)
if words rhyme, they end with the same sound: *"Weigh" rhymes **with** "play."*

rhythm /'rɪðəm/ *noun*
a regular sound like a drum in music: *I like to dance to music with a good rhythm.* | *African drum music has an exciting rhythm that can keep you dancing all night.*

rib /rɪb/ *noun*
one of the narrow bones that go around your chest —see picture at SKELETON

rib·bon /'rɪbən/ *noun*
a long narrow piece of cloth used for tying things and making them look pretty: *She has a ribbon in her hair.*

rice /raɪs/ *noun* [U]
a white or brown grain grown in a wet field and eaten as food

rich /rɪtʃ/ *adjective*
1 having a lot of money ≫ compare POOR
2 rich foods contain a lot of oil, sugar, butter etc. and make you feel full very quickly —**richness** *noun* [U]

rich·es /'rɪtʃɪz/ *plural noun*
money and goods: *She gave away all her riches.* | *All the riches of the world could not compare with his love for his family.*

rid /rɪd/
get rid of something to throw away or remove something or someone you do not want: *He got rid of his old shirts.*

rid·den /'rɪdn/
the PAST PARTICIPLE of the verb **ride**

rid·dle /'rɪdl/ *noun*
an amusing question that you must guess the answer to, often making people laugh

ride¹ /raɪd/ *verb* (**riding**, *past tense* **rode** /roʊd/, *past participle* **ridden** /'rɪdn/)
to sit or travel in a vehicle or on an animal: *She is riding her bicycle.* | *They rode horses on the mountain.*

ride² *noun*
a trip in a vehicle or on an animal, often for pleasure: *We **gave** him **a** ride to work.* | *Do you want to **go for a** ride?*

rid·er /'raɪdə/ *noun*
someone who rides a horse, bicycle etc.: *The rider was thrown off his horse.*

ridge /rɪdʒ/ *noun*
a long narrow raised part of something such as the top of a mountain

ri·dic·u·lous /rɪ'dɪkyələs/ *adjective*
very silly: *What a ridiculous thing to say!*

ri·fle /'raɪfəl/ *noun*
a long gun that you hold up against your shoulder to shoot

right[1] /raɪt/ *adjective*
1 correct or true: *Do you know the right time? | She was right to tell the police.* ≫ compare WRONG[1]
2 on the right side, that is, the hand with which most people write: *Take the next right turn. | He broke his right arm.* ≫ compare LEFT[3]
3 used for saying that you agree with someone, or for asking if someone agrees with you: *You wanted coffee, right?*

right[2] *noun*
1 [U] behavior that is, fair and good. *You must learn the difference between right and wrong.* ≫ compare WRONG[3]
2 what is or should be allowed by law: *We must work for equal rights for everyone.*
3 [U] the side of your body that has the hand with which most people write: *The school is on the left of the street, and his house is on the right.* ≫ compare LEFT[2]

right[3] *adverb*
1 exactly in a particular position or place: *That's our house right there. | He's right behind you!*
2 immediately; happening now: *I'll be right there. | I need the report right away.*
3 correctly: *Did they spell your name right?* ≫ compare WRONG[2]
4 toward the right side: *Turn right at the corner.* ≫ compare LEFT[4]
5 completely; all the way: *I read right to the end of the book.*

right an·gle /ˌ. '../ *noun*
the shape made when two sides of a square meet at a corner; there are 90 degrees in a right angle

right-hand·ed /ˌ. '..ɪ/ *adjective*
using your right hand for things such as writing
≫ opposite LEFT-HANDED

rig·id /'rɪdʒɪd/ *adjective*
1 stiff and not easy to bend: *I need a box with rigid sides.*
2 not easy to change; strict: *He has rigid ideas about what women can do.*

rim /rɪm/ *noun*
the outside edge of something: *She broke the rim of her glasses.*

rind /raɪnd/ *noun*
the hard outer skin of fruit, cheese etc.

ring[1] /rɪŋ/ *noun*
1 a piece of jewelry that you wear on your finger: *She has a gold wedding ring.* —see picture at JEWELRY
2 a circle: *There was a ring of fire around the house.*
3 the sound made by a bell

ring[2] *verb* [*past tense* **rang**, *past participle* **rung**]
to make a bell make a sound: *I heard the telephone ringing.*

rinse /rɪns/ *verb* (**rinsing, rinsed**)
to use water to remove soap, dirt etc. from something: *I rinsed the sand off my feet.*

ri·ot[1] /'raɪət/ *noun*
a violent fight by an angry crowd of people: *News of the leader's death caused riots in the streets.*

riot[2] *verb*
if a crowd of people riots, they fight in a violent way

rip /rɪp/ *verb* (**ripping, ripped**)
to tear something: *I ripped my pants on a nail.*

ripe /raɪp/ *adjective*
ready to be eaten: *This fruit isn't ripe yet.*

ripple
ripple

rip·ple[1] /'rɪpəl/ *noun*
a small wave on the surface of a liquid

ripple² *verb*
(**rippling, rippled**)
to move in small waves: *I can hear the water rippling over the rocks.*

rise¹ /raɪz/ *verb*
(**rising,** *past tense* **rose** /roʊz/, *past participle* **risen** /'rɪzən/)
1 to increase in number, value etc.: *Oil prices are rising.* ≫ compare FALL¹
2 to go up: *Smoke rose from the chimney.*
3 to stand up: *He rose **to his feet**.* ≫ compare SIT
4 to appear in the sky: *The sun rose at seven o'clock.* ≫ compare SET²
5 to become more important or powerful: *When did he rise to power?*

rise² *noun*
an increase in number, amount etc.: *We had a rise **in** prices.* ≫ compare FALL²

ris·en /'rɪzən/
the PAST PARTICIPLE of the verb **rise**

risk¹ /rɪsk/ *verb*
to put something in a situation where it could be lost, damaged, or harmed: *He risked his **life** in saving the child. | You risk losing all your money.*

risk² *noun*
the chance that something bad will happen: *He **took a risk** in buying the old car.*

ri·val /'raɪvəl/ *noun*
a person, company etc. that tries to do better than someone else: *She is his business rival.*

ri·val·ry /'raɪvəlri/ *noun* (*plural* **rivalries**)
a competition between people, companies etc. who want to do better than each other

riv·er /'rɪvər/ *noun*
a continuous flow of water that goes into the ocean or a lake: *The longest river in Africa is the Nile.* —see color picture on page 188

road /roʊd/ *noun*
1 a hard wide surface on which vehicles can travel: *Where's the best place to cross the road?* ≫ compare STREET —see color picture on page 188
2 **on the road** traveling for a long distance: *We've been on the road since this morning.*

roam /roʊm/ *verb*
to walk or travel in a place: *Bears roamed through the woods.*

roar¹ /rɔr/ *verb*
to make a deep loud noise, like a lion

roar² *noun*
a deep loud noise: *You could hear the roar of the crowd.*

roast¹ /roʊst/ *verb*
to cook food over a fire or in an OVEN

roast² *adjective*
cooked over a fire or in an OVEN: *Do you like roast chicken?*

rob /rɑb/ *verb* (**robbing, robbed**)
to take something from a person, bank etc. that is not yours: *They planned to rob the bank.*

NOTE: Compare **rob** and **steal**. Someone **robs** a person or an organization, but **steals** things such as money: *I've been robbed! He was sent to prison for robbing a bank. Someone stole my bag. She stole the money.*

rob·ber /'rɑbər/ *noun*
someone who steals something from a person, bank etc.

rob·ber·y /'rɑbəri/ *noun* (*plural* **robberies**)
the crime of stealing something from a person, bank etc.: *He was charged with **armed** robbery* (=using a gun).

robe /roʊb/ *noun*
a long loose piece of clothing that covers most of your body

rob·in /'rɑbɪn/ *noun*
a common wild bird with a red chest

ro·bot /'roʊbɑt, -bʌt/ *noun*
a machine that moves and works instead of a person

rock¹ /rɑk/ *noun*
1 [U] stone that forms part of the Earth's surface
2 a large piece of stone: *The ship hit a rock during the storm.*
3 [U] a type of popular modern music with a strong beat, played on electric instruments

rock² *verb*
to move gently from one side to the other: *Susan is rocking the baby to sleep.*

rock·et /'rɑkɪt/ *noun*
1 a machine used for carrying something from the ground into space —see color picture on page 192

rock·et /'rɑkɪt/ *noun*
1 a machine used for carrying something from

rocket

the ground into space —see color picture on page 192

2 an explosive that goes high into the air and explodes into many bright colors

rock·ing chair /'.. ,./ *noun*
a chair with two pieces of curved wood under it, so that it moves gently backward and forward

rock·y /'raki/ *adjective* (**rockier, rockiest**)
covered with rocks: *The beach is rocky and wet.*

rod /rad/ *noun*
a long thin pole or stick: *I bought a new fishing rod.*

rode /rood/
the PAST TENSE of the verb **ride**

ro·de·o /'roodi,oo, roo'deioo/ *noun*
a competition in which people ride wild horses, and catch cattle with ropes

role /rool/ *noun*
1 the position or job that someone has in a situation or activity: *The country plays a major role in keeping the peace.*
2 a character in a play or movie: *He played the role of the old king in our play.*

roll¹ /rool/ *verb*
1 to move by turning over and over, or on wheels: *A ball rolled under the table. | The car rolled backward.*
2 (*also* **roll up**) to make a round shape by turning something over and over: *Roll up the carpet so we can carry it. | Roll the string into a ball.*
3 (*also* **roll out**) to make something flat and straight: *Roll out your sleeping bag on the floor.*
4 **roll over** to turn your body so you are lying in a different position: *Roll over. You're crowding me!*

roll² *noun*
1 something rolled up into a long round shape like a tube: *A roll of coins fell off the table.*
2 a small round piece of bread
3 an official list of people's names

Roll·er·blade /'roolɚ,bleid/ (*trademark*) *noun*
a special boot with a row of wheels attached under it

roller coast·er /'.. ,../ *noun*
a long track with steep slopes and curves on which people ride in special cars

roller skate /'.. ,./ *noun*
a boot with four wheels attached under it

Roman Cath·o·lic /,roomən 'kæθlik/ *adjective*
relating to the church whose leader is the Pope

ro·mance /'roomæns, roo'mæns/ *noun*
1 a relationship between two people who love each other
2 a story about love between two people

ro·man·tic /roo'mæntik/ *adjective*
showing strong feelings of love —**romantically** *adjective*

roof /ruf, rʊf/ *noun*
the top surface of a building, car etc.: *There's a cat on our roof.*

room /rum, rʊm/ *noun*
1 one of the parts of a building that has walls and doors: *The house has six rooms.*
2 [U] enough space: *There isn't enough room for anyone else in the car.*

room·mate /'rum meit/ *noun*
someone who shares a room or house with someone else

room·y /'rumi, 'rʊmi/ *adjective* (**roomier, roomiest**)
with plenty of space

roost·er /'rustɚ/ *noun*
a male chicken

root /rut, rʊt/ *noun*
the part of a plant that grows under the ground

rope /roop/ *noun*
a strong thick string

rose¹ /rooz/
the PAST TENSE of the verb **rise**

rose² *noun*
a beautiful flower with a sweet smell

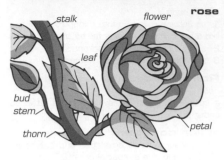

stalk · flower · **rose** · leaf · bud · stem · thorn · petal

rot /rɑt/ verb (rotting, rotted)
to go bad and soft because of being old, wet etc.: *The fruit began to rot.* | *Sugar will rot your teeth.* ≫ compare DECAY¹

ro·tate /ˈroʊteɪt/ verb (rotating, rotated)
to go around like a wheel: *Rotate the handle to the left.*

ro·ta·tion /roʊˈteɪʃən/ noun
a movement around and around like a wheel

rot·ten /ˈrɑtˈn/ adjective
1 bad and soft because old or wet; decayed: *The rotten fish smelled terrible!*
2 very bad or unpleasant: *The way he treated her was really rotten.*

rough /rʌf/ adjective
1 not even or smooth: *Can your car travel over a rough road?* ≫ compare SMOOTH
2 using force or violence; not gentle: *The sea was rough because of the storm.*
3 not exact: *Do you have a rough **idea** of when you will leave?*

rough·ly /ˈrʌfli/ adverb
1 about; not exactly: *We sailed roughly twenty miles.* ≫ compare APPROXIMATELY
2 not gently or carefully

round¹ /raʊnd/ adjective
like a ring or circle: *They sat at a large round table.*

round² noun
1 a number of events that are related: *The latest round **of** meetings went very well.*
2 one of the parts or periods of time in a sports competition: *The boxing match is ten rounds long.*

round³ verb
to go around something such as the corner of a building: *The car rounded the corner going too fast.*

round-trip /ˌ. ˈ.◂/ adjective
a round-trip ticket is for taking a trip from one place to another, then going back again

route /rut, raʊt/ noun
the way from one place to another, especially on a map: *What's the shortest route from here to Boston?*

rou·tine /ruˈtin/ noun
the normal or usual way of doing things: *I don't like anything that upsets my daily routine.*

row¹ /roʊ/ noun
a line of things or people: *I walked past a row **of** houses.* | *She sat **in the front** row.* (=the first line of seats)

row² verb
to make a boat move through the water using OARs (=long sticks with a flat end)

row·boat /ˈroʊboʊt/ noun
a small boat that you move through the water using OARs (=long sticks with a flat end) —see color picture on page 187

roy·al /ˈrɔɪəl/ adjective
relating to or belonging to a king or queen: *Did you see the royal family?*

roy·al·ty /ˈrɔɪəlti/ noun [U]
members of the family of a king or queen

rub /rʌb/ verb (rubbing, rubbed)
to move your hand, a cloth etc. over a surface while pressing against it: *She rubbed cream into her hands.* | *Can you rub my back? It's sore.*

rub·ber /ˈrʌbɚ/ noun [U]
a soft substance that comes from a tree and is used for making boots, tires etc.

rubber band /ˌ.. ˈ., ˈ.. ˌ./ noun
a thin piece of rubber like a circle that is used for keeping things together

ru·by /ˈrubi/ noun (plural rubies)
a dark red jewel, or the color of this jewel

rude /rud/ adjective
saying or doing bad things that are not polite or nice: *Don't be so rude **to** your father.* ≫ compare POLITE

rug /rʌg/ noun
a thick cloth that you put on the floor as a decoration ≫ compare CARPET

rug·ged /ˈrʌgɪd/ adjective
rough, uneven and full of rocks

ru·in¹ /'ruɪn/ *verb*
to destroy or spoil something: *I spilled ink on my dress and ruined it.*

ruin² *noun*
1 [U] a situation in which something is damaged or destroyed: *The company faces financial ruin.*
2 ruins the part of a building that is left after the rest has been destroyed: *We saw the ruins of the old church.*

rule¹ /rul/ *verb* (**ruling, ruled**)
1 to have power in a country and to control it: *The country is ruled by a king.*
2 to make an official decision about something: *The judge ruled that he was guilty.*

rule² *noun*
1 a law; something that tells you what you can or cannot do: *It's **against the** rules to pick up the ball.*
2 [U] the government of a country by a particular group: *The city is under military rule.*

rul·er /'rulə/ *noun*
1 someone who controls a country
2 a piece of wood or plastic with a straight edge used for measuring things and for drawing straight lines

rum /rʌm/ *noun* [U]
a strong alcoholic drink made from sugar

rum·ble /'rʌmbəl/ *verb* (**rumbling, rumbled**)
to make a long low noise —**rumble** *noun*

ru·mor /'rumə/ *noun*
something that people tell each other but that may not be true: *Have you heard the rumor about John?*

run¹ /rʌn/ *verb* (**running,** *past tense* **ran** /ræn/, *past participle* **run**)
1 to move very quickly using your legs: *He ran across the road.*
2 to control or operate a business, company etc.: *There is not enough money to run the hospital. | She runs a clothing store in the city.*
3 to work or be working: *He left the engine running. | The radio runs on batteries.*
4 to go somewhere quickly, either walking or in a car: *I need to run into town to get some things. | Can you run to the store for me?*
5 to be in a particular place or continue in a particular direction: *The road runs along the river bank. | A path runs between the houses.*
6 to try to get elected: *She is running for President.*

7 to take people from one place to another: *The trains run every hour.*
8 to flow: *Who left the water running?*
9 run away to go away from a place because you are unhappy: *He ran away **from home** when he was thirteen.*
10 run someone down to hit or injure a person or an animal with a car
11 run into someone or something (a) to hit someone or something with a car or other vehicle: *I ran into a tree.* (b) to meet someone by chance: *I didn't think I would run into you here.*
12 run off to run away from a place or person when you are not supposed to: *Our dog keeps running off.*
13 run out of something to use all of something so there is none left: *The car has run out of gas.*

run² *noun*
1 an act of running: *I always **go for a** run before breakfast.*
2 a point in a baseball game
3 in the long run from now until a time far into the future: *In the long run, I think our plan will work.*
4 on the run trying to hide or escape from someone, especially the police: *He has been on the run for a year.*

run·a·way /'rʌnə,weɪ/ *noun* (*plural* **runaways**)
someone, especially a child, who has left the home where he or she is supposed to be

rung¹ /rʌŋ/
the PAST PARTICIPLE of the verb **ring**

rung² *noun*
one of the steps on a ladder

run·ner /'rʌnə/ *noun*
someone who runs, especially as a sport or for exercise

run·ning¹ /'rʌnɪŋ/ *noun* [U]
the activity of running as a sport or for exercise: *How often do you **go** running?*

running² *adjective*
running water water that comes from a pipe in your home .

run·ny /'rʌni/ *adjective* (**runnier, runniest**)
1 not solid or thick enough: *This paint is too runny to use.* ⟫ compare THICK
2 a runny nose has liquid coming out of it because you are sick

ru·ral /ˈrʊrəl/ *adjective*
relating to the country, not the city: *Farm animals are kept in rural areas.* ≫ compare URBAN

rush¹ /rʌʃ/ *verb*
to move or do something quickly: *She rushed into the room to tell us the news.*

rush² *noun* [U]
a sudden fast movement of people or things: *Everyone **made a** rush for the door.*

rush hour /ˈ. ./ *noun*
the time of day when there are a lot of vehicles on the road because people are going to or from work

rust¹ /rʌst/ *noun* [U]
a red-brown substance that forms on iron when it has been wet: *The old car has a lot of rust.*

rust² *verb*
to become covered with RUST: *The lock is rusted shut.*

rus·tle¹ /ˈrʌsəl/ *verb* [rustling, rustled]
if leaves or papers rustle, they make a light sound as they rub together: *The leaves rustled in the wind.*

rustle² *noun* [U]
a light sound made when something RUSTLEs

rust·y /ˈrʌsti/ *adjective* [rustier, rustiest]
covered with RUST: *I found a box of rusty nails.*

rut /rʌt/ *noun*
1 a deep narrow track made by a wheel in soft ground
2 **in a rut** living or working in a situation that does not change and is boring

S s

's /z, s, ɪz/
1 is: *What's your name?*
2 has: *She's been here before.*
3 us: *Let's go, or we will be late.*
4 used for showing who owns something:
Those are Tom's books. (=those books belong to Tom)

NOTE: When there is more than one owner, write **s'**, not **'s**: *the boy's books* (=1 boy), *the boys' books* (=several boys).

sack /sæk/ *noun*
a large bag made of thick strong material: *The truck carried sacks of rice.*

sa·cred /'seɪkrɪd/ *adjective*
relating to a god or religion: *A church is a sacred building.*

sac·ri·fice¹ /'sækrə,faɪs/ *noun*
1 something that you decide not to have or do so that you can have something more important: *Her parents made a lot of sacrifices so that she could go to college.*
2 an object or animal that is offered to a god

sacrifice² *verb* (**sacrificing, sacrificed**)
1 to not have or do something so that you can have something more important: *She sacrificed her job to take care of her children.*
2 to offer something to a god: *They sacrificed a goat.*

sad /sæd/ *adjective* (**sadder, saddest**)
unhappy: *She looks very sad.* | *I was sad to leave my job.* —**sadly** *adverb*

sad·dle /'sædl/ *noun*
1 a seat made of leather that you put on a horse's back
2 a seat on a bicycle or MOTORCYCLE

sa·fa·ri /sə'fɑri/ *noun*
a trip through a place to look at wild animals

safe¹ /seɪf/ *adjective*
1 not in danger of being harmed or destroyed: *This town is very safe at night.* | *Do you feel safe driving home alone?*

2 not likely to cause injury or harm: *Is it safe to swim here?* —**safely** *adverb*

safe² *noun*
a strong metal box or cupboard with a lock on it, where you keep money and important things

safe·ty /'seɪfti/ *noun* [U]
the state of being safe from danger or harm: *Some parents are concerned about safety at the school.*

safety pin /'.. ,./ *noun*
a bent metal pin with a cover that its point fits into, so that it cannot hurt you

sag /sæg/ *verb* (**sagging, sagged**)
to hang or bend down away from the usual position: *The bookshelf sagged in the middle.*

said /sɛd/
the PAST TENSE and PAST PARTICIPLE of the verb say

sail¹ /seɪl/ *noun*
a large cloth fastened to a boat so that the wind will push the boat

sail

sail² *verb*
1 to travel on water in a boat or ship: *His ship sails today.*
2 to direct the movement of a boat or ship: *She sailed the boat without any help.*

sail·or /'seɪlər/ *noun*
1 someone who works on a ship
2 someone who is in the navy

saint /seɪnt/ *noun*
someone who has lived a very good and religious life

sake /seɪk/ *noun*
1 **for someone's sake** in order to help or please someone: *Please be nice to your sister, for my sake.*
2 **for goodness' sake** said when you are annoyed or surprised: *Oh, for goodness' sake, hurry up!*

sal·ad /'sæləd/ *noun*
a mixture of raw vegetables

salad dress·ing /'.. ,../ *noun*
a mixture of liquids that you put on a SALAD to give it a special taste

sal·a·ry /'sæləri/ *noun* (*plural* **salaries**)
money that you receive as payment for the job you do » compare PAY[2]

sale /seɪl/ *noun*
1 the act of giving something to someone for money: *The sale of cigarettes is controlled by the law.*
2 a time when stores sell things at lower prices: *They are having a sale this week.*
3 for sale available to be bought: *Is this table for sale?*

sales clerk /'. ./ *noun*
someone whose job is to sell things in a store

sales·man /'seɪlzmən/ *noun* (*plural* **salesmen**)
a man whose job is to sell things

sales·person /'seɪlz,pɚsən/ *noun*
someone whose job is to sell things

sales·wom·an /'seɪlz,wʊmən/ *noun* (*plural* **saleswomen**)
a woman whose job is to sell things

salm·on /'sæmən/ *noun* (*plural* **salmon**)
a large river and ocean fish that you can eat

salt /sɔlt/ *noun* [U]
a white mineral that is added to food to make it taste better

salt·y /'sɔlti/ *adjective* (**saltier, saltiest**)
tasting like salt, or containing salt

sa·lute[1] /sə'lut/ *verb* (**saluting, saluted**)
to hold your right hand to your head to show respect to someone in the military: *The soldier saluted the officer.*

salute[2] *noun*
an act of holding your right hand to your head to show respect to someone in the military

same /seɪm/ *adjective, pronoun*
1 the same (a) like each other in one or many ways: *Your pen is the same as mine.* | *They all look the same to me.* **(b)** one particular thing, and not a different one: *We go to the same place every year for vacation.* » compare DIFFERENT
2 used for saying that a particular person or thing does not change: *The machine kept playing the same song.*

sam·ple[1] /'sæmpəl/ *noun*
a small part of something that shows what the whole thing is like: *I need to see a sample of his work.*

sample[2] *verb* (**sampling, sampled**)
to taste a food or drink to see if you like it: *I sampled several different ice creams.*

sand /sænd/ *noun* [U]
very small grains of rock, often found next to the ocean and in deserts

san·dal /'sændl/ *noun*
an open shoe that you wear in warm weather

sand·wich /'sændwɪtʃ/ *noun* (*plural* **sandwiches**)
two pieces of bread with cheese, meat etc. between them: *I had a chicken sandwich for lunch.*

sand·y /'sændi/ *adjective* (**sandier, sandiest**)
covered with sand: *We walked on the sandy beach.*

sane /seɪn/ *adjective*
able to think in a normal and reasonable way » opposite INSANE

sang /sæŋ/
the PAST TENSE of the verb **sing**

sank /sæŋk/
the PAST TENSE of the verb **sink**

San·ta Claus /'sæntə ,klɔz/ *noun* (*also* **Santa**)
an old man with red clothes and white hair who children believe brings them presents at Christmas

sap /sæp/ *noun* [U]
the liquid inside a plant that carries food through it

sap·phire /'sæfaɪɚ/ *noun*
a bright blue jewel

sar·cas·tic /sɑr'kæstɪk/ *adjective*
using words in an unkind way to show that you are annoyed: *Don't be so sarcastic!*

sar·dine /sɑr'din/ *noun*
a small fish that is eaten as food

sat /sæt/
the PAST TENSE and PAST PARTICIPLE of the verb **sit**

Sa·tan /'seɪt⁻n/ *noun*
the devil; an evil spirit considered to be the main evil power in the world

sa·tan·ic /sə'tænɪk, seɪ-/ *adjective*
relating to Satan or the devil, or treating the devil like a god

satellite

sat·el·lite /'sætḷ,aɪt/ *noun*
1 an object sent into space to receive signals from one part of the world and send them to another: *The television broadcast came from Europe by satellite.* —see color picture on page 192
2 a moon that moves around a PLANET: *The moon is a satellite of the Earth.*

sat·is·fac·tion /ˌsætɪs'fækʃən/ *noun* [U]
a feeling of pleasure because you have done something or got what you wanted: *I get great satisfaction from working with children.*

sat·is·fac·to·ry /ˌsætɪs'fæktəri, -tri/ *adjective*
good enough: *Are the students making satisfactory progress?* » opposite UNSATISFACTORY

sat·is·fied /'sætɪs,faɪd/ *adjective*
pleased because something has happened in the way that you want: *I am satisfied with my test results.* | *We want everyone to be a satisfied customer.* » opposite DISSATISFIED

sat·is·fy /'sætɪs,faɪ/ *verb* (**satisfying, satisfied**)
to make someone happy by giving what he or she wants or needs: *It is very difficult to satisfy my boss.* —**satisfying** *adjective*

Sat·ur·day /'sætə·di, -,deɪ/ *noun*
the seventh day of the week

sauce /sɔs/ *noun*
a liquid that you add to food to give it a particular taste

sauce·pan /'sɔs-pæn/ *noun*
a deep round metal container with a handle, used for cooking —see picture at PAN

sau·cer /'sɔsə·/ *noun*
a small plate on which you put a cup

sau·na /'sɔnə/ *noun*
a room in which you sit, that is filled with steam to make it very hot

sau·sage /'sɔsɪdʒ/ *noun*
a mixture of meat cooked inside a skin shaped like a tube

sav·age /'sævɪdʒ/ *adjective*
wild and violent: *The lion can be a savage animal.*

save /seɪv/ *verb* (**saving, saved**)
1 to make someone or something safe from danger or harm: *I saved the animals **from** the flood.* | *Peter saved my life.*
2 (*also* **save up**) to keep money so that you can use it later: *How much did you save this month?* | *She is saving up to buy a car.*
3 to use less of something so that you do not waste it: *We'll save time if we take this road.*
4 to make a computer keep the work that you have done on it: *Did you save your file?*

sav·ings /'seɪvɪŋz/ *plural noun*
all the money that you have saved, especially in a bank: *He used his savings to buy a car.*

sav·ior /'seɪvyə·/ *noun*
someone or something that saves you from difficulty or danger

saw¹ /sɔ/
the PAST TENSE of the verb **see**

saw² *noun*
a tool with a flat blade with sharp metal points, used for cutting wood

saw³ *verb* (*past tense* **sawed**, *past participle* **sawn** /sɔn/ *or* **sawed**)
to cut something using a SAW: *He sawed the wood into three pieces.*

sax·o·phone /'sæksə,foʊn/ *noun* (*also* **sax**)
a metal musical instrument that you play by blowing into it and pressing buttons on it

say¹ /seɪ/ *verb* (**saying**, *past tense* **said** /sɛd/, *past participle* **said**)
1 to speak words: *He said that he wanted to go to town.* | *I didn't understand what she was saying.* » compare SPEAK
2 to give information in writing, pictures, or numbers: *What time does the clock say?*

NOTE: Compare **say** and **tell** in these sentences: *She said something. She told me something. He said he was busy. He told me he was busy.* **Say** never has a person as its object (to say sth **to sb**), but **tell** often has a person as its object (to tell **sb** sth).

say² *noun* [U]

the right to help decide something or give your opinion about something: *It is important to* **have a** *say in your child's education.*

say·ing /'seɪ-ɪŋ/ *noun*

a statement that most people believe is true and wise

scab /skæb/ *noun*

a hard layer of skin that grows over a cut or wound

scaf·fold /'skæfəld, -foʊld/ *noun*

a structure built next to a building for people to stand on while they work on the building

scald /skɔld/ *verb*

to burn yourself with steam or hot liquid: *She scalded her tongue on the hot coffee.*

scale /skeɪl/ *noun*

1 a machine for weighing someone or something: *Put the bananas on the scale.*

2 [U] the size or level of something, especially when compared to what is usual: *The large scale of the project surprised me.*

3 a set of marks on an instrument used for measuring something: *I need a ruler with a metric scale.*

4 the relationship between the size of a map or drawing and the size of the actual place: *The scale of this map is one inch to the mile.* [=one inch equals one mile]

5 a series of musical notes going higher or lower in order

6 one of the flat hard pieces of skin that cover the body of a fish, snake etc.

scalp /skælp/ *noun*

the skin on the top of your head

scan·dal /'skændl/ *noun*

something that has happened that people think is very bad or shocking: *The scandal involved several politicians.*

scan·ner /'skænɚ/ *noun*

a piece of computer equipment that copies a picture or words from paper onto the computer

scar¹ /skɑr/ *noun*

a mark left on your skin by a wound or cut

scar² *verb* [scarring, scarred]

to have a mark on your skin from a wound or cut: *His face was badly scarred after the accident.*

scarce /skɛrs/ *adjective*

if something is scarce, there is not enough of it: *Food becomes scarce during a war.*

scarce·ly /'skɛrsli/ *adverb*

almost not at all: *She scarcely said a word all evening.*

scare¹ /skɛr/ *verb* [scaring, scared]

to make someone feel afraid: *The strange noise scared me.* » compare FRIGHTEN

scare² *noun*

a sudden feeling of fear: *You gave me a scare last night.*

scare·crow
/'skɛrkroʊ/ *noun*
an object that looks like a person, that you put into a field to keep birds away

scared /skɛrd/
adjective
feeling afraid or nervous about something: *I was scared* **that** *something bad would happen to her.* » compare AFRAID

scarf /skɑrf/ *noun* [plural **scarves** or **scarfs**]

a piece of cloth that you wear around your neck or head to keep warm or as a decoration —see color picture on page 190

scar·let /'skɑrlɪt/ *adjective, noun* [U]

a very bright red color

scar·y /'skɛri/ *adjective* [scarier, scariest]

very frightening: *I hate scary movies!*

scat·ter /'skæt̮ɚ/ *verb*

1 to move or be made to move in different directions: *The crowd scattered into the streets.*

2 to throw or drop things over a wide area: *My clothes were scattered all over the floor.*

scene /sin/ *noun*

1 a view of a place as you see it, or as it appears in a picture: *He painted a lovely country scene with trees and a river.*

2 the place where something happens: *Police arrived quickly* **at the** *scene of the accident.*

3 a part of a play or movie in which the action happens in one place or at one time: *This play is divided into three acts, and each act has three scenes.*

sce·ner·y /'sinɚi/ *noun* [U]

1 the natural things that you can see in a place such as trees, mountains etc.: *The scenery here is very beautiful.*

2 the painted pictures at the back of a theater stage

scent /sɛnt/ *noun*
1 a pleasant smell: *The scent of flowers filled the room.*
2 the smell left behind by a person or animal: *The dogs picked up his scent.*

sched·ule /ˈskɛdʒəl, -dʒul/ *noun*
1 a plan of what you will do and when you will do it: *My schedule is very busy this week.*
2 a list of times when buses, trains etc. arrive or leave a place

scheme¹ /skim/ *noun*
a plan, especially to do something that is not honest: *He thought of a scheme to get some money.*

scheme² *verb* (**scheming, schemed**)
to make plans, especially to do something that is not honest: *They are scheming to steal money from the bank.*

schol·ar /ˈskɑlɚ/ *noun*
1 someone who knows a lot about a particular subject
2 a student who has been given money to study at a college

schol·ar·ship /ˈskɑlɚˌʃɪp/ *noun*
money given to a student to pay for his or her education: *She won a scholarship to Harvard.*

school /skul/ *noun*
1 a place where children go to learn: *Which school do you go to?* | *I'm learning Spanish in school.*
2 [U] the time someone is at school: *What are you doing after school?*

sci·ence /ˈsaɪəns/ *noun*
the study of nature and the way things in the world are made or behave, or the knowledge gained by this

science fic·tion /ˌ.. ˈ../ *noun* [U]
(*also* **sci-fi**) books and stories about imaginary things in science such as space travel

sci·en·tif·ic /ˌsaɪənˈtɪfɪk/ *adjective*
relating to science: *He is doing a scientific study on tigers.*

sci·en·tist /ˈsaɪəntɪst/ *noun*
someone who studies or works in science: *Scientists were discussing the problem of global warming during an international conference on the environment.*

scis·sors
/ˈsɪzɚz/ *plural noun*
an instrument with two sharp blades joined together used for cutting paper, cloth etc.: *Hand me a pair of scissors, please.*

scold /skoʊld/ *verb*
to tell a child in an angry way that he or she has done something wrong: *My mother scolded me for dropping the plates.*

scoop¹ /skup/ *verb*
to pick up something with your hands, a spoon etc.: *She scooped some flour out of the bag.*

scoop² *noun*
a big spoon for picking up food such as flour and ICE CREAM

scoot·er /ˈskutɚ/ *noun*
1 a light small MOTOR-CYCLE
2 a board with two small wheels and a handle that children ride by standing on it with one foot while the other foot pushes against the ground

score¹ /skɔr/ *noun*
1 the number of points that you get in a game or test: *The final score was 35–17.*
2 **keep score** to write down how many points each person or team has in a game

score² *verb* (**scoring, scored**)
1 to win points in a game or test: *How many points did you score?*
2 to give a particular number of points in a game or test

scor·pi·on /ˈskɔrpiən/ *noun*
a small creature that stings with its tail

scowl¹ /skaʊl/ *verb*
to look at someone in an angry way: *She scowled at me because I was late.*

scowl² *noun*
an angry look on someone's face

scram·ble /ˈskræmbəl/ *verb* (**scrambling, scrambled**)
to move over something quickly but with difficulty: *The children scrambled up the hill.*

scram·bled eggs /ˌskræmbəld 'ɛgz/
plural noun
eggs that have had their white and yellow parts
mixed together and then cooked

scrap /skræp/ *noun*
a small piece of paper, cloth etc.: *There were
scraps of paper on the floor.*

scrap·book /'skræpbʊk/ *noun*
a book of empty pages in which you can put pictures and pieces of writing that you want to
keep

scrape /skreɪp/ *verb* [scraping, scraped]
to remove something using the edge of a knife,
stick etc.: *Scrape the mud off your boots.*

scratch¹ /skrætʃ/ *verb*
1 to rub a part of your body· with your
FINGERNAILs: *Can you scratch my back?*
2 to make a small cut on a surface using
something sharp: *The cat scratched the chair.*

scratch² *noun* [*plural* scratches]
a small cut or mark made by something sharp:
She has a scratch on her hand.

scream¹ /skrim/ *verb*
to make a loud, high noise with your voice
because of fear or excitement: *"Look out!" she
screamed.*

scream² *noun*
a loud, high·noise that you make with your voice
when you are afraid, injured etc.

screech /skritʃ/ *verb*
to make a loud, high, unpleasant sound: *The
car screeched around the corner.* —**screech**
noun

screen /skrin/ *noun*
1 a flat square glass part of a television or
computer
2 a large flat white surface on which movies
are shown
3 a piece of material on a frame used for dividing one part of a room from another: *The doctor asked him to undress behind the screen.*

screw¹ /skru/ *noun*
a small pointed piece of metal that you push
and turn to fasten pieces of wood together
—see picture at SCREWDRIVER

screw² *verb*
1 to fasten two objects together with a screw
using a screwdriver: *He screwed the mirror to
the wall.*

2 to fasten or close something by turning it:
Screw the lid on tightly.

screwdriver

screwdriver

screw

screw·driv·er /'skru,draɪvɚ/ *noun*
a tool with a long thin metal end used for turning screws

scrib·ble /'skrɪbəl/ *verb* [scribbling,
scribbled]
to write quickly and carelessly: *I'll scribble a
note to say when we'll come home.*

scrip·ture /'skrɪptʃɚ/ *noun*
1 the holy writings of a particular religion
2 (*also* the Holy Scripture) the Bible

scroll /skroʊl/ *verb*
to move information up or down a computer
screen to read it

scrub /skrʌb/ *verb* [scrubbing, scrubbed]
to rub something hard to clean it, especially
using a brush

sculp·tor /'skʌlptɚ/ *noun*
an artist who makes shapes and objects from
wood, stone, or metal

sculp·ture /'skʌlptʃɚ/ *noun*
1 objects made from wood, stone, or metal
2 [U] the art of making objects from wood,
stone, or metal

sea /si/ *noun*
1 a large area of salty water that is smaller
than an ocean: *We sailed the Mediterranean
Sea.*
2 another name for the ocean: *The ship was
heading out to sea.*

sea·food /'sifud/ *noun* [U]
ocean animals that can be eaten: *We eat a lot
of seafood.*

sea·gull /'sigʌl/ *noun*
a common bird that lives near the ocean and
has a loud cry

seal¹ /sil/ *noun*
1 an animal that has smooth fur, eats fish, and lives near the ocean
2 an official mark that is put on a document to prove that it is real

seal² *verb*
(*also* **seal up**) to close something tightly: *She sealed the envelope and put a stamp on it.*

seam /sim/ *noun*
a line where two pieces of cloth are joined together

search¹ /sɔtʃ/ *verb*
to look carefully in a place because you want to find something: *Police searched the house. | I've searched everywhere for my keys.*

search² *noun* (*plural* **searches**)
an attempt to find something: *After a long search, they found the lost child.*

sea·shell /'siʃɛl/ *noun*
the hard shell that covers some ocean creatures

sea·shore /'siʃɔr/ *noun* [U]
the land along the edge of the ocean

sea·sick /'si,sɪk/ *adjective*
feeling sick because of the movement of a boat on the water: *I felt seasick because the ocean was very rough.*

sea·son /'sizən/ *noun*
1 one of the four parts of the year; spring, summer, fall, or winter: *Summer is the hottest season.*
2 a time of the year during which something usually happens or is done: *The football season begins soon.*

seat /sit/ *noun*
1 a place to sit, or a thing to sit on: *I could not find a seat on the bus.*
2 **take a seat, have a seat** to sit down: *Please, come in and take a seat.*

seat belt /'. ./ *noun*
a belt attached to a seat in a car or airplane, that you fasten around yourself for protection in an accident

sec·ond¹ /'sɛkənd/ *adjective, adverb*
2nd; after the first one: *This is the second time I have met him. | I came in second in the race.*

second² *noun*
a very short period of time; there are 60 seconds in one minute

secondary school /'.... ,./ *noun*
a school for children over 11 or 12 years old after ELEMENTARY SCHOOL

se·cret¹ /'sikrɪt/ *noun*
an idea, plan etc. that you do not tell other people about: *Don't tell anyone about this. It's a secret. | Can you **keep a secret**?* (=not tell anyone else)

secret² *adjective*
not known about by other people: *There is a secret plan to attack the country.* —**secretly** *adverb*

sec·re·tar·y /'sɛkrə,tɛri/ *noun* (*plural* **secretaries**)
1 someone whose job is to answer the telephone, write letters etc. in an office
2 a government official

sec·tion /'sɛkʃən/ *noun*
one of the parts of something: *One section of the bookcase had records on it. | The machine was built in sections.*

se·cure /sɪ'kyor/ *adjective*
1 not likely to change; safe: *She has a secure job with the bank.*
2 fastened firmly so it will not move or be harmed: *The boat will be secure here.*

se·cu·ri·ty /sɪ'kyorəti/ *noun* [U]
the state of being safe and protected: *The government is responsible for the security of the country.*

see /si/ *verb* (*past tense* **saw** /sɔ/, *past participle* **seen** /sin/)
1 to use your eyes to notice something: *I can't see without my glasses. | Have you seen the new movie?*
2 to understand something: *Do you see what I mean? | I could see that she didn't like me.*
3 to meet or visit someone: *I'll see you outside. | You should see a doctor.*
4 to find out information or a fact: *Go and see how many people have arrived. | I'll see if anyone wants a cup of coffee.*
5 to experience something: *I have seen a lot of things in my life.*
6 **see you, see you later** used for saying goodbye to someone: *"Goodbye, Bill." "See you later, Terry."*
7 **let's see** said when you are thinking about something, or trying to remember something:

Let's see. How many people are coming?

8 see to something to deal with something or make sure that it happens: *I will see to it that she gets home safely.*

9 I'll see, we'll see said when you want to think about something before making a decision: *"Can I use the car this Saturday?" "We'll see."*

seed /sid/ *noun* [*plural* **seed** *or* **seeds**]
a small grain from which a new plant grows

seek /sik/ *verb* [*past tense* **sought** /sɔt/, *past participle* **sought**]
to try to find or get something: *We sought a peaceful answer to the problem.*

seem /sim/ *verb*
to appear to be: *Your sister seems very nice.* | *There seems to be a problem with the car.*

seen /sin/
the PAST PARTICIPLE of the verb **see**

see·saw /'sisɔ/ *noun*
a long piece of wood balanced in the middle, so that when one end goes up the other end comes down, for children to play on

seize /siz/ *verb* [**seizing, seized**]
to take hold of something quickly and firmly: *A woman seized his arm.*

sel·dom /'sɛldəm/ *adverb*
only a few times; not often: *Bill seldom eats lunch.* ≫ compare RARELY

se·lect /sɪ'lɛkt/ *verb*
to choose something or someone: *I was selected for the team.*

se·lec·tion /sɪ'lɛkʃən/ *noun*
the act of choosing someone or something, or the person or thing that you choose: *Did you make a selection?*

self /sɛlf/ *noun* [*plural* **selves** /sɛlvz/]
the type of person you are, especially your character, abilities etc.: *Caroline seemed like her old self today.* (=seemed normal again)

self-con·fi·dent /ˌ. '.../ *adjective*
being confident about your appearance or abilities, not shy or nervous —**self-confidence** *noun* [U]

self-con·trol /ˌ. .'./ *noun* [U]
the ability to control your feelings and behavior even when you are angry or upset

self-de·fense /ˌ. .'./ *noun* [U]
the use of force to protect yourself from attack or harm

self·ish /'sɛlfɪʃ/ *adjective*
caring only about yourself and not other people: *Don't be so selfish with your toys!*

self-serv·ice /ˌ. '...⁀/ *adjective*
getting things for yourself, rather than being served by someone: *self-service gas stations*

sell /sɛl/ *verb* [*past tense* **sold** /soʊld/, *past participle* **sold**]
1 to give something in exchange for money: *She sold her bicycle to me.* | *Do you sell milk?* ≫ compare BUY
2 sell out to sell all of something so that there is none left: *We've sold out of newspapers.*

se·mes·ter /sə'mɛstɚ/ *noun*
one of two periods of time into which a year at college is divided

sem·i·cir·cle /'sɛmiˌsɚkəl/ *noun*
half a circle

sem·i·co·lon /'sɛmiˌkoʊlən/ *noun*
the mark ";" used in writing to separate parts of a sentence: *It was a long walk; I'm very tired.*

sem·i·fi·nal /'sɛmiˌfaɪnl, 'sɛmaɪ-, ˌsɛmi'faɪnl/ *noun*
one of two games whose winners then compete against each other to decide who wins the whole competition

sen·ate /'sɛnɪt/ *noun* [*also* **Senate**]
one of the groups in a government that make the laws in some countries such as the U.S.

sen·a·tor /'sɛnəṭɚ/ *noun*
a member of a SENATE

send /sɛnd/ *verb* [*past tense* **sent** /sɛnt/, *past participle* **sent**]
1 to cause a thing to go or be taken somewhere: *She sent me a present.* | *Did you send him a letter?*
2 to make someone go somewhere: *They sent their children to school in Massachusetts.* | *We had to send in the soldiers to stop the fighting.*
3 send for someone to ask someone to come to you: *She is sick, so her mother sent for the doctor.*

Senior /'sinyɚ/ *adjective*
used after the name of a man who has the same name as his son ≫ compare JUNIOR

sen·ior¹ *adjective*
1 older: *She teaches a senior class.* ≫ compare JUNIOR²
2 higher in position or importance: *She is now a senior officer in the army.*

senior² *noun*
a student who is in the last year of high school or college

sen·ior cit·i·zen /ˌ.. '.../ *noun*
an old person

sen·sa·tion /sɛn'seɪʃən/ *noun*
1 the ability to feel, or a feeling that you have: *She felt a burning sensation on the back of her neck.*
2 excitement or a lot of interest: *The new show caused a sensation.*

sense¹ /sɛns/ *noun*
1 [U] good understanding and judgment: *She has enough sense to call us if she needs to.*
2 a feeling about something: *I felt a strong sense of pride when I won the race.*
3 one of the five natural abilities to hear, see, taste, feel, or smell: *He has a good sense of smell.*
4 **make sense** to have a meaning that you can understand: *Does this sentence make sense to you?*

sense² *verb* (sensing, sensed)
to feel that something is true without being told: *The dog sensed that I was afraid.*

sense·less /'sɛnslɪs/ *adjective*
1 happening or done for no good reason or purpose: *The crime was completely senseless.*
2 not conscious: *The punch knocked him senseless.*

sen·si·ble /'sɛnsəbəl/ *adjective*
having or showing good sense; reasonable: *Tom is a sensible man. | I think we made a sensible decision.*

sen·si·tive /'sɛnsətɪv/ *adjective*
able to understand the feelings or problems of other people: *You need to be sensitive to your wife's needs.*

sent /sɛnt/
the PAST TENSE and PAST PARTICIPLE of the verb **send**

sen·tence /'sɛntˀns, -təns/ *noun*
a group of words that makes a statement or asks a question ≫ compare CLAUSE

sep·a·rate¹ /'sɛprɪt/ *adjective*
1 not touching each other or connected to each other; apart: *They have gone to separate places. | We sleep in separate beds.*
2 different: *The word has three separate meanings.*

sep·a·rate² /'sɛpəˌreɪt/ *verb* (separating, separated)
1 to move people or things apart: *The teacher separated the class into four groups.*
2 to be between two things and keep them apart: *A fence separated the cows from the pigs.* —separation *noun*

Sep·tem·ber /sɛp'tɛmbɚ/ *noun*
the ninth month of the year

se·quence /'sikwəns/ *noun*
a series of related events or actions that have a particular result: *A sequence of events led to the murder.*

ser·geant /'sɑrdʒənt/ *noun*
an officer in the army or the police

se·ri·al /'sɪriəl/ *noun*
a story that is told or written in parts

se·ries /'sɪriz/ *noun* (plural series)
a group of events or actions that happen one after the other: *There has been a series of accidents on this road.*

se·ri·ous /'sɪriəs/ *adjective*
1 thinking carefully about what you say or do: *He is serious about finding a new job.*
2 very bad or dangerous and making you worry: *My father has a serious illness.*
3 important and deserving your attention: *We had a serious conversation about our future.*

se·ri·ous·ly /'sɪriəsli/ *adverb*
1 in a bad or dangerous way that makes you worry: *He is seriously ill.*
2 **take something seriously** to think that something is important: *The police are taking the threats seriously.*

ser·mon /'sɚmən/ *noun*
a talk about a religious subject given in a church

serv·ant /'sɚvənt/ *noun*
someone whose job is to work for someone in his or her house

serve /sɚv/ *verb* (serving, served)
1 to give someone food or drinks as part of a meal: *Dinner will be served at eight o'clock.*
2 to work or do a particular job: *He served in the army for 15 years.*
3 to be used for a particular purpose: *This sofa also serves as an extra bed.*
4 to provide someone with something that is useful or necessary: *The food from the farm serves our needs.*
5 **it serves you right** said when you think someone deserves the bad thing that has hap-

pened to him or her: *He didn't do well on the test, but it serves him right for not studying.*

serv·ice /ˈsɚvɪs/ *noun*
1 [U] the help that people who work in a restaurant or store give to you: *The service in the new restaurant is very slow.*
2 the work that you do for someone else: *She retired after twenty-five years of service.*
3 something useful that the public can use to help them: *Is there a regular bus service from here?*
4 a religious ceremony, usually in a church: *We went to the morning service.*

ses·sion /ˈsɛʃən/ *noun*
a meeting for a particular purpose: *Court is now in session.* (=beginning the meeting)

set¹ /sɛt/ *noun*
1 a group of things that belong together: *She has a beautiful set of dishes.*
2 a television or radio: *We have a color TV set.*
3 the place where a movie or television program is acted and filmed

set² *verb* (setting, *past* set)
1 to put something somewhere carefully: *She set the flowers on the table.*
2 when the sun sets, it goes down in the sky until you cannot see it: *The sun is setting.* ≫ compare RISE¹
3 if a movie or story is set in a place, the events happen there or at that time
4 **set an example** to behave in a way that you want other people to behave: *Parents should set a good example for their children.*
5 **set fire to something, set something on fire** to make something start to burn
6 **set someone free** to let a prisoner go free
7 **set the table** to put plates, knives etc. on the table so they can be used
8 **set up** (a) to start a company, organization etc.: *The government has set up a special program for young mothers.* (b) to build something or put it somewhere: *Police set up a roadblock to stop traffic.*
9 **set off** to make something start happening: *When he came into the building, he set off an alarm.*
10 **set out to do something** to start doing something: *He set out to make a movie about the war.*

set³ *adjective*
1 a set time, price etc. has been arranged and cannot be changed: *We meet at a set time each week.*

2 ready to do something: *If everyone is set, we'll begin.*

set·tle /ˈsɛtl/ *verb* (settling, settled)
1 to begin to live in a new place: *My son settled in Los Angeles.*
2 to end an argument by agreeing to do something: *We settled our disagreement without a fight.*
3 to rest on something in a comfortable position: *I settled back on the chair and relaxed.*
4 **settle a bill** to pay the money that you owe for something
5 **settle down** to become calmer and less noisy: *It took the children a while to settle down.*
6 **settle in** to become happier in a new place or job: *How are you settling in at the school?*
7 **settle for something** to accept something that is less than what you wanted: *Most of the tickets were gone, so we had to settle for what we could get.*

set·tle·ment /ˈsɛtlmənt/ *noun*
an official decision or agreement that ends an argument: *The two sides have reached a settlement.* (=made an agreement)

sev·en /ˈsɛvən/ *adjective, noun*
the number 7

sev·en·teen /ˌsɛvənˈtin/ *adjective, noun*
the number 17

sev·enth /ˈsɛvənθ/ *adjective, noun*
7th

sev·en·ty /ˈsɛvənti/ *adjective, noun*
the number 70

sev·er·al /ˈsɛvrəl/ *adjective*
more than two, but not many: *She has several friends in the town.* | *I've talked to Pam several times on the phone.* ≫ compare FEW

se·vere /səˈvɪr/ *adjective* (severe, severest)
1 very bad or serious: *He has severe head injuries.*
2 not kind or friendly: *The criticism of her work was severe.*

sew /soʊ/ *verb* (past tense sewed, past participle sewn /soʊn/ or sewed)
to join pieces of cloth together or attach something to a piece of cloth using a needle and thread: *He sewed a button on his shirt.* ≫ compare KNIT

sew·ing /ˈsoʊɪŋ/ *noun* [U]
the activity of joining pieces of cloth together or attaching something to a piece of cloth using a

needle and thread: *My sister is very good at sewing.*

sewing machine /'.. ,../ *noun*
a machine used for sewing pieces of cloth together

sex /sɛks/ *noun*
1 [U] the activity that a male and female do together to produce children or for pleasure
2 [C] being male or female: *What sex is your cat?*

sex·ism /'sɛk,sɪzəm/ *noun* [U]
the belief that one sex is weaker, less intelligent, or less important than the other

sex·ist /'sɛksɪst/ *adjective*
relating to SEXISM: *The book is full of sexist opinions.*

sex·u·al /'sɛkʃuəl/ *adjective*
relating to sex: *The movie examines sexual attraction.* —**sexually** *adverb*

sex·y /'sɛksi/ *adjective* (**sexier, sexiest**)
sexually exciting or sexually attractive

shab·by /'ʃæbi/ *adjective* (**shabbier, shabbiest**)
old, dirty, and in bad condition: *A man in shabby clothes got on the bus.*

shade

shade¹ /ʃeɪd/ *noun*
1 [U] an area that is cooler and darker because it is away from sun: *They sat in the shade of the tree.*
2 a cover that you pull across a window to block the light: *Can you close the shades, please?*
3 a particular type of a color: *I want a darker shade of blue.*

shade² *verb* (**shading, shaded**)
to protect something from the sun or light: *I shaded my eyes with my hand.*

shad·ow /'ʃædoʊ/ *noun*
a dark shape made when something is between

a surface and the light: *The sun behind us cast our shadows on the wall.*

shad·y /'ʃeɪdi/ *adjective* (**shadier, shadiest**)
protected from the sun: *It's cool and shady under the tree.*

shake /ʃeɪk/ *verb* (**shaking,** *past tense* **shook,** *past participle* **shaken**)
1 to move quickly from side to side, or up and down: *My hands were shaking from the cold.* | *She shook the rug to remove the dirt.*
2 shake hands to hold someone's hand in yours and move it up and down when you meet him or her
3 shake your head to move your head from side to side to say "no"

shall /ʃəl; *strong* ʃæl/ *verb*
used with I and we in questions when asking or suggesting something: *Shall I help you with that?*

shal·low /'ʃæloʊ/ *adjective*
going down only a short distance from the top or surface of something; not deep: *The swimming pool is shallow here.* ≫ compare DEEP

shame /ʃeɪm/ *noun* [U]
1 the feeling of being guilty or embarrassed when you have done something wrong: *The argument left me with a deep sense of shame.*
2 what a shame, it's a shame said when something is sad or disappointing, and you wish it were different: *What a shame that Mary could not be here!*
3 shame on you said when telling someone that he or she should be ashamed for doing something: *Shame on you for not helping him.*

sham·poo /ʃæm'pu/ *noun*
a liquid soap used for washing your hair

shape

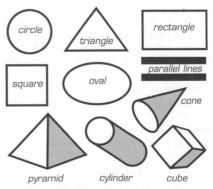

circle triangle rectangle

parallel lines

square oval cone

pyramid cylinder cube

shape¹ /ʃeɪp/ *noun*
1 the form of something: *She made a cake in the shape of a heart.*
2 the condition or health of something: *Our car is not in good shape.* | *I want to get back in shape.* (=become more healthy)

shape² *verb* (**shaping, shaped**)
to make something have a particular form: *He shaped the clay into a pot.*

share¹ /ʃɛr/ *verb* (**sharing, shared**)
1 to have or use something together with other people: *I share a house with two other girls.*
2 to divide something between two or more people: *We shared the cookies with them.*

share² *noun*
the part of something that is owned, done, or used by you: *What happened to my share of the money?*

shark /ʃɑrk/ *noun*
a large sea fish with a lot of sharp teeth

sharp

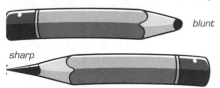

blunt

sharp

sharp /ʃɑrp/ *adjective*
1 having an edge that can cut things easily: *You need a sharp knife to cut the vegetables.* ≫ compare DULL
2 having a thin point: *My pencil is not sharp.*
3 a sharp change is very sudden and big: *There was a sharp increase in oil prices.*
4 able to think and understand things quickly: *He is a very sharp student.*
5 able to see or hear things that are far away: *An eagle has sharp eyes to help it find food.*
6 wearing good, clean clothes: *You look sharp today.*

sharp·en /'ʃɑrpən/ *verb*
to make something sharp: *Sharpening a knife takes time.*

sharp·en·er /'ʃɑrpənɚ/ *noun*
a tool or machine that makes knives, pencils etc. sharp

sharp·ly /'ʃɑrpli/ *adverb*
changing suddenly: *Prices have risen sharply.*

shat·ter /'ʃætɚ/ *verb*
to break suddenly into small pieces: *The glass fell to the floor and shattered.*

shave¹ /ʃeɪv/ *verb* (**shaving, shaved**)
to cut off hair very close from your face, legs, or body: *My father shaves every day.*

shave² *noun*
an act of shaving: *I need a shave.*

shav·er /'ʃeɪvɚ/ *noun*
a tool used for removing hair from your face, legs, or body

she /ʃi/ *pronoun*
the female person or animal that the sentence is about: *My sister's name is Lora, and she is nine years old.*

shear /ʃɪr/ *verb* (*past tense* **sheared**, *past participle* **shorn** or **sheared**)
to cut the wool off a sheep

shears /ʃɪrz/ *plural noun*
a tool like a large pair of scissors

she'd /ʃid/
1 she had: *I went to her house, but she'd already left.*
2 she would: *She'd like to meet you.*

shed¹ /ʃɛd/ *noun*
a small building in which you keep things

shed² *verb* (**shedding**, *past tense* **shed**, *past participle* **shed**)
to allow something to fall off, usually as part of a natural process: *Snakes shed their skin.*

sheep /ʃip/ *noun* (*plural* **sheep**)
a farm animal that is kept for its meat and wool

sheer /ʃɪr/ *adjective*
1 sheer joy, sheer luck etc. joy, luck etc. with no other feeling mixed with it: *The people were singing with sheer joy.*
2 very steep: *The ocean was a sheer drop from where we stood.*

sheet /ʃit/ *noun*
1 a thin flat piece of something: *I need a sheet of paper to write on.*
2 a large piece of thin cloth that you put on a bed

shelf /ʃɛlf/ *noun* (*plural* **shelves** /ʃɛlvz/)
a long flat board attached to a wall, on which you put or store things: *He took a cup from the shelf.*

she'll /ʃɪl, ʃil/
she will: *She'll be here at ten o'clock.*

shell /ʃɛl/ *noun*
the hard outer covering of a nut, egg, animal etc.

shel·ter¹ /'ʃɛltɚ/ *noun*
a place that protects you from bad weather or danger, or the protection that is given to you: *We took shelter in the basement from the storm.*

shelter² *verb*
to protect someone or something from bad weather or danger, or to stay in such a place: *The wall sheltered us **from** the wind.*

shep·herd /'ʃɛpɚd/ *noun*
someone who takes care of sheep

sher·iff /'ʃɛrɪf/ *noun*
the chief police officer in a COUNTY

she's /ʃiz/
1 she is. *She's very tall.*
2 she has: *She's got a new car.*

shield¹ /ʃild/ *noun*
something that protects someone or something from danger or harm: *The police carried large metal shields.*

shield² *verb*
to protect someone or something from being hurt or damaged: *He shielded his eyes **from** the sun.*

shift¹ /ʃɪft/ *verb*
to move something or to change your body's position: *She shifted in her chair.*

shift² *noun*
1 one of the periods in a day in which people are at work: *I'm on the night shift at the hospital.*
2 a change in the way people think about something: *A shift in public opinion surprised the government.*

shin /ʃɪn/ *noun*
the front part of your leg between your knee and your foot

shine /ʃaɪn/ *verb* (**shining**, *past tense* **shone** /ʃɑn/, *past participle* **shone**)
1 to produce light: *The sun is shining.*
2 to look bright and smooth: *The water shone in the moonlight.*
3 to point a light toward a particular place or direction: *Shine the light over here so I can see.*

shin·y /'ʃaɪni/ *adjective* (**shinier, shiniest**)
bright and smooth looking: *He wore a pair of shiny black boots.*

ship¹ /ʃɪp/ *noun*
a large boat that carries things on the ocean —see color picture on page 187

ship² *verb* (**shipping, shipped**)
to deliver goods to a place: *We can ship this anywhere in the country.*

ship·ment /'ʃɪpmənt/ *noun*
a load of goods being delivered, or the act of sending them

shirt /ʃɚt/ *noun*
a piece of clothing that covers the upper part of your body and your arms, and has buttons down the front —see color picture on page 190

shiv·er /'ʃɪvɚ/ *verb*
to shake because you are cold or afraid: *A dog shivered in the cold.*

shock¹ /ʃɑk/ *noun*
1 an unpleasant event that makes you very upset: *It was a great shock for him when his wife died.*
2 [U] the feeling of surprise or worry that you have when something unpleasant happens: *Everyone was in shock at the news of the flood.*
3 a painful feeling caused by electricity passing through your body: *The bad wires gave me a shock.*

shock² *verb*
to make someone feel very surprised or upset: *I was shocked when I heard about your accident.*

shock·ing /'ʃɑkɪŋ/ *adjective*
very upsetting and wrong: *We read about the shocking crime in the newspaper.*

shoe /ʃu/ *noun*
something you wear to cover your foot: *She gave me a pair of brown leather shoes.* —see color picture on page 190

shoe·lace /'ʃuleɪs/ *noun*
a long piece of string that you use to make your shoes fit tightly on your feet

shone /ʃoʊn/
the PAST TENSE and PAST PARTICIPLE of the verb **shine**

shook /ʃʊk/
the PAST TENSE of the verb **shake**

shoot¹ /ʃut/ *verb* (*past tense* **shot** /ʃɑt/, *past participle* **shot**)
1 to kill or injure someone or something with a gun: *Four people were shot in the attack.*
2 to fire a weapon at something or someone: *They were shooting into the crowd.*

3 to move quickly, or make something do this: *A severe pain shot through my leg.* | *The ball shot past my head.*

shoot² *noun*
a new part of a plant that is just starting to grow

shoot·ing /'ʃutɪŋ/ *noun*
the act in which someone is killed or injured by a gun

shop¹ /ʃɑp/ *noun*
a small store that sells a particular type of goods

shop² *verb* (**shopping, shopped**)
to go to stores to buy things: *We often shop at the mall.*

shop·ping /'ʃɑpɪŋ/ *noun* [U]
the activity of going to stores to buy things: *I like shopping for clothes.*

shopping mall /'.. ,./ *noun*
a very large building with a lot of stores inside it

shore /ʃɔr/ *noun*
the land at the edge of a large area of water: *We walked along the shore.*

short /ʃɔrt/ *adjective*
1 not long, a small distance from one end to the other: *He has short black hair.* ≫ compare LONG¹ —see picture at LONG¹
2 happening for only a little time, or for less time than usual: *The meeting was very short.*
3 not as tall as most people: *She's the short-est girl in the class.* ≫ compare TALL —see color picture on page 191
4 **be short of something** to not have enough of something: *I'm short of money right now.*

short·age /'ʃɔrtɪdʒ/ *noun*
a situation in which there is not enough of something: *The war led to a food shortage.*

short cut /'. ./ *noun*
a quicker way to do something or go some-where: *I know a short cut to the store.*

short·en /'ʃɔrtˀn/ *verb*
to become shorter, or make something short-er: *Do you want to shorten this dress?* ≫ compare LENGTHEN

short·ly /'ʃɔrtli/ *adverb*
very soon: *They should be here shortly.*

shorts /ʃɔrts/ *plural noun*
pants that end at or above the knee —see color picture on page 190

shot¹ /ʃɑt/
the PAST TENSE and PAST PARTICIPLE of the verb **shoot**

shot² *noun*
1 the act of firing a gun: *I heard two shots in the street.*
2 the act of putting medicine into your body using a needle: *Did you get your flu shot?*
3 a photograph: *He took a shot of the sunset.*
4 the act of throwing, hitting, or kicking a ball toward the place where you get a point in a game: *That was a good shot.*

shot·gun /'ʃɑtˀgʌn/ *noun*
a long gun, used for shooting animals and birds

should /ʃəd; *strong* ʃʊd/ *verb*
1 used when saying what your opinion is, or for asking for advice: *You should call him now.* | *Should I buy this bag?*
2 used for saying what you think will happen or what you think is true: *They should arrive soon.* | *It should be a good movie.*
3 used in sentences like **if** to say what may happen: *Should you buy the house, we can help you pay for it.*

shoul·der /'ʃoʊldɚ/ *noun*
one of the two parts of your body on each side of your neck where your arm is connected: *She put her head on his shoulder.*

shoulder bag /'.. ,./ *noun*
a small bag that hangs from your shoulder

should·n't /'ʃʊdnt/
should not: *You shouldn't eat so much chocolate.*

should've /'ʃʊdəv/
should have: *You should've told me that you would be late.*

shout¹ /ʃaʊt/ *verb*
1 to say something in a loud voice: *"Help! Help!," he shouted.*
2 **shout at someone** to say something in a loud voice to someone because you are angry: *Stop shouting at the children!*

shout² *noun*
a loud cry or call: *I heard a shout from the next room.*

shove /ʃʌv/ *verb*
to push someone or something using your hands: *He shoved the little girl and she fell over.*

shov·el¹ /'ʃʌvəl/ *noun*
a tool with a long handle and a wide end, used for digging or moving earth

shovel² *verb*

to dig or move earth using a shovel

show¹ /ʃoʊ/ *verb* (*past participle* **shown** /ʃoʊn/)

1 to let someone see something: *He showed me his new computer.*

2 to make it clear that something is true by giving facts or information: *The report shows that crime is rising.*

3 to tell someone how to do something: *Can you show me how to play the game?*

4 to go with someone and guide them to a place or around a place: *Thank you for showing us around the museum.*

5 if something shows, it can be seen or is easy to notice: *Don't worry, the stain on your dress doesn't show.*

6 to let other people notice something, for example your feeling or your knowledge: *Men aren't supposed to show their feelings.*

7 **show off** to try to make people notice or admire you: *No one likes him very much because he's always showing off.*

8 **show up** to arrive at a place where someone is waiting for you: *She showed up late for the game.*

9 **show something off** to make people notice something you have, especially because you are proud of it: *He drove to school to show off his new car.*

show² *noun*

1 a performance in a theater or on television that people watch: *This is my favorite TV show.*

2 a lot of things gathered together for people to see: *Many people went to the flower show.*

3 **for show** if you do something for show you do it in order to impress other people

show·er /ˈʃaʊə/ *noun*

1 when you wash yourself while standing under running water: *He's taking a shower.*

2 a thing that you stand under to wash yourself in running water, or the place where you get washed in this way: *The phone always rings when I'm in the shower.*

3 a short period of rain: *We may have some showers today.* —**shower** *verb*: *She showered and had breakfast.*

shown /ʃoʊn/

the PAST PARTICIPLE of the verb **show**

show-off /ˈ. ./ *noun*

someone who tries to make people notice or admire them: *He seemed only interested in impressing other people – even some of his friends now regard him as a show-off.*

shrank /ʃræŋk/

the PAST TENSE of the verb **shrink**

shred /ʃrɛd/ *noun*

a small piece that is cut or torn off something: *Michael tore the letter to shreds.* (=into small pieces)

shrewd /ʃrud/ *adjective*

good at understanding people and situations, so that you can get advantages for yourself

shriek /ʃrik/ *verb*

to make a high, loud sound because you are afraid, excited, or angry: *The crowd shrieked with delight.* —**shriek** *noun*

shrill /ʃrɪl/ *adjective*

unpleasant because it is too loud and high: *The teacher had rather a shrill voice.*

shrimp /ʃrɪmp/ *noun*

a small pink sea animal that you can eat

shrine /ʃraɪn/ *noun*

a holy place

shrink /ʃrɪŋk/ *verb* (*past tense* **shrank**, *past participle* **shrunk**)

to become smaller, or make something do this: *You shouldn't wash the dress in hot water. It'll shrink.*

shrub /ʃrʌb/ *noun*

a small bush

shrug /ʃrʌg/ *verb* (**shrugging, shrugged**)

to move your shoulders up and down to show that you do not know something or do not care about something: *When I asked Katie if she liked her new school, she just shrugged her shoulders.*

shrunk /ʃrʌŋk/

the PAST PARTICIPLE of the verb **shrink**

shud·der /ˈʃʌdə/ *verb*

when you shake especially because you are frightened, or cold: *The thought of going back there again made him shudder.*

shut /ʃʌt/ *verb* (**shutting**, *past tense* **shut**, *past participle* **shut**)

1 to close something, or to become closed: *Please shut the door.* | *The little boy shut his eyes and went to sleep.* ≫ compare OPEN²

2 **shut up!** a rude way of telling someone to stop talking: *Shut up! I'm trying to think!*

3 **shut (something) down** to stop working or operating, or make something stop working or operating: *A lot of factories have had to shut down.*

shut·ter /'ʃʌtɚ/ *noun*
one of a pair of covers on the outside of a window

shut·tle /'ʃʌtl̩/ *noun*
1 a vehicle that can fly into space and return to Earth, and can be used more than once
2 an airplane or bus that makes regular short trips between two places

shy /ʃaɪ/ *adjective* (**shier, shiest**)
nervous and embarrassed about talking to other people: *The child was shy and hid behind his mother.*

sick /sɪk/ *adjective*
1 not healthy; having a disease: *My father got sick last night.*
2 **be sick** to make food come up from your stomach and out of your mouth; VOMIT: *She was sick all over the floor.*
3 **feel sick** to feel that food might start coming up from your stomach and out through your mouth: *When the ship started to move I suddenly felt sick.*
4 **be sick of something** to be angry about something that has been happening for a long time: *I'm sick of having to clean up after him!*
5 **make someone sick** to make someone feel very angry and annoyed: *You make me sick! I hate you!*

sick·ness /'sɪknɪs/ *noun* [U]
the condition of being or feeling sick: *The people suffered from hunger and sickness.*

side /saɪd/ *noun*
1 one of the two parts that something is divided into: *the left side of the brain | They live on the other side of the town.*
2 the part of something that is not its front, back, top, or bottom: *He walked around to the side **of** the house.*
3 one of the flat surfaces of something: *Write on both sides **of** the paper. | A cube has six sides.*
4 the part of your body from your shoulder to the top of your leg: *I have a pain in my side.*
5 one of two people, teams, countries etc. in a game, argument, war etc.: *Neither side wants to give in.*
6 **by the side of** next to something: *She lives by the side of a big lake.*
7 **side by side** next to each other: *We sat side by side in the car.*

side·walk /'saɪdwɔk/ *noun*
a hard surface or path that you walk on next to a street: *Don't ride your bike on the sidewalk.*

side·ways /'saɪdweɪz/ *adverb*
1 toward one side: *He stepped sideways to let me pass.*
2 if something is facing sideways, the side is at the front: *We turned the table sideways for more room.*

sigh /saɪ/ *verb*
to breathe out loudly and slowly because you are tired, sad etc. —**sigh** *noun*

sight /saɪt/ *noun*
1 [U] the ability to see: *My grandmother is losing her sight.*
2 [U] when you see something: *I can't stand the sight of blood.*
3 something that is interesting to see because it is beautiful, large, unusual etc.: *The Space Needle is one of the most famous sights in Seattle.*
4 **catch sight of someone/something** to suddenly see someone or something: *She caught sight of him as she was walking past a restaurant.*

sight·see·ing /'saɪt,siɪŋ/ *noun* [U]
the activity of going to see famous or interesting places when you are visiting somewhere on vacation

sign¹ /saɪn/ *noun*
1 a piece of paper, metal etc. with words or pictures on it in a public place, that gives you information or instructions: *The sign said, "No Smoking." | He ignored the "stop" sign.*
2 a picture or shape that has a particular meaning: *A dollar sign looks like "$."*
3 something that shows that something exists, is starting to happen etc.: *Scientists believe they may have found signs **of** life on Mars.*

sign² *verb*
to write your name, for example at the end of a letter

sig·nal¹ /'sɪgnəl/ *noun*
a sound, action, or movement that tells you to do something: *Don't start until I give the signal.*

signal² *verb*
to make a movement or sound that tells someone to do something

sig·na·ture /'sɪgnətʃɚ/ *noun*
your name written in the way that you usually write it, for example on a letter, check etc.
≫ compare AUTOGRAPH

sig·nif·i·cance /sɪg'nɪfəkəns/ *noun*
the meaning or importance of something: *an*

event **of great** political significance (=very important)

sig·nif·i·cant /sɪg'nɪfəkənt/ adjective
noticeable and important: *There's been a significant change in people's attitudes to marriage.* —**significantly** adverb

sign lan·guage /'. ,../ noun [U]
a language that uses hand movements instead of spoken words, used by people who cannot hear

sign·post
/'saɪnpoʊst/ noun
a road sign that says which direction a place is in, or how far it is

AMERICAS EUROPE
NORTH POLE

si·lence
/'saɪləns/ noun [U]
when there is no sound and everything is completely quiet. *They worked in silence.*

si·lent /'saɪlənt/ adjective
not saying anything or not making any sound: *Simon was silent for a moment.* —**silently** adverb

silk /sɪlk/ noun [U]
a soft shiny cloth made from thin threads: *a silk shirt*

sil·ly /'sɪli/ adjective (sillier, silliest)
not serious or sensible: *What a silly question!* | *Don't pay attention to her. She's just being silly.* ≫ compare STUPID

sil·ver /'sɪlvɚ/ noun [U]
1 a soft shiny white metal used for rings, jewelry etc.
2 the color of this metal

sim·i·lar /'sɪmələ/ adjective
almost the same, but not exactly the same: *Our dresses are similar.* | *His interests are similar to mine.* ≫ compare ALIKE

sim·i·lar·i·ty /ˌsɪmə'læɹəti/ noun (plural similarities)
something that is the same about two people or things: *There are many similarities between English and German.* ≫ compare DIFFERENCE

sim·ple /'sɪmpəl/ adjective (simpler, simplest)
1 easy to understand: *The instructions are very simple.* ≫ compare DIFFICULT
2 not having a lot of decoration; plain: *She wore a simple blue dress.*

sim·pli·fy /'sɪmplə,faɪ/ verb (simplifying, simplified)
to make something easier to understand or do: *a simplified version of the book*

sim·ply /'sɪmpli/ adverb
1 only; just: *I simply wanted to help.*
2 used when you want to emphasize what you are saying; really: *What she said simply isn't true!*
3 in a way that is easy to understand: *Let me explain it simply.*

sin /sɪn/ noun
something that you should not do especially because it is against religious rules

since /sɪns/ adverb, preposition
at or from a time in the past until now: *I've been here since six o'clock.* | *She arrived in 1991 and has lived here ever since.* ≫ compare AGO, FOR

NOTE: Compare **for** and **since**. Use **for** when you are talking about a period of time such as a week, a month, a year, etc.: *I've been studying English for 3 years. I lived there for 6 months* (but I don't live there any more). Use **since** when you are talking about the exact moment in the past when something began: *I've been studying English since 1998.* **Since** always refers to something which began in the past but continues until now, so you must use it with the PRESENT PERFECT tense, not the past tense: *I've lived here since October.* (=I came to live here in October and I am still living here)

sin·cere /sɪn'sɪr/ adjective
honest and really meaning what you say: *Do you think he was being sincere?*

sin·cere·ly /sɪn'sɪrli/ adverb
1 in a true and honest way: *I sincerely hope that you succeed.*
2 **Sincerely,** something you write at the end of a formal letter before you write your name

sing /sɪŋ/ verb (past tense **sang** /sæŋ/, past participle **sung** /sʌŋ/)
to make musical sounds with your voice: *She sang a song.* | *I can hear the birds singing.*

sing·er /'sɪŋɚ/ noun
someone who sings: *an opera singer*

sin·gle¹ /'sɪŋgəl/ adjective
1 only one: *We lost the game by a single point.*

2 not married: *Are you married or single?*
3 for one person only: *a single room* ≫ compare DOUBLE[1] —see picture at BED
4 in single file in a line with one person behind the other: *Walk in single file, please.*

single[2] *noun*
a record with one song on each side: *Michael Jackson's latest single*

sin·gu·lar /'sɪŋgyələ/ *noun*
the singular the form of a word for only one person or thing: *"Dog" is the singular of "dogs".* ≫ compare PLURAL

sink[1] /sɪŋk/ *verb* (*past tense* **sank**, *past participle* **sank** *or* **sunk**)
1 if a ship or an object sinks, it moves down below the surface of the water toward the bottom: *The ship is sinking.* ≫ compare FLOAT
2 to move to a lower level: *The sun sank behind the mountain.*

sink[2] *noun*
a container in a kitchen or bathroom that you fill with water in which you wash dishes

sip[1] /sɪp/ *verb* (**sipping, sipped**)
to drink something slowly in small amounts: *She sipped her hot tea.*

sip[2] *noun*
a very small amount of a drink

sir /sə/ *noun*
1 a polite way to speak to a man whose name you do not know: *Can I help you, sir?*
2 Dear Sir used at the beginning of a formal letter to a man whose name you do not know

si·ren /'saɪrən/ *noun*
a thing that makes a loud warning sound, used on police cars, fire trucks etc.

sis·ter /'sɪstə/ *noun*
1 a girl who has the same parents as you: *My sister's much taller than I am.* ≫ compare BROTHER
2 a NUN

sister-in-law /'.. . ,./ *noun* (*plural* **sisters-in-law**)
1 the sister of your husband or wife
2 the wife of your brother

sit /sɪt/ *verb* (**sitting**, *past tense* **sat**, *past participle* **sat**)
1 to rest your body on something such as a chair: *Come and sit here.* | *The children sat around her in a circle.* ≫ compare RISE[1]
2 sit down to rest your body on something

such as a chair after you have been standing up: *Would you like to sit down?*
3 sit up to move into a sitting position after you have been lying down: *I sat up in bed when I heard the noise.*
4 sit around to rest for a long time and not do anything useful: *He just sits around the house and does nothing.*

site /saɪt/ *noun*
1 a place where something important or interesting happened: *the site of the battle*
2 a place where a building is being built or will be built: *a construction site*

sit·u·at·ed /'sɪtʃu,eɪṭɪd/ *adjective*
be situated to be in a particular place: *The hotel is situated next to the airport.*

sit·u·a·tion /,sɪtʃu'eɪʃən/ *noun*
the things that are happening at a particular time and place: *The political situation in the country is very dangerous.*

six /sɪks/ *adjective, noun*
the number 6

six·teen /,sɪk'stin‹ / *adjective, noun*
the number 16

sixth /sɪksθ/ *adjective, noun*
1 6th
2 one of six equal parts

six·ty /'sɪksti/ *adjective, noun*
the number 60

siz·a·ble /'saɪzəbəl/ *adjective* (*also* **sizeable**)
fairly large: *A sizable crowd turned up for the show.*

size /saɪz/ *noun*
how big or small something or someone is: *His room is the same size as mine.* | *Do you have any shoes in a size 5?*

skate[1] /skeɪt/ *verb* (**skating, skated**)
to move smoothly over ice or over ground wearing SKATEs: *She skated over the ice toward us.*

skate[2] *noun*
a special shoe with wheels or a blade fixed under it: *roller skates* | *ice skates*

skate·board /'skeɪtˈbɔrd/ *noun*
a short board with wheels under it that you stand on and ride along the ground for fun —see color picture on page 185

skat·ing /'skeɪṭɪŋ/ *noun* [U]
the activity or sport of moving over ice or over the ground wearing SKATEs: *Do you want to **go** skating with us?* —see color picture on page 184

skel·e·ton
/'skɛlətˀn/ *noun*
all the bones in an
animal or person

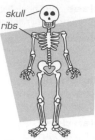

skull
ribs

the human skeleton

sketch¹ /skɛtʃ/
noun (plural
sketches)
a quick drawing that
does not have a lot of
details

sketch² *verb*
to draw a picture quickly and without a lot of
details

ski¹ /ski/ *noun (plural* **skis**)
one of a pair of long, narrow pieces of wood or
plastic that you wear on your boots to move
easily over snow

ski² *verb* (**skiing**, *past tense* **skied**, *past participle* **skied**)
to move over snow on SKIs: *We're* ***going*** *skiing
on Saturday.*

skid /skɪd/ *verb* (**skidding**, **skidded**)
to slide sideways suddenly on a wet surface:
The car skidded on the ice.

ski·ing /'ski-ɪŋ/ *noun* [U]
the activity or sport of moving over snow on
SKIs: *Do you like skiing?* —see color picture on
page 184

skill /skɪl/ *noun*
an ability to do something very well, especially
because you have learned it: *Everyone should
have some basic computer skills.*

skilled /skɪld/ *adjective*
having the knowledge or training to do something well: *skilled workers*

skill·ful /'skɪlfəl/ *adjective*
good at doing something well: *a skillful driver*
—**skillfully** *adverb*

skin /skɪn/ *noun*
the outer covering of a person, animal, vegetable, or fruit: *The drums are made from ani-
mal skins.* | *She has pale skin.* | *a banana skin*
≫ compare FLESH

skin·ny /'skɪni/ *adjective* (**skinnier**,
skinniest)
very thin or too thin: *Larry was very skinny as a
child.* ≫ compare SLIM

skip /skɪp/ *verb* (**skipping**, **skipped**)
1 to move forward with quick jumps from one

foot to the other: *The two girls were skipping
down the street.* —see color picture on page
189
2 to not do something that you should do: *Let's
skip that question and go on to the next one.*

skirt /skɚt/ *noun*
a piece of a woman's clothing that hangs down
from her waist and covers part of her legs
≫ compare DRESS² —see color picture on
page 190

skull /skʌl/ *noun*
the bones of a person's or animal's head —see
picture at SKELETON

sky /skaɪ/ *noun (plural* **skies**)
the space above the Earth where the sun,
moon, and stars are: *The sky is blue.*

skyscraper

sky·scrap·er /'skaɪˌskreɪpɚ/ *noun*
a very tall building in a city

slab /slæb/ *noun*
a large flat piece of something hard: *a concrete
slab*

slack /slæk/ *adjective*
1 hanging loosely: *The rope around the horse's
neck was slack.* ≫ compare TIGHT¹
2 not busy: *We're having a slack period at
work.*

slam /slæm/ *verb* (**slamming**, **slammed**)
to shut a door or window with a loud noise, or
to become shut: *He slammed the door angrily.* |
I heard the door slam.

slang /slæŋ/ *noun* [U]
informal spoken words used especially by a particular group of people, for example young people or people in the army

slant¹ /slænt/ *verb*
to slope to one side

slant² *noun*
a sloping position or angle: *The house sits on a
slant.*

slap¹ /slæp/ *verb* [slapping, slapped]
to hit someone or something with the flat inside part of your hand ≫ compare PUNCH¹

slap² *noun*
a quick hit with the flat inside part of your hand: *She gave him a slap on his face.*

slash /slæʃ/ *verb*
to cut something violently: *He slashed her throat with a knife.*

slaugh·ter¹ /'slɔtɚ/ *noun* [U]
1 when a lot of people are killed in a cruel way
2 when animals are killed for food

slaughter² *verb*
1 to kill a lot of people in a cruel way
2 to kill an animal for food

slave¹ /sleɪv/ *noun*
someone who is owned by another person and is not allowed to be free: *Millions of Africans were taken to America as slaves.*

slave² *verb*
to work very hard: *I spent all day slaving in the kitchen.*

slav·er·y /'sleɪvəri/ *noun* [U]
when people are kept as slaves and are not allowed to be free: *laws against slavery*

sled /slɛd/ *noun*
a small vehicle used, especially by children, to slide over snow

sleep¹ /slip/ *verb* [past tense slept /slɛpt/, past participle slept]
1 to rest with your eyes closed: *Did you sleep well last night?* —see also ASLEEP
2 **sleep together, sleep with someone** to have sex with someone you are not married to: *Are you sure they are sleeping together?*

sleep² *noun*
1 when you are resting with your eyes closed: *I need to get some sleep.* | *Sometimes he talks in his sleep.* (=while he is sleeping)
2 **go/get to sleep** to start sleeping: *It took me a long time to get to sleep.*

sleeping bag /'.. ,./ *noun*
a large warm bag for sleeping in, especially in a tent. —see color picture on page 188

sleep·less /'sliplɪs/ *adjective*
sleepless night a night when you cannot sleep because you are worried

sleep·y /'slipi/ *adjective* [sleepier, sleepiest]
tired and wanting to sleep: *I felt sleepy all day.*

sleet /slit/ *noun* [U]
a mixture of rain and snow

sleeve /sliv/ *noun*
the part of a piece of clothing that covers your arm: *shirts with short sleeves*

sleigh /sleɪ/ *noun*
a large vehicle pulled by animals, used for moving over snow

slen·der /'slɛndɚ/ *adjective*
thin in an attractive way: *long, slender arms*

slept /slɛpt/
the PAST TENSE and PAST PARTICIPLE of the verb sleep

slice¹ /slaɪs/ *noun*
a flat piece or bread, meat etc. cut from a larger piece: *a thin slice of cheese*

slice² *verb* [slicing, sliced]
(*also* **slice up**) to cut something into thin flat pieces: *I sliced the bread.*

slick /slɪk/ *adjective*
1 good at persuading people, often in a way that is a little dishonest: *a slick salesperson*
2 smooth and slippery: *The roads are slick with ice.*

slide¹ /slaɪd/ *verb* [sliding, past tense slid /slɪd/, past participle slid]
to move smoothly over a surface: *She slid across the ice.*

slide² *noun*
1 a tall structure with a slope for children to slide down
2 a small piece of film in a frame that shows a picture on a screen when you shine a light through it

slight /slaɪt/ *adjective*
small and not very important or serious: *There will be a slight delay.* | *a slight problem*

slight·ly /'slaɪtli/ *adverb*
a little: *He moved his head slightly.*

slim /slɪm/ *adjective* [slimmer, slimmest]
1 thin in an attractive way: *I wish I was as slim as Jackie.* —see colour picture on page 191
2 very small: *We have a slim chance of success.*

slime /slaɪm/ *noun* [U]
a thick slippery substance that looks or smells bad

sling /slɪŋ/ *noun*
a piece of cloth tied around your neck to sup-

port your arm when it is injured: *His arm has been **in a sling** for two weeks.*

slip¹ /slɪp/ *verb* (**slipping, slipped**)

1 to accidentally slide so that you fall: *He slipped on the ice and fell.*

2 to slide out of the correct position, or out of your hand: *The knife slipped and cut her finger.*

3 to put something somewhere quickly and without people seeing it: *He slipped the money into his pocket.*

4 **slip out/in/off** etc. to move somewhere quickly or quietly: *Casey slipped out of the room when no one was looking.*

5 **slip up** to make a mistake: *Someone slipped up and gave him the wrong medicine.*

slip² *noun*

1 a small piece of paper: *I have a slip of paper with her phone number on it.*

2 a piece of clothing that you wear under a dress or skirt

slip·per /'slɪpɚ/ *noun*

a soft shoe that you wear inside your house: *a pair of slippers*

slip·per·y /'slɪpəri/ *adjective*

smooth or wet and difficult to walk on or hold: *Be careful! The floor is very slippery.*

slit¹ /slɪt/ *noun*

a narrow cut in something

slit² *verb* (**slitting,** *past tense* **slit,** *past participle* **slit**)

to make a narrow cut in something: *I slit open the letter with a knife.*

slo·gan /'sloʊɡən/ *noun*

a short phrase that is easy to remember, used in advertisements and in politics

slope¹ /sloʊp/ *noun*

a surface that is higher at one end than the other: *a ski slope*

slope² *verb* (**sloping, sloped**)

if a surface slopes, it is higher at one end than the other: *The hill slopes down to the road.*

slop·py /'slɑpi/ *adjective* (**sloppier, sloppiest**)

1 not careful or neat enough: *Her writing is very sloppy and hard to read.*

2 very loose and not looking neat: *Wayne likes wearing big sloppy shirts.*

slot /slɑt/ *noun*

a long narrow hole in something: *Put the coins in this slot.*

slot ma·chine /'. .,./ *noun*

a machine in which you put a coin in order to play a game on it

slow /sloʊ/ *adjective*

1 not moving or happening quickly: *The bus travels at a slow speed.* » compare FAST¹

2 a clock or watch that is slow shows a time that is earlier than the correct time: *My watch is five minutes slow.*

slow down /,sloʊ 'daʊn/ *verb*

to go less fast than before: *Slow down. You're driving too fast!*

slow·ly /'sloʊli/ *adverb*

at a slow speed: *He writes very slowly.*

slug /slʌɡ/ *noun*

a small creature with a soft body and no legs, like a SNAIL —see picture at SNAIL

slug·gish /'slʌɡɪʃ/ *adjective*

moving or working more slowly than usual

slum /slʌm/ *noun*

an area of a city with old buildings in bad condition and many poor people

slump /slʌmp/ *verb*

to be sitting with the top part of your body leaning forward: *He slumped in the corner and slept.*

slur /slɚ/ *verb* (**slurring, slurred**)

to speak in a way that is not clear: *He was drunk and slurred his words.*

sly /slaɪ/ *adjective* (**slier, sliest**)

good at deceiving people to get what you want

smack /smæk/ *verb*

to hit someone with your open hand, especially as a punishment: *Be quiet or I'll smack you!* —**smack** *noun* » compare SLAP¹

small /smɔl/ *adjective*

1 not large in size or amount; little: *He lives on a small farm. | This bag is too small.* » compare BIG, LARGE

2 not important or serious: *There is a small problem with the tire.*

3 small children are very young —see color picture on page 191

smart /smɑrt/ *adjective*

intelligent; able to make good decisions: *He is a smart politician.*

smash /smæʃ/ *verb*

1 to break into small pieces, or make something do this: *The plate smashed to the floor. |*

The crowd smashed the windows of the store.
2 to hit something in a violent way: *He smashed his fist against the door.*

smear¹ /smɪr/ *verb*
to spread something sticky, dirty, or oily on something else: *The child's face was smeared with chocolate.*

smear² *noun*
a mark that is left when a substance is spread on something: *He had a black smear on his pants.*

smell¹ /smɛl/ *verb*
1 to have a particular smell: *The food smells good.* | *It smells like cigarettes in here.*
2 to use your nose to notice something: *He smelled the flowers.* | *I can smell gas.*

smell² *noun*
something that you notice using your nose: *There's a bad smell in here.* | *I like the smell of fresh bread.*

smell·y /'smɛli/ *adjective* (**smellier, smelliest**)
having a bad smell

smile¹ /smaɪl/ *verb* (**smiling, smiled**)
to show that you are happy or pleased by making the corners of your mouth turn up: *The baby smiled at me.*

smile² *noun*
an expression of happiness on your face

smoke¹ /smoʊk/ *noun* [U]
the white or black gas made by something burning

smoke² *verb* (**smoking, smoked**)
1 to breathe in smoke from a cigarette or PIPE: *Do you smoke?*
2 to make smoke: *The fire is still smoking.*

smok·er /'smoʊkɚ/ *noun*
someone who smokes cigarettes or a PIPE: *This part of the restaurant is for smokers.*

smok·ing /'smoʊkɪŋ/ *noun* [U]
the activity of using cigarettes or a PIPE: *Smoking is not allowed in school.*

smok·y /'smoʊki/ *adjective* (**smokier, smokiest**)
full of smoke: *We sat in a smoky room.*

smol·der /'smoʊldɚ/ *verb*
to burn slowly without a flame but with some smoke

smooth /smuð/ *adjective*
1 having a flat even surface: *She has very smooth skin.* ≫ compare ROUGH
2 without problems or difficulties: *We had a smooth trip all the way.*

smooth·ly /'smuðli/ *adverb*
well and without problems or difficulties: *Everything went smoothly at work.*

smoth·er /'smʌðɚ/ *verb*
1 to stop someone from breathing by putting something on his or her face
2 to put a large amount of something on something else: *The cake was smothered in chocolate.*

smudge¹ /smʌdʒ/ *noun*
a dirty mark —**smudgy** *adjective*

smudge² *verb*
if a substance such as ink or paint smudges or is smudged, it becomes messy or unclear because someone has touched or rubbed it: *Now look, you've smudged my drawing!* | *Your lipstick is smudged.*

smug·gle /'smʌgəl/ *verb* (**smuggling, smuggled**)
to take something secretly and illegally from one place to another, especially into another country: *They were trying to smuggle cocaine into the U.S.*

smug·gler /'smʌglɚ/ *noun*
someone who SMUGGLEs something: *Police caught the drug smugglers.*

snack¹ /snæk/ *noun*
a small amount of food that you eat between meals: *During the long journey, the children ate so many snacks, that they lost their appetite even for desserts.*

snack² *verb*
to eat a small amount of food between meals: *You'll get fat if you snack on cookies all the time.*

snack bar /'. ./ *noun*
a place where you can buy SNACKs

snag /snæg/ *noun*
a small difficulty or problem: *It's a great car, but the snag is, I can't afford it right now.*

snail /sneɪl/ *noun*
a small creature with a soft body and no legs, that has a round shell on its back

snail

snail   slug

snake /sneɪk/ *noun*
a long thin animal with no legs that slides across the ground —see color picture on page 183

snap¹ /snæp/ *verb* (**snapping, snapped**)
1 to break with a short loud noise: *The branch snapped under his foot.*
2 to suddenly speak to someone in an angry way: *I am sorry that I snapped **at** you.*
3 if a dog snaps at you, it tries to bite you

snap² *noun*
a short loud noise of something breaking: *I heard a snap, and the tree fell over.*

snarl /snɑrl/ *verb*
1 if an animal snarls, it makes a low angry sound and shows its teeth: *The two dogs snarled at each other, and then started fighting*
2 to say something in an angry way

snatch /snætʃ/ *verb*
to take something away from someone quickly and using force: *She snatched the book **from** my hands.*

sneak /snik/ *verb* (*past tense and past participle* **sneaked** *or* **snuck**)
to go somewhere quietly because you do not want people to see or hear you: *The boys sneaked out of school and went to the park.*

sneak·er /'snikɚ/ *noun*
a kind of light soft shoe used for sports —see color picture on page 190

sneer /snɪr/ *verb*
to smile or talk about someone in a way that shows you have no respect for them: *She sneered **at** the mention of his name.*

sneeze /sniz/ *verb* (**sneezing, sneezed**)
to suddenly make air come out of your nose and mouth, for example when you have a cold ≫ compare COUGH² —**sneeze** *noun*

sniff /snɪf/ *verb*
1 to take air into your nose in short breaths because you are sick or have been crying: *Stop sniffing and blow your nose!*
2 to smell something by taking air into your nose: *The dog sniffed the bone.*

snob /snɑb/ *noun*
someone who thinks he or she is better than other people who are not as rich or important

snooze¹ /snuz/ *verb* (**snoozing, snoozed**)
to sleep for a short time; DOZE: *Dad was snoozing in front of the fire.*

snooze² *noun*
a short, light sleep

snore /snɔr/ *verb* (**snoring, snored**)
to make a loud noise each time you breathe when you are sleeping

snow¹ /snoʊ/ *noun* [U]
soft white pieces of frozen water that fall from the sky when it is cold

snow² *verb*
if it snows, snow falls from the sky: *Look, it's snowing!*

snow·ball /'snoʊbɔl/ *noun*
a small ball made out of snow: *The children were throwing snowballs at each other.*

snow·board·ing /'snoʊ,bɔrdɪŋ/ *noun* [U]
a sport in which you travel on snow with your feet on a wide board. —see color picture on page 184

snow·flake /'snoʊfleɪk/ *noun*
a soft, white piece of frozen water that falls from the sky

snowflake/snowman

snow·man /'snoʊmæn/ *noun* (*plural* **snowmen**)
a figure like a man made out of snow

snow·y /'snoʊi/ *adjective* (**snowier, snowiest**)
snowing, or having a lot of snow: *The snowy weather will continue.*

snug /snʌg/ *adjective*
warm and comfortable

so /souː/ *adverb, adjective*
1 used to emphasize what you are saying: *The party was so boring! | You have been so nice to me!*
2 also: *Ann was there, and so was Mary.*
3 therefore: *I was very hungry, so I ate the cake.*
4 in order to do something or make something happen: *We got up early so we could go swimming.*
5 used for showing agreement: *"Look, it's raining!" "So it is."*
6 used when you are going to ask someone a question, or when you want to get someone's attention: *So, when did you move to Denver?*
7 so ... that used to emphasize something and say that is the reason for something else: *I was so tired that I fell asleep on the bus.*
8 or so used when you are not giving an exact number or amount: *The trip takes an hour or so. | She left a week or so ago.*
9 say so/tell someone so used to say that this is what someone says: *"How do you know?" "Peter told me so."*
10 so long used to say goodbye: *So long, John, I'll see you next week.*
11 and so on used after a list to say that there are other things that you have not mentioned: *My husband does all the cooking, cleaning and so on.*

soak /souk/ *verb*
1 to leave something in a liquid: *She soaked the dirty clothes in water*
2 to make something very wet: *The rain soaked through our coats.*

soaked /soukt/ *adjective*
very wet: *I am absolutely soaked!*

soak·ing /'soukɪŋ/ (also **soaking wet**) *adjective*
very wet: *My clothes are soaking wet.*

soap /soup/ *noun* [U]
a substance that you use with water to wash yourself: *She washed her hands with a bar of soap.*

soap op·e·ra /'. ,../ *noun*
a story on television about the lives and problems of a group of people

soar /sɔr/ *verb*
1 to fly high in the air

2 to rise quickly to a high level: *Prices are soaring again.*

sob /sab/ *verb* (**sobbing, sobbed**)
to cry while breathing in short sudden breaths

so·ber /'soubər/ *adjective*
not drinking too much alcohol; not drunk
≫ compare DRUNK[1]

soc·cer /'sakər/ *noun*
a game in which two teams of eleven players try to kick a ball between two posts at either end of a field. —see color picture on page 184

so·cia·ble /'souʃəbəl/ *adjective*
someone who is sociable is friendly and enjoys being with other people

so·cial /'souʃəl/ *adjective*
1 relating to the people who live in a place and the way they live together: *Social problems such as crime and jobs are not easy to solve.*
2 relating to the things that you do with other people for fun: *He has a lot of friends and a good social life.* —**socially** *adverb*

so·cial·ize /'souʃə,laɪz/ *verb* (**socializing, socialized**)
to spend time with other people in a friendly way

Social Se·cu·ri·ty /,.. .'.../ *noun* [U]
money paid by the government to people who are old or who cannot work

so·ci·e·ty /sə'saɪəṭi/ *noun* (*plural* **societies**)
a large group of people who live together and share the same laws, religions, ways of doing things etc.: *We're living in a multi-racial society.*

sock /sak/ *noun*
a soft piece of clothing you wear on your foot inside your shoe ≫ compare SHOE —see color picture on page 190

sock·et /'sakɪt/ *noun*
a place in the wall where you connect a piece of equipment to the electricity

so·fa /'soufə/ *noun*
a long comfortable chair on which two or more people sit

soft /sɔft/ *adjective*
1 not hard or firm, but easy to press: *The bed is nice and soft. | a soft cushion* ≫ compare HARD[1]
2 smooth and pleasant to touch: *She has very soft skin.*
3 quiet and pleasant: *He played some soft music on the guitar.*
4 not too bright: *I need a dress with soft colors.*

soft·ball /'sɔftbɔl/ *noun* [U]
a game similar to baseball, but played with a larger and softer ball

soft drink /'. ./ *noun*
a sweet drink that has BUBBLEs in it but no alcohol

soft·en /'sɔfən/ *verb*
to become softer, or make something do this: *This lotion will soften your skin.*

soft·ly /'sɔftli/ *adverb*
quietly; not too loud: *She spoke softly to him.*

soft·ware /'sɔft-wɛr/ *noun* [U]
a set of instructions that tells a computer what to do: *What type of software do you use?*
≫ compare HARDWARE

sog·gy /'sɑgi/ *adjective* (**soggier, soggiest**)
very wet and soft in a way that seems unpleasant: *The ground was very soggy.*

soil /sɔil/ *noun* [U]
the earth in which plants grow

so·lar /'soulər/ *adjective*
relating to the sun or the sun's power: *The building is heated using solar energy.*

solar sys·tem /'.. ,../ *noun*
the Earth and all the moons and PLANETs that move around the sun

sold /sould/
the PAST TENSE and PAST PARTICIPLE of the verb sell

sol·dier /'souldʒər/ *noun*
someone in the army

sole¹ /soul/ *noun*
the bottom of your foot or shoe

sole² *adjective*
only: *She is the sole owner of the company.* | *John was the sole survivor of the accident.*

sole·ly /'souli/ *adverb*
only; not involving anyone else: *I am solely responsible for the mistake.*

sol·emn /'sɑləm/ *adjective*
very serious or sad: *The funeral was a solemn event.* —**solemnly** *adverb*

sol·id¹ /'sɑlɪd/ *adjective*
1 hard and firm with no holes: *We had to dig through solid rock.* ≫ compare HOLLOW
2 made of one material all the way through: *The ring is solid gold.*

solid² *noun*
a substance that is hard, not a liquid or gas

so·lo /'soulou/ *adjective*
done alone, without anyone else helping you

so·lu·tion /sə'luʃən/ *noun*
the answer to a problem or question: *Has anyone found a solution **to** the problem?*

solve /sɑlv/ *verb* (**solving, solved**)
to find the answer to something: *Police are working to solve the crime.* (=to find out who did it)

some /səm; *strong* sʌm/ *pronoun, adverb*
1 an amount or number of something. Use "some" when you do not need to say exactly how much of something there is: *She opened the candy and gave me some.* | *Would you like some coffee?* ≫ compare ANY¹
2 a few of the people or things in a group: *Some girls are dancing; others are talking.* | *Some of my friends liked the movie.*
3 a little more or a little less than a particular amount or number: *The fire spread some twenty miles in two days.*

some·bod·y /'sʌm,bɑdi, -,bʌdi/ *pronoun*
another word for SOMEONE

some·how /'sʌmhau/ *adverb*
1 in some way, although you do not know how: *We will get the money somehow.*
2 for some reason that you do not understand: *Somehow, I do not trust him.*

some·one /'sʌmwʌn/ *pronoun*
1 used to mention a person, without saying who the person is: *Be careful! Someone could get hurt.*
2 **someone else** a different person: *I thought that was Gary, but it was someone else.*
≫ compare ANYBODY

somersault

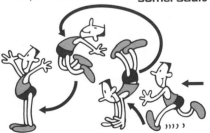

som·er·sault /'sʌmər,sɔlt/ *noun*
when you turn your body in the air so that your feet go over your head and then touch the ground —see color picture on page 189

some·thing /'sʌmθɪŋ/ *pronoun*
a word you use to talk about a thing without saying its name, or without saying exactly what it is: *There is something in my eye.* | *She bought something to eat.* ≫ compare ANYTHING

some·time /'sʌmtaɪm/ *adverb*
at some time in the past or the future: *I hope I'll see you again sometime.*

some·times /'sʌmtaɪmz/ *adverb*
at some times, but not always: *Sometimes I help my mother clean the house.*

some·where /'sʌmwɛr/ *adverb*
in or to a place: *At last we found somewhere to park the car.* | *Ellen's looking for somewhere to live.* ≫ compare ANYWHERE

son /sʌn/ *noun*
your male child: *I have a son and a daughter.*

> NOTE: The word **son** is used when you are talking about a male child only. Compare the questions: *Do you have any sons?* (=do you have any male children) and *Do you have any children?* (=do you have any sons or daughters)

song /sɔŋ/ *noun*
a piece of music: *What's your favorite song?*

son-in-law /'. . ,./ *noun* (*plural* sons-in-law)
the husband of your daughter

soon /sun/ *adverb*
1 in a short time from now: *Dinner will be ready soon.* | *Come and see me soon.*
2 as soon as immediately after something has happened: *I called as soon as I heard the news.* | *She came as soon as she had finished work.*
3 as soon as possible as quickly as possible: *I'll get the car fixed as soon as possible.*
4 sooner or later said when you think something will definitely happen: *Sooner or later, he will find out the truth.*
5 too soon too early: *It's too soon to know if she will get better.*

> NOTE: Compare these sentences: *I should go to bed* **soon** (=in a short time from now). *I should go to bed* **early** (=before the usual time). Compare also **soon** and **quickly**: *Do it* **soon** (=do it in a short time from now). *Do it* **quickly** (=do it fast).

soot /sʊt/ *noun* [U]
the black powder left by smoke when something burns

soothe /suð/ *verb* (**soothing, soothed**)
1 to make someone feel less worried or angry: *She did her best to soothe their fears.*
2 to make something less painful: *The medicine will soothe a sore throat.*

so·phis·ti·cat·ed /sə'fɪstə,keɪt̬ɪd/ *adjective*
designed in a skillful and often complicated way: *sophisticated weapons*

soph·o·more /'safmɔr/ *noun*
a student in the second year of high school or college

sore¹ /sɔr/ *adjective*
painful: *My feet are sore.*

sore² *noun*
a painful place on your skin, especially one caused by a disease

sor·ry /'sari, 'sɔri/ *adjective* (**sorrier, sorriest**)
1 used when you feel ashamed or unhappy about something bad that you have done: *I'm sorry that I lied to you.*
2 used when you have touched or interrupted someone by mistake: *I'm sorry, did I step on your foot?*
3 disappointed about something, or wishing that something had not happened: *I'm sorry that you can't come to the party.*
4 feel sorry for someone to feel pity for someone because he or she is in a bad situation: *I couldn't help feeling sorry for her.*

sort¹ /sɔrt/ *noun*
1 a type of person or thing etc.: *What sort of material is it made of?*
2 sort of a little; slightly: *I feel sort of tired today.*

sort² *verb*
1 to put things in a particular order or group: *Letters are sorted according to where they are being sent.*
2 sort something out (a) to find an answer to a problem: *We have a few problems to sort out.* (b) to organize something that is messy or in the wrong order

so-so /'. ./ *adjective, adverb*
neither very good nor very bad: *"Did you like the book?" "So-so."*

sought /sɔt/
the PAST TENSE and PAST PARTICIPLE of the verb
seek

soul /soʊl/ *noun*
the part of a person that contains their deepest
thoughts and feelings, which many people
believe continues to exist after death

sound¹ /saʊnd/ *noun*
something that you hear: *the sound of birds
singing* » compare NOISE

NOTE: **Sound** is the general word for
anything that you hear, e.g. *the sound of
music, the sound of a baby crying*. A **noise**
is usually something which is loud and not
nice: *Stop making that terrible noise!*

sound² *verb*
1 to seem: *That sounds like a good idea.* | *It
sounds like you are upset.*
2 to make a sound: *The bells sounded.*

sound³ *adjective*
1 practical and based on good judgment: *a
sound decision*
2 in good condition: *The floor of the old house
was perfectly sound.*

sound⁴ *adverb*
sound asleep completely asleep: *The baby is
sound asleep.*

sound·ly /ˈsaʊndli/ *adverb*
sleep soundly to sleep well without waking up

soup /sup/ *noun*
a hot liquid food with pieces of meat, fish, or
vegetables in it

sour /saʊɚ/ *adjective*
1 having a strong taste like LEMON or VINEGAR
2 not fresh, having a bad smell: *The milk has
gone sour.*

source /sɔrs/ *noun*
the person, place etc. where something comes
from: *The river is the source of all our water.* |
Her book is a good source of information.

south /saʊθ/ *noun, adjective, adverb*
the direction that is opposite of north: *Mexico
is south of the U.S.* | *We live on the south side
of the city.* | *South America*

south·east /ˌsaʊθˈist◂/ *noun, adjective,
adverb*
the direction that is between south and east:
The wind is coming from the southeast.
—southeastern *adjective*

south·ern /ˈsʌðɚn/ *adjective*
in or from the south part of an area, country
etc.: *southern California* | *Do you like southern
cooking?*

South Pole /ˌ. ˈ./ *noun*
the South Pole the place that is the most
southern point in the world, where it is very cold

south·west /ˌsaʊθˈwɛst◂/ *noun,
adjective, adverb*
the direction that is between south and west:
The town is southwest of here. **—southwestern**
adjective

sou·ve·nir /ˌsuvəˈnɪr, ˈsuvəˌnɪr/ *noun*
something that you buy or keep to help you
remember a place or an event

sow /soʊ/ *verb (past participle* **sown** /soʊn/ *or*
sowed)
to put seeds in the ground so that they will grow
into plants

space /speɪs/ *noun*
1 [U] the empty area away from the Earth,
where the sun and stars are
2 an empty area that can be used for something: *There is not enough space for more fur-
niture.* | *I need to find a parking space for the
car.*

space·craft /ˈspeɪs-kræft/
(*also* **spaceship**) *noun*
a vehicle that can travel in space

space shut·tle /ˈ. ˌ./ *noun*
a type of space vehicle that can carry people
into space and then return to the Earth to be
used again

spa·cious /ˈspeɪʃəs/ *adjective*
having a lot of space for you to use: *The car is
big and spacious.*

spade /speɪd/ *noun*
a tool with a short handle and a flat metal end
used for digging

spa·ghet·ti /spəˈgɛti/ *noun* [U]
an Italian food that consists of long thin pieces
of food, which look like strings

span¹ /spæn/ *noun*
the amount of time during which something
exists or happens: *The library was built over a
span of two years.*

span² *verb* [**spanning, spanned**]
to include all of a particular period of time: *Her
singing career spanned the 1970s.*

spank /spæŋk/ *verb*
to hit a child on the BUTTOCKs with an open hand

spare¹ /spɛr/ *adjective*
1 a spare key, tire, room etc. is an extra one that you keep or have in case you need it: *a spare tire* | *You can stay in the spare bedroom.*
2 something that is spare is not being used and is available for another person to use: *Are there any spare seats?*
3 spare time time when you are not working or busy: *He paints pictures in his spare time.*

spare² *verb* (**sparing, spared**)
to be able to give or lend something: *Can you spare me ten dollars?*

spark /spɑrk/ *noun*
a very small piece of fire that comes from a larger fire

spar·kle /'spɑrkəl/ *verb* (**sparkling, sparkled**)
to shine with bright points of light: *The diamond sparkled in the light.*

spar·row /'spæroʊ/ *noun*
a small common brown bird

spat /spæt/
the PAST TENSE and PAST PARTICIPLE of the verb **spit**

speak /spik/ *verb* (*past tense* **spoke** /spoʊk/, *past participle* **spoken** /'spoʊkən/)
1 to say words to someone: *I need to speak to you about something.* | *She could hardly speak.*
2 to be able to talk in a particular language: *He speaks English and German.*
3 speak up to say something more loudly: *Could you speak up, please?*

speak·er /'spikɚ/ *noun*
1 someone who talks to a large group of people about something: *Most of the speakers at the meeting were women.*
2 the part of a radio, television etc. where the sound comes out

spear /spɪr/ *noun*
a long thin weapon with a pointed end, which you throw

spe·cial /'spɛʃəl/ *adjective*
1 better or more important than ordinary things: *She wants to go someplace special on her birthday.*
2 different from what is usual, and intended for a particular purpose or person: *a special school for deaf children*

spe·cial·ist /'spɛʃəlɪst/ *noun*
someone who knows a lot about a particular subject: *a heart specialist*

spe·cial·ize /'spɛʃə,laɪz/ *verb* (**specializing, specialized**)
to limit your study, business etc. to one particular type of thing, so that you know a lot about it: *She specializes in children's diseases.*

spe·cial·ly /'spɛʃəli/ *adverb*
1 for one purpose: *The car is specially made to carry a lot of weight.*
2 more than usual; especially: *I wanted to go there specially for you.*

spe·cies /'spiʃiz, -siz/ *noun* (*plural* **species**)
a group of plants or animals of the same type

spe·cif·ic /spɪ'sɪfɪk/ *adjective*
1 a particular type of person or thing: *What are the specific issues we need to discuss?*
2 saying clearly and exactly what you mean: *Can you be more specific about your plans?*

spe·cif·i·cal·ly /spɪ'sɪfɪkli/ *adverb*
1 for a particular type of person or thing: *The movie is specifically for children.*
2 clearly and exactly: *I specifically told you not to do that.*

spec·i·men /'spɛsəmən/ *noun*
a small amount of something that is used as an example of what the whole thing is like: *The doctor took a specimen of blood from her arm.*

speck /spɛk/ *noun*
a very small piece of something: *I have a speck of dust in my eye.*

spec·tac·u·lar /spɛk'tækyəlɚ/ *adjective*
very impressive or exciting: *There's a spectacular view of the mountains.*

spec·ta·tor /'spɛkteɪtɚ/ *noun*
someone who watches a game, event etc.

sped /spɛd/
the PAST TENSE and PAST PARTICIPLE of the verb **speed**

speech /spitʃ/ *noun*
1 (*plural* **speeches**) a talk given to a group of people: *The President gave a speech to Congress.*
2 [U] the ability to speak, or the way someone speaks: *She lost the power of speech.* (=she became unable to speak)
3 freedom of speech/free speech the right to say or write what you want

spider

speed¹ /spid/ *noun*
how fast something moves: *The car was traveling at a high speed.* (=very fast)

speed² *verb* [*past tense and past participle* **speeded** *or* **sped** /spɛd/]
1 to move quickly: *The car sped off into the distance.*
2 **speed up** to move or happen faster: *We had to speed up to pass the slower cars.*
3 **be speeding** to be driving a vehicle faster than the legal limit

speed·boat /'spidboʊt/ *noun*
a small boat that can go very fast

speed lim·it /'. ,../ *noun*
the fastest speed that you are allowed to travel on a particular road: *There is a 40 mile an hour speed limit here.*

spell¹ /spɛl/ *verb* [*past tense* **spelled** *or* **spelt** /spɛlt/]
to say or write the letters of a word in the correct order: *How do you spell "embarrassed"?*

spell² *noun*
a set of magic words used for making something happen

spell·ing /'spɛlɪŋ/ *noun*
1 the ability to spell words correctly: *My spelling's terrible.* (=I am very bad at it)
2 the correct way of writing a word: *The American spelling is different from the British one.*

spend /spɛnd/ *verb* [*past tense* **spent**, *past participle* **spent** /spɛnt/]
1 to use your money to buy or pay for something: *How much money do you spend each week?*
2 to use time doing something: *I spent an hour writing this letter.*

sphere /sfɪr/ *noun*
a solid round shape like a ball

spice /spaɪs/ *noun*
a seed, root, powder etc. from a plant, used for giving a strong or hot taste to food: *The sauce had lots of spices in it.* ≫ compare HERB

spic·y /'spaɪsi/ *adjective* [**spicier**, **spiciest**]
having a strong, hot taste: *I don't like spicy food.* ≫ compare MILD

spi·der /'spaɪdɚ/ *noun*
a small creature with eight legs, that uses threads from its body to make a WEB (=a kind of net for catching other insects)

spied /spaɪd/
the PAST TENSE and PAST PARTICIPLE of the verb **spy**

spike /spaɪk/ *noun*
a thin sharp piece of metal: *The fence has spikes on the top.*

spill /spɪl/ *verb*
if a liquid spills or you spill it, it goes over the edge of a container: *I spilled coffee all over my shirt.*

spin /spɪn/ *verb* [**spinning**, **spun** /spʌn/]
1 to turn around very fast: *The wheels were spinning around.*
2 to make thread by twisting cotton, wool etc. together

spin·ach /'spɪnɪtʃ/ *noun* [U]
a vegetable with large dark green leaves

spine /spaɪn/ *noun*
the bones of your back —**spinal** *adjective*

spinning wheel /'.. ,./ *noun*
a wheel used in past times to make thread from wool

spi·ral /'spaɪrəl/ *noun*
a shape that goes around and around as it goes up

spir·it /'spɪrɪt/ *noun*
1 a person's mind, including attitudes, thoughts and feelings: *I'm 85, but I still feel young in spirit.*
2 **spirits** a strong alcoholic drink such as WHISKEY
3 a thing like a person which does not have a physical body, for example a ghost: *the spirits of the dead*

spir·i·tu·al /'spɪrɪtʃuəl, -tʃəl/ *adjective*
relating to the spirit and not the body or mind

spit /spɪt/ *verb* [**spitting**, *past tense* **spat** *or* **spit**, *past participle* **spat** /spæt/]
to force a small amount of liquid or food out of your mouth: *He spat on the floor.*

spite /spaɪt/ *noun* [U]

1 in spite of something although something else is happening or is true: *We went out in spite of the rain.*

2 the feeling of wanting to hurt or annoy someone: *She refused to see him out of spite.*

splash¹ /splæʃ/ *noun* (*plural* **splashes**)

the sound made by something falling into or hitting water: *She jumped into the river with a big splash.*

splash² *verb*

to move or hit water in a noisy way and make someone or something wet: *The children were splashing each other in the pool.*

splen·did /'splɛndɪd/ *adjective*

excellent or impressive: *We have a splendid view from our window.*

splin·ter /'splɪntɚ/ *noun*

a small sharp piece of wood, glass, or metal: *I have a splinter in my finger.*

split¹ /splɪt/ *verb* (**splitting,** *past tense* **split,** *past participle* **split**)

1 to tear or break something, especially from one end to the other: *We split the wood into thin pieces.* | *My pants split when I sat down.*

2 (*also* **split up**) to divide something into parts: *We split the money between us.*

split² *noun*

a long straight hole in something: *I have a split in my dress.*

spoil /spɔɪl/ *verb*

1 to damage something so that it is less useful or enjoyable: *His actions spoiled our evening.*

2 to be too kind to a child and give him or her too much attention so that he or she behaves badly: *You should not spoil the children.*

spoiled /spɔɪld/ *adjective*

rude and behaving badly because of being given too much money, attention etc.: *Tim is a very spoiled boy.*

spoke¹ /spoʊk/

the PAST TENSE of the verb **speak**

spoke² *noun*

one of the thin metal pieces that join the outer ring of a wheel to the center

spok·en /'spoʊkən/

the PAST PARTICIPLE of the verb **speak**

sponge /spʌndʒ/ *noun*

a soft sea animal, or a substance like it used for washing something

spool /spul/ *noun*

an object like a small wheel around which you put thread, wire etc.

spoon /spun/ *noun*

an instrument with a handle and a round end used for eating liquids, cooking etc.: *You eat soup with a spoon.*

spoon·ful /'spunfʊl/ *noun* (*plural* **spoonsful** *or* **spoonfuls**)

the amount that a spoon holds: *You must take two spoonfuls of medicine.*

sport /spɔrt/ *noun*

a game or competition in which you use your body, such as tennis or baseball: *What is your favorite sport?* | *I'm no good at sports.*

sports car /'. ./ *noun*

a fast car, often with a roof that can open

spot¹ /spɑt/ *noun*

1 a small mark on something: *I see spots of paint on the floor.*

2 a small round area of color: *Our dog is brown with black spots.*

3 a place: *It's a very pretty vacation spot.*

spot² *verb* (**spotting, spotted**)

to see or notice someone or something: *I spotted you at the party.*

spot·less /'spɑtlɪs/ *adjective*

completely clean: *She keeps her room spotless.*

spout /spaʊt/ *noun*

an opening in a container through which liquid comes out

sprain /spreɪn/ *verb*

to damage a part of your body by turning it suddenly: *He sprained his ankle when he fell.*

sprang /spræŋ/

the PAST TENSE of the verb **spring**

spray¹ /spreɪ/ *verb* (**spraying, sprayed**)

to make a liquid come out of something in very small drops: *He sprayed water on the flowers.*

spray² *noun* (*plural* **sprays**)

liquid that comes out of a container in small drops: *Can I use your hair spray?*

spread /sprɛd/ *verb* (spreading, spread)
1 (*also* **spread out**) to open something so that it covers a wide area: *Spread out the map on the table.*
2 to get bigger by having an effect on a larger area: *The disease spread through the town.*
3 to make something known to a lot of people: *The news of her death spread quickly.*
4 to cover something thinly: *She spread butter on the bread.*

spring¹ /sprɪŋ/ *noun*
1 the season between winter and summer, when plants start to grow again: *The show opens in the spring.*
2 a place where water comes up from the ground
3 a twisted piece of metal wire that will return to its usual shape after it is pressed

spring² *verb* (past tense **sprang** /spræŋ/, past participle **sprung** /sprʌŋ/)
to jump suddenly: *The cat sprang out of the chair.*

sprin·kle /'sprɪŋkəl/ *verb* (sprinkling, sprinkled)
to let small drops or pieces fall on the surface of something: *She sprinkled sugar on the cake.*

sprout¹ /spraʊt/ *verb*
to start to grow: *The seeds are beginning to sprout.*

sprout² *noun*
a new growth on a plant

sprung /sprʌŋ/
the PAST PARTICIPLE of the verb **spring**

spun /spʌn/
the PAST TENSE and PAST PARTICIPLE of the verb **spin**

spy¹ /spaɪ/ *noun* (plural **spies**)
someone whose job is to watch people secretly in order to discover facts or information about them: *Everyone was surprised to find there was a spy among them.*

spy² *verb* (spying, spied)
to watch people secretly in order to discover facts or information about them: *She's been spying on the neighbors.*

square¹ /skwɛr/ *noun*
1 a shape with four straight sides of equal length —see picture at SHAPE¹
2 an open place in a town with buildings all around it

square² *adjective*
having four straight sides of equal length: *The window was square.*

squash¹ /skwɑʃ, skwɔʃ/ *noun*
1 a large fruit such as a PUMPKIN, eaten like a vegetable
2 [U] an indoor game played with a ball and RACKETs

squash² *verb*
to press something flat, often causing damage: *The fruit at the bottom had been squashed.*

squeak /skwik/ *verb*
to make a short high noise: *My chair is squeaking.* —**squeak** *noun*

squeal¹ /skwil/ *verb*
to make a long loud cry or sound: *Pigs squeal.*

squeal² *noun*
a long loud cry: *She gave a squeal of surprise.*

squeeze /skwiz/ *verb* (squeezing, squeezed)
1 to press something firmly, especially with your hand: *He squeezed an orange to get the juice out.*
2 to try to make a person or thing fit into a small space: *We can squeeze one more person into the car.* —**squeeze** *noun*

squid /skwɪd/ *noun*
a sea creature with a long soft body and ten arms

squir·rel /'skwɚəl, 'skwʌrəl/ *noun*
a small gray or brown animal with a thick hairy tail, that lives in trees and eats nuts

squirt /skwɚt/ *verb*
to make a liquid come out of a narrow hole quickly: *He squirted the sauce from a bottle.*

St.
1 a short way to write the word SAINT
2 a short way to write the word **street**

stab /stæb/ *verb* (stabbing, stabbed)
to push a sharp object into someone or something using force: *He stabbed her with a knife.*

sta·ble¹ /'steɪbəl/ *noun*
a building where horses are kept

stable² *adjective*
not likely to move or change; steady: *Is the ladder stable?* | *We need a stable government.*

stack¹ /stæk/ *noun*
a neat pile of things: *A stack of books is by the door.*

stack² *verb*
to put things into a neat pile: *Stack the dishes in the sink.*

sta·di·um /'steɪdiəm/ *noun*
a large outdoor sports field with many rows of seats around it: *Have you seen the football stadium?*

staff /stæf/ *noun*
a group of people who work together for an organization: *All the staff members of the school came to the meeting.*

stage /steɪdʒ/ *noun*
1 a particular time or state in a long process: *The next stage is getting the book to the printer.* | *The disease is still in its early stages.*
2 the part of a theater where the actors stand and perform

stag·ger /'stægɚ/ *verb*
to walk in an unsteady way, as if you are going to fall: *The old man staggered down the street.*

stain¹ /steɪn/ *verb*
to make a mark on something that is difficult to remove: *The coffee stained his shirt.*

stain² *noun*
a mark on something that is difficult to remove: *I have grass stains on my pants.*

stair·case /'sterkeɪs/ *noun*
a set of stairs inside a building: *She sat at the top of the staircase.*

stairs /sterz/ *plural noun*
a set of steps that go from one level of a building to another: *He ran up the stairs.*

stale /steɪl/ *adjective*
not fresh, tasting old and dry: *No one eats stale bread.*

stalk /stɔk/ *noun*
the tall, main part of a plant —see picture at ROSE²

stall /stɔl/ *noun*
a small enclosed area in a room, for washing or using the toilet

stam·mer /'stæmɚ/ *verb*
to repeat the first sound of a word because you speak with difficulty: *"Th-th-thank you," he stammered.* ≫ compare STUTTER

stamp¹ /stæmp/ *noun*
1 a small piece of paper that you stick on an envelope or a package to show how much you have paid to send it —see picture at ENVELOPE

2 an instrument that you press onto paper to make a mark, or the mark that is made

stamp² *verb*
1 to lift your foot and put it down hard on something: *He stamped on the insect.*
2 to put a word or sign on something using a special tool

stand¹ /stænd/ *verb* (*past* **stood** /stʊd/)
1 to be upright on your feet: *I had to stand all the way home on the bus.*
2 to move so that you are on your feet: *All the children stood up.* | *Please stand for the reading.*
3 to be in a certain place: *The house stands at the top of the hill.*
4 to not change, to remain in a particular state or condition: *We are standing firm in our decision.*
5 to be able to accept and deal with something difficult: *I can't stand the pain.*
6 **stand back, stand aside** to stand farther away from something: *She stood back to let me pass.*
7 **can't stand** to dislike something or someone very much: *I can't stand getting up early.* | *We can't stand him!*
8 **stand by** (a) to do nothing to help someone or to stop something unpleasant from happening: *Most people stood by and watched the attack.* (b) to be ready to help if someone needs you: *Doctors are now standing by.*
9 **stand for something** to be a short form of a word or phrase: *What does PLO stand for?*
10 **stand up for someone or something** to say that someone or something is good or right: *You should always stand up for yourself.*

stand² *noun*
a small piece of furniture used for supporting something: *Where is my music stand?*

stan·dard¹ /'stændɚd/ *noun*
1 a level of quality or skill that is considered acceptable: *Your work must be of a high standard.*
2 the idea of what is normal, used for making comparisons to something else: *By American standards, this is a small house.*

standard² *adjective*
usual or normal: *Is this a standard practice?*

stank /stæŋk/
the PAST TENSE of the verb **stink**

sta·ple¹ /'steɪpəl/ *noun*
a small thin piece of metal with ends that bend around, used to hold pieces of paper together

staple² *verb*
to fasten papers together with a STAPLE

star¹ /stɑr/ *noun*
1 a bright point of light that you can see in the sky at night —see color picture on page 192
2 a shape with five or six points, used as a sign
3 a famous actor, singer etc.: *I want to be a movie star.*

star² *verb* (**starring, starred**)
to act as the most important person in a movie etc.: *We saw a movie starring Charlie Chaplin.*

stare /stɛr/ *verb* (**staring, stared**)
to look at someone or something for a long time without moving your eyes: *Are you staring **at** me?*

start¹ /stɑrt/ *verb*
1 to begin doing something: *If you are ready, you can start your work.* | *The children started singing.* ≫ compare FINISH¹, STOP¹
2 start over to begin doing something again from the beginning so you can correct what you did wrong the first time

start² *noun*
the beginning of an activity, event, or situation: *I don't want to miss the start of the show.*

start·le /'stɑrtl/ *verb* (**startling, startled**)
to make someone suddenly surprised or shocked: *You startled me when you shouted.*

star·va·tion /stɑr'veɪʃən/ *noun* [U]
death or feeling very weak caused by not having enough to eat

starve /stɑrv/ *verb* (**starving, starved**)
1 to die or suffer because you do not have enough to eat ≫ compare FAST³
2 be starving to be very hungry: *I'm starving! When is dinner?*

state¹ /steɪt/ *noun*
1 the condition of something; how good, bad etc. it is: *He's **in a state of** shock.*
2 one of the areas of a country that has a government: *There are 50 states in the U.S.*
3 a country or its government: *The heads of state will meet tomorrow.*

state² *verb* (**stating, stated**)
to say something in a formal way or on a formal occasion: *He stated that he had never seen the woman before.*

state·ment /'steɪtmənt/ *noun*
something that is said in a formal way or on a formal occasion: *The man **made a** statement **to** the police.*

states·man /'steɪtsmən/ *noun* (*plural* **statesmen** /-mɛn/)
an important leader in a government

sta·tion /'steɪʃən/ *noun*
1 a place where buses or trains stop: *I'll meet you at the bus station.*
2 a building for a particular type of work: *There is always someone at a police station.*

sta·tion·a·ry /'steɪʃəˌnɛri/ *adjective*
not moving; still: *The car was stationary when the accident happened.*

sta·tion·er·y /'steɪʃəˌnɛri/ *noun* [U]
paper that is used for writing letters

stat·ue /'stætʃu/ *noun*
a shape of a person or animal made of stone, metal, or wood

stay /steɪ/ *verb* (**staying, stayed**)
1 to continue to be in a particular place, state, job etc.: *Stay here. I'll be right back.* | *It stayed cold all night.*
2 to live in a place as a guest for a short time: *They're staying at a hotel.*

stead·i·ly /'stɛdɪli/ *adverb*
at a speed or level that does not change very much: *We drove steadily at 30 miles an hour.*

stead·y /'stɛdi/ *adjective, adverb* (**steadier, steadiest**)
1 firmly in one place; not moving: *Hold the chair steady while I stand on it.*
2 staying at the same level, speed etc. over a period of time: *He has a steady job.*

steak /steɪk/ *noun*
a thick flat piece of meat or fish

steal /stil/ *verb* (*past tense* **stole** /stoʊl/, *past participle* **stolen** /'stoʊlən/)
to take something that does not belong to you, without asking for it: *Who stole my money?*

steam¹ /stim/ *noun* [U]
the gas that water becomes when it boils: *There was steam coming from the engine.*

steam

steam

steam² *verb*
1 to send out steam
2 to cook something using steam

steel /stil/ *noun* [U]
a strong hard metal made from iron, used for knives, machines etc.

steep /stip/ *adjective*
having a slope that is high and difficult to go up: *The car rolled down a steep hill.*

stee·ple /'stipəl/ *noun*
a tall pointed tower on a church

steer /stɪr/ *verb*
to direct or guide a vehicle: *He steered the car carefully into the garage.*

steering wheel /'.. ,./ *noun*
the wheel that you turn to make a vehicle move to the left or right

stem /stɛm/ *noun*
the long thin part of a plant from which the leaves or flowers grow —see picture at ROSE²

step¹ /stɛp/ *verb* (**stepping, stepped**)
to move one foot up and put it down in front of the other: *He stepped over the dog. | What did you step in?*

step² *noun*
1 the act of moving one foot up and putting it down in front of the other: *He took a step toward the door.*
2 one action in a series that you do to get a particular result: *The first step in an accident is to call for help.*
3 one part of a set of stairs: *She sat on a step and waited.*
4 the sound you make when you take a step: *I heard steps outside.*

step-by-step /,. . '.◄ / *adverb*
carefully; doing one thing at a time: *He showed us how to repair the car step-by-step.*

step·fa·ther /'stɛp,faðər/ *noun*
a man who marries your mother, but is not your father

step·moth·er /'stɛp,mʌðər/ *noun*
a woman who marries your father, but is not your mother

ster·e·o /'stɛri,oʊ, 'stɪr-/ *noun*
a machine for playing records, CDs, etc., that produces music

stew¹ /stu/ *noun*
food made of meat and vegetables, cooked slowly in liquid

stew² *verb*
to cook food slowly in liquid

stew·ard·ess /'stuərdɪs/ *noun*
a woman who takes care of passengers on a ship or plane

stick¹ /stɪk/ *noun*
1 a long thin piece of wood
2 a thin piece of wood or metal used for a particular purpose: *Can I borrow your hockey stick?*

stick² *verb* (*past* **stuck** /stʌk/)
1 to attach something to something else using a sticky substance like GLUE: *I stuck a stamp on the letter.*
2 to put something pointed into something else: *She stuck her fork into her food.*
3 to become or stay firmly in one place and difficult to move: *The car is stuck in the mud.*
4 to put something somewhere: *Just stick that in the corner until we need it.*
5 **stick by someone** to continue to support someone: *She has always stuck by me.*
6 **stick something out** to make something come forward or out: *She stuck her foot out and caused him to fall.*

stick·y /'stɪki/ *adjective* (**stickier, stickiest**)
covered with or containing something that sticks to surfaces: *My hands are sticky.*

stiff /stɪf/ *adjective*
not easy to move or bend: *The cards are made of stiff paper. | My leg muscle is stiff.*

still¹ /stɪl/ *adverb*
1 up to a particular point in time: *Do you still play tennis?*
2 even more than something else, or even longer than you expect: *The weather is still colder than last week.*
3 in spite of someone or something else: *It was raining, but she still went out.*

still² *adjective*
1 not moving: *Sit still while I comb your hair.*
2 quiet: *The ocean was calm and still.*

sting¹ /stɪŋ/ *verb* (*past* **stung** /stʌŋ/)
1 to hurt someone using a sharp point: *The bee stung her leg.*
2 to feel a sharp pain: *My eyes are stinging because of the smoke.*

sting² *noun*
a pain or wound made when something stings you

stink¹ /stɪŋk/ *verb* (*past tense* **stank** /stæŋk/, *past participle* **stunk** /stʌŋk/)
to have a very unpleasant smell

stink² *noun*
a very bad smell —**stinky** *adjective*

stir /stɚ/ *verb* [**stirring, stirred**]
1 to mix a liquid or food by moving a spoon around in it: *He put sugar in his coffee and stirred it.*
2 to move a little: *The leaves stirred in the wind.*

stitch¹ /stɪtʃ/ *noun* [*plural* **stitches**]
1 one of the small lines of thread where you sew a cloth: *The dress was sewn with small stitches.*
2 a small circle of wool that you make while KNITTING

stitch² *verb*
to sew something

stock¹ /stɑk/ *noun*
1 a supply of something in a store: *We have large stocks of canned goods.*
2 **in stock** ready for sale in a store: *Are there any more boots in stock?*
3 **out of stock** not in the store or not ready for sale: *Red boots are out of stock.*

stock² *verb*
to have something for sale in a store: *Do you stock any fishing equipment?*

stock·ing /'stɑkɪŋ/ *noun*
a very thin piece of clothing that women wear on their legs and feet

stole /stoul/
the PAST TENSE of the verb **steal**

sto·len /'stoulən/
the PAST PARTICIPLE of the verb **steal**

stom·ach /'stʌmək/ *noun*
the part of your body where food goes when you swallow it

stomachache /'stʌmək,eɪk/ *noun*
a pain in your stomach: *I have a stomachache.*

stone /stoun/ *noun*
1 a piece of rock: *The boys threw stones into the lake.*
2 [U] rock: *The walls are made of stone.*
3 a piece of colored rock of great value; a jewel

stood /'stud/
the PAST TENSE and PAST PARTICIPLE of the verb **stand**

stool /stul/ *noun*
a chair without a back or sides —see picture at CHAIR

stoop /stup/ *verb*
to bend your body over forward and down: *He had to stoop to get through the door.*

stop¹ /stɑp/ *verb* (**stopping, stopped**)
1 to end an activity, event, movement etc.: *We stopped eating.* | *The rain has stopped.*
≫ compare START¹
2 to prevent someone from doing something: *They stopped me from going out of the door.*
3 to pause during an activity, trip etc. so you can do something: *We had to stop for gas.*
4 **stop it, stop that** said when you want to tell someone not to annoy or upset you: *Stop it. That hurts!*

stop² *noun*
1 an action of stopping or being stopped: *The car came to a stop.*
2 a place where a bus or train stops for people: *We waited at the bus stop.*

stoplight /'stɑplaɪt/ *noun*
a set of red, yellow, and green lights that tell cars when they can go and when they must stop

store¹ /'stɔr/ *noun*
a large room or building where goods are sold: *I'm going to the grocery store.*

store² *verb* (**storing, stored**)
to put something away or keep it so you can use it later: *My old clothes are stored in those boxes.*

storm /stɔrm/ *noun*
a time of bad weather when there is a lot of wind and rain

storm·y /'stɔrmi/ *adjective* (**stormier, stormiest**)
full of rain, wind, or snow: *The stormy weather will continue.*

sto·ry /'stɔri/ *noun* [*plural* **stories**]
1 a description of an event that can be real or imaginary: *Please read us a story!* | *Did you see the story in the newspaper?*
2 [*also* **storey**] a floor or level in a building: *She lives on the third story.*

stove /stoov/ *noun*
a piece of equipment in the kitchen, on which you cook food —see color picture on page 188

straight¹ /streɪt/ *adjective*
1 not bending or curved: *My sister has straight hair.* | *Can you draw a straight line?*
2 level or upright; not leaning: *The picture isn't straight. Move the left side up.*

3 honest: *Give me a straight answer.*
4 one after the other: *We won three straight games!*

straight² *adverb*
1 in a line which does not bend or curve: *The car went straight down the road.*
2 immediately and directly; without any delay: *He went straight to his friend to ask for help.*
3 happening one after the other: *I was working for four days straight.*

straight·en /'streɪt⁊n/ *verb*
1 to become straight, or make something straight: *She straightened the picture on the wall.*
2 (*also* **straighten up**) to clean something that is messy: *Straighten up your room now!*

strain /streɪn/ *verb*
1 to injure a part of your body by stretching it too much: *I strained my back when I lifted the box.*
2 to use a lot of effort to do something: *She was straining to hear me.*
3 to take out solid things from a liquid by pouring it through a cloth or other object

strait /streɪt/ *noun*
a narrow piece of water that joins two larger areas of water

strand /strænd/ *noun*
a long thin piece of thread, hair, wire etc.

strand·ed /'strændɪd/ *adjective*
needing help because you cannot move from a particular place: *I was stranded after the car broke down.*

strange /streɪndʒ/ *adjective* (**stranger, strangest**)
1 unusual, surprising, or difficult to understand: *I heard a strange noise from the next room.*
2 not what you expect; not familiar: *We visited a strange city.*

strang·er /'streɪndʒɚ/ *noun*
someone you do not know

stran·gle /'stræŋgəl/ *verb* (**strangling, strangled**)
to kill someone by tightly pressing his or her throat with your hands or a rope

strap /stræp/ *noun*
a narrow piece of leather, cloth, etc. that is attached to something so that it does not fall down or fall off

straw /strɔ/ *noun*
1 [U] the dry stems of wheat or other plants used for making something: *Do you like my straw hat?*
2 a thin tube used for sucking liquid from a bottle: *He drank the milk through a straw.*
3 a single dry stem of wheat or other plants

straw·ber·ry /'strɔˌbɛri/ *noun* (*plural* **strawberries**)
a sweet red fruit —see picture at FRUIT

stray¹ /streɪ/ *adjective*
a stray animal is lost and has no home

stray² *verb* (**straying, strayed**)
to move away from a safe place without intending to: *She strayed **from** the road and got lost.*

streak /strik/ *noun*
a long thin line of color: *There is a streak **of** paint on the wall.*

stream /strim/ *noun*
1 a small river —see color picture on page 188
2 a long line of people, vehicles, events etc.: *A stream **of** cars came down the road.*

street /strit/ *noun*
a road in a town or city with buildings next to it: *The library is across the street from the school.* | *Robert lives on Main Street.*
≫ compare AVENUE, ROAD

street·light /'strit-laɪt/ *noun*
a light on a tall pole that is next to the street

strength /strɛŋkθ, strɛnθ/ *noun* [U]
1 the power or ability to move heavy things: *He didn't have the strength to get up.*
2 the power of an organization, country, relationship etc.: *The country wants to build its military strength.*

strength·en /'strɛŋkθən, 'strɛnθən/ *verb*
to make someone or something stronger: *Exercise will strengthen your arms.*

stress¹ /strɛs/ *noun*
1 [U] the feeling of being worried because of difficulties in your life: *He is **under** a lot of stress at work.*
2 [U] special attention or importance given to an idea, activity etc.
3 (*plural* **stresses**) the force that you use when you say a word or part of a word

stress² *verb*
1 to give special attention or importance to a fact, idea etc.: *I must stress that we don't have much time.*

2 to say a word or part of a word with more force ≫ compare EMPHASIZE

stress·ful /'strɛsfəl/ *adjective*
making you worry a lot: *She has a very stressful job.*

stretch /strɛtʃ/ *verb*
1 to become larger or longer by pulling, or make something do this: *She stretched the rope between the two poles.* | *Rubber stretches easily.*
2 to reach out your arms or legs to their full length: *He stretched his legs out in front of him.* —see color picture on page 189
3 to spread out or cover a large area: *The forest stretched for miles.*

stretch·er /'strɛtʃɚ/ *noun*
a frame on which you carry someone who is sick or injured

strict /strɪkt/ *adjective*
making sure that rules are obeyed: *She is very strict with her children.*

strict·ly /strɪktli/ *adverb*
1 exactly and correctly: *What he says is not strictly true.*
2 in a way that must be obeyed: *Smoking is strictly illegal in this building.*

strike¹ /straɪk/ *verb* (**striking, struck** /strʌk/, *past participle* **struck** *or* **stricken** /'strɪkən/)
1 to hit someone or something: *The car was struck by a tree.*
2 to stop working, usually because you want more money
3 to suddenly have a particular thought or idea. *He struck me as being a very nice man.*
4 if a clock strikes, it makes a sound to show what time it is: *The clock struck three.* (=3 o'clock)
5 to attack quickly and suddenly: *When will the killer strike again?*

strike² *noun*
a time when people stop working, usually because they want more money: *The workers are on strike.*

string /strɪŋ/ *noun*
1 a strong thread with which you can tie things: *I tied a string around the box.*
2 a long thin piece of wire used in some musical instruments, such as a VIOLIN

strip¹ /strɪp/ *noun*
a long narrow piece of cloth, paper etc.

strip² *verb* (**stripping, stripped**)
1 to remove the outer covering of something: *He stripped the paper off the wall.*
2 to take off your clothes: *John stripped off his shirt.*

stripe /straɪp/ *noun*
a long thin line of color: *A tiger has dark stripes.*

striped /straɪpt, 'straɪpɪd/ *adjective*
having long thin lines of color: *He wore a striped shirt.* —see picture at PATTERN

stroke¹ /stroʊk/ *noun*
1 a sudden illness in your brain: *She had a stroke last year.*
2 a movement with your arms when you are swimming
3 a single movement of a pen or brush, or a line made by this

stroke² *verb* (**stroking, stroked**)
to move your hand over something gently: *He stroked her hair gently.*

stroll¹ /stroʊl/ *verb*
to walk slowly: *We strolled through the park.*

stroll² *noun*
a slow walk for pleasure: *We went for a stroll in the evening.*

stroll·er /'stroʊlɚ/ *noun*
a small chair on wheels, in which you can push a small child

strong /strɔŋ/ *adjective*
1 having a lot of power or force: *He is a strong man.* | *She is a strong swimmer.* ≫ compare WEAK
2 not easy to break or damage: *I need a strong rope.*
3 having a lot of power or influence: *Is he a strong leader?*
4 strong feelings, ideas etc. are very important to you
5 a strong smell, taste, color etc. is easy to notice —**strongly** *adverb*

struck /strʌk/
the PAST TENSE and PAST PARTICIPLE of the verb **strike**

struc·ture /'strʌktʃɚ/ *noun*
1 a building, or something that is being built: *The bridge is a very tall structure.*
2 the way in which something is arranged: *The structure of the company will not change.*

strug·gle¹ /ˈstrʌgəl/ *verb* (**struggling, struggled**)
1 to fight someone: *I struggled **to** get free.*
2 to try to do something that is difficult: *He struggled **to** learn English.*

struggle² *noun*
a fight: *The men were involved in a struggle.*

stub·born /ˈstʌbən/ *adjective*
not willing to change your ideas easily: *She never listens. She's just being stubborn.*

stuck /stʌk/
the PAST TENSE and PAST PARTICIPLE of the verb **stick**

stu·dent /ˈstudnt/ *noun*
someone who studies in a school or college

stu·di·o /ˈstudiˌoʊ/ *noun*
1 a place in which movies, or radio and television shows are made
2 a room in which a painter or photographer works

stud·y¹ /ˈstʌdi/ *verb* (**studying, studied**)
1 to learn about something by reading, going to classes etc.: *I am studying art. | Brad needs to study **for** his English test.*
2 to look at something carefully: *Before we go, we'll have to study the map.*

study² *noun* (*plural* **studies**)
1 the activity of studying, or a piece of work about this: *He is doing a study **on** crime in the city.*
2 a room in which you work or study

stuff¹ /stʌf/ *noun* [U]
any substance or material: *There's some white stuff on the floor.*

stuff² *verb*
1 to fill something with a substance: *The bed was stuffed **with** cotton.*
2 to push something into something else quickly: *She stuffed the letter **into** her pocket.*

stuff·ing /ˈstʌfɪŋ/ *noun* [U]
material that is put inside something

stuff·y /ˈstʌfi/ *adjective* (**stuffier, stuffiest**)
not having enough clean air: *Open a window. The room is stuffy.*

stum·ble /ˈstʌmbəl/ *verb* (**stumbling, stumbled**)
to almost fall down while you are walking: *She stumbled coming out of the door.*

stump /stʌmp/ *noun*
a part that is left when the rest is cut off: *He sat on a tree stump.*

stung /stʌŋ/
the PAST TENSE and PAST PARTICIPLE of the verb **sting**

stunk /stʌŋk/
the PAST TENSE and PAST PARTICIPLE of the verb **stink**

stu·pid /ˈstupɪd/ *adjective*
not having good sense; not intelligent: *How could you be so stupid?*

stu·pid·i·ty /stuˈpɪdəti/ *noun* [U]
behavior that shows that someone does not have good sense or is not intelligent

stur·dy /ˈstədi/ *adjective* (**sturdier, sturdiest**)
strong and not likely to break: *a sturdy table*

stut·ter /ˈstʌtə/ *verb*
to speak with difficulty, repeating the first sound of a word or phrase: *"I ca-ca-can't help it,"* she stuttered. ≫ compare STAMMER

style /staɪl/ *noun*
1 a particular way of behaving, working, or doing something: *I like his style **of** writing.*
2 a way of dressing, painting etc. that everyone likes at a particular time: *Her dresses are always **in** style.*

sub·ject /ˈsʌbdʒɪkt/ *noun*
1 something that you study at a school: *English is one my favorite subjects.*
2 something that you talk or write about: *Don't try to **change the** subject.* (=talk about something else)
3 the person or thing that does the action of a verb; the noun that usually goes in front of the verb: *In the sentence, "Jane bought the bread", "Jane" is the subject.* ≫ compare OBJECT¹

submarine

sub·ma·rine /ˈsʌbməˌrin, ˌsʌbməˈrin/ *noun*
a ship that can travel under water —see color picture on page 187

sub·stance /'sʌbstəns/ noun
a liquid, solid, or powder that you can touch:
There is a poisonous substance in the water.

sub·sti·tute¹ /'sʌbstə,tut/ noun
someone who does someone else's job while he
or she is away, sick etc.: *We had a substitute
teacher today.*

substitute² verb
to use something new or different instead of
something else: *You can substitute margarine
for butter in the recipe.*

sub·tract /səb'trækt/ verb
to take one number from a larger one: *If you
subtract 3 from 5, you get 2.* ≫ compare ADD

sub·trac·tion /səb'trækʃən/ noun
the taking of one number from a larger one
≫ compare ADDITION

sub·urb /'sʌbɚb/ noun
an area away from the center of a city: *He lives
in a suburb of Houston.* —**suburban** adjective

sub·way /'sʌbweɪ/ noun (plural **subways**)
a railroad that is under the ground in a city:
Sally rides the subway to work.

suc·ceed /sək'sid/ verb
1 to do well, to do what you tried to do: *If you
try hard, you'll succeed.* ≫ compare FAIL
2 to have the result or effect something is
intended to have: *He succeeded in selling his
house.*

suc·cess /sək'sɛs/ noun
1 [U] the act of doing what you tried to do or
want to do: *Have you had any success in finding her?* ≫ compare FAILURE
2 (plural **successes**) someone or something
that pleases people or does very well: *Her party
was a big success.*

suc·cess·ful /sək'sɛsfəl/ adjective
having done well or pleased people: *She has a
successful business.* —**successfully** adverb
≫ opposite UNSUCCESSFUL

such /sʌtʃ/
1 like the one you have just mentioned: *What
would you do in such a situation?*
2 used for making what you say stronger: *It's
such a lovely day.* ≫ compare SO
3 **such as** for example: *I like sports, such as
tennis.*

suck /sʌk/ verb
to pull liquid into your mouth with your lips: *The
baby is sucking milk from the bottle.*

sud·den /'sʌdn/ adjective
1 done or happening quickly or without being
expected: *Her death was a sudden shock.*
2 **all of a sudden** quickly and with no warning:
All of a sudden, the lights went out.

sud·den·ly /'sʌdnli/ adverb
quickly and without being expected: *Suddenly,
everyone ran out of the room.*

sue /su/ verb
to try to make someone pay you money in a
court of law, because they have harmed you in
some way

suede /sweɪd/ noun [U]
soft leather with a slightly rough surface

suf·fer /'sʌfɚ/ verb
to be in pain or trouble: *She suffers from
headaches.*

suf·fer·ing /'sʌfərɪŋ/ noun
great pain or trouble that you experience:
Suffering is a part of life.

suf·fi·cient /sə'fɪʃənt/ adjective
enough: *The amount of food is sufficient to feed
four people.*

suf·fix /'sʌfɪks/ noun (plural **suffixes**)
letters that you add to the end of a word to
make a new word, such as adding "ness" to the
word "kind" to get "kindness" ≫ compare PRE-
FIX

sug·ar /'ʃʊgɚ/ noun [U]
a substance made from some plants, used for
making food sweet

sug·gest /səg'dʒɛst, sə'dʒɛst/ verb
to tell someone that something is a good idea:
I suggested that we meet for lunch.

sug·ges·tion /səg'dʒɛstʃən, sə'dʒɛs-/
noun
an idea or plan that you mention: *Can I make a
suggestion?*

su·i·cide /'suə,saɪd/ noun
the act of killing yourself: *Alan's brother com-
mitted suicide.*

suit¹ /sut/ verb
to be right or acceptable for someone: *"Can
you come tomorrow?" "That suits me fine."*

suit² noun
1 a set of clothes made from the same material, including a short coat and pants or a skirt:
I want a dark gray suit. —see color picture on
page 190

2 a problem that someone brings to a court of law to be settled

suit·able /'suṭəbəl/ *adjective*
right or acceptable for a particular purpose: *This toy is not suitable **for** young children.* —**suitably** *adverb* » opposite UNSUITABLE

suit·case /'sut¬keɪs/ *noun*
a large bag with a handle, in which you carry clothes » compare BRIEFCASE

sum /sʌm/ *noun*
1 an amount of money: *We spent a large sum of money on the computer.*
2 the sum of the total when you add numbers: *The sum of 5 and 5 is 10.*

sum·mer /'sʌmɚ/ *noun*
the season between spring and fall, when it is warmest: *What are you doing this summer?* » compare WINTER

sum·mit /'sʌmɪt/ *noun*
the top of a mountain

sum·mon /'sʌmən/ *verb*
to order someone to come to a place: *They were summoned **to** the governor's office.*

sun /sʌn/ *noun*
1 the large ball of fire in the sky that gives us light and heat » compare MOON —see color picture on page 192
2 [U] the light and heat from the sun: *We went to the beach to lie in the sun.*

sun·bathe /'sʌnbeɪð/ *verb* (**sunbathing, sunbathed**)
to lie in the sun to make your skin brown

sun·burn /'sʌnbɚn/ *noun* [U]
the condition of having sore, red skin from spending too much time in the sun —**sunburned** *adjective* » compare SUNTAN

Sun·day /'sʌndi, -deɪ/ *noun*
the first day of the week

sung /sʌŋ/
the PAST PARTICIPLE of the verb **sing**

sun·glass·es /'sʌn,glæsɪz/ *plural noun*
dark glasses that you wear to protect your eyes when the sun is bright

sunk /sʌŋk/
the PAST TENSE and PAST PARTICIPLE of the verb **sink**

sun·light /'sʌnlaɪt/ *noun* [U]
natural light from the sun: *Plants need sunlight to grow.*

sun·ny /'sʌni/ *adjective* (**sunnier, sunniest**)
full of bright light from the sun: *The day was bright and sunny.*

sun·rise /'sʌnraɪz/ *noun*
the time in the morning when the sun first appears

sun·set /'sʌnsɛt/ *noun*
the time when the sun disappears and night begins

sun·shine /'sʌnʃaɪn/ *noun* [U]
the light and heat from the sun: *I enjoy walking in the sunshine.*

sun·tan /'sʌntæn/ *noun*
(*also* **tan**) skin that is brown because of spending a lot of time in the sun » compare SUNBURN

su·per /'supɚ/ *adjective*
very good or nice: *We had a super time on vacation.*

su·perb /sʊ'pɚb/ *adjective*
very good or fine; excellent: *The food here is superb.*

su·pe·ri·or /sə'pɪriɚ, sʊ-/ *adjective*
better than other things; extremely good » compare INFERIOR

su·per·la·tive /sə'pɚləṭɪv, sʊ-/ *noun, adjective*
a word or a form of a word that shows that something is the best, worst, biggest, smallest etc.; "fastest" is the superlative form of "fast" » compare COMPARATIVE

su·per·mar·ket /'supɚ,mɑrkɪt/ *noun*
a large store that sells food and things that people need for the house —see color picture on page 193

su·per·son·ic /,supɚ'sɑnɪk◂/ *adjective*
faster than the speed of sound

su·per·sti·tion /,supɚ'stɪʃən/ *noun*
a belief that some things are lucky and some are not: *It is only a superstition that the number 13 is unlucky.* —**superstitious** *adjective*

su·per·vise /'supɚ,vaɪz/ *verb* (**supervising, supervised**)
to watch people to make sure that they do the right things while they work

su·per·vi·sion /,supɚ'vɪʒən/ *noun* [U]
the activity of watching people to make sure that they do the right things while they work: *We were under her supervision.*

su·per·vis·or /'supɚˌvaɪzɚ/ *noun*
someone who watches other people while they work to make sure they do the right things

sup·per /'sʌpɚ/ *noun*
an evening meal ≫ compare DINNER

sup·plies /sə'plaɪz/ *plural noun*
things that you need for daily life: *Supplies are difficult to find in the desert.*

sup·ply¹ /sə'plaɪ/ *noun* (*plural* **supplies**)
an amount of something that you can use when it is needed: *The country has a large supply of oil.*

supply² *verb* (**supplying, supplied**)
to give or sell something to someone who needs it: *We supply paper to the company.*

sup·port¹ /sə'pɔrt/ *verb*
1 to hold something so that it does not fall: *These poles support the roof.*
2 to say that you agree with an idea, person etc. and you want them to succeed: *Which political group do you support?*
3 to give money, food etc. for someone to live: *She supports her family by working two jobs.*

support² *noun*
1 [U] encouragement and help: *Thank you for your support.*
2 something that holds something else so that it does not fall

sup·pose¹ /sə'pouz/ *verb* (**supposing, supposed**)
1 **be supposed to do something** used for saying what someone should do, or what should happen: *You are supposed to stop at a red light.* | *When is the movie supposed to start?*
2 **be supposed to be something** to be believed to be true or real: *It's supposed to be a good book.*
3 to think that something is probably true or that it might happen: *I suppose that he went home.* | *He'll come with us, I suppose.*

suppose²
used for saying what might happen: *Suppose someone found out about our plan. What would you do?*

su·preme /sə'prim, su-/ *adjective*
highest, best, or most important: *The most important court in the country is called the Supreme Court.*

sure¹ /ʃʊr, ʃɚ/ *adjective*
1 certain about something: *I am sure that I put the money in the bank.*

2 **make sure (a)** to be certain that something is true or has been done: *I'll make sure that the car is locked.* **(b)** to do something so that you are certain something will happen: *We'll make sure that we get there early.*

sure² *adverb*
1 used for saying yes to someone: *"Will you come to the party?" "Sure!"*
2 used for adding force to something you are saying: *It sure is cold today!*

sure·ly /'ʃʊrli, 'ʃɚli/ *adverb*
used for saying that you think something must be true: *Surely you're not serious!*

surf¹ /sɚf/ *noun* [U]
white waves that come onto the beach

surf

surf² *verb*
to ride on ocean waves while being on a special board

sur·face /'sɚfəs/ *noun*
the outside or top part of something: *Don't scratch the surface of the table.*

surf·board /'sɚfbɔrd/ *noun*
a long narrow piece of wood or plastic on which you lie or stand to ride ocean waves

surf·ing /'sɚfɪŋ/ *noun* [U]
the activity or sport of riding on ocean waves on a special board

sur·geon /'sɚdʒən/ *noun*
a doctor who cuts open someone's body to fix or replace something inside

sur·ger·y /'sɚdʒəri/ *noun* [U]
the act of cutting open someone's body to fix or replace something inside: *Beth had surgery on her knee.*

sur·prise¹ /sɚ'praɪz, sə'praɪz/ *noun*
1 something that is not expected or usual: *What a surprise to see you here!*
2 [U] the feeling that you have when something unexpected or unusual happens: *I could see the surprise in her eyes.*

3 take someone by surprise to happen in an unexpected way: *When he offered me the job, it took me completely by surprise.*

sur·prise² /sə'praɪz/ *verb* [surprising, surprised]
to make someone have a feeling of surprise: *His gift surprised me. I didn't expect anything from him.*

sur·ren·der /sə'rɛndər/ *verb*
to stop fighting because you know that you cannot win

sur·round /sə'raʊnd/ *verb*
to be or go all around something: *The school is surrounded by a fence.*

sur·round·ings /sə'raʊndɪŋz/ *plural noun*
all the things that are around you: *How do you like your new surroundings?*

sur·viv·al /sə'vaɪvəl/ *noun* [U]
the state of continuing to live after a difficult or dangerous time: *His **chances of** survival are not good.*

sur·vive /sə'vaɪv/ *verb* [surviving, survived]
to continue to live after an accident, illness etc.: *Three people survived the car accident.* —**survivor** *noun*

sus·pect¹ /sə'spɛkt/ *verb*
1 to think that someone may be guilty of a crime: *She is suspected of murder.*
2 to think that something is true, especially something that is bad: *I suspect that he is not telling the truth.*

suspect² /'sʌspɛkt/ *noun*
someone who may be guilty of a crime: *The police have the suspect now.*

sus·pend /sə'spɛnd/ *verb*
1 to stop or delay something from continuing: *The weather caused the airport to suspend travel.*
2 to hang something from something else: *The lamp was suspended **from** the ceiling.*

sus·pend·ers /sə'spɛndərz/ *plural noun*
two cloth bands that go over your shoulders and are attached to your pants to hold them up —see color picture on page 190

sus·pense /sə'spɛns/ *noun* [U]
a feeling of not knowing what is going to happen next: *Don't **keep** us **in** suspense. Tell us what happened!*

sus·pi·cion /sə'spɪʃən/ *noun*
a feeling or belief that something may be true: *I'm not sure who did it, but I have my suspicions.*

sus·pi·cious /sə'spɪʃəs/ *adjective*
1 not willing to trust someone or something: *I am suspicious **of** her plans.*
2 making you think that something bad or wrong is happening: *The man in the corner looks suspicious.*

swal·low¹ /'swɑloʊ/ *verb*
to make food or drink go down your throat: *She swallowed some milk.*

swallow² *noun*
a small bird with a tail that has two points

swam /swæm/
the PAST TENSE of the verb **swim**

swamp /swɑmp, swɔmp/ *noun*
land that is always soft and very wet —**swampy** *adjective*

swan /swɑn/ *noun*
a large white water bird with a long curved neck

swap /swɑp/ *verb* [swapping, swapped]
to exchange something you have for something that someone else has: *Can I **swap** seats **with** you?* —**swap** *noun*

swarm¹ /swɔrm/ *noun*
a large group of insects: *A swarm **of** bees lives in the tree.*

swarm² *verb*
to move in a large group: *The crowd swarmed into the building.*

sway /sweɪ/ *verb* [swaying, swayed]
to move slowly from one side to the other: *The trees swayed in the wind.*

swear /swɛr/ *verb* [past tense **swore** /swɔr/, past participle **sworn** /swɔrn/]
1 to say very bad words: *Don't swear in front of the children.*
2 to make a serious promise or threat: *Do you swear to tell the truth? | I swear I'll kill him!*

sweat¹ /swɛt/ *noun* [U]
water which comes out of your skin when you are hot or afraid: *Sweat poured down his face as he ran.* —**sweaty** *adjective*

sweat² *verb*
to have water coming out through your skin because you are hot or afraid: *She was sweating when she reached the top of the hill.*

sweat·er /'swɛtɚ/ *noun*
a piece of clothing, usually made of wool, that covers the top part of your body —see color picture on page 190

sweats /swɛts/ *plural noun*
1 a set of clothes made of thick soft cotton, usually worn for playing sports
2 pants of this type —see color picture on page 190

sweat·shirt /'swɛtʃɚt/ *noun*
a soft thick shirt, usually worn for playing sports

sweep /swip/ *verb (past swept /swɛpt/)*
1 to clean the dirt from something using a brush: *I swept the floor.*
2 to move quickly: *The crowd swept **through** the gates.*

sweet /swit/ *adjective*
1 containing or tasting like sugar: *I don't like sweet foods.*
2 pleasant, kind, and friendly: *What a sweet smile she has!* —**sweetly** *adverb*

sweet·heart /'swithɑrt/ *noun*
someone that you love

swell /swɛl/ *verb (past participle swollen /'swoʊlən/)*
to become larger: *I injured my hand and it is swelling up.* | *After the rain, the river swelled.*

swell·ing /'swɛlɪŋ/ *noun*
a place on your body that is larger than usual because of injury or sickness: *I have pain and swelling in my knee.*

swept /swɛpt/
the PAST TENSE and PAST PARTICIPLE of the verb **sweep**

swerve /swɚv/ *verb (swerving, swerved)*
to turn suddenly to one side when you are moving quickly: *The car swerved to avoid hitting the dog.*

swift /swɪft/ *adjective*
happening or moving very fast: *She is a swift runner.*

swim¹ /swɪm/ *verb (swimming, swam /swæm/, past participle swum /swʌm/)*
to move through the water by using your legs and arms: *He swam across the river.*

swim² *noun*
an act or time when you swim: *Would you like to **go for a** swim after work?*

swim·mer /'swɪmɚ/ *noun*
someone who swims: *Gina is a good swimmer.*

swim·ming /'swɪmɪŋ/ *noun [U]*
the activity of moving through the water using your arms and legs: *Swimming is my favorite exercise.* —see color picture on page 184

swimming pool /'.. ,./ *noun*
a POOL

swim·suit /'swɪmsut/ *noun*
a piece of clothing that you wear for swimming

swing¹ /swɪŋ/ *verb (past swung /swʌŋ/)*
to move backward and forward while hanging from a particular point: *The boy swung on the rope tied to a tree.* | *The door is swinging in the wind.* —see color picture on page 189

swing

swing² *noun*
a seat hanging from ropes or chains, on which children swing

switch¹ /swɪtʃ/ *noun (plural switches)*
the part of a machine that you press or turn to make it start or stop working

switch² *verb*
1 to change from one thing to another: *I studied English, but then I switched **to** history.*
2 switch something off, switch something on to make a machine stop or start working by pressing or turning part of it: *Switch off (=turn off) the lights.* | *Can you switch the television on? (=turn it on)*

swol·len /'swoʊlən/
the PAST PARTICIPLE of the verb **swell**

swoop /swup/ *verb*
to move downward through the air very quickly: *The bird swooped down to catch a fish.*

sword /sɔrd/ *noun*
a weapon that you hold in your hand, with a long sharp blade like a long knife

swore /swɔr/
the PAST TENSE of the verb **swear**

sworn /swɔrn/
the PAST PARTICIPLE of the verb **swear**

swum /swʌm/
the PAST PARTICIPLE of the verb **swim**

swung /swʌŋ/
the PAST TENSE and PAST PARTICIPLE of the verb **swing**

syl·la·ble /'sɪləbəl/ noun
a part of a word that contains one vowel sound: There are two syllables in "window": "win" and "dow."

sym·bol /'sɪmbəl/ noun
a picture, letter, or sign that means or shows something else: The symbol **for** a church on the map is a cross.

sym·pa·thet·ic /ˌsɪmpə'θɛtɪk/ adjective
nice and understanding about someone else's hurt or sadness: She is a very sympathetic friend.

sym·pa·thy /'sɪmpəθi/ noun (plural sympathies)
a feeling of understanding and support for someone's hurt or sadness: I have a lot of sympathy **for** people who have sick children.

symp·tom /'sɪmptəm/ noun
a sign of something, especially a disease: Fever is a symptom **of** many diseases.

syn·a·gogue /'sɪnə,gɑg/ noun
a building where Jewish people go for religious services

syn·o·nym /'sɪnə,nɪm/ noun
a word with the same meaning as another word: "Mad" and "angry" are synonyms.

syn·thet·ic /sɪn'θɛtɪk/ adjective
not natural; made by people in a factory: My sweater is made of synthetic material.

sy·ringe /sə'rɪndʒ/ noun
a hollow tube and needle used for giving people medicine through their skin —see picture at NEEDLE

syr·up /'sɚəp, 'sɪrəp/ noun [U]
a thick liquid made from sugar

sys·tem /'sɪstəm/ noun
a group of things that work together for a particular purpose: We have a large system **of** highways. | The company needs a new computer system.

ta·ble /'teɪbəl/ *noun*
1 a piece of furniture with a flat top and three or four legs: *The family is **sitting at the** kitchen table.*
2 set the table to put plates, spoons, etc. on the table before a meal

ta·ble·cloth /'teɪbəl,klɔθ/ *noun*
a cloth used for covering a table

ta·ble·spoon /'teɪbəl,spun/ *noun*
a large spoon used for serving food

tab·let /'tæblɪt/ *noun*
a small round piece of medicine that you swallow ≫ compare PILL

table ten·nis /'.. ,../ *noun* [U]
PING-PONG

tack·le /'tækəl/ *verb* (**tackling, tackled**)
1 to begin to work on a difficult problem: *I must tackle that report this evening.*
2 to try to stop someone from running in a sports game: *He was tackled on the play.*

tact·ful /'tæktfəl/ *adjective*
careful not to say or do something that will upset or embarrass someone: *He gave a tactful response to her question.*

tad·pole /'tædpoʊl/ *noun*
a small creature that lives in the water and becomes a FROG or TOAD

tag /tæg/ *noun*
a small piece of paper, plastic etc. that is put on something and gives information about it: *Is there a price tag on this?*

tail /teɪl/ *noun*
the part at the back of an animal that can move: *The dog is wagging its tail.*

tai·lor /'teɪlɚ/ *noun*
someone whose job is to make suits, coats, etc.

take /teɪk/ *verb* (**taking, took** /tʊk/, *past participle* **taken** /'teɪkən/)
1 to move someone or something to another place: *I'll take you **to** the hospital. | He is taking some work home with him.*

2 used for showing that something is being done: *Can you **take a picture** for me? | I need to take a shower.* (=have a shower)
3 to accept or receive something: *Are you going to take the job? | Will the store take a check?*
4 to need something in order for something else to happen: *The trip to Boston takes three hours. | What kind of gas does the car take?*
5 to steal something: *They took all her jewelry.*
6 to study a particular subject: *I took four years of Spanish. | She wants to take some guitar classes.*
7 to swallow medicine: *I took some medicine for my cough.*
8 to remove something from a place: *Take the meat **out of** the oven.*
9 to travel in a vehicle or on a particular road: *I took the bus home. | Take the first right.*
10 to decide to buy something: *I'll take two pizzas with extra cheese. | He gave me a good price on the car, so I said I'd take it.*
11 take something off to remove something: *He took his coat off. | My name was taken off the list.*
12 take off to leave the ground and rise into the air: *The plane takes off in an hour.*
13 take place to happen: *The accident took place on Saturday night.*
14 take something back to return something to the store where you bought it: *If the dress doesn't fit, take it back.*
15 take someone out to go with someone to a restaurant, movie etc.: *I am taking Sharon out tonight.*
16 take up something to begin doing an activity or job: *We've taken up painting this year.*
17 take after someone to look or behave like someone else: *He takes after his father.*

tak·en /'teɪkən/
the PAST PARTICIPLE of the verb **take**

take·out /'teɪk-aʊt/ *noun*
1 a meal that you buy from a restaurant and eat somewhere else
2 a place that sells this food

tale /teɪl/ *noun*
a story about events that are not real

tal·ent /'tælənt/ *noun*
the ability to do something well: *My sister has a talent **for** singing.*

tal·ent·ed /'tæləntɪd/ *adjective*
able to do something well: *He is a talented actor.*

talk¹ /tɔk/ *verb*
1 to say things to someone; speak: *The baby is just starting to talk.* | *I talked **to** Janet today.*
2 talk back to someone to say rude things to someone: *Don't talk back to your father!*

talk² *noun*
1 a conversation: *We had a long talk.*
2 a speech to a group of people: *She is **giving** a talk **on** how to find a job.*

talk·a·tive /ˈtɔkətɪv/ *adjective*
liking to talk a lot

tall /tɔl/ *adjective*
1 higher than other people or things: *James is the tallest boy in our class.*
2 having a particular height: *He is 6 feet tall.* | *How tall are you?* —see color picture on page 191

tame¹ /teɪm/ *adjective* (**tamer, tamest**)
a tame animal is trained to live with people: *She has a tame monkey for a pet.* ≫ compare WILD

tame² *verb* (**taming, tamed**)
to train a wild animal to live with people

tan¹ /tæn/ *noun*
(*also* **suntan**) the darker skin that you get when you have been out in the sun: *I want to **get a** tan this summer.*

tan² *adjective*
pale brown in color: *He was wearing a tan jacket.*

tan·ger·ine /ˌtændʒəˈrin/ *noun*
a sweet fruit like a small orange

tan·gled /ˈtæŋgəld/ *adjective*
twisted together into knots: *The poor girl has tangled hair.*

tank /tæŋk/ *noun*
1 a large container for holding liquid or gas: *Our car's gas tank leaks.*
2 a heavy military vehicle with guns on it, used in battle

tank·er /ˈtæŋkɚ/ *noun*
a very large ship that carries oil or other liquids

tap¹ /tæp/ *verb* (**tapping, tapped**)
to hit your finger or foot against something gently: *She tapped me on the shoulder.* | *I'm tapping my foot in time to the music.*

tap² *noun*
1 an act of hitting something gently: *I felt a tap on my arm.*
2 a piece of equipment at the end of a pipe that controls the flow of water, beer etc.

tap danc·ing /ˈ. ˌ../ *noun* [U]
a type of dancing in which you wear special shoes that make a sound when you dance

tape¹ /teɪp/ *noun*
1 a long thin band of plastic inside a small case, on which you can record sound or pictures: *Which tape* (=of music) *should we listen to next?*
2 a thin narrow band of sticky material, used for sticking things together

tape² *verb* (**taping, taped**)
1 to record music or a movie on a TAPE: *If we tape the movie, we can watch it later.*
2 to stick something onto something else using TAPE: *She closed the box and taped it.*

tape re·cord·er /ˈ. .ˌ../ *noun*
a machine which records and plays music and other sounds

tar /tɑr/ *noun* [U]
a thick black sticky substance that is used in making roads

tar·get /ˈtɑrgɪt/ *noun*
an object, person, or place that you attack or shoot at

task /tæsk/ *noun*
a job or piece of work that must be done: *He has the dangerous task of trying to stop the fire.* ≫ compare JOB

taste¹ /teɪst/ *noun*
1 the feeling that is produced when your tongue touches a particular food or drink: *My sense of taste isn't very good; I have a cold.* | *Chocolate has a sweet taste.*
2 the particular type of clothes, music etc. that someone likes: *I do not share her taste **in** clothes.*
3 a small amount of food or drink that you eat to find out what it is like: *Here, **have a** taste **of** this soup.*

taste² *verb* (**tasting, tasted**)
1 to put a small amount of food or drink into your mouth to find out what it is like: *Can I taste your drink?*
2 to have a particular taste in your mouth: *This wine tastes sweet.*

tast·y /ˈteɪsti/ *adjective* (**tastier, tastiest**)
having a good taste: *We had some tasty fish for lunch.*

tat·too /tæˈtu/ *noun*
a picture or word that is put on someone's skin using a needle and colored ink

taught /tɔt/
the PAST TENSE and PAST PARTICIPLE of the verb **teach**

tax¹ /tæks/ noun (plural **taxes**)
money that you must pay the government from the money that you earn

tax² verb
to make someone pay a particular amount of money to the government

tax·i /'tæksi/ noun
a car with a driver whom you pay to take you somewhere: I'll take a taxi home. —see color picture on page 187

tea /ti/ noun
1 [U] a drink made by pouring boiling water onto dry leaves: Will you make a pot of tea?
2 dry leaves or flowers used for making a hot drink: She likes mint tea.

teach /titʃ/ verb (past **taught** /tɔt/)
1 to give lessons in a subject in a school or college: Mr. Jones teaches history.
2 to show someone how to do something: Who taught you to ride a bicycle?

teach·er /'titʃɚ/ noun
someone whose job is to teach

teacher's pet /,.. './ noun
a name for a student that the teacher likes a lot, especially one that the other students do not like

team /tim/ noun
1 a group of people who play a sport or game against other groups: Mike is **on the** tennis team.
2 a group of people who work together to do something: A team of writers wrote the words for the movie.

tea·pot /'tipɑt/ noun
a pot used for pouring tea

tear¹ /tɪr/ noun
a drop of water that comes from your eyes when you cry

tear² /tɛr/ noun
a hole in something where it has torn: I have a tear **in** my pants.

tear³ verb (past tense **tore** /tɔr/, past participle **torn** /tɔrn/)
1 to put a hole in something by pulling it very hard or touching it with something sharp: She tore her dress on the chair. | I tore the envelope **open**.

2 to remove something roughly from a place: Did the wind tear the door off?
3 **tear something up** to destroy something such as paper by pulling it into little pieces: She tore up the letter.
4 **tear something down** to destroy a building: They tore the old school down a year ago.
5 **tear someone apart** to make someone feel very upset and unhappy: It is tearing me apart to see her suffer.

tease /tiz/ verb (**teasing, teased**)
to annoy or embarrass someone by making jokes about him or her: You shouldn't tease your little sister.

tea·spoon /'tispun/ noun
a small spoon used for mixing sugar or milk in coffee, tea etc.

tech·ni·cal /'tɛknɪkəl/ adjective
relating to the skill or knowledge used in a particular science or machine

tech·ni·cian /tɛk'nɪʃən/ noun
someone whose job uses skill or knowledge about a particular science or machine: Anne is training to be a medical technician.

tech·nique /tɛk'nik/ noun
a special way of doing something: He wants to try some new teaching techniques.

tech·nol·o·gy /tɛk'nɑlədʒi/ noun [U]
all the knowledge and equipment used in science, the making of machines etc.: Modern technology has made many jobs easier.

ted·dy bear /'tɛdi ,bɛr/ noun
a soft toy that looks like a bear

teen·ag·er /'ti,neɪdʒɚ/ noun
someone who is between 13 and 19 years old ≫ compare ADOLESCENT —see color picture on page 191

teens /tinz/ plural noun
the period of time when you are between 13 and 19 years old: She got married **in her** teens. —see picture at HEAD¹

teeth /tiθ/
the plural of **tooth**

tel·e·com·mu·ni·ca·tions
/,tɛləkə,myunə'keɪʃənz/ noun [U]
the activity or business of sending and receiving information by telephone, radio etc.

tel·e·phone¹ /'tɛlə,foʊn/ noun
PHONE

telephone² verb (telephoning, telephoned)
PHONE

telephone number /'... ,../ noun
PHONE NUMBER

tel·e·scope
/'telə,skoup/ noun
an object that you look through to see things that are very small or far away >> compare BINOCULARS

tel·e·vi·sion
/'telə,vɪʒən/ noun
(also **TV**)
1 a machine shaped like a box on which you can watch pictures and hear sound: *Turn the television on.* —see color picture on page 187
2 [U] the pictures and sounds that you can watch and listen to on a television: *We are **watching** television.*
3 **on television** shown on the television: *What's on television tonight?*

tell /tel/ verb (past **told** /toʊld/)
1 to speak to someone and give facts or information about something: *Tell me what happened.* >> compare SAY¹
2 to say that someone must do something: *I told him **to** see a doctor about the pain.* | *Dad told me **to** be home by 10 o'clock.*
3 to be able to recognize or judge something correctly: *I can always tell when he is lying.*
4 **tell someone off** to talk to someone in an angry way because he or she did something wrong: *My mother told me off **for** swearing.*
5 **I told you so** said when someone does something that you warned him or her not to do

tem·per /'tempə/ noun
1 the way you feel, especially when you are angry: *He is not able to control his temper.*
2 **lose your temper** to become very angry suddenly

tem·per·a·ture /'temprətʃə/ noun
1 how hot or cold something is: *Water freezes at a low temperature.*
2 **have a temperature** to have a higher body temperature than usual, especially because you are sick

tem·ple /'tempəl/ noun
1 a holy building
2 the flat part of your head between your eye and your ear

tem·po·rar·i·ly /,tempə'rerəli/ adverb
for a short time only: *The school is temporarily closed.*

tem·po·rar·y /'tempə,reri/ adjective
existing or happening for a short time only: *This is only a temporary job.* >> compare PERMANENT

tempt /tempt/ verb
1 to make someone want to do or have something even if it is wrong or bad: *Can I tempt you with another piece of cake?*
2 **be tempted to do something** to think about doing something that may not be a good idea: *I was tempted to sell my car for the money.*

temp·ta·tion /temp'teɪʃən/ noun
a strong desire to have or do something even if it is wrong or bad

ten /ten/ adjective, noun
the number 10

ten·ant /'tenənt/ noun
someone who pays money to live in a house or room

tend /tend/ verb
tend to do something to be likely to do something: *She tends to cry at weddings.*

tend·en·cy /'tendənsi/ noun (plural tendencies)
something that usually happens: *Chuck **has a** tendency **to** talk too much.*

ten·der /'tendə/ adjective
1 easy to cut and eat: *The meat was nice and tender.* >> compare TOUGH
2 kind and gentle: *He has a tender look on his face.*

ten·nis /'tenɪs/ noun [U]
a game played by two or four people in which you hit a ball over a net using a RACKET —see color picture on page 184

tennis shoe /'.. ,./ noun
a light shoe used for sports

tense¹ /tens/ adjective
1 nervous and worried: *You seem tense. Is anything wrong?* >> compare RELAXED
2 tight and stiff, not able to relax: *The muscles in my back are tense.*

tense² noun
the form of a verb that shows whether the action of the verb happens in the past, now, or in the future: *"I am looking" is in the present tense, "I looked" is in the past tense, and "I will look" is in the future tense.*

tent /tɛnt/ *noun*
a shelter made of thick cloth supported by poles
—see color picture on page 188

tenth /tɛnθ/ *adjective, noun*
1 10th
2 one of ten equal parts

term /tɜm/ *noun*
1 a word or expression that has a particular meaning: *What is the correct term **for** a baby duck?*
2 a period of time, especially in politics or a school: *There are three terms in our school year.*

ter·mi·nal /'tɜmənəl/ *noun*
a place where you can get on a bus, plane, or ship

ter·mite /'tɜmaɪt/ *noun*
an insect that eats wood from a tree or building

terms /tɜmz/ *plural noun*
the things that you must agree to or accept, especially in a contract

ter·race /'tɛrɪs/ *noun*
1 a flat area cut out of the side of a hill
2 a flat area outside a house where you can eat, relax etc.

ter·ri·ble /'tɛrəbəl/ *adjective*
1 very serious and causing harm or damage: *They were in a terrible accident.*
2 very bad: *Your writing is terrible.*

ter·ri·bly /'tɛrəbli/ *adverb*
1 very; extremely: *I'm terribly sorry to hear about your loss.*
2 very badly: *We played terribly and lost the game.*

ter·rif·ic /tə'rɪfɪk/ *adjective*
very good; enjoyable: *What a terrific party!*

ter·ri·fy /'tɛrə,faɪ/ *verb* (**terrifying, terrified**)
to make someone very afraid: *I was terrified by the storm.*

ter·ri·to·ry /'tɛrə,tɔri/ *noun* (*plural* **territories**)
1 land that is controlled by a government: *This island is British territory.*
2 an area of land of a particular type: *Wild animals will protect their territory.*

ter·ror /'tɛrɚ/ *noun* [U]
great fear, or something that causes this: *She ran away **in** terror.*

ter·ror·ist /'tɛrə,rɪst/ *noun*
someone who uses violence to try to make a government do something

test¹ /tɛst/ *verb*
1 to look at something to see what it is like or to find out something: *The weapons will be tested by the army.*
2 to ask someone questions to see if he or she knows the answers: *We will be tested on American history.*

test² *noun*
a set of questions used for measuring how much someone knows about something: *How well did you do **on the** math test?*

test tube /'. ./ *noun*
a small glass container like a tube that is used in scientific tests

text /tɛkst/ *noun* [U]
the writing in a book

text·book /'tɛkstbʊk/ *noun*
a book that contains information about a particular subject

tex·ture /'tɛkstʃɚ/ *noun*
the way that a surface or material feels when you touch it

than /ðən, ðɛn; *strong* ðæn/
used when you are comparing two things: *My brother is older than me.* | *Mary sings better than anyone else in the class.*

thank /θæŋk/ *verb*
1 to tell someone that you are pleased or grateful: *I thanked her for the gift.*
2 **thank you** (*also* **thanks**) said to someone to show you are grateful for something: *Thank you **for** helping us.* | *"Would you like another cup of coffee?" "No, thank you."*

thank·ful /'θæŋkfəl/ *adjective*
very glad: *I was thankful that the children were safe.* —**thankfully** *adverb*

thanks /θæŋks/ *plural noun*
1 the things you say to show that you are grateful: *He sent a letter of thanks to everyone who came.*
2 **thanks to someone** because of: *Thanks to Peter, we won the game.* | *We missed the train, thanks to you.*

Thanks·giv·ing /,θæŋks'gɪvɪŋ/ *noun* [U]
a holiday in November when families have a large meal together, to show their thanks for food, health, families etc.

that /ðæt/
1 (*plural* **those** /ðoʊz/) the one over there; the one farther away than this one: *They don't live in this house; they live in that one.*
2 used when talking about something that has been mentioned: *Did you bring that picture I wanted?* | *I called her, and we met for lunch later that day.*
3 (/ðət/; *strong* /ðæt/) used instead of **who, whom, which**: *He's the man that sold me the bicycle.*
4 (/ðət/; *strong* /ðæt/) used for joining two parts of a sentence: *I think that it will rain tomorrow.* | *Did you get the letter that I sent to you?*
5 so; very: *I can't walk that fast!* | *I really don't care that much.*
6 that is used for giving more information about something, or for correcting something: *Paul said his family can come; that is, his wife and two kids can come.*
7 that's that said when something is finished, or when a decision will not be changed: *You're not going to the party and that's that!*

thaw /θɔ/ *verb*
to become soft or liquid, after having been frozen: *The ice began to thaw.*

the /ðə; *before a vowel* ði; *strong* ði/
1 used before another word to show that you are talking about a particular person or thing: *That is the dress that I want.* | *Hand me the red book.*
2 used in front of the names of some things: *We flew over the Mediterranean Sea.* | *He lives in the United States.*
3 used in front of the name for a class or group of people: *The rich* (=rich people) *should help the poor.* (=poor people) | *The library provides books for the blind.* (=people who cannot see)
4 used when talking about a particular time or date: *Today is Tuesday, the fifth of May.* | *They were popular back in the '50s.* (=the 1950s)
5 used instead of "each" or "every": *Our car gets 30 miles to the gallon.* (=for each gallon of gas)
6 used for saying that something is important or famous: *It is the movie to see this year.*

the·a·ter /ˈθiətər/ *noun*
a building in which plays are performed, or where movies are shown

theft /θɛft/ *noun*
1 [U] the crime of stealing: *He was put in prison for car theft.*

2 the act of stealing something: *We told the police about the theft of our bags.*

their /ðər; *strong* ðɛr/
belonging to the people or things that have been mentioned: *The children carried their bags to school.*

theirs /ðɛrz/
something that belongs to people or things that have been mentioned: *They looked at our pictures, but they didn't show us theirs.*

them /ðəm, əm; *strong* ðɛm/
the people or things that have been mentioned: *We gave them some food.* | *I can't find my shoes; have you seen them?*

theme /θim/ *noun*
the main idea or subject in a book, movie, speech etc.

them·selves /ðəmˈsɛlvz, ðɛm-/
1 the same people, animals, or things that the sentence is about; the same people as "they" in the sentence: *The tigers washed themselves in the river.* | *They bought themselves a new car.*
2 used for giving **they** a stronger meaning: *They painted the house themselves.*
3 by themselves (a) without help from anyone else: *The children did the drawing by themselves.* **(b)** alone: *They spent the day by themselves.*
4 to themselves for their own use: *They had the pool to themselves.*

then /ðɛn/ *adverb*
1 after something has happened; next: *We watched a movie and then went to bed.*
2 at a particular time in the past or future: *He lived in another city back then.*
3 if one thing is true, the other is also true: *"I lost my ticket." "Then you must get another one."*

the·o·ry /ˈθiəri, ˈθiri/ *noun* (*plural* **theories**)
an idea that tries to explain something, but it may not be true

there¹ /ðɛr/ *adverb*
in or near a particular place: *Don't sit there by the door; come and sit here.* | *Look at that man over there.* ≫ compare HERE

there²
there is, there are used for showing that someone or something exists or that something happens: *There is a letter for you.* | *Are there any questions?*

there·fore /ˈðɛrfɔr/ *adverb*
for that reason that has been mentioned: *He broke his leg, and therefore he cannot walk.*

ther·mom·e·ter /θəˈmɑmətə/ *noun*
an instrument that measures heat and cold: *The doctor used a thermometer to find out my temperature.*

Ther·mos /ˈθəməs/ (*trademark*) *noun*
a special type of bottle that keeps hot drinks hot, or cold drinks cold

these /ðiz/
the ones here; the ones nearer than that one: *I don't like these books; those are better.*

they /ðeɪ/
the people, animals, or things that have been mentioned: *My friends are coming, and they want you to come too. | I stopped at their house, but they were not home.*

they'd /ðeɪd/
1 they had: *They'd already left the house.*
2 they would: *They said they'd help.*

they'll /ðeɪl, ðɛl/
they will: *They'll probably arrive tomorrow.*

they're /ðə; strong ðɛr/
they are: *They're very nice people.*

they've /ðeɪv/
they have: *They've been shopping.*

thick /θɪk/ *adjective*
1 having a large distance between one side and the other: *The house is surrounded by thick walls.* ≫ compare THIN
2 filling the air and difficult to see through: *I couldn't see them through the thick smoke.*
3 not having a lot of water in it: *This soup is too thick.*
4 growing very close together so there is not much space in between: *She has thick black hair.*

thief /θif/ *noun* (*plural* **thieves** /θivz/)
someone who steals something: *The car thief was sent to prison.* ≫ compare ROBBER

thigh /θaɪ/ *noun*
the top part of your leg above your knee

thin /θɪn/ *adjective* (**thinner, thinnest**)
1 having a small distance between one side and the other; narrow: *She gave me a thin slice of cheese.* ≫ compare THICK
2 not having much fat on your body: *You should eat more; you're too thin.* ≫ compare FAT[1] —see color picture on page 191

3 having a lot of water in it so that it flows easily

thing /θɪŋ/ *noun*
1 an object: *What is that thing you are carrying?*
2 an act, idea, action or event: *That was a silly thing to do. | A funny thing happened last week.*

things /θɪŋz/ *plural noun*
1 life in general, and the way it affects someone: *How are things with you? | Things can be hard living on your own.*
2 the objects that you own, or that you are carrying: *They lost all their things in the fire. | Just put your things there for now.*

think /θɪŋk/ *verb* (*past* **thought** /θɔt/)
1 to use your mind to decide something, have ideas, or solve problems: *Think carefully before you decide. | What are you thinking **about**?*
2 to have an opinion or belief about something: *Do you think it will rain? | I think that is a good idea.*
3 **think of something, think up something** to have a new idea, plan, or suggestion: *We need to think of a way to earn more money. | He thought up another answer to the problem.*
4 **think something over** to consider something carefully before making a decision: *Have you had enough time to think over our offer?*
5 **think back** to remember something from the past: *Think back to the time you were a boy.*

thin·ly /ˈθɪnli/ *adverb*
in a way that leaves a small distance between one side and the other: *Spread the butter thinly on the bread.*

third /θəd/
1 3rd
2 one of three equal parts

thirst /θəst/ *noun* [U]
the feeling of wanting or needing to drink something ≫ compare HUNGER

thirst·y /ˈθəsti/ *adjective* (**thirstier, thirstiest**)
feeling that you want to drink something: *Can I have some water? I'm very thirsty.* ≫ compare HUNGRY

thir·teen /ˌθəˈtin/ *adjective, noun*
the number 13

thir·ty /ˈθəti/ *adjective, noun*
the number 30

this /ðɪs/ (*plural* **these** /ðiz/)
1 the one here; the one nearer than that one:

This is my bowl; that bowl is yours. | *He gave me this ring.*
2 used when talking about something that has been mentioned: *This is the third time I've called.* | *We took these pictures on our vacation.*
3 so; very: *I didn't expect it to be this expensive.* | *We never stayed up this late before.*
4 nearest to the present time: *Should we go there this Friday?*

this·tle /'θɪsəl/ *noun*
a wild plant with leaves that have sharp points

thorn /θɔrn/ *noun*
a sharp point that grows on a plant —see picture at ROSE²

thor·ough /'θɚ·oʊ, 'θʌroʊ/ *adjective*
complete and careful, including every detail: *The police made a thorough search of the house.* —**thoroughly** *adverb*

those /ðoʊz/
the ones over there; the ones farther away than this or these ones: *Should we give them these cards, or those that John is holding?*

though /ðoʊ/
1 even if; in spite of: *Though he was poor, he was happy.*
2 but: *I bought it here, though it is probably cheaper somewhere else.* ⟫ compare ALTHOUGH
3 **as though** as if: *She looked as though she had been crying.*

thought¹ /θɔt/
the PAST TENSE and PAST PARTICIPLE of the verb **think**

thought² *noun*
1 [U] the act of thinking: *After much thought, he decided not to buy the car.*
2 an idea or opinion that you think of: *She's very quiet and doesn't share her thoughts.*

thought·ful /'θɔtfəl/ *adjective*
serious and quiet because you are thinking about something: *He has a thoughtful look on his face.* —**thoughtfully** *adverb* —**thoughtfulness** *noun* [U]

thou·sand /'θaʊzənd/ *adjective, noun*
1 the number 1,000: *She lived over one thousand years ago.*
2 **thousands of something** a lot of: *There were thousands of people at the game.*

thou·sandth /'θaʊzəndθ/ *adjective, noun*
1,000th

thread¹ /θrɛd/ *noun*
a long single piece of cotton, silk, or other material that you use to sew clothes

thread² *verb*
to put a thread through a hole: *Can you thread this needle for me?*

threat /θrɛt/ *noun*
a warning that someone will hurt you if you do not do what he or she wants: *He **made a threat** against my family.*

threat·en /'θrɛt⌐n/ *verb*
to say that you will hurt another person if he or she does not do what you want

three /θri/ *adjective, noun*
the number 3

threw /θru/
the PAST TENSE of the verb **throw**

thrill¹ /θrɪl/ *verb*
to make someone feel strong excitement and pleasure: *David thrilled us with his stories.*

thrill² *noun*
a strong feeling of excitement or pleasure

thrilled /θrɪld/ *adjective*
very excited, pleased, or happy

thrill·ing /'θrɪlɪŋ/ *adjective*
exciting and interesting: *It was a thrilling game!*

throat /θroʊt/ *noun*
1 the part at the back of your mouth, where you swallow: *I can't speak. I have a sore throat.*
2 the front outside part of your neck: *He grabbed me by the throat.*

throne /θroʊn/ *noun*
the chair on which a king or queen sits

through¹ /θru/ *preposition*
1 into one side or end of something and out the other end or side: *The nail went through the wood.* | *He climbed in through the window.* —see color picture on page 194
2 by means of, or because of someone or something: *We solved the problem through discussion.*
3 during and to the end of a period of time: *She slept through the night.*

through² *adjective*
be through with something to have finished using something: *Are you through with the phone?*

through·out /θru'aʊt/ *preposition*
1 in every part of something: *He is famous throughout the world.*
2 during all of a period of time: *It rained throughout the night.*

throw¹ /θroʊ/ *verb* (**throwing**, **threw** /θru/, *past participle* **thrown**)
1 to send something through the air by moving your arm and pushing the thing out of your hand: *He threw the ball to me, and I caught it.* —see color picture on page 189
2 **throw something away** to get rid of something you do not want or need: *Did you throw the newspaper away?*
3 **throw something out** to get rid of something you do not want or need
4 **throw someone out** to force someone to leave a place: *He was thrown out of the restaurant for being drunk.*

throw² *noun*
an act of throwing something such as a ball

thrown /θroʊn/
the PAST PARTICIPLE of the verb **throw**

thrust /θrʌst/ *verb* [*past* **thrust**]
to push something somewhere suddenly and hard: *He thrust his hands into his pockets.*

thud /θʌd/ *noun*
a low sound made by something heavy hitting something else: *He fell and landed with a thud.*

thug /θʌg/ *noun*
a violent person

thumb /θʌm/ *noun*
the short, thick finger on your hand that helps you hold things —see picture at HAND¹

thumb·tack /'θʌmtæk/ *noun*
a short pin with a round, flat top used for attaching papers to a wall

thun·der /'θʌndɚ/ *noun* [U]
the loud sound that you hear in the sky during a storm

thun·der·storm /'θʌndɚˌstɔrm/ *noun*
a storm with heavy rain, loud noises, and bright flashes of light

Thurs·day /'θɚzdi, -deɪ/ *noun*
the fifth day of the week

tick¹ /tɪk/ *noun*
the short sound made by a watch or clock

tick² *verb*
if a clock ticks, it makes a short sound

tick·et /'tɪkɪt/ *noun*
a small piece of paper that shows that you have paid to do something: *Do you have your plane ticket?*

tick·le /'tɪkəl/ *verb* (**tickling**, **tickled**)
to move your fingers lightly on someone's body and make him or her laugh: *I tickled her under her arms.*

tic·tac·toe /ˌtɪk tæk 'toʊ/ *noun* [U]
a game in which two players draw the letters X and O in a pattern of nine squares

tide /taɪd/ *noun*
the rise and fall of the level of the ocean

ti·dy /'taɪdi/ *adj*
NEAT

tie¹ /taɪ/ *verb* (**tying**, **tied**)
1 to fasten something with a string or rope: *She tied the dog **to** the fence.*
2 to make a knot in a rope or string: *Can you tie your shoes?*
3 **be tied** to have the same number of points in a game: *The score is tied.*
4 **tie something up** to fasten something using a string or rope: *Tie the package up with some string.*

tie² *noun*
1 a narrow piece of cloth that you wear around your neck, tied in a knot outside your shirt —see color picture on page 190
2 the result of a game in which no one wins because both sides have the same number of points

ti·ger /'taɪgɚ/ *noun*
a large strong wild cat that has yellow fur with black lines —see color picture on page 183

tight¹ /taɪt/ *adjective*
1 pulled or stretched closely together: *Make the knot very tight.* ≫ compare SLACK
2 fitting part of your body very closely: *These shoes are too tight.* ≫ compare LOOSE

tight² *adverb*
very firmly or closely: ***Hold on** tight and don't let go of my hand.*

tight·en /'taɪt n/ *verb*
to close or fasten something firmly: *I need to tighten this screw. It's very loose.* ≫ compare LOOSEN

tight·ly /'taɪtli/ *adverb*
firmly: *Tie the string tightly.*

tile /taɪl/ *noun*
a flat thin piece of baked clay used for covering floors or walls

till¹ /tɪl, tl/
until: *I was up till 1:00 a.m. studying for my test.*

till² /tɪl/ *noun*
CASH REGISTER

tim·ber /ˈtɪmbɚ/ *noun* [U]
trees that are cut down and used for building things

time¹ /taɪm/ *noun*
1 [U] something that is measured in minutes, hours, days, years etc.: *How do your **spend** your time at home?*
2 [U] a particular point in time shown on a clock in hours and minutes: *What time is it?*
3 an occasion when something happens: *We'll go by car **next** time. | When was the last time you saw your sister?*
4 [U] the amount of time that you need to do something: *It takes a long time to learn a new language. | I don't have time to stop now.*
5 used for showing how often something happens: *I go swimming three times a week. | One time (=once) we went to Australia.*
6 a particular period in history: *This road was built during the time of the Romans.*
7 **on time** at the right time; not early, not late: *The train arrived on time.*
8 **in time** early or soon enough to do something: *We arrived in time **to** see her sing.*
9 **it's time, it's about time** said when you think something should be done or should happen soon: *She said it was time to go.*
10 **all the time** continuously; often: *It rained all the time in Portland. | I used to play tennis all the time.*
11 **at a time** in one group; together: *She can only have two visitors at a time.*
12 **at times** sometimes: *I hated my job at times.*
13 **in no time** soon or quickly: *We will be there in no time.*
14 **for the time being** for now; for a short while: *You can live with us for the time being.*
15 **have a good time** to enjoy yourself: *Have a good time at the party.*
16 **ahead of time** before an event, or before you need to do something: *We should arrive ahead of time to get a good seat.*
17 **take your time** to do something slowly and carefully without hurrying: *There's no hurry. Take your time.*

18 **from time to time** sometimes, but not very often: *We go to the theater from time to time.*

time² *verb* (timing, timed)
1 to do something or arrange for something to happen at a particular time: *The bomb was timed to go off at 4 o'clock.*
2 to measure how long it takes to do something

time off /ˌ. ˈ./ *noun* [U]
time when you are allowed not to be at work

times /taɪmz/ *preposition*
multiplied by: *2 times 2 is 4.*

tim·id /ˈtɪmɪd/ *adjective*
not brave; shy

tin /tɪn/ *noun* [U]
a soft white metal used for making cans

ti·ny /ˈtaɪni/ *adjective* (tinier, tiniest)
very small

tip¹ /tɪp/ *verb* (tipping, tipped)
1 (also **tip over**) to fall or turn over, or make something do this: *I tipped the box over and the papers fell out.*
2 to lean at an angle, or to make something do this: *I tipped the table and the glasses fell off.*
3 to give a small amount of money to someone for his or her service: *How much did you tip him?*

tip² *noun*
1 the pointed end of something: *I cut the tip **of** my finger.*
2 a small amount of money that you give to someone for his or her service: *Did you leave a tip?*
3 a useful piece of advice: *He **gave** me some tips **on** choosing a good car.*

tip·toe¹ /ˈtɪptoʊ/ *verb* (tiptoeing, tiptoed)
to walk on your toes, especially when you do not want to make any noise: *I tiptoed past the sleeping child.*

creak!

tiptoe² *noun*
on tiptoe standing on your toes, with the rest of your foot off the ground: *Let's walk on tiptoe so they don't hear us.*

tire¹ /taɪɚ/ *noun*
a thick round piece of rubber that fits around the wheel of a car, bicycle etc.

tire² /verb/ (tiring, tired)
to feel that you need to rest, or to make someone feel this: *Even a short walk would tire her out.*

tired /taɪəd/ *adjective*
1 feeling that you need to rest or sleep: *I felt tired after work.*
2 **be tired of something** to be bored with something or annoyed by it: *I am tired of listening to her stories.*
3 **be tired out** to be completely tired

tis·sue /'tɪʃu/ *noun*
a thin soft piece of paper used for blowing your nose

ti·tle /'taɪtl/ *noun*
1 the name of a story, book, movie etc.
2 a word used in front of someone's name: *Doctors have the title "Dr." in front of their name.*

to /tə, before vowels tʊ; strong tu/ *adverb, preposition*
1 in the direction of; toward: *He ran to the door.* | *We are driving to town.*
2 in order to be in a particular state, place etc.: *I couldn't get to sleep last night.* | *Are you going to the wedding?*
3 used for showing the position of something: *The water came up to our knees.*
4 used for showing who receives or owns something: *Give the book to her.* | *The ring belongs to her mother.*
5 used for showing why you do something: *She worked hard to earn some money.*
6 used after a verb to show the INFINITIVE: *Does anyone want to go?*
7 used for saying how many minutes there are until the next hour: *It's ten to nine.* (=10 minutes before 9 o'clock)
8 **from something to something** starting with one thing or place and ending with another: *I can count from 1 to 100.* | *It's twenty miles from here to the city.*

toad /toʊd/ *noun*
an animal like a large FROG

toast /toʊst/ *noun* [U]
bread that is heated until it is brown and hard: *I had a **piece of** toast for breakfast.*

toast·er /'toʊstə/ *noun*
a machine that is used for making TOAST

to·bac·co /tə'bækoʊ/ *noun* [U]
the dried leaves of a plant that are smoked in cigarettes

to·day /tə'deɪ/ *noun, adverb*
1 the day that is happening now: *Today is Monday.*
2 the present time: *Many of today's students use computers at school.*

toe /toʊ/ *noun*
one of the five parts on the end of your foot
—see picture at FOOT

toe·nail /'toʊneɪl/ *noun*
the hard flat part that covers the top end of your toe

tof·fee /'tɔfi, 'tɑfi/ *noun*
a sticky brown candy made from sugar and butter, or a piece of this

to·geth·er /tə'gɛðə/ *adverb*
1 forming a single group, mixture, or object: *Can you add these numbers together?* | *I stuck the two pieces of paper together.*
2 at the same time: *The two letters arrived together.*
3 with or next to each other: *We went to school together.*

toi·let /'tɔɪlɪt/ *noun*
a container that you sit on to get rid of waste from your body

toilet paper /'.. ,../ *noun* [U]
thin soft paper which you use to clean yourself after you get rid of waste from your body

to·ken /'toʊkən/ *noun*
1 a piece of metal like a coin that you use in some machines
2 something that represents a feeling, event, fact etc.: *We shook hands as a token **of** our friendship.*

told /toʊld/
the PAST TENSE and PAST PARTICIPLE of the verb **tell**

toll¹ /toʊl/ *noun*
1 the number of people killed or injured at a particular time: *The **death toll** has risen to 83.*
2 **take its toll (on)** to have a bad effect on someone or something over a long period of time: *Smoking has taken its toll on his health.*
3 the money you have to pay to use a particular road, bridge etc.

toll² *verb*
if a bell tolls, or you toll it, it keeps ringing slowly

to·ma·to /tə'meɪtoʊ/ *noun* (plural **tomatoes**)
a soft round red fruit that you can eat raw or cooked —see picture at FRUIT

tomb /tum/ *noun*
a grave above the ground in which a dead person is put

tom·boy /'tɑmbɔɪ/ *noun* (*plural* **tomboys**)
a girl who likes to play the same games as boys

to·mor·row /tə'mɑroʊ, -'mɔr-/ *noun, adverb*
1 The day after today: *It's too late to do it now. Let's do it tomorrow.* ≫ compare YESTERDAY
2 the future: *We are building the computer of tomorrow.*

ton /tʌn/ *noun*
1 a measure of weight equal to 2,000 pounds
2 a very large amount or weight: *We ate tons of food! | This box weighs a ton!*

tone /toʊn/ *noun*
1 the way your voice sounds that shows how you are feeling: *I could tell that she was angry by the tone of her voice.*
2 the sound of a musical instrument

tongs /tɑŋz, tɔŋz/ *plural noun*
a tool made of two narrow pieces of metal joined at one end, used for picking things up: *He picked up the hot metal with a pair of tongs.*

tongue /tʌŋ/ *noun*
1 the part inside your mouth that moves when you speak
2 **hold your tongue, bite your tongue** not to speak: *I wanted to shout at him, but I had to bite my tongue.*

to·night /tə'naɪt/ *adverb, noun*
the night or the evening at the end of today: *We are going to a party tonight.*

too /tu/ *adverb*
1 also: *I want to come too. | "I'm hungry." "I am too!"*
2 more than is needed or wanted: *He drives too fast. | She drinks too much.*
3 very: *You shouldn't have to wait too long for the bus.*

took /tʊk/
the PAST TENSE of the verb **take**

tool /tul/ *noun*
something that helps you build or repair things

tooth /tuθ/ *noun* (*plural* **teeth** /tiθ/)
1 one of the white hard objects in your mouth that you use to bite your food: *You should **brush your** teeth after every meal.*
2 one of the sharp pointed parts on a comb or SAW

tooth·ache /'tuθeɪk/ *noun*
a pain in a tooth

tooth·brush /'tuθbrʌʃ/ *noun*
a small brush for cleaning your teeth —see picture at BRUSH¹

tooth·paste /'tuθpeɪst/ *noun* [U]
a substance used for cleaning your teeth

tooth·pick /'tuθ,pɪk/ *noun*
a small pointed piece of wood used for removing pieces of food from between your teeth

top¹ /tɑp/ *noun*
1 the highest part of something: *He climbed to the top of the hill.* ≫ compare BOTTOM
2 the flat upper surface or cover of something: *My table has a glass top. | He took the top off the box.*
3 clothing that you wear on the upper part of your body: *I need a new top to wear with this skirt.*

top² *adjective*
1 highest: *Put it in the top drawer.*
2 best or most successful: *It was the top movie of the week!*

top³ *verb* (**topping, topped**)
to be higher, better, or more than something: *Our sales topped $1,000,000 this year!*

top·ic /'tɑpɪk/ *noun*
something to talk or write about

torch /tɔrtʃ/ *noun* (*plural* **torches**)
a long stick that you burn at one end for a light

tore /tɔr/
the PAST TENSE of the verb **tear**

torn /tɔrn/
the PAST PARTICIPLE of the verb **tear**

tor·na·do /tɔr'neɪdoʊ/ *noun* (*plural* **tornadoes** or **tornados**)
a storm with strong winds that spin very fast

tor·pe·do /tɔr'pidoʊ/ *noun* (*plural* **torpedos**)
a weapon that is fired under the surface of the ocean from one ship at another

tor·toise /'tɔrtəs/ *noun*
a land animal that moves very slowly, with a hard shell covering its body

tor·ture¹ /'tɔrtʃɚ/ *verb* (**torturing, tortured**)
to make someone suffer pain so that he or she will give information

torture² *noun*
the act of making someone suffer pain so that he or she will give information

toss /tɔs/ *verb*
1 to throw something: *They tossed the ball to each other.*
2 **toss something out** to get rid of something: *"Where's the newspaper?" "I tossed it out."*

to·tal¹ /'toʊtl/ *noun*
the final number after everything has been added together: *Add up these numbers and tell me the total.*

total² *adjective*
complete; including everything: *The total cost of the building is not yet known.*

to·tal·ly /'toʊtl-i/ *adverb*
completely: *I totally agree with you.*

touch¹ /tʌtʃ/ *verb*
1 to put your finger, hand etc. on something so that you feel it: *Don't touch the paint. It's still wet.*
2 if two things are touching, there is no space between them: *Are the wires touching?*

touch² *noun*
1 the action of putting your finger, hand etc. on something: *I felt the touch of his hand.*
2 [U] the sense that you use to feel something by putting your finger, hand etc. on it
3 **get in touch** to write to someone or to telephone him or her: *I've been trying to get in touch with you all day.*
4 **keep in touch, stay in touch** to speak or write to someone regularly: *Do you still keep in touch with John?*

tough /tʌf/ *adjective*
1 difficult and needing a lot of effort: *She has a tough job.* | *Moving here was a tough decision.*
2 not easy to cut or bite; hard: *This meat is tough.* ≫ compare TENDER
3 very strict: *There are tough laws against smoking.*

tour¹ /tʊr/ *noun*
1 a trip during which you visit different places: *They have gone on a tour of Egypt.*
2 a short trip through a place to see the things in it: *We went on a tour of the museum.*

tour² *verb*
to visit a place during a trip: *We toured a candy factory.*

tour·ism /'tʊrɪzəm/ *noun* [U]
the business of having places for people to stay and things for them to do while on vacation

tour·ist /'tʊrɪst/ *noun*
someone who travels for pleasure

tour·na·ment /'tʊrnəmənt, 'tɚ-/ *noun*
a sports competition

tow /toʊ/ *verb*
to pull a vehicle or ship using a rope or chain: *We towed the car to the garage.*

to·ward /tɔrd, tə'wɔrd/ (*also* **towards**) *preposition*
1 in the direction of: *She walked toward me.* | *The storm was moving toward the city.* | *He lives down toward San Diego.* —see color picture on page 194
2 just before a particular time: *I felt tired toward the end of the day.*
3 concerning someone or something: *How do you feel toward her?*

tow·el /'taʊəl/ *noun*
a piece of cloth used for drying something

tow·er /'taʊɚ/ *noun*
a tall narrow building or part of a building

town /taʊn/ *noun*
a place with many houses and stores where people live and work ≫ compare CITY

town hall /,. './ *noun*
a building used for a town's local government

toy /tɔɪ/ *noun* [*plural* **toys**]
an object made for children to play with

trace¹ /treɪs/ *noun*
a small sign that shows that someone or something has been in a place: *We found no trace of them in the building.*

trace² *verb* (**tracing, traced**)
1 to copy a picture, plan etc. by putting a piece of paper over it and drawing the lines that you can see
2 to try to find someone or something by looking carefully: *They are trying to trace the missing child.*

track /træk/ *noun*
1 a road or path with a rough surface
2 the two metal lines along which a train rolls: *We walked across the railroad tracks.*
3 **tracks** [*plural*] a series of marks made on the ground by an animal, person, or vehicle: *The hunter followed the animal's tracks.*

4 keep track of to know where something is and what is happening: *It is hard to keep track of everyone's names.*

5 lose track of to not know where something is, or not know what is happening: *I've lost track of when the meeting is.*

track and field /ˌ. . './ *noun* [U]
all the sports that involve running races, jumping, and throwing things —see color picture on page 184

trac·tor /'træktɚ/ *noun*
a large vehicle used for pulling farm equipment —see color picture on page 187

trade¹ /treɪd/ *noun*
1 [U] the activity of buying and selling goods: *Trade with other countries is important.*
2 an exchange of one thing for another: *I made a trade for his baseball.*
3 a particular job: *She's a dressmaker by trade.*

trade² *verb* (**trading, traded**)
1 to buy and sell goods: *We trade with other countries.*
2 to exchange one thing for another: *I'll trade my candy for your book.*

trade·mark /'treɪdmɑrk/ *noun*
a special name or mark on a product that shows that it is made by a particular company

trad·er /'treɪdɚ/ *noun*
someone who buys and sells goods

tra·di·tion /trə'dɪʃən/ *noun*
a belief or custom that has existed for a long time: *Telling stories at Christmas is an old family tradition.*

tra·di·tion·al /trə'dɪʃənl/ *adjective*
being done in a particular way for a long time: *We sing a traditional song at family birthdays.* —**traditionally** *adverb*

traf·fic /'træfɪk/ *noun* [U]
1 the cars and people moving on a particular road: *The city streets are full of traffic.*
2 the movement of airplanes, ships, or trains from one place to another

traffic jam /'.. ˌ./ *noun*
a long line of vehicles that cannot move, or that move slowly on a road

traffic lights /'.. ˌ./ *plural noun*
lights that change color to direct the movement of traffic

trag·e·dy /'trædʒədi/ *noun* (*plural* **tragedies**)
1 an event that causes a lot of sadness: *Her son's death was a great tragedy.*
2 a serious play with a sad ending

tra·gic /'trædʒɪk/ *adjective*
very sad: *She had a tragic accident.*

trail /treɪl/ *noun*
1 a series of marks on the ground that show where someone or something has been: *The man left a trail of blood on the floor.*
2 a path across open country, or through mountains or woods

trail·er /'treɪlɚ/ *noun*
a vehicle that can be pulled by a car —see color picture on page 187

train¹ /treɪn/ *noun*
1 a number of railroad cars pulled by an ENGINE —see color picture on page 187
2 by train on a train: *We traveled by train.*

train² *verb*
1 to teach someone or be taught to do a particular job or activity: *She is training to become a nurse.*
2 to prepare for a sports event by exercising: *I am training for the Olympics.*

train·ee /treɪ'ni/ *noun*
someone who is being taught how to do a job

train·ing /'treɪnɪŋ/ *noun* [U]
1 the process of being taught how to do a particular job: *Do you have any training in computers?*
2 special activities or exercises that you do for a sport

trai·tor /'treɪtɚ/ *noun*
someone who is not loyal to his or her friends or country: *The traitor was sent to prison.*

trans·fer¹ /'trænsfɚ, træns'fɚ/ *verb* (**transferring, transferred**)
to move from one place or job to another: *His company transferred him to another office. | I want to transfer some money into my bank account.*

transfer² *noun*
the act of moving someone or something from one place to another

trans·form /træns'fɔrm/ *verb*
to change the appearance or character of something or someone completely: *The country transformed itself into a world power.*

tran·si·tive /ˈtrænˌzətɪv/ *noun, adjective*
a transitive verb has an object: *In the sentence I gave the book to Jane, "gave" is a transitive verb.* ≫ compare INTRANSITIVE

trans·late /ˈtrænzleɪt, ˌtrænzˈleɪt/ *verb*
(translating, translated)
to give the meaning of words of one language in another language: *He translated the speech from Spanish into English.* —**translator** *noun* ≫ compare INTERPRET

trans·la·tion /trænzˈleɪʃən/ *noun*
1 something that has been changed from one language into another
2 [U] the activity or job of changing the words of one language into another

trans·par·ent /trænsˈpærənt, -ˈpɛr-/ *adjective*
clear and easy to see through: *Glass is transparent.*

trans·plant /trænsˈplænt/ *verb*
to move something from one place to another

trans·port /trænsˈpɔrt/ *verb*
to move or carry goods or people from one place to another: *The coal was transported by train.*

trans·por·ta·tion /ˌtrænspərˈteɪʃən/ *noun* [U]
the process or business of moving people or goods from one place to another: *Buses are an important form of public transportation.*

trap¹ /træp/ *noun*
1 a piece of equipment for catching an animal: *Did you buy a mouse trap?*
2 a plan to catch someone: *The police set a trap for the thieves.*

trap² *verb*
(trapping, trapped)
1 **be trapped** to not be able to escape from a dangerous or unpleasant place: *She was trapped in the burning house.*
2 to catch an animal in a trap: *He is trapping rabbits.*

trash /træʃ/ *noun*
waste material such as old food and dirty paper, or the container that this is put into: *Throw this in the trash for me.*

trash can /ˈ. ./ *noun*
GARBAGE CAN

trav·el¹ /ˈtrævəl/ *verb*
1 to make a trip from one place to another: *I want to travel around the world.*
2 to move at a particular speed, or go a particular distance: *What speed is he traveling?* | *We traveled 200 miles today.*

travel² *noun* [U]
the activity of traveling: *The rain is making travel difficult.*

travel a·gen·cy /ˈ.. ˌ.../ *noun* (*plural* **travel agencies**)
a business that arranges travel and vacations

travel a·gent /ˈ.. ˌ../ *noun*
someone who works in a TRAVEL AGENCY

trav·el·er /ˈtrævələ/ *noun*
someone who is on a trip

traveler's check /ˈ... ˌ./ *noun*
a special check that you take to another country to get money in that country

tray /treɪ/ *noun* (*plural* **trays**)
a flat piece of wood, metal, or plastic that is used for carrying food, plates etc.

treas·ure /ˈtrɛʒə/ *noun* [U]
gold, silver, jewels, money etc.: *They found the treasure buried under a tree.*

treat¹ /trit/ *verb*
1 to behave toward someone in a particular way: *He treats his dog very badly.* | *At work she treats everyone the same.*
2 to consider something in a particular way: *The subject of crime must be treated carefully.*
3 to give someone medical attention for an injury or sickness: *The children were treated for burn injuries.*
4 to give someone something special: *I'm going to treat my mother to a new hat.*

treat² *noun*
something special that you give to someone or do for someone: *As a treat, I bought her some ice cream.*

treat·ment /ˈtritˀmənt/ *noun*
1 a way of making someone who is sick or injured better: *The hospital is trying a new treatment for bone disease.*
2 [U] the way you behave towards someone: *He did not receive any special treatment.*

trea·ty /'triti/ *noun* (*plural* **treaties**)
a formal written agreement between two or more countries: *Both countries signed the* **peace** *treaty.*

tree /tri/ *noun*
a large plant with branches, leaves, and a thick TRUNK (=main stem)

trem·ble /'trɛmbəl/ *verb* (**trembling, trembled**)
to shake because you are afraid, upset, or angry: *Her lips are trembling with fear.*

tre·men·dous /trɪ'mɛndəs/ *adjective*
1 very great in size, amount, or power: *A tremendous explosion destroyed the building.*
2 very good or wonderful: *The plan was a tremendous success.* —**tremendously** *adverb*

trench /trɛntʃ/ *noun* (*plural* **trenches**)
a long narrow hole that is dug in the earth

trend /trɛnd/ *noun*
the way that a situation develops or changes

tres·pass /'trɛspæs/ *verb*
to go onto someone else's land without permission

tres·pass·er /'trɛspæsɚ, -'pəsɚ/ *noun*
someone who goes onto someone else's land without permission

tri·al /'traɪəl/ *noun*
1 the process in which a court of law decides whether someone is guilty of a crime: *The trial lasted a month.* | *She is* **on** *trial* **for** *murder.*
2 a test to know if something is good or bad: *The trials for the new drug are going well.*

tri·an·gle /'traɪˌæŋgəl/ *noun*
a flat shape with three straight sides and three angles —**triangular** *adjective* —see picture at SHAPE[1]

trib·al /'traɪbəl/ *adjective*
relating to a tribe: *I collect tribal art.*

tribe /traɪb/ *noun*
a group of people of the same race, language, customs etc. that live in one place

trib·ute /'trɪbyut/ *noun*
something that you say, do, or give to show your respect or admiration for someone: *The movie is a tribute* **to** *their courage.*

trick¹ /trɪk/ *noun*
1 something that you do to deceive someone: *He got the money from me by a trick.*

2 a set of actions done to entertain people: *I can* **do** *magic tricks.*
3 **play a trick on someone** to surprise someone and make other people laugh: *She played a trick on her brother.*

trick² *verb*
to deceive or cheat someone: *He tricked me* **into** *giving him my money.*

trick·le /'trɪkəl/ *verb* (**trickling, trickled**)
if a liquid trickles, it flows in drops or a thin stream: *Blood trickled from the wound.*

trick·y /'trɪki/ *adjective* (**trickier, trickiest**)
difficult to deal with: *This is a tricky job.*

tri·cy·cle /'traɪsɪkəl/ *noun*
a small vehicle with one wheel at the front and two at the back, usually for children

tried /traɪd/
the PAST TENSE and PAST PARTICIPLE of the verb **try**

trig·ger /'trɪgɚ/ *noun*
a small part of a gun that you press with your finger to fire it

trim /trɪm/ *verb* (**trimming, trimmed**)
to make something neater by cutting a small amount off it: *She trimmed his hair.*

trip¹ /trɪp/ *noun*
an occasion when you go from one place to another: *She is* **on a** *business trip to New York.*

trip² *verb* (**tripping, tripped**)
to hit your foot against something so that you fall or nearly fall: *Be careful! Don't trip over that box.*

tri·umph /'traɪəmf/ *noun*
a victory or a success: *Winning the race is a great triumph for our team.*

trol·ley /'trɑli/ *noun* (*plural* **trolleys**)
a vehicle that carries people along the street on metal tracks

troops /trups/ *plural noun*
groups of soldiers

tro·phy /'troʊfi/ *noun* (*plural* **trophies**)
a prize given to someone for winning a game or race

trop·i·cal /'trɑpɪkəl/ *adjective*
1 coming from or existing in the hottest parts of the world: *The coconut is a tropical plant.*
2 very hot: *I am not used to tropical weather.*

trop·ics /'trɑpɪks/ *plural noun*
the tropics the hottest wettest parts of the world

trou·ble¹ /'trʌbəl/ *noun*

1 [U] problems that make something difficult: *I'm **having** some trouble **with** the car.*

2 [U] a difficult or dangerous situation: *Visitors to the country could be **in** trouble.*

3 [U] a problem that you have with your health: *He has heart trouble.*

4 a situation in which someone is angry with you and wants to punish you: *Is she **in** trouble **with** the police again?*

5 the effort and time that is needed to do something: *He **took the** trouble **to** explain it to me.* | *It's **no** trouble (=no difficulty) to help you.*

6 a situation in which people argue or fight with each other

7 the trouble with someone or something used when saying what is not good about someone or something: *The trouble with her is she always criticizes people.*

trouble² *verb* (**troubling, troubled**)
to ask someone to do something for you, especially when it is difficult: *I'll not trouble you again.*

trou·bled /'trʌbəld/ *adjective*
having many emotional problems

trough /trɔf/ *noun*
a long narrow open container that holds food or water for animals

truck /trʌk/ *noun*
a large vehicle used for carrying heavy loads —see color picture on page 187

true /tru/ *adjective* (**truer, truest**)

1 correct, real, and based on facts: *I will tell you a true story.* ≫ compare FALSE, UNTRUE

2 come true if dreams or wishes come true, they happen: *His wish of writing a book finally came true.*

tru·ly /'truli/ *adverb*
really; in a way that is true: *I am truly grateful for all your help.*

trum·pet /'trʌmpɪt/ *noun*
a musical instrument that you blow into, shaped like a bent metal tube that is wide at one end

trunk /trʌŋk/ *noun*

1 the thick wooden stem of a tree

2 an enclosed space at the back of a car in which you can carry tools, bags etc.

3 a large box in which you carry or store clothes

4 the long nose of an ELEPHANT

5 the human body without the head, arms, or legs

trunks /trʌŋks/ *plural noun*
a piece of clothing like short pants, that men wear when they swim

trust¹ /trʌst/ *verb*

1 to believe that someone is honest and good and will not hurt you: *I don't trust her since she lied to me.*

2 to depend on something: *You can trust him to do his best.*

trust² *noun* [U]
the belief that someone is good and honest and will not hurt you: *You have to be careful who you put your trust in.*

trust·wor·thy /'trʌst,wɚði/ *adjective*
able to be trusted or depended on: *Let Paul have the money; he's trustworthy.*

truth /truθ/ *noun* [U]
what is true; the correct facts: *You should always tell the truth.* ≫ compare LIE²

truth·ful /'truθfəl/ *adjective*
giving the true facts about something: *The statement is truthful.* —**truthfully** *adverb*

try¹ /traɪ/ *verb* (**trying, tried**)

1 to attempt to do something: *He tried to climb the tree, but he could not.* | *Please try not to be late.*

2 to do something or test something to find out if it is suitable or good: *Try another match to see if it lights.* | *Are you going to try out your new radio?* | *I want to try another piece of cake.*

3 to examine and judge someone in a court of law: *He is being tried for the crime.*

4 try something on to put on a piece of clothing to see if it fits you: *Can I try this shirt on?*

try² *noun* (*plural* **tries**)
an attempt to do something: *If you can't open the box, let me have a try.*

T-shirt /'ti ʃɚt/ *noun*
a light shirt with short sleeves —see color picture on page 190

tub /tʌb/ *noun*

1 a bathtub

2 a round container used for holding things: *A tub of ice sat outside.*

tube /tub/ *noun*

1 a hollow pipe made of metal, plastic, glass, or rubber

2 a long round container for a soft substance: *We need to buy a tube **of** toothpaste.* —see picture at CONTAINER

tuck /tʌk/ *verb*
1 to push the edge of a piece of clothing into something else: *Tuck your shirt into your pants.*
2 tuck someone in to make someone comfortable in bed by pulling the covers over him or her
3 to put something into a small space or a safe place: *She tucked the money into her pocket.*

Tues·day /'tuzdi, -deɪ/ *noun*
the third day of the week

tug¹ /tʌg/ *verb* (**tugging, tugged**)
to pull something hard: *The child tugged at my hand.*

tug² *noun*
1 a sudden strong pull: *I gave the rope a tug.*
2 (*also* **tug boat**) a small powerful boat used for pulling ships to or from a place

tug-of-war /ˌ. . './ *noun*
a competition in which two groups of people pull on opposite ends of a rope

tu·lip /'tulɪp/ *noun*
a tall brightly colored flower shaped like a cup

tum·ble /'tʌmbəl/ *verb* (**tumbling, tumbled**)
to fall or roll suddenly: *She tumbled down the stairs.*

tum·bler /'tʌmblɚ/ *noun*
a glass with a flat bottom and straight sides

tum·my /'tʌmi/ *noun* (*plural* **tummies**)
your stomach: *Mommy, I have a tummy ache.*

tu·na /'tunə/ *noun*
a large common ocean fish, or the meat from this fish, usually sold in cans

tune¹ /tun/ *noun*
a series of musical notes that are pleasant to listen to: *The song has a happy tune.* ≫ compare SONG

tune² *verb* (**tuning, tuned**)
1 to make small changes to the strings of a musical instrument so that it gives the correct sound: *When was the last time the piano was tuned?*
2 tune in to watch or listen to a particular television or radio program: *Millions of people tuned in to watch the game.*

tune-up /'. ./ *noun*
an occasion when someone fixes and cleans your car's engine

tun·nel¹ /'tʌnl/ *noun*
a passage through a mountain or under the ground, for cars or trains

tunnel² *verb*
to dig a passage through a mountain or under the ground

tur·ban /'tɚbən/ *noun*
a long piece of cloth that is worn around the top of your head

tur·key /'tɚki/ *noun* (*plural* **turkeys**)
1 a large farm bird that is used for food
2 [U] the meat of this bird: *We had roast turkey for dinner.*

turn¹ /tɚn/ *verb*
1 to move so that you are looking in a new direction: *She turned to look behind her.* | *He turned over in the bed.*
2 to go in a new direction, or make something do this: *She turned left at the end of the road.*
3 to go around and around, or make something do this: *The wheels are turning.* | *Turn the wheel to the right.*
4 to become a particular age: *He just turned 40.* | *When does she turn 21?*
5 to move an object so that it is facing a new direction: *I turned the box over to see the bottom.*
6 turn something down (a) to make a machine produce less sound, heat etc.: *Turn the television down. It's too loud.* (b) (*also* **turn someone down**) to say no to an offer or request: *He turned down the new job.*
7 turn something off to make something stop working: *Turn the radio off.*
8 turn something on to make something start working: *Turn the heater on.*
9 turn up (a) to make a machine produce more sound, heat etc.: *Please turn up the TV. I can't hear it!* (b) to arrive at a place: *He turned up late.*
10 turn a page to move a page so that you can see the next one
11 turn something out if you turn out a light, you push a button to make it stop shining

12 turn something over to give someone the right to own something or be responsible for something: *He turned the business over to his children.*

13 turn to to try to get help from someone or something: *He turned to his parents for advice.*

14 turn out to happen in a particular way, or have a particular result: *How did the meeting turn out?*

15 turn something into something to become something different, or make something do this: *She turned her bedroom into an office.*

16 turn someone against someone or something to make someone stop liking or agreeing with someone or something: *My bad experiences turned me against the job.*

turn² *noun*
1 the time when it is your chance to do something: *It's my turn to choose a movie.*
2 take turns to do something that a group of people are doing, one after the other: *We took turns driving the children to school.*
3 the act of moving an object or your body so that it faces a different direction: *Give the wheel another turn.*
4 a change in the direction you are moving: *Make a right turn at the end of the road.*
5 a place where a road joins another road: *We missed our turn and had to stop the car.*

turn sig·nal /'. ,../ *noun*
one of the two lights on a car that are used for showing that the car is going to turn left or right

tur·tle /'tɔtl/ *noun*
an animal with a hard shell over its body, that lives mainly in the water —see color picture on page 183

tusk /tʌsk/ *noun*
one of two very long pointed teeth that grows out of the mouth of an animal such as an ELEPHANT

tu·tor¹ /'tutɚ/ *noun*
someone who teaches only one or a few students in a particular subject: *Her French tutor teaches her at home.*

tutor² *verb*
to teach someone a particular subject: *He tutored me in English.*

TV /ˌ. './ *noun*
1 a television: *Turn on the TV.*
2 on TV shown on the television: *There's a good movie on TV tonight.*

tweez·ers /'twizɚz/ *plural noun*
a small tool made of two thin pieces of metal joined at one end, used for pulling out single hairs

twelfth /twɛlfθ/ *adjective, noun*
12th

twelve /twɛlv/ *adjective, noun*
the number 12

twen·ty /'twɛnti/ *adjective, noun*
the number 20

twice /twaɪs/ *adverb*
two times: *You've asked me that question twice.*

twig /twɪg/ *noun*
a very small branch on a tree

twin /twɪn/ *noun*
one of two children who are born to the same mother at the same time

twin bed /ˌ. './ *noun*
a bed for one person

twin·kle /'twɪŋkəl/ *verb* (twinkling, twinkled)
to shine while changing from bright to dark: *The stars twinkled in the sky.*

twist¹ /twɪst/ *verb*
1 to turn something together or around something else: *She twisted her hair around her fingers.*
2 to turn around or bend a part of your body: *I twisted my ankle when I fell.*
3 to have a lot of curves and change directions: *The path twisted up the hill.*

twist² *noun*
1 a shape made by twisting something: *There are several twists in the rope.*
2 a sudden change in a story or situation: *Her information put a new twist on things.*
3 a bend in a road or river

twitch /twɪtʃ/ *verb*
to move suddenly and quickly without control: *The cat's tail twitched several times.* —**twitch** *noun*

two /tu/ *adjective, noun*
the number 2

ty·ing /'taɪ-ɪŋ/
the PRESENT PARTICIPLE of the verb **tie**

type¹ /taɪp/ noun
a particular kind of person or thing: *A rose is a type of flower.* ≫ compare KIND¹

type² verb (typing, typed)
to write something using a machine such as a computer: *Are you finished typing the letter?*

type·writ·er /'taɪp,raɪtə/ noun
a machine used for writing letters onto paper

typ·i·cal /'tɪpɪkəl/ adjective
having the usual qualities of a particular group, person, or thing: *A typical day at work goes by very slowly.*

typ·i·cal·ly /'tɪpɪkli/ adverb
in the way that something usually happens: *Prices typically fall when there is too much of a product.*

typ·ing /'taɪpɪŋ/ noun [U]
the activity of writing using a machine such as a computer or TYPEWRITER

UFO /ˌyu ɛf 'oʊ/ *noun*
an object in the sky that you do not recognize; some people think it might be a space vehicle from another world —see color picture on page 192

ug·ly /'ʌgli/ *adjective* (**uglier, ugliest**)
very unpleasant to look at: *The little dog has an ugly face.*

um·brel·la /ʌm'brɛlə/ *noun*
a piece of plastic stretched over a frame, that you can hold over your head to protect you from the rain

um·pire /'ʌmpaɪɚ/ *noun*
someone who makes sure that the rules are obeyed in a sports game

un·a·ble /ʌn'eɪbəl/ *adjective*
not able to do something: *She was unable **to** attend the meeting because she was sick.* ≫ opposite ABLE

un·ac·cept·a·ble /ˌʌnək'sɛptəbəl/ *adjective*
so wrong or bad that it should not continue: *Your behavior is totally unacceptable!*

u·nan·i·mous /yu'nænəməs/ *adjective*
a unanimous decision is one on which everyone agrees

un·armed /ˌʌn'ɑrmd◂/ *adjective* ≫ opposite ARMED
not carrying a gun or other weapon

un·at·trac·tive /ˌʌnə'træktɪv◂/ *adjective*
not beautiful or attractive: *The company is in an unattractive area of the city.* ≫ opposite ATTRACTIVE

un·bear·a·ble /ˌʌn'bɛrəbəl/ *adjective*
too painful or unpleasant for you to be able to deal with it: *The pain in my leg is unbearable.*

un·be·liev·a·ble /ˌʌnbɪ'livəbəl/ *adjective*
very surprising: *It's unbelievable how strong she is.* ≫ opposite BELIEVABLE

un·cer·tain /ʌn'sɚt̚n/ *adjective*
not sure or certain about something: *He was*

uncertain what to buy for her. | Our plans are still uncertain.

un·cle /'ʌŋkəl/ *noun*
the brother of one of your parents, or the husband of the sister of one of your parents ≫ compare AUNT

un·clear /ˌʌn'klɪr◂/ *adjective*
difficult to understand or be sure about: *Her instructions were unclear.*

un·com·fort·a·ble /ʌn'kʌmftəbəl, ʌn'kʌmfɚtəbəl/ *adjective*
1 not feeling relaxed, or not pleasant to sit on, lie on, or wear: *The large chair was uncomfortable.*
2 embarrassed or worried; not happy: *I feel uncomfortable talking about my personal life.*

un·com·mon /ʌn'kɑmən/ *adjective*
rare or unusual ≫ compare RARE

un·con·scious /ˌʌn'kɑnʃəs◂/ *adjective*
not able to see, hear, or move because you are not conscious: *The fall knocked her unconscious for several minutes.* ≫ opposite CONSCIOUS

un·con·trol·la·ble /ˌʌnkən'troʊləbəl/ *adjective*
not able to be stopped or controlled: *He was in a state of uncontrollable anger.*

un·cov·er /ʌn'kʌvɚ/ *verb*
1 to remove a cover from on top of something else: *He uncovered the dish and showed us the food.*
2 to discover a fact, event etc. that was secret or hidden: *The police uncovered their plan to steal the money.*

un·der /'ʌndɚ/ *preposition, adverb*
1 in or to a lower place that is below something: *She sat in the shade under a tree. | My shoes are under the bed.* —see color picture on page 194
2 less than a particular number, age, amount etc.: *The ticket was under ten dollars.* [=cost less than $10] | *All the children are under twelve years old.*
3 controlled or governed by a system, government etc.: *The country is under military rule.*
4 having a lower position in a job, company etc.: *She has three people under her at work.*
5 under way happening or being done: *The project is already under way.*

un·der·go /ˌʌndɚ'goʊ/ *verb*
(*present participle* **undergoing,** *past tense* **underwent** /ˌʌndɚ'wɛnt/, *past participle* **undergone** /ˌʌndɚ'gɔn/)

to experience something that is unpleasant or hard to deal with: *He underwent two operations on his foot.*

un·der·grad·u·ate /ˌʌndə'grædʒuɪt/ *noun*
a student in the first four years of college

un·der·ground /'ʌndə,graʊnd/ *adjective*
under the ground; under the earth's surface: *There is an underground tunnel to the house.*

un·der·line /'ʌndə,laɪn, ˌʌndə'laɪn/ *verb* (**underlining, underlined**)
to draw a line under a word or words: *This sentence is underlined.*

un·der·neath /ˌʌndə'niθ/ *adverb, preposition*
below or under something: *We turned the rock over to see what was underneath.*

un·der·pants /'ʌndə,pænts/ *plural noun*
a short piece of underwear that you wear on the lower part of your body

un·der·pass /'ʌndə,pæs/ *noun*
a road that goes under another road

un·der·shirt /'ʌndə,ʃət/ *noun*
a piece of underwear that you wear under a shirt

un·der·stand /ˌʌndə'stænd/ *verb* (**understanding, understood** /ˌʌndə'stʊd/)
1 to know the meaning of words or ideas: *Do you understand what I am saying? | She understands Japanese.*
2 to know how someone feels and why he or she behaves the way he or she does: *Michael just doesn't understand me. | Believe me, I understand how you feel.*

un·der·stand·ing¹ /ˌʌndə'stændɪŋ/ *noun* [U]
1 knowledge about something: *He has a good understanding of English.*
2 sympathy or pity for someone: *I appreciate your understanding.*

understanding² *adjective*
showing sympathy and pity for someone: *She was very understanding when I told her my problem.*

un·der·stood /ˌʌndə'stʊd/
the PAST TENSE and PAST PARTICIPLE of the verb **understand**

un·der·take /ˌʌndə'teɪk/ *verb* (*present participle* **undertaking**, *past tense* **undertook**, *past participle* **undertaken**)

1 to start to do something such as a piece of work: *He has undertaken the job of writing the report.*
2 **undertake to do something** to promise or agree to do something: *She undertook to pay the money back before July.*

underwater

un·der·wa·ter /ˌʌndə'wɔtə, -'wɑ-/ *adjective*
below the surface of the water: *Can you swim underwater? | I have an underwater camera.*

un·der·wear /'ʌndə,wɛr/ *noun* [U]
clothes that you wear next to your body under your other clothes: *You should **change your underwear** (=put on clean underwear) every day.*

un·der·went /ˌʌndə'wɛnt/
the PAST TENSE of the verb **undergo**

un·did /ʌn'dɪd/
the PAST TENSE of the verb **undo**

un·do /ʌn'du/ *verb* (*present participle* **undoing**, *past tense* **undid** /ʌn'dɪd/, *past participle* **undone** /ʌn'dʌn/)
to try to remove the bad effects of something: *You won't be able to undo your mistakes.*

un·done /ˌʌn'dʌn/ *adjective*
1 not finished or completed: *The work on the bridge is still undone.*
2 not tied or closed: *My shirt button is undone.*

un·dress /ʌn'drɛs/ *verb*
to take your clothes off, or take someone else's clothes off: *The doctor asked me to undress. | She undressed the baby.* » opposite DRESS¹

un·dressed /ʌn'drɛst/ *adjective*
not wearing any clothes: *I got undressed and went to bed.*

un·eas·y /ˌʌn'izi/ *adjective* (**uneasier, uneasiest**)
feeling anxious, afraid, or embarrassed in a situation: *I had an uneasy feeling that someone was watching me.*

un·em·ployed /ˌʌnɪm'plɔɪd/ *adjective*
without a job: *He was unemployed for two months.*

un·em·ploy·ment /ˌʌnɪm'plɔɪmənt/
noun [U]
1 the condition of not having a job: *The city has* **high** *unemployment.* (=a lot of people do not have jobs) ≫ opposite EMPLOYMENT
2 money that the government pays to people who do not have jobs: *My brother is* **drawing** *unemployment.* (=receiving money)

un·e·ven /ʌn'ivən/ *adjective*
not level, flat, or smooth: *It is difficult to run across uneven ground.* ≫ opposite EVEN[1]

un·ex·pect·ed /ˌʌnɪk'spɛktɪd/
adjective
not what you think will happen; surprising: *We had an unexpected visitor.*

un·fair /ˌʌn'fɛr/ *adjective*
not treating people equally; not right or fair: *It's unfair to pay me less than her.* ≫ opposite FAIR[1]

un·faith·ful /ʌn'feɪθfəl/ *adjective*
having a sexual relationship with someone who is not your usual partner

un·fa·mil·iar /ˌʌnfə'mɪlyə/ *adjective*
not what is known to you; strange: *I am unfamiliar* **with** *her writing.*

un·fash·ion·a·ble /ʌn'fæʃənəbəl/
adjective
not popular at the present time ≫ opposite FASHIONABLE

un·fa·vor·a·ble /ʌn'feɪvərəbəl/ *adjective*
unfavorable events or conditions are not as good as you want them to be: *We wanted to go to the beach, but the weather was unfavorable.*

un·fin·ished /ʌn'fɪnɪʃt/ *adjective*
not complete yet; not finished: *I am working on an unfinished painting.*

un·fit /ʌn'fɪt/ *adjective*
not suitable or not good enough to be used for something: *The food is unfit* **for** *small children.* ≫ opposite FIT[2]

un·fold /ʌn'foʊld/ *verb*
to open something that was folded: *She unfolded the letter carefully.*

un·for·tu·nate /ʌn'fɔrtʃənɪt/ *adjective*
having bad luck; unlucky: *He had an unfortunate accident.* ≫ opposite FORTUNATE

un·for·tu·nate·ly /ʌn'fɔrtʃənɪtli/
adverb
used when you are sorry or disappointed about something: *Unfortunately, I can't come to your party.* ≫ opposite FORTUNATELY

un·friend·ly /ʌn'frɛndli/ *adjective*
(unfriendlier, unfriendliest)
not nice or pleasant ≫ opposite FRIENDLY

un·hap·py /ʌn'hæpi/ *adjective* **(unhappier, unhappiest)**
sad or worried; not happy: *She felt unhappy* **about** *her marriage.* ≫ opposite HAPPY

un·health·y /ʌn'hɛlθi/ *adjective*
(unhealthier, unhealthiest)
1 not in good health; not physically healthy: *The child is thin and unhealthy.* ≫ opposite HEALTHY
2 likely to cause bad health or harm: *It's unhealthy to eat so much fat.*

unhelpful /ʌn'hɛlpfəl/ *adjective*
not helping someone else; not helpful

u·ni·form /'yunəˌfɔrm/ *noun*
special clothing that you wear for a job, at a school etc.: *The police wear dark blue uniforms.*

un·im·por·tant /ˌʌnɪm'pɔrt nt/
adjective
not causing you to worry; not important: *All these small details are unimportant.*

un·in·ter·est·ing /ʌn'ɪntrɪstɪŋ/
adjective
not interesting ≫ compare DULL, BORING

un·ion /'yunyən/ *noun*
1 (*also* **labor union**) a group of workers who have joined together to protect their pay and working conditions: *Have you joined the union?*
2 the act of joining two or more things together: *The country was formed by a union of states.*

u·nique /yu'nik/ *adjective*
1 the only one of its type: *Her collection of ancient coins is unique.*
2 very special and good: *I have a unique opportunity to hear him perform in person.*

u·nit /'yunɪt/ *noun*
1 someone or something that is a whole part of something larger: *The family is a basic social unit.* | *She works in the emergency unit at the hospital.*
2 an amount or quantity used as a standard of measurement: *The dollar is the unit* **of** *money in the U.S.*

u·nite /yu'naɪt/ *verb* (uniting, united)
to join together with other people and act as one group: *The threat of an attack united the country.*

United Na·tions /.ˌ.. '../ *noun*
the United Nations (*also* UN) an organization of countries that tries to find solutions to world problems

u·ni·ver·sal /ˌyunə'vɚsəl / *adjective*
concerning all the people in a group or the world: *We want to start universal health care.*

u·ni·verse /'yunə,vɚs/ *noun*
the universe all the space, stars etc. that exist

u·ni·ver·si·ty /ˌyunə'vɚsəti/ *noun* (*plural* universities)
a school at the highest level, where you study for a DEGREE: *Which university did you go to?*
≫ compare COLLEGE

un·kind /ˌʌn'kaɪnd◂ / *adjective*
cruel or not nice: *She made some unkind remarks about me.* ≫ opposite KIND²

un·known /ˌʌn'noʊn◂ / *adjective*
not known about by most people: *The cause of the disease is unknown.*

un·lead·ed /ˌʌn'lɛdɪd◂ / *adjective*
unleaded gas does not contain any LEAD³

un·less /ən'lɛs, ʌn-/
used for saying what will happen or be true if something else does not happen: *Unless you leave now, you'll be late.*

un·like /ˌʌn'laɪk◂ / *adjective, preposition*
1 different from someone or something else: *I've never known two brothers to be so unlike one another.*
2 not typical of someone: *It is unlike John to be so violent.*

un·like·ly /ˌʌn'laɪkli◂ / *adjective*
not likely to happen: *The plane is unlikely to leave in this weather.* ≫ opposite LIKELY

un·load /ʌn'loʊd/ *verb*
1 to take goods off of a vehicle: *He quickly unloaded the truck.* ≫ opposite LOAD²
2 to take film out of a camera, or bullets out of a gun

un·lock /ʌn'lɑk/ *verb*
to open a lock on a door, box etc.: *She unlocked the door and went in.* ≫ opposite LOCK²

un·luck·y /ˌʌn'lʌki◂ / *adjective* (unluckier, unluckiest)
having bad luck; not lucky: *Some people think that 13 is an unlucky number.* | *I was unlucky to have missed the bus.* ≫ opposite LUCKY

un·mar·ried /ˌʌn'mærid◂ / *adjective*
not married; SINGLE

un·nat·u·ral /ˌʌn'nætʃərəl/ *adjective*
not what is usual, expected, or normal; not natural: *It's unnatural for a child to be so quiet.*

un·nec·es·sar·y /ˌʌn'nɛsə,sɛri/ *adjective*
not needed: *He made a lot of unnecessary changes to the plans.* ≫ opposite NECESSARY

un·pack /ʌn'pæk/ *verb*
to take things out of a suitcase or box: *I'm going to unpack my suitcase.* ≫ opposite PACK¹

un·pleas·ant /ʌn'plɛzənt/ *adjective*
not nice or enjoyable: *There's an unpleasant smell in the house.* ≫ opposite PLEASANT

un·plug /ʌn'plʌg/ *verb* (unplugging, unplugged)
to remove a PLUG from the wall and stop a piece of electrical equipment from working

un·pop·u·lar /ʌn'pɑpyələ/ *adjective*
not liked by most people ≫ opposite POPULAR

un·real /ˌʌn'ril◂ / *adjective*
very strange; not relating to real situations or experiences: *The whole trip seems so unreal.*

un·rea·son·a·ble /ʌn'rizənəbəl/ *adjective*
wrong, or not fair and acceptable: *He's making unreasonable demands on our time.* ≫ opposite REASONABLE

un·re·lat·ed /ˌʌnrɪ'leɪtɪd◂ / *adjective*
not connected with something else

un·re·li·a·ble /ˌʌnrɪ'laɪəbəl◂ / *adjective*
not able to be trusted or depended on: *The information that I have is unreliable.* ≫ opposite RELIABLE

un·roll /ʌn'roʊl/ *verb*
to open something that is curled into a tube and make it flat: *He unrolled the blanket and sat down on it.*

un·ru·ly /ʌn'ruli/ *adjective*
behaving in an uncontrolled or violent way: *The unruly crowd began to shout.*

un·safe /ʌn'seɪf/ *adjective*
dangerous; not safe

un·sat·is·fac·to·ry /ˌʌnsæʈɪs'fæktəri/ *adjective*

not good enough: *Your written work is unsatisfactory.* ≫ opposite SATISFACTORY

un·screw /ʌn'skru/ *verb*

to open or undo something by twisting it: *Unscrew the light bulb and put in this one.*

un·stead·y /ʌn'stɛdi/ *adjective*

shaking when you move; not firm, and likely to fall: *My legs are unsteady.*

un·suc·cess·ful /ˌʌnsək'sɛsfəl/ *adjective*

not doing what you wanted to achieve: *He is an unsuccessful writer.* ≫ opposite SUCCESSFUL

un·suit·a·ble /ʌn'suʈəbəl/ *adjective*

not good for a particular purpose or person: *The movie is unsuitable for young children.* ≫ opposite SUITABLE

un·sure /ˌʌn'ʃʊr/ *adjective*

not certain about something, or about what you have to do: *I am unsure about the rules of the game.*

un·tie /ʌn'taɪ/ *verb* (**untying, untied**)

to take apart a knot or something that is tied: *She untied her shoes and took them off.*

un·til /ən'tɪl, ʌn-/ *preposition*

up to the time when something happens: *We can't go until Thursday.* | *I couldn't read until I was six years old.*

un·true /ʌn'tru/ *adjective*

not correct or true; false ≫ opposite TRUE

un·used /ˌʌn'yuzd/ *adjective*

not being used: *The old houses sit dark and unused.*

un·u·su·al /ʌn'yuʒuəl, -ʒəl/ *adjective*

not usual or ordinary; strange. *I have an unusual request.*

un·u·su·al·ly /ʌn'yuʒuəli, -ʒəli/ *adverb*

more than usual: *It was an unusually hot day.*

un·well /ʌn'wɛl/ *adjective*

not well; sick

un·will·ing /ʌn'wɪlɪŋ/ *adjective*

not wanting to do something: *He is unwilling to start over.*

un·wind /ʌn'waɪnd/ *verb* (*past* **unwound** /ʌn'waʊnd/)

1 to relax, not be anxious or worried: *A hot bath will help you unwind.*

2 to undo something that is twisted or

wrapped around something: *She unwound the yarn from the ball.*

un·wise /ˌʌn'waɪz/ *adjective*

not reasonable or wise: *The company has made some unwise decisions.*

un·wound /ʌn'waʊnd/

the PAST TENSE and PAST PARTICIPLE of the verb **unwind**

un·wrap /ʌn'ræp/ *verb* (**unwrapping, unwrapped**)

to remove the covering off something: *She unwrapped her presents.* ≫ opposite WRAP

un·zip /ʌn'zɪp/ *verb* (**unzipping, unzipped**)

to open a piece of clothing that had been fastened with a ZIPPER: *She unzipped her jacket.*

up /ʌp/ *adverb, preposition, adjective*

1 toward or in a higher place or position: *She climbed up the tree.* | *Go up the hill and turn right.* ≫ compare DOWN¹ —see color picture on page 194

2 increasing in loudness, strength, heat etc.: *Turn up the TV, please.* | *Sales are up this year.*

3 awake or out of bed: *Are you up yet?*

4 near or toward someone or something: *He came up to me and asked my name.*

5 into an upright or raised position: *The hair on my neck stood up.* | *He sat up and talked to me.*

6 completely: *The car is full up.* | *Eat your food up.*

7 above and including a particular number: *The program is for children aged 10 and up.*

8 up and down (a) higher and lower: *The kids were jumping up and down on the bed.* (b) in one direction and then in the opposite direction: *She walked up and down the street looking for the house.*

9 be up to something (a) to be doing something, often something secret: *I think he is up to something.* (b) to be good enough or well enough to do something: *Are you up to a walk along the beach?*

10 up to as much or as many as: *The room can hold up to 200 people.*

11 what's up? used for greeting someone, or for asking if there is a problem: *Hi Bill, what's up?*

12 be up against something to have to deal with a difficult problem or situation: *Our company is up against some strong competitors.*

up·com·ing /'ʌpˌkʌmɪŋ/ *adjective*

happening soon: *Are you voting in the upcoming election?*

up·date /ˈʌpdeɪt, ˌʌpˈdeɪt/ *verb*
(updating, updated)
to add new information to something: *We need to update our computer files.*

up·grade /ˈʌpgreɪd, ˌʌpˈgreɪd/ *verb*
(upgrading, upgraded)
to improve something, or change it for something better: *My ticket was upgraded to first class for the flight.*

up·hill /ˌʌpˈhɪl◂/ *adverb*
toward the top of a hill: *It is difficult walking uphill.* ≫ compare DOWNHILL

up·on /əˈpɑn, əˈpɔn/ *preposition*
on: *The village stands upon a hill.*

up·per /ˈʌpɚ/ *adjective*
1 in a higher position; near the top: *He had burns on the upper part of his body.* | *The upper floors in the building are more expensive.*
2 more important or higher in rank: *She works in upper management.*

up·per case /ˌ.. ˈ.◂/ *noun* [U]
letters written in their large form, such as A, B, D, G, J etc. ≫ compare LOWER CASE

upper class /ˌ.. ˈ.◂/ *noun*
the group of people in the highest and richest social class

up·right /ˈʌp-raɪt/ *adjective*
straight up: *Stand the bottle upright on the table.*

up·set¹ /ˌʌpˈsɛt◂/ *adjective*
feeling unhappy or worried about something: *She was upset because he wouldn't talk to her.*

upset² *verb* **(upsetting, upset)**
1 to make someone feel unhappy or worried: *It upset me when I found out how sick she was.* ≫ compare OFFEND
2 to change a plan and cause problems: *The bad weather upset our plans for a party.*

up·side down /ˌʌpsaɪd ˈdaʊn/ *adverb*
in a position with the top at the bottom and the bottom at the top

up·stairs /ˌʌpˈstɛrz◂/ *adjective, adverb*
on an upper floor in a building, or going toward the upper floor of a building: *Our office is upstairs.* | *The upstairs bathroom is very small.* ≫ compare DOWNSTAIRS

up·to·date /ˌ.. . ˈ.◂/ *adjective*
modern and new: *Are your records up-to-date?*

up·ward /ˈʌpwɚd/ *adverb*
1 from a lower place or position to a higher one: *The plane moved gently upward.* ≫ compare DOWNWARD
2 increasing to a higher level or amount: *The cost of the project is moving upward.*

ur·ban /ˈɚbən/ *adjective*
relating to a town or city: *Most people live in urban areas.* ≫ compare RURAL

urge¹ /ɚdʒ/ *verb* **(urging, urged)**
to try very hard to persuade someone to do something: *He urged her **to** find another job.*

urge² *noun*
a strong wish or need: *She suddenly **had an urge to** go back to New York.*

ur·gent /ˈɚdʒənt/ *adjective*
very important and needing to be done without delay: *I have an urgent message for you.*

U.S. /ˌyu ˈɛs/ *noun*
a short way to write or say the United States: *He is moving back to the U.S.*

us /əs; *strong* ʌs/
the person who is speaking and some other person or people: *The teacher told us* (=me and the other students) *to be quiet.* | *Give us another chance.*

us·age /ˈyusɪdʒ/ *noun* [U]
the way that something is used, or the amount that is used

use¹ /yuz/ *verb* **(using, used)**
1 to do something with something or put it into action: *What do you use this **for**?* | *Do you know how to use a sewing machine?*
2 (*also* **use something up**) to take something until it is all gone: *You used all the toothpaste up.* | *My car uses a lot of oil.*

use² /yus/ *noun*
1 the act of using something: *Do you approve of the use **of** force?* | *The machine is now **ready for** use.*
2 a way in which something is used, or the purpose for which it is used: *The computer has many educational uses.*
3 [U] the right to use something: *He gave me **the** use **of** his car.*
4 it's no use said when you stop doing something because you do not think it will be successful: *It's no use. I can't fix it.*

used /yuzd/ *adjective*
used cars, clothes etc. are not new and have already had an owner

used to[1] /'yustə; *final or before a vowel* 'yustu/ *adjective*
be used to something be familiar with something or someone so that it does not seem strange, unusual, or difficult: *He's used to traffic because he drives all the time.*

used to[2] *verb*
used with another verb to show that something was done often in the past, but is not done now: *He used to play football every Saturday.* | *She never used to smoke.*

NOTE: The NEGATIVE of **used to** is **didn't use to** or **used not to**: *I used not to like fish. I didn't use to like fish.* The question form of **used to** is **did you/he/she use to ...?**: *Did you use to go there often?*

---

use·ful /'yusfəl/ *adjective*
helping you do or get what you want: *She gave me some useful information.*

use·less /'yuslɪs/ *adjective*
not helpful or useful: *This knife is useless. The handle's broken!*

us·er /'yuzə/ *noun*
someone who uses a product, service etc.: *Prices are falling for telephone users.*

u·su·al /'yuʒuəl, -ʒəl/ *adjective*
1 done or happening most often, or as expected: *We had lunch at the usual place.*
2 as usual in the way that happens most of the time: *As usual, he arrived late.*

u·su·al·ly /'yuʒuəli, -ʒəli/ *adverb*
used when describing what happens most of the time; generally: *I'm usually at school early, but today I was late.*

u·ten·sil /yu'tɛnsəl/ *noun*
a tool or object with a particular use: *He bought some new kitchen utensils.*

u·til·i·ty /yu'tɪləti/ *noun* (*plural* **utilities**)
a service such as water, electricity, or gas that is provided for people to use: *How much do you pay for utilities?*

U-turn /'yu tərn/ *noun*
a turn that you make in a vehicle in which you go back in the opposite direction: *He made a U turn in the middle of the highway.*

va·can·cy /ˈveɪkənsi/ *noun* (*plural* vacancies)
1 a room in a hotel or house that is not being used: *I saw a sign that said, "No vacancies."*
2 a job that is available for someone: *They are advertising a vacancy for a driver.*

va·cant /ˈveɪkənt/ *adjective*
1 empty and available to be used or lived in: *We looked all over town for a vacant room.*
2 a vacant job is available for someone to do

va·ca·tion /veɪˈkeɪʃən, və-/ *noun*
a time away from work and school when you can relax: *We are on vacation for the next five days.*

vac·ci·nate /ˈvæksəˌneɪt/ *verb* (vaccinating, vaccinated)
to put a substance into someone's body to protect him or her from a disease

vac·ci·na·tion /ˌvæksəˈneɪʃən/ *noun*
a substance put into someone's body to protect him or her from a disease

vac·uum[1] /ˈvækyum/ *noun*
1 a space that is empty of all gas or air
2 a VACUUM CLEANER

vacuum[2] *verb*
to clean a floor using a VACUUM CLEANER: *Are you finished with the vacuuming?*

vacuum clean·er /ˈ.. ˌ../ *noun*
a machine that cleans a floor by sucking up the dirt from it

vague /veɪg/ *adjective* (vaguer, vaguest)
not clear in your mind because of not having enough details: *I have only a vague idea where the house is.*

vague·ly /ˈveɪgli/ *adverb*
slightly; a little: *She looks vaguely familiar.*

val·en·tine /ˈvælənˌtaɪn/ *noun*
a card that you give to someone on VALENTINE'S DAY

Valentine's Day /ˈ... ˌ./ *noun*
a holiday on February 14, on which someone gives a card, flowers, or candy to someone that he or she loves

val·id /ˈvælɪd/ *adjective*
officially legal and acceptable: *Do you have a valid passport?*

val·ley /ˈvæli/ *noun* (*plural* valleys)
an area of lower land between two lines of hills or mountains —see color picture on page 188

val·u·a·ble /ˈvælyəbəl, -yuəbəl/ *adjective*
1 worth a lot of money: *Is the ring valuable?*
2 very useful: *Your help has been very valuable.*

val·ue[1] /ˈvælyu/ *noun*
1 the amount of money that something is worth: *What is the value of your house?*
2 [U] the importance or usefulness of something: *Your advice has been of great value to me.*

value[2] *verb* (valuing, valued)
1 to think that something is important or useful to you: *I value your friendship.*
2 to say how much something is worth: *The book was valued at $1,000.*

val·ues /ˈvælyuz/ *plural noun*
principles about what is right, wrong, or important: *I believe in having strong family values.*

valve /vælv/ *noun*
a part of a pipe that opens and closes to control the flow of liquid, air, or gas passing through it

vam·pire /ˈvæmpaɪɚ/ *noun*
an imaginary creature that looks like a person and sucks the blood from someone's neck

van /væn/ *noun*
a vehicle like a small truck with an enclosed back, used for carrying goods

van·dal /ˈvændl/ *noun*
someone who damages or destroys public property intentionally

van·dal·ism /ˈvændlˌɪzəm/ *noun* [U]
the crime of intentionally damaging public property

van·dal·ize /ˈvændlˌaɪz/ *verb* (vandalizing, vandalized)
to damage or destroy public property intentionally: *All the public telephones had been vandalized.*

va·nil·la /vəˈnɪlə/ *noun* [U]
a sweet liquid from the bean of a plant, that is added to foods: *Do you like vanilla ice cream?*

van·ish /'vænɪʃ/ *verb*
to disappear suddenly in a way that cannot be explained easily: *Police said that the man vanished into thin air.*

van·i·ty /'vænəţi/ *noun* [U]
being too proud of yourself, especially your appearance or abilities

va·por /'veɪpɚ/ *noun*
a lot of small drops of liquid that float in the air: *Steam is nothing more than water vapor.*

va·ri·e·ty /və'raɪəţi/ *noun*
1 [U] the differences within something that make it interesting: *You need some variety in your life.*
2 [U] a lot of things of the same type that are different from each other in some way: *These shirts come in a variety of colors.*
3 [plural **varieties**] a type of something that is different from others in the same group: *He is growing a new variety of beans.*

var·i·ous /'vɛriəs, 'vær-/ *adjective*
different: *There are various colors to choose from.*

var·nish¹ /'vɑrnɪʃ/ *noun* [plural **varnishes**]
a clear liquid that is put onto wood to give it a shiny surface

varnish² *verb*
to put a clear liquid on wood to give it a shiny surface

var·y /'vɛri, 'væri/ *verb* (**varying, varied**)
1 to change often: *The weather varies from day to day.*
2 to be different from others of the same type: *The wines vary in quality.*

vase /veɪs, veɪz, vɑz/ *noun*
a container used for decoration or for holding flowers

vast /væst/ *adjective*
extremely large: *The middle of the country is covered in vast deserts.* ⟫ compare HUGE, ENORMOUS

vault /vɔlt/ *noun*
1 a room with thick walls where money, jewels etc. are kept for safety
2 a room where people are buried

VCR /ˌvi si 'ɑr/ *noun*
a machine that is used for recording television programs or watching a VIDEOTAPE: *While we were away, the VCR had recorded Louise's favorite movie.*

've /v, ɛv/
have: *I've never felt better! | So we've decided to sell the car.*

veal /vil/ *noun* [U]
meat from a young cow

vegetable

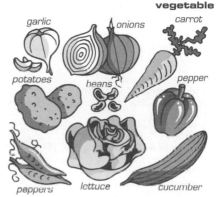

garlic, onions, carrot, potatoes, beans, pepper, peppers, lettuce, cucumber

veg·e·ta·ble /'vɛdʒtəbəl/ *noun*
a plant such as corn or potatoes, that is grown to be eaten

veg·e·tar·i·an /ˌvɛdʒə'tɛriən/ *noun*
someone who does not eat meat or fish

ve·hi·cle /'viɪkəl/ *noun*
something such as a bicycle, car, or bus that is used for carrying people or goods

veil /veɪl/ *noun*
a thin piece of material that covers a woman's face

vein /veɪn/ *noun*
one of the tubes in your body that carry blood to your heart

vel·vet /'vɛlvɪt/ *noun* [U]
a type of cloth with a soft surface

vend·ing ma·chine /'vɛndɪŋ məˌʃin/ *noun*
a machine from which you can buy candy, drinks, cigarettes etc.

vent /vɛnt/ *noun*
a hole or pipe through which air, gas, smoke etc. can go in or out

ven·ti·late /'vɛntlˌeɪt/ *verb* (**ventilating, ventilated**)
to let fresh air into a room or building

ve·ran·da /və'rændə/ *noun*
a PORCH

verb /vɚb/ *noun*
a word that describes an action, experience, or state: *In the sentence, "She wrote a letter", "wrote" is a verb; it is the past tense of the verb "write".*

ver·bal /'vɚbəl/ *adjective*
spoken: *We had a verbal agreement.*

ver·dict /'vɚdɪkt/ *noun*
an official decision made by a court of law: *Has the jury reached a verdict?* (=made a decision)

verge /vɚdʒ/ *noun*
be on the verge of something to be about to do something: *She was on the verge of tears.* (=about to cry)

verse /vɚs/ *noun*
1 [U] words that have a musical beat and a RHYME
2 a set of lines that forms one part of a poem or song

ver·sion /'vɚʒən/ *noun*
1 a copy of something that has been slightly changed: *I have the latest version of the software.*
2 a story that is told by one person: *Is that your version of what happened?*

ver·sus /'vɚsəs/ *preposition*
against each other in a sports competition or court case: *It should be a great game. It's the Bulls versus the Lakers.* | *The case I am referring to is Brown versus the State of Florida.*

ver·ti·cal /'vɚṭɪkəl/ *adjective*
pointing straight up; upright: *A vertical line is drawn up and down.* ≫ compare HORIZONTAL

ve·ry /'vɛri/ *adverb*
1 used for emphasizing another word: *It's very hot in this room.* | *Open the box very carefully.*
2 **not very** used before another word to mean the opposite of that word: *She is not very happy.* (=she is sad or angry) | *He is not very tall.* (=he is short)
3 **very much** a lot: *The book didn't cost very much.* | *Thank you very much for your help.*

vest /vɛst/ *noun*
1 a piece of clothing with no SLEEVEs, that you wear over a shirt
2 special clothing with no SLEEVEs, that you wear to protect your body —see color picture on page 190

vet /vɛt/ *noun*
1 a VETERINARIAN
2 a VETERAN

vet·er·an /'vɛṭərən/ *noun*
someone who has been a soldier in a war

vet·er·i·nar·i·an /ˌvɛṭərə'nɛriən, ˌvɛtrə-, ˌvɛt⁻n-/ *noun*
a doctor who takes care of sick animals

ve·to /'vitoʊ/ *verb*
to refuse officially to allow something to happen, especially in a government: *The President vetoed the plan.*

vi·a /'vaɪə, 'viə/ *preposition*
traveling through a place to another place: *I flew from New York to Miami via Washington.*

vi·brate /'vaɪbreɪt/ *verb* (**vibrating, vibrated**)
to shake quickly with small movements: *The house was vibrating with the music.*

vi·bra·tion /vaɪ'breɪʃən/ *noun*
a continuous slight shaky movement: *Touch the engine and you'll feel the vibration.*

vice /vaɪs/ *noun*
1 [U] crime that involves sex or drugs
2 a bad habit: *Smoking is my only vice.*

vice pres·i·dent /ˌ. '...◂/ *noun*
the person who is next in rank to the president in a government or company

vi·cin·i·ty /və'sɪnəṭi/ *noun* [U]
the area around a place: *The boy was found in the vicinity of* (=near) *the park.*

vi·cious /'vɪʃəs/ *adjective*
dangerous and violent and likely to hurt people: *He suffered a vicious attack last night.*

vic·tim /'vɪktɪm/ *noun*
someone who has been hurt or killed by someone or something: *She was the victim of a car accident.*

vic·to·ry /'vɪktəri/ *noun* (*plural* **victories**)
the act of winning a battle, game etc.: *Our party is hoping for victory in the next election.* ≫ compare DEFEAT²

vid·e·o /'vɪdioʊ/ *noun*
1 a copy of a movie or television program that is on a VIDEOTAPE: *We have a video of the wedding.*
2 a VIDEOTAPE: *Do you have a blank video I can borrow?*

video cas·sette re·cord·er
/ˌ.... .'. .ˌ../ *noun*
a VCR

video game /'... ,./ noun
a game in which you press buttons to move special pictures on a screen

vid·e·o·tape¹ /'vɪdioʊˌteɪp/ noun
a long narrow band of material in a plastic container on which movies and television programs can be recorded

videotape² verb (videotaping, videotaped)
to record something on a VIDEOTAPE

view /vyu/ noun
1 an opinion or belief about something: *What's your view on school prayer?*
2 the ability to see something from a particular place: *The tall man blocked my view of the stage.*
3 the things that you can see from a particular place: *The view from the top of the hill was lovely.*

view·er /'vyuɚ/ noun
someone who watches television

vig·or·ous /'vɪgərəs/ adjective
very active or strong: *She enjoys vigorous exercise.*

vil·lage /'vɪlɪdʒ/ noun
a very small town

vil·lain /'vɪlən/ noun
1 the bad character in a movie or play
2 a bad person; criminal

vine /vaɪn/ noun
a plant with long stems that climb on other plants, buildings etc.

vin·e·gar /'vɪnɪgɚ/ noun [U]
a very sour liquid made from wine, used in preparing food

vine·yard /'vɪnyɚd/ noun
a piece of land where vines are grown for producing wine

vi·o·lence /'vaɪələns/ noun [U]
1 behavior that hurts someone in a physical way: *There is too much violence on television.*
2 very great force: *The violence of the storm was surprising.*

vi·o·lent /'vaɪələnt/ adjective
1 using force to hurt someone: *He is a violent man who attacked his wife.*
2 having great force: *a violent earthquake*

vi·o·let¹ /'vaɪəlɪt/ noun
1 a small purple flower with a sweet smell
2 the color of the violet; purple

violet² adjective
having a color that is a mixture of blue and red

vi·o·lin /ˌvaɪə'lɪn/ noun
a musical instrument with four strings, that you play by pulling a special stick across the strings

vi·o·lin·ist /ˌvaɪə'lɪnɪst/ noun
someone who plays the violin

vir·gin /'vɚdʒɪn/ noun
someone who has never had sex

virtual re·al·i·ty /ˌ... .'.../ noun [U]
an environment produced by a computer that looks and sounds real

vir·tue /'vɚtʃu/ noun
a good quality of someone's character: *Honesty is a virtue.*

vi·rus /'vaɪrəs/ noun
1 a very small living thing that causes illnesses, or the illness caused by this
2 a dangerous set of instructions secretly put into a computer to damage the information stored in the computer

vi·sa /'vizə/ noun
an official mark put into a PASSPORT giving someone permission to enter, pass through, or leave a country: *Do Americans need a visa to visit Canada?*

vis·i·ble /'vɪzəbəl/ adjective
able to be seen: *The smoke from the fire was visible from the road.* ≫ compare INVISIBLE

vi·sion /'vɪʒən/ noun
1 [U] sight; the ability to see: *She has good vision.*
2 something that you imagine could happen: *I have a vision of a better future for my children.*

vis·it¹ /'vɪzɪt/ verb
1 to go and see a person or place: *We visited our friends in town.*
2 to talk to someone in a friendly way: *I visited with Kathy for an hour.*

visit² noun
the act of going and seeing a person or place: *We had a visit from your teacher.*

vis·i·tor /'vɪzɪtɚ/ noun
someone who goes and sees a person or place

vis·u·al /'vɪʒuəl/ *adjective*
relating to seeing or your sight

vi·tal /'vaɪtl/ *adjective*
very important or necessary: *The information is vital for our success.*

vi·ta·min /'vaɪtəmɪn/ *noun*
a chemical substance in food that is important for growth and good health: *Oranges contain vitamin C.*

viv·id /'vɪvɪd/ *adjective*
1 producing clear pictures in your mind: *She gave a vivid description of the accident.*
2 vivid colors are very bright and strong

vo·cab·u·lar·y /vou'kæbyə,lɛri, və-/ *noun (plural vocabularies)*
1 all the words you know and use: *He has a very large vocabulary.* (=he knows a lot of words)
2 [U] all the words in a particular language: *We learned some new vocabulary today.*

vo·cal /'voukəl/ *adjective*
relating to the voice: *He is doing vocal exercises.*

voice /vɔɪs/ *noun*
1 the sound that you make when you speak or sing: *We could hear the children's voices in the garden.* | *She spoke in a loud voice.*
2 **raise your voice** to speak in a loud angry way
3 **lose your voice** to not be able to speak

voice mail /'. ./ *noun* [U]
a system that records telephone calls so that you can listen to them later

vol·ca·no /vɑl'keɪnou/ *noun (plural volcanoes or volcanos)*
a mountain with a hole at the top from which come burning rock and fire

vol·ley·ball /'vɑli,bɔl/ *noun*
1 [U] a game in which two teams hit a ball across a net with their hands and try to not let it touch the ground
2 the ball used in this game

volt /voult/ *noun*
a measure of electricity

vol·ume /'vɑlyəm, -yum/ *noun*
1 [U] the amount of space that something contains or fills: *What is the volume of this bottle?*

2 [U] the amount of sound that something produces: *She turned down the volume on the radio.*
3 a book, especially one of a set of books

vol·un·tar·y /'vɑlən,tɛri/ *adjective*
done willingly, without being forced or paid: *She's a voluntary worker at the hospital.*
—**voluntarily** *adverb*

vol·un·teer[1] /,vɑlən'tɪr/ *noun*
someone who offers to do something without expecting to be paid: *We need volunteers to deliver food to people's homes.*

volunteer[2] *verb*
to offer to do something without expecting to be paid: *I volunteered to help out at the camp.*

vom·it /'vɑmɪt/ *verb*
to bring food up from your stomach: *The child vomited after eating the bad meat.*

vote[1] /vout/ *verb* (**voting, voted**)
to mark a piece of paper or raise your hand to show who you want to elect or which plan you support: *Who did you vote for?* | *Most people voted against the plan.*

vote[2] *noun*
a choice or decision that you make by voting: *There were seven votes for the plan and three votes against it.*

vot·er /'voutɚ/ *noun*
someone who votes or has the right to vote

vow /vau/ *noun*
a serious promise: *We wrote our own marriage vows.*

vow·el /'vauəl/ *noun*
one of the written letters **a, e, i, o,** or **u,** and sometimes **y** ≫ compare CONSONANT

voy·age /'vɔɪ-ɪdʒ/ *noun*
a long trip, especially by ship or in a space vehicle

vs. /'vɚsəs/
a short way to write the word **versus**

vul·gar /'vʌlgɚ/ *adjective*
vulgar language or behavior is rude and offensive, often relating to sex

vul·ture /'vʌltʃɚ/ *noun*
a large wild bird that eats dead animals

wad /wɑd/ *noun*
a thick pile of something: *He had a wad **of** dollar bills in his pocket.*

wade /weɪd/ *verb* (**wading, waded**)
to walk through water that is not very deep: *We waded across the stream.*

waf·fle /'wɑfəl/ *noun*
a flat bread with a pattern of square holes in it, eaten for breakfast

wag /wæg/ *verb* (**wagging, wagged**)
to move something from side to side: *The dog wagged its **tail**.*

wage /weɪdʒ/ *noun*
the amount of money that you earn for doing a job; usually you are paid for each hour that you work: *What is your hourly wage?*

wag·es /'weɪdʒɪz/ *plural noun*
the money that you get each day, week, or month for doing a job

wag·on /'wægən/ *noun*
1 a vehicle with four wheels, usually pulled by horses
2 a small vehicle with four wheels and a long handle, pulled by children as a toy

wail /weɪl/ *verb*
to cry with a long loud sound because you are sad or in pain

waist /weɪst/ *noun*
the narrow part around the middle of your body: *Ann has a slim waist.*

wait¹ /weɪt/ *verb*
1 to not do something until someone comes or something happens: *Wait here until I come back. | We're waiting around for his plane to arrive. | I was waiting **for** the bus.*
2 **wait on someone** to serve food to someone's table at a restaurant: *Have you been waited on?*
3 **wait up for someone** to stay awake until someone returns: *Don't wait up for me, I'll be late.*

wait² *noun*
a time when you do nothing until someone comes or something happens: *We had a long wait **for** the train.*

wait·er /'weɪtər/ *noun*
a man who serves food in a restaurant

waiting room /'.. ,./ *noun*
a room in which people wait, for example to see a doctor

wait·ress /'weɪtrɪs/ *noun* (*plural* **waitresses**)
a woman who serves food in a restaurant

wake /weɪk/ *verb* (**waking,** *past tense* **woke** /woʊk/, *past participle* **woken** /'woʊkən/)
1 (*also* **wake up**) to stop sleeping, or make someone stop sleeping: *I woke early this morning. | Don't wake the baby!*
2 **wake up** to start paying attention to something: *Hey, wake up when I'm talking to you!*
3 **wake up to something** to start to realize a danger, or understand an idea: *Our company is waking up to the fact that it is losing money.*

walk¹ /wɔk/ *verb*
1 to move forward by putting one foot in front of the other: *We walk **to** school each day.*
2 **walk away from something** to leave a situation without caring what happens: *You can't just walk away from your problems!*
3 **walk in on someone** to go to a place and interrupt someone when he or she did not expect you. *I accidentally walked in on her while she was dressing.*

walk² *noun*
the time or the distance that you travel when you walk: *Do you want to **go for a** walk? | The store is a ten minute walk from here.*

walk·er /'wɔkər/ *noun*
a metal frame used for helping old or sick people to walk

walk·ie-talk·ie /,wɔki 'tɔki/ *noun*
a small radio that you carry and use to speak to someone else who has the same type of radio

Walk·man
/'wɔkmən/ (*trademark*) *noun*
a small machine that you can carry, that plays music and has special equipment that you wear over your ears —see color picture on page 185

wall /wɔl/ *noun*
1 one of the sides of a room or building: *We painted all the walls white.*
2 a structure made of bricks or stones that divides one area from another: *A high wall surrounds the prison.*

wal·let /'wɑlɪt, 'wɔ-/ *noun*
a small flat case for cards or paper money, usually carried in a pocket

wall·pa·per /'wɔl,peɪpə/ *noun* [U]
paper used as a decoration to cover the walls of a room

wall-to-wall /ˌ. . '. ◂ / *adjective*
covering all the floor: *The house has wall-to-wall carpeting.*

wal·nut /'wɔlnʌt/ *noun*
a large light brown nut, or the tree on which this grows

waltz /wɔlts/ *noun* (*plural* **waltzes**)
a slow dance with a pattern of three beats, or the music for this dance —**waltz** *verb*

wan·der /'wɑndə/ *verb*
1 to move or travel with no particular purpose: *They wandered **around** the shopping mall all day.*
2 (*also* **wander off**) to move away from where you are supposed to be or stay: *Don't wander off alone.*

want[1] /wʌnt, wɑnt, wɔnt/ *verb*
1 to have a desire or need for something: *I want a bicycle for my birthday.* | *He wants you **to** call him.*
2 **if you want** if you would like that: *I can pick you up later if you want.*

want[2] *noun* [U]
something that you desire or need but do not have: *The children were in want of food.*

want ad /'. ./ *noun*
an advertisement in a newspaper for a job or something to sell

war /wɔr/ *noun*
1 a time of fighting between countries: *Did your father fight in the war?* ≫ compare BATTLE
2 **at war** fighting: *The two countries have been at war for years.*
3 **declare war** to start a war: *One country declared war **on** another.*
4 **go to war** to begin fighting: *The country is preparing to go to war.*

war·den /'wɔrdn/ *noun*
someone who is in charge of a prison

war·drobe /'wɔrdroʊb/ *noun*
the clothes that someone has

ware·house /'wɛrhaʊs/ *noun* (*plural* **warehouses** /-haʊzɪz/)
a large building used for storing things

wares /wɛrz/ *plural noun*
things that you can buy: *The man spread his wares on the table.*

war·fare /'wɔrfɛr/ *noun* [U]
the fighting that happens in a war

warm[1] /wɔrm/ *adjective*
1 slightly hot, but not too hot: *The water was nice and warm.*
2 able to keep in heat and keep out cold: *I need some warm clothes.*
3 friendly: *She always greets you with a warm smile.*

warm[2] *verb*
1 (*also* **warm up**) to make or become hotter: *The hot drink warmed him.* | *Warm yourself by the fire.*
2 **warm up** to do gentle exercises before doing a more difficult activity: *He is warming up before the race.*

warmth /wɔrmθ/ *noun* [U]
1 the feeling of being warm: *The warmth of the sun felt wonderful!*
2 friendliness: *the warmth of her welcome*

warn /wɔrn/ *verb*
to tell someone about something bad so that he or she can avoid it: *She warned me about walking home alone.*

warn·ing /'wɔrnɪŋ/ *noun*
something that tells you about something bad so that you can avoid it: *Cigarette packs have a warning printed on the side.*

war·rant /'wɔrənt, 'wɑ-/ *noun*
an official paper that allows the police to do something: *The police have a warrant for his arrest.*

war·ran·ty /'wɔrənti, 'wɑ-/ *noun* (*plural* **warranties**)
a written promise that a company will fix something if it breaks after you buy it

war·ship /'wɔrʃɪp/ *noun*
a large ship used for war

was /wəz; *strong* wʌz, wɑz/ *verb*
the PAST TENSE of the verb **be** that we use with **I**, **he**, **she**, and **it**: *I was angry.*

wash¹ /wɑʃ, wɔʃ/ *verb*
1 to make something clean using water and soap: *Did you wash your hands?*
2 to flow over or against something: *The waves washed against the shore.*
3 wash up to clean your hands: *Be sure to wash up before supper.*
4 wash off if a substance washes off, it can be removed from something else

wash² *noun*
1 [U] clothing, sheets etc. that have been or need to be cleaned: *Hang the wash out when it is finished.*
2 in the wash being washed or waiting to be washed: *Your shirt is in the wash.*

wash·cloth /'wɑʃklɔθ/ *noun*
a cloth with which you wash yourself

wash·er /'wɑʃɚ/ *noun*
a washing machine

washing ma·chine /'.. .,./ *noun*
a machine used for washing clothes

was·n't /'wʌzənt, 'wɑzənt/
was not: *I wasn't in school yesterday.*

wasp /wɑsp, wɔsp/ *noun*
a flying insect that stings like a BEE

waste¹ /weɪst/ *verb* (wasting, wasted)
to use something in a way that is not effective, or to use too much of it: *I waste a lot of my time on the phone.*

waste² *noun* [U]
1 the use of something in a way that is not effective or sensible: *The meeting was a complete waste of time.*
2 things that are left after something has been used, or things that you do not want: *There are laws for getting rid of nuclear waste.*

waste·bas·ket /'weɪst,bæskɪt/ *noun*
a container into which you put paper and other things that you want to get rid of

wast·ed /'weɪstɪd/ *adjective*
useless: *All my time working with him was just wasted effort.*

watch¹ /wɑtʃ, wɔtʃ/ *noun* (plural **watches**)
1 a small clock that you wear on your wrist
2 keep watch to look out for danger: *You keep watch for now, and I'll sleep.*

3 keep a watch on something to keep looking at something carefully: *Police kept a close watch on the house.*

watch² *verb*
1 to look at something and pay attention to it: *Do you watch a lot of television?* ≫ compare LOOK¹
2 to take care of someone or something: *Will you watch the baby? | The older kids watch over the younger ones.*
3 to be careful about something, or about how you use it: *I am trying to watch my weight.* (=be careful not to get fat) | *Watch your language!* (=be careful about what you say)
4 watch out to be careful and pay attention to what you are doing: *Watch out for the cars when you cross the street.*
5 watch for something to look for something so that you will be ready to deal with it: *Doctors are watching for any signs of the disease.*

> NOTE: Compare **watch**, **see** and **look at**. **See** is the general word for what you do with you eyes: *I can't see – it's too dark. | We saw them standing outside the school.* If you **look at** something, you move your eyes toward it because you want to see it: *Look at me! | They were looking at the pictures.* If you **watch** something, you move your eyes toward it and pay attention to it for a long time. Use **watch** when you are talking about something such as a TV program or sports event where things are changing or moving: *We watched a movie on TV. | He goes to watch a football game every Saturday.*

watch·man /'wɑtʃmən/ *noun* (plural watchmen /-mɛn/)
someone whose job is to guard a place

wa·ter¹ /'wɔtɚ, 'wɑ-/ *noun* [U]
the clear liquid in rivers, lakes, and oceans, or that falls as rain: *Would you like a glass of water?*

water² *verb*
to pour water on a plant or seeds in the ground

wa·ter·col·or /'wɔtɚ,kʌlɚ/ *noun*
a paint mixed with water, or a painting made with this paint

wa·ter·fall /'wɔtɚ,fɔl/ *noun*
water that falls down over rocks or from a high mountain —see color picture on page 188

water foun·tain /ˈ.. ˌ../ *noun*
a piece of equipment in a public place that produces water that you can drink

wa·ter·mel·on /ˈwɔtɚˌmɛlən/ *noun*
a large round green fruit with red juicy flesh and black seeds

wa·ter·proof /ˈwɔtɚˌpruf/ *adjective*
not allowing water to go through: *She has a new waterproof jacket.*

watt /wɑt/ *noun*
a measure of electrical power: *Do you have a 60 watt light bulb?*

wave¹ /weɪv/ *noun*
1 an area of raised water that moves on the surface of the ocean
2 a movement of your hand from side to side: *She gave a wave as she left the house.*
3 a sudden increase in an activity, emotion etc.: *What is the cause of the recent crime wave?*

wave² *verb* (**waving, waved**)
1 to move your hand from side to side as a signal or greeting: *We waved goodbye **to** them.*
2 to move or cause to move from side to side or up and down: *The flag waved in the wind.*

wav·y /ˈweɪvi/ *adjective* (**wavier, waviest**)
having waves or curved shapes in it: *She has beautiful wavy blond hair.*

wax¹ /wæks/ *noun* [U]
the hard substance that candles are made of

wax² *verb*
to put WAX on something, especially to polish it

way /weɪ/ *noun* (*plural* **ways**)
1 a road or path: *Can you tell me the way **to** the school? | Which way should we go?*
2 a particular direction: *Look both ways before you cross the **street**. | Take two steps this way.*
3 a method of doing something: *Is there any way **to** solve this problem? | He has a funny way **of** talking.*
4 the distance or time between two places or events: *We have to go **a** long way to get there.*
5 **in a way, in some ways** used for saying that something is partly true: *In some ways, I wouldn't mind working there.*
6 **have your way, get your way** to do what you want, especially if someone else wants to do something different: *She always gets her own way!*
7 **by the way** said when you want to talk about a new subject: *Oh, by the way, your Mom called earlier.*

8 **No way!** said when you will not do something, or when you are very surprised by something: *"Will you help me clean my room?" "No way!" | "She said she likes you!" "No way!"*
9 **in the way** in a position that stops you from going somewhere: *I can't drive through there. The bus is in the way.*
10 **on the way, on my way** while going somewhere: *I can drop you off at the store. It's on my way.*
11 **out of the way** not in a position that stops you going somewhere: *Get out of my way!* (= move to the side)
12 **under way** happening or moving: *Our plan is under way.*
13 **way around** in a particular position or place: ***Which** way around does this skirt go?*
14 **way to go!** said to someone who has done something very well or very good: *"I passed my science test!" "Way to go!"*

we /wi/ *pronoun*
the person who is speaking and one or more other people: *We go to the same school.*

weak /wik/ *adjective*
1 not strong in body: *She was weak after her illness. | He has a weak heart.* ≫ compare STRONG
2 not strong in character: *He is a weak leader.*
3 containing a lot of water, or not having much taste: *I don't like weak tea.*

weak·en /ˈwikən/ *verb*
to become less strong, or make someone or something do this: *The disease weakened her lungs.*

weak·ness /ˈwiknɪs/ *noun* (*plural* **weaknesses**)
1 a fault in someone's character, a company, a plan etc.: *Spending too much money is her weakness.*
2 [U] the state of lacking strength in your body

wealth /wɛlθ/ *noun* [U]
a large amount of money, land etc. that someone owns: *She passed on the family's wealth to her children.*

wealth·y /ˈwɛlθi/ *adjective* (**wealthier, wealthiest**)
having a lot of money; very rich ≫ compare POOR

weap·on /ˈwɛpən/ *noun*
something that you use to fight with, such as a gun or knife

wear¹ /wɛr/ *verb* (*past tense* **wore** /wɔr/, *past participle* **worn** /wɔrn/)

1 to have something on your body, especially clothes: *She wore a pretty dress.*
2 to weaken or damage something because of continued use: *You've worn a hole in your sock.*
3 to have your hair in a particular style: *He wears his hair short.*
4 wear well to remain in good condition after a period of time: *These shoes have worn well. They still look new.*
5 wear off to become less and less: *The effect of the drug is wearing off.*
6 wear out to become weak, broken, or not good enough to use: *The batteries are worn out.*
7 wear down to become smaller or weaker because of being used: *The heels on my shoes are worn down.*

wear² *noun* [U]
normal damage cause by continued use of something: *The tires are showing signs of wear.*

wea·ri·ly /'wɪrəli/ *adverb*
in a tired way: *"I can't help you any more," she said wearily.*

wea·ry /'wɪri/ *adjective* (**wearier, weariest**)
very tired: *I felt weary after working all day.*

weath·er /'wɛðɚ/ *noun* [U]
the temperature and the state of the wind, rain, sun etc.: *I don't like cold weather.* | *The weather has been dry this week.*

weave /wiv/ *verb* (**weaving**, *past tense* **wove** /woʊv/, *past participle* **woven** /'woʊvən/)
to make threads into cloth, by moving one thread over and under another on a special machine

weav·ing /'wivɪŋ/ *noun* [U]
the activity of making cloth

web /wɛb/ *noun*
1 a net of sticky thin threads made by a SPIDER
2 the Web the WORLD WIDE WEB

web·site /'wɛbsaɪt/ *noun*
a program on a computer that gives information about a product or subject on the INTERNET

we'd /wid/
1 we would: *I thought we'd never get here.*
2 we had: *We didn't go because we'd seen the movie before.*

wed·ding /'wɛdɪŋ/ *noun*
a ceremony in which a man and a woman get married: *I've been invited to their wedding.*
≫ compare MARRIAGE

Wednes·day /'wɛnzdi, -deɪ/ *noun*
the fourth day of the week

weed¹ /wid/ *noun*
a wild plant that grows where you do not want it

weed² *verb*
to remove WEEDs from a place: *I am busy weeding the garden.*

week /wik/ *noun*
1 a period of time equal to seven days, especially from Sunday through Saturday: *I play tennis twice a week.* | *Will you come and see us next week?*
2 (*also* **work week**) the part of a week when you work on a job, usually from Monday to Friday: *I don't have much free time during the week.*

week·day /'wikdeɪ/ *noun* (*plural* **weekdays**)
any day except Saturday or Sunday

week·end /'wikɛnd/ *noun*
Saturday and Sunday: *What did you do over the weekend?*

week·ly /'wikli/ *adjective, adverb*
happening once a week, or every week: *The weekly newspaper is printed on Fridays.*
≫ compare DAILY

week·night /'wiknaɪt/ *noun*
any night except Saturday or Sunday

weep /wip/ *verb* (*past tense* **wept** /wɛpt/, *past participle* **wept**)
to cry: *She wept when she heard the news.*

weigh /weɪ/ *verb*
1 to measure how heavy something is: *He weighed the apples.*
2 to have a particular weight: *The fish weighed two pounds.*
3 to consider something carefully: *You should weigh all the options before deciding.*

weight /weɪt/ *noun* [U]
1 how heavy something is: *The baby's weight was ten pounds.*
2 the fact of being heavy, or something that is heavy: *I can't lift heavy weights with my bad back.*

weird /wɪrd/ *adjective*
strange and unusual: *I've had a weird feeling all day.* ≫ compare ODD

wel·come¹ /'wɛlkəm/ *adjective*
1 wanted; happy to be accepted: *You are*

always welcome in my home. | *She made a welcome suggestion.*

2 you're welcome said as a polite reply to someone who has thanked you for something: *"Thanks for the coffee." "You're welcome."*

welcome² *verb* (**welcoming, welcomed**)
1 to say hello to someone who has just arrived: *He welcomed everyone at the door.*
2 to gladly accept an idea or suggestion: *I would welcome your comments on the plan.*

welcome³ *noun*
a greeting that you give to someone when he or she arrives: *We were given a warm welcome.*

wel·fare /'wɛlfɛr/ *noun* [U]
1 money that is given by the government to poor people: *They can't afford a car because they are on welfare.*
2 your health, comfort, and happiness: *We're all concerned about your welfare.*

we'll /wɪl; *strong* wil/
we will: *We'll see Jane tomorrow.*

well¹ /wɛl/ *adverb* (**better, best**)
1 in a good or satisfactory way: *Mary can read very well.* | *Did you sleep well last night?*
2 completely; thoroughly: *Mix the paint well before you begin.*
3 as well also: *I'd like a cup of coffee and some cake as well.*
4 as well as and also; in addition to: *I'm learning French as well as German.*

well² *adjective* (**better, best**)
in good health: *Call me when you're well enough to go out.*

well³
1 used for pausing before you say something, or to show surprise: *Well, I suppose we should go now.* | *Well, I never thought she would admit to the crime!*
2 (*also* **oh, well**) said when you accept a situation even though it is not a good one: *Oh, well, there's nothing we can do about it.*

well⁴ *noun*
a deep hole in the ground from which water or oil is taken

well-be·ing /ˌ. '../ *noun* [U]
a feeling of being comfortable, happy, and healthy

well-known /ˌ. '. ◂/ *adjective*
known by a lot of people: *A well-known writer lives here.*

well-off /ˌ. '. ◂/ *adjective*
having enough money to live in comfort

went /wɛnt/
the PAST TENSE of the verb **go**

wept /wɛpt/
the PAST TENSE and PAST PARTICIPLE of the verb **weep**

we're /wɪr/
we are: *We're in the same class in school.*

were /wɚ/ *verb*
the PAST TENSE of the verb **be**, that is used with **you**, **we**, and **they**: *Where were you born?*

weren't /wɚnt, 'wɚ-ənt/
were not: *You weren't here yesterday, were you?*

west /wɛst/ *noun, adjective, adverb*
1 in or toward the direction where the sun goes down: *We traveled west for two days.* ≫ compare EAST
2 the West the countries in North America and the western part of Europe
3 the west the western part of a state, country etc.

west·ern /'wɛstɚn/ *adjective*
1 in or from the west
2 Western in or from the countries in North America and the western part of Europe

west·ward /'wɛstwɚd/ *adverb, adjective*
toward the west: *The ship sailed westward to Hawaii.*

wet¹ /wɛt/ *adjective* (**wetter, wettest**)
1 covered with or containing liquid: *My hair is wet.* ≫ compare DRY¹
2 rainy: *It looks like another wet day.*
3 not yet dry: *Don't touch the wet paint.*

wet² *verb* (**wetting, wet** *or* **wetted**)
to make something wet ≫ compare DRY²

we've /wiv/
we have: *We've missed our flight!*

whale /weɪl/
noun
a very large animal that lives in the ocean and breathes through a hole in the top of its head: *A whale was seen ahead of the ship.*

what /wʌt, wɑt; *weak* wət/ *pronoun*
1 used when asking about something that you do not know: *What is your name?* | *What time is it?*
2 said when you did not hear what someone has said: *"Is it hot?" "What?" "I said, is it hot?"*
3 used for talking about things or for giving information: *She told me what to do.* | *I didn't know what happened.*
4 used for showing surprise or for emphasizing what you are saying: *What a stupid thing to do!* | *What a great guy!*
5 what for used for asking the reason for something; why: *What do you use this for?* | *"Can I have this?" "What for?"*
6 what about ...? said when you want to suggest something: *What about trying some new medicine?*

what·ev·er /wɑt'ɛvɚ/ *pronoun*
1 any or all of the things that are needed or wanted: *Take whatever you need.*
2 no matter what: *Whatever I do, it's going to be wrong.*
3 said when it does not matter what happens: *"Do you want a pizza?" "Oh, whatever."*

wheat /wit/ *noun* [U]
a plant with grain that is made into flour

wheel /wil/ *noun*
1 one of the round things under a vehicle that turns around and around and allows it to move
2 a STEERING WHEEL

wheel·bar·row /'wil,bærou/ *noun*
an object with one wheel at the front and two handles at the back, used for carrying things

wheel·chair /'wil-tʃɛr/ *noun*
a chair with wheels, used by people who cannot walk —see picture at CHAIR

when /wɛn/ *adverb*
1 at what time: *When will the bus come?*
2 at a particular time: *I lived in this house when I was a boy.*
3 used for saying what was happening when another event happened: *When the phone rang, I was in the shower.*

when·ev·er /wɛ'nɛvɚ, wə-/ *adverb*
1 at any time; every time: *Please come to see me whenever you can.* | *Whenever I see him, I talk to him.*
2 used for saying that it does not matter when something happens: *"What time should I arrive?" "Oh, whenever. I'll be there all day."*

where /wɛr/ *adverb*
1 in or to what place: *Where do you live?* | *Do you know where Brenda is?*
2 used for asking or talking about the state of something: *Where do you go from here?* | *Where will it all end?*

wher·ev·er /wɛr'ɛvɚ/ *adverb*
at or to any place: *I will drive you wherever you want to go.* | *Sit wherever you like.*

wheth·er /'wɛðɚ/
if: *I don't know whether he'll come or not.*

which /wɪtʃ/ *pronoun*
1 what person or thing: *Which of you is bigger: Mary or Jane?* | *Which one of these do you want?*
2 used for adding more information to a sentence: *We went to Plano, which is just outside Dallas.* » compare THAT

while¹ /waɪl/
1 during the time that something is happening: *I met her while I was in college.* | *While I ate dinner, I watched the game on TV.*
2 in spite of the fact; though: *While she seemed like a nice person, I just didn't trust her.*

while² *noun*
a while a period of time, usually short: *After a while she fell asleep.* | *I'll be back in a little while.*

whim·per /'wɪmpɚ/ *verb*
to make low crying sounds: *The dog whimpered in the corner.*

whine¹ /waɪn/ *verb* (**whining, whined**)
1 to complain about something in an annoying voice: *Stop whining, or we'll turn around and go back!*
2 to make a long high sound because of sadness or pain: *A dog was whining at the door.*

whine² *noun*
a long high sound: *The whine of the engine was very loud.*

whip¹ /wɪp/ *noun*
a long piece of leather or rope with a handle, used for hitting animals or people

whip² *verb* (**whipping, whipped**)
1 to hit a person or an animal with a whip: *He whipped the horse to make it run faster.*
2 to defeat someone easily: *We were whipped 35–0.*
3 to move something suddenly: *He whipped a gun out of his pocket.*
4 to quickly mix cream or the clear part of an egg until it becomes stiff

whirl /wɚl/ *verb*
to spin around very fast, or make something do this: *The wind whirled the leaves into the air.*

whisk·er /'wɪskɚ/ *noun*
one of the long stiff hairs that grow near the mouth of a dog, cat etc.

whisk·ers /'wɪskɚz/ *plural noun*
the hair that grows on a man's face

whis·key /'wɪski/ *noun* (*plural* **whiskeys**)
a strong alcoholic drink made from grain, or a glass of this drink

whis·per¹ /'wɪspɚ/ *noun*
a very quiet voice: *She spoke in a whisper.*

whisper² *verb*
to speak very quietly: *What are you whispering about?*

whis·tle¹ /'wɪsəl/ *noun*
1 a small object that makes a high sound when you blow into it: *The teacher blew a whistle to start the race.*
2 a high sound made blowing air through your lips: *When he gave a whistle, his dog ran to him.*

white¹ /waɪt/ *adjective*
1 having a color like snow, clouds, or the paper in this book
2 with lightly colored skin: *Some of the children were white, and others were black.*

white² *noun*
1 [U] a white color: *She was dressed in white.*
2 someone who has lightly colored skin
3 the white part of your eye, or of an egg
—see picture at EGG

White House /'. ./ *noun*
1 the official home in Washington, D.C. of the President of the U.S.
2 [U] the President of the U.S., and the people who advise him or her: *The White House has no comment on the issue.*

who /hu/ *pronoun*
1 used for asking about a person or group of people: *Who gave you that book? | Who are those people?*
2 used for adding information about someone: *The man who lives there is my uncle.*

who'd /hud/
1 who had: *She asked who'd seen the film.*
2 who would: *He wanted to know who'd be able to help him.*

who·ev·er /hu'ɛvɚ/ *pronoun*
1 used for talking about someone whose name you do not know: *Whoever those people are, I don't want to see them.*
2 used for saying that it does not matter which person does something: *Whoever arrives first can get the tickets.*

whole¹ /hoʊl/ *adjective*
1 all of something; total: *They told me the whole story.*
2 **the whole thing** everything about a situation: *The whole thing just makes me mad!*

whole² *noun*
1 complete amount or thing: *Two halves make a whole.*
2 **the whole of something** all of something: *He spent the whole of the morning cleaning the car.*
3 **on the whole** in general: *On the whole, I agree with you.*
4 **as a whole** considering all the parts of something: *I think that, as a whole, the plan is a good one.*

whole·sale /'hoʊlseɪl/ *adjective*
relating to selling goods in large amounts to stores and people who then sell the goods to other people

who'll /hul/
who will: *Who'll be here tomorrow?*

whom /hum/ *pronoun*
what person or people, used when it is the object of a verb: *Whom did you see?*

who's /huz/
1 who is: *Who's coming to the party?*
2 who has: *Who's eaten my apple?*

whose /huz/ *pronoun*
1 used for asking which person or people something belongs to: *Whose coat is that?*
2 used for showing the relationship between a person and something that belongs to that person: *That is the woman whose house burned down.*

who've /huv/
who have: *There are some people who've already left.*

why /waɪ/ *adverb*
1 for what reason: *Why is she crying? | No one knows why the plan did not work.*
2 **why not?** **(a)** used for asking someone why he or she has not done something: *"I'm not finished yet." "Why not?"* **(b)** used for agreeing to

do something: *"Do you want to come with us?"* *"OK, why not?"*

wick·ed /'wɪkɪd/ *adjective*
very bad; evil: *The story was about a wicked witch.*

wide¹ /waɪd/ *adjective* (**wider, widest**)
1 measuring a large distance from side to side; broad: *The flood affected a wide area.* ≫ compare NARROW —see picture at NARROW
2 from many people: *The news story received wide attention.*
3 a wide range of something a large variety of something: *The store offers a wide range of shoes.*

wide² *adverb*
1 completely: *The door was wide open.* | *I am wide awake.* | *His legs were wide apart.*
2 away from the place at which you were aiming: *My shot went wide to the left.*

wide·ly /'waɪdli/ *adverb*
1 in a lot of different places or by a lot of people: *His books are widely read.* | *The product is widely available.*
2 to a large degree; a lot: *Taxes vary widely from state to state.*

wid·ow /'wɪdoʊ/ *noun*
a woman whose husband is dead

wid·ow·er /'wɪdoʊɚ/ *noun*
a man whose wife is dead

width /wɪdθ, wɪtθ/ *noun*
the distance from one side of something to the other; how wide something is: *The window has a width of five feet.* ≫ compare LENGTH —see picture at LENGTH

wife /waɪf/ *noun* (*plural* **wives** /waɪvz/)
the woman to whom a man is married ≫ compare HUSBAND

wig /wɪg/ *noun*
a cover for your head, made from people's hair

wild /waɪld/ *adjective*
1 not trained to live with people: *We saw some wild horses.* ≫ compare TAME¹
2 living in its natural condition: *We picked the wild flowers on the hill.*
3 showing a lot of emotion such as anger or excitement: *She has a wild look in her eyes.*
4 exciting, interesting, or unusual: *We went to a wild party!*

wil·der·ness /'wɪldɚnɪs/ *noun* [U]
a large natural area of land where there have never been buildings or farms

wild·life /'waɪldlaɪf/ *noun* [U]
animals and plants in their natural condition

will¹ /wəl, əl, l; *strong* wɪl/ *verb*
1 used with other verbs to say that something is going to happen: *It will probably rain tomorrow.*
2 used when asking someone to do something: *Will you help me, please?*
3 used for saying that you are willing to do something: *I will do whatever you want.*
4 used for showing what is possible: *This car will seat six people.*

will² *noun*
1 [U] the power to do exactly what you have decided to do: *He has lost the will to live.*
2 a legal document that says to whom you want to give your money and property after you die: *The man left his farm to his son in his will.*

will·ing /'wɪlɪŋ/ *adjective*
1 ready to do something: *Are you willing to help?*
2 eager or wanting to do something

win¹ /wɪn/ *verb* (**winning**, *past tense* **won** /wʌn/, *past participle* **won**)
1 to be first or do best in a competition, race, or fight: *Who won the race?* ≫ compare LOSE
2 to earn something at a race or competition: *He won $500 at the race track.*

win² *noun*
a victory or success, especially in a sport

wind¹ /wɪnd/ *noun*
air that moves quickly: *The wind blew the leaves off the trees.*

wind² *verb* (*past tense* **wound** /waʊnd/, *past participle* **wound**)
1 (*also* **wind up**) to turn a handle around and around to make a machine, toy etc. work: *Can you wind the clock for me?*
2 to turn or twist something around something else: *She wound the string into a ball.*
3 to bend and curve many times: *The path wound along the side of the river.*
4 wind down to become slower or less active: *The party is winding down.*
5 wind up (a) to do something or become involved in something: *Most of the men wound up without jobs.* (b) to end an activity or meeting: *It's about time to wind things up.*

wind·mill /'wɪndmɪl/ *noun*
a tall building with sails that are turned around by the wind, used for producing power or crushing grain

win·dow /'wɪndoʊ/ *noun*
an opening with glass across it in the wall of a building or vehicle, used for allowing light and air to enter

win·dow·sill /'wɪndoʊˌsɪl/ *noun*
a flat shelf at the bottom of a window

wind·shield /'wɪndʃild/ *noun*
the piece of glass across the front of a car, bus, or airplane

windshield wip·er /'.. ˌ../ *noun*
a long thin piece of metal with a rubber edge, used for removing water from a WINDSHIELD

wind·y /'wɪndi/ *adjective* (**windier, windiest**)
with a lot of wind blowing

wine /waɪn/ *noun* [U]
an alcoholic drink made from fruit such as GRAPEs

wing /wɪŋ/ *noun*
1 the part of a bird's or insect's body used for flying
2 one of the two flat parts on the side of an airplane that help it fly —see picture at AIRPLANE

wink /wɪŋk/ *verb*
to close and open one eye quickly: *He winked at me.* —**wink** *noun* ≫ compare BLINK

win·ner /'wɪnɚ/ *noun*
someone who wins a competition, race, or fight

win·ter /'wɪntɚ/
the season between fall and spring, when the weather is coldest ≫ compare SUMMER

wipe /waɪp/ *verb* (**wiping, wiped**)
1 to remove dirt, water etc. from something with a cloth or your hand: *She wiped the tears from her eyes.*
2 to clean something by rubbing it: *Wipe your shoes before coming in.*
3 **wipe something out** to remove or destroy someone or something completely: *Fire wiped out most of the city.*

wire /waɪɚ/ *noun*
1 [U] thick metal thread: *I put up a wire fence.*
2 a piece of thin metal used for carrying electricity

wis·dom /'wɪzdəm/ *noun* [U]
good judgment and knowledge gained through experience

wise /waɪz/ *adjective*
1 based on good judgment and experience: *I want to make a wise decision.*
2 able to make good decisions and give good advice: *He is a wise leader.*

wish¹ /wɪʃ/ *verb*
1 to want or hope for something, even though it is not likely to happen: *I wish I had a million dollars.*
2 **wish someone something** to hope that someone has something: *We wish you success in your new job.* | *Wish me luck!*

wish² *noun* (*plural* **wishes**)
1 the act of hoping for or wanting something: *She had a wish to be a famous singer.*
2 something that you hope for or want: *Did you get your wish?*

wit /wɪt/ *noun* [U]
the ability to say things that are funny or interesting

witch

witch /wɪtʃ/ *noun* (*plural* **witches**)
a woman who is believed to have magic powers

with /wɪθ, wɪð/ *preposition*
1 together or near each other: *She walks to school with her sister.*
2 using something: *He opened the door with his key.* | *Steve ate the soup with a spoon.*
3 having a particular quality: *She has a white dress with red stripes.*
4 because of something: *They smiled with pleasure.* | *The room was bright with light.*
5 including: *The computer comes with free software.*
6 used for saying what covers or fills something: *His hands were covered with blood.*
7 relating to someone or something: *What's wrong with the TV?*
8 against someone: *He always fights with his sister.*

with·draw /wɪθ'drɔ, wɪð-/ *verb* (*past tense* **withdrew** /wɪθ'dru/, *past participle* **withdrawn** /wɪθ'drɔn/)
1 to take money out of a bank account: *She withdrew all her money from the bank.*
2 to stop being involved in something, or to make someone do this: *He had to withdraw from the race with an injury.*

3 to move out of a place, or to make someone do this: *The soldiers decided to withdraw.*

with·draw·al /wɪθ'drɔəl/ *noun*
the action of taking money out of your bank account: *I'd like to **make a** withdrawal, please.*

with·er /'wɪðər/ *verb*
to become drier and smaller, and then to die: *The plants withered in the heat.*

with·in /wɪ'ðɪn, wɪ'θɪn/ *adverb, preposition*
1 during a particular period of time: *He learned to speak English within six months!*
2 inside a particular area or distance: *Within the old walls, there was once a town.*
3 inside an organization, company, or group: *We are looking for a new leader from within our own team.*

with·out /wɪ'ðaʊt, wɪ'θaʊt/ *adverb, preposition*
1 not having or doing something: *I can't see anything without my glasses. | He left without saying goodbye.*
2 not being with someone or not having someone to help you: *We can't leave without the children.*
3 go without something, do without something to not have something that you need or want: *I had to go without food for three days.*

wit·ness /'wɪt⸌nɪs/ *noun (plural witnesses)*
someone who sees something happen: *She was a witness to the accident.*

wit·ty /'wɪt̬i/ *adjective (wittier, wittiest)*
using words in a funny or interesting way: *She is a very witty person.*

wives /waɪvz/
the plural of **wife**

wiz·ard /'wɪzərd/ *noun*
a man who is believed to have magic powers

wob·ble /'wɑbəl/ *verb (wobbling, wobbled)*
to move in an unsteady way: *The table wobbles.*

woke /woʊk/
the PAST TENSE of the verb **wake**

wo·ken /'woʊkən/
the PAST PARTICIPLE of the verb **wake**

wolf /wʊlf/ *noun (plural wolves /wʊlvz/)*
a wild animal similar to a dog

wom·an /'wʊmən/ *noun (plural women /'wɪmɪn/)*
an adult female person ≫ compare MAN

won /wʌn/
the PAST TENSE and PAST PARTICIPLE of the verb **win**

won·der¹ /'wʌndər/ *verb*
1 to think about something and to want to know what is true about it: *I wonder **if** she ever thinks about me.*
2 to be surprised by something: *We wondered why she waited for so long.*

wonder² *noun*
1 [U] a feeling of surprise and admiration: *The music filled us with wonder.*
2 no wonder it is no surprise: *No wonder he's not hungry. He only ate an hour ago.*
3 someone or something that makes you feel great admiration: *The wonders **of** modern medicine are amazing.*

won·der·ful /'wʌndərfəl/ *adjective*
very good: *The birth of your son is wonderful news.*

won't /woʊnt/
will not: *We won't be late home.*

wood /wʊd/ *noun* [U]
the material of which the trunks and branches of trees are made

wood·en /'wʊdn/ *adjective*
made from wood: *He sat on a wooden box.*

woods /wʊdz/ *plural noun*
a small forest: *We took a walk **in the** woods.*
—see color picture on page 188

wool¹ /wʊl/ *noun* [U]
1 the soft thick hair of sheep
2 the thread or material made from the hair of sheep: *The dress was made of wool.*

wool² *adjective (also **woolen**)*
made from wool: *I saw a wool blanket on the bed.*

word /wɜrd/ *noun*
1 a letter or letters, used for making phrases and sentences: *What's the French word for "cheese"? | I wrote a 1,000 word paper.*
2 [U] a promise: *I give you my word that I will return.*
3 something that you say or write: *I **didn't hear a** word she said. | I **won't say a** word about what happened.*
4 a short important statement or discussion: *Peter, could I **have a** word **with** you?*
5 [U] information, news, or a message: *Send me word as soon as you get home.*

6 in other words a phrase you use before you repeat the same thing using different words

7 in your own words saying what you think, not repeating what someone else has said: *Tell me what happened in your own words.*

8 take someone's word for it to believe what someone says about something

9 word for word said or written with exactly the same words in the same order

word pro·cess·or /'. ,.../ *noun*

a computer used for writing letters and storing information

wore /wɔr/

the PAST TENSE of the verb **wear**

work¹ /wɚk/ *verb*

1 to do a job: *He works for a shoe company.* | *Where does your mom work?*

2 to make a machine do something: *Can you work the printer?* | *The radio isn't working.*

3 to do an activity using time and effort: *I've been working to improve my cooking.*

4 to be effective or successful: *It looks like your plan is going to work.*

5 work out (a) if a problem works out, it stops being a problem: *I'm sure everything will work out in the end.* **(b)** to do a set of exercises for your body regularly: *I work out with weights twice a week.*

6 work something out to find an answer to a problem: *She worked the problem out for herself.*

7 work on something to try to repair, complete, or improve something: *He's still working on his degree.*

NOTE: Compare **work** and **job**. **Job** is a noun which has a plural (=jobs). **Work** has the same meaning, but has no plural: *He is trying to find* **a** *job. He's trying to find* **some** *work.* **Work** can be used as a general word when you are talking about several different jobs. If you say, "I've got a lot of work to do," it could mean either that you have one big job to do, or lots of different jobs.

---

work² *noun*

1 [U] an activity that uses a lot of time and effort: *Dad's doing some work on the car.*

2 [U] a job or the place where you do your job: *Sometimes it is difficult to arrive at work on time.*

3 [U] the things that you produce while studying, writing etc.: *The teacher is pleased with my work.*

4 the things that an artist makes while doing something: *The museum has great works of art.*

5 at work doing a job or activity

6 out of work with no job but wanting a job: *I've been out of work for 6 months.*

7 set to work, get to work to start doing something: *They set to work on the building.*

work·er /'wɚkɚ/ *noun*

someone who does a particular job: *There were several workers who lost their jobs.* ≫ compare LABORER

work·ing /'wɚkɪŋ/ *adjective*

1 having a job: *Working mothers have to balance their jobs and family.*

2 relating to work or used for work: *The working conditions at the factory are very poor.*

work·man /'wɚkmən/ *noun* [plural **workmen** /-mɛn/]

a man who works with his hands, especially building or repairing things

work·out /'wɚk-aut/ *noun*

a period of time when you do a lot of exercise, especially for a sport

world /wɚld/ *noun*

1 the Earth on which we live: *They went on a trip around the world.*

2 all people or countries on the Earth: *The world is working for peace.*

3 in the world used for emphasizing something that you are saying: *You're the best dad in the whole world.* | *What in the world were you thinking?*

world·wide /ˌwɚld'waɪd◂/ *adjective, adverb*

everywhere in the world, or within the whole world: *The company has 500 stores worldwide.*

World Wide Web /ˌ. ,. './ *noun* [also **the Web**]

a system that makes it easy for you to see and use information on the INTERNET

worm /wɚm/ *noun*

a long thin creature with a soft body and no legs, that lives in the ground

worn /wɔrn/

the PAST PARTICIPLE of the verb **wear**

worn out /ˌ. '.◂/ *adjective*

1 very tired: *I am worn out after work.*

2 too old or damaged to be useful: *My shoes are worn out.*

wor·ried /ˈwɔːid, ˈwʌrid/ *adjective*
unhappy or anxious because you are worrying about something: *He seems worried **about** something.* | *She has a worried look on her face.*

wor·ry¹ /ˈwɔːi, ˈwʌri/ *verb* (**worrying, worried**)
to feel unhappy, upset, or anxious when thinking about someone or something: *My parents worry **about** me if I come home late.*

worry² *noun*
1 [U] the feeling of being unhappy or anxious about something: *The worry showed on her face.*
2 (*plural* **worries**) a problem or bad situation that makes you feel anxious: *My father has a lot of worries.*

worse¹ /wɔːs/ *adjective, adverb*
1 not as good; more unpleasant: *Traffic is worse on Fridays.* ≫ compare BETTER¹
2 sicker, in a less good condition: *She was not feeling well, and now she's worse.*
3 in a more severe way than before: *The pain feels worse.*
4 not as well, less successful: *He draws even worse than I do.*

worse² *noun* [U]
something worse: *The new job was **a change for the worse**.*

wors·en /ˈwɔːsən/ *verb*
to become worse, or make something do this: *His condition worsened over the weekend.*

wor·ship¹ /ˈwɔːʃɪp/ *verb* (**worshipping, worshipped**)
to show great respect to a god, especially by praying

worship² *noun* [U]
a strong feeling of love and respect for someone, especially a god

worst /wɔːst/ *adjective, adverb, noun*
1 worse than anything else: *That was the worst movie I've ever seen!* ≫ compare BEST¹
2 **worst of all, the worst** someone or something that is worse than other people, results etc.: *Four people were in the accident, but she was injured worst of all.*
3 **at worst** as bad as something can be: *It'll cost $200 at worst to replace the tires.*

worth¹ /wɔːθ/ *adjective*
1 having a particular value: *How much is this ring worth?* | *Each question is worth ten points.*

2 good enough or useful enough for something: *The book is really worth reading.*

worth² *noun* [U]
an amount of something based on how much it cost or how much time you use it: *I bought $20 worth **of** food.* | *He won a year's worth of gas.*

worth·less /ˈwɔːθlɪs/ *adjective*
not valuable, important, or useful

worth·while /ˌwɔːθˈwaɪl◂ / *adjective*
worth all the effort, money, or time needed to get something

wor·thy /ˈwɔːði/ *adjective* (**worthier, worthiest**)
good enough to deserve respect or admiration: *He is worthy **of** our trust.*

would /wəd, əd, d; *strong* wʊd/ *verb*
1 used for **will** when saying what someone has said: *They said they would play on Saturday.*
2 used for saying that you expect something to happen or to be true: *I thought she would be happy for me, but she wasn't.*
3 **Would you?** used as a polite way of asking someone something: *Would you like some help?*
4 used for saying that something happened regularly in the past: *Edward would come over to play games with us.*

would·n't /ˈwʊdnt/
would not: *I knew she wouldn't come.*

would've /ˈwʊdəv/
would have: *I would've come if I'd had time.*

wound¹ /waʊnd/
the PAST TENSE and PAST PARTICIPLE of the verb **wind**

wound² /wund/ *verb*
to injure or hurt someone: *Was he badly wounded?*

wound³ /wund/ *noun*
an injury on your body, especially caused by a knife or gun

wove /woʊv/
the PAST TENSE of the verb **weave**

wo·ven /ˈwoʊvən/
the PAST PARTICIPLE of the verb **weave**

wrap /ræp/ *verb* (**wrapping, wrapped**)
1 (*also* **wrap something up**) to fold paper, cloth etc. around something to cover it: *I haven't wrapped your birthday gift yet.* ≫ opposite UNWRAP

2 wrap your arms around someone to hold someone or something by putting your arms around him, her, or it
3 be wrapped up in something to pay too much attention to someone or something: *He is too wrapped up in his work to notice her.*

wrap·per /'ræpɚ/ *noun*
the paper, plastic etc. that covers something, especially food: *Where is your bubble gum wrapper?*

wreath /riθ/ *noun*
a decoration made from flowers or plants, shaped like a circle

wreck¹ /rɛk/ *noun*
1 a ship, car, plane etc. that is so damaged that it cannot be used
2 a bad accident involving vehicles or planes: *He was in a car wreck.*

wreck² *verb*
to destroy or ruin something: *The ship was wrecked on the rocks.* | *He ended up wrecking their marriage.*

wreck·age /'rɛkɪdʒ/ *noun* [U]
the broken parts of a car, plane, building etc.: *Two people were recovered from the wreckage.*

wrench¹ /rɛntʃ/ *noun*
a metal tool with a round end used for turning things that are tight

wrench² *verb*
to pull or turn something suddenly and with force: *He wrenched the door open.*

wres·tle /'rɛsəl/ *verb* (**wrestling, wrestled**)
to fight by holding someone and trying to push or pull him or her to the ground

wres·tler /'rɛslɚ/ *noun*
someone who WRESTLES as a sport

wres·tling /'rɛslɪŋ/ *noun* [U]
a sport in which you try to push or pull someone to the ground

wrig·gle /'rɪgəl/ *verb* (**wriggling, wriggled**)
to twist from side to side with small quick movements: *The snake wriggled through the grass.*

wring /rɪŋ/ *verb* (*past tense* **wrung** /rʌŋ/, *past participle* **wrung**)
(*also* **wring out**) to twist wet clothes to remove water from them

wrin·kle /'rɪŋkəl/ *noun*
1 a line in cloth caused by crushing or folding it: *Can you iron the wrinkles out of this shirt?*
2 a line on your skin, especially when you are old —see color picture on page 191

wrist /rɪst/ *noun*
the joint between your hand and your arm —see picture at HAND¹

wrist·watch /'rɪst-wɑtʃ/ *noun*
a watch that you wear around your wrist

write /raɪt/ *verb* (**writing,** *past tense* **wrote** /rout/, *past participle* **written** /'rɪt⌐n/)
1 to make letters or words on paper, using a pen or pencil: *The children are learning to write.* | *Write your name here.*
2 to produce a letter and send it to someone: *He writes **to** me every day.*
3 to produce a new book, play, song etc.: *She's written several books.*
4 **write back** to answer a letter by sending one to whoever sent one to you
5 **write something down** to put information on a piece of paper so you do not forget it: *Did you write down her phone number?*

writ·er /'raɪtɚ/ *noun*
someone who writes books, especially as a job

writ·ing /'raɪtɪŋ/ *noun* [U]
1 the activity or job of writing books or stories, or the books and stories that are written: *I enjoy the humorous writing of Mark Twain.*
2 words that are written or printed, or the style in which this is done: *What beautiful writing!* | *I can't read your writing.*
3 **in writing** a promise, agreement etc. that is written and official: *Can I have that promise in writing?*

writ·ten /'rɪt⌐n/
the PAST PARTICIPLE of the verb **write**

wrong¹ /rɔŋ/ *adjective*
1 not good or acceptable; bad: *Telling lies is wrong.*
2 not correct: *I gave the wrong answer.* ⪢ compare RIGHT¹
3 not suitable: *This is the wrong time to visit her.*
4 **what's wrong?** (a) said when asking someone what the problem is: *What's wrong? Aren't you feeling well?* (b) said when asking someone

wring

why something is not working: *Hey, John, what's wrong **with** the TV?*

wrong² *adverb*

1 not in the correct way: *You spelled the word wrong.* ≫ compare RIGHT³

2 get something wrong to make a mistake or not get the correct answer

3 go wrong to have problems and not be successful: *If anything goes wrong, we'll fix it for free!*

wrong³ *noun [U]*

behavior that is bad, incorrect, or unacceptable: *Some children do not know the difference between right and wrong.* ≫ compare RIGHT²

wrote /roʊt/

the PAST TENSE of the verb **write**

wrung /rʌŋ/

the PAST TENSE and PAST PARTICIPLE of the verb **wring**

www

the short way to write WORLD WIDE WEB

X·mas /'krɪsməs, 'ɛksməs/ *noun [U]*
a short way to write the word CHRISTMAS

x-ray

x-ray¹ /'ɛks-reɪ/ *noun (plural* **x-rays***)*
a photograph of the inside of your body, taken with a special light that cannot be seen, used by a doctor to see an injury: *The x-ray showed two broken bones.*

x-ray² *verb* (**x-raying, x-rayed**)
to photograph a part of someone's body using an X-RAY

yacht /yɑt/ *noun*
a large expensive boat, used for sailing or racing

yam /yæm/ *noun*
SWEET POTATO

yank /yæŋk/ *verb*
to pull something quickly and with force: *The little boy yanked my hair.*

yard /yɑrd/ *noun*
1 the land around a house, usually covered with grass: *We have a swimming pool in the back yard.*
2 a measure of length, equal to three feet or 0.9 meters

yard sale /'. ./ *noun*
a sale of old clothes, furniture, toys etc. in someone's yard

yarn /yɑrn/ *noun*
a thick thread used by someone to KNIT something

yawn¹ /yɔn/ *verb*
to open your mouth wide and breathe deeply because you are tired or bored: *I felt so sleepy, I couldn't stop yawning.*

yawn² *noun*
an act of YAWNing

yd. *noun*
a short way to write the word **yard** used as a measurement

yeah /yɛə/
used for saying "yes": *"Do you like ice cream?" "Yeah!"*

year /yɪr/ *noun*
1 a period of time equal to 365 days or 12 months, beginning on January 1 and ending on December 31: *She is seven years old. | The agreement is good for another year.*

2 years, in years, for years many years; a long period of time: *I haven't seen her in years.* | *It's been years since I rode a horse.*

year·book /'yɪrbʊk/ *noun*
a book printed once a year by a high school or college, about its students, sports events, clubs etc. during that year

year·ly /'yɪrli/ *adjective, adverb*
happening or done every year or once a year

yeast /yist/ *noun* [U]
a living substance used for making bread rise and for producing alcohol

yell /yɛl/ *verb*
to shout or say something very loudly

yel·low /'yɛloʊ/ *adjective, noun*
having the color of the sun, or the middle part of an egg: *The park was full of yellow flowers.*

Yellow Pag·es /,.. '../ *(trademark)*
plural noun
a book that has the telephone numbers of the businesses in a particular area

yes /yɛs/ *adverb*
1 said when giving a positive reply to a question: *"Will you call me tomorrow?" "Yes, I will."* ≫ compare NO
2 said when agreeing with a statement: *"It is a beautiful day." "Yes, it is."*
3 said when you do not agree completely with a statement: *"He doesn't love me any more." "Yes he does!"*
4 said when you are excited about something: *Yes! Yes! Yes! We won!*

yes·ter·day /'yɛstɚdi, -,deɪ/ *adverb, noun*
the day before today: *It was very hot yesterday.* ≫ compare TOMORROW

yet /yɛt/ *adverb*
1 used in questions and negative statements to say whether something that you expect to happen has happened: *Did he come yet?* | *I don't think she is awake yet.*
2 at some time in the future; still: *She may come yet.*
3 in addition to what you have already done or gotten: *I made yet another mistake.* | *I will try to help her yet again.*

NOTE: Use **yet** in questions and NEGATIVE sentences: *Are you finished yet? I'm not ready yet.* In other types of sentence, use **already**: *I am already finished.*

yield /yild/ *verb*
1 to allow yourself to be persuaded to do something: *The government yielded to public demands for lower taxes.*
2 to allow the cars from another road to go first
3 to produce fruit, vegetables etc.: *The trees yielded a large crop of fruit.*

YMCA /,waɪ ɛm si 'eɪ/ *noun*
an organization, especially in large cities, that provides places to stay and sports activities for young people

yo·gurt /'yoʊgɚt/ *noun* [U]
a thick liquid food made from milk, that has a slightly sour taste

yolk /yoʊk/ *noun*
the yellow part in the center of an egg —see picture at EGG

you /yə, yʊ; *strong* yʊ/ *pronoun*
1 the person or people that someone is talking to: *You can swim fast.* | *I can't hear you.*
2 people in general: *You can't believe anyone these days.* | *It's not good for you to smoke.*

you'd /yəd, yʊd; *strong* yud/
1 you had: *You'd already left when I called.*
2 you would: *If you brushed your hair, you'd look better.*

you'll /yəl, yʊl; *strong* yul/
you will: *You'll get it tomorrow.*

young¹ /yʌŋ/ *adjective*
not old; not having lived very long: *She was with a young child.* ≫ compare OLD —see color picture on page 191

young² *plural noun*
1 the young young people as a group: *The music is directed at the young.*
2 young animals: *Animals protect their young.*

your /yɚ; *strong* yʊr, yɔr/
belonging to the person or people you are speaking to: *Put your books on your desks.* | *Is that your mother?*

you're /yɚ; *strong* yʊr, yɔr/
you are: *You're late again!*

yours /yʊrz, yɔrz/
1 something belonging or relating to you: *Are these pencils yours?* | *Is he a friend of yours?*
2 yours, yours sincerely a phrase you write at the end of a letter before you sign your name

your·self /yɚ'sɛlf/ *(plural* **yourselves** /yɚ'sɛlvz/)

1 the same person as the one that someone is talking to: *Look at yourself in the mirror.* | *Make yourself at home.*

2 used for emphasizing the word "you": *You told me the story yourself.*

3 by yourself (a) without help: *You can't lift that by yourself!* (b) alone: *Do you live by yourself?*

4 to yourself for your own use: *You will have the house to yourself this week.*

youth /yuθ/ *noun*

1 [U] the time when someone is young: *In his youth, he was a singer.*

2 (*plural* **youths**) a young man: *Two youths were involved in the accident.*

3 (*plural*) young people in general: *The youth of the country suffered the most.*

you've /yəv, yʊv; *strong* yuv/
you have: *You've forgotten your coat.*

yo-yo /'youyou/ *noun*
a toy that you hold in your hand, and make it go up and down on a string

yup·pie /'yʌpi/ *noun*
someone who is only interested in earning a lot of money and buying a lot of expensive things

zebra

ze·bra /'zibrə/ *noun*
a wild animal in Africa like a horse, that has black and white lines on its body —see color picture on page 183

ze·ro /'zirou, 'zirou/ *noun* (*plural* **zeros** or **zeroes**)
the number 0

zig·zag /'zɪgzæg/ *noun*
a pattern like a long line of Z's joined together —see picture at PATTERN

zip /zɪp/ *verb* (**zipping, zipped**)
(*also* **zip up**) to fasten something using a ZIPPER: *She zipped up her dress.*

zip code /'. ./ *noun*
a number that you write below the address on an envelope so that it can be delivered quickly

zip·per /'zɪpɚ/ *noun*
a fastener on clothes, bags etc. that has two lines of metal or plastic teeth and a sliding piece that joins the lines together —see picture at FASTENER

zo·di·ac /'zoudi,æk/ *noun*
the zodiac an imaginary circle in space that the sun, moon, and PLANETs follow as a path, which some people believe influences people's lives

zone /zoun/ *noun*
part of an area used for a particular purpose: *This is a no-parking zone.*

zoo /zu/ *noun*
a place where many different animals are kept so that people can look at them

Irregular verbs

Here are a few simple rules to help you find the correct ending for different verbs:

A. Verbs which end in a consonant and a silent "e", such as like, hope, create, advise, amuse

1. In the **present** tense, you add "**s**" to the **he**, **she**, or **it** forms:
She **likes** cheese.
He **loves** her.

2. In the **past** tense, you add "**d**" to all forms:
She **created** a terrible noise.
They **liked** the movie.
He **hoped** to win a prize.

3. In the **continuous** tenses, you take away the "**e**" and add "**ing**."
She's **hoping** to pass the test.
I was just **admiring** your new car.

B. Verbs which end in "y" (NOT verbs which end in -ay, -oy, -uy, -ey)

1. In the **present** or **past** tenses, you change "**y**" into "**ie**."

cry — The baby **cries** a lot.
She **cried** all night.
worry — It **worries** me.
He **worried** his mother.

2. In the **continuous** tenses, you do not change the "**y**". You add "**ing**" to the "**y**."

dry — She's **drying** her hair.
hurry — He's **hurrying** to work.
fry — She's **frying** an egg.

C. Verbs which double the consonant

1. If a verb has one syllable and ends in a single vowel and a consonant, such as **hit**, **clap**, **plan**, **pin**, the consonant is usually doubled:

clap — She **clapped** her hands.
plan — I'm **planning** to go home tomorrow.

2. If a verb has more than one syllable, but ends in a single vowel and a consonant, and has the stress on the last syllable, the consonant is usually doubled:

begin — I'm **beginning** to understand.
upset — She's really **upsetting** me.

3. If a verb has more than one syllable and the stress is **not** on the last syllable, the last consonant is not usually doubled:

offer — She **offered** me some coffee.
open — He **opened** the door.

4. If the last vowel sound of a verb is written with two letters, you do **not** double the final consonant:

heat — I'm **heating** the soup.
cook — He **cooked** our dinner.

Table of irregular verbs

verb	present participle	past tense	past participle	verb	present participle	past tense	past participle
arise	arising	arose	arisen	breed	breeding	bred	bred
be	being	was	been	bring	bringing	brought	brought
bear	bearing	bore	borne	broadcast	broadcasting	broadcast	broadcast
beat	beating	beat	beaten	build	building	built	built
become	becoming	became	become	burn	burning	burned	burned
begin	beginning	began	begun	buy	buying	bought	bought
bend	bending	bent	bent	catch	catching	caught	caught
bet	betting	bet	bet	choose	choosing	chose	chosen
bind	binding	bound	bound	cling	clinging	clung	clung
bite	biting	bit	bitten	come	coming	came	come
bleed	bleeding	bled	bled	cost	costing	cost	cost
blow	blowing	blew	blown	creep	creeping	crept	crept
break	breaking	broke	broken	cut	cutting	cut	cut

verb	present participle	past tense	past participle	verb	present participle	past tense	past participle
deal	dealing	dealt	dealt	panic	panicking	panicked	panicked
die	dying	died	died	pay	paying	paid	paid
dig	digging	dug	dug	picnic	picnicking	picnicked	picnicked
do	doing	did	done	put	putting	put	put
draw	drawing	drew	drawn	quit	quitting	quit	quit
dream	dreaming	dreamed or dreamt	dreamed or dreamt	read	reading	read	read
				repay	repaying	repaid	repaid
drink	drinking	drank	drunk	ride	riding	rode	ridden
drive	driving	drove	driven	ring	ringing	rang	rung
eat	eating	ate	eaten	rise	rising	rose	risen
fall	falling	fell	fallen	run	running	ran	run
feed	feeding	fed	fed	saw	sawing	sawed	sawn
feel	feeling	felt	felt	say	saying	said	said
fight	fighting	fought	fought	see	seeing	saw	seen
find	finding	found	found	seek	seeking	sought	sought
fly	flying	flew	flown	sell	selling	sold	sold
forbid	forbidding	forbade	forbidden	send	sending	sent	sent
forget	forgetting	forgot	forgotten	set	setting	set	set
freeze	freezing	froze	frozen	sew	sewing	sewed	sewn
get	getting	got	gotten	shake	shaking	shook	shaken
give	giving	gave	given	shear	shearing	sheared	shorn
go	going	went	gone	shed	shedding	shed	shed
grind	grinding	ground	ground	shine	shining	shone	shone
grow	growing	grew	grown	shoot	shooting	shot	shot
hang	hanging	hung or hanged	hung or hanged	show	showing	showed	shown
				shrink	shrinking	shrank	shrunk
have	having	had	had	shut	shutting	shut	shut
hear	hearing	heard	heard	sing	singing	sang	sung
hide	hiding	hid	hidden	sink	sinking	sank	sunk
hit	hitting	hit	hit	sit	sitting	sat	sat
hold	holding	held	held	sleep	sleeping	slept	slept
hurt	hurting	hurt	hurt	slide	sliding	slid	slid
keep	keeping	kept	kept	sling	slinging	slung	slung
kneel	kneeling	knelt	knelt	slit	slitting	slit	slit
know	knowing	knew	known	sow	sowing	sowed	sown
lay	laying	laid	laid	speak	speaking	spoke	spoken
lead	leading	led	led	speed	speeding	sped or speeded	sped or speeded
leave	leaving	left	left				
lend	lending	lent	lent	spend	spending	spent	spent
let	letting	let	let	spin	spinning	spun	spun
lie1	lying	lay	lain	spit	spitting	spit or spat	spat
lie2	lying	lied	lied	split	splitting	split	split
lose	losing	lost	lost	spring	springing	sprang	sprung
make	making	made	made	stand	standing	stood	stood
mean	meaning	meant	meant	steal	stealing	stole	stolen
meet	meeting	met	met	stick	sticking	stuck	stuck
mistake	mistaking	mistook	mistaken	sting	stinging	stung	stung
mow	mowing	mowed	mowed or mown	stink	stinking	stank	stunk
				stride	striding	strode	stridden
outgrow	outgrowing	outgrew	outgrown	strike	striking	struck	struck
overhear	overhearing	overheard	overheard	swear	swearing	swore	sworn
oversleep	oversleeping	overslept	overslept	sweep	sweeping	swept	swept
overtake	overtaking	overtook	overtook	swell	swelling	swelled	swollen

verb	present participle	past tense	past participle	verb	present participle	past tense	past participle
swim	swimming	swam	swum	unwind	unwinding	unwound	unwound
swing	swinging	swung	swung	upset	upsetting	upset	upset
take	taking	took	taken	wake	waking	woke	woken
teach	teaching	taught	taught	wear	wearing	wore	worn
tear	tearing	tore	torn	weave	weaving	wove	woven
tell	telling	told	told	weep	weeping	wept	wept
think	thinking	thought	thought	wet	wetting	wet *or* wetted	wet *or* wetted
throw	throwing	threw	thrown				
thrust	thrusting	thrust	thrust	win	winning	won	won
tie	tying	tied	tied	wind	winding	wound	wound
undergo	undergoing	underwent	undergone	withdraw	withdrawing	withdrew	withdrawn
understand	understanding	understood	understood	wring	wringing	wrung	wrung
undertake	undertaking	undertook	undertaken	write	writing	wrote	written
undo	undoing	undid	undone				

The Longman Defining Vocabulary

Words used in the definitions in this dictionary

All the definitions in this dictionary have been written using the words on this list. If a definition includes a word that is not on the list, that word is shown in SMALL CAPITAL LETTERS.

The Defining Vocabulary has been carefully chosen after a thorough study of all the well-known frequency lists of English words. Furthermore, only the most common and "central" meanings of the words on the list have actually been used in definitions. We have also used a special computer program that checks every entry to ensure that words from outside the Defining Vocabulary do not appear in definitions.

Word class restrictions

For some words in the list, a word class label such as *n* or *adj* is shown. This means that this particular word is used in definitions only in the word class shown. So **age**, for example, is used only as a noun and not as a verb. But if no word class is shown for a word, it can be used in any of its most common word classes: **answer**, for example, is used in definitions both as a noun and as a verb.

Compound words

Definitions occasionally include compound words formed from words in the Defining Vocabulary, but this is only done if the meaning is completely clear. For example, the word **businessman** (formed from **business** and **man**) is used in some definitions.

Prefixes and suffixes

The main list is followed by a list of common prefixes and suffixes. These can be added to words in the main list to form derived words, provided the meaning is completely clear. For example, the word **walking** (formed by adding **-ing** to **walk**) is used in some definitions.

Phrasal verbs

Phrasal verbs formed by combining words in the Defining Vocabulary (for example, **put up with something**) are NOT used in definitions in the dictionary, except in a very small number of cases where the phrasal verb is extremely common and there is no common equivalent. So, for example, **give something up** (as in **give up smoking**) and **take off** (as in **the plane took off**) are occasionally used.

Proper nouns

The Defining Vocabulary does not include the names of actual places, nationalities, religions, and so on, which are occasionally mentioned in definitions.

A	actor, actress	after *adv, conj, prep*	along
a	actual	afternoon	alphabet
abbreviation	add	afterward	already
ability	addition	again	also
able	address	against	although
about	adjective	age *n*	always
above *adv, prep*	admiration	ago	among
abroad	admire	agree	amount *n*
absence	admit	agreement	amuse
absent *adj*	adult	ahead	amusement
accept	advanced	aim	amusing
acceptable	advantage	air *n*	an
accident	adventure	aircraft	ancient
according (to)	adverb	airport	and
account *n*	advertise	alcohol	anger *n*
achieve	advertisement	alive	angle
acid	advice	all *adv, determiner,*	angry
across	advise	*predeterminer,*	animal
act	affair	*pron*	announce
action	affect	allow	announcement
active	afford	almost	annoy
activity	afraid	alone	another

answer
anxiety
anxious
any
anymore
anyone
anything
anywhere
apartapartment
appear
appearance
apple
appropriate
approval
approve
area
argue
argument
arm
army
around
arrange
arrangement
arrival
arrive
art
article
artificial
artist
as
ash
ashamed
ask
asleep
association
at
atom
attach
attack
attempt
attend
attention
attitude
attract
attractive
authority
available
average *adj, n*
avoid
awake
away
awkward

B
baby
back *adj, adv, n*
background
backward(s) *adv*
bad
bag *n*
bake
balance
ball

band *n*
bank *n*
bar *n*
barely
base *n, v*
baseball
basic
basket
basketball
bath
bathtub
battle *n*
be
beach
beak
beam *n*
bean
bear
beard
beat
beautiful
beauty
because
become
bed
beer
before
begin
beginning
behave
behavior
behind *adv, prep*
belief
believe
bell
belong
below *adv, prep*
belt *n*
bend
beneath
berry
beside(s)
best *adj, adv, n*
better *adj, adv*
between
beyond *adv, prep*
bicycle *n*
big
bill *n*
bird
birth
bite
bitter
black
blade
blame
bleed
blind
block
blood
blow
blue
board

boat
body
boil
bomb
bone
book *n*
boot *n*
border
bored
boring
born
borrow
both
bottle
bottom *n*
bowl *n*
box *n*
boy
brain
branch
brave
bread
break *v*
breakfast
breast
breath
breathe
breed
brick
bridge *n*
bright
bring
broad *adj*
broadcast
brother
brown *adj, n*
brush
bucket
build *v*
building
bullet
bunch *n*
burn
burst
bury
bus *n*
bush
business
busy
but *conj*
butter *n*
button *n*
buy *v*
by

C
cake
calculate
call
calm
camera
camp
can *n, v*

candy
cap *n*
capital
car
card
care
careful
careless
carriage
carry
case *n*
castle
cat
catch *v*
cattle
cause
ceiling
celebrate
cell
cent
center *n*
centimeter
central
century
ceremony
certain
chain
chair
chance
change
character
charge
chase *v*
cheap
cheat *v*
check
cheek
cheerful
cheese
chemical
chemistry
  chest
chicken
chief
child, children
chin
chocolate
choice
choose
church
cigarette
circle n
circular
citizen
city
claim
class
clay
clean
clear
clerk
clever
cliff

climb v
clock
close
cloth
clothes, clothing
cloud
club
coal
coast n
coat
coffee
coin
cold
collar
collect v
college
color
comb
combination
combine v
come
comfort
comfortable
command
committee
common
communicate
communication
company
compare
comparison
compete
competition
competitor
complain
complaint
complete
compound n
computer
concern v
concerning
concert
condition n
confidence
confident
confuse
connect
connection
conscious
consider
consist
container
continue
continuous
contract n
control
convenient
conversation
cook
cookie
cool
copy
corn

corner n
correct adj
cost
cotton
cough
could
council
country
courage
course
court
cover
cow
crack
crash
crazy
cream
creature
crime
criminal
criticism
criticize
crop n
cross n, v
crowd n
cruel
crush v
cry
cup
cupboard
cure
curl
current n
curtain
curve
customer
cut

D
daily adj, adv
damage
dance
danger
dangerous
dark
date n
daughter
day
dead
deal n
deal with
death
debt
decay
deceit
deceive
decide
decision
decorate
decoration
decrease
deep
defeat

defense
defend
definite
degree
delay
deliberate
delicate
deliver
demand
department
depend
dependent
depth
describe
description
desert
deserve
design
desirable
desire
desk
destroy
destruction
detail n
determination
determined
develop
dictionary
die v
difference
different
difficult
difficulty
dig
dinner
dip v
direct
direction
dirt
dirty
disappoint
discover
discovery
discuss
discussion
disease
dish
dismiss
distance n
distant
divide v
do
doctor
document
dog
dollar
door
double adj, v
doubt
down adv, prep
draw v
drawer
dream

dress
drink
drive
drop
drug
drum n
drunk past participle, adj
dry
duck n
dull
during
dust n
duty

E
each
eager
ear
early
earn
earth
east
eastern
easy
economic
edge
educate
educated
education
effect
effective
effort
egg
eight
eighth
either
elbow
elect
election
electric
electricity
electronic
else
embarrass
emotion
emphasize
employ
employer
employment
empty
enclose
encourage
end
enemy
energy
engine
engineer
enjoy
enjoyable
enjoyment
enough

enter
entertain
entertainment
entrance
envelope
environment
equal
equipment
escape
especially
establish
even *adj, adv*
evening
event
ever
every
everyone
everything
everywhere
evil
exact
examination
examine
example
excellent
except *conj, prep*
exchange
excite
excited
exciting
excuse
exercise
exist
existence
expect
expensive
experience
explain
explanation
explode
explosion
explosive
express *v*
expression
extreme
eye
eyelid

F
face
fact
factory
fail
failure
faint *adj, v*
fair *adj*
fairly
faith
faithful
fall
false
familiar
family

famous
far
farm
farmer
farther
farthest
fashion
fashionable
fast *adj, adv*
fasten
fat
father
fault *n*
favorable
favorite
fear
feather
feature
feed *v*
feel *v*
feeling(s)
female
fence
fever
few
field *n*
fierce
fifth
fight
figure *n*
fill *v*
film
final *adj*
finally
financial
find *v*
find out
fine *adj*
finger
finish
fire
firm *adj, n*
first *adv, determiner*
fish
fit *adj, v*
five
fix
flag
flame
flash
flat
flesh
flight
float
flood
floor
flour
flow
flower
fly
fold
follow
food

foot *n*
football
for *prep*
forbid
force
foreign
forest
forever
forget
forgive
fork
form
formal
former
fortunate
forward(s) *adv*
four(th)
frame *n*
free
freedom
freeze
frequent *adj*
fresh
friend
friendly
frighten
frightening
from
front *adj, n*
fruit
full
fun
funeral
funny
fur
furniture
further
future

G
gain
gallon
game
garage
garden
gas
gasoline
gate
gather
general
generally
generous
gentle
get
gift
girl
give
glad
glass
glue
go
goat
god, God

gold
good
goodbye
goods
govern
government
graceful
grade
gradual
grain
gram
grammar
grand *adj*
grandfather
grandmother
grandparent
grass
grateful
grave *n*
gray *adj, n*
great
green
greet
greeting
ground
group *n*
grow
growth
guard *v*
guess *v*
guest
guide
guilty
gun

H
habit
hair
half
hall
hammer *n*
hand *n*
handle
hang
happen
happy
hard
hardly
harm
harmful
hat
hate *v*
hatred
have
he
head *n*
health
healthy
hear
heart
heat
heaven
heavy

heel
height
hello
help
helpful
her(s)
here
herself
hide *v*
high
high school
hill
him
himself
his
historical
history
hit *v*
hold
hole
holiday
hollow *adj*
holy
home *adv, n*
honest
honor *n*
hook *n*
hope
hopeful
horn
horse *n*
hospital
host
hot
hotel
hour
house *n*
how
human
humorous
humor
hundred(th)
hungry
hunt *v*
hurry
hurt
husband

I
ice *n*
idea
if
ignore
ill
illegal
illness
image
imaginary
imagination
imagine
immediate
immediately
importance

important
impressive
improve
improvement
in *adv, prep*
inch
include
including
income
increase
independent
indoor(s)
industrial
industry
infect
infection
infectious
influence
inform
information
injure
injury
ink
inner
insect
inside
instead
institution
instruction
instrument
insult *v*
insurance
insure
intelligence
intelligent
intend
intention
interest
interesting
international
interrupt
into
introduce
introduction
invent
invitation
invite
involve
inward(s)
iron *adj, n*
island
it
its
itself

J
jaw
jewel
jewelry
job
join
joint
joke

judge
judgment
juice
jump
just *adv*
justice

K
keep *v*
key *n*
kick
kill
kilogram
kilometer
kind
king
kiss
kitchen
knee
kneel
knife
knock
knot
know *v*
knowledge

L
lack
lady
lake
lamb
lamp
land
language
last *adv, determiner*
late
lately
laugh
laughter
law
lawyer
lay
layer *n*
lazy
lead *v*
leaf
lean
learn
least
leather
leave
left
leg
legal
lend
length
less
lesson
let
let go of
let out
letter
level *adj, n*

library
lid
lie
lie down
life
lift
light
like *prep, v*
likely
limit
line *n*
lion
lip
liquid
list *n*
listen
literature
liter
little
live *v*
load
loaf *n*
local
lock
lonely
long
look
look for
loose
lose
loss
lot
loud
love
low *adj*
lower *v*
loyal
loyalty
luck
lucky
lung

M
machine
machinery
magazine
magic
mail
main
make
make into
make up
male
man
manage
manager
manner
many
map
march
mark *n*
market *n*
marriage

married
marry
match
material
mathematics
matter
may
me
meal
mean *v*
meaning
means
measure
meat
medical
medicine
meet
meeting
melt
member
memory
mental
mention *v*
mess
message
messy
metal
method
meter
middle *adj, n*
might *v*
mile
military *adj*
milk
million(th)
mind
mine *n, pron*
mineral
minister
minute *n*
mirror
miss
mist
mistake
mix *v*
mixture
model *n*
modern
moment
money
monkey
month
monthly
moon
moral *adj*
more
morning
most
mother
motor
mountain
mouse
mouth

move *v*
movement
much
mud
multiply
murder
muscle
music
musician
must
my
mysterious
mystery

N
nail
name
narrow
nasty
nation
national
natural
nature
navy
near *adj, adv, prep*
nearly
neat
necessary
neck
need
needle
negative
neither
nerve
nervous
nest
net
network
never
new
news
newspaper
next
nice
night
nine
ninth
no *adv, determiner*
noise
none
nonsense
no one
nor
normal
north
northern
nose
not
note
nothing
notice
noun
now

nowhere
number *n*
nurse
nut

O
obey
object *n*
obtain
occasion
ocean
o'clock
odd
of
off *adv, prep*
offense
offend
offensive *adj*
offer
office
officer
official
often
oil *n*
old
old-fashioned
on *adv, prep*
once
one
onion
only
onto
open *adj, v*
operate
operation
opinion
opponent
opportunity
oppose
as opposed to
opposite
opposition
or
orange
order
ordinary
organ
organize
organization
origin
original
other
ought
our(s)
out *adj, adv*
outdoor(s)
outer
outside
over *adv, prep*
owe
own *determiner*
owner
oxygen

P
pack *v*
package
page *n*
pain
painful
paint
painting
pair *n*
pale
pan
pants
paper
parallel
parent
park
part *n*
particular
partly
partner
party *n*
pass *v*
passage
passenger
past
path
patience
patient *adj*
pattern *n*
pause
pay
payment
peace
peaceful
pen
pencil
people
pepper
per
perfect *adj*
perform
performance
perhaps
period
permanent
permission
person
personal
persuade
pet *n*
photograph
phrase
physical
piano
pick *v*
pick up
picture *n*
piece *n*
pig
pile *n*
pilot *n*
pin
pink

pipe *n*
pity
place
plain *adj, n*
plan
plane
plant
plastic
plate
play
pleasant
please
pleased
pleasure
plenty
plural
pocket
poem
poet
poetry
point
pointed
poison
poisonous
pole
police
polish
polite
political
politician
politics
pool *n*
poor
popular
population
port
position *n*
positive
possess
possession
possible
possibility
possibly
post
pot *n*
potato
pound *n*
pour
powder *n*
power *n*
powerful
practical
practice
praise
pray
prayer
prefer
preparation
prepare
present *adj, n*
preserve
president
press *v*

pressure *n*
pretend
pretty *adj*
prevent
previous
previously
price *n*
priest
prince
principle
print
prison
prisoner
private *adj*
prize *n*
probably
problem
process *n*
produce *v*
product
production
profession
profit *n*
program
progress *n*
promise
pronounce
pronunciation
proof
property
proposal
protect
protection
protective
protest
proud
prove
provide
public
publicly
pull
pump
punish
punishment
pure
purple
purpose
push
put

Q
quality
quantity
quarrel
quarter *n*
queen
question
quick
quiet *adj, n*

R
rabbit
race

radio
railroad
rain
raise *v*
range *n*
rank *n*
rapid
rare
rat
rate *n*
rather
raw
reach
react
reaction
read *v*
ready
real
realize
really
reason
reasonable
receive
recent
recently
recognize
record *n, v*
red
reduce
reduction
refusal
refuse *v*
regard *v*
regular
related
relative
relation
relationship
relax
religion
religious
remain
remark *n*
remember
remind
remove
rent
repair
repeat *v*
reply
report
represent
representative *n*
request *n*
respect
responsible
rest
restaurant
restrict
result
return
reward
rice

rich
rid
ride
right
ring
ripe
rise
risk
river
road
rob
rock *n*
roll *v*
romantic *adj*
roof
room
root
rope
rose
rough
round *adj*
row
royal
rub
rubber
rude
ruin
rule
ruler
run
rush *v*

S
sad
safe *adj*
safety
sail
salary
sale
salt
same
sand *n*
satisfaction
satisfactory
satisfy
save
say *v*
scale *n*
scatter
scene
school
science
scientific
scientist
scissors
screen
screw
sea
search
season *n*
seat
second *adv, deter-
    miner, n*

secrecy
secret
secretary
see
seed
seem
seize
sell
send
sensation
sense
sensible
sensitive
sentence
separate
serious
seriously
servant
serve
service
set
settle
seven(th)
several
severe
sew
sex
sexual
shade
shadow
shake
shame n
shape
share
sharp
she
sheep
sheet
shelf
shell n
shelter
shine v
shiny
ship n
shirt
shock
shoe
shoot
shop
shore
short
shot
should
shoulder
shout
show
shut
shy
sick
sickness
side
sideways
sight n

sign
signal
silence n
silent
silk
silly
silver
similar
similarity
simple
since
sincere
sing
single
singular
sink v
sister
sit
situation
six(th)
size n
skill
skillful
skin
skirt
sky
slave
sleep
slide v
slight
slip v
slippery
slope
slow
small
smart
smell
smile
smoke
smooth
snake
snow
so
soap
social
society
sock
soft
soil
soldier
solid
solution
solve
some determiner,
  pron
somehow
someone
something
sometimes
somewhere
son
song
soon

sore adj
sorrow
sorry
sort n
soul
sound n, v
soup
sour
south
southern
space n
spade
speak
special adj
specific
speech
speed n
spell v
spend
spin v
spirit
in spite of
split
spoil
spoon
sport(s)
spot n
spread v
spring
square
stage n
stair
stamp
stand v
standard
star n
start
state
statement
station
stay
steady
steal
steam
steel
steep
stem
step
stick
sticky
stiff
still
sting
stitch
stomach
stone
stop
store
storm n
story
straight
strange
stranger

stream n
street
strength
stretch
strict
strike v
string n
strong
structure n
struggle
student
study
stupid
style n
subject n
substance
subtract
succeed
success
successful
such
suck
sudden
suffer
sugar
suggest
suit
suitable
suitcase
sum
summer
sun
supper
supply
support
suppose
sure
surface
surprise
surround
swallow v
swear
sweep
sweet
swell
swim
swing
sword
sympathetic
sympathy
system

T
table
tail
take
take care of
talk
tall
taste
tax
taxi
tea

teach	toe	universal	weather
team	together	universe	weave
tear	toilet	university	wedding
technical	tomorrow	unless	week
telephone	tongue	until	weekly
television	tonight	up	weigh
tell	too	upper	weight
temper	tool	upright	welcome
temperature	tooth	upset *v, adj*	well
temporary	top *adj, n*	upside down	west
ten(th)	total *adj, n*	upstairs	western *adj*
tend	touch	urgent	wet
tendency	tour	us	what
tennis	tourist	use	whatever
tense	toward	useful	wheat
tent	tower	useless	wheel
terrible	town	usual	when
terror	toy		whenever
test	track	**V**	where
than	trade *n*	vacation	whether
thank	tradition	valley	which
that	traditional	valuable	whichever
the	traffic	value *n*	while *conj*
theater	train	variety	whip
their(s)	training	various	whisper
them	translate	vegetable	whistle
then	transparent	vehicle	white
there	trap	verb	who
therefore	travel	very	whole
these	treat *v*	victory	whose
they	treatment	view *n*	why
thick	tree	violence	wide
thief	tribe	violent	width
thin	trick	visit	wife
thing	trip *n*	voice	wild *adj, adv*
think	tropical	vote	will
third	trouble	vowel	willing
this	truck		win *v*
thorough	true	**W**	wind *n, v*
those	trunk	wages	window
though	trust	waist	wine
thought	truth	wait *v*	wing
thousand(th)	try *v*	wake	winter
thread	tube	walk	wire
threat	tune *n*	wall	wisdom
threaten	turn	wander	wise
three	twice	want	wish
throat	twist	war	with
through	two	warm	within *prep*
throw	type *n*	warmth	without *prep*
thumb	typical	warn	witness *n*
ticket		warning	woman
tie	**U**	wash	wood
tiger	ugly	waste	wooden
tight	uncle	watch	wool
time *n*	under *prep*	water	word *n*
tire *v*	understand	wave	work
tired	underwear	way	world
tiring	undo	we	worm
title	uniform *n*	weak	worry
to	union	wealth	worse
tobacco	unit	weapon	worst
today	unite	wear	worth

would
wound
wrap *v*
wrist
write
wrong *adj, adv, n*

Y
yard
year
yearly
yellow
yesterday
yet
you
young
your(s)
yourself

Z
zero

Prefixes and suffixes that can be used with words in the Defining Vocabulary

-able	-ess	-ly
-al	-ful	-ment
-an	-ible	mid-
-ance	-ic	mis-
-ar	-ical	-ness
-ate	im-	non-
-ation	in-	-or
dis-	-ing	-ous
-ed	-ion	re-
-en	ir-	-ry
-ence	-ish	self-
-er	-ist	-ship
-ery	-ity	-th
	-ive	un-
	-ization	-ward(s)
	-ize	-work
	-less	-y
	-like	